# If Not Us, Who?

# If Not Us, Who?

*William Rusher,* National Review,
*and the Conservative Movement*

## David B. Frisk

Wilmington, Delaware

Library of Congress Cataloguing-in-Publication Data

Frisk, David B.
      If not us, who? : William Rusher, National Review, and the
      conservative movement / David B. Frisk.

      p. cm.
      Includes bibliographical references and index.
      ISBN 978-1-935191-45-2

      1. Rusher, William A., 1923–2011. 2. Intellectuals—United States—
Biography. 3. Conservatives—United States—Biography. 4. National Review. 5. Conservatism—United States. I. Title.

JC573.2.U6F74 2011
320.52092—dc22
   [B]                                          2010020120


ISI Books
Intercollegiate Studies Institute
3901 Centerville Road
Wilmington, Delaware 19807-1938
www.isibooks.org


Manufactured in the United States of America

*To all who ask: "If not us . . . ?"*

# Contents

# If Not Us, Who?

# Introduction

# "The Most Underrated Major Conservative Leader"

Untold stories can place the familiar ones in a new light. William Rusher was a centrally situated conservative leader and "wise man" who advised his colleagues, at *National Review* and elsewhere, on how they might respond to the challenges facing the conservative movement. As publisher of the Right's leading magazine from 1957—two years after its founding—all the way through 1988, Rusher was not mainly an executive or manager, as his title suggests. He was a political intellectual, tactician, and strategist who also held business responsibilities there.

When Rusher was away from the job, he was still on the job as he understood it: meeting with fellow movement leaders, speaking to a conservative conference or a liberal college audience, debating, attending a Republican national convention. At work he shared his news, his reflections, and often his recommendations. When he wrote to editor William F. Buckley Jr. or the senior editors, his usual topic was either current political opportunities and anxieties or how *NR* could best aid and influence conservatism while remaining a healthy magazine. "I don't think there was ever a situation in which I felt myself . . . incommunicado from his thinking," Buckley recalls. "In the first place, he didn't prefer that to happen."[1]

Rusher had a major although not exclusive theme. Year after year, he urged Buckley and others to consider themselves the leaders of a movement, and to ensure that *NR* maintained and cultivated its activist side. This position was not always received favorably. But the insights behind it were welcome, for colleagues especially valued Rusher as an analyst of the political world.

"Bill knew a great deal more about the insides of politics than most of the rest of us did, and it was much more important to him," says Priscilla Buckley, whose time as managing editor overlapped closely with his thirty-one years as publisher. He "added a tremendous amount of political sophistication to [our] analysis of what was going on in this country," and could do that because he kept in touch with political events and the people behind them.[2] He was an indispensable link between the *National Review* theorists and the Right's practitioners. As his friend and early political partner F. Clifton White wrote more than a generation ago: "Bill Rusher is that rarest of all combinations, an intellectual with a sure instinct for both business and practical politics."[3] He was "an amphibian" who moved comfortably between politics and the conservative intellectual milieu, suggests political consultant Jeffrey Bell, a protégé beginning in the early 1960s. Rusher was "at home in both worlds . . . an instigator and a militant in both worlds." Unlike some, he didn't think it was enough for conservatives to be an influence on the culture. "He felt you had to try to win."[4]

Without Rusher, *NR* might have reviewed the nation and era from a less political, more intellectual, more ideologically inclusive perspective. That was the approach urged by his frequent opposite, the more scholarly senior editor James Burnham. Buckley respected Burnham enormously and felt drawn toward his position. Yet Rusher—allied with another senior editor, Frank Meyer, until the latter's death in 1972 and carrying on thereafter—kept up a constant counterpoint in the spirit of the maxim attributed to Ronald Reagan: "If not us, who? If not now, when?"

He prodded his colleagues to make the magazine helpful to political causes and insisted it seize such opportunities. He argued that it should be the leader, or a major leader, of conservatism—not just an example of it or a spokesman for the Right's ideas. In regard to public policy and candidates, Rusher believed the magazine should uphold a strongly although not rigidly ideological position. With Buckley's permission from the start, he insisted on sharing his views in memos and the many editorial meetings. He had the privilege of speaking out on any subject. Armed with a wealth of knowledge and a powerful wit, Rusher expressed himself frequently and memorably. With two exceptions, he conceded little to the editor, founder, and owner. Those exceptions were his belief that Buckley was an indispensable conservative leader, and his recognition that Buckley was the indisputable boss at *NR*.

"Bill Rusher is every bit as vital to *National Review* as I am," Buckley told the audience at the magazine's twentieth-year celebration in 1975. "Tonight he has been trenchant, which he always is; and diplomatic, which usually he isn't. In contrast to his generous performance tonight, at *National Review* he exhibits no respect for me whatever; and that is very good for me, and therefore for my beloved *National Review*. I don't know what I would do without the disrespect regularly shown towards me. You will be reassured that there is no prospect of a national shortage."[5]

Among the *NR* leadership, it was Rusher and Meyer who cared the most about immediate—elective and practical, not necessarily short-term—politics. It was Rusher who knew the most about immediate politics and also had the most experience and contact with the Republicans and conservatives who were building the movement so it could (through Ronald Reagan in 1980, as it turned out) take significant political power. But like Burnham and Meyer, and unlike Buckley, he stood at the edge of the limelight. In the growing number of books on modern American conservatism, Rusher is never considered at length or even fully described, although he is usually an acknowledged player and some of his actions and advocacies are recorded.

In reality, he was more important than that. "Bill was a *character*," Buckley recalls, "and anyplace . . . that gave him license to establish his character ended up reflecting him in part. So I think that a lot of whatever can be deemed as the success of *National Review* is attributable to his contributions to it." In addition, he was of great help to *NR* in an operational sense. Rusher is, according to Buckley, "an important figure in the evolution of the right wing at several levels."[6]

William Rusher's political career began long before he came to *NR*, and it continued well after he retired from the magazine. In the Young Republican National Federation in the 1950s, he helped Clif White to build, coach, and deploy internally a large cadre that won the organization's national conventions for years. Many of its members became dedicated conservatives, some of whom would form the nucleus of the Draft Goldwater campaign. Rusher was central to the Goldwater drive—even helping start it in mid-1961—although White, by then an established political consultant and presidential-campaign veteran, was in charge. In addition, he helped to found and guide Young Americans for Freedom (YAF) and the American Conservative Union (ACU) in the 1960s. He attained wider fame in the early 1970s on a successful public-television debate program, *The Advocates*, compiling an impressive record of victories in its viewer ballots.

Rusher was central to post-1964 conservative organizing. "Nobody, but nobody, was more at the heart of this," says Richard Viguerie, active in the movement since the early 1960s and the main developer of direct-mail fundraising on the Right. "Rusher's fingerprints were everywhere—and not just involved, but you get a feeling that he was pulling an awful lot of the strings."[7] He was present "at every way station—and integral to what was going on at every stage," recalls M. Stanton Evans, a former ACU chairman who began his career as a movement journalist in the 1950s. In Evans's opinion, Rusher is "probably the most underrated major conservative leader." With a versatility perhaps unmatched among top movement figures, he "had more things going for him than almost any other conservative leader that I can think of."[8] According to Eugene Meyer, Frank Meyer's younger son and president of the Federalist Society, Rusher is "an unsung hero of the conservative movement."[9]

At the thirtieth-anniversary *National Review* banquet in 1985, President Reagan, in a readily understood reference to Buckley's prop on his TV show *Firing Line*, called the editor "our clipboard-bearing Galahad." For Rusher one hears less dramatic words: catalyst, unifier, strategist, broker, consigliere. After retiring from the magazine, he sometimes introduced himself simply as a "conservative activist."[10] Those terms are true but incomplete. In *The Making of the American Conservative Mind: "National Review" and Its Times* (2005), former senior editor Jeffrey Hart offered a good one-sentence summary: "The ultimate cosmopolitan, he nevertheless was one of the architects of the disaster that overtook the Establishment, which he only seemed to embody."[11] Buckley needed a political counselor and a political eyes-and-ears. In Rusher, *National Review* had a worldly political professional or near professional, yet at the same time a dedicated conservative.

An only child whose parents were solid Republicans but lacked his intense political interest, Rusher built up a little machine in high school. He flouted the country-club culture at his college, Princeton, by being at least as politically active there. In the Young Republicans in Manhattan in the early 1950s, he was a founder and leader of the Action Faction, its name chosen to implicitly criticize two other factions as "stuck-in-the-muds who weren't doing anything."[12] Soon, in national Young Republican politics, he helped run the organization's predominant and increasingly conservative alliance, which rivals eventually labeled as the Syndicate—a name Rusher gladly accepted. A graduate of Harvard Law School, he used his legal training at a major Wall Street law firm for several years but considered this "golden rut" insufficiently worthy of his energies. So in 1956, he joined the Senate Internal Security Subcommittee staff to investigate communist subversion, the topic of his first book a decade later.[13] Adhering in the 1940s to the Republican Party's moderate "eastern establishment," Rusher became, mainly from concern about communism, a militant conservative and thus an antagonist to that establishment by the mid-1950s.

In addition to his *NR* work and early movement organizing, Rusher became a public speaker and debater and a frequent radio guest, well known among conservatives in the New York area by the early 1960s, then nationally famous within a decade. In 1973, he began writing a syndicated column,

The Conservative Advocate, which would continue until early 2009, when he decided he could no longer write it at eighty-five. A serious prospect for a conservative third party arose in the 1970s amid the ideologically unsatisfying presidency of Gerald Ford, the GOP's 1974 electoral rout, and persisting dismay over several Nixon administration "betrayals" of conservative principles. Rusher spent well over a year as one of the main organizers of this project while continuing to work at *NR*. The party's failure to launch, owing mainly to Reagan's lack of interest, came as a great disappointment to him. Much happier with the state of things by 1984, satisfied that the movement had succeeded to a great extent, he wrote an early history called *The Rise of the Right*.[14]

Although born in Chicago, Rusher grew up in the New York City area and would be a devotee of fine food, fine wine, opera, and world travel while still identifying with Middle America. In the words of Kevin Lynch, a former junior colleague at the magazine, he was "defiantly square" in his personal style. He stood apart from the pranks, the capers, the bohemian insouciance that enlivened the *National Review* atmosphere and image. "I'm trying to remember," says former managing editor Linda Bridges, who has known Rusher since she started at *NR* more than forty years ago. "Have I ever seen him without a tie? I don't think so. Have I ever seen him without a jacket? I don't think so."[15] The formality coexisted with considerable charm. "He was a great person to talk to, to spend an evening with," notes senior editor Richard Brookhiser. "He was very gracious. Neither writers nor political types are necessarily gracious."[16]

Rusher's relationship with Buckley, just slightly younger than himself, was complex: "I've often said, 'Thank God the *Communist Manifesto* wasn't really well-written. We would have lost Buckley early on.'"[17] Neither seriously meant nor accurate, the jest is still indicative. Buckley placed a great emphasis on style and on *NR*'s obligation to, as he put it, "think." More than anyone else, for longer than anyone else, Rusher tethered the magazine to the political world. In that realm, ideology can take precedence over style and the need to win trumps independent thought. The tension between politicians and intellectuals, however much they agree on policy, is inevitable, rooted in the natures of both. Without Rusher and his two-way ambassadorship—explaining practical politics to the editors and urging them to consider it more, symbolizing the magazine's intellectual concerns and love of principle to those in the political world—*National Review* would have had the depth it always sought and usually achieved, but might have influenced the period less.

The publisher's importance in conservative politics depended largely on his place at *National Review* but was neither exhausted nor wholly defined by it. He became a substantial voice in his own right. Fascinated all his life by the internal workings and prospects of the Republican Party, Rusher sketched a good part of its future well in advance. His widely distributed 1963 article "Crossroads for the GOP," for example, made a cogent case that the Republicans, at least if led by a conservative, had vast potential in what remained basically the one-party South. Barry Goldwater's success there in the 1964 general election, in retrospect a decisive event in American history, proved Rusher correct less than two years later. The party's new strength in the region continued to grow for decades, leading to some presidential victories and augmenting others, also creating Republican majorities in both houses of Congress in 1994. Rusher accurately predicted the upsetting of what had been the nation's political geography for a century, closely tying his prediction to a conservative brand of Republicanism.

In the 1970s, inspired partly by the research of political analyst Kevin Phillips, he promoted an alliance between the economic conservatives, nearly all Republicans, and the social conservatives, often Democrats who found their party an increasingly uncomfortable home. Rusher saw the basic division in American society as one between "producers and non-producers." It cut across class lines, uniting some of the upper-middle class with much of the lower-middle and working classes. Such a view represented a kind of populism—a concept Rusher hoped conservatives would snatch from the Left. He urged the organized Right, and Republican leaders who would listen, to see the socially conservative elements of the working class in middle-class terms and to embrace social-conservative causes. Reagan's message, and the voters known as Reagan Democrats in the 1980s, fulfilled this vision. So does the current "red-America, blue-America" divide.

Appropriately for one who had helped lead an Action Faction, Rusher was always quick to spot new talent at all levels, often willing to mentor younger activists. Movement veteran and historian Lee Edwards remembers him as "a natural teacher in all things, not just politics," and as a leader who "was always available." He was "far more than just an activist. This was somebody who was also principled and well-founded."[18] Another characteristic was a bias toward moving sooner rather than later. At least once, he was willing to think radically indeed. Much as he admired Reagan, promoting him for the presidency as early as the beginning of 1967, Rusher found the weak, centrist Republican Party of the mid-1970s unacceptable since it had, he thought, become useless as a vehicle for movement principles. Wasting no time, he churned out a book proposing that activists immediately—not someday—start a "new majority party" uniting economic and social conservatives. It also explained in relatively realistic terms how this might be done.[19]

Although he strongly hoped Reagan would lead such a party, Rusher would have backed even a modest effort by a lesser conservative had it occurred. But ever since Reagan's resoundingly successful 1980 candidacy, the former scourge of the Republican hierarchy has been a down-the-line party loyalist. At a quarterly *NR* board meeting in mid-2000, Buckley asked whether the magazine should enthusiastically support presidential nominee George W. Bush, who was not a movement conservative, or pressure him. Rusher recalls: "I got up and said, 'For Christ's sake,' or words to the same effect, 'wait till after November to pressure him. But for the time being, get in there and push!'"[20]

While hoping and planning for big things, he tried not to expect too much. "Politicians are the grease on which society's wheels turn," Rusher says. "And they can't be better, most of the time, than a sort of low competence and honor."[21] Similarly, he met the conservative movement's (which is every ideological movement's) endless dilemma, the choice between realism and idealism, not with a standing commitment to either but with a constant balancing act. His great hero in American politics was Reagan: the most successful example, many would say, of that balancing act in recent times. Of Richard Nixon, whom he refused to support in the 1960 and 1972 general elections, Rusher says: "He was an interesting man, and a complex man—and not in any sense of the word an evil man. I think he was, however, rather devoid of any moral appreciation of politics. I think he regarded it all as a tremendously complicated game. To me it was not a game."[22]

Rusher became significant not only because he sat in the right place at the right time but also because he was, though disinclined from a young age to seek office himself, unusually well-suited to politics in the broad sense. In his lecture "Politics as a Vocation," the great social theorist Max Weber spoke of it as "a strong and slow boring of hard boards" that "takes both passion and perspective." In addition to demanding sometimes contradictory qualities, politics can be heartbreaking and exasperatingly difficult. Few people, Weber implied, can really make it a lifelong calling.[23] Rusher could and he did. Stamina took the place of star power. His half century of labor for conservatism, described in this book, is a tale of dogged persistence through its many turns of fortune. "That's his faith," Buckley explains. "That's what he lives for."[24]

But it is worth seeing as well the simplicity of his motives. "Our friend is a man of most meticulous habits," Buckley said at a 1969 dinner held in Rusher's honor, "and it is a miracle, of the kind that providence less and less frequently vouchsafes us, that he should have endured for so long the disorderly habits of his colleagues."[25] The truth is less poetic. Rusher endured at *NR* for the same reason he left a Wall Street law firm to join what remained of the unfashionable congressional investigations into domestic communism more than fifty years ago. He believed it was the best available use for his zeal and his talents. "I think he liked the controversy too," Priscilla Buckley notes.[26]

Rusher's biography is an extended study in political choice and judgment, beginning with a speech recorded at the World's Fair in 1940 urging American entry into the war and a college thesis praising Wendell Willkie and other "progressive" Republicans of that distant time. The choices and judgments of the leading politicians, and of the animating spirits like Buckley, matter greatly. But those of the less-obvious leaders can tell us much.

# 1

# Enter This War Now

The Great Neck High School yearbook of 1940 puckishly listed a quality each senior would leave to someone else. For William Rusher the entry was a silly prediction: "leaves for the Senate." At sixteen he wanted to be a political operative or a highbrow columnist. But to most classmates, such aspirations and the Senate might have meant the same thing. A year and a half before, Bill had won a newspaper essay contest on the Constitution. "After all," he told the *New York Journal and American* for its brief write-up, "we students should be Constitution-conscious. We are going to grow up and be the people who run the nation."[1]

The war came to Western Europe during his last weeks of high school as Nazi Germany invaded several countries with little resistance. In Philadelphia the Republican National Convention was coming up. Bill glued his ears to the radio and eventually heard the news he was hoping for. After a dramatic six ballots, Wendell Willkie clinched the presidential nomination. For the young listener it was early proof that an insurgent campaign could win. With the world in crisis, a well-organized groundswell had brought an unlikely newcomer into the game.

Most delegates still preferred Senator Robert Taft of Ohio or the youthful district attorney of New York, Thomas Dewey—not Willkie, a utility executive who had recently left the Democratic Party and was making his first run for office. But the Republicans were meeting just after France had surrendered to Germany, and England might be next. The specter of Hitler haunted the convention as its "uninvited guest."[2] The Republican Party, Bill had written a month earlier, was "left high and dry on the stationary promontory of its principles, while the world rushed by below it, toward a new conception of international affairs."[3]

Willkie, the only candidate urging immediate aid for Britain, looked like the man of the hour to the fledgling pundit and to enough of the delegates. The greater man of the hour was the defiant new prime minister, Winston Churchill, whose speeches Bill heard when they were broadcast across the Atlantic. "Well, if you have to have a hero," his father said, "I guess you've picked a good one." On a visit to the nearby World's Fair that summer, the young admirer of Churchill and Willkie recorded as a keepsake his own prointervention speech: "Consequently I think we should enter this war now, with all our heart and with all our soul." In September, Rusher entered Princeton University and the Reserve Officer Training Corps.[4] It was the beginning of an ambiguous relationship with the "eastern establishment," one that would shape his political career and thereby influence the conservative movement.

## Parents and Upbringing

Although Bill spent most of his childhood in the New York area, the family had lived in Chicago until 1930. As a boy in the East, he would explain later in an autobiographical sketch, he became "self-consciously a midwesterner-in-exile—swelling with pride when we studied Chicago in geography class, rooting for the Cubs though I was largely uninterested in baseball."[5]

His parents were "a fairly typical midwestern couple, both from Methodist backgrounds," successful enough when Evan Rusher had his better jobs, but not wealthy. The elder Rusher was a solid but not a passionate Republican, conservative but not in his son's recollection "right wing." He worried about the country's direction under President Franklin Roosevelt, generally agreed with the anti–New Deal radio commentary, and followed the news closely without being politically active. A sales manager and executive who put great energy into his work, Evan thought little of politics as a career. He seemed not to welcome Bill's inclination toward it. "His first reaction was rather dismissive," Rusher recalls. When they visited Washington once, about 1937 and probably at Bill's urging, they spent a lot of time in the hotel's air-conditioned restaurant.[6]

Evan Rusher came from tiny Hymera, Indiana, near Terre Haute. The son of a socialist coal-mine foreman, he had only a high-school education. He volunteered for the Army shortly after American entry into World War I. Serving in the field artillery, he trained in France and was promoted to second lieutenant. He never saw combat but was evaluated as "a hard and most willing worker . . . very satisfactory." After discharge, Evan was hired as a traveling salesman by the Chicago-based Standard Advertising Company. He would spend a decade with the firm, which sold advertising and promotional services to retail stores and newspapers around the country.[7] On his route he met Verna Rae Self, an elementary-school teacher in Independence, Kansas, whose father kept a store. Evan wrote her daily for a year and they married in December 1920. After a year and a half on the road, both in their midtwenties, they settled in Chicago.[8]

William Allen Rusher, born there on July 19, 1923, was their only child. It was a difficult birth at which multiple doctors had to assist. Verna, who got a dangerous abdominal infection for a few weeks, told her son many years later: "We had the best of care or we wouldn't be here."[9] The young family lived in an apartment near the University of Chicago, in the Hyde Park neighborhood. Later they would move often, Bill attending different schools around New York. They were able to hire a live-in maid for some years but usually occupied a comfortable apartment or a rented house, not their own home. There were no expensive vacations and no luxuries to speak of. But when the family listened to *Hawaii Calls*, a musical program broadcast from a hotel at Waikiki Beach to the accompaniment of the Pacific waves, Bill fell under its spell.[10]

The maid was a middle-aged black woman named Sarah, of whom he saw "a good deal more . . . that I did of my parents." Evan and Verna considered her practically one of the family and would innocently ask her, perhaps with some "unconscious patronization" as Rusher reflected later, to the living room so everyone could listen to *Amos 'n' Andy*. Large-figured in a black dress and white apron with matching cap, she chuckled softly at the program's humor. Sarah was uneducated and "highly skeptical. When I ran to her with the news, gleaned from a children's encyclopedia, that the sun was 93 million miles away, she refused to believe it, and told me, 'The man just put that in the book to make money.'" At the same time, he appreciated Sarah's excellent memory for short poems and the variety of "arcane lore" she shared with him. "I loved her dearly."[11]

Bill's parents did not attend church but sent him to a Sunday school when they lived long enough in one place. "Methodist or Presbyterian," Rusher recalls. "Anything reasonably moderate would do." Verna, a stay-at-home mother, was a graduate of a teacher's college and thus had more formal education than her husband. Deeply devoted to her boy, she had one other strong interest: the piano-accordion, then a popular instrument, at which she became as proficient as she could. "I think she would have liked, had she been in a position, to have had a career in that," Rusher says. "She was very good at it."[12] But her husband jealously forbade her to perform outside their home. For years, Verna played the "splendid Wurlitzer" in her bedroom every afternoon. Evan was "an authoritative, distinguished type." In the sales world, he had to convince people he knew what he was talking about. One of his closest associates later claimed he could sell glasses to a blind man. The young Rusher experienced something similar in a talk about his future:

> Once, probably in my early teens—when I hadn't decided what I wanted to do as a career, or where I wanted to go to college—my father put up the idea that . . . science or technology . . . was the way to go, and MIT was the school to go to. And he had me absolutely convinced at the end of the day, on both scores. Looking back on it, I think he was doing nothing but just exercising his salesmanship that day. I don't think there was the slightest expectation that I would take his advice. But he felt like selling somebody on something, and he did it very fast.[13]

Evan Rusher was also tenacious, self-confident, and naturally analytical. By about 1927, he had become president of the company that hired him in 1919. He then struck out on his own. Not long before the Depression, Rusher developed a strategy for independent stores. The Standard Plan, as he called it, enabled them to compete better with the already-threatening chains by purchasing as a group, consulting with an expert staff, and delegating functions like cost control and sales planning to a company in New York. Rusher headed the firm, Standard Store Service, which in 1931 occupied three floors of a Broadway building and employed one hundred people.[14] It is unclear what happened to the company. But Evan would recall that he "spent ten years following sound rules for building a strong financial foundation" after the war, "only to have it all swept away in the crash of 1929–30." In the next several years "I was able to keep my earnings at their normal level but, through reaction, I largely threw them away in an exaggerated form of living."

Hit by the Depression, he took pride in earlier successes. A well-designed flier he prepared when seeking better work in 1933 said he had traveled some five hundred thousand miles as a salesman in the past thirteen years and had never missed a quota.[15] Soon he was the sales manager for a hosiery company, and apparently a forceful one. In its newsletter, Evan exhorted the staff in early 1934:

> Thousands of dollars worth of business is getting away in almost all of your territories, that YOU COULD GET if you planned your work right and *then went after it* . . . You have proven since January

1st, that you were only scratching the surface up to that time and I say to you, that you can have and this Company must have far more business . . . Some of this may sound like strong language, but it's written for the good of all of us . . . If you could see the composite, cross-section picture that I see, you would know d— well that I am right and would DO MORE ABOUT IT.[16]

At *National Review*, his son would sometimes write comparably urgent memos, although more sophisticated ones, about politics.

The elder Rusher eventually got an untitled position with the *New York Herald Tribune*. The family moved to an apartment in Great Neck, near Queens, because its high school had an excellent academic reputation. The *Trib* initially paid $100 a week, roughly half of what Evan had earned in the mid-1920s. But he soon doubled his starting pay and would spend three years there as head of its retail merchandising service, promoting the paper to potential advertisers. He was later hired as president of National Merchandise News, which served papers around the country. Although his career was promising again, it didn't last. Chest pains, which Evan had developed by 1937, became bad enough that a doctor told him in 1941 to quit work indefinitely. After a year and a half of rest, divorced and now living in Oklahoma, he took a less-demanding job at a large retail store.[17]

In his college yearbook, Bill would describe his father as "semi-retired." But Evan wanted to pass along what he had learned. In 1947, he published four pamphlets for salesmen that drew heavily on his experience. His message was tough but optimistic. Over the years he had "learned a highly significant and basic fact . . . that *the average person does not try very hard to succeed in his or her job.*" To try hard, a salesman must think seriously about his humble occupation and about people. "Most of your prospective customers will have in mind an unsatisfied desire, or an unspoken wish, which can be fulfilled through the purchase of one or more items of merchandise. However . . . they will vary widely as to type and you will use different tactics in serving them."[18]

Despite Evan's good sense of humor, he and Verna were unhappy together. Their son remembers much arguing, "always a Mexican standoff" that neither parent won, and believes Evan was probably a borderline alcoholic. The marital problems, Rusher suspects, were worsened by his father's frequent absences on the road and the likelihood he was "meeting young ladies along the way—as salesmen do from time to time," perhaps the exaggerated living he regretted later. The couple considered going their separate ways as early as 1931, when Bill turned eight. By the time they brought him to Princeton in 1940, they were in the process of divorce.[19] "He saw how his

*Watton Studios, Oklahoma City, with permission of Research Division, Oklahoma Historical Society*

*Sarony, New York*

*Evan and Verna Rusher*

parents did not get along," according to Judy Fernald, a close friend since the early 1950s, "and I think it scarred him for marriage."[20]

There was probably also an ironic value, as it turned out, in Bill's troubled family life. An admiring talk-show host once asked how he became such a good debater. He thought it had much to do with growing up in that kind of home, Rusher told Barry Farber. Hearing as a child such "constant arguing and taking advantage of the other person's weakness, coming down hard on targets of opportunity," he learned a lot about how to debate.[21] Although his parents treated him kindly, their arguments were "severe and painful to have to watch," Rusher recalled in an interview in the late 1990s. He also learned to appreciate "how peaceful an otherwise empty apartment could be"—which might, he added, explain why he remained a lifelong bachelor.[22]

With few close friends, Bill kept tropical fish, dabbled in magic, and read the newspaper quite a bit.[23] He took piano lessons for a time with "lamentably brief" interest, but the pet fish would be a lasting hobby. At a piano recital when he was eleven, his teacher had given prizes to everyone. Bill received a goldfish in a bowl and would keep three tanks while in high school.[24] As a teen he also had a little dog, a Scotty, whose death would be cause for genuine grief. Bill had "found real love" in the dog, Fernald recalls. "He could talk about him in such tender terms."[25]

The Rushers took the *Herald Tribune*—Evan's employer, but more importantly a leading voice of the Republican establishment, which was driven from power by the election and success of President Roosevelt but still had impressive media resources. The *Trib* was not only a Republican presence in the New York of the 1930s but also a genteel one that provided outstanding cultural coverage. No other American paper matched its "stringency of critical standards, quality of critical writing, or range of critical assessment."[26] Appropriately for a *Herald Tribune* family, Verna would introduce Bill to a lifelong enjoyment of the opera by taking him on New Year's Day 1940 to a matinee performance of *Rigoletto* at the Old Met starring Lily Pons, Lawrence Tibbett, and Jussi Björling. "I was knocked out by it," Rusher remembers. "I just loved it. And I got the Red Seal Victor recordings and branched out, and got to know a little bit more about Italian opera, and have loved it ever since."[27]

## Behind-the-Scenes Skills

By 1936, when Bill began paying close attention to politics, the *Herald Tribune* had toned down the Republican bias in its news pages. But stories about GOP presidential candidate Alf Landon tended to get better placement than ones about Roosevelt, and the paper ran a column by one of Landon's organizers. With gentle yet "unmistakably" barbed ridicule, notes Richard Kluger in his history of the *Trib*, its Pulitzer Prize–winning cartoonist "continually chided the Roosevelt administration for alleged shackling of big business, subservience to organized labor, handouts to the idle and undeserving, and usurpation of libertarian values."[28] The paper also featured the column of the classic pundit-intellectual Walter Lippmann. Bill followed it devoutly and thought he might try to become another Lippmann if he didn't go into politics. More broadly, he accepted the *Trib*'s editorial line: mild conservatism on domestic issues plus an internationalism at odds with midwestern Republican isolationism. He developed a sense that the world was in deep trouble, along with a desire to express himself publicly. By 1938, he was writing "Americanism editorials" for the school paper.[29]

Rusher's first real political memory is the 1936 election. His father believed the badly mistaken *Literary Digest* poll, betting a hat on Landon, the Kansas governor whom the Republicans had nominated, while many of the town's residents wore Landon buttons. Roosevelt's forty-six-state triumph hit Bill hard, especially since the candidate came from his mother's hometown. The next day he could barely drag himself to school. "I guess," Rusher said more than sixty years later, "I'm still fighting the election of 1936 in some ways."[30]

Great Neck, a respectable suburb on the north side of Long Island, was strongly Republican. Bill enrolled in its high school at age thirteen in the fall of 1936. He was a year younger than most freshmen, having skipped second grade, but more adult in his interests.[31] Another freshman, Tom Farmer, also thirteen, shared his fascination with politics. Tom was a staunch liberal Democrat, one of the school's few, but the boys had a lot in common. They were both "very much eggheads," Farmer recalls, and there was "nobody else I had ever met who was that focused on ideas and on moving toward certain targets." They became friends and allies, with an emphasis on the latter. Although Farmer remembers "a lot of time talking about what was happening in Europe, arguing about the New Deal, and maneuvering our various little high-school schemes," he didn't hear about Bill's family difficulties, meet his parents, or visit his home. His friend was "very private . . . We had no social contact other than that. Maybe strange, but that's the way it was."[32]

The schemes were mostly to influence whoever their classmates might elect to student office. Neither of them tried to become class president. "I think we both realized that our skills were sort of behind-the-scenes skills . . . and we both knew we weren't the kind of person that people would vote for." Instead, according to Farmer, they provided the candidates with a kind of "intellectual mentorship." They campaigned for people, "got them to be somewhat indebted to us, and then helped tell them what the issues were."[33] Bill became secretary-treasurer of the school debating society, called the Filibusters; president of the student bank; and active in the student senate.[34] Alongside his Democratic buddy, he coedited the school paper, produced by "a good bunch of kids," Farmer recalls, who "worked like hell." Eager to raise the intellectual quality of the *Great Neck Guidepost*, they learned a political lesson when they decided football belonged in the sports section at the end. After the story on the Great Neck–Port Washington game was placed on the back page, a "public outcry" made them restore sports to the front. "There was always a somewhat anti-establishment view in Bill . . . even in high school. Because we were clearly not 'establishment.' The establishment was the football team and the cheerleaders . . . and Bill was always quite 'anti' that."[35]

Rusher took something of a lead in their partnership. "I think Bill was the teacher, but I was an eager student," Farmer says, "and my mother thought he was a bad influence on me—that he was too Machiavellian and too scheming." It was from a teenaged Rusher that he first heard the saying "An honest politician is one who, when bought, stays bought." Bill said it "without any sort of disapproval. And that made a big impression on me. My father was very idealistic and never talked about politics in those terms."[36]

The 1940 yearbook described Bill as "eloquent . . . intelligent . . . an unwavering Republican" with a "natural aversion to radicals." Although he was busy with extracurricular activities and doesn't believe he worked espe-

cially hard in classes, he once surprised a teacher by translating the Gettys-
burg Address into Latin. Rusher's grades were very strong, and he got into
Princeton without legacy status, choosing it over Colgate in upstate New
York, the only other university to which he applied.[37]

## An Air of Affairs

Although Great Neck High had an impressive reputation, very few of its
alumni attended the most prestigious Ivy League institutions, which were
still "considered too upper-upper class," Farmer notes. "Great Neck was
not Greenwich." Others went to the Princetons and Harvards, but nearly
all were from prep schools, and "we'd never meet them."[38] Rusher's college
years were a financially difficult time for his father given Evan's heart condition and semiretirement, the divorce, a remarriage in 1942, and his move
to Oklahoma. He had to borrow about $1,000 from two business associates
to help with tuition the first year, asking Bill to visit the men's Manhattan
office and thank them. Rusher also had a student loan, and he earned a little
as a freshman "probably selling hot dogs at football games."[39]

Princeton would provide his first sense of an upper class. Seventy to
90 percent of entering students came from private schools. Still for men
only, Princeton was heavily dominated by "old-stock" Americans despite its
proximity to New York.[40] The full Princeton experience, many thought, was
available only to students in the distinctive eating clubs, where upperclass-
men were served by waiters, hosted sometimes lavish parties, and bonded
with companions of similar identity: bluebloods, athletes, aesthetes. Alumnus F. Scott Fitzgerald's popular 1920 novel *This Side of Paradise*, centered
on the campus, introduced it through the main character, Amory: "I think
of Princeton as being lazy and good-looking and aristocratic—you know,
like a spring day."[41]

The country-club aspects weren't the whole story. Princeton took pride
in its "preceptorial method," introduced by its then president, Woodrow
Wilson, in 1905 as an attempt to stress faculty contact with students, guarantee many small classes, and emphasize readings at least as much as lectures. Another reformist president, Harold Dodds, wanted more students
from public schools, so in 1940 objective tests replaced the old curriculum-
based admission exams, improving public-school applicants' chances.[42] The
university was also intimately tied to the American founding. Princeton in
its early days was led by the Reverend John Witherspoon, a signer of the Declaration of Independence. Owing partly to Witherspoon's emphasis on public life, the College of New Jersey, as it was originally named, produced many

high officeholders. The Constitutional Convention included nine alumni, more than from any other college. Princeton then seemed to be "a seminary of statesmen rather than a quiet seat of academic learning," Wilson said in an address at the 150th-anniversary ceremonies, and if it was to serve the nation well in modern times too, "an air of affairs should be admitted to all its classrooms."[43] In keeping with Wilson's vision, Princeton set up the School of Public and International Affairs in 1930, its goal to prepare students for public careers.

Rusher enrolled there, majoring in politics. He became active in the distinguished American Whig–Cliosophic Society, which included a senate, a guest speakers' program, and the debate team. But such interests brought little popularity at Princeton. "Everybody was a Republican to speak of, but you didn't do much about it. It 'wasn't done' to be as involved in politics as I was, either in national politics or simply Whig-Clio and its machinations internally . . . That was disapproved." As classmate Ted Meth recalls: to be on a debate team, in the student senate, or in Whig-Clio at all was "either déclassé or on the edge of it."[44]

Conformity and not getting excited were powerful traditions. "There was an expression at Princeton at the time," Meth notes. "The person that was favored had a kind of 'studied ease,'" a demeanor also known as white-shoe. Meth complied, while "Bill was . . . more powerfully inner-directed than to do that."[45] Many years later, Rusher ran across a quotation of Napoleon's "which I sort of adopted: '*Je n'aime pas beaucoup les femmes, ni les jeux . . . Je suis tout à fait un être politique.*'" In English: "I'm not very fond of women or games . . . I am entirely a political being," or as Rusher translates it: "I am 100 percent a political animal." In his sophomore year, the mysterious selection process for eating clubs produced only an invitation from the not very prestigious Court Club. He accepted and took his meals there.[46]

In terms of his overriding interest, Rusher thrived at Princeton even though he was not a big man on campus in the sense of having a large number of friends. In some respects, Princeton was a difficult match, but he remained mostly undiscouraged. "He was sort of a loner in a way, and yet he reached out in a political sense and made friends there," notes Konrad Mueller, a roommate their junior year. "The more I got interested in these things," Rusher says, "the harder I tried to persuade people and the more people I managed to persuade."[47]

Despite an antipolitical mind-set among most students, Princeton offered good opportunities to the politically inclined. Debate had a long heritage and sizable participation. Whig-Clio was the oldest debating club in the United States, descended from the American Whig Society founded in 1769 and the Cliosophic Society formed a year later. The young James

Madison honed such skills at Princeton. The organization met in Whig Hall, a late-nineteenth-century neoclassical building that resembled a Greek temple.[48] The senate's self-chosen membership gathered weekly in this august setting. Rusher was its majority leader as a sophomore and junior. He functioned well as a student legislator, according to Mueller, and could deal with situations effectively as they arose.[49] A profile of him the semester before graduation claimed that a Whig-Clio rival, Wally Williamson, had established a club for Rusher's "former foes," now in the lowly status of "museum piece politicians."[50]

Meth remembers Rusher as a "stupendously good debater" although irritatingly rigid: "If the proposition he is favoring is 'All ships should have sails'—god damn it, that is it." Actual subjects included socialized medicine, "the union question," Lend-Lease, and international relations after the war.[51] Princetonians competed with teams from colleges along the East Coast, including Harvard and Yale in a yearly Triangular Debate. Rusher performed well from the beginning, winning top honors in the freshman competition. Later he was the First Junior Orator Medalist, a member of the Woodrow Wilson Honorary Debate Panel, and the manager of the Princeton debate team. As a finalist in the National Intercollegiate Radio Prize Debates, he got early experience speaking to the general public.[52]

Rusher also served as executive secretary of Whig-Clio and headed its speakers' panel, in addition to becoming vice president of the student senate. Before graduation, the Class of 1944 chose him as Biggest Politician. He was a politician in the loose sense only, however. Trying for the highest spot, senate president, he made the mistake of letting his ambition show. "I didn't have any knack for saying: 'I don't know if I really want this job,' and the other thing, 'I want to spend more time with my family,' that politicians say. I just went out gung-ho, and that generated opposition."[53]

As a freshman in 1940, Rusher was in good company backing Willkie for president. Eighty-three percent of the undergraduates preferred the challenger to Roosevelt in a *Daily Princetonian* straw ballot. Rusher's vigorously interventionist stance, which went beyond the "aid short of war" position taken by Roosevelt and Willkie, was controversial. When the war started in 1939, he "became a passionate 'interventionist,' eager for America to enter the fray." In 1940, he joined the Committee to Defend America by Aiding the Allies. In 1941, finding the organization to be disappointingly "pallid stuff," Rusher switched to the Fight for Freedom Committee.[54] Isolationist Princetonians, meanwhile, sometimes joined the America First Committee. When a large anti-intervention rally addressed by Socialist Party leader Norman Thomas and Republican senator Gerald Nye of North Dakota, two of the most prominent isolationists, was held on campus in February 1941,

Rusher attended the lively "battery and counter-battery" event, "booing and asking difficult questions."[55] Late in life, Rusher would explain that he believed America should enter the war "before Hitler consolidated his hold on the continent and, with the help of the Japanese, penned us in the Western hemisphere and began nibbling away at Argentina and Chile, both of which were rife with Nazi sympathizers."[56]

The interventionist position was less common at Princeton than support for Willkie. Insistent hawkishness, even strong empathy with Britain, were far from prevalent at the mostly WASP institution. Ironically, Rusher's paternal ancestry, like all of Wendell Willkie's, was German. The keenly felt division over war policy at the time produced no simple pattern, despite the mostly isolationist views among Republicans and the issue's ethnic and cultural overtones. Although isolationism is often associated with pre–Cold War conservatives, many liberals and leftists opposed intervention, while many moderate Republicans favored it.[57] Opinions on the issue did not predict later foreign-policy standpoints. William F. Buckley Jr. (two and a half years younger than Rusher) was an isolationist, as were his parents and siblings. Among Rusher's other near contemporaries who supported the isolationist cause were John F. Kennedy, Gerald Ford, Sargent Shriver, and Gore Vidal.[58]

Rusher had other minuses at Princeton in addition to his political intensity and public-school background. "Many people felt, and I did too, that he often was pompous," Meth recalls. "He chose his words with care, but he appeared to be doing that . . . This was an environment where you weren't supposed to be making an effort."[59] A middle-aged Rusher would admit that in his college years, he had been the "'common Whig-Clio type—largely humorless, politics-absorbed, officious, over-mature, and detached from the life of the masses.'"[60] At the same time, he cultivated a youthful version of the high tastes for which he was later noted among conservatives—also taking up cigarettes in his second year at the rate of two packs a day. Rusher wasn't stylish in dress but was nonetheless "born a Tory," Meth remembers. "He liked the world of red baize and polished brass." Also notable was an aptness for the right words at the moment. In a billiard game once, Meth missed a three-cushion shot he confidently expected to make. "Brilliantly conceived, miserably executed," Rusher announced. It was an uplifting barb, characteristic of Bill, that "gave a certain elegance to the whole thing."[61]

In a similar spirit, perhaps, Rusher had close friends somewhat to his left. In his sophomore year he roomed with Stan Cleveland, a graduate of Andover and a fellow politics major active in Whig-Clio and the senate leadership. Another friend who considered himself a Democrat was Konrad Mueller, who came from Germany and had a Jewish mother, experiencing the anti-Semitic discrimination of the Nazi regime as a child. The family knew it should leave, and in 1936 his father, who worked for I. G. Farben, arranged a transfer to New York. Mueller was a history major, a Whig-Clio member, and president of the International Relations Club. Another commonality with Rusher was his conviction that the United States should get involved in the war.[62]

On Sunday, December 7, 1941, Rusher lay on a couch in his room in Brown Hall, reading *The Bottlenecks of Business* by Thurman Arnold, a book assigned for his economics class. "The guys next door had tuned their radio to a football game, which was annoying but endurable." An announcer kept interrupting to say something about Pearl Harbor. Rusher finally turned on his own radio and heard the news.[63] As Republican leader in the campus senate and chairman of its foreign-relations committee, he introduced a resolution to declare war on "the Empire of Nippon," which passed unanimously. He also offered the same resolutions against Germany and Italy, which hadn't yet declared war on the United States, but those were defeated.[64] The senior yearbook eventually made light of it all:

> It must be admitted . . . that Pearl Harbor offered a sparkling contrast to a rather drab football season. There was no marked hysteria, but the occasion presented a golden opportunity to burn Economics textbooks. According to the *Daily Prince*, the war bonfire was the biggest since the previous spring. So it can be seen that the event did have some effect on campus life. Nor can we forget that the Princeton Senate called an emergency meeting and declared war even before the United States.
>
> Hardly anybody in the class left college immediately. We were too busy with preparations for joining eating clubs.[65]

Within days, Princeton officials drew up a wartime plan that compacted four years of study into three, adding summer courses and more work during the regular terms. Rusher would graduate in 1943 with what was called the Class of 1944, just short of his twentieth birthday. He had experienced no special inspirations among the professors and no dramatic intellectual turning points. His best grades were in politics, history, and English, often ranking in the first group out of seven (Princeton having no letter grades at the time). He did not excel in the ROTC military-science classes, earning only "fair" and "passing" marks.[66] Princeton annals would set him down as a jawing politico. In the Class Day variety show at commencement time:

> Stan Cleveland and Bill Rusher held forth in their favorite sport of oratory (or shooting off the mouth, depending on which side of the

fence you are) on the subject "What is Love?" About the middle of
Rusher's gallant plea for the platonic conception, both were firmly
gagged and shot through the heart, to the consternation of none
save themselves. Whig-Clio lodged a protest and called a special
meeting of the Senate immediately. Quicker than after Pearl Harbor, no kiddin'.

Rusher seems not to have overreacted to this kind of ribbing. "My feeling is that he was bothered by it," Meth says, "but that he had bigger things
to do with his life than to let that bother him altogether." As Mueller puts it,
"He was his own man."[67]

## Progressive Republican

It was at Princeton that Rusher wrote his first sustained political analysis, a
senior thesis titled "The Progressive Element in the Republican Party From
1936 to the Present." He began by asserting a point that would later prove
fundamental to both his public commentary and the perspective he urged
upon *National Review* colleagues. A democratic people's political direction,
Rusher wrote, must stem from the "practical convictions of its major parties" rather than "lofty ideals proclaimed in the pulpit or on the rostrum."
He believed the Republicans' convictions had proved badly impractical in
recent years, not only detached from public opinion, but a threat to their
survival as a major party. Fortunately, the GOP recognized its problem and
became "progressive," moving from electoral disaster to renewed vigor after
1936 in a "long and toilsome climb back to national respect."[68]

The "ideological revolution" it had taken to accomplish that, according
to Rusher, was a return to the honorable Republican tradition of progressivism. This was not Theodore Roosevelt's Progressive Party or the broader
movement under that label. It was not a movement but simply the concept of
looking ahead and responding realistically to things. Theoretically a conservative could also be a progressive, because progressivism defied placement
on the right-left spectrum. "It is not a political standpoint at all," Rusher
explained, "but a state of mind." Progressivism "favors moral and material
progress. It connotes activity, movement forward, constructive processes."
The most progressive periods in Republican history were the party's greatest
ones, coinciding with its support for the westward movement, the Panama
Canal, and America's assumption of world-power status.[69]

A long time had passed since these greatest periods. The victories of
Warren Harding, Calvin Coolidge, and Herbert Hoover in the 1920–28

presidential elections had "effectively silenced the progressive Republicans." Even after the electoral collapse of 1932, which brought in FDR and a heavily Democratic Congress, "ultra-conservative elements" still held much power in the party. A nonprogressive outlook plus "aging and inadequate leadership" caused an even worse performance in 1936, when the Republicans sank to historic lows in the presidential vote and the legislative branch.[70]

Rusher—who had excitedly followed the Landon campaign seven years before—now wrote with more detachment that Landon's "picayune criticisms and petty carping" got him nowhere. Roosevelt and the Democrats racked up enormous majorities because the people were generally well pleased "with four years of the New Deal, and unsatisfied with petty Republican quibbling as a substitute for a forthright alternative program." To satisfy this electorate, the party needed to shake off a "poisonous paralysis." By 1943, it had done so—with huge gains in the last two midterm elections, many forward-looking Republicans now holding office, and the progressive Willkie's inspiring presidential campaign, which won far more votes than Landon's. Rusher dedicated his thesis to Willkie, "the tireless and far-seeing statesman under whose leadership the Republican Party found itself again."[71]

In seeming contrast to his view that progressivism was nonideological, Rusher said the party in the 1930s had needed "a more liberal domestic policy." On the merits as well as for political reasons, he urged that Republicans seek to "preserve and expand the opportunities for economic betterment without which liberty is at best a hollow prize." American foreign policy should help in "constructing a world in which peace and prosperity can prevail," so Republicans should "become the standard-bearers" of international progress as well. Arguing more pragmatically, Rusher cited a 1939 Gallup poll in which 55 percent of Republican voters said the GOP should take a more "liberal" position in the next campaign than it had in 1936.[72] He also pointed out that in early 1940, the party's designated Program Committee had issued a document conceding that Roosevelt's expanded government must be accepted at least in the broadest sense, while criticizing much of the New Deal and proposing various partial alternatives. It was a "competent summary of the things all intelligent Republicans had come to accept and indeed to espouse."[73]

Rusher, who had preferred Willkie for the nomination largely on foreign policy grounds, says he would, if old enough, have voted reluctantly for Roosevelt if someone else were the Republican candidate. But he saw much to like in Thomas Dewey, just thirty-eight years old in 1940 and already nationally known as a gangster-busting district attorney. Dewey "prosecuted the New Deal as though it were a criminal," Rusher wrote, "piling up irresistible mountains of logic, lancing it with swift strokes of sarcastic humor, annihilating it with cavalry charges of oratory. Under his spell Republicans felt the thrill of the chase again—they lifted their heads high as they had not done for older and more experienced leaders in years." He also credited Willkie as a good partisan for waging "an offensive against the whole philosophy underlying the New Deal."[74]

The latter comment is no longer obvious, and some Republicans would have disputed it even then. Willkie is sometimes remembered as a "me-too" liberal Republican who disagreed little with Roosevelt on either domestic or foreign policy. But to an extent, this inaccurately reads his post-1940 politics into his presidential campaign. In 1940, he made substantial anti–New Deal arguments.

In a widely noticed magazine article, Willkie charged that the New Deal had "extended government power far beyond the limits carefully worked out by the founders" of America's constitutional system. This "huge centralized government" was not progressive but primitive, a dangerous throwback. The worse abuses often came from the new federal executive commissions—unelected bodies with "literally immeasurable power." It was a troubling new system in which a small number of bureaucrats "make the laws for industry, prosecute the violaters [sic] of the laws, and sit as judges over the violations." Such amalgamated authority went against the Constitution's fundamental separation-of-powers principle. It also meant businessmen needed the "personal good will of commissioners," with government now "depending upon the caprice and favor of a few men." That was Willkie's conservative side. But along with his constitutionalist critique was a belief that American government had become "obsolete" and now needed a "businesslike approach . . . generating opportunities for private enterprise." And his liberal tendencies appeared clearly enough when he urged Americans to accept the welfare state in principle: "Government, either state or federal, must be responsible not only for the destitute and the unemployed, but for elementary guarantees of public health, the rehabilitation of farmers, rebuilding of the soil, preservation of the national forests, clearance and elimination of city slums, and so forth."[75]

In foreign policy, Willkie urged a massive defense buildup, helped win passage of authorization for a draft, and refrained from opposing the "destroyers-for-bases" deal with Britain. But he also said Roosevelt's failure to consult Congress on the agreement made it "the most arbitrary and dictatorial action ever taken" by a president. Late in the campaign, he also muddled his interventionist position by telling audiences: "I want to lead the fight for peace" and "Our boys shall stay out of Europe."[76] In his thesis, Rusher noted with implicit approval that Willkie had tended to support Roosevelt's specific war policies tacitly, not too vocally. More direct agreement with the president, the young political observer judged, would have cost Willkie many votes from isolationists.[77]

Willkie represented a slight parallel to Rusher. Both were midwesterners who moved to New York and became part of it, although Willkie was from a small town. Derided by Roosevelt operative and cabinet member Harold Ickes as "the simple, barefoot Wall Street lawyer," he was, in truth, a strikingly Middle American figure despite his acceptance into the establishment. The wife of a key Willkie backer remembered him as "a big, shambling, rumpled, overweight, carelessly dressed man" with a "stunning combination of intellect and homely warmth." He spoke in "a rumbling bass voice, grating down hard on the vocal cords as many mid-western Americans do," and had "a delightful, instantly responsive chuckle."[78] Much of his appeal in 1940 stemmed not only from his independence of political orthodoxies but also from his basic candor. Roosevelt acknowledged Willkie as his most formidable opponent in thirty years of politics. "The people like him very much," the president told columnist Walter Winchell. "His sincerity comes through with terrific impact . . . We are going to have a heck of a fight on our hands with him."[79]

In certain respects, Willkie had the strengths and weaknesses of another Rusher favorite, Barry Goldwater. His successful drive for the nomination was far shorter in length than the sustained campaign Clif White, Rusher, and others organized for Goldwater. It depended to a large extent on the mobilized resources of the eastern financial and media elites, including the Henry Luce publishing empire consisting of *Time, Life*, and *Fortune*. But it also owed a lot, like Goldwater's, to spirited and often self-starting volunteers guided by confident, resourceful leadership that initially had to work without a declared candidate. Both were straightforward and outspoken, but troublingly proud and stubborn as well. After the convention, Willkie ran a disorganized campaign and tended to work poorly with the regular party, to which he remained an outsider, more so than Goldwater.[80]

Willkie is known also for a classic internationalist tract, which Rusher applauded in his thesis. The book grew out of an extraordinary trip in 1942. With Roosevelt's enthusiastic approval, Willkie flew around the world in seven weeks, visiting mainly the Middle East, the Soviet Union, and China. The journey and the thoughts it inspired were recorded in his hugely successful bestseller *One World*. The vast "reservoir of good will" for America that he found everywhere was "the biggest political fact of our time," Willkie wrote, and this auspicious mood "must be used to unify the peoples of the earth in the human quest for freedom and justice." They had faith in American ideals and methods, but the moment might be lost, as it was after World War I. The United States must show its sincerity by promoting two things in particular: an anticolonialist policy and "the economic freedom on which all lasting self-government inevitably rests." Willkie also advocated that the United States and the Soviet Union—despite Russia's admittedly unfree, undemocratic system—work together "for the economic welfare and the peace of the world."[81] Most of Willkie's recommendations in *One World* were fuzzy. But its thrust was unmistakable. In these new times, international cooperation should be given the highest priority. "Wendell Willkie," Rusher enthused, "was becoming a world citizen." He had

> demonstrated that the horizons of his mind were capable of encompassing an equally great conception of liberty on the world stage . . . [including] social liberty, and social equality—the concept of mankind as one race, instead of a hundred quarreling nations, or five skin-distinct tribes. And it was that concept which added the capstone to the philosophy of progressive Republicanism.

But Rusher added a caveat to this praise. As he saw it, Willkie proposed a "middle ground" between the national interest and the agenda of the most liberal internationalists. Not a "global New Deal."[82]

Rusher wrote his thesis as Willkie, though certainly "tireless" and in some ways "far-seeing," continued to lose steam in his adopted party. Despite his nomination in 1940, most Republicans in Congress voted, often overwhelmingly, against the main interventionist measures. After Pearl Harbor, Willkie turned naturally to support of the war effort. But he also frequently and openly made what many Republicans considered arrogant, uncompromising demands that the party shrug off national-interest foreign-policy principles, even risk national sovereignty, to meet global postwar needs. In addition to his unpopularity with most party leaders, Willkie lost many Republican voters during the war years despite his buoyant personality, strenuous speechmaking schedule, and near-constant public commentary.[83]

Although his "energetic activity" didn't "suit the party bosses," Rusher wrote, it was admirable in "a man who, by all the laws of politics, was dead." By mid-1944, Willkie was probably finished as a GOP leader. Having ended his candidacy for that year's presidential nomination, he was considering the possibility of combining liberal Republicans and liberal Democrats in a new party after the war. Roosevelt too was interested in the idea. But both leaders would be gone within a year. When Willkie died unexpectedly of heart disease a month before the 1944 election, he hadn't endorsed either Roosevelt or the Republican candidate, Dewey. Rusher, by then in the armed services, was not aware of his largely unpublicized interest in a new party. "Willkie would have lost me very fast if I had known it."[84]

## A Quiet War

World War II was mostly uneventful for Rusher. Despite repeated attempts to pass the eye exam, inadequate vision of 20/100 and 20/200 prevented him from joining the Army field artillery as he had hoped to, as his father had done, and as the Princeton ROTC specialized in. "If I can't fight this war," he thought, "I'm going to enjoy it." Among the officer training programs he was qualified for—many sounded dull—Rusher chose Air Force administration. After graduating from college in May 1943, he entered the Officer Candidate School of the Army Air Forces in Miami Beach. Completing it that November, he was commissioned a second lieutenant. Rusher served at Tyndall Field in Panama City, Florida, then at a subbase in nearby Apalachicola as adjutant to the commander, then back at Tyndall Field in the Special Service, where he handled informational materials. Soon the AAF sought Special Service officers with "excellent" and "superior" ratings to send overseas.[85]

Rusher volunteered, leaving at the end of June 1944 on the USS *General A. E. Anderson*. The men were told to prepare for a country with a hot climate. The forty-day voyage in stifling heat on the packed transport ship took them sixteen thousand miles through the Caribbean and the Panama Canal, across the South Pacific, down to Melbourne, south around Australia, up the Indian Ocean. Rusher turned twenty-one as the ship passed between the two islands of New Zealand.[86]

At first he was delighted to be sent to India, having seen only Canada previously. Its exotic quality struck him immediately. "I remember leaning over the side of the ship and watching as we got to Bombay. The pilot came out—the harbor pilot, an Englishman—and he was being rowed in a rowboat by a group of lascars, who have a peculiar kind of fez they wear. And this was the first introduction I had to the caste system." The officers soon learned that Westerners in India had servants known as "bearers" who took care of laundry, made beds, and the like. "I didn't mind it, and I think I handled it very well," Rusher recalls. "But I noticed that a good many of the Americans, who had never had a servant in their lives, really became quite addicted to the system . . . A lot of the Americans tended to boss them around and so on. I didn't."[87]

Rusher was assigned to the Air Force Headquarters, India-Burma Theater, a joint U.S. and British facility near Calcutta. Supervised by Major Layden, "sort of a cracker from Alabama," Lieutenant Rusher worked mainly at a desk. Running a warehouse, he helped to provide troops around the theater with leisure items such as athletic supplies, movies, and music speakers. "What that meant," he explained to a friend many years later, "was that no ping-pong ball moved from Rangoon to Calcutta without my knowledge and approval."[88]

The Japanese had rather ineffectively bombed Calcutta twice earlier in the war. By the time Rusher arrived in September 1944, they were withdrawing from Burma, and the Calcutta area was no longer seriously threatened. Various Allied military headquarters had been moved there from New Delhi because Calcutta, a major seaport, was much nearer Burma and China. The command occupied an old jute mill sixteen miles north of the city, a makeshift headquarters sometimes improbably called the Little Pentagon.[89]

Rusher remembers a mostly relaxed, mostly unenjoyable year at Hastings Mill. He had to sleep under mosquito netting but says a more telling illustration of the experience was that a mess officer there was awarded a Bronze Star for providing shrimp cocktail once a week.[90] The treat came from the States, and had Rusher been in Calcutta a bit earlier in the war, it might have been delivered by an amused Captain Barry Goldwater, who piloted transport planes on the Fireball and Crescent routes from the eastern U.S. When one flight arrived, Goldwater told Rusher decades later, "there wasn't enough whiskey on it to get *me* drunk. That's about the way it was. We knew that you fellows had a luxury run there, so we used to borrow little items from it all the time."[91]

Because Lieutenant Rusher could fly to the forward bases in his supply work, he saw other parts of easternmost India and areas in Burma the Allies had retaken. But during his ten months outside Calcutta, "the theater wasn't any more active than we were. A friend of mine—Paul Martin, a warrant officer, a very witty guy—after one dinner party . . . came up to me the next day and said: 'I have decided what our slogan is.' I said: 'What is it?' 'Dance to Victory.' And that's about the mood a sarcastic guy would have. There wasn't a lot going on, no enemy to speak of."[92]

From the personal collection of William Rusher

*At the "Little Pentagon" near Calcutta*

Although he later became a dedicated world traveler with an admiration for East Asian cultures, Rusher was unimpressed, "putting it mildly," with what he saw of India and would return there only once, in 1964. He recalls an example in wartime Calcutta. Half of the headquarters's drivers were Chinese and half were Indians. The Indians tended to fear driving and wouldn't pass a truck, let alone a sacred cow. The Chinese, who plowed right ahead undeterred, were more to his liking.[93] Rusher's reaction was common. Others, including Captain Goldwater, developed a similar opinion of Indian labor. American servicemen tended to be "alienated by [the] poverty, hunger, disease, dirt, and general behind-handedness," a city planner who had been stationed in India with the Army engineers observed not long after the war. There was a "lack of understanding" of the country plus "general boredom, disillusion, homesickness."[94]

In a letter to his father in May 1945, shortly before leaving the Calcutta headquarters on June 29, Rusher told excitedly of a visit he had just made to Burma: "At Meiktila, I found a real souvenir—a Japanese helmet, with a bullet-hole in it! I'll bring it home to prove that I really was in this war."[95]

# 2

# Young Republican

The next decade prepared Rusher for his role in the conservative movement's early leadership. When the war ended, he was a twenty-two-year-old junior officer who had a Princeton degree, a fascination with public life, and the skills needed to break into it—but in an undetermined way, probably part-time. By 1957, he would find himself strategically situated with an ambitious new magazine called *National Review*. Bridging the gap were his experience as a national leader in the Young Republicans, his deepening commitment to anticommunism, and his growing sense that he was an ideological conservative.

Rusher returned to the United States in the summer of 1945, serving for a time at the Air Force Overseas Replacement Depot in Greensboro, North Carolina. Curious about psychology, he became friends with a neurologist and psychologist there, Dr. Albert Rosner. When his conservative tendencies came up as a topic, the doctor suggested they owed much to a yearning for order that stemmed from an unstable childhood. Rusher thought it was "a shrewd insight" and remembered it. In February 1946 he left the Air Force as a captain, a rank he received upon discharge.[1]

By now he had chosen direct political action over punditry: "I was not going to write, I was going to participate." But assuming it wasn't possible to make an honest living from politics, Rusher decided the law made sense as an occupation. After all, it seemed "most politicians were lawyers." Although he never developed a zeal for the law, he valued his legal education and several years of corporate practice. "Law is an interesting and challenging discipline, and you learn a lot and you learn a way to think. Two lawyers, afterward, one will say of another: 'He's a lawyer,' and they know what he means. It tells you something about the guy. He's not going to make certain types of mistakes." Rusher applied to Harvard Law School and was accepted.[2]

Unlike Princeton, postwar Harvard proved congenial to his activist bent. With a large number of veterans aided by the GI Bill, the campus seemed to have more "social and economic democracy" plus an "extraordinary . . . cross-fertilization of ideas," an instructor there noted in Rusher's final year. The diverse new crop of students, knowing the world was in a mess, energetically organized and attended lectures and discussions. A *Harvard Crimson* writer saw an environment "stirred . . . to a nervous tension reflected in spontaneous action committees, rallies, and pamphlets which bury the average undergraduate under a confusing and conflicting mass of ideologies."[3]

Rusher soon entered into such activity, founding the Harvard Republican Open Forum, part of a national organization launched by presidential aspirant Harold Stassen. The young recent governor of Minnesota, who briefly inherited Willkie's title to progressive leadership in the party or shared it with Dewey, idealistically suggested that the GOP could become a majority through "specific policies developed by an informed citizenry." The Forum would stimulate and channel discussion among rank-and-file Republicans about the positions the party should take on an assigned monthly topic. A major goal was to bring in new voters, independents, and dissatisfied Democrats.[4]

The somewhat passive project didn't hold Rusher's interest for long but did introduce him to a political ally and lifelong friend. At its first Harvard meeting in November, "I said: 'Anybody who wants to join, please leave your name with the secretary' . . . I was talking with somebody, and I heard over my shoulder this West Virginia twang: 'Put my name down there. It's McWhorter. Republicanism is mah religion!' I thought: 'There's a good man.'" Charlie McWhorter signed up with the Forum, joined Rusher's Harvard Young Republican Club a year later, and succeeded him as president of the latter group.[5]

Republican politics in the late 1940s were more promising than they had been for years. But even as President Roosevelt's death opened things up politically, he cast a long shadow, having redefined politics and government in a lasting way. Somewhat demoralized by his hold on vast segments of the public, the Right also took pride in seeing through and resisting its larger-than-life antagonist, whom it perceived as a habitually dishonest demagogue with dictatorial leanings. "The figure of Roosevelt exhibited before the eyes of our people is a fiction," wrote the isolationist, anti-FDR commentator John T. Flynn. Many Americans considered him a "noble . . . combination

of philosopher, philanthropist and warrior." It was a false image, "fabri-
cated out of pure propaganda" and used by a "small collection of dangerous
cliques . . . to advance their own evil ends."[6] Many Republicans thought
Roosevelt had not only manipulated the United States into the European war
but also provoked or even knowingly permitted the Japanese attack. In addition, many believed he had allowed the Russians to establish military dominance, leading to communist political control, in half of Europe toward the
end of the war. In regard to domestic issues, Republicans saw Roosevelt and
the Democrats as agitators and exploiters of un-American class warfare, as
ruthless imposers of vast new federal power, confiscatory taxation, and an
arrogant new bureaucracy. The growing power of an aggressive labor movement worried them as well.

Within a year after Harry Truman became president in April 1945, problems of transition to a normal peacetime economy shaped domestic politics,
disastrously for the Democrats. Also helpful to Republicans in the midterm
election were the first stirrings of serious anticommunism among the general public, as the peace quickly soured and America's recent ally showed
itself in a new light. The war had brought a strangely unquiet peace. A Soviet
Union as brutal in most ways as Nazi Germany wielded its own massive
military machine, perhaps unanswerable except with the horrifying atomic
bomb. It not only controlled much of Europe but also seemed expansionist.

The darkening world climate had its counterpart in fears of domestic
treason. Soviet spies, and American communists who whether party members or not were ultimately under Kremlin direction, had infiltrated deeply
into the U.S. government and civil society for the past decade. In the 1946
congressional elections, the successful Republican campaign included the
issues of Russian imperialism, apparent American weakness with Stalin at
the Yalta conference of 1945, and the toleration of domestic communists by
the Roosevelt administration. Over the ensuing decade, such issues became a
vital stimulus to an increasingly coherent Right and did much to distinguish
ideological conservatives from mere Republicans. Conservatives believed
they simply knew more about communist dangers than did most liberals
and most Americans. Strengthened documentation, however, arrived only
much later. In the immediate postwar period, counterintelligence officers
had become increasingly convinced there was "a covert assault on the United
States," according to historians John Earl Haynes and Harvey Klehr. "The
Soviet espionage offensive, in their minds, indicated that the Cold War was
not a state of affairs that had begun after World War II but a guerrilla action
that Stalin had secretly started years earlier. They were right."[7]

Among the direst voices on foreign policy was one of Rusher's future
colleagues, James Burnham, who would play a central role for decades at

*National Review*. In the 1930s, Burnham had been a leading American communist of the Trotskyist, anti-Stalin variety. In 1941, as a nonideological ex-communist, he had published *The Managerial Revolution*, a widely respected book interpreting new conditions in capitalist society and geopolitics. An ardent Cold Warrior as early as 1946, Burnham now portrayed a challenge to America as grim as the one Churchill's Britain had faced several years earlier. This time it was worldwide in scope. The postwar situation admittedly seemed confusing. Some observers, in the globalist vein of Willkie a few years before, stressed that Americans must develop unprecedented knowledge of many peoples. Burnham demanded instead that his ill-prepared and reluctant countrymen fight a new conflict the Soviets had thrust upon them. Deadly serious although not yet a shooting war, it would determine the fate of all mankind. The contrast between Burnham's *The Struggle for the World* and Willkie's optimistic wartime book, *One World*, was stark.[8]

Rusher too saw communism as a menace and would become impassioned on the subject in the coming years. But Republican renewal, the apparent opportunity to undo Roosevelt's political revolution, was his main interest until the early 1950s. Not a moderate in regard to the Democrats, he could express a fiery partisanship. After the powerful labor boss Sidney Hillman, the subject of FDR's famous request that the Democratic National Committee chairman "clear everything with Sidney" about the 1944 vice-presidential nomination, passed away two years later, Rusher penned an anti-Roosevelt limerick John T. Flynn would have applauded:

A statesman of dubious kidney / Once told us to Clear It With Sidney / But the statesman departed / And Sidney, outsmarted / Went right down there after him, didn't he?[9]

Within his party, Rusher still preferred the East Coast–oriented elite to the Middle American, small-town Republicans. He did not see the GOP establishment as liberal. On domestic issues, New York governor Dewey and most other eastern party leaders stood "well to the right" of the Democrats. In foreign policy they were committed to a hawkish position. Just as he had favored entry into World War II long before the United States was attacked, Rusher now accepted America's new international role at a time when many former isolationists remained uncomfortable with it. Faced with a new threat to the nation, eastern Republicans and their adherents upheld what he considered the more responsible foreign-policy tradition, much as the interventionist Willkie had done in 1940–41. This "tendency to involvement in world affairs," Rusher thought, "dovetailed with Cold War activism rather better than the views of Robert Taft and his followers."[10] As in his college thesis, he also favored significant concessions to economic liberalism—thinking, for example, that "Social Security was probably economically unsound, but that we were a rich country and could probably afford it, and politically had to." Rusher judged possible Republican standard-bearers by their potential with voters, not ideology. "My idea of what was most important in a president or a candidate was whether he could win."[11]

## Harvard Law School

By early 1947, Rusher had lost interest in the Open Forum method of building the party. Passing through Washington while returning from a visit to his mother that spring, he met with the Republican National Committee chairman, Congressman B. Carroll Reece, who urged him to start a more partisan organization in keeping with a drive to create more GOP clubs at colleges. Rusher agreed and rounded up the "most activist-minded" Republicans on campus, introducing the Harvard Young Republican Club on November 4.[12] In a statement announcing their kickoff, the HYRC's founders signaled a distinctly ideological approach. Moderate socialism, as could now be seen in Europe, was really a "monotonous prelude" to totalitarianism. Harvard would now have "an organization around which can rally those students— and there are many—who have 'had enough' of Communist disloyalty and socialist drivel." Quoting the incendiary passages, the slightly disrespectful *Crimson* news blurb added: "The club will also attempt to arouse interest in the ideals of the Republican Party."[13]

The HYRC quickly established a vigorous presence, overshadowing the Conservative League, which became virtually extinct, and a study group called the Free Enterprise Society. It also looked beyond Harvard, encouraging students to form Republican clubs on other New England campuses. Rusher, not one to think small when he could think big, is said to have called it the "West Point of Republican Politics."[14] The club was open to all Harvard students and consisted mostly of undergraduates. Although it had issued a vehement opening statement and pledged "active opposition to Communists and Socialists," its president wanted mostly to introduce young Republicans to professional politics. "We don't believe in rallies and telegrams," Rusher told a *Crimson* interviewer. "We want concrete and useful political action." As the paper said, it was "a Party subsidiary, not a philosophic group."[15]

By the spring of 1948, about four hundred students had joined the Republican Club, reportedly making it larger than all other Harvard political outfits combined. It had a "complicated hierarchy of officers," as well as an agent at each residential house who was expected to find new members and keep current ones interested. It regularly hosted talks by some-what prominent Republican figures, published a twice-monthly newsletter, and participated in a local radio forum.[16] Rusher urged members to pro-mote their favorite presidential candidates as the election year got under way, observing: "It does them good to let off steam." Much effort went into staging a realistic Republican convention in a Harvard lecture hall, which featured state delegations and nominating speeches, drawing five to six hun-dred students. The delegates chose Senator Arthur Vandenberg of Michigan, who had dropped his isolationist views and become a leading Republican advocate of Cold War internationalism. "I'm rather surprised that I didn't, now that I think of it, arrange for Dewey to win," Rusher says. "But maybe I just sort of rolled with the punch and let it be Vandenberg."[17]

The club saw itself as competing with, not just opposing, the liberals. On one occasion its leaders showed up at a Harvard Young Democrats meet-ing to signal its presence and laugh at them. An item in the club's newslet-ter proudly cited the growth in membership, adding: "Have you asked your room-mate, your Republican friends and acquaintances, the man who sits next to you in class? Others have, and that's why the score is rising. But to keep the HYRC ahead, *you* must do your share." When a new liberal group claimed over four hundred, slightly surpassing the Young Republicans if the number was true, Rusher accused the *Crimson* of, in the writer's words, "neglecting to mention too many salient, arguable points."[18]

At least once, Young Republican action spoke louder than words. Rusher managed to plant a spy in the Democratic club shortly after it was formed. He summoned two of his new undergraduate members, told them to keep their HYRC identity secret, then sent them to join the other club. They were to "keep their heads low, attend its meetings, and report to me weekly." One persevered, making new friends in the Democratic group and furtively visit-ing Rusher at night to tell him the latest. In April, Rusher felt speechless for one of the few times in his life when the mole, William Oppenheim, called to say the Young Democrats had just elected him president. Seeing an oppor-tunity, he told his spy to be a good president, but not too good, while await-ing further instructions.[19] At the height of the 1948 campaign, Oppenheim denounced President Truman's "ineptitude" and resigned, adding piously: "I'm still a democrat with a small d." Unaware of the incident's true nature, the Young Democrats took it quite seriously, saying they would bring nine articles of impeachment against their faithless leader. In Rusher's opinion the Democrats "went out of their minds," considering the additional articles their feverish response generated in the *Crimson*. Oppenheim played it cool, admitting that he should have notified the Democratic club before announc-ing his switch to the Young Republicans but expressing disappointment that his resignation "could not be accepted in good faith." In the summer of 1973, with Watergate dominating the headlines, Rusher had the perfect topic for his first regular newspaper column: "I Confess."[20]

Rusher's political focus caused his academic work to suffer, and it "became a serious problem: whether I was really a Young Republican at Harvard, or whether I was studying law." The second-year exams "were tough . . . so be prepared for anything," he wrote his father in October 1947. "But I've given up prophecy, ever since I passed Remedies and Contracts and flunked Torts." The next day—"I thought you'd like to know right away"— he reported his second-year average of 68, a high C. This improved upon his first-year average of 63, placing him "definitely in the upper half of the class." A few weeks later, Evan Rusher, although he and Bill had seen each other only a little since the divorce, visited the law school while on a cross-country trip. When Bill explained his coursework and the cases he was briefing, his father gave him a terse compliment: "Well, it seems to me that somebody has finally succeeded in putting you to work."[21]

It was their last chance to talk. Evan had been a good high-school basketball player but developed unhealthy habits. In addition to drinking heavily, he smoked, enjoyed rich breakfasts, and didn't care to exercise. Once, when a doctor gave him a list of steps to improve his health, he tore it up and threw it away, exclaiming, "Hell, that's not living!"[22] After visiting Bill, he continued with his second wife on the car trip, which doubled as a promotional effort for his salesmen's booklets. On November 8, Evan wrote from Roanoke, Virginia: "I expect the mental excitement of coming East was a little hard on me . . . [but] have felt better and am taking less pills since I left New York. From now on, I believe I will continue to enjoy the trip and get along OK." The next day, he had a fatal heart attack in Knoxville, Tennessee, at age fifty-two.[23]

Rusher graduated in October 1948, after slightly more than two years rather than the usual three because the law school's schedule was year-round in the hectic postwar period. His class rank was 183rd out of 336. Just before graduating, he felt tempted by a job notice from a law firm in Honolulu but made the conventionally ambitious choice to seek employment in New York. "There, in both law and politics, were the highest mountains," Rusher recalled later for *National Review*. "I was only 25, and curious to know if I could scale them."[24] Of the many Wall Street firms he visited, only two showed interest. One was Shearman & Sterling & Wright, the largest and one of the oldest firms there. "The man who headed the litigation department, John Wilson, was . . . to some degree an orator. He liked my background in public speaking and one thing and another, so I had a little leg up in that regard. It certainly wasn't my marks, I don't think."[25]

## Dewey's Party

To Rusher's regret, his job would not include courtroom practice. "The cases were so large that we couldn't possibly afford to risk losing them in a jury verdict, so they were always settled." The most time-consuming was a complicated lawsuit involving a large prewar debt owed by Tabacalera, the tobacco monopoly in the Philippines, to the Manila branch of the National City Bank of New York. As Shearman & Sterling's fact man on the case—the firm obtained more than 1,200 documents from the plaintiff—Rusher had it "in the forefront of my mind" for at least three of his seven years there. Things turned out "magnificently well" for City Bank, their client, when Tabacalera's $2.2 million suit was settled in favor of the bank for half a million dollars, five-sixths of its counterclaim.[26]

Rusher remembers his colleagues as "very professional, smart, able men—all much more dedicated than I was to becoming partners and participating in what was called the Golden Rut." He considered himself competent as a lawyer but didn't work as hard as advancement called for. "The others were working terrible hours; I was doing the minimum." Eventually, Rusher knew he "had not put in the performance" necessary to become a partner. "He didn't care about the practice of law at all," according to Frank Shepherd, a Florida state judge who has been a close friend since the late 1960s. Rusher once noted that he "didn't want to get to the end of his life, and be somebody who was the best-known estate lawyer in the country or something like that."[27]

The young attorney lived inexpensively at the Princeton Club, an old brownstone at Park Avenue and 39th Street near the Empire State Building, for the entire time he was at Shearman & Sterling. He earned enough to become interested in good restaurants and wine, studying the latter subject a bit on his own. He also resumed his tropical-fish hobby, setting up three tanks as he had in high school. Rusher spent a lot of time feeding the "lively, colorful" creatures and maintaining their aquariums. "After a day reading or writing legal briefs, it was immensely relaxing."[28] Common sense told him smoking was unhealthful, and he tried to quit around the end of 1952 but failed after six weeks when he was given a copy of a new complaint against one of the firm's clients. "I looked at the damned thing, and it could have been the Chinese constitution as far as I was concerned. I couldn't make it out." Realizing his mind was "going on strike," he rang his secretary, also a smoker, who gave him a cigarette to resolve the crisis. He was able to read the complaint and kicked the habit permanently a year later.[29]

In his spare time, Rusher participated in the New York Young Republican Club and the local party apparatus, experiences that would acquaint him more deeply with the establishment-type Republicanism he initially preferred but later turned against. After Tom Dewey was elected governor in 1942, the state GOP became a model of strict, top-down organization. Ideologically, it was characterized by the moderation he favored in public policy. Dewey worked hard to manage the state's already sizable bureaucracy and its complex political structure efficiently and honestly while maintaining a good business climate. He slashed taxes and debt but also increased spending substantially on education, public assistance, public employees, and localities. When he ran as the Republican challenger to Roosevelt in 1944, the state branch of the American Federation of Labor endorsed FDR but assured its members Dewey was "no enemy" of the workingman.[30]

As the former district attorney, he had a base in New York City, and his ability to win votes there solved an old problem for the Republicans statewide. But Dewey was in the city, not really of it. Raised in Owosso, Michigan, the grandson of a man who had attended a founding meeting of the Republican Party in 1854, he saw himself as "the talented and sophisticated but nonetheless faithful representative of the men who in the natural order of the world ran things in the small towns and cities" of the Northeast and Midwest. He believed the Republicans were America's natural majority party—and that, as he once said, "the heart of this nation is the rural small town."[31]

Rusher had admired Dewey since he first sought the GOP nomination in 1940. He saw the governor as Truman's strongest opponent in 1948 while also appreciating a kindred spirit. "Temperamentally, I think we had a lot in common. If he had been at *National Review*, he would have lent a certain 'astringency' to the situation there. He was rather meticulous in his dressing, and in his speaking, and in his behavior generally . . . I liked what he said, [but] the very fact that he was as buttoned-up as he was rather appealed to me, I think." Still in law school that June, Rusher attended the Republican National Convention in Philadelphia, where Dewey was nominated, and "cheered him to the rafters."[32]

Best known today for losing an election he seemed sure to win, Dewey was among the most accomplished politicians and public servants of his time. He was a legendary fighter against organized crime in the nation's largest city, then the successful governor of its largest, wealthiest, and most complicated state. In government and in campaigns, he devoted himself intensely to detail. Dewey was the first presidential candidate to have his own polling unit, was a pioneer in the use of advance men, and had already become interested in the political uses of television. As a communicator he was not just articulate but precise. He spoke better English than any other American politician of the time, admitted H. L. Mencken, the curmudgeonly critic who enjoyed covering presidential campaigns. His voice was "cultured and silken, trained by hours of listening to recordings of itself in earlier radio appearances," according to a subsequent biographer, "capable of giving resonance and freshness to the most banal pleasantry—and holding the magical Franklin Roosevelt to a radio draw."

But Dewey had inhibitions and a good deal of stubbornness as well. With damaged front teeth and an overbite, he found it hard to smile fully. Although his neatly trimmed mustache was a political liability, he kept it because his wife liked it. In public appearances he seemed tightly wound, short of warmth. Seeing him at his desk in shirtsleeves, a friend suggested that perhaps the governor should try the more casual look elsewhere. Dewey replied: "There's a dignity that comes with this job. If you lose that, then the office isn't worth having."[33]

Against President Truman's emotional and demagogic rhetoric, he did little to defend himself or convey much empathy with the people. Essentially a "rationalist . . . in an intuitive profession," Dewey believed government and politics were a science. His guiding axiom was: "Good government is good politics." He ran as a uniter who championed a common good that transcended economic interests and identity groups; he also largely ignored domestic communism, although his campaign manager and longtime associate, Herbert Brownell, had publicly said it would be the most important issue of 1948. Meanwhile, Truman consistently slammed his opponent and the Republican Congress as greedy, coldhearted authoritarians who aimed to destroy the young welfare state and would deliberately ruin workers and farmers. In the Midwest, where Truman was gaining, a Republican foot soldier urged the challenger to respond to such accusations. Dewey told him: "Nobody believes that stuff anyway."[34]

Confidence about Dewey's chances was pervasive. Every pollster had called the election for him, and fifty columnists, queried in early October, all predicted he would win easily. Rusher was "astonished" by his defeat. "I went back to Harvard to be with my Young Republicans when he won. It was a ghastly evening."[35] The club had arranged a victory party in Memorial Hall, equipped with two television sets and a loudspeaker. More than one thousand "students and college girls" showed up. But Rusher's successor as YR president, Charlie McWhorter, had promised to let the Liberal Union take over the festivities if Truman was leading at midnight. As Rusher remembers: "*Bom, bom, bom*—here came a drum and a conga line of Democrats. And we stood there, with our beer in our hands, while they snaked around our room. We didn't say a thing. We just watched. It was terrible." The *Crimson* noticed "a small crowd of Young Republicans and their girls, formally dressed, drinking champagne, and never a one of them cracking a smile."[36]

The Republicans had blown their shot at the presidency and lost Congress—which, under their control for the first time since 1930, was probably conservative enough on economic issues to hurt Dewey's chances. Recriminations came from both sides of the party. The defeat was "a good thing," the moderate RNC chairman, Congressman Hugh Scott of Pennsylvania, told reporters as the news sank in. The conservatives on Capitol Hill "wouldn't listen to me. They had to learn their lesson. Now maybe they'll go out and pass some good social legislation." On the right, popular novelist Clarence Budington Kelland, an outspoken Republican national committeeman from Arizona, lamented: "Dewey's campaign was smug, arrogant, stupid and supercilious . . . It was a contemptuous campaign, contemptuous alike to our antagonists and to our friends." His inner circle seemed to be "geniuses in the art of stirring up an avalanche of lethargy. No issue was stated or faced."[37]

This dilemma—too conservative? too moderate?—would fuel endless debate in the Republican Party and on the organized Right. But the 1948 shocker may have shown the importance of running a candidate who could connect better with the public. In a memorial piece on Dewey, Rusher later wrote: "When the voters picked Truman instead, something snapped deep in the heart of the GOP. Evidently sheer ability wasn't going to be enough."[38] For the next few years, though, Governor Dewey remained the most powerful figure in the national party. He continued as leader and symbol of its eastern establishment for somewhat longer.

Manhattan, where Rusher now lived, was a reasonably good place to be a Republican. The local party, noted a writer on New York state politics, got substantial patronage from the Dewey administration and had also, by 1948, become "more alive and alert than it was." Rusher served as an election-district captain, basically a precinct captain, in the 1st Assembly District, an East Side seat the GOP held for many years by maintaining a solid organization. His most important duty was to circulate nominating petitions for the higher-ups' approved candidates. Because this meant a lot of door knocking, he became a somewhat familiar face in his small territory. Although he doubts the grassroots experience was really formative, "you learn a little bit about what Republicans think and how they react."[39]

Activity in the Young Republicans would launch Rusher's political career—and for the better part of a decade, that still meant party, not ideology. The city's YRs in the late 1940s and early 1950s weren't even split into political camps. "Nobody was wildly conservative or Taftite. We were all sort of Dewey people. Nobody was wildly liberal either, I must say." But the club had a sociological and stylistic divide, captured in nicknames, which inspired a political opportunity. The White Shoes, who often worked at large law firms, "tended to be rather suave, and like my prewar Princetonians, just a little bit above it all." The Dirty Necks, sometimes Jewish, were from less-prestigious Midtown law firms and businesses. Neither of these rivals had a particular mission.

Rusher and his fellow Harvard Law alumnus McWhorter "promptly started a third group, which McWhorter brilliantly denominated the Action Faction." It was "more militant . . . not necessarily more conservative, but militant, in our Republicanism. We were more self-aware. I doubt the White Shoes would have admitted that there was such a thing as the White Shoes. I'm sure the Dirty Necks didn't want to admit there was such a thing as the Dirty Necks. We didn't mind saying, at all, that there was such a thing as the Action Faction, [which] implicitly criticized them as stuck-in-the-muds who weren't doing anything."[40] Rusher and McWhorter aggressively sought additional support. Leon Weil later joined the YR club largely because he didn't know many people in New York. "I went there cold," he recalls, "and when I got out of the elevator on the floor where the meeting was supposed to be, there were a couple of guys prowling around looking for new faces like mine . . . They were very nice to me, and we became friends."[41]

In late 1948, Rusher had met a second political comrade, F. Clifton White. Before long, they would lead a small group of kingmakers in the Young Republican National Federation. White came from the small town of Earlville in upstate New York. Five years older than Rusher and a graduate of Colgate, he too had been a college debater. During the war, he was a captain and lead navigator in a B-17 unit that flew missions over Germany, earning the Distinguished Flying Cross. "Watching my friends being shot down in flaming bombers almost every day," White recalled later, "I made a private vow that, if I were lucky enough to get home alive, I would do whatever I could . . . to prevent another era of appeasement that would lead to a third world war." Back home he began teaching at Cornell University and Ithaca College, also becoming caught up in politics.[42]

White's first political effort was heading his county chapter of the American Veterans Committee, a nonpartisan but liberal organization advocating the interests of ex-servicemen. With social-democratic activist Gus Tyler of the International Ladies Garment Workers Union, he also fought communist influence in the AVC and formed units throughout the upstate region.

In 1946, White ran for a congressional nomination. Undiscouraged by his loss, he started building a political base in Ithaca and Tompkins County. He became heavily involved in the state and national Young Republicans— groups Dewey considered important to his political clout—and simultaneously continued his progression in the senior party. As a member of the Youth for Dewey national board, White organized the governor's floor demonstration at the 1948 Republican convention. By 1952, he would serve as an Eisenhower delegate to the national convention and as the state Republican committee's acting executive secretary. He was also a Dewey appointee in the Department of Motor Vehicles. Thirteen of Ithaca's fourteen aldermen in the early 1950s were Republicans, "handpicked by me."[43]

After volunteering for "every job imaginable" in politics, White had seen "exactly what could and could not be accomplished on each level of government" and decided that the real action lay in organizing, not running for office. "My eyes were opened wide when I found out that elected politicians, for the most part, did not know the fundamentals of practical politics . . . Real power rested with the people behind the scenes who planned and orchestrated the entire event. This was perhaps the most important lesson I learned in all my years in politics." White also came to feel a strong sense of responsibility for the survival of America's constitutional system and economic freedom.[44] As a principled conservative who was also steeped in New York's machine-like Republican politics, he was gradually becoming an invaluable resource.

The friendship between White and Rusher may have thrived on their contrasts. Ned Cushing, a Kansan who was elected national YR chairman with their assistance in 1959 and later helped them launch the Goldwater draft, considered White "a little more lighthearted than Bill." Although not a loud man, he seemed "much more animated," more comfortable with the glad-handing side of politics. White was "very nonthreatening" and could always manage people smoothly, Rusher's YR friend Judy Fernald recalls. He could work a crowd without being obvious about it, with a graceful body language reminiscent of Fred Astaire. "I don't know anyone who didn't like him." In contrast, Rusher "could be a lightning rod at times" and had "a more authoritarian mannerism: 'This is the way it is and always was.'" Fernald remembers them as loyal, honorable, and a good team. "I can't think of Bill ever doing anything dishonest, nor Clif."[45]

They became such close friends partly because, as Rusher later explained, in comparison with most of his Young Republican colleagues, "I almost qualified as an intellectual." His undergraduate specialty in American politics had acquainted him with the writings of such leading political scientists as Charles Merriam and Harold Lasswell. Rusher and White, with his quasi-academic background, shared a "common fund of knowledge and interest" that fueled leisurely, wide-ranging conversations during the latter's visits to the city. They also shared a Dewey-like quest for precision and discipline. "We both viewed politics as at least potentially a science," thinking and talking "long and hard about how to conduct scientifically the bid for political leadership that we were—of course—planning to make."[46]

Despite his modest personality, White soon made himself familiar to

Young Republicans throughout the state. In 1949, within months after they met, he and Rusher led an alliance between an upstate YR network and a minority of the city membership. At the 1950 statewide convention, the new coalition won, with White elected president and Rusher becoming chairman of the board. Their vice president was Wilma Sievertsen, like Rusher a city-based member of the alliance. The three officers, she recalls, would sometimes sit up all night "talking about what we were going to do."[47] In 1951, Rusher helped White to elect the new national YR chairman, Herbert Warburton of Delaware, over the opposition of Washington-based party leaders. The first of their five biennial wins in the organization, it was in the service of a higher authority. As White would later illustrate the relationship: "I called Dewey to report on our victory, and he said 'Fine.' That was it, nothing else. No 'Thank you for a job well done.' As far as the governor was concerned, I had done what was expected of me. Anything less would have been unacceptable to him; Tom Dewey did not keep people who disappointed him around very long."[48]

Unsentimental though it often was, politics could also produce and sustain friendship. In YR culture the two weren't easily distinguished. Assembly-district Republican committees in the New York area, for example, held annual dances. "You had to go to these things," Judy Fernald (then Judy Gregg) recalls, "and you had to have somebody take you." They featured big-band orchestras in spacious hotel ballrooms, "lovely big places," and the dress was tuxedos and evening gowns. Judy was often a convenient date for Rusher. But after sharing one dance, she and Bill circled the room in opposite directions, taking many partners. It was a time for "politicking."[49]

## "I Was a *Conservative*"

Playing politics with increasing seriousness and earning a living in corporate law, Rusher gave little thought to the political principles of which he and White spoke reverently in their lengthy discussions. Before 1953, his commitment to the Republican viewpoint was "comprehensive but shallow." But he already knew there was an intellectual perspective, not just a position, to his right. The first such figure with whom he came into contact was the libertarian writer Rose Wilder Lane. As a finalist in the national collegiate radio debates during his last year at Princeton, he made a mild-mannered case for free enterprise. Lane heard it and began a correspondence that continued until Rusher went to India in 1944, expressing a "defiant contempt for the Leviathan state" that was "wholly new in my experience and made a powerful impression on me."

From that point, he found himself interested in the Right's growing theoretical manifestations. Especially significant was *The Road to Serfdom* by Friedrich Hayek, which introduced Rusher to "rigorous classical liberalism" when he read it not long after its 1944 publication and reread it, with a social-democratic response he found impressive for its intellectual honesty, in a jurisprudence course taught by Professor Lon Fuller at Harvard. Also influential was Russell Kirk's history of the traditionalist heritage, *The Conservative Mind*, published in 1953, and his more topical *Academic Freedom*, which came out in 1955. Some of the other leading conservative works remained unfamiliar to Rusher. When Buckley's *God and Man at Yale* appeared in 1951, he read reviews but probably not the book itself.[50]

What captured his interest most strongly was communism. He had considered its psychology at least briefly during the war, upon becoming acquainted with another young officer who was "a big left-winger" and may previously have been in the Communist Party. As they sat in the officers' club in Bombay one evening, his friend reciting poetry, Rusher thought for half an hour and crafted an appropriate sonnet:

> A man cannot know himself, and that is well
> for men are strange, and seldom what they seem.
> Our deepest thoughts are not for us to tell;
> our inward vision is a fitful gleam.
> No star is so remote as to escape
> the restless roving of the human eye,
> yet we cannot discern the very shape
> of that within us which must touch the sky.
> I know a man who sees the world too well,
> pities its poverty and hates its pelf;
> who sees on every hand the signs of hell,
> but dreams not of the devil within himself.
> He has the heart of Abel, who was slain.
> He is a son of Adam, and of Cain.[51]

The lines could have been written by Whittaker Chambers, whose great memoir of communism and anticommunism, *Witness*, had an "immense" effect on Rusher when it was published in 1952. He read it eagerly and "digested it thoroughly." Most striking to him wasn't the author's account of his conversion to communism, his description of life in the party and its underground, or the story of his break from communism. Nor was it the confrontation between Chambers and his former comrade Alger Hiss. Even more potent, Rusher thought, was the "Letter to My Children" with which *Witness* began.[52]

Here Chambers presented a challenging, and to many people unfamiliar, perspective on the world situation. Communism and freedom were "irreconcilable faiths," so radically at war that "the history of our times . . . can end only in the destruction of one or both of the contending forces." If one saw its essence, Chambers wrote, communism was not a peculiarly modern problem but really "man's second oldest faith . . . whispered in the first days of the Creation . . . 'Ye shall be as gods.'" This atheistic vision was far more powerful than the communists' relatively small numbers in the Free World would suggest, since millions of others shared it and thus formed "part of Communism's secret strength." Chambers believed the West had been wracked for decades by a fundamental crisis because to a great extent it was "indifferent to God," actually sharing communism's "materialist interpretation of history, politics and economics." He saw in communism "the focus of the concentrated evil of our time," yet it also had a "profound appeal to the human mind." It was "the central experience of the first half of the 20th century, and may be its final experience."[53]

Rusher already agreed on the importance of fighting communism, but unlike Chambers he had "no coherent world view and no religious beliefs," merely a "respectful agnosticism." But *Witness* was beautifully written and argued, impressing him as "the Alpha and Omega . . . of a true insight into the mind of an American Communist." It defined the philosophical case against communism so well as to make "brilliantly clear why a thoughtful individual might well devote his life to resisting" its triumph. Rusher was also fascinated by the Hiss-Chambers case, reading every published account of the ex–State Department official's two trials.[54] Still, his deepening anticommunism did not lead to a sectarian position at first. His highest priority remained the election of a Republican president, which meant attracting voters in the middle. In the legendary Taft-Eisenhower battle at the 1952 convention, Rusher rooted enthusiastically for Ike. This was "no year to take chances."[55]

Taft's liabilities included his identification with the Republican Eightieth Congress of 1947–48, which Truman had run against so effectively. For the past decade, the Ohio senator had played two roles in the party. He was its most important leader in Congress. He also represented the midwestern, relatively rural, conservative, isolationist, and ex-isolationist side of the GOP. Willkie had defeated him for the nomination in 1940, then Dewey had beaten him in 1948. Although Taft and Dewey led opposite camps in the party, both had built reputations for exceptional integrity and dedication to public service. Both were workhorses, could seem arrogant, and tended to lack the common touch. Taft was conceded to be an especially able and well-informed legislator, much as Dewey was seen as a governor. But campaigning did not suit him well. In contrast with Dewey's polish and Eisenhower's relaxed public geniality, he came across as awkward and shy. It wasn't unusual for an ill-considered comment to get him in trouble. "He still found it hard to chatter, tell stories, unbend with reporters, even to accept the plaudits of a crowd," remaining an "enigmatic politician who could at once display becoming modesty and breathtaking curtness and self-assurance."[56]

The senator's supporters believed it was their man's turn, and theirs. The establishment was equally determined to nominate Eisenhower. Taft complained privately that "the main Eisenhower men seem to be the international bankers, the Dewey organization allied with them, Republican New Dealers, and even President Truman. Apparently they want to be sure that no matter which party wins, they win." In addition to their confidence that Eisenhower would carry the election for the Republicans, establishmentarians also thought the general was a safer bet to continue Truman's internationalist and hawkish foreign policies. Much as it helped to sell many Republicans on Willkie in 1940, a unified eastern faction in 1952 hammered home the slogan "Taft Can't Win."[57]

But many party regulars felt a deep loyalty to Taft, and he was slightly ahead before the Chicago convention. The outcome hung on disputes over the legitimacy of three southern delegations. The Eisenhower forces successfully insisted that the convention adopt a "Fair Play Amendment" and thus resolve these contests in their favor. Dewey handled the New York delegates on the key vote like a true machine politico—first pointing out that he would be governor for two and a half more years, "and remember that." He called the roll, asking each delegate to identify himself and the number of patronage jobs he controlled, then warned that a vote against Fair Play would cost them these jobs.

The Taft enthusiasts targeted Dewey, more than Eisenhower, as their enemy. One of their official fliers urged delegates: "End Dewey's Control of Our Party. Eight Years of *Deweyism and Defeat.*" The governor was "the most cold-blooded, ruthless, selfish political boss in the United States today. He stops at nothing to enforce his will."[58] Senator Everett Dirksen of Illinois, a leading Taft supporter, addressed a "special word to my good friends from the Eastern seaboard" before a crucial vote. Asking the New York and Pennsylvania delegates to raise their hands, he urged from the rostrum: "Reexamine your hearts before you take this action . . . We followed you before and you took us down the path to defeat." Dewey people shouted in protest, and there were fights on the floor. In the gallery, Rusher "booed so long and loud that I had to go to the hospital to be treated for polyps on my throat."[59]

Although President Eisenhower would become a symbol of postwar consensus for many Americans, he was nominated by the most angrily divided Republican convention since 1912. Taft's admirers tended to think their favorite, "Mr. Republican," had been wronged—and more, that their party betrayed itself by rejecting the candidate who so obviously deserved the nomination. There was added poignancy in the fact that Taft died of cancer only a year after the convention. In a novel Buckley later wrote about the early movement, *Getting It Right,* a lonely conservative professor looking back in 1956 tells himself the party had "repudiated . . . its organic leader." [60]

Rusher was a young party activist, not an old academic. When Eisenhower won the presidency and brought in a very narrowly Republican Congress, he experienced "a sense of joy I had not previously known" in sixteen years of watching politics. But the chance to work in the new administration wasn't a sufficient attraction when an official of the Manhattan Republican Party asked if he would be interested in a job with the Securities and Exchange Commission. Increasingly, Rusher focused on anticommunism. It was Robert Morris, a fellow attorney with whom he shared mutual friends in city Republican politics, who precipitated this "sea-change" in his life. [61]

Morris had begun his anticommunist career in 1940 as an assistant counsel to the Rapp-Coudert Committee, a state legislative panel that examined communist influence in the New York City schools. He then entered the Navy, where he did counterintelligence work on the East Coast during World War II, observing what he later called a "gradual national letting-down of our guard toward Communism." Morris met Whittaker Chambers as early as 1941, seven years before the latter testified in public. The ex-communist, then an editor at *Time* magazine, became "a trusted friend" and pointed him toward key evidence against Alger Hiss. Morris warned the Navy, and the recipients of its counterintelligence information, that the seemingly respectable bureaucrat had been a Soviet agent. But notwithstanding "the most precise and definitive reports from us," Hiss remained in a major State Department position. This convinced Morris that his work was generally futile. He quit the Navy at the end of 1945 and resumed legal practice. [62]

In 1950, he became counsel to the Republican minority on the Tydings Committee, which had been set up to investigate Senator Joseph McCarthy's recent charges that the State Department was full of communists. Despite what they saw as the Democratic majority's anti-McCarthy manipulations, Morris and the Republican senators were able to establish a record showing to their satisfaction that the committee investigation hadn't been "seriously undertaken." In 1951, he worked as special counsel for the probe of the left-wing Institute of Pacific Relations led by Senator Pat McCarran of Nevada, a conservative Democrat who headed the new Senate Internal Security Subcommittee (ISSC).

After a year in private law practice in New York, Morris returned to Washington in 1953 and served as the ISSC's chief counsel under its new Republican chairman, William Jenner. A friend of McCarthy's, he had been offered the same position with the investigatory panel of the Government Operations Committee, which McCarthy was about to chair. Morris refused because he was already committed to the ISSC job but repeated his earlier recommendation that Justice Department attorney Roy Cohn be given the chief counselship, also suggesting that another candidate for it, Robert Kennedy, be hired in another capacity. McCarthy said that was what he would do.[63]

Although his committee positions were short term, Morris took them very seriously. In terms of helpful anticommunist investigation, no less an authority than Chambers would observe: "Bob Morris really accomplished most of what the Senator [McCarthy] is credited with."[64] Lee Weil, who met him through Rusher on various occasions, remembers that there was "a cachet" about Morris. "Bill promoted that, actually." Rusher later described his friend as resembling a "typical stage Irishman" with a "hearty, genial manner . . . humorous remarks, extravagant compliments and infectious laughter" despite occasional periods of depression.[65]

Through Morris, Rusher was invited to consider a job with the ISSC or the House Committee on Un-American Activities in early 1953. He found himself strongly tempted, but Shearman & Sterling wouldn't allow such a junior associate to take a long leave, at least for internal security work in Washington. After being elected later that year as a municipal judge in New York, Morris kept in touch with ex-communists and others knowledgeable on the subject whom he had gotten to know. In 1954 and 1955, Rusher met many of them at Morris's East 64th Street apartment, in conversations that lasted late into the evening. They were people who believed communism must be "fought hard and completely. They were not in favor of compromise."[66]

Rusher freely voiced the same view. Tom Farmer recalls that the two old friends, both with major law firms in the city, got into a "rather acrimonious argument" at dinner at his apartment in Brooklyn Heights over McCarthy and "whether I was naïve or not" about communist subversion. It was his wife's first encounter with Rusher, and she became "very angry." Farmer, a veteran of the World War II infantry and of military intelligence, had more recently worked at the Central Intelligence Agency for Allen Dulles, the agency's deputy director at the time. Rusher insisted he was "just blind" and that "the CIA was also soft on communism." Although Rusher doesn't remember such an argument, he agrees he "certainly could have said that." When expressing his vigorously anticommunist opinions, he also defended McCarthy to an extent. "I certainly thought, and said, that the job the liberals were doing on McCarthy was outrageous and I disapproved of it. And I still disapprove of it. I still think it was a thoroughly malignant business."[67]

About 1953, the Young Republican Club invited a liberal guest to speak at its regular luncheon, held at Schwartz's Restaurant near Wall Street. Retired brigadier general Telford Taylor, known as a prosecutor of Nazi war criminals at the Nuremberg trials, now practiced law in the city. Addressing the audience, he referred peevishly to "*your* party" and spoke patronizingly of McCarthy. The senator's conduct had become somewhat better, Taylor noted, "rather like the boy at camp who got the medal for having 'improved most' during the summer." Rusher stood up in the question period and asked:

> General Taylor, we have all enjoyed your witty remarks on the vicissitudes of "our party," and the medal you evidently feel Senator McCarthy has earned for his recent behavior. To keep the record in balance, though, I thought it would be well to recall that the last time *your* party was in power the Director of the Office of Special Political Affairs of the Department of State was a Russian spy, and the Deputy Chief of the Presentation Division of the Office of Strategic Services was a secret Communist, and the secretary of the National Labor Relations Board was a secret Communist. And I was just wondering, General, what medals you are handing out for that performance, and whether you have anything witty to say about it?[68]

A year into the first Republican presidency in two full decades, Rusher was disappointed not so much at seeing Eisenhower leave the New Deal intact—no realist, he thought, could actually expect otherwise—but at the president's failure to seriously challenge the Democratic Party's later "redistributionist and collectivist tendencies." Eisenhower had also accepted a stalemate in the Korean War. Even worse, he wasn't anticommunist enough at home.[69] "My disaffection," Rusher explains, "came largely over his treatment of the McCarthy issue. And the communist issue generally—Eisenhower just seemed, to me, to do nothing about it." The president did try to remove communists and their fellow travelers from the executive branch but chose to "let the liberals off" despite the fact that many, during the Democratic years, had "acquiesced all too easily in the presence of Communists among their colleagues." Rusher also opposed his "quiet participation" in the liberal onslaught against McCarthy.[70]

Among his most vivid memories from the period would be a speech by Vice President Richard Nixon that drew a distinction between Eisenhower Republicans and McCarthyites. The senator exhausted Eisenhower's relative

patience with him in early 1954 by aggressively pursuing Army officials for
allegedly going soft on communists and ignoring a possible espionage ring
at the ultrasensitive Signal Corps research laboratories at Fort Monmouth,
New Jersey.[71] Nixon's nationwide address on March 13 came in response to
an attack by Adlai Stevenson, the previous Democratic presidential nominee,
which claimed the Republican Party couldn't govern because it was divided
between Eisenhower and McCarthy. Much of the vice president's speech
dealt with internal security. Unlike the Truman administration (which had
in fact removed communists too), "this Administration," Nixon said, "recognizes the danger of Communist infiltration in the United States," and
in the past year many people apparently guilty of "subversive activities or
associations" had resigned or been fired. But he then drew a sharp contrast
between responsible and irresponsible means:

> When you go out to shoot rats, you have to shoot straight, because
> when you shoot wildly it not only means that the rat may get away
> more easily, you make it easier on the rat. But you might hit some-
> one else who's trying to shoot rats too. And so we've got to be fair.
> For two very good reasons: One, because it's right, and two, because
> it's the most effective way of doing the job . . . When we use unfair
> methods for fighting Communists we help to destroy freedom itself
> . . . In recent weeks . . . men who have in the past done effective
> work exposing Communists in this country have, by reckless talk
> and questionable methods, made themselves the issue rather than
> the cause they believe in so deeply.[72]

That evening, McCarthy was addressing the Junior Chamber of Commerce in Manitowoc, Wisconsin. He declined to comment on Nixon's
speech but told the audience: "It's a difficult job to pick these slimy creatures
without getting rough. If someone can tell me the gentlemen's way to dig out
Communists, I invite them to come on in, the water's fine."[73]

Rusher was returning to Manhattan from a day in Westhampton, Long
Island, with other politically minded friends. The car radio was on. Thirty
years later, he described his reaction to the vice president's address:

> Usually, on those long car rides, I was a dependable source of enter-
> tainment, often leading the conversation with a series of jokes,
> anecdotes, and more serious discussion topics. But that night, when
> Nixon had finished, I settled into a silence not so much gloomy as
> utterly empty. My friends did their best to rouse me, but without
> success. To me, the speech seemed to say clearly that my whole

eighteen-year commitment to the Republican party had been a mistake, that I would have to cut deeper, and altogether elsewhere, if I wanted to influence my country's destiny in the ways I believed to be desirable.

Such reflections caused Rusher to become emotionally separated from more routine political concerns. By mid-1954 he understood himself not merely as a partisan Republican, to the right of the Democrats, and a staunch anticommunist, but as something new and distinct from any of these. "I was a *conservative.*"[74]

In the next several months, Rusher watched as McCarthy's clout collapsed. On December 2, 1954, the Senate voted to censure him for contemptuous behavior toward a Senate committee that examined his conduct of the Army investigation. All of the Democrats present, and half of the forty-four voting Republicans, supported the censure. Rusher felt so "bitterly opposed" to these Republicans that he clipped a list of their names from the newspaper, vowing not to rest until every one of them had departed from the Senate. Clif White, disagreeing with this reaction, "just shook his head sadly . . . He forgave them. He understood politics better than I did, I guess."[75] Rusher had come a long way from Dewey Republicanism, and Farmer wasn't the only old acquaintance taken aback. "I regarded Bill in those years as a fascist," recalls college classmate Ted Meth, who as a lawyer sometimes represented targets of the Un-American Activities Committee.[76]

A more cheerful occasion came two months after the McCarthy vote. At a Young Republican national executive committee meeting in February 1955, Rusher heard Barry Goldwater speak for the first time. He was inspired when the freshman senator addressed the YR officials at the Broadmoor Hotel in Colorado Springs. Goldwater "clearly represented conservatives like myself, who had supported Eisenhower over Taft in 1952 but now felt acutely unrepresented in the higher levels of the administration." He also came from the West, where "my deepest political instincts told me the future of Republicanism, and in many respects the seedbed of conservatism, lay." Rusher, by now the New York State YRs' general counsel and a more senior figure among them, "alarmed" their leaders by insisting Goldwater be invited to address the upcoming state convention and threatening to resign if he wasn't. They reluctantly agreed. But out of concern for political balance, they had Jacob Javits, New York's liberal Republican attorney general, speak as well.[77]

Another significant event in 1955 was the chance to direct an anticommunist investigation, requiring a short leave from Shearman & Sterling. "I don't think it did me any good at the firm, because they liked to have you exclusively dedicated to it," Rusher notes. "But the idea of working for the Republican State Senate of New York was more than I could resist, and on this subject above all else." At the behest of Majority Leader Walter Mahoney, the Senate Finance Committee was to investigate two appointees of Averell Harriman, the new Democratic governor. On Bob Morris's recommendation, Rusher was hired to run the probe, which soon focused entirely on Isador Lubin, a former New Dealer who had been named to head the state Labor Department.[78]

The nominee had impressive credentials, most notably as the federal Commissioner of Labor Statistics from 1933 to 1946. In that position, Lubin oversaw the government's Consumer Price Index and made it familiar to the public. He was also sent by President Truman to Moscow, where he sat as a representative on the international commission that negotiated German war reparations. From 1946 to 1953, he served on United Nations economic panels. The *New York Times* called him "one of the country's most respected economists."[79]

The investigation developed "substantial evidence connecting Lubin to both Communists and Communist causes," according to Rusher. He was "very nervous" under questioning and "forgot everything, professed that he didn't know this and that."[80] The committee hearing occurred behind closed doors. The *Times* vaguely explained that the objections against Lubin were based on articles he had written during the 1920s in which he favored "nationalization of several natural resources," plus concern that he had been "associated with left-wing organizations" at the time. The Democrats countered with "evidence that he is a firm adherent of the free enterprise system" and had headed several successful private businesses. They also presented letters from Eisenhower and UN representative Henry Cabot Lodge Jr. commending him for his governmental service. Rusher, in contrast, recalls a 1929 article from the Communist Party's *Daily Worker* in which Lubin, back from a trip to Moscow, was reported as speaking at a rally for the CP and blasting "fakers who back the imperialist war plans against the Workers' Republic."[81]

Most of the Republican senators retreated from their intention to reject Lubin, but only after political maneuvers by several powerful figures on his behalf in addition to three caucus meetings. Assembly Speaker Oswald Heck, state attorney general Javits, and two of the party's main local leaders argued that a refusal to confirm him would "do irreparable harm to the Republican cause in any state-wide elections," the *Times* reported. Although seven of the senators still voted against Lubin, none spoke in opposition or publicly explained their objections. The outcome seemed to be a serious blow to Majority Leader Mahoney's prestige. An editorial the next day contended that Speaker Heck, Javits, and others "saved the Republican party, somewhat belatedly and somewhat incompletely, from disgrace."[82] Mahoney was "furious" about the impending confirmation but knew he couldn't stop it. Rusher tried to philosophize, telling committee chairman Austin Erwin: "Remember, Senator, in the long run the truth will come out." Erwin agreed, adding a cautionary note: "Yes, in the long run the truth will come out. But sometimes it takes a long, long time."[83]

Rusher doubted whether he would have a long time. His father had lived only to fifty-two, an uncle to fifty-six, his grandfather to fifty-eight. "Rushers had heart attacks like other people had colds—and they died of them." One pleasant evening in the middle of the decade after a Republican social event, he was walking up Fifth Avenue with Judy Gregg for a snack at Reuben's. Telling of his father's heart attack, Bill suggested that an early death "might be his lot in life too." He further confided to Judy that he would never marry, since things had gone so badly between his parents. It was an unusual glimpse into major personal fears. "I don't think he ever opened up that way again."[84]

But if he had trouble opening up, he had little difficulty in making friends. Young people with similar politics were often drawn to him. Judge Diarmuid O'Scannlain of the Ninth Circuit Court of Appeals first met Rusher while a student at St. John's University in New York. O'Scannlain was from a traditionalist Irish Catholic family, and his father had voted Republican for president since 1940. He had read *Witness* and been greatly impressed. Professors at St. John's inspired a compelling sense of America's positive role in the world and of the need to stop, if possible roll back, international communism. Rusher, who seemed to tie these influences neatly together, was an "extremely impressive guy: articulate, focused, probably the most gifted logician I've ever known either then or since." In addition, he was "always there—incredibly gracious in returning phone calls, being available to meet for lunch or dinner or whatever, always available to talk strategy on almost any front."[85]

Along with his political involvement in the city, Rusher kept in close touch with the Harvard YRs, a significant presence in the national federation. Now in his early thirties, he could provide a big brother's guidance as well as political comradeship. John Thomson, who became president of the Harvard club, met him as a freshman in the fall of 1953 and saw him regularly over the next four years. "Whether it was the choice of college subjects, New York restaurants or what to wear on a date, Rusher always had a pithy suggestion."

Savoring small pleasures like good food, cigars, and conversation, the youthful mentor had also developed a somewhat aggressive nose for quality. At the Detroit YR convention in 1955, where Charlie McWhorter was elected national chairman, the White-Rusher team went through days of "seemingly endless" meetings and caucuses. Late one afternoon, Thomson recalls, it was time for an overdue lunch. "Bill asked if any of us knew of a good restaurant, and I piped up that I had seen a Brass Rail nearby." The one in New York seemed fine. But Rusher, thinking of his own experiences with pub food, remained doubtful: "Thomson, your future culinary reputation rests on this. It better be good." Their meal was a failure, with roast beef like shoe leather. Rusher never let him choose a restaurant again.[86]

# 3

# Investigating Communism

In March 1956, Rusher moved from Wall Street to Washington and the anticommunist major leagues. Again it was thanks to Morris, who was still compelled toward such work: "When an issue grabbed him," notes Lee Weil, "he was very forceful."[1] As a judge in New York, Morris found time for several speaking engagements a month in which he stressed that "the communists were winning." Invited back to the ISSC as chief counsel, he was unimpressed by advice that he cling to the job security of his judgeship. Given Soviet advances in recent years and what he viewed as the inadequate American response, Morris seriously questioned whether "we would even survive as a nation" by his term's end in 1964.[2] Deciding to take the ISSC position, he asked Rusher to be associate counsel, the panel's only other lawyer and in essence its deputy director. Rusher gladly accepted. Especially with his strong convictions about defeating communism, ordinary legal practice even at a high-end firm seemed unrewarding. He wanted to "fight my own battles, not somebody else's."[3]

As much as he loved a good meal and bottle of wine, Rusher was now advocating a demanding level of political idealism when given a chance. A few months before, Thomson had invited him to Thanksgiving with family friends in Scarsdale, New York. Also present was Paul Lockwood, who had been a key aide to Dewey throughout the governor's three terms and was important in his presidential campaigns. After dinner, a discussion arose about the great dilemma in politics. As the others listened closely, Lockwood and Rusher dominated the spontaneous debate. Rusher was "very, very respectful but very, very firm," Thomson recalls, as he held his ground with the Dewey lieutenant. "Lockwood contended, endlessly it seemed to me, that the priority was to be elected 'because the individual can do nothing unless and until he holds office.' Rusher . . . took the position that politicians without principles were at best technicians and at worst susceptible to unprincipled positions if not corrupt temptations."[4]

Considering Morris's offer, Rusher knew he felt unfulfilled by work at Shearman & Sterling, which he later described as "the sedate conferences behind paneled doors; the delicately nuanced letters and affidavits; the silent victories and muted defeats of corporate law practice." He reflected on the fact that just after the war, one of his friends, previously a professor at a small midwestern college, had seen the forced repatriation of anticommunist Russians who had fought with the invading Germans against Stalin. With American and Allied cooperation, they were "herded into trucks and shoved . . . into Stalin's waiting grasp. Some—the lucky ones—had managed to slit their wrists in time, with broken pieces of glass. The rest were never heard from again. 'I knew then,' said my friend, 'that I couldn't spend the rest of my life footnoting Chaucer.'" Similarly, Rusher wouldn't spend his own life "disentangling the silken ropes that cumbered American business." When he told Thomson he expected to take the ISSC job, the younger man remarked that it was politically risky. He hadn't even considered this, Rusher said. "It's the right thing to do."[5]

Rusher believed the communist threat, at least internationally, was getting worse. Although the congressional probes into domestic communism had passed their peak and the American people were obviously tired of the issue, it remained worthy of his best efforts. He was aware that the anticommunist investigators in Congress were caricatured as "smear artists," but he "knew the truth: that men like Bob Morris were veritable connoisseurs of Communism, able to distinguish between the subtlest shades of the numerous creeds sheltered in that vast temple." They also had "a profound compassion for human frailties." Rusher told himself the congressional red-hunters were still "arming America with a priceless knowledge of its foe—'building a record,' as lawyers would say, on which all could draw—contemporary America, if it chose to do so; history, if it did not." That seemed reason enough to join them. "It was late, but I would do what I could."[6] Sixteen years after his high-school yearbook made its prediction, Rusher left for the Senate.

## Associate Counsel

In 1956, the ISSC was the main Senate panel addressing domestic communism. Its official mandate was to look into the administration, operation, and enforcement of all laws that dealt with "espionage, sabotage, and infiltration by persons who are or may be under the domination of the foreign government or organizations controlling the world Communist movement or any other movement seeking to overthrow the Government of the United States by force and violence."[7] The subcommittee's chairmen and staff understood its charter as authorizing investigation into communist penetration of any American institution, not only government.

Most recently, in terms of high-profile work, the ISSC had investigated the presence of communists in the press during the 1930s and 1940s. Radio and television commentator Winston Burdett, a former war correspondent, testified the previous year about his former communist activity and his availability to spy for the Russians in 1940–42. Morris, who was not with the ISSC at the time, advised him to testify and helped to arrange the testimony—also persuading network officials not to fire him for his communist past or for failing to disclose it to them until some years later. Burdett named about two dozen people in the media whom he knew or strongly suspected had been communists. In all, the ISSC subpoenaed nearly four dozen witnesses in July and November 1955, many of them past or present *New York Times* employees. Most witnesses were uncooperative, and many refused to answer key questions by taking the Fifth Amendment. Several journalists were fired as a result of these hearings. The *Times* gave the story extensive coverage, and in January 1956, just weeks before Rusher joined the subcommittee, ran an editorial accusing the ISSC of singling it out partly because of the paper's vigorous opposition to "McCarthyism and all its works." Newspapers around the country applauded the editorial.[8] The 32-year-old attorney would be professionally associating himself not only with internal security controversies but with an investigative body that had recently been burned by bad publicity.

In Rusher's seventeen months with the ISSC in 1956–57, it conducted a wide range of inquiries. He helped to interview Harry Gold, who had transmitted atomic-bomb secrets to the Soviet Union and been a key witness in the Julius and Ethel Rosenberg case; worked on an investigation of communism in Hawaii; and traveled to Europe on a sensitive mission after the failed Hungarian revolution. The ISSC also probed communist influence in New Orleans and looked into possible flirtations with communist political support a decade earlier by New York's Jacob Javits, who would soon be elected to the Senate. It studied the newly available Morgenthau Diary, an extensive document kept by the wartime treasury secretary that shed light on communist agents' mishandling or thwarting of American aid to the struggling Nationalist Chinese government. Other objects of investigation during Rusher's stint were communist control of a major communications industry union in New York, the activities of the Soviet news agency Tass and its employees in America, and "J. Peters," formerly the Kremlin's top spy in the United States.[9]

Rusher and Morris worked in the Senate Office Building, known today as the Russell Building. With their two secretaries, they shared a small room on the mezzanine level by the main entrance while the ISSC researchers, clerks, and a tiny staff of investigators had somewhat more spacious quarters on the ground level. Despite "distressingly casual" methods of questioning at times, Rusher would recall in *Special Counsel*, a memoir of his ISSC experience, Morris kept a pace that exhausted both the senators and the targets. Careful to avoid needlessly dangerous ground, he also had an "unerring nose for the key point in . . . heterogeneous information" and was well able to sense where new and valuable insights might be obtained. The ISSC's research director, Ben Mandel, had long been a leading investigator of domestic communism as well. Having served on the party's central committee decades before, he could talk with special understanding to other ex-communists called as witnesses.[10]

Unlike McCarthy's hearings and the Tydings Committee, the ISSC experienced no serious ideological divisions. The Democrats had retaken control of Congress in 1955, but the conservative Senator James Eastland of Mississippi chaired the panel and ran it in a bipartisan manner. Although this allowed Morris to be hired as chief counsel despite his Republican affiliation, it was not the most cordial relationship. Rusher noticed that Eastland, usually "taciturn and gruff," tended to stare noncommittally in a disconcerting way, and he smoked continually, leaving a large ring of cigar ashes around the swivel chair in his office. Yet he could be genuinely kind in his actions, never spoke ill of anyone, and was "imperturbable" with hostile witnesses. More than once, when Rusher and Morris urgently needed to see Eastland, they learned he had left suddenly to attend a secret meeting with southern colleagues. Also chairman of the full Judiciary Committee, he ranked among the most powerful opponents of civil-rights bills. He voted for the McCarthy censure in 1954 but had come to regret this and by 1956 was actually a good friend of McCarthy's.

Rusher saw some panel members more than others, acquiring an impression of most. The "craggy, humorless" Democrat John McClellan of Arkansas spent little time on Internal Security matters, but was an exceptionally able and hardworking senator. Ranking minority member and former chairman William Jenner of Indiana was the leading presence among the Republicans. A "short, wiry man with piercing black eyes," the zealous anticommunist coupled his hot temper with "one of the gamiest vocabularies" in the Senate. As with Eastland, appearance and reality could differ. Republican

Arthur Watkins of Utah was "grave and dignified," with what were probably quite conservative instincts, but Rusher concluded that political opportunism or necessity made him "painfully subservient to the Eisenhower administration and . . . the liberal pressures that rain down constantly upon every senator." Watkins, it seemed to Rusher, would often stall important votes in full Judiciary meetings so he could get instructions from the White House. More impressive was Roman Hruska, a Nebraska Republican who joined the committee in January 1957. The quiet, modest "square-jawed prairie lawyer with the deliberate manner and the easy smile" worked major investigations "with consummate care and skill . . . laying the legal foundations for his questions like a master mason laying stones."[11]

Largely unconnected in Washington, Rusher lived in a small Capitol Hill apartment just east of the Senate Office Building. In the spring of 1956 he met L. Brent Bozell Jr., a close college friend of Buckley's who had married one of the Buckley sisters. Bozell, with his brother-in-law two years earlier, had cowritten *McCarthy and His Enemies*, a book defending the senator while acknowledging he was guilty of some flaws and excesses. He now worked as a speechwriter for McCarthy. Soon Rusher was spending a fair amount of time with Bozell and his family, otherwise feeling socially bored. But the job fascinated him.[12]

Rusher enjoyed the right to approach a senator in the chamber when business required it, known as the privilege of the floor, and after a while he was "striding quite casually" around the Senate side of the Capitol. Despite its somewhat languid atmosphere, he found the Senate "a busy and knowing place" that moved through its day like a "huge, well-run luxury liner." He looked forward to the irresistible rum pie served in its staff dining room once a week. For dinner he usually ate a "good meal" at the Capitol Hill Club, a Republicans-only facility near the House office buildings. As he walked home, Rusher would often detour slightly, enjoying the terraces and view along the Capitol's western front. Looking toward the Mall, the Washington Monument, and the Lincoln Memorial at sunset, he found it "impossible not to feel . . . a profound sense of obligation." Two and a half months after starting at the subcommittee, he wrote to J. Anthony Panuch, a New York attorney and former security director for the State Department, that he considered it "a high privilege" to be assisting Morris in "one of the many jobs that need so desperately to be done."[13]

Among his responsibilities was assisting at the ISSC hearings, which were covered regularly by every wire service and usually by several print reporters as well. The most newsworthy hearings still drew something of a crowd, including curious Washington residents and tourists. Well-known communists could expect a cheering section and were opposed by a "booing corps," as the Capitol police kept order. In addition, Rusher presented for committee approval the contempt citations against uncooperative witnesses who hadn't chosen to protect themselves with the Fifth Amendment. He also helped with proposed legislation. It was an "awesome duty" to deliver ISSC reports to the full Judiciary committee in executive sessions, where he briefly described a bill and answered senators' questions about it.[14]

Along with the exciting aspects of the job, Rusher was getting his first close-up exposure to media bias. The young Robert Novak, a new reporter in town, was told by a United Press veteran that ISSC investigations were best ignored: "With Internal Security, we never write anything except what happens in open hearing. We never, ever interview Morris . . . Because nothing they do deserves it."[15] Rusher once asked whether their work had any point, given the media's ability to conceal and distort ISSC findings. Morris explained that each subcommittee report went to the hundreds of libraries designated as federal depositories. "When some doctoral candidate a hundred years from now wants the truth," he said, "it will be there."[16]

At the same time, Rusher experienced both the dangers and the paranoiac fringe of anticommunist vigilance when he screened letters and calls from people who claimed they were victimized by internal-security procedures or who told of unlikely conspiracies. He found some cases in the first category troubling, as with two ex-CIA employees who said they had been fired unjustly. Although they seemed to be "quarrelsome personalities and quite possibly near-unemployable neurotics," it bothered Rusher that the vague grounds for discharge—"the good of the service," which in these situations wrongly suggested a security risk—would make it almost impossible to get a good job elsewhere. In addition, the agency's review process, emphasizing secrecy, seemed biased against employees. But more common than contacts from fired employees were pleas from "true psychotics." Almost daily, there came a letter or call from someone convinced he was "the victim of a monstrous plot, usually Communist in origin, and that we alone could save him . . . They would write us (for example) on paper towels filched from washrooms of Veterans Administration hospitals, begging to be saved from a gigantic conspiracy of Communists and psychiatrists." Many claimed they were being assaulted with mysterious electronic vibrations.[17]

In the early autumn of 1956, Rusher and ISSC investigator Frank Schroeder flew to San Francisco and sailed from there to Hawaii. Because of their strategic naval position, the islands had long been a major communist target. The largest factor in this subversion, according to Rusher, was the International Longshoremen's and Warehousemen's Union, "solidly dominated" by communists and led by the procommunist Harry Bridges. For ten days, he and Schroeder spoke with local experts and civic leaders about red activities in Hawaii, working in the basement of the old Iolani Palace, seat of its territorial government. There they reviewed previous investigations, studied reports on activities of communists and communist sympathizers, and prepared subpoenas. Despite the ILWU's great power and a "liberal supply of cowards" who were unwilling to offend the union, the two Senate staff members got many business and political figures to cooperate. These local witnesses would testify about communist influence at hearings the ISSC held several weeks later.[18]

Rusher would not be in Hawaii for the hearings but in the heart of Europe. After the attempted Hungarian revolution and the Soviets' slaughter of the patriots that fall, many anticommunist refugees fled across the border to Austria. Among them was John Santo, who had been a communist and a significant labor leader in New York. He was deported to his native Hungary in 1949, served in its communist government, and had now escaped to Vienna. The ISSC sent Rusher and investigator Ed Duffy there in "that cold, gray November" for two purposes. It wanted them to debrief Santo and also to seek out possible Soviet defectors among the Hungarian refugees. Upon his arrival, Rusher was installed in a fancy hotel room that "might as well have been the set for a Strauss operetta."

At a small coffeehouse just off the Ringstrasse, he and Duffy spent many hours over several days talking with Santo, who feared for his life and his family's at the hands of the communists. Quickly convincing him they were "neither bigots nor fools" and could listen sympathetically, the Americans heard the story of his early communism and U.S. labor activity, followed by his deflated hopes to do meaningful work for the Hungarian people's republic. A post in the communist bureaucracy and life in Budapest had been a "long lesson in disillusion." Now Santo wished to return to America and tell its working class that communism was a fraud, a betrayal. He didn't wish to name names but eventually decided he would. The ISSC staffers promised to recommend strongly that he be allowed back into the United States at least for subcommittee testimony. Then, perhaps, he could get permanent residency.

Rusher thought Santo's information about communist activity in American labor some fifteen years before was just marginally useful. But he had been a major communist, and he was eager to denounce his former ideology. Like Duffy and later Morris, Rusher believed "the door should not be slammed shut against such a man. Not only for his sake, but as an example to all the others like him who might ... be watching his case and assessing developments in it as a guide to their own conduct." Santo was finally permitted to return in 1963. Speaking at length to HUAC about his years in the Hungarian regime, he was almost totally silent about his communist career in the U.S.[19]

As for Russians, might there be some—deserting soldiers or political commissars, perhaps—who crossed the border with the fleeing Hungarians? The American intelligence chief in Vienna said there was only one Soviet defector, a Red Army draftee who knew nothing of interest. The investigators visited the opera, the cathedral, and the imperial palace outside the city but continued to take in the unforgettable situation around them. As Rusher wrote a decade later: "Vienna . . . throbbed with sympathy for the thousands upon thousands of refugees who clogged its bureaucratic hallways, its charities and its makeshift soup kitchens—families and broken pieces of families, often with no clothes other than those on their backs, and hungry, always hungry."

They embarked on a tour of refugee camps. At one, Traiskirchen, Rusher noted the lightbulbs hanging limply from the ceiling of the dormitory, where in "row upon row of triple-decker bunks . . . the refugees were preparing to settle down for the night: men, women and children all scrambled together, clutching what few pitiful belongings they had been able to bring with them from Hungary." When the Americans' driver got into a conversation with one of them, Rusher thought it crystallized the escape from totalitarianism. "'Pretty rough here, isn't it?' he had asked, waving his hand around the hall. 'I mean—the light, the noise, the crowding.' But the old gentleman was having none of that. 'Listen,' he snapped, 'this is the first decent night's sleep anybody here has had in years.'" Rusher soon heard a convincing explanation of why there had been no Russians in Vienna. An American aid official told him: "No Russian soldier would have had a chance among these refugees, no matter how hard he protested he was on their side. Just his uniform—or even his accent—would have been enough to set them off. They would have killed him first and asked questions afterward."[20]

Near the end of Rusher's time at the ISSC, in April 1957, the panel was plunged into a crisis that would sharpen his sense of belonging, as an active anticommunist, to a beleaguered minority. Morris had been investigating John K. Emmerson, a career diplomat who was then the deputy chief of mission at the U.S. embassy in Lebanon and temporarily assigned to a sensitive post with the American delegation to the UN. After the Japanese surrender in 1945, Emmerson had been a political adviser to General Douglas MacArthur, who headed the Allied occupation authority in the country. He was not an alleged communist but a possible sympathizer. The subcommittee was especially interested, according to Rusher, in the fact that Emmerson had, in late 1944, written a memorandum to higher-ups that suggested a communist-controlled organization be used in, as the memo put it, "reestablishing order" in postwar Japan. In his ISSC testimony, Emmerson admitted having known then that the Japanese Peoples Emancipation League was communist—a fact his memo seemingly was worded to deny: "Its declared principles are democratic. It is not identified with the Communist Party." In his defense, he told the subcommittee it had been written "in the atmosphere of our great concentration upon the war effort against Japan, and our general desire to get collaboration and cooperation wherever it might be found . . . I was not aware [of] . . . the risks which would be involved in collaboration, close collaboration, with the Communists . . . I think that there was a general feeling among many quarters, and some perhaps high statesmen, that collaboration with the Communists was possible."[21]

Emmerson had been a friend of E. Herbert Norman, a prominent scholar of Japanese history and culture who was formerly chief of the American and Far Eastern division in the Canadian foreign ministry and was now, in 1957, Canada's ambassador to Egypt and minister to Lebanon. They had also met once for lunch in Beirut in the fall of 1956, precisely at the time of the Suez crisis. Norman, too, had served with the occupation authority in Japan after the war. In its 1951 Institute of Pacific Relations investigation, the ISSC, under Bob Morris's direction, had taken testimony about his communist associations, and his alleged communism, while a graduate student in the U.S. in 1938. Now it wanted to know not only about Emmerson's policy recommendations but also about his relationship with Norman. The topic was included in the first hearing with the American diplomat, held in executive session on March 12.

It was in this context that Morris entered into the record what the ISSC had learned about Norman over the years, including (without identifying the source) the substance of a 1950 Royal Canadian Mounted Police memorandum. In addition, the panel voted on March 14 to make public the transcript of Emmerson's testimony, and on March 28 it released the transcript of the second Emmerson hearing, also a closed-door proceeding. In addition, the ISSC, seeking to learn more about Norman, took executive-session and public testimony from a Japanese economist who was then in the U.S. This was followed, Rusher later wrote, by "an explosive reaction in Japan, fully reported and ably exploited" by critics of the subcommittee. All of this had the effect of publicizing the ISSC's interest in Norman and various evidence against him. On April 4, the panel planned to question another witness, likely to be uncooperative.

Brushing his teeth at his apartment that morning, Rusher heard on a radio newscast that the ambassador had thrown himself off the top of a building in Cairo. Competing thoughts jammed together in his mind. Norman had been "my enemy, and the enemy of all who love freedom"—placing his charm, intelligence, and learning "at the disposal of a murderous [Soviet] dictatorship." Yet the suicide was certainly a personal tragedy. Perhaps he had killed himself for reasons quite apart from the ISSC investigation. In any case, the crisis was clear. "Would our friends rally to [us] now, or desert us? Would our foes play fair, or strike for the jugular?" Hurrying to work, Rusher visualized "that grim scene in a Cairo street. Now, and no fooling, the fat was in the fire."[22]

Over the past year, he had become optimistic about the subcommittee's ability to avoid major attacks, partly because some otherwise critical observers had commended Morris as a fair investigator and partly because the chief counsel was indeed careful. But the Norman controversy would lead him to conclude that many other liberals were just waiting for it to make a mistake, since they quickly sought to savage Morris and destroy the ISSC. Rusher and his boss now wrote a bland press statement, cleared with Senators Eastland and Jenner, that said the panel could not fulfill "our obligation of presenting a record to the United States Senate" if it "deleted references to foreign nationals" who evidence indicated had engaged in communist activity in the U.S. Morris stepped into the Senate Office Building rotunda and faced a "hostile mob" of reporters. He read the statement and distributed it under a barrage of questions, stoically refusing all comment.

In the United States, Canada, and around the world, the message from "hundreds of liberal megaphones" was that Norman had been hounded to death by the ISSC. Preaching at the Episcopal Cathedral of St. John the Divine in New York, Dean (later Bishop) James Pike accused it of "assassination by insinuation." In the *Washington Post*, cartoonist Herblock portrayed the subcommittee as a "grinning figure with a death's head." The accompanying lead editorial contended the ISSC was "directly responsible for the persecution which may have led to Ambassador Norman's death," adding that the Senate should "at last . . . put an effective check" on its irresponsibility. For a week after the diplomat's suicide, "scarcely a word concerning his published record of Communist activity" reached the public, and even among leading conservative commentators and members of the subcommittee, Rusher noticed a troubling silence. Chairman Eastland suspended the hearings until the crisis was over. But the atmosphere in the office was "feverish . . . The phone rang incessantly, like some crazy klaxon. Friends passed and repassed, with words of encouragement and advice, most of the latter contradictory."[23]

The Canadian foreign minister, Lester Pearson, had stated angrily in March that Norman was previously "subjected . . . to a special and exhaustive security check" that had done nothing to undermine his government's confidence in his loyalty. But vindication for the subcommittee, Rusher believed, began a week later when the Progressive Conservative opposition leader asked a simple question in Parliament. With an election coming up,

John Diefenbaker, who on April 4 had been severely critical of the ISSC, demanded to know whether the government would repeat its earlier expressions of confidence that Norman was innocent. Pearson, once the diplomat's mentor and now the Liberal candidate for prime minister, wasn't easily pinned down but conceded that Norman had once associated with communists or people believed to have been communists.

Within a few days, friends in the media began to tell the subcommittee's side of the story. In addition, Pearson revealed that the ISSC summary about Norman, released the previous month, had been based on the earlier Canadian memo and that the police agency had received a tip about Norman in 1940 from an informant in the Communist Party. As the public could now see, the Norman inquiry was not a smear, nor was it originally the ISSC's issue. The subcommittee and Morris could continue. In addition, it later developed, U.S. intelligence sources in Cairo had reported almost immediately after the suicide that Norman told a friend the night before that if made to testify in a possible Canadian investigation, he would have to implicate sixty or seventy people from both countries—and would rather kill himself. But in the 1960s, the actual subject of the ISSC investigation, John Emmerson, would become the number-two official at the American embassy in Japan.[24]

The Senate job also led to an acquaintance with Senator McCarthy. Rusher met him on about half a dozen occasions, sometimes with Morris at the McCarthys' house on Capitol Hill and other times at the Bozell home in Chevy Chase, Maryland. His first impression in May 1956 was of a "pleasant, soft-spoken, almost shy" manner. McCarthy expressed no bitterness toward political enemies but rather "bewilderment, both amused and slightly sad, at the ferocity of his liberal foes, and at the security policies they endorsed." A gregarious man who had a sense of fun and habitually invited friend or foe to share a drink with him, McCarthy was "a typical politician in his readiness to check his razor (figuratively speaking) at the door before entering any party." The key to his character, Rusher would conclude, was an "ingenuous stubbornness" or admirable naïveté already noticeable on their first visit. "Most politicians, after all, are pretty adept at sensing when to stop riding an issue . . . When it stops paying dividends, when on straight pleasure-pain principles it ceases to yield a sufficient return in praise, all but the most exceptional politicians will quietly drop it. McCarthy wouldn't; and, studying him that evening, I slowly came to understand the origin of his intransigence . . . [It] was a strange and ultimately fatal innocence."[25]

Rusher's last real contact with McCarthy occurred on the day of the second Eisenhower inauguration in January 1957. He had worked most of the morning at the office, "ostentatiously ignoring" the ceremonies a few hundred feet away on the Capitol steps. That afternoon, the Morrises and Rusher decided to "cap our defiance of Eisenhower Republicanism" by visiting McCarthy. The senator and his wife, Jeanie, were in their living room watching the inaugural parade on television. McCarthy mentioned that he had listened to Eisenhower's speech, including "the part about Hungary and how brave those people had been, and how we can never turn our backs on them," then continued sadly: "I thought of how he had let the Russian tanks roll over 'em last November." He "paused, shook his head, and was silent."[26]

Rusher would live to witness a more thorough exposure of communism than the ISSC and other congressional panels could achieve. He noted with great interest that with the opening of Soviet archives by the postcommunist Russian government in the 1990s, recognized scholars were able to document a surprisingly extensive network of Soviet spies and agents in the American government during World War II and the immediate postwar eras. They had learned much more than the various congressional investigators could. "The trouble with McCarthy was, he didn't know the half of it," Rusher says. "And none of us did. When I was with the Internal Security Subcommittee we didn't. It's fascinating to see . . . how thorough the penetration was."[27]

## The Syndicate

Although Rusher took much satisfaction from his Senate work, his Young Republican sideline was a thrill. Right-wingers in the party had remained frustrated and angry in the years after Eisenhower defeated Taft for the nomination. As General Robert Wood, the recently retired chairman of Sears, Roebuck and former head of the prewar America First Committee, told such an audience in Chicago in 1955: "The trouble is that Eastern Republicans and Middlewestern Republicans don't talk alike, don't think alike and don't act alike. All of us here despise Dewey, and there aren't many leaders east of the Alleghenies we do like."[28] But Rusher, White, and Charlie McWhorter were now working across just such geographical lines in the YR federation.

In the early 1950s, the trio put together a new nationwide coalition joining New York delegates with ones from Ohio and other states that had tended to favor Taft. Although White was the architect of this alliance, he agreed with Rusher's insistence that the New York YRs should reach out to these states as allies.[29] It wasn't always easy. "New York Republicans were not well liked nationally," according to White, because Dewey and others by association with him were considered arrogant and autocratic. But White and his two comrades had many "can openers"—informed, well-connected YR friends—around the country. Several years later, the alliance's opponents would call it the Syndicate, a name its leadership and followers gladly adopted. Syndicate candidates, or initially White's candidates, won the national chairmanship at every convention from 1949 through 1959. White and his team took care about where those candidates were from. "One was from South Dakota," Rusher explains, "one was from Delaware. Little states that didn't have any harsh edges to them in anybody's mind."[30]

On similar principles, the Syndicate headquarters were always "rather decorous," banning alcohol in favor of New York apple juice. "Somebody went into the New Jersey headquarters, and everybody was lying around drunk. They allowed alcohol. Like hell. I mean, you can't win a Young Republican National Convention with that kind of thing." Meanwhile, a special control room facilitated calm but timely decisions. "Removed from the headquarters, on another floor . . . there would be a quiet suite where White and McWhorter and I would be. And we would run the convention from there, and do the quiet thinking and the reasoning, and bring in people to talk to and to bargain with . . . It was a very efficient system, and it was well worked-out."[31]

In 1955, Rusher sought a meeting with Dewey's former right-hand man Herbert Brownell, whom Eisenhower had appointed attorney general, in order to acquaint him with the New York–based members of the Syndicate and with ex–Young Republicans who supported them. The group, he explained to an aide of Brownell's, had furnished much of the state and national YR leadership for the past six years. It had "no special ideological flavor, other than loyalty to President Eisenhower and to the general principles of the Republican Party." The second part of that description was soon outdated. In his capacity as YR chairman after being elected that year, McWhorter appointed John Ashbrook, leader of the Ohio Young Republicans, to run the national organization's campaign efforts in the upcoming presidential race.[32] In 1957, the Syndicate got Ashbrook, later one of the first Draft Goldwater organizers and a leading conservative congressman, elected YR chairman. That year's convention in Washington proved something of a milestone in conservative history.

The delegates put on a tribute to Eisenhower, and the 1,500 attendees "whooped and hollered" a welcome to Vice President Nixon, chanting: "We want Dick." But the next day, Rusher and platform chairman Don Bostwick got them to take some important positions. "Mindful of the inevitable connection between subsidization and control," in the words of one such item, delegates opposed the president's proposals to introduce federal aid for school construction. Departing again from the politically cautious Eisenhower, they also urged in their platform that the Taft-Hartley Act be amended to ban compulsory union membership—meaning Congress should pass a national right-to-work law, a position loudly rejected at the last YR gathering in 1955.[33]

The main goal of the conservative activists was to elect Ashbrook, not to make policy statements. Their platform victory, Rusher would admit, was a "maraschino on the sundae," and most delegates probably hadn't thought much about it. But however inadvertently, the junior Republicans had made an apparent declaration of independence from their president. On the next day's front page, people at the White House would read: YOUNG G.O.P. HITS EISENHOWER STAND ON 4 OF 5 ISSUES. As Rusher and company learned later, the president was "mad as a wet hen, and he had a good denunciatory answer ready with his next press conference. Unfortunately, no reporter asked him."[34]

## "Be Part of It"

Charlie McWhorter actually moved closer to the Republican establishment that year when he became a legislative assistant to Nixon. If White was more lighthearted than Rusher, McWhorter was more colorfully so. An accomplished pianist, he was also a jazz and classical-music aficionado. He knew many important artists and spent his vacations at Interlochen, a prestigious summer school for young musicians in Michigan, later becoming a generous patron of the facility and of the jazz scene. There was a "pixieish" quality to him, recalls John Thomson of the Harvard YRs. "He was a genuinely sweet personality. He didn't have an ideological bone in his body." McWhorter expressed his partisan identity with a certain whimsy, collecting elephant figures in many poses and displaying them centrally in his New York apartment for visitors. Eventually they would number in the hundreds.[35]

Thomson, in contrast, had begun to consider what he really owed the party. In early 1956, having been appointed to supervise the young pages at the Republican National Convention, he wondered how he could bring himself to support Eisenhower. Over dinner in Washington, Rusher sympathized with such doubts, noting that he had spoken similarly to Senator Jenner a few days ago. Jenner's response was that Eisenhower would be a lame duck from the moment of his second inauguration. Rusher drew the lesson that conservatives could begin focusing entirely on 1960 once the president was reelected. He also told his younger friend that Ike was certainly preferable to Adlai Stevenson, the former Illinois governor, 1952 Democratic nominee, and likely Democratic candidate in 1956. Rusher, Thomson notes, "just despised" what Stevenson seemed to represent: "the airy, academic, egghead approach to government."[36] Although he successfully advised Thomson to take part in the convention and campaign, Rusher felt alienated enough from Eisenhower and the party establishment that he chose to disenfranchise himself by moving his legal residence from New York to the District of Columbia, which was still excluded from presidential elections. "I didn't have to vote for Jacob Javits either. I had a double bonus that year."[37]

Tom Dewey would not have been pleased. But Rusher's attitude was becoming more common among conservatives, who increasingly felt politically homeless. "Why . . . has the Right scarcely a voice that speaks for it with authority and conviction," Whittaker Chambers had asked a friend in 1954, "or without the curse of faint apology?" The anticommunist icon also complained a few years later to Bill Buckley, to whom he had grown close, about "the sense of unreality and pessimism on the Right, running off into all manner of crackpotism."[38] Self-conscious conservatives also perceived the liberals as having a virtual monopoly on public discourse. "So long as they control the means of communication, they don't have to worry too much about a slight set-back in Washington," publisher Henry Regnery remarked in 1953, implicitly dismissing the new Republican presidency and Republican Congress. Buckley was similarly restless. He had been thinking of establishing or buying a magazine at least since 1952, hoping to lend conservatism a new vitality. The Right lacked even one weekly journal of opinion, while the liberals had eight. "They know the power of ideas," Buckley wrote, "and it is largely for this reason that socialist-liberal forces have made such a great headway in the past thirty years."[39]

In the summer of 1955, Rusher learned *National Review* was in the works while sharing a drink with Lyle Munson, a former CIA agent he had met through Morris. He signed up as a charter subscriber. By happenstance, he came to Buckley's attention early. Roger Allan Moore of the Harvard YRs asked him to write a piece for their new paper. Since Rusher had mentioned Buckley was starting a magazine, Moore sent *National Review* a copy after it ran in early November, a few weeks before the magazine's first issue.[40] The essay in the *Harvard Times-Republican*, titled "Cult of Doubt," impressed Buckley enough—"very well-worded," he recalls—that he was moved to quote several excerpts in his *NR* column on academe, where he cited it as a heartening example of a new disdain for liberalism among many students and recent graduates (although its author was seven years out of law school). Introducing the long quotation, Buckley urged readers: "Get a load of this."

Rusher warned: "The one sin for which nature exacts the supreme penalty of national extinction is a failure on the part of the members of a society to believe [in] its inherent worth." A person need not be actively disloyal, like the communists, to warrant this accusation. Throughout society and in both parties, too many citizens were now "indifferent or hostile" to their country's tenets. Denying it their moral support, they were unfit to lead it. Rusher contrasted them with the "great majority" who were "now convinced that the struggle for survival must not be led, on behalf of the American society, by some doubt-ridden egghead exquisitely poised between Yea and Nay. The world will go—and perhaps rightly—to those who want it most. If it is to go to the defenders of freedom, they must want that freedom not merely in order to doubt, but to believe."[41]

Buckley sent the author a copy of the forthcoming column along with a note requesting "an opportunity to talk with you." They met in January 1956 at the University Club, where Rusher had first heard of the magazine over drinks. Buckley "tried to get me to write articles on legal subjects—the Supreme Court and things like that. I couldn't tell him I was already being vetted for the Internal Security Subcommittee, which I went to in March. Then I called him and told him I was going to Washington. He said, 'Well, consider us thoroughly exploitable.'" Shortly before he was sent to Vienna in November, Rusher accepted Buckley's last-minute invitation to stay at his home in Stamford, Connecticut, on the weekend of the Princeton-Yale football game. Yale won by a sorry score of 42–20, but introductions to Buckley's "spectacularly beautiful and intelligent" wife, Pat, and to fellow Princetonian Frank Meyer, one of the magazine's intellectual stars, more than compensated.[42]

Rusher was increasingly primed for the opportunity to join *National Review* that came several months later. In addition to his "Cult of Doubt" piece, he had written, at the beginning of 1956, an essay called "The Rebellion Against the Eggheads" that extended its theme beyond politics. In it, Rusher suggested there was a causal connection between moral relativism and statism. Most American intellectuals, he wrote, had lost the conception of "a divinely-ordained Natural Law that does not change or pass" and had also abandoned their country's distinctive "contribution to that tradition—the superb declaration that all men are endowed by their Creator with certain unalienable rights, to secure which governments are instituted among men."

In recent years, however, the citizenry had intuitively come to see "the perilous inadequacy of the Liberal philosophy." It was now rebelling against liberal trends in religion, jurisprudence, literature, and the arts. Rusher drew a sharp contrast between the Depression era, which "temporarily paralyzed the critical faculty of the American mind" because people were desperate for solutions, and the 1950s, a time of public awakening.[43]

Among people he knew, there proved to be an appetite for such analyses. Frank Barnett, later the founding president of the defense-oriented National Strategy Information Center, thought the *Times-Republican* piece was a "splendid philosophical essay" and urged his friend to continue writing similar material—especially since "conservative 'metaphysicians' are in desperately short supply." New York State assemblyman Malcolm Wilson, a conservative who eventually succeeded Nelson Rockefeller as governor, wrote that he was "profoundly impressed" and wished to distribute copies "in places where I think they will do some good." Representative Alvin Bentley, a Michigan Republican, placed the essay in the *Congressional Record*.

Manhattan attorney Anthony Panuch, the former State Department security director, wrote that in view of the threat from the "Fifth Column" in America: "The country is fortunate that the post war vintage of true Republicans includes articulate young men of your patriotism and crusading energy who are spearheading the renascence of the enduring values that made this nation great. Keep punching."[44] In a lighter spirit, a former Shearman & Sterling colleague saw the excerpt from "Cult of Doubt" in *NR* and, he teased Rusher, was sufficiently moved by its criticism of intellectuals that he "resolved at once to become less cerebral." Rusher told another friend he had had "no idea the article would stimulate as much interest as it has . . . Apparently I accidentally managed to say some things a lot of people had been thinking and feeling."[45]

Another factor in what turned out to be his transition to *National Review* was his decision, at some point in the latter half of 1956, to drop any ambition for a political career. "For the first 33 years of my life," Rusher later explained to *NR* contributor Ernest van den Haag, "I more or less assumed that the mercantile ethic ('the customer is always right') was both valid and applicable to me. I wanted to get into politics, and (so help me God) I can even remember practicing my smile before a mirror." But ultimately he decided that politics "in the candidatorial sense, or in the more general sense of trying to be 'appealing' or 'persuasive,' was just not for me. I began doing and saying what I wanted to do and say, and immediately experienced a great sense of liberation."[46]

The following spring, before he was offered the publisher's job at the magazine, Rusher tried to recruit McWhorter, a friend since Harvard Law School, into movement conservatism. A decade later, coming upon handwritten notes prepared for their talk, he typed a copy and sent it to McWhorter as evidence of his strong attempt to do so.

Rusher began by observing that their common viewpoint, insofar as they developed one, had been "a mature and sophisticated version of the Liberal Republican tradition." Both of them were smart, ambitious, hardworking young men. "Being sophisticated, we coupled [liberal Republicanism] with some pretty shrewd and diligent politics. No wonder Dewey was our god! So, for a number of years, we ran with the hares, successfully. I do not say we were wrong; still less do I say Taft (e.g.) was right. We were immersed in our milieu; we absorbed this over-all concept of the world through every pore; our very intelligence made us the more vulnerable to its persuasiveness. Those who bucked it were either dumb or Catholic; we were neither."

But prevailing ideas, Rusher continued, were usually the product of a passing age. The liberal philosophy was superficial, with only shallow historical roots. "In the great systole and diastole of events, we are about to witness . . . a powerful surge forward and upward, deriving its impetus from ancient and powerful truths that Liberalism has forgotten. And the highest (as well as politically the soundest) function we can perform—indeed, our moral obligation—is to spend our lives bringing this to birth and giving it a healthy political expression."

Rusher didn't claim greater natural insight into the tantalizing situation, merely an ability to step back and notice it. McWhorter, more concerned with daily politics, understandably had "listened less carefully for the first signs of change." Ideological conservatism, Rusher suggested, was the "uniform response of your close colleagues" and hence deserved serious consideration. Furthermore, McWhorter's satisfaction with the GOP was mistaken. "The Republican-Democratic battle is real, but it is far from being the whole story . . . Realists, engaging in the struggle that counts, must deal with the parties instrumentally." In other words, ideologically committed people must use parties to advance what was higher, their principles. "If, at the last, I prove politically wrong, still we can die confident in the knowledge that we were morally right."[47]

Shortly after this searching conversation took place in April 1957, Rusher was "profoundly shocked" by the death of Joe McCarthy, not knowing how ill he had been. He paid his respects at the funeral home and a few days later attended the Senate service, having finally obtained a hard-to-get ticket through Brent Bozell. Rusher noticed McCarthy's friends and foes among the senators, with their "varying records, varying memories, varying regrets." Nixon took a chair at the front of the chamber, FBI director J. Edgar Hoover was in the gallery somewhere in front of Rusher, and in another row Bozell sat with Buckley. The voice of a young priest filled the chamber with the Roman Catholic funeral oration, six full-dress Marines brought the casket out through the doors, and McCarthy left the Senate forever.[48]

Also leaving the Senate, or rather its staff, was Morris, who intended to run for a seat himself. Rusher knew it would be a different job, almost a different subcommittee, with his friend and supervisor gone. He planned a return to private legal practice and began putting out feelers. He knew the Buckley family was in the oil business and wondered whether their company needed a young lawyer. Invited to the Stamford house for lunch one Sunday in June, Rusher raised the issue. "The window had a view of Long Island Sound, and Bill took his time. He said: 'How would you like to come to *National Review?*' And I thought: 'What would they need a lawyer for?' I said: 'As what?' And he looked out the window . . . and thought long and hard, and then he said: 'As publisher.'"[49]

Buckley, who was still the publisher in addition to the editor and owner, recognized that the first of these positions required someone to take it over: "As the magazine evolved, it became plain that it was a full-time job—especially for an enterprise that lost money, as we did." There was a business manager, Arthur Harris, who according to both men was not performing well. "Buckley was planning to get rid of him, I think," Rusher says, "and I think he probably first thought of me as a replacement for Harris. Then when he looked out the window, he thought: 'No, that's not going to sell, and I don't really need these two jobs.' . . . So then he said: 'As publisher.' I think that's probably the way it happened."[50]

The offer was especially attractive because Buckley indicated Rusher would not only supervise the magazine's business side but also participate in all major editorial conferences and decisions. Still, the choice was not easy. Rusher considered *NR* "the most important and responsible voice" in the conservative movement and the most significant development in current political thinking. But the hard fact was that he would have to quit a profession to which he had given nine years. *National Review* was losing money "at a rate that suggested it was not long for his world," and Rusher knew it lacked any great source of income to keep it going in the event of disaster. He also had "an uncomfortable, vaguely Calvinistic feeling that anything I wanted to do so much must be bad for me."[51]

Countering his doubts was the chance to participate in a promising new movement as it was taking shape. In April he had pitched conservatism to McWhorter as a rising force. Here was a chance to do what he had, in effect, urged: "Get with it and be part of it." Halfway through Rusher's several weeks of deliberations, Buckley called and increased the pay. Clif White advised against taking the job; his friend would sacrifice too much by abandoning his legal career, and it sounded like a risky venture. But Rusher "felt I didn't have a lot to lose, that I didn't have a wife and children that I had to feed and educate and so on. I could afford to take a chance. If it didn't work out, I could go back to the practice of the law and do something else." As Buckley recalls: "In his careful way, he looked into all aspects of the situation and came aboard—happily aboard."[52]

Having accepted the offer, Rusher attended his last session of the Internal Security Subcommittee on July 23. Before it adjourned, Senator Hruska, who for the next two decades would be among the most stalwart conservatives in Congress, noted his resignation and plans to enter a new field. "Do you want to tell us what it is, Mr. Rusher?" he asked. "Publisher of the

*National Review* magazine, in New York City," answered the young counsel. "Well," the senator said, "that is fine . . . I have been very gratified [by your work] . . . We are sorry you are leaving. We hope you will find your new job both beneficial and interesting." Late the next morning, Rusher boarded the northbound train. On his first day at the magazine, July 25, 1957, he met Buckley for breakfast at the University Club, and they took a taxicab to *NR*. Rusher would remember the editor announcing "in a sepulchral tone: 'This is your office.'"[53]

# 4

# The Right Publisher

Assigned to one of the two usable offices at *National Review*, Rusher could work more comfortably than the editors in their cubicles at the sides of the room. The magazine was still at its first location, 211 East 37th Street near the Midtown Tunnel—"about as un-chic a business address as it was possible to have"—and Rusher would remember its work space as a "rabbit hutch."[1] It was unclear how long *NR* would survive. There wasn't enough advertising, the subscriptions and deliveries didn't function smoothly, and paid circulation was just 16,500. Four months after the first issue appeared in November 1955, senior editor Willmoore Kendall joked that the business manager, advertising manager, and bookkeeper thought *NR* was actually producing shoes and were "waiting to see them before going out to sell." Of the financial situation, the bookkeeper would say: "Don't worry. Mr. Buckley will find the money."[2]

In reality, a larger financial base was needed. Asking for money, Buckley told *NR* donor Gerrish Milliken in 1958, was "easily the most unpleasant job . . . in the world today." The editor probably figured his new publisher would find it easy to solicit potential donors, Rusher suggests, "because he couldn't. He found out I couldn't either. We're both awful at it . . . but I did my best."[3] Despite his lack of fund-raising talent and his unfamiliarity with publishing, Rusher soon made a difference in the magazine's operations. As Buckley later attested, he "began to impose order on our affairs."[4] He did so with the help of a good assistant. When Jim McFadden said that first day that "we might want to try some direct mail," Rusher "nodded gravely" without knowing what it was. "I kept my mouth shut, and slowly—thanks largely to Jim—learned the ropes."[5]

*NR*'s public side came more naturally to Rusher. Having recently worked at the Internal Security Subcommittee, he didn't mind being in another hot seat. Even as most conservatives took only a mild interest in *National Review*, liberal opinion journalists tended to jeer. Murray Kempton had quickly dismissed it as a "national bore." It promoted "radicalism," not real conservatism, explained John Fischer of *Harper's*. In *Commentary*, Dwight Macdonald lamented what he found to be its demagogic ideas and style, characteristic of "the *lumpen*-bourgeoisie, the half-educated, half-successful provincials . . . who responded to Huey Long, Father Coughlin, and Senator McCarthy." The long piece, titled "Scrambled Eggheads on the Right," was especially obnoxious to Buckley, who considered it an attempt to personally discredit him.[6] But *NR* was making its mark elsewhere. In October 1957 a city post of the Catholic War Veterans presented its annual Americanism Award to the magazine—praising its "intellectual, factual, courageous and candid writings," its "articulate pen," and its "dedication to patriotism [that epitomizes our motto] . . . For God For Country For Home." Rusher would accept the award at the group's annual ball.[7]

## Disparate Talents

*NR*'s best asset was its founder and editor. His deeply ingrained sense of humor, pugnacity, and willingness to take risks helped to strengthen the spirit of his colleagues. "Buckley ran a very relaxed, good-humored shop," Rusher recalls. "He liked a lot of laughter, had a terribly low threshold for boredom."[8]

The magazine aimed at intellectual sophistication, and Buckley could insist on it because he was a good example of it himself. He took a more complex view of his liberal opponents than most other conservatives, had more fun as he denounced them. He was young and determined to seize the future, aggressive yet well-bred. He tended to make a lasting impression: "a flashing smile, a rapier mind, bright blue eyes, and a half-British, half-southern drawl." Buckley knew how to surprise, how to ridicule, how to use long words. Another trait was his combination of pride and humility; yet another was his ability to make crucial distinctions. "I don't think I have an exceptionally powerful mind," he once told Rusher, "but I do think I have an exceptionally quick one."[9] Like most conservatives, Buckley spoke as a moralist. More than most, he saw modern liberalism as not only wrong but a stifling orthodoxy; conservatism as not only correct but visionary and more intelligent. As he became known to the public, his distinctive qualities challenged the assumption that the Right was "stupid, and inarticulate, and Lord knows not witty."[10]

Buckley's training in controversial speech began in childhood at his family dinner table, where a capable defense of one's opinions was expected. It continued at Yale after the war, where he edited the *Daily News* and was a champion debater. As a freshman in 1946–47, Buckley represented the campus political union's Conservative Party in opposition to U.S. adoption of the controversial United Nations Declaration on Human Rights. His main opponent in the debate was the great liberal heroine of the time, Eleanor Roosevelt.[11] Only twenty-nine when he founded the magazine and thirty-one when Rusher arrived, Buckley had marginal job experience: teaching Spanish part-time at Yale, minor work with the CIA in Mexico, then writing for the conservative *American Mercury* and *Freeman*. He had never run a business or been involved in practical politics, but two books put him on the conservative map. *God and Man at Yale* (1951) was a passionate exposé of what he believed to be a pervasive bias against religion and free enterprise at his alma mater; it also suggested that these problems were common in academe as a whole. *McCarthy and His Enemies*, published in 1954 and written with Brent Bozell, was more judiciously composed but equally bold, defending the politician most hated by liberals.

The topics of Buckley's books reflected his deepest concerns: Christian orthodoxy, anticommunism, antistatism, and a critique of elite liberalism that seemed to flow naturally from these positions. He explicitly rejected the moderate politics of the 1950s, in which the differences between legitimate conservatives and legitimate liberals were thought to be small. In the first issue of *National Review*, Buckley's opening statement did more than make the point, now universally quoted, about standing athwart the forces of history and yelling, "Stop." In a more political and practical vein, it distinguished sharply if rather cryptically between a "well-fed Right," whom Buckley accused of "ignorance and amorality," and the "radical conservatives," with whom *NR* identified. He told readers that serious conservatives, although disregarded and even humiliated by many of their establishmentarian distant cousins, now had a voice undeterred by "the Liberals, who run this country." While painting a bleak political scene, Buckley added that his team was starting out with a certain optimism, based solidly on the fact that the magazine had been successfully launched.[12]

The editor and his colleagues knew the cautionary example of a project recently gone awry. The *Freeman*, founded in the 1920s, was refounded in 1950 by John Chamberlain and Suzanne La Follette, both experienced journalists, and free-market author Henry Hazlitt. They hoped it would become a highly engaged opinion journal, the classical-liberal counterpart to the *New Republic* and the *Nation*. But the *Freeman* was beset with factional squabbling that reflected, in Rusher's words, "the disorderly every-man-for-himself intellectual atmosphere" of conservatism early in the decade.[13] When its board chose to make no endorsement rather than support Robert Taft for the 1952 Republican nomination, Chamberlain and La Follette resigned. Under new ownership, the *Freeman* then focused on economic philosophy.[14] The expansively defined purpose of *Modern Age*, an academic conservative periodical founded in mid-1957, was "to stimulate discussion of the great moral and social and political and economic and literary questions of the hour" and was not "to pick quarrels, but to bring about a meeting of men's minds."[15] The *American Mercury*, which enjoyed its heyday under the editorship of H. L. Mencken in the twenties, had become political and conservative, but it was a monthly and therefore less immediately topical. Thus, while other conservative intellectual magazines existed in the late 1950s, only *NR* confronted the political scene as directly as Buckley wished to. Rusher and senior editor Frank Meyer would work to shape and sustain that confrontation.

Family wealth was essential to *National Review* in its gestational period and early years; it had received $100,000 in startup money from the editor's father, self-made oil entrepreneur William F. Buckley Sr. But the enterprise depended equally on the young man's ability to impress those he met. "He is something special," Whittaker Chambers told his wife after Buckley first visited their Maryland farmhouse in 1954. "He was born, not made, and not many like that are born in any time."[16] As a supporter of the magazine told Rusher several years later: "It seems that everyone in Wisconsin who had the good fortune to hear WFB Jr. was thoroughly entranced. Conservatives badly need the assurance that competence gives them."[17] Another audience was developing, too, as Buckley became a fixture in New York and was admired by many who opposed his politics. A liberal writer noticed him with other journalists covering a 1960 campaign rally in a hotel ballroom: "tall and elegant, surveying the scene with a happily jaundiced eye and those large, knowing winks for everyone, his casual greetings rolling out like oratorical gems."[18] For a fighter and rebel, he got along remarkably well with others. Rusher would stress his "great gift for pulling disparate people together." Maintaining a strong sense of common enterprise at the magazine, as Buckley did, was "a tremendous diplomatic achievement."[19]

To pull the disparate talents together, a clear line of authority was drawn at the outset. Buckley owned all of the voting stock. As Rusher later observed, this allowed people to acquiesce easily when decisions went against them, because they were merely respecting his rights as the owner, not conceding that their judgments were wrong. Over the years, then, conflicts about editorial decisions and issues never became "power struggles."[20] But to control policy certainly wasn't to control the senior editors and Rusher, who spoke their minds and expected to be heard. The publisher's job, as offered in 1957, included the right to attend editorial meetings and to give an opinion on anything, and Buckley kept his word. It was a substantial promise, for in the frequent meetings and memos at *National Review*, there was much that required deliberation. Rusher enjoyed this and signaled immediately that he expected to. For the issue coinciding with his arrival in late July, he wrote a "Report from the Publisher." Without saying much about himself or what he hoped *NR* would do, he suggested that continued self-appraisal would be necessary: "'The unexamined life,' said Socrates, 'is not worth living.' This is as true for nations—and magazines—as for individuals."[21] The piece foreshadowed one of Rusher's main roles at *NR*, that of internal critic, while also hinting at the discretion he tried to bring to it.

The several editors, now joined by a full-time publisher, had differences among themselves ranging from a generational gap to philosophical ones. Buckley, Rusher, and Brent Bozell were the young men while James Burnham, Willmoore Kendall, and Meyer were about fifteen to twenty years older. Their political backgrounds varied. Burnham and Meyer had once been communists, and Kendall had been associated less formally with the far Left. Buckley, in contrast, was a lifelong conservative, and Rusher a lifelong Republican who started out as a moderate but was never a liberal. Bozell, formerly Buckley's debate partner at Yale, was an intense convert to Roman Catholicism who had been more liberal in his college years.[22] The editors' interests also diverged considerably. Rusher once said "the difference between Frank Meyer and Jim Burnham was: Meyer wanted to know what the relationship of virtue was to freedom. Burnham wanted to know what the noted Kurd leader Salid Bhagdash was doing in Damascus last week."[23] There were diverse temperaments, hot and cool. Most important of all, there were differing attitudes toward political action—and divergent understandings of *NR*'s ideal voice and role.

Although the magazine was just a year and a half old when Rusher arrived, it already had a bit of history. The founding of *National Review* was no easy thing for Buckley, even conceptually. He needed encouragement. Much of it came from Willi Schlamm, an Austrian émigré who had been a communist in his youth and was later a prominent anti-Nazi and anti-Stalinist newspaper editor in Berlin and Prague. He left for the United States in 1938, doubtful that European democracy had a future. During the war, he became the foreign-policy adviser and assistant to Henry Luce, the demanding and generally conservative editor in chief of *Time, Life,* and *Fortune,* publications that collectively reached an enormous audience. After a period of "intellectual Americanization," as Schlamm called it, he struck out on his own in 1951 and helped to edit the *Freeman* for a few years. He met Buckley in 1952, was deeply impressed, and persistently urged the young man to start a journal of conservative opinion.[24] Buckley later reflected gratefully to Burnham: "it was Willi who dreamed of the magazine, and who persuaded me to make the effort to launch it . . . It took the prodding of Willi, his generosity and that of yourself and of others, to convince me that, for one or another reason, the idea of such a magazine was not grotesque; that the magazine was desprately [sic] needed; and, even, that the magazine might succeed."[25]

At *NR*, they found it hard to get along. Although it was Schlamm who had suggested Buckley should be the sole owner, he disliked it when the younger, less-experienced editor made decisions he disagreed with. Buckley also rejected several of his editorials, in part for being too melodramatic, and found Burnham's writing more professional. Schlamm was uncomfortable with the growing influence his colleague had on Buckley and wanted the magazine to be, as one of its early writers would put it, "more crusading." He continued to talk against Burnham, and then against Buckley as well. Eventually he agreed to substantial restrictions, such as not discussing *NR* matters away from work. But when the editor decided the newly hired Rusher should have the office Schlamm was using just one or two days a week, he gathered his personal items and walked out.[26]

An earlier inspiration for Buckley was Kendall, his intellectual mentor at Yale. A political theorist concerned with the analysis and preservation of constitutional democracy, Kendall was a dedicated but disputatious teacher, more than willing to make both students and fellow professors uncomfortable for the sake of clear thinking. In class he was heard admonishing the young Buckley: "You don't know a damn thing about economics." A janitor he had just spoken with, Kendall told Yale colleagues on another occasion, understood the proper democratic response to domestic communism much better than they did.[27]

After graduation, Buckley met Burnham, then an early Cold Warrior, who would play a large role in the founding of *NR* and would become the leading influence on Buckley's editorial decisions. In a former life, Burnham had been a leader in the Socialist Workers Party, a communist but anti-Stalin movement that looked to the exiled Russian Revolution leader Leon Trotsky as its living prophet. In the second stage of his career, having abandoned communism but still fascinated by power of all types, he wrote books on industrial society, what he favorably termed "Machiavellian" political thought, and the struggle with the Soviet Union. He was also a philosophy professor at New York University until the early 1950s, when he decided "twenty years of teaching is enough." Burnham now identified wholeheartedly with the basics of the postwar conservative cause: intense anticommunism, individual liberty, constitutionalism, capitalism, the belief in social stability. His style of thinking, on the other hand, retained a class-minded and deterministic element owing to European social theory. This contributed to the large differences between the Burnham vision and the Meyer-Rusher vision of *National Review*.

Buckley had met Frank Meyer when both were writing for the *Freeman*. Formerly a significant leader in the Communist Party, Meyer was now a learned libertarian essayist who sought to define the new conservative movement's beliefs more precisely. Although he earned Buckley's profound admiration, he would have less than the broad, consistent influence that Burnham developed.

Each of these senior editors was given a column in which to analyze a side of politics that especially interested him. Kendall wrote The Liberal Line, monitoring the daily "operations of the Liberal propaganda machine."[28] Burnham's column on international events, diplomacy, and defense was called The Third World War. Meyer had a largely theoretical column, "Principles and Heresies," discussing conservative precepts and potentially dangerous deviations from them. Burnham had two great advantages at *NR*: his especially strong relationship with Buckley and the fact he was assigned to write many of the editorials. Meyer's institutional strength was his editorship of the book-review section, which also brought him into closer contact with intellectuals around the country, allowing him to publicize their work and to influence them. While Burnham's clout gradually increased at *National Review*, Meyer did more public speaking and assisted in political organizing. That made him a conservative leader, not just a conservative writer, and was one of the common grounds between him and Rusher.

Kendall never had a Burnham- or Meyer-like niche at *NR*. He regretted his lesser clout but was mainly concerned with developing his own thinking and became increasingly interested in the great works of political philosophy. Most of his influence on the editor had come previously. Four years after graduating from Yale, Buckley noted: "I attribute whatever political and philosophical insights I have to his tutelage and his friendship," also acknowledging that Kendall helped "a great deal" with his two early books.[29] In one sense, their friendship was more unusual than that of Buckley and the polished, worldly Burnham. A native Oklahoman, Kendall disliked the Northeast and didn't particularly adapt to it, considering himself an "Appalachians to the Rockies" patriot.

Self-consciously a man of the people, Kendall wanted conservatives to be as specifically American in their thinking as he was, Constitution-minded and democratic. His deepest intellectual commitments were to the concept of "public orthodoxy," meaning enforceable bounds to political and cultural dissent, and to what he regarded as the heart of American constitutionalism—federalism, majority rule, and congressional rather than presidential power—more than to tradition, small government, or individual freedom. The welfare state, which had been legislated democratically, was less troubling to him than in Buckley's or Meyer's case. Although he was passionately anticommunist like everyone else at *NR*, Kendall focused on the nationalizing and undemocratic regime he thought the liberals were striving to impose, especially through the Supreme Court. He believed the principles of majority rule and federalism were under determined assault, but also that they were surviving reasonably well. He attributed the slow progress of the liberal offensive to two factors: the constitutional design of the founders, which tended to allow only gradual change in policy, and the political soundness of average Americans, which also kept things gradual. His populist tendencies contributed to a relatively optimistic outlook on current politics. They also made him a key source for what became practically a doctrine of the Right, and a main theme of Rusher's, beginning in the late 1960s: faith in the existence of a conservative "silent majority."

Unlike Kendall, Burnham had completed his intellectual journey. He spent just two days a week at the magazine, commuting from the scenic countryside near Kent, Connecticut, not far from Sharon, where the Buckleys had grown up. He was undistracted by the restless thinking-through of the meaning of American conservatism that preoccupied Kendall, seemingly free of the inner turmoil Kendall suffered. Burnham ended up sharing an office with Priscilla Buckley, whose calm personality meshed well with his, when she was promoted to managing editor in 1959. After a week of the new arrangement, he said: "I think that I could be content here."[30] It was true of his attitude toward *National Review* as well.

Burnham came from a privileged background like Buckley but carried much weightier experiences. As a young academic edging into left-wing political activism, he had traveled through the industrial Midwest in 1933, perceiving amid an extremely desperate economy a class struggle that seemed to define the new times. The "real world," he decided, "was the world of strikes, organizing, and labor violence." To Burnham, Marxist-Leninism was the available means of saving modern civilization. The communists had the unity and discipline, the "effective centralized structure" as he called it, without which ideas were mere "talk" and could never change things.[31] Eventually, however, it was his belief in communism that proved unsustainable. Given his analytical and thoughtful nature, it was difficult for Burnham to remain a leader or member of any doctrinaire, revolutionary party. Trotsky himself, although they never met, denounced him as an "educated witch-doctor," a "strutting petty-bourgeois pedant," and an "intellectual snob."[32]

Burnham's first book, *The Managerial Revolution: What Is Happening in the World* (1941), gave him the status of a major pundit often asked by the media for comment on current issues. But to some critics, it also made him look like a power worshiper. In his antitotalitarian novel *1984*, George Orwell featured the book under a more sinister title: *The Theory and Practice of Oligarchic Collectivism* by a Trotsky-like Emmanuel Goldstein.[33] Orwell had been especially offended by Burnham's prediction, in *Managerial Revolution*, that Nazi Germany would defeat the Soviet Union, and by his prophecy late in the war that Russia would conquer all of Europe. At each point, he remarked in a critical essay, "Burnham is predicting a continuation of the thing that has been happening. Now the tendency to do this is not simply a bad habit . . . It is a major mental disease, and its roots lie partly in cowardice and partly in the worship of power, which is not fully separable from cowardice." Orwell also associated Burnham with unfortunate American tendencies to "admire size for its own sake" and to "feel that success constitutes justification."[34]

Whatever truth there might have been in these accusations, Burnham was, from the immediate postwar period at least, second to none in his enmity toward communism and the Soviet Union, and in his desire for Western victory. He worked eagerly to spread his views through book luncheons, radio forums, and speeches to public-affairs clubs. But he saw it as duty, not pleasure. Although politics was "the most important activity of our time," he found it "the least personally rewarding."[35] To Burnham, as to Buckley, political activity was really an obligation one must accept in such grave times. In this attitude they differed from Rusher, who enjoyed politics. It was a difference that would do much to fuel dynamic disagreements and arguments at *NR* throughout the publisher's three decades there.

In 1950, Burnham was a major player in the founding of the International Congress for Cultural Freedom, the leading organization of anticommunist Western intellectuals. From 1949 to the early 1950s, he worked on psychological warfare for the CIA's Office of Policy Coordination, a semi-independent covert-action branch—thinking that propaganda, disinformation, and bribery directed by agencies like the CIA could spark trouble in the Soviet system and inspire defections to the West. Soon, though, Burnham came to doubt that Washington had enough expertise or commitment for such a strategy. He believed the governing class and the rest of the American elite were too soft, too confident that deals could settle all conflicts.[36] As his hopes for decisive action against international communism faded, Burnham's remaining ties to the Left grew weaker. They ended in 1953, when the editors of the prestigious democratic-socialist journal *Partisan Review* asked him to leave its board because readers considered him a McCarthyite.[37]

The separation from *Partisan Review* did nothing to lessen Burnham's long-standing interest in magazines. In *The Coming Defeat of Communism*, which Buckley would recall reading on his honeymoon, Burnham had proposed that there be at least one periodical, newspaper, and publishing house in each country to express the viewpoint of the "world anti-communist offensive." In the United States, the most urgently needed of these was an opinion journal—actually several of them, broadly antiliberal rather than narrowly conservative.[38] Buckley easily persuaded Burnham, then professionally homeless, to join his venture despite its more directly ideological character, and the famous recruit helped considerably in the practical preparations for the magazine.

Rusher's *National Review* hero was Meyer, even before they first met in 1956. He had sometimes called him the Master, envisioning a "magisterial white-haired eminence," and was surprised to meet "this little Jewish elf." Meyer helped to shape Rusher's perspective "from the very beginning, when I started reading him," and they would be permanent allies at *NR*. "My notion of what conservatism was about, what it was good for it to do, what it might hope to accomplish—all of those things were influenced by Meyer."[39]

The two were "our purists," Brent Bozell remarked to the editors in 1961, "forever hitting the rest of us over the head for subordinating 'principle' to politics." By this, Bozell meant not that they cared little about conservatives winning office and power, but that they didn't want the magazine to settle too easily in politics. Despite strikingly different styles, Meyer and Rusher both had a keen appetite for political activity and tended to react strongly to the latest political news, characteristics neither Burnham nor Buckley shared. Conservative journalist M. Stanton Evans, who considered Meyer one of his closest friends, remembers him as a true political strategist and "a master of maneuver." As a University of Wisconsin student in the mid-1960s, American Conservative Union chairman David Keene got to know Meyer. Keene would occasionally travel to New York and take a long bus trip, arriving exhausted in the early evening, the beginning of Meyer's day. Back home, in the dead of night, he might get a call from Meyer to follow up on their last discussion: "You were liable to . . . get busted out of bed to find out what you were doing, and 'Why hadn't you done this?' or 'Why hadn't you done the other thing?'" Meyer "had been a militant communist," Rusher notes, "and I had been a militant Republican. They're not all that far apart, except in what they believe."[40]

Meyer converted to Marxism while a graduate student at Oxford in the early 1930s. He became an organizer for the Young Communist League and later in the decade was a regional educational director for the Communist Party, also serving as the director of its Chicago Workers School. Meyer broke from the party in 1945 and was briefly a liberal anticommunist. A Truman Democrat in 1948, he supported the New Deal as well as containment. But he grew uneasy with liberals, deciding that too many were relativists who denied objective good and evil, right and wrong. Meyer thought liberal anticommunism had allowed, among other disasters, the fall of China to Mao Tse-tung in 1949. Unlike Burnham, he worried equally about liberal domestic policies. Friedrich Hayek's foreboding analysis of the welfare state in *The Road to Serfdom* led him to attack the New Deal as a stage in the eventual development of totalitarianism. In the early 1950s, he contacted journalists and authors on the Right, hoping to become active in the nascent conservative movement. He began writing for the *Freeman* and the *American Mercury*.[41]

By the time Meyer joined *NR*, he was already a rising spokesman for libertarian conservatism and something of an intellectual knife thrower. In a 1955 review that denounced one of the movement's founding texts, *The Conservative Mind* by Russell Kirk, he argued that the systematic deference to tradition that Kirk presented as the essence of conservatism was really "collectivism rebaptized" under a nicer name.[42] But within several years, Meyer became the leading advocate of "fusionism," a belief he was largely responsible for articulating and that he shared with Buckley and Rusher. According to the fusionists, both traditionalism—especially with its emphasis on virtue and restrained conduct—and libertarianism were necessary to a correct philosophy of society. Together, they defined both the true American heritage and the true heritage of Western civilization.[43]

Meyer clung to his rural home in Woodstock, New York, a longish distance from the city, and kept a nocturnal schedule that made it impossible to work at the office. Retiring in the early morning, waking in the late afternoon, he communicated with fellow conservatives by running up enormous telephone bills and hosting all-night visitors. At these sessions and elsewhere, Rusher later recalled, he "talked loudly and extensively and authoritatively."[44] With visitors he was typically in motion—pacing, smoking, drinking bourbon. The special blend of physical and mental energy, according to a later colleague, Jeffrey Hart, "could be overwhelming." Meyer's commitment to a life of learning was as strong as his personality. In the house he shared with his wife, Elsie, and their home-schooled boys John and Eugene, books covered every wall, in every room. Rusher would remember a cheap wine Meyer provided on an all-night visit: "He didn't have a lot of money, and that was what he could afford." It was the only such visit for Rusher. Although he respected Meyer to the point of awe, he was a man of habit who craved order in all things.[45]

Meyer would not have fit in at the office, according to Priscilla Buckley. With a magazine to produce, the staff "didn't have the time to listen" to him, "the energy to fight every point, or the inclination to make high drama of any given point."[46] He was a cauldron of argumentative energy. "If he'd been there all the time," recalls his older son, John Meyer, "there might have been a blowup."[47] It was possible to take him for a mere eccentric. Chambers once mocked him for unwillingness to engage with the political world as it really was. He compared Meyer, then only forty-nine, to an old man who might be seen in "one of those dark little shops . . . fingering for his own pleasure" left-over segments of nineteenth-century cloth which he wasn't even interested in selling. But Chambers soon noticed an impressive ability to explain *National Review*'s and American conservatives' philosophical identity. About a year after writing his dismissive comment, he conceded to Buckley that Meyer was "emerging clearly as the Voice . . . this, I gather from stray *NR* readers, is just what they want to hear."[48] Rusher has suggested another metaphor for Meyer: "the intellectual engine of the conservative movement."[49]

About a year after he became publisher, Rusher met Chambers, whose book *Witness* several years earlier had deepened his anticommunism. Chambers was already writing articles for *NR* and now decided to work for it more directly. In the late summer and fall of 1958, he arrived by train every other week, hurriedly in time to share an editorial lunch. He wrote for an afternoon, then helped with production work the following morning. Like others at *National Review*, Rusher was surprised that the living legend seemed so friendly, a "great corpulent ho-ho sort of guy."[50] While talking avidly with his new colleagues on any number of subjects, Chambers also "listened superbly," Buckley noted. The visits, requiring a long trip from his home in rural Maryland, ended when he suffered another heart attack that November.[51] But a close friendship and a thoughtful, probing correspondence with Buckley made Chambers a continuing part of *NR* in the few years left to him.

Like Burnham, he tended toward a moderate, antisectarian viewpoint. Buckley cites Chambers's early importance "in giving me the notion that we should avoid denominationalism, and seek to come up with a product that was useful on a very wide scale."[52] He also had a prophetlike quality. At times he rejected not only political theory but even expressly conservative political action as futile. Buckley would praise his spiritual depth—"speaking to our time from the center of sorrow, from the center of the earth"—and wept upon hearing of his death in 1961. In Rusher's experience over the decades, Chambers and Burnham were almost the only people to whom Buckley, in a general sense, would intellectually defer.[53]

Chambers's political thoughts were a curious mixture of distanced pessimism and pragmatism—including a belief that the Republicans must "create a program that means something to masses of people." He told Buckley he felt a kinship with Burnham, since both tried to grasp "the reality of the desperate forces" of the age. He claimed, questionably, that he had almost nothing in common with the theoretical analyses of Meyer and Kirk. However logically presented, he found them "by contrast with the total reality" to be "chiefly an irrelevant buzz." Chambers did not deny the intellectual value of their writings. "There will be a time when the mode that preoccupies them may again be relevant," he acknowledged. "But, unless I am greatly mistaken, that time lies on the far side of unimaginable changes, which must be assimilated and generalized before a new synthesis can have any wide meaning." He meant that forces greater than philosophy were at work. "We are in the middle of a universal earthquake," Chambers told Buckley. "If we survive it, then there will be something to reflect on. It is perfectly clear that we may not survive. At that point, I lose interest."[54]

Yet another figure in Buckley's intellectual formation was the radically libertarian social critic Albert Jay Nock (1870–1945), a friend of his father's and an occasional guest at the family home.[55] Nock had been the founder of the original *Freeman*, but his political alienation exceeded that of Chambers while his elitism surpassed Burnham's. Nearly all government, he contended, was a rather thuggish conspiracy against private property. That wasn't about to change, because only a small fraction of society had either intelligence or political virtue. The only good use of a conservative's or libertarian's time was to preach to this minority. Had he lived longer, Nock might well have encouraged the young Buckley to start a magazine. He would not have encouraged hopes that the Right could take power, let alone Rusher's campaign to make *National Review* into a spearhead of conservative politics.

Nock-style conservatism rejected politics as an incurable realm of exploitation and tyranny, unworthy of the wise, moral minority. The problem was human nature, not wrong ideas or election results. The state was antisocial, weakening society, yet its growth resulted from an age-old "iron law . . . that man tends always to satisfy his needs and desires with the least possible exertion." Essentially, people could either work or steal. Work, the "economic means," was harder and therefore less attractive. More attractive was the "political means," which meant taking what others produced. Men would try this whenever they could; thus the state's constant growth. What could be done about it? "Simply nothing," Nock answered. Like a man "in a row-boat on the lower reaches of the Niagara," civilization was drifting inevitably toward catastrophe.[56]

Nock divided humanity into "mass-men" and the "Remnant." The masses lacked the intelligence to grasp the principles that produced the good life; they also lacked the character to consistently follow these principles. The Remnant were the minority who could do both. But they couldn't take power. Nock's model was the prophet Isaiah in ancient Israel, who cared only for the integrity of his message, not its ability to change things. "He knew that the Remnant would listen, and knowing also that nothing was to be expected of the masses under any circumstances, he made no specific appeal to them, did not accommodate his message to their measure in any way, and did not care two straws whether they heeded it or not. As a modern publisher might put it, he was not worrying about circulation or advertising."[57]

Rusher's attitude was entirely different from those of Chambers and Nock. To wait for "the far side of unimaginable changes" or to "lose interest" was impossible for anyone so fascinated by politics, so confident that political ideas—and action informed by them—mattered greatly. Whittaker Chambers was a great anticommunist hero, a moral exemplar, but no guide to politics. Rusher shared little of his sense of resignation and none of his detachment. If liberals were to be replaced at the heights from which they ran the country, high-quality preaching by *National Review* could be only a start. No Remnant could elect a president.

From Rusher's activist standpoint, the immediately problematic influence at *NR* was Burnham. While Rusher was fascinated by electoral politics, Burnham focused on what he saw as the real power, the elite: how it was formed, how it changed over time, how it shaped things. The elite was simultaneously governmental and economic, social and intellectual. Government by itself, therefore, was not the determining factor in society, nor was it a more important target than the elite as a whole. According to this view, socioeconomic factors, not elections and more than ideas, set the nation's course.

Kendall, in contrast, thought conservative academics and writers were too susceptible to defeatism, once scoffing that their "favorite battle-cry . . . is: 'We are losing! We are losing! But in how noble, how fine, how glorious a cause!'" Many conservatives unfortunately thought in terms "of storming American public opinion from without, of conquering the hearts and minds of an essentially hostile because already Left-wing people, ready always to sell its votes" to the highest bidder.[58] Although Kendall's more democratic perspective was closer to that of Rusher and Meyer, they wouldn't have his backing in editorial disagreements, because for complicated reasons including alcoholism, he gradually became alienated from Buckley and *NR* in the early 1960s. His quarrelsome personality diminished what could have been a larger role at the magazine. The man who was probably its "most original and adventurous thinker," according to Jeffrey Hart, also "carried turbulence with him" everywhere he went.[59]

Rusher remembers Kendall as a difficult man but also "a lot of fun." They had numerous conversations and "no trouble of any kind."[60] But Kendall became increasingly discontented, deciding the magazine wasn't living up to its founding ideal. According to Rusher, there was also a specific difficulty with Buckley, his former student. "Willmoore did not have any children of his own, and I'm inclined to think that this had a psychological effect." Buckley had "adopted him as practically a father" while at Yale, and Kendall "perceived in Bill, I think, the son he never had." Being in a position to help his former teacher have an influence on American society, the young editor represented Kendall's "second chance." Rusher doubts Buckley understood the situation. "I don't think he ever perceived that this was happening . . . and yet at the same time, I think Buckley encouraged it very much."[61]

Buckley's growing independence in *National Review*'s early years provoked Kendall to take it personally when the editor differed with his opinion or didn't consult him.[62] The political theorist also complained about "the general collapse of conversation in the *National Review* crowd, all of whom except Frank Meyer are too busy-busy for anything so old-fashioned." Neither at Yale nor at *NR* could he "talk about the things that interest me."[63] After leaving his Yale professorship in frustration, Kendall became permanently estranged from Buckley while writing in Spain and teaching in California. He officially left the magazine in 1963 and passed away in 1967. His last years were spent happily as a popular professor at the University of Dallas—where he finally felt he was "home," having escaped from the "world of the Buckleys."[64]

Burnham's clout only grew, in part because of a gentlemanly self-control that Kendall and Schlamm often lacked. In Buckley's increasingly frequent absence, he was the closest thing to a final authority on-site. Colleagues were impressed by his intellectual coolness and personal warmth. Burnham was "never too busy to give reasons for thinking as he did," Buckley would recall, "or too harassed to interrupt his own work to help others with theirs." He worked closely but gently with the younger writers, weeding out emotionalism and abstractions from their copy, minimizing fancy language.[65] At the same time, his erudition was formidable. Once, according to Priscilla Buckley, "he started to recite Horace in Latin at an editorial lunch to show that in *Lolita*, Nabokov had plagiarized some classical rhythms."[66] His outlook remained unsentimental. Around the office, several of his hardheaded sayings became known as Burnham's Laws: "Who says A, must say B." "Just as good, isn't." "If there's no alternative, there's no problem." "You cannot invest in retrospect." "No excuse, sir."[67]

Akin to Burnham in approach to the magazine and in personality was the managing editor, known as "Pitts" to her family and to senior people at *NR*. Buckley's older sister Priscilla came on board in early 1956, after a career with the United Press wire service at which she did "rewrite" in New York and then was a general correspondent in Paris. Between stints she had worked in Washington for the CIA. Buckley hired her with the thought, as he told Priscilla, that he had lots of professors and needed a real journalist.[68] She was a calming influence as well. With "her basic common sense," Rusher recalls, "her good nature, her general understanding of people—everybody respected Priscilla." The "ego tantrums and funk" to which journalists could be susceptible "seemed merely ridiculous in her presence," Hart later wrote. "So did fanaticism."[69]

Rarely if ever would Priscilla Buckley, who replaced Suzanne La Follette as managing editor in 1959, use the position for an ideological or strategic purpose. Her job was to strive for professionalism in each edition, ensure it was produced on schedule, and make it look serious but attractive. "When she did take a stand on something," according to Rusher, "whatever Priscilla said, and meant, turned out to be the law even where Bill was concerned." She truly "understood journalism, and as managing editor she kept the magazine together. There's no question about it at all. She saved Bill the problem of putting out the magazine—*she* put it out."[70]

Rusher's assistant, James McFadden, had joined NR a year before his new boss. A former newspaperman, he arrived fresh out of Army service in Europe, having discovered the magazine at a USO canteen. Reading every issue, savoring *National Review*'s conservatism and its Catholic tinge, McFadden decided to work there himself. Just off his troop ship, he walked in seeking a position preferably as a writer or editor but willing to take "any job you give me, Mr. Buckley." Noting his "pleasant unmistakably Irish face" and his "cocky, jaunty air," Priscilla found him "immediately likeable." Bill Buckley would recall McFadden as "middle-sized, brown-eyed, always with his horn-rimmed glasses and his pipe," a young man who "punctuated his conversation about the Soviet enterprise and creeping European socialism with cackles of laughter." He could see the funny side to everything while remaining "deadly serious" about his political beliefs, his faith, and his country: "He was the prime exhibit of [essayist] G. K. Chesterton's dogged insistence that piety and laughter are inseparable, and indefeasibly the work of God."[71]

McFadden had been the assistant to Buckley, and upon Rusher's arrival became the assistant to the new publisher—presumably, Rusher notes, "not his highest ambition." His job was mainly the direct oversight of circulation and promotion. He got on well at the magazine, and Rusher remembers him as "a very hard worker, a very able man in his field" who did "a tremendous amount for *National Review*." But their personal relationship was distant. "He adored Buckley. The sun just rose and set behind Bill Buckley, as far as McFadden was concerned . . . We got along, but we were never great buddies temperamentally." The publisher thought him "a rather prickly man, at least toward me."[72]

Rusher has often said he "lived happily ever after" at *National Review*. But his new environment, sometimes lax and sometimes raucous, was also an imperfect fit. His old law firm Shearman & Sterling, like the Senate, resembled "a huge ocean liner in which everything ran just according to form."[73] *NR* was no ocean liner, and there was a sense that a new sort of hire had been made. Buckley remembers that when he "timidly" asked Rusher to join the magazine, Rusher "instinctively reached into his pocket and pulled out his notebook, presumably to see whether his notebook had any objections."[74] Priscilla heard from her brother-in-law Brent Bozell and her sister Patricia that he was "a very good guy indeed," based on the couple's friendship with him in Washington. Meeting Rusher for the first time upon returning from a vacation, she found his manner "a little stiff." A subtle condolence appeared when she mentioned him in a light piece on the office and its characters for *NR*'s fifth-anniversary edition. "He claims to be happy," wrote the managing editor, "and certainly his presence makes us happy; but we suspect every now and then he is nostalgic for the old serenity" of his Senate job. There the main worries were hostile columnist Drew Pearson and "table-pounding Fifth Amendment Communists."[75]

## A Complicated Job

In Rusher's previous settings—the Internal Security Subcommittee, the Wall Street law firm, the Young Republicans—the purpose of the institution was more limited and perfectly clear. In contrast, the high command at *National Review* often had to improvise as history unfolded. Rusher, who preferred well-defined projects and predictability, also found himself dealing with more fluid responsibilities: the financial jitters at *NR*, the magazine's duties to conservatism and conservatives, the constant stream of events it must or could address. Although he had "almost qualified as an intellectual" in leisurely talks with Clif White several years before, he was now surrounded by intellectuals, not attorneys focused on a case or party activists preparing for a convention. And along with his business tasks (not "all that colossal," according to Rusher), it was necessary to reflect on the political messages *NR* was conveying, alert colleagues to how they were being received, and suggest ways in which these messages could help the magazine and the conservative cause.[76]

*National Review* was an in-between product, neither wholly contemplative like *Modern Age* nor entirely news-oriented like *Human Events*, the conservative weekly founded in 1944. It was both contemplative and news-oriented; an opinion journal necessarily was. As such, it faced a special difficulty. The magazine aimed, in part, to intellectualize politics. But intellectuals, more than the congressional aides, junior party activists, and young lawyers with whom Rusher had worked, prized their freedom to respond to things on their own terms.

By claiming the high ground in the battle of ideas, *NR* had confronted liberals with a new challenge. To advance the challenge politically was a harder task. Conservatives agreed with Buckley that the liberals ran the country but disagreed among themselves on what should be done about it. Conservative intellectuals might ignore the very question. Many of them "didn't have any political ideas," according to Rusher, and "didn't much want any political ideas. If they had, [they] didn't know how to create them—nor what to do with them if they got them." Since intellectuals dealing with politics knew both more and less than they needed to, their theoretical precision might combine awkwardly with practical naïveté. Rusher once heard Revilo Oliver, a classics professor and extraordinarily gifted linguist who was then a prominent figure on the Right, make the observation: "Now, it is probable that the Republican Party will have a presidential candidate in 1960. It is not certain. But it is probable."[77] The publisher felt a continuing responsibility to remind colleagues that the Republicans would certainly have a presidential candidate, that political processes like nomination contests began sooner rather than later, and that *NR* should participate in them.

After the magazine moved to a new headquarters a few blocks away in 1958, it became a more attractive place to work, although its atmosphere remained idiosyncratic. The small former apartment building at 150 East 35th Street still had claw-footed bathtubs that had never been removed. Rusher would later have to remind landlord Frederick Scholem, a Manhattan attorney, of poor building maintenance and slow repairs. Over the years he also wrote many notes to the staff urging a security-conscious attitude. Although the quiet residential neighborhood was nice enough, items were sometimes pilfered because doors often went unlocked.[78]

College students and recent graduates, excited about the lively new magazine and thrilled to be at one of the centers, perhaps *the* center, of the conservative renaissance, now came in as temporary or short-term staff. Burnham once joked that *NR* was actually "Miss Buckley's finishing school for young ladies and gentlemen of conservative persuasion." It was, Priscilla recalls, "a social club as well as a work situation." With the sandwich lunches, after-work drinks on press day, and invitations to editorial dinners at Buckley's townhouse, new people were "brought into the family . . . and Rusher was very good at that also." His conversation topics at Tuesday-night dinners with senior editors, initially held at small French bistros and later at Nicola Paone, an Italian restaurant near the magazine, were social rather than political. A frequent subject might be his travels, especially the "good food and drink aspects."[79]

One evening in the early sixties, staff and editors began discussing Rusher's orderly habits after he left early to pack for a trip to Asia. William Rickenbacker, a new senior editor, came up with an idea. Everything in the publisher's office would be changed, but only a little. His stacked magazines and the leaves in his desk calendar were placed in reverse chronological order. Every picture on the wall was moved just a bit to the right. The buzzer was fixed so that Rusher would reach the wrong people when he pushed its buttons. His efficient secretary Ann Turner, whom he liked, was persuaded to leave a note saying: "Dear Mr. Rusher. I find I am a Democrat so I must resign."

When he returned to his apartment after the long flight from Taiwan, Rusher found most of it covered in dust sheets because a repainting job wasn't finished. Crying out in dismay, he dropped his luggage and went to the office, only to encounter the irritating confusion that was carefully set up for him. He "staggered out to the street," Priscilla later recalled, "hailed a taxi, and ordered the driver to take him to the University Club." From there he called Ann Turner, telling her to let him know when everything was restored so he could get to work. But she forgot a slightly risqué drawing, similar to the innocuous original, that one of the magazine's cartoonists had prepared as part of the hoax. It hung on the wall for months before it was discovered—by which time Rusher had "regained his sunny good humor" and could laugh along with everyone else.[80]

The informality came with disadvantages. *National Review* "has not really had an editor the last couple of years," Burnham warned in early 1963. Buckley was away at least half the time, leaving nobody in charge. With no official distinction among the editors, Burnham pointed out to the vacationing Buckley, "each feels he has as much right as any other to determine policy; resents changes; takes advantage of being last man [handling] the copy, etc. . . . rather silly and childish, but that's the way people are." Employees arrived late, took overlong lunches, did too much "yakking," left early, and tended to put off chores.[81] Rusher disdained this as well. He was also, like Burnham, uncomfortable with raised voices and emotional venting (except, within reason, in editorial meetings). "He didn't like that at all," Priscilla remembers.[82]

The publisher was determined that his colleagues know the business facts of their decidedly nonprofit enterprise. Believing in planning and solid data, he drew up charts for factors like circulation totals and promotional costs. Not everyone cared for this. "Bill, there is no proposition so simple that it cannot be rendered unintelligible to me by putting it on a graph,"

Kendall complained in a protest that failed to move Rusher. "The graphs go on," Buckley noted at a 1969 dinner in the publisher's honor, "and, for those who have the stomach for it, they will give you a synoptic understanding of the financial record of *National Review* over the last twelve years."[83]

The unglamorous side of the job was partly responsible for the respect in which Rusher was held. He had to "find the money," Priscilla Buckley notes, and "deal with the printers, and the paper people, and the people who were not being paid within thirty days—more likely ninety days." Things were "so disorganized" at the time. "We didn't worry about formalities or procedures, particularly. We just got the job done." Rusher "wanted us to do it in a more methodical, organized fashion."[84] Junior staff members had an office pool each year, betting on how many secretaries he would hire and fire. But when really difficult situations arose, they would respectfully admit they needed the publisher's help. In a play on his initials, he was known as "the WAR department."[85] Rusher's painstaking ways could also end up making others feel better. Priscilla admired his thoroughness and fairness in settling the "innumerable small fights" about matters under his authority. Since he was "always just" in these situations, everybody respected his nonpartisanship. "It was a very good talent, and very much needed."[86] His unwillingness to endorse a business-related proposal unless he was convinced it made sense for the magazine served as "a very good restraint on some of the blither spirits around"—including Bill Buckley, "who sometimes had impractical ideas."[87]

Rusher's work at the law firm had helped to prepare him for such roles. "What the experience lacked in breadth," he recalled in *Special Counsel* in 1968, "it more than made up in depth—in precision, in thoughtfulness, in care." At *NR*, he not only introduced more professionalism into the business practices but also helped the editors understand the workings of government. "I think it was important training," Buckley says, "because much of our time was given over to analysis. That analysis—of proposed legislation, for instance—is enhanced by a knowledge of the law, and of procedure and of evidence, and Bill was proficient in his knowledge of those fields."[88] The lawyer's perspective was also evident in his concern about libel. "Effective immediately," Rusher told the staff on one occasion, "please try strenuously to avoid the phrase 'an identified Communist.' This may be the last word in literary excellence, but it will get us into trouble just as sure as shooting. It requires us to be prepared to prove, on our own, that the person in question is in fact a Communist, and not merely that he has been identified as one by a witness before a Congressional committee. This is a deadly serious matter, and I would appreciate it if you will all burn this message into your brains."[89]

Within months after Rusher started at *NR*, Buckley told the editors he had "so effectively relieved me of a mountain of troubles." The appreciation was similar four years later. "You are most welcome back. We all missed you dreadfully," he noted after the publisher returned from a trip. "I tried to hang the organization together in your absence, but did so quite unconvincingly."[90] Like his sister, Buckley knew Rusher wasn't wholly comfortable at the magazine. "I don't know how to communicate to you the impression you have made on everyone concerned at *NR*," the vacationing editor wrote from a hotel in Barcelona. "In many ways it is a very difficult community to penetrate. But you have done so, and in full measure, and you are alone responsible. As far as I am myself concerned, suffice it to say that this entire jaunt would have been unthinkable but for you."[91]

## Rusher and Buckley

Rusher communicated his views in meetings but also on paper. Many of his memos and letters were sent to Buckley alone, while most others went to the senior editors as a whole. An average memo to Buckley when he was on his long annual working vacation might include details about circulation, a report that an employee was or wasn't following through on a task, an idea for correcting a recent production glitch, and a judgment about how the latest issue looked. Then, often at length, Rusher would typically share his insights about the immediate political scene, or perhaps on the next step in *NR*'s relationship with an organization. He might go into soul-searching speculations about the conservative movement's prospects and how best to respond to them. Typically he would include a bit of humor, which could be at his own expense or almost anyone's. These memos were grouped in numbered sections that each contained as many as several paragraphs—"very orderly," Buckley notes.[92]

When discussing politics, Rusher even in his thirties frequently adopted the tone of a seasoned elder who had seen a lot. His reflections on the conservative movement often conveyed a strong sense of hope or anxiety, going well beyond basic analysis. To Buckley he normally wrote in the style of a subordinate, but a subordinate who thought he had better knowledge of most things he was covering. It was common for Rusher to step back momentarily from his advocacy, conceding his own fallibility or acknowledging the impressions others might get. Of his repeated insistence that *NR* was disengaged from its obligations as a movement leader, he admitted to Buckley in 1962: "I plead guilty to being positively tedious about this."[93] In addition to political and journalistic analysis, Rusher sometimes offered the editor personal advice if it was professionally relevant. During Buckley's vacations, a six-page single-spaced memo from Rusher wasn't unusual, and four more pages might follow a week later. The editor responded from Switzerland just as if he were in New York. "He wanted me to be aware of all of his thoughts," Buckley recalls. "I was very grateful for what he did, and I felt very keenly informed about what he did."[94]

Rusher was not a general intellectual influence on Buckley, as Burnham was or Kendall had been, but he strengthened the editor's political knowledge and contacts. Although "deeply interested in politics," Buckley did not have "an instinctive natural political sense." He was "quite willing to be introduced by me to figures, and to ideas, and to practices in the political scene . . . It didn't mean that he agreed to be guided by me. He's not that kind of a fellow. But he was grateful, I think, for the input."[95] David Franke, who was a junior *NR* staffer and a Young Americans for Freedom leader in the early 1960s, remembers Rusher as "Bill's emissary to the political world."[96]

One of their earliest disagreements involved the place of political anger. Buckley did not share Rusher's wish to see all twenty-two Republicans who had voted for the McCarthy censure gone from the Senate. "I thought it was a little Bolshevik in its totality. We didn't ask our readers, or suggest to our readers, that they take lifelong vows to bury those people. I can't even remember who they were, but I'm sure some of them were pretty good soldiers in later years."[97]

In late 1957, Ralph de Toledano, a conservative journalist who was a close friend of Richard Nixon, passed along an invitation for Buckley to interview the vice president. Given Nixon's early front-runner status for the next presidential nomination and Buckley's stature as a highly visible conservative spokesman, the meeting, as Rusher later described it, would be something of an "encounter between a candidate and a political bloc that might or might not decide to support him." Wanting to have some tough questions ready, Buckley asked Rusher for suggestions. Rusher figured Nixon would deal easily with questions that called for a choice between ordinary conservative and liberal positions. Seven times out of ten, he would give a moderately conservative response for Buckley; the other three times, he would give a liberal answer. While tending to satisfy people on the Right, this wouldn't threaten whatever interest liberals had in Nixon as a candidate. Rusher preferred a question that would pressure the vice president to choose between the liberals and Eisenhower, and he came up with one. In 1954, a special panel under former Army secretary Gordon Gray had revoked the security clearance of nuclear physicist J. Robert Oppenheimer, given evidence of his earlier Communist sympathies and connections. Now, with liberals urging the reversal of that decision, Nixon should be asked whether he supported this or preferred to maintain the revocation. Rusher knew that Eisenhower both agreed with the panel's judgment and hadn't yet made his actual decision. In addition, Nixon had said nothing about the issue, and it was a major one for many liberals.[98]

At the meeting, Buckley asked the suggested question. "I have the highest confidence in the integrity of the Gray Board," Nixon replied. Rusher, who was not present, remained impressed even many years later by the answer's "deceptive polish." While sounding anti-Oppenheimer, it left open the possibility that the committee was honest but wrong. Buckley repeated the question, and Nixon evasively "went off over high hills and dales." Finally cornered and forced to choose, he agreed with Eisenhower but still couldn't say it plainly. To Rusher this showed the essential Nixon, "always bucking and dodging and weaving . . . all things to all men."[99] Buckley, however, seemed satisfied when he printed the response in *National Review*: "We are glad to report . . . from the Vice-President's own mouth . . ." Writing Nixon to thank him for his time, he observed that a little "tension" between political leaders and conservative intellectuals was healthy, adding: "But I hope you know that we mean well, and well by you." Rusher had caused Nixon a bit of trouble but may also have offended him. A Nixon aide whom he knew, perhaps Charlie McWhorter, noted: "Buckley didn't do himself any good with the boss by printing that paragraph."[100]

Despite their strong relationship as colleagues and their nearly complete political agreement, Buckley and Rusher didn't develop the kind of tight personal friendship for which the editor became famous. "They were, I think, very close in the first few years," Priscilla Buckley recalls. The gloomy business picture required that they work closely together, but as these immediate pressures diminished, their need for shop talk lessened. Well acquainted with his publisher by then, Buckley "pretty much knew what Bill Rusher's reaction would be to anything," and Rusher knew the same of Buckley. Each had also "developed a persona," different interests, different circles of friends.[101]

Among Buckley's hobbies were sailing and skiing. Within several years after founding *National Review*, he was also enjoying friendships with celebrities and well-known intellectuals outside its immediate crowd. Rusher "didn't solicit the kind of life that I went in for." As Buckley once teased the publisher from Switzerland in the early years: "I pray you won't think I have wasted my time when I get back. Have you ever tried skiing?"[102] In November 1962 they visited southern Africa together as journalists. About ninety minutes after takeoff, Buckley recalls, "we were told that we had an engine problem. Bill was very nervous about that. It infuriated him that I continued typing while we clambered back to New York to get a fresh plane."[103]

Rusher, on the other hand, sometimes sought to bolster Buckley's politically aggressive side. One of the editor's best academic friends was the conservative scholar Gerhart Niemeyer, a political science professor at Notre Dame. In 1958, Niemeyer was spending a year teaching at the National War College, and Buckley gave a lecture there. According to Niemeyer, the lecture provoked hostility among much of the audience. A civil war atmosphere was in the air that day, he told Buckley, in what should have been a relatively sympathetic audience. Niemeyer urged Buckley to "touch common ground" in future presentations. Buckley forwarded the letter to Rusher and asked for his thoughts.[104] Rusher responded that Niemeyer was raising a problem "we are going to face for the rest of our lives."

He began his long commentary by noting that the talk might have been either "too elliptical for the military mind" or too "irreverent" toward President Eisenhower to be well received by "men who . . . derive their prestige and paychecks from appointments they hold during his pleasure." But the real question wasn't whether the audience liked what Buckley had said. Even if the result really was something of a civil-war atmosphere, Rusher thought this hardly proved "that you 'failed to communicate'—quite the contrary. A true failure to communicate tends to produce apathy, not hysteria." What Niemeyer really meant was that Buckley "failed to *persuade*." Rusher then gave his view of how persuasion worked.

As relevant experience, he pointed to his own rightward journey within the Republican Party and the fact that friends had moved in the same direction. From it, he had learned that "nobody *ever* surrendered—visibly and all at once—a tenaciously-held opinion on an important subjective question." When someone admitted that an argument impressed him, Rusher found, this was "solid evidence that he was either predisposed in the same direction, or genuinely undecided, before the discussion began." When a person truly disagreed with what he heard, "a powerful argument's first effect was always to *shake* him," and such a reaction would either be concealed or take the form of irritation, silence, or evasive humor. Only later, perhaps months or years later, would he notice a change in the friend's position. True persuasion developed like a "classic syndrome—outrage, silence, assent, enthusiasm. In that order."

Buckley's lecture would have "a profound effect," Rusher continued. It would "rattle around at the base of their brains, unforgettable and unassimilable, long after the pablum that preceded and followed it has been eliminated from their memories." Buckley had criticized "the established order" that day, and the audience's instinct was to "identify themselves with it and defend it," Rusher explained. "But to many of them, some day soon, there will come a moment when some particular Liberal inanity becomes too much to bear; and then they will try to remember what it was you said, and will wish desperately they had your wit and panache." That would mark "the beginning of another trouble-maker for Liberalism."

Rusher next aimed a shot at Niemeyer. "There is nothing wrong with his low-pressure technique of disputation, save that it doesn't accomplish anything. He may think he is slowly gaining converts to conservatism, but I will bet (perhaps Burnham could check this) that he has already been measured and discounted at the National War College, and will soon be forgotten altogether." Finally, Rusher issued Buckley this challenge: "I recently read somewhere a little homily to the effect that, if a person makes us *think* we're thinking, we love him; but if he makes us *think*, we hate him. Take your choice—and then make up your mind to take the consequences."[105]

*Moderating a* National Review *Forum debate at Hunter College between Buckley and* New York Post *editor James Wechsler—"Resolved: That Liberalism Should Be Repudiated"*

Buckley remained aggressive on the public stage. But he also aimed for a pleasing cultural product, not just political advocacy, at the magazine. "What was most important to Bill in editing *National Review* was that the writing be distinguished," Priscilla later explained. "It seemed to him more important that a writer write beautiful prose than . . . be a movement conservative."[106] Although Rusher looks back on the hiring of young writers (among them John Leonard and Joan Didion) without knowing whether they were conservatives as "a bad habit" of Buckley's, he became friends with one in particular.

Garry Wills was unformed politically when he came to *NR* in the summer of 1957 but could "go along" with its politics, Rusher recalls. He was "single and young and hungry, and I needed people to go out to restaurants with me." As "great friends," they had many conversations, often about God or philosophy. Rusher would remember one, "the kind of thing we were always discussing," about the role of the actor in the theater. "At some point I said to Wills, and nearly reduced him to tears of laughter: 'Let us take the hypothetical case of the malignant Hamlet.'" They exchanged letters for a while after Wills left to begin graduate work in classics at Yale. When he married not long thereafter, Rusher and Buckley were ushers at the wedding.[107] Wills told Rusher: "You are able justly to call more people 'the nicest (young couple, fellow, people, etc.) I know' than anyone I ever met." He had assumed "you merely had some trick of *finding* them," but "on second thought, I believe you have an alchemistry of your own for *making* them so."[108]

The magazine's reputation was naturally of great importance to Buckley, whether in the interest of political impact or in terms of the intrinsic value of work well done. Looking back half a century later, he would reflect: "*National Review* became, very quickly, the organ of the literate and concerned body of libertarian and conservative thought in America. It became their spokesman—and that happened quite early on, in the late fifties. One published in *National Review*, or in effect nowhere else . . . That gave it a kind of standing which I guess I would point to as supremely satisfying."[109]

Major right-of-center intellectuals, though, weren't always impressed. T. S. Eliot told Russell Kirk, in the first months of publication, that he thought it was "too consciously the vehicle of a defiant minority." Unless a reader shared all of Buckley's opinions, Eliot admonished, he might "gradually get the impression that it was a vehicle of prejudice, and that all issues were decided in advance." Kirk, who wrote a column on higher education for *NR* and wished the magazine well but always kept a distance from it, had already admitted to Eliot that he found it gave off "too much Yale undergraduate spirit."[110] The French political philosopher Bertrand de Jouvenel told Buckley that although "I often appreciate the talent of [your] contributors, I nearly always deplore the tone, which is a sort of clawing." Anyone engaged in politics should assume the "good faith and honesty of opponents" and speak with the greatest possible civility. To preserve and indeed elevate the tone of debate, Jouvenel urged, was a "special obligation" of the Right and was also in its self-interest. Buckley answered: "What you object to is what the English would call cheekiness, the Americans smart-aleck. I tire of it myself, although our bumptiousness is first-rate, by and large." It was necessary "precisely because we have needed to inspirit our people, and show that there is [still] wit and trenchancy" even in allegedly simplistic conservatives. The magazine's "tonal vibrancy," Buckley added, had "caught the ear of a great many young people . . . [and]

caused them to stop a minute in what otherwise would have been a headlong plunge into liberalism."[111]

*National Review* was also criticized from the opposite direction, as seeming aloof and elitist. E. F. Hutton, one of its few early donors in big business, observed that the magazine didn't "speak the homely language of Americans . . . on the farms and factories" and concluded it was therefore "too highbrow to be effective." Buckley agreed with the first point but not the second. The magazine was more intellectual than average readers, he knew, but that didn't make it ineffective. As he explained to columnist Ruth Alexander, who shared Hutton's concerns, *NR* must avoid "the popular and cliché ridden appeal to the 'grassroots'" if it hoped to revive conservatism. It was "very consciously aiming at thoughtful people, at opinion makers."[112]

Rusher's sympathies on the issue were with Hutton and Alexander. Admitting he was "a complete neophyte" in opinion journalism, he made a few suggestions even in his first months at *National Review.* The magazine, he told Buckley, must be "more readable." Much of it certainly was, but some of it "verged on obscurantism." Both the language and the concepts in *NR* could lack clarity. More thought should be given to the reader. "I remind you of *Time*'s famous literary convention . . . that it would be written 'as if *by* one man *to* one man.' On another level, consider the *New Yorker,* whose writers uniformly toe a single line as to what its readers are expected to know, find amusing and just generally like." Although Rusher wasn't seeking "such rigid conformity" as that, the editors should have a "reasonably uniform mental image of the person, or at least of the spectrum of types of person to whom the magazine is addressed."[113]

Buckley wanted high quality in both the intellectual analysis and the political coverage, also wishing to keep a distance from conservative writing of a lower class. Several months after joining *NR,* Rusher on a friend's suggestion sent copies of *Nine Men Against America* by Rosalie Gordon, an attack on the Supreme Court, to more than one hundred law-school deans and requested comments on it that the magazine might run. Erwin Griswold at Harvard replied "promptly, fully and vehemently," Rusher noted.[114] "It makes me rather sad," Dean Griswold wrote, "that you should apparently feel that this pamphlet is a helpful contribution towards better understanding in this important area. The bias and unfairness of the pamphlet are, of course, readily disclosed by its title. Do you really think that Earl Warren and John M. Harlan, to take two examples, are 'against' America? . . . To suggest, as this pamphlet repeatedly does, that they are not patriotic, conscientious Americans, is not worthy of you." The respectability of the author was questionable as well. "At no point is her identity or background disclosed. What are her qualifications for passing such definite judgment on such important matters?" Griswold also found the booklet full of interpretive and factual errors. Another law-school dean was outraged. "Miss Gordon stimulates a kind of anger in me," wrote Vernon Miller of Catholic University. "I do not want to . . . stoop to epithets because I might be more extravagant than she. After I put aside the brochure, I could not wash my mind, but I did wash my hands."[115]

Buckley more or less sided with Griswold and Miller. "Given the fact that *National Review* has an uphill fight for intellectual recognition," he told Rusher and Bozell (who wrote on legal as well as political affairs), "it is my very strong opinion that we must be extremely careful in all our dealings with academic luminaries. I think we made a mistake in accosting—in many cases for the first time—the deans of the law schools to ask their opinion of Miss Gordon's pamphlet." The book was "not by any stretch of the imagination a piece of legal analysis," Buckley added. "It is a political polemic, parts of it very shoddy indeed, parts of it resourceful and lively, but not the kind of thing that entitles us to arrest the attention of men professionally engaged in the analysis of law." *National Review* had probably "damaged our reputation by even so aloof a sponsorship of this pamphlet," especially among "deans who are searching for a concrete impression of N.R. without reading it."[116]

## Developing *National Review*'s Base

Three weeks after Buckley's anxious warning about *Nine Men Against America*, Rusher enthusiastically told Garry Wills how impressed he was by the number and type of people who read the magazine. His old political mentor Tom Curran, leader of the Manhattan Republican Party, "gave three gift subscriptions last Christmas!" Archbishop (soon Cardinal) Cushing of Boston was a subscriber and donor. Los Angeles–area subscribers included everyone "from the Board Chairman of Southern California Edison and the President of Union Oil to the owner of the Santa Anita racetrack!"[117] Various senators and congressmen had made their mailing lists available. The journal of the Daughters of the American Revolution sometimes ran excerpts from *National Review*. Rusher thanked U.S. Steel for deciding to donate one hundred free subscriptions to employees. *NR* made a special effort to become known among conservative Catholics—repeatedly mailing promotional write-ups to lists of priests, the memberships of Catholic and Irish-American groups, and readers of church publications, in addition to advertising in the *Tablet*, the church's Brooklyn newspaper. By 1961, *NR* had "many loyal friends in the Irish community."[118]

A sense of family was building among subscribers. An elderly woman in Washington was thrilled with her copy of the magazine's first anthology, the *National Review Reader*, where her viewpoints were "so much better analysed and expressed than I am capable of." The autographs included in the volume were "heart-warming. They give me a happy sense of belonging and being a part of an effort that will be sure to continue after I am gone. I am eighty-four, and my later years are not made happy by the state of the country I have loved all my life. Incidentally, I have already saved my second contribution to the cause to send you next Spring or whenever you need it."[119]

In addition to gratitude and word-of-mouth support, such people came through with money. When *NR* faced an especially acute financial crisis in 1958, it was solved partly by reducing the frequency of publication from weekly to every other week, and partly by a plea for medium-sized donations.

*National Review* was initially envisioned as a profit-making enterprise, with a break-even point predicted in its third year and a $100,000 profit in its fourth. But as readers were told in the magazine's newsletter, profits from KOWH, an Omaha radio station Buckley had purchased to produce income for *NR*, were much less than the expected $20,000 in monthly revenue. Advertising was also quite disappointing due to various factors: "fear of association with an independent conservative weekly," failure to understand the role *NR* could play in "generating an atmosphere conducive to freedom and free enterprise," and the business rules common among advertising executives—such as not buying in small magazines.[120]

*NR* was losing $100,000 a year, and the $5,000 and $10,000 contributions from members of the Buckley family couldn't keep it going indefinitely. Fortunately, the plea for donations worked. The editors and staff "watched with growing joy and relief," Rusher would recall in 1984, "as a bar graph set up in the central editorial room . . . inched upward toward our goal." Thereafter, a fund appeal went to subscribers each year, always remaining a crucial resource. The magazine's survival over the next two and a half decades was "directly traceable to the support of several thousand people whose confidence in it never wavered. All honor to them."[121]

Another positive development was the new *National Review Bulletin*, a supplement that briefly reported and reacted to the latest political and world news. An admirer anonymously provided gift subscriptions of the *Bulletin* to every senator and congressman. Eight months before he was hired, Rusher had given a *NR* subscription to his college friend, William Runyeon, a doctor in eastern Pennsylvania and a firmly moderate Republican at the time. A year later, calling it "the most important magazine in America," Runyeon signed up his father for *National Review*. In 1958 the elder Runyeon donated one hundred dollars to the ailing journal and, Rusher was told, was giving eight or ten subscriptions to friends.[122]

As of September 1957, about two months after Rusher arrived, *NR* had about 17,000 paid subscribers. A year later it had more than 23,000. Then, in the fall of 1958 alone, subscriptions rose to more than 27,000, largely because of Jim McFadden's direct-mail solicitations.[123] In 1960 circulation reached 34,000. After a stagnant period in 1962–63, rapid progress continued. Thanks partly to the grassroots mobilization associated with the Goldwater campaign, circulation in 1964 climbed to 90,000. The magazine faced little competition in its niche. It also switched to better-quality paper and full-color covers in the early sixties, improving visual appeal. Growing interest in the movement among young people proved helpful as well. High school and college students like himself, recalls American Conservative Union chairman David Keene, "counted down the hours" for their new issue of *NR*.[124]

Just as not every Buckley admirer was on the Right and not everybody on the Right was thrilled by the magazine, not all readers were conservatives. Advertising director Mike Mooney could report in mid-1962: "It is now hip in the book trade, in Greenwich Village, The New York Post and other such homes of the latest fad, to read National Review (and hate it)."[125]

Meanwhile, Rusher's political and other activities may have cut into his oversight responsibilities as publisher. In 1962, a long report from a business staff member—written after a note from Buckley to the effect that something seemed "gravely wrong with the circulation department"—described what a mess it had been in for the past year.[126]

Eventually, the drought in display advertising eased when more ads began running from larger companies, sources that previously showed little interest in *NR* for both economic and political reasons. Even after almost seven years of growth, however, true financial stability remained a dream. In early 1964, Rusher told Buckley the picture was "relatively (though only relatively) good, thanks to the false dawn provided by the fund appeal." *NR* was sixty to ninety days behind on most bills.[127]

# 5

# Speaker, Debater, Advocate, Mentor

In his first several years at the magazine, Rusher's political activity shifted toward speechmaking, radio appearances, and debating, even as he remained quietly involved in the Young Republicans. After the 1957 YR convention, Rusher and White largely "faded away" as open players, according to their Syndicate ally Ned Cushing. Sensitive to accusations that their preferred candidates were pawns, they tried to stay inconspicuous at the 1959 convention in Denver, where they helped Cushing narrowly win election as national chairman, but they were "always in the background." As the Syndicate's candidate for cochairman (in effect vice chairman) at the same convention, Judy Fernald had a supposedly more conservative opponent. As people asked "all kinds of questions" at a meeting of a delegation that was leaning against her, movement journalist Stan Evans "stood up at the back of the room and said: 'Isn't Bill Rusher one of your best friends?' I said: 'Oh yes, he is,' and the caucus went for me immediately."[1]

Despite Rusher's disinclination to run for office, his experience as a Young Republican leader and as a college debater made it easy to give well-received speeches, and soon many groups were hearing him. "He was always compelling when he was on a public podium," Buckley recalls.[2] Given his recent background and his route into ideological conservatism, Rusher was especially eager to address the cold-war issues then dominant on the Right. Answering a local Democratic club's invitation, he admitted: "I know very little about economics and dislike what little I know. Why not assign me to talk on some aspect of the Communism question?"

Rusher's intensity was well suited to the anxiously questing mood that became prevalent among conservatives in his first years at *NR*. After a speech to the National Society of New England Women titled "Eleventh Hour for America," he was praised for articulating "a message of real Americanism" that made the ladies "more determined than ever to be alert" to communist efforts.[3] Thanking him for his talk to a Young Republican group in Brooklyn, its president reported that the "discussion and arguments" continued for hours after Rusher left around 10:30 P.M.—and that *NR* would have some new subscribers as a result of his visit. Of the three talks at an event shortly after the disastrous 1958 midterm election, noted Mrs. M. N. Bonbrake, a friend of *NR*, she and many others had enjoyed his the most: "You managed to give your listeners a note of hope . . . At this moment bitter cynicism is not what people need . . . While still hopeful, you were honest and factual and did not pull your punches."[4]

Rusher became a frequent guest on the New York radio programs hosted by Barry Farber, Barry Gray, and "Long John" Nebel. Well-prepared and aggressive, he impressed Farber as "a combination laser beam, Swiss watch, and steel trap." Opponents seemed sincerely indignant, scolding him and calling him names, but he conceded nothing and ably turned negatives around. In an early appearance on the program, Farber recalls, Rusher answered one objection by saying: "No, I *haven't* been to South Africa. But you *must* have been to South Africa, or you wouldn't be making such heavy weather of it. Now, what did you learn in South Africa that you think is so important for us to know?'" A disarmament activist mentioned that he and his son had just visited Hiroshima, where they saw the continued human devastation from the atomic bomb. "Dr. Jack," Rusher said, "I wonder if on your way to Hiroshima, you happened to stop off at Pearl Harbor, where 3,000 American servicemen are buried . . ." At parties, Farber was often asked to do imitations of his sharp-tongued guest.[5]

For those already on his side, Rusher had a strong appeal. Pleased by his deft handling of two "leftist . . . creeps" on the Gray program, a local business owner wrote: "We in Amityville never fail to listen to you, but last night you were at your best. You have millions behind [*sic*], keep the ball rolling, we can't be stopped now. God bless you."[6] The Nebel show was a particular challenge, requiring a pair of guests to debate all night, with food provided by the Carnegie Delicatessen and Restaurant. Columbia student Jeff Bell, later a leading conservative activist and political consultant, heard Rusher on the program, enjoyed his "very unapologetic" style, and contacted him for an interview that ran in his short-lived campus journal.[7]

One evening at Mamma Leone's, an Italian restaurant on West 48th Street from which Farber broadcast at the time, Rusher debated Socialist

Party leader and perennial presidential candidate Norman Thomas. Reaching back to the isolationist rally at Princeton he had attended as a heckler in 1941, he highlighted Thomas's contention that America could be defended from the Nazis at "the bulge of Brazil" if necessary. "It wasn't a very pleasant evening for Thomas," according to Rusher, who used the point to roll over him "like a truck, again and again and again"—in retrospect, he adds, perhaps too harshly with the old man. Afterward, Thomas turned to Rusher and said: "A unique experience."[8] A woman in the live audience, a left-wing friend of Farber's, applauded the socialist after the debate ended. Rusher was uncharacteristically rattled: "Look, Barry. It's hard enough being a conservative without having Screaming Mimis like this." But in fact, "he did roll over him like a truck."

Although debates were the show's regular format in these years, no one developed a reputation as a good liberal opponent. "I was waiting for a nemesis to appear," Farber recalls, "but none ever did." After five decades as a radio host, he still considers his shows with Rusher "the best of my best broadcast days."[9]

## A Movement Magazine?

When Nikita Khrushchev came to the United States for a tour in September 1959, it was the first visit to America by any Soviet premier. Outraged that President Eisenhower had invited him, Buckley thought up an attention-getting mass rally to show opposition. He got Rusher and Marvin Liebman, a tireless anticommunist organizer and fund-raiser in New York, to form a Committee Against Summit Entanglements for this purpose. Rusher would remember that the necessary tasks—which Buckley, despite his warning to the contrary, had breezily estimated as just "a couple of phone calls"—took up the time of most *NR* staff members for nearly three weeks. Irritated by "hints that he wasn't shouldering his share of the burden," Buckley helped by finding an organist.

To Rusher's chagrin, the noted musician followed Buckley's classical tastes and played a Bach fugue that evening. Based on his experience of many political rallies, he had wanted something more like "a loud brass band . . . to set a crowd's pulses pounding." The rally was a notable success anyway. Filling Carnegie Hall to capacity were 2,500 people wearing black armbands and waving black flags to recognize communism's tens of millions of victims. As master of ceremonies, Rusher opened by asking the audience to rise and sing "that outmoded classic, 'The Star-Spangled Banner.'"[10]

Taking minor swipes at Buckley when recounting the episode in *Rise of the Right* a quarter-century later, Rusher also stressed his admiration for the editor's concluding address by quoting several paragraphs. "Khrushchev is *not* aware that the gates of hell shall not prevail against us," Buckley said. "Even out of the depths of despair, we take heart in the knowledge that it cannot matter how deep we fall, for there is always hope. In the end, *we* will bury *him*." Rusher added proudly: "In such terms did conservatism, in that year of Our Lord 1959, defy the conventional wisdom of the day."[11]

Although Buckley could be an eloquent speaker and the eager catalyst for an event like the anti-Khrushchev rally, he also sympathized with tendencies by some on the Right to remain aloof from political struggle. To Buckley, Rusher recalls, organized conservatism's thin political presence around 1960 was "not all that undesirable a situation. He was a literary man. He was doing a literary thing. He didn't have, I'd say at some level knew he didn't have, a lot of political instincts—and therefore, starting a political movement was not really what he was about. It was very much what I was about."[12]

Buckley certainly felt less strongly than Rusher about conservative organizing and did not naturally enjoy it, but his attitude was more than literary or elitist. Not known for avowals of populism, he nonetheless placed a certain faith in the majority's good sense, as had his teacher Willmoore Kendall. In a 1963 newspaper column, Buckley said conservatives should join Parent-Teacher Associations, professional groups, the conservative National Association of Manufacturers, the Republican Party, even the Democratic Party in places where it was "salvageable." Agreeing that there was "every reason to fight hard through organizations," he added that one should also celebrate Americans' "decent conservative instincts." These were, he believed, a force substantial enough to continue effective resistance to liberalism even if political activity on the Right should disappear: "Abolish every single conservative organization in America—every one of them; and still the Liberals' way is not cleared. Because deep within us . . . is an unquenchable desire for freedom, and for a sense of order rooted in the Christian ethic. They may take it away from us by attrition—I fear that they will. But . . . they must go against the grain of the American personality, which is the secret weapon of American conservatives."[13]

In memos and in thrice-yearly deliberative meetings known as "The Agony," *NR* editors considered the magazine's policies. As voices in this running seminar, Rusher and Meyer sought more direct political involvement by the magazine, and a more obviously right-wing identity for it, than Burnham and Buckley preferred. Largely agreeing with them was a more recently appointed senior editor, Bill Rickenbacker, adopted son of Eddie Rickenbacker, the legendary World War I pilot. Managing editor Priscilla Buckley, however, tended toward her brother's and Burnham's view.

Meyer, Rusher, and Rickenbacker valued the long Agony meeting, held either at the Buckleys' Manhattan townhouse or at their home in Stamford, as an important chance to counter Burnham. About 1960, they successfully insisted that Buckley begin to schedule it three times a year, rather than once or twice a year as the editor preferred. As Rickenbacker later explained, they "felt a need to combine our forces to hold the line" against Burnham and therefore "decided to . . . let Bill see that JB's opposition on the board was organized and not inconsiderable."[14]

Rusher's emphasis on tangible political results clashed with Burnham's stress on cultural evolution driven by economics and by the thought patterns of the American elite. While Burnham advised a gradual attempt to persuade that elite away from liberalism, Rusher urged that *NR* take a leading role in forming a doctrinally sound movement of political activists—as distinct from the conservative intellectual movement, to which it was already central. Almost by definition, a political movement would consist mainly of people who wanted to get something done.

Meyer's battle at *NR*, his son John remembers, was "to prevent it from becoming what he called 'the right wing of the establishment.' He wanted it to continue a head-on challenge to the establishment." He tried to "keep it from basking in the recognition of: 'Oh, you're the intelligent conservatives,'" believing Buckley was "prone to that tendency" because of his increasing connections in high society. After the magazine's first five years or so, Meyer felt he was constantly struggling against such an attitude—and not necessarily winning. It was "an ongoing battle that he expected to be fighting forever." His father both liked and disliked working with Buckley, according to John Meyer, complaining at times that the editor "doesn't have a political bone in his body." In addition, he and Burnham had "knockdown, drag-out" arguments about the latter's belief that forces, rather than people, determined history.[15]

Burnham's position derived from a keen sense of the weight of the "establishment," from a belief that American society would not fundamentally change unless the elite changed, since the people did not really rule. Also important was his great concern for quality. "Priscilla and I take a more professional point of view toward NR," he told Buckley, adding:

> We want simply to have the best magazine in the world, assuming a general (not too sharply defined) conservative and anti-communist point of view. Frank, Bill R. and Bill R. also want a good magazine, of course, but they first of all want a crusade, a political party and a kind of ersatz church, and they want NR itself to be all these things or at least organically and intimately a part of all three, rather than

a magazine-as-magazine which would have a certain aloofness from crusades, parties and churches, even if it altogether agreed with them.[16]

In addition to his distaste for the concept of *NR* as a movement builder and his relative political moderation, Burnham had more doubts about the public than did Meyer and Rusher. He warned of the extent to which liberalism not only misled Americans but also appealed to them. "Perhaps a majority is liberal," he wrote in 1964, "but that is hard to determine accurately." In any case, liberalism had a "profound and widespread influence, to which very few citizens of the Western nations are altogether immune." It exerted such an influence because it "fulfilled a pervasive and compelling need." It could, Burnham explained, "comfort us in our afflictions" by offering "a transcendental world, where the soul may take refuge from the prosaic, unpleasant world of space and time."[17]

Meyer and Rusher saw not a continuum, as Burnham suggested, but what Meyer called a "profound chasm . . . between the beliefs and instincts of the solid citizenry" and the liberalism that characterized most intellectual and high-level governmental leaders. The liberal elite, he observed in a 1962 essay, held power in two ways: by a "quasi-monopolistic control of the channels of communication" and by advocating "speciously attractive" programs. But it hadn't yet succeeded in "seriously establishing its ideology in the minds and souls of the American people." This unpersuaded public, Meyer believed, included both average citizens and "the great majority of professionals and businessmen and community leaders, of Congressmen and . . . legislators and municipal officials." Although powerful, the liberal establishment was really a "limited and shallow stratum" in whose outlook most Americans refused to "acquiesce."

But Meyer also thought conservatives were in a race against time. "The problem can be stated in the starkest terms: Can the men of the rising conservative movement . . . expel the dominant Establishment from its positions of control before they succeed in bringing about the corruption of the American people in the image of their own corruption?" The struggle was "a confrontation at every level: intellectual, moral, social, political. The conservative task would seem to be a heroic task."[18]

The disputes between Burnham and Meyer led to endless rivalry for Buckley's agreement. This rivalry was difficult for Meyer and his allies because of the special respect the editor accorded Burnham. Buckley had acquired a great admiration for him through his writings, by noting the regard others expressed for him, and from the fact that "his deportment was always so perfect." Burnham, he recalls, impressively combined "an absolute maintenance of his own editorial integrity" and his "reputation as a very thoughtful philosopher" with an "occasional appetite for combat," which appeared in the strong editorials he often wrote.[19]

In early 1964, with Rusher and Burnham predictably at odds over the Goldwater candidacy, Buckley cautioned the publisher: "I rate your political knowledge and shrewdness very high indeed, and I listen intently to everything you have to say. I think you would be wiser still if you permitted yourself every now and then to reflect on the fact that some very profound and shrewd political observers and philosophers have assessed James Burnham's political mind as being among the half dozen shrewdest of this century." Burnham was, Buckley affirmed decades later, unquestionably "the dominant intellectual influence in the development of this journal."[20]

Jeff Bell, who worked as an intern at *NR* in 1963 and was on the staff for several months after graduating from college in 1965, describes the relationship between Rusher and Burnham as "cold." Discussing the magazine with him over lunch as they sometimes did, the publisher and Bill Rickenbacker seemed of two minds about their older colleague. Although they showed great respect for him and "helped me understand how important a figure he was in the 20th century," they also talked about "their war with Burnham, and how he was corrupting Bill Buckley" in an intellectual sense. Rusher worried, as much as anything, about a reluctant attitude toward politics. "He thought Buckley, and in a weird way Burnham . . . lacked self-confidence."

It was, Bell suggests, a plausible insight. "Burnham understood the extent of the Left, and how pervasive it was, and what a threat it was to traditional America. But he knew so much about it . . . that he almost couldn't help but be pessimistic about the conservatives." Buckley was similarly "insecure about what conservatives could do, how they could overcome marginalization." Both "felt surrounded—by the strength of the Left in Europe, and Marxism and all the rest—and they were pessimistic."[21]

Rusher also believed Burnham was too willing to accommodate currently powerful figures, too unwilling to back political revolt: "I think his ideal would be for *National Review* to have become the intellectual cabinet of Nelson Rockefeller. He believed in power, he believed that power was associated with money, he knew the Rockefellers had money, and he was interested in cultivating them and being cultivated by them." Burnham did not envision a mass movement based on principles, and his conservatism was, in Rusher's view, "more the agreed dominance of an elite." Meyer, who advocated a movement that would challenge liberals directly in the political arena and work to unseat them, had "ultimately more consequence."[22]

Substantive differences among the senior editors and Rusher weren't always easy to separate from personality clashes. "A certain amount of

Burnham was a tease," Buckley notes. "He liked to tease, especially Frank Meyer, and there was a ritual reenactment of this at every one of our [quarterly] editorial meetings. After two or three hours of this, that and the other, we were about ready to go—and Burnham would say: 'I think we ought to reconsider the length of the book section.' It always had a predicted effect. Frank Meyer would rise up with his cigarette in his hand, and declaim the rightness of his approach, and everybody else would just be sort of quietly amused."[23] Meyer was "very easy for Burnham to bait," Rusher agrees. "I had to warn him once: 'Don't you realize that Burnham is just saying these things to get your goat?' It hadn't occurred to him. After that, he tamed down a little bit, but Burnham would always tweak him and be gratified by the explosion."[24]

Meyer had a particular dislike for Burnham, "relentlessly and snidely criticizing him in conversations with other NR personnel" and even calling him "the Enemy" at times, according to biographer Kevin Smant. Rusher remembers the Meyer-Burnham conflict as "a true struggle" and his own relationship with Burnham as better. "There was never the slightest hostility; certainly not anything that lasted. We respected each other, we got along, we saw a great many things the same way. I admired him enormously."[25]

Much of the conflict between Rusher and Burnham is best understood as a difference in focus and intellectual habit, according to Priscilla Buckley. "Bill knew a great deal more about the insides of politics than most of the rest of us did, and it was much more important to him." He also "liked to win battles" and was more aggressive in the meetings, "readier for a fight than Burnham was." In contrast, Burnham emphasized "the global place in which the United States sat and its influence." He enjoyed "analyzing the causes behind an event: who the players were, and what the pressures on them were . . . what the happening meant." He also liked "confronting a proposition and being able to tear it down, as an intellectual practice."[26]

With the second annual rally of Young Americans for Freedom coming up in 1962, Rusher couldn't resist reporting one of Burnham's reactions to Buckley: "Jim expressed great shock" that the young people "might actually boo the name of President Kennedy—their sovereign!" Showing such disdain for lesser figures like UN ambassador Adlai Stevenson was acceptable to Burnham, but the president was another matter. "It took some time to convince him that you can hardly expect 17,000 . . . enthusiasts to miss a chance like that to boo Kennedy."[27]

Rusher's major editorial theme in meetings was "right-wing militance," Buckley recalls. "He was always very distressed by anything that was heretical, or quasi-heretical, or leaned in that direction." A typical point might be that a senator made an "idiotic speech last weekend" and that the magazine should have mentioned it. "Very often, he was absolutely right." Comments from Rusher were "received as interesting and relevant. Every now and then, there would be a discreet yawn if he brought up something which was a King Charles's head with him. But he was an active, resourceful, and well-read contributor in everything that had to do with what the magazine was interested in."[28]

The publisher spoke in a vigorous, projecting baritone voice and often seemed to be delivering a speech. "Bill Rusher's perorations at [the weekly] editorial meetings could be absolutely extraordinary," Priscilla remembers. "He's a born orator, and very funny. We'd all sit back and just enjoy the performance." Burnham, in contrast, tended to state his own opinion briefly, commenting more on others' remarks and asking quiet questions. He listened carefully but was "less interested, some thought, in a colleague's argument than in the underlying motives that had led him to advance it."[29] Yet Burnham remained patient with the publisher's themes. He "listened to Rusher respectfully" and "never dismissed him," Priscilla recalls. He was "always interested in anyone's mode of analysis, and I think he was quite prepared to learn from Bill Rusher. He would often, when we were talking about it in our little office afterwards, say: 'You know, Rusher has a very good point there.'"[30]

## A Publisher's Concerns

Whether *National Review* wished to shape and lead a movement or not, holding such a visible place among conservatives sometimes required it to make judgments about them—and to decide whether and how strongly to judge. The first major instance was the *American Mercury* controversy in 1959. The journal's owner, Russell Maguire, had included anti-Semitic writings in the *Mercury* over the past few years and now ran an editorial endorsing the belief in a Jewish conspiracy to control the world. Two of Buckley's friends on the Right, Morrie Ryskind and Alfred Kohlberg, urged him to disassociate *NR* from the *Mercury*.

When the possibility of a public stand against the magazine came up in a directors' meeting, Rusher and Mrs. Bonbrake, a local activist who sat on the board as a grassroots representative, opposed the idea, cautioning that *NR* might lose hundreds or even thousands of subscriptions. With Burnham's support, however, Buckley chose a moderate but clear condemnation, telling readers: "*National Review* will not carry on its masthead the name of any person whose name also appears on the masthead of the *American Mercury*. The editors of *National Review* have individually resolved not to write for

*The Mercury* until management changes hands." This led other prominent conservatives to disassociate themselves from the journal as well. Whittaker Chambers praised Buckley's step as a "liberation," and cancellations were fewer than Rusher and Bonbrake feared.[31]

More politically significant than the *Mercury's* drift into bigotry was the rise of a vigorous new organization of conspiracy believers, the John Birch Society, founded in 1958 by businessman Robert Welch and firmly controlled by him. The JBS was named after an American missionary-turned-soldier in China who was killed by communist partisans at the end of World War II; Welch honored him as the first casualty of the Cold War. "Birchers," as they were known, had an impassioned commitment to publicizing and confronting an internal communist conspiracy they believed was close to controlling American government and society and already had great influence on both.

Organized in deliberately small chapters to guard against penetration and maximize trust among members, they also ran campaigns to impeach the liberal chief justice Earl Warren and *"Get US Out of the UN!"* The Birch Society industriously opened bookstores in many communities as well. Its founder and leader said—although later, in 1963, he publicly repudiated the claim—Eisenhower had long been a knowing instrument of the Soviet conspiracy. Although JBS members were not expected to repeat or required to believe it, and in many cases weren't even aware of it, Welch's accusation was becoming known because it was in a book he wrote and circulated on a limited basis, *The Politician*. Among the major anticommunist leaders on the Right who distanced themselves from Welch were Fred Schwarz of the Christian Anti-Communism Crusade and former Minnesota congressman Walter Judd.[32]

Yet the Birch Society was able to enroll a substantial number of members who were well respected by prominent conservatives who knew them, and *NR* could not wisely or fairly disregard this. In New Orleans, Phoenix, and Dallas, Meyer spoke to groups in which, he reported, "three-fourths of the best people I met were John Birch members." In a January 1962 meeting with Buckley and others, Senator Goldwater said he wouldn't categorically condemn the society, since its membership included "nice guys" as well as "kooks."[33] In addition, various people who had been close to the magazine sat on the Birch Society's national council. Willi Schlamm and *NR* contributor Medford Evans, Stan Evans's father, were on the editorial board of the Birch journal *American Opinion*. One of *National Review's* top donors, textile manufacturer Roger Milliken, belonged to the organization.

In early 1961, Rusher and Meyer opposed Buckley's plan to run an editorial against the JBS.[34] Instead, Rusher called for an editorial "(1) praising the public aims of the John Birch Society, (2) carefully describing and sorrowfully deploring the simplistic aims of Welch personally with respect to Communist subversion and especially Eisenhower's supposed role in it, and (3) piously expressing the hope that Welch, 'or the Society,' will soon make it clear that such damaging views are no part of the Society's basic doctrine."

To say more than that, Rusher warned the editors, would "injure NR seriously" in ways barely considered "in the rush to get into print." If Welch told his supporters to stop taking the magazine, the publisher and Jim McFadden thought, cancellations could easily be in the low thousands. Furthermore, the Milliken brothers' annual contributions, in one form or other, equaled about 40 percent of the operating deficit expected for the year. The survival of the magazine wasn't at stake even so, Rusher conceded, but his greater worry was "what an injudicious editorial will do to NR's position *as a leader of conservative opinion* in this country." Since the rumor began that it was about to criticize the JBS, letters, telegrams, and calls had poured in—nearly all contending that although Welch had been "mistaken in major particulars," it was unnatural "for NR to 'join the rat pack' in attacking him or his Society."[35]

Buckley didn't run an editorial at the time, choosing instead to moderately criticize Welch in a question-and-answer piece he wrote about the Birchers. Rusher described it several months later as "a masterpiece, winning the approval of everybody from *Life* magazine to Welch himself"—and after it ran, he noted, it seemed that efforts were made in the JBS national council to limit and reform Welch's role.[36]

When the issue arose again in early 1962, Meyer told colleagues, in an argument similar to one of Rusher's points a year before, that the main thing to consider was the question of establishing "responsible leadership over the conservative movement—or, more precisely, over those who in one way or another regard themselves as conservative." He added: "*Communications have to be kept open and authority developed.* Criticism of a demagogic leader (or of an opportunistic politician) should be conducted in such a way that their followers will still listen to us." An excessively strong editorial, Meyer thought, would be "disastrous . . . in terms of our remaining ability to speak over Welch's head to the vital hard-right forces."[37] Rusher again joined Meyer in opposition, as did Rickenbacker and Brent Bozell, but the decision to run an anti-Welch editorial had support from Burnham and Priscilla. The Birch Society leader, the editorial explained, was damaging the anticommunist cause by persisting "in distorting reality and in refusing to make the crucial moral and political distinction . . . between 1) an *active pro-Communist*, and 2) an *ineffectually anti-Communist liberal*."[38]

After the editorial was published, it seemed to Rusher that responses from many readers confirmed fears he had cited in 1961. He made it a point to review all of this mail, much of which came from non-Birch-ers. "One recurrent theme," he told Buckley, "is the suspicion that you personally are jealous of Welch, and launched the attack because you disliked to have your own prominence in the conservative movement threatened." People were also expressing their dismay to others. John Ashbrook, the former YR comrade of Rusher's who was now a congress-man, said he heard uniformly negative reactions to the editorial when giving Lincoln Day talks to Republicans around the Midwest, although most seemed sad rather than angry. Ashbrook qualified as an objective source, since he was "a thoroughly professional politician," conservative "but by no means Birchite."

In conclusion, Rusher told Buckley the anti-Welch editorial was "a wrenching break with a simplistic segment of *National Review*'s, and your own personal, following." Judging by the letters the editorial provoked, "it seems perfectly clear that the after-effects of that break will leave scars upon the future—in the form of questions after lectures, and muffled criticisms, and unvoiced doubts—for long years after we have drained the last drop of excitement, or even of calm nobility, out of the gesture."[39]

Buckley remained confident that his decision made sense both morally and politically, not just for *NR* but for the Right as a whole. While Rusher and Meyer worried about the conservative base, he worried about others who might or might not be won to it. Answering one critical letter, Buckley explained: "It was precisely my desire to *strengthen* the ranks of conserva-tism that led me to publish the editorial. Our movement has got to govern. It has got to expand by bringing into our ranks those people who are, at the moment, on our immediate left—the moderate, wishy-washy conservatives: the Nixonites . . . If they are being asked to join a movement whose leader-ship believes the drivel of Robert Welch, they will pass by crackpot alley, and will not pause until they feel the warm embrace of those way over on the other side, the Liberals."[40] Still, Meyer's and Rusher's fears were partly borne out. *National Review* received hundreds of negative letters, a significant number of cancellations, and numerous losses of $100-plus donors. Rusher's old friend Lewis Kirby, a major *NR* contributor, stopped his donations to the magazine and did not seek reelection to its board. Buckley had a painful phone conversation with Roger Milliken, who nonetheless maintained his very generous level of support.[41]

Rusher also voiced concern for readers' reaction after *National Review*, in mid-1961, opposed an encyclical of Pope John XXIII as "a venture in trivial-ity." *Mater et Magistra*, its title emphasizing the church as both a mother and a teacher to the faithful, was denounced by *NR* for focusing on Third World problems while barely mentioning "the continuing and demonic successes of the Communists." In the next issue of *National Review*, the witty grab-bag column For the Record reported that Catholic conservatives had been saying "*Mater si, Magistra no.*" The liberal Jesuit weekly *America* demanded that *NR* apologize to its Catholic readers, calling the jest "slanderous."[42]

It was a sensitive area because the Buckley family was strongly Catholic, *NR*'s content and language were influenced by Catholicism, and more than half of its readership was Catholic.[43] Whatever these readers and donors thought of the church's more liberal positions, they had been taught to respect its hierarchy long before they started reading the new magazine. An outsider to this demographic, Rusher still felt he could bring useful insight to the question. "There has never been a social [issues] encyclical," he told Buckley, "out of which even the gloomiest Catholic conservative could not extract considerable comfort if he concentrated on the right passages." Thus, even if *NR* believed the pope was simply wrong, it would have been better to respond "in a prudently obfuscatory manner, rather than disagree with him publicly." Proceeding otherwise, *NR* had incurred the hostile reaction from the Jesuit magazine. As a Protestant, Rusher added, he wasn't bothered by this himself. But as publisher, he worried about the controversy's effect on "the undiscriminating laymen and the more pronouncedly ultramontane clergy among our heavy proportion of Catholic readers (and our even heavier proportion of Catholic financial supporters)."[44]

By the end of 1961, *NR*'s paid circulation stood at what Rusher called a "very respectable" fifty-five thousand. Even more important, the publisher thought, was that advertising had grown impressively under Mike Mooney's direction. But many subscribers weren't renewing now, and circulation seemed likely to drop below 50,000. Rusher blamed the incipient or imminent decline on two factors. The year 1962 was lean for conservative causes in general—*Human Events*, for instance, had suffered as well. Rusher suspected that the major media's "furious concentration . . . on the 'ultra-Right'" had made it "temporarily harder . . . to persuade marginal prospects to risk trial subscriptions to allegedly 'Right-wing' publications."

Raising the Birch Society issue again, Rusher also complained that *NR* had chosen to "alienate" much of the conservative movement at this sensitive juncture by running the anti-Welch editorial in February 1962. Subscription renewals had come in at a disappointing rate ever since, which suggested the Birch controversy was still "an open wound" for the magazine. Furthermore, Welch might have as many friends on the conservative lists to which *NR* was mailing in search of new subscribers as he seemed to have among the people who had been solicited for renewal. If so, the editorial might well have turned off some prospective readers in addition to current ones. The publisher thought the pro-Welch "extremists" (as he too called them) were probably going to the Birch magazine *American Opinion* and to *Human Events*, which had adopted a more popular tabloid format.

Given the recent stagnation in subscriptions, Rusher feared that "in due course *National Review* will settle down to being a nice little publication for perhaps 40,000 die-hards." With "no advertising to speak of," it could expect a permanent operating deficit of about $100,000 a year, "made up by its friends in the false hope that the road will have a turning." Rusher suggested that *NR*'s marketing had become insufficiently aggressive. He thought it had been a bad idea to stop soliciting new prospects by direct mail—a decision that resulted from what he saw as an underestimation of the size of *NR*'s potential readership. Rusher suspected that Buckley, in cutting back on direct mail, had pessimistically assumed there was an upper limit on the number of people able to read the magazine and willing to pay for it. Such an assumption seemed hard to believe. There must be numerous lists full of conservatives whom *NR* had never known about: "My God, with a year-long national Goldwater campaign directly ahead of us, how could there fail to be?"

A much higher subscription level of 75,000 or even 100,000 was quite possible, Rusher told the editor. But that couldn't happen, nor could recent losses be reversed, without an "emotional commitment" from Buckley. "If you secretly do not think it can be done, or just don't care, your attitude will subtly but inevitably communicate itself" to McFadden. For the attempt to find new readers in the tens of thousands that Rusher sought, his assistant needed "the stimulus of your potential approval, even enthusiasm."[45]

The publisher further admonished that "vigorous cooperation" from Buckley was necessary in a more general sense as well. In particular, Rusher wanted a clearer sense of the magazine's objectives—about which he was "beginning to feel rather disoriented." Buckley shouldn't "merely treat the whole matter as a problem in Morale Therapy . . . My morale doesn't need a cent spent on it, but I do desperately need to know where you think *National Review* is going, if anywhere, so I can resume helping it get there."[46]

## Mentor

Regardless of what might be decided at *NR*, Rusher continued to form friendships with many young conservatives, developing a distinctive reputation among them. Many people considered it a treat to know him or have significant contact with him. Apologizing for a small turnout at his latest talk at Harvard in early 1961, YR club president Hugh Barber noted that the chance to share dinner and a late-evening discussion with Rusher was "the kind of cement that holds the organization together." His visits were educational, "influencing younger men who *need* good influence." Rusher answered warmly: "I enjoy these get-togethers every bit as much as you do, and wouldn't miss one for the world. To heck with the attendance!"

*With Diarmuid and Maura O'Scannlain on their wedding day*

Always quick to uphold his aesthetic standards, however, he added that future talks could be scheduled in a nicer room, "redolent of leather and wood paneling."[47]

Rusher lived just a few blocks from work, at 30 East 37th Street, next to the Union League Club. His small apartment was immaculate, Judy Fernald recalls, with "everything in its place, no book out of alignment." It had no real view and little natural light, but the nice living room and smaller bedroom seemed adequate for a single man. "I don't think he needed more."[48] An unusual coffee table, with tiles forming a world map, reflected his increasingly extensive travels. Cemented into it were polished rocks from countries he had visited. Rusher would tell visitors about the stones, remembering where he had picked them up.

Tom Van Sickle, a Young Republican who worked as the YR chairman's administrative assistant in Washington in 1959–61 and could easily visit New York, was "transfixed" on his visits with Rusher. He planned on a legal career, and here was "a Harvard lawyer . . . not just any lawyer." As Rusher told stories about his work on the Senate subcommittee, Van Sickle "sat on the edge of my seat."[49] For many youthful conservatives in the city, he provided an introduction to higher culture. As Jeff Bell remembers: "He showed you the world, the big world out there. 'This is Western civilization, and it's a great thing. And you have to understand it, because people aren't getting this in the schools anymore . . . This is what we're trying to preserve and keep alive.'"[50]

When Anne Edwards came to New York at age nineteen, not having attended college, she considered the city "my campus" and Rusher became one of her teachers. "I thought he was English at first, because of the way he dressed. It just tickled me so much to see him like that." After Edwards joined the Young Republican women's club and began writing for its newsletter, she "kept getting in trouble . . . because I was conservative. The Rockefeller people didn't like that." When more knowledgeable members "realized they were going to have to put up with me, I think they called Rusher. I needed a lot of schooling." Once she became the group's president, Edwards was strategically situated in youth politics because of its eleven votes in the state Young Republican federation. Rusher sometimes took her to dinner at expensive restaurants while patiently advising her on how to cast them. He would also explain the wines to her, recording their names in a little notebook and giving each a grade. Edwards learned "all about wines and Armagnac—oh, I loved Armagnac. All that was from Bill. I don't know if it was good for my liver, but he was fun."[51]

Another young acquaintance of Rusher's in the early sixties was Richard Viguerie, then "a green kid from Houston," later the leading direct-mail fund-raiser for grassroots causes on the Right. Viguerie had always been a zealous conservative and anticommunist, "consumed with politics" even as a child, although his blue-collar parents weren't highly political. Like Rusher, he had chosen sides within the Republican Party. As chairman of the Harris County YRs in the late 1950s, he found the Texas GOP largely a "patronage club" that grated on his activist instincts. Viguerie was a protégé of Thad Hutcheson, a prominent Houston lawyer whom he recalls as exemplifying the state party's passive style: "You didn't break into a sweat. You didn't roll up your sleeves and get your hands dirty. You didn't attack Democrats." The mentorship ended abruptly at a county convention when Viguerie "sided with the populist conservatives against Thad . . . It was just like water off a duck's back, no big deal." After all, he was a populist himself.[52]

In 1961, Viguerie saw a classified ad in NR circumspectly announcing the availability of a national position with a conservative organization. Rusher liked his response, checked out his credentials and reputation, and recommended that New York's ubiquitous movement activist Marvin Liebman, both a fund-raiser and a kind of senior supervisor for the recently founded Young Americans for Freedom, should see him. Viguerie first met Rusher one Saturday on the sidewalk outside *National Review.* Wearing a bowler hat and carrying an umbrella, recognizing the young man instantly from a picture attached to his résumé, Rusher began: "Mr. Viguerie, I presume?"[53]

Soon, working under Liebman, he was YAF's executive secretary. Like Anne Edwards, Viguerie saw the New York conservative scene as an educational, not just political experience. With fellow YAF activists David Franke and Don Shafto, he would sometimes eat dinner, then attend a Rusher debate or sit in on one of his radio appearances. Struck by his ability in such settings, he couldn't get enough: "It blew me away, just blew me away." For a year and a half, Viguerie read as much as possible, hoping he might eventually compete with people like Rusher or participate in high-level conservative dialogue. He decided he couldn't catch up.[54]

Like Viguerie, Franke came from a humble background in Texas; his parents had not completed grade school. Editing the paper at his community college, he got a break when *Human Events* ran several of his editorials. Franke landed a job with the conservative newsweekly and came to Washington. Upon returning to school there, he edited the College Republicans' national publication while working as a *Human Events* writer. With activist Douglas Caddy, he cofounded the National Student Committee for the Loyalty Oath in 1959. By 1960, having impressed Buckley in particular, Franke was brought to *National Review.*[55]

He had already met Rusher before joining the magazine. As managing editor at *Human Events,* Stan Evans taught journalism and political strategy to its younger writers at work, at Harrigan's bar in Southwest Washington, and at the back of Martin's Tavern in Georgetown. Martin's had been a favorite of younger New Dealers in the 1930s. Knowing this, Franke and his comrades were "fancying ourselves" in a similar role, "planning the next revolution." Rusher would sometimes join them if he was in town. Once, the talk turned to Barry Goldwater as a great conservative leader. As Evans got louder with each round of beers, a fed-up patron called Goldwater a fascist, igniting a minor brawl. "Rusher was obviously traumatized by this. It was not his lifestyle." Similarly, when they went to German pubs and to his first opera in New York, Franke appreciated it but noticed a formal, "at arm's length" quality to such occasions. With Buckley, "you could really let your hair down."[56]

Stanley Goldstein, then active with the Young Republicans in the city and later *NR*'s outside accountant, fondly recalls Rusher as "very articulate, very well-informed, very fussy—an old bachelor before his time." Meeting him as national YR chairman, the small-town Kansan Ned Cushing found him a bit intimidating, also noticing a tendency to keep his mouth tight when he spoke. "When he told me he didn't have a driver's license and never owned an automobile, I thought: 'I can't believe this guy.'" Among

Goldstein's Republican acquaintances, Rusher was not unanimously popular, and those who disliked him would often associate his "eccentricities"
with what they considered his outside-the-mainstream views. But to others,
he was endearing. "Those who loved him, liked to make fun of him."[57]

An unambiguous advantage for Rusher was his verbal exactitude combined with a forceful voice. As Goldstein notes, "the cadence of his language
was so precise, so careful, as if he'd rehearsed it for hours." When people
first heard him in conversation, they usually "sat up and took notice," recalls
former congressman Robert Bauman, then active in Young Americans for
Freedom. "It was in sharp contrast to Bill Buckley's slow sort of delivery."
Rusher was "very crisp, very to the point, and very emphatic . . . In fact, it
got to be a joke with a lot of us. We'd imitate him to his face." He often came
up with a quotation on the spur of the moment, drawing upon an apparently vast mental inventory. With a strong, disciplined tone and a sense of
"assured ideas" behind it, Rusher, like his father the salesman, sounded as if
he knew what he was talking about. He also seemed like "a guy who means
business." Bauman got the impression he had an extra ten hours a day.[58]

## Rusher and Young Americans for Freedom

In the next two decades, much of Rusher's contact with junior conservatives would be with members of Young Americans for Freedom, which was
founded in September 1960 and immediately became the main youth organization on the Right. Buckley, Rusher, and other movement leaders considered it a high priority to keep YAF in good shape—setting themselves what
proved to be a challenging task.

The idea of such an organization came from Marvin Liebman and former
New Jersey governor Charles Edison, the inventor's youngest son and a key
backer of Liebman's anticommunist projects. YAF grew out of separate but
kindred, unofficial campaigns at the 1960 Republican convention that aimed
to nominate Goldwater and Congressman Walter Judd, respectively, for vice
president. Before leaving Chicago, Liebman and Edison called a meeting of
Youth for Goldwater members, in particular, and urged them to start conservative clubs at their colleges. Doug Caddy, who had cofounded the Loyalty Oath committee with David Franke a year before, played an especially
important part in planning the founding conference that would be held at
Great Elm, the Buckleys' family home in rural Connecticut. Invitations went
to 120 "outstanding youth leaders" known to be active and influential on the
Right. Rusher had previously recommended Caddy as a "strong-minded and
able young man, militantly and intelligently conservative."[59]

That weekend, the "older generation"—Buckley, Meyer, Bozell, Rusher, former governor Edison, and himself—were "resolved to give no advice unless it was asked for," Liebman later recalled, and to "keep our mouths shut."[60] Rusher didn't like the acronym YAF, especially when Liebman quipped that people like themselves would be Old Americans for Freedom, or OAFs. But he was impressed by the group's manifesto, known after the town where they were meeting as the Sharon Statement, which Stan Evans had written. It was a succinct yet comprehensive description, Rusher thought, of "what modern American conservatism was all about."[61]

After a slow start, YAF became a dynamic group, strenuously activist in orientation. It also took ideas seriously, competing boldly with liberals and radicals for the minds of the rising generation. Its existence encouraged others on the Right and could make liberals anxious. The first large YAF rally was held in March 1961 at the Manhattan Center, with Senator Goldwater as the main speaker. The arena filled to capacity with 3,200 people; another 6,000 had to be turned away. A *New York Times* editorial warily suggested: "something is afoot which could drastically alter our course as a nation." Columnist Murray Kempton was skeptical on that count, as he had shrugged off the new *NR*. "We must assume that the conservative revival is *the* youth movement of the 60s," he wrote after the rally, "and may even be as important to its epoch as the Young Communist League was to the 30s, which was not very."[62]

Kempton's guess to the contrary, the new organization heightened conservatism's profile among young people and the public, also providing a training ground for political activism and even—as Rusher found especially satisfying—an early start to many political careers. YAF's imaginative demonstrations and boycotts were a new thing on the Right, in some ways foreshadowing the leftist youth rebellion that erupted later in the decade. As another liberal writer later observed, after the quieter 1950s, many in the press were "eager for something new and colorful to come along," and YAF was "good at providing it." In addition, the organization often attracted a new breed to conservative politics. Franke would proudly recall the sometimes unconventional membership of the chapters he oversaw in the New York area: "I had Teamsters, I had longshoremen, I even had a motorcycle gang from the Bronx. They had New York accents. None of the Young Republicans had New York accents."[63]

With Buckley a kind of "removed presence," Rusher was the "ambassador" between *National Review* and the YAF leaders, according to Bob Bauman, and they took him quite seriously. "When you got a memo from Rusher in the mail, it was a big deal." Working in the opposite direction, he would "tell Buckley what he thought had to be done; and when it was required on high, Buckley would make a speech or write a column . . . or let us use Great Elm."[64]

Junior conservatives in YAF and the YRs saw the two senior figures very distinctly as "the two Bills," recalls Lee Edwards, who was founding editor of YAF's publication the *New Guard*. They would look to Buckley for "inspiration," modeling themselves upon him both intellectually and personally, trying to "drawl like him and use the same kind of language . . . write like him, dress like him." But for "instruction" and "political guidance," they looked to the other Bill, who was happy to provide it. Rusher "obviously responded to young people," and they "responded to him because he was interested in them." They noticed his quirks but could respect them too. "We all made jokes about the black book and crossing out names," as Rusher did when an appointment was over. "We all knew that he was obsessive about things being on time, taking advantage of time. He was very meticulous in all matters—the way he talked, the way he dressed, the way he operated. For young people to emulate that is pretty difficult. But we still could, in a sense, admire it."[65]

YAF's early leaders, as one of them puts it, were "aggressive . . . full of testosterone," and a year after its founding, the group was riddled with intense disputes at the highest level. In order to protect YAF, Rusher recalled later, he was "phoning, conferring, pleading, politicking, *ad nauseam*."[66] Trouble began as early as May 1961 with a conflict between Caddy, YAF's first national director, and Franke, coordinator of the chapters in metro New York. Rusher became convinced that Caddy was seeking to control the organization.[67]

After this dispute was resolved, Caddy was accused of moving to keep control of YAF in his absence, through six months of Army duty, by appointing William Cotter, a Fordham University undergraduate, to stand in for him as acting national director. Supporting them against Rusher and Marvin Liebman, and the Rusher-Liebman or *"National Review"* faction, were YAF leaders Robert Schuchman, a Yale law student and the group's first chairman; Howard Phillips, eventually a top New Right organizer and third-party presidential candidate; and Scott Stanley, later associated with the John Birch Society. The faction was also highly critical of YAF's dependence on Liebman, who called Rusher and expressed alarm at the situation. The creation of the new post of "executive secretary" in 1961, and the hiring of Richard Viguerie for it, was part of the senior figures' attempt to maintain clout in the organization.

Rusher and Liebman unquestionably had more political experience, in addition to their value to YAF as important members of the *National Review* family and as people close to Buckley. For these reasons, they had a claim to legitimate authority in the YAF equation. The dissenting faction, Bill Cotter says, "had access to that and we listened to it, but we just didn't want them to be the puppeteers. We were intelligent guys—young, not experienced, but we'd done things in our lives."[68]

To Caddy, the questions at stake in his opposition to the older duo's heavy involvement were YAF's strategy and its ability to be an independent, and thus more effective, organization. Even as YR president in the District of Columbia, he had thought the conservative movement must "appeal to union members, and to southerners, and all sorts of people. And that was the purpose of YAF . . . to have its own identity, and to bring in these people that would not want to be associated with the Republican Party or with the Young Republicans." Caddy thought his view of political organizing as a more open process was incompatible with Rusher's narrower YR orientation and background, in which the "whole philosophy . . . is to keep your cards very close to your vest." In addition, Caddy believes, his faction was up against a craving for backstage power: "Rusher liked to control things."[69] According to Howard Phillips, for example, Rusher tried unsuccessfully to withhold thousands of dollars Phillips had raised for his political efforts at a National Student Association convention in Madison, Wisconsin, unless he voted correctly at an upcoming YAF board meeting. As for Liebman, Caddy contended at the time that he was financially exploiting the organization in his role as chief fund-raiser for it.[70]

Rusher thought established conservatives, himself included, had failed to anticipate YAF's predictable problems. Admitting this to *NR* colleagues, he took for granted their right to play a major role: "All of us simply overlooked, when we encouraged the formation of YAF a year ago, the transcendently important fact that we were bringing into existence a social organization . . . composed of real people, who have to be dealt with in the old-fashioned political mode. Instead, we tended to spoil these young men with too many credit cards, etc., while remaining totally ignorant of the inevitable development of political leaders and factions in their midst." But Rusher asserted that the group's health and future, not his own power, was his motivation—telling a YAF board member, William Madden, in mid-1962 that his concern was its ability to be effective for the movement. He was especially worried about Caddy's "unwarranted," counterproductive claims about the organization's alleged financial problems and irregularities.[71]

There was also an ideological aspect to the conflict. Rusher warned that Caddy and others were edging YAF toward Governor Rockefeller, the nation's leading liberal Republican and highly ambitious for the presidency. He also charged that board member Scott Stanley was steering it toward the Birch Society. In a September 1961 memo to *National Review* colleagues, Rusher reported that Caddy, Cotter, Phillips, and Bob Schuchman had "formed themselves into a well-disciplined clique, harassed their rivals nearly out of the organization, gone into barely concealed opposition to Marvin Liebman (who had been YAF's indispensable mentor), and even formed a stealthy liaison (though apparently more social than political—so far)" with a Rockefeller aide.

Already, at a national board meeting of the organization on September 2, Rusher had threatened to withdraw Liebman's and *National Review*'s support from YAF. The meeting, held at Liebman's office near the magazine, lasted twelve or thirteen hours despite the sweltering heat that resulted from failed air conditioning. Rusher, Lee Edwards recalls, instructed their faction to keep the meeting going, keep the doors locked, and keep everyone in the room until it got the vote it wanted. As Rusher reported to *NR*, "we succeeded in beating the Caddy bloc and reestablished working control of YAF," but they "had the unfortunate presence of mind not to resign" and were now alienated.[72] Thus it seemed to be only a temporary win. "We have scotched the snakes, not killed them," he explained to Buckley, Liebman, and Meyer. It would be necessary to "find friendly forces" in YAF, strong enough to fight Caddy and his allies.[73]

In warning of a stealthy liaison between YAF leaders and a gubernatorial aide, Rusher was referring to what he called Rockefeller's "Vice President in Charge of Capturing Conservatives"—Martin McKneally, a past national commander of the American Legion who became friends with Caddy and Cotter. McKneally was "consciously wooing us," Cotter acknowledges, and his job was indeed to "work with conservatives and bring them into the Rockefeller fold, or at least neutralize them" in that sense. But he doesn't remember his even suggesting anything YAF could do for his boss. When some of the organization's leaders were invited to meet with the governor, "I said: 'Sure, what the hell, why not? Famous guy.'"

The August 1 meeting at the Rockefeller offices at 22 West 55th Street had no positive impact on him, according to Cotter. "I remember my comment going out of there. I said: 'This is the most arrogant man I've ever met in all my life.'"[74] Another participant in the meeting, Carol Dawson of the anti-Caddy and pro-Rusher faction, has a similar recollection that it was inconsequential: "Rockefeller tried to assure us that he did not want to preside over the decline of the system that built his wealth—or words to that effect—but he influenced no one." The context of the outreach, she suggests, was really that the governor felt "somewhat unnerved" by the YAF activists in New York.[75]

But Rusher feared Rockefeller could gain traction among impressionable young people, despite his general liberalism, at least partly by using his reputation as a foreign-policy hard-liner. The governor had tried this in the recent meeting with the YAF leaders, Rusher told *National Review* colleagues. He had said, for example, that as president he would have invaded Hungary in order to save its democratic revolution in 1956—and that he also favored equipping a liberation force, with air and sea cover, to oust the communist Fidel Castro regime in Cuba. This approach troubled Rusher, who figured Rockefeller would probably follow "a relatively 'hard' line on a fairly wide range of subjects" once he was reelected in 1962 and began to run for president. If a relationship developed between him and YAF, Rusher warned, it would weaken the growing conservative activity around the country, activity which although promising remained fragile.[76]

In addition, Edwards recalls, the fact that Caddy was or soon would be working for the governor in Manhattan was "anathema to us." But although Caddy was employed at the Rockefeller offices, he actually worked for Lieutenant Governor Malcolm Wilson, a conservative. The Rockefeller people there "viewed me with suspicion," Caddy says, and the governor was surprised to learn, some months later, that he was on staff there.[77] The alleged Bircher, Stanley, was in fact given the editorial responsibilities for Robert Welch's publications. He was brought to Welch's attention, however, by two JBS board members who had been impressed by his presentation at a National Association of Manufacturers event. Stanley has denied he ever joined the Birch Society, explaining that he was merely made an honorary member in 1964 at the earliest.[78]

Rusher's anti-Rockefeller vigilance, according to Caddy, was "a wasted effort" in regard to YAF: "I can't think of anybody who would have supported him for any national ambitions." The new national chairman Rusher helped to elect in 1962, Bob Bauman, agrees: "I don't think there was ever a chance of YAF being taken over by the Rockefeller forces or the Birchers."[79] An expert on YAF, historian Gregory Schneider, later concluded that the charges about a possible drift into the Rockefeller orbit and a possible takeover by the Birch Society "rested on flimsy evidence and represented means by which the [Caddy] faction could be eliminated rather than real dangers to the organization's vitality"—but also that Rusher was right, given the "disastrous" implications for the conservative movement if YAF *should* somehow ally with Rockefeller, to insist the group maintain ideological cohesion even if this meant less autonomy.[80]

The factionalism went on in 1962 after the Caddy-Cotter group, as Rusher had cautioned it would, tried to retake control. The publisher now suggested that his own faction cut off the salaries of the other side's two most crucial supporters by pleading a lack of money. He also favored ending the post of organizing director, a job he said regional and state-level people could handle. Rusher was successful in these objectives as the YAF board eliminated the two salaries and the organizing position. With his support, Buckley urged several changes in the bylaws to reduce political infighting.

In addition, Rusher recruited successful candidates for YAF offices in 1962, including Bauman for national chairman. By the end of that summer, all members of the Caddy faction had been removed from the leadership. Bauman, elected at the first national convention that September, envisioned an ambitious agenda for YAF including a radio and television program, a speakers' bureau, and a move to Washington. Nearly five hundred members attended the convention, held in New York. Delegates passed resolutions urging a blockade of Cuba and opposing the recent Supreme Court ruling that outlawed officially sponsored prayer in the public schools. Rusher joined Burnham on a panel about American strategy in the Cold War.[81]

The most significant fact about Rusher's role in the YAF conflicts may be his undisputed will and ability to win, including his ability to direct one of the group's factions, rather than the disputed soundness of his contentions about possible dangers it faced. He commanded a special respect, according to Viguerie, who saw Rusher in YAF meetings, in discussions during the same period about founding the Conservative Party of New York, and in other such settings over the years. Although not much older than many others or necessarily the oldest person in the room, he "had the maturity, he had the experience, he had the gravitas—and that was a lot: the gravitas. People would defer to Bill Rusher, and they had confidence in him. Of course, Bill Buckley was the one who was ten feet tall. But Bill would not get in there and mix it up politically. He wouldn't roll up his sleeves and slug it out with everybody . . . When Rusher mixed it up, his gravitas—and his experience and knowledge, and toughness and determination—invariably would carry the day."

Because he focused so intently, like a busy lawyer, on whatever needed doing at the moment, Viguerie suggests, Rusher didn't necessarily have to spend a large amount of time on it. David Franke got the impression, from his vantage point at *NR* and elsewhere, "that he was the most organized man in the movement."[82]

## Leaders or Tablet-Keepers?

Despite YAF's troubles, 1961 was a year of increasing hope for Rusher because of his involvement, starting in July, in the earliest planning for the Draft Goldwater campaign and also because of what he was seeing in general. As he told Buckley, Meyer, and Bozell a few weeks after his faction's victory in the drawn-out YAF meeting in early September, he was seeing "a truly remarkable upsurge of conservative interest and activity." At the same time, he was deeply worried.[83]

There had recently been a round of memos about the movement's direction. In July, Gerhart Niemeyer, the Notre Dame political science professor and friend of Buckley's, sent the editor an analysis of the situation facing conservatives. Described as a more-or-less open letter, it was distributed to Meyer, Rusher, Bozell, and Willmoore Kendall. Niemeyer warned against any "elation" about conservative progress that might weaken the right kind of momentum. Conservatism, he thought, would certainly gain more political influence in coming years. But a conservative presidency was unlikely, especially since that would require a truly conservative party. There was no likelihood of such, because any American political party was essentially a coalition of viewpoints.

Making a few suggestions for strengthening the movement organizationally, Niemeyer advised that the current public interest in conservatism should be used "not to prepare an immediate change" in politics or policy, but rather to "broaden the base of conservative influence, to strengthen the network of conservative organizations, and to clarify conservative thinking." *National Review*, especially, should forget about "short-range exploitation of conservative strength." Its proper role was working toward "long-range change" in general public attitudes. This would mean articles of greater depth, and fewer "delightfully flippant" editorials. The magazine "should become more grave," Niemeyer counseled, "even at the expense of circulation."[84]

Writing in response, Meyer welcomed the call for deeper discourse in the movement and especially in *NR*. But he told fellow editors that Niemeyer was badly wrong in his major claim: the idea that only the long term was truly important. "To forget long-range principle is to be opportunistic," Meyer agreed, "but to 'renounce the short range' is to be abstract, utopian, aridly ideological." Rusher applauded Niemeyer for calling attention to the serious problem of "*National Review*'s . . . failure to think through the problems of mobilizing and thereafter controlling the conservative upsurge that we all seem to foresee." But otherwise, he told Buckley, the analysis and suggestions were wrong. Political upsurges "do not 'come' and then 'go,'" Rusher wrote, but were "incorporated into the history of their time and into the fabric of events, and nothing is ever quite the same again." In addition, Niemeyer's organizational proposals didn't seem very original; and such steps were results of political strength, not causes of it. They would follow from "the ripening of an initiating cause . . . by events, not by academicians at the Hoover Institution," where Niemeyer was a visiting scholar.[85]

Two weeks later, at the end of September, Rusher added more thoughts on the state of the movement. He was becoming increasingly anxious about what he considered *NR*'s lack of true political leadership. The magazine's great progress in circulation during the past year, from less than 33,000 to nearly 50,000 subscribers, reflected an increased "awareness of *National Review* as a conservative spokesman"—resulting from "all the debates, etc., that Bill and the other editors and I have been on over radio and TV in recent years." Rusher was also struck by a growing willingness among well-established individuals he knew to make large sacrifices for the cause. Also impressive was the fact that seemingly limited issues could get so many average citizens interested. A suburban YAF chapter had recently invited him as a warm-up for its main speaker, city manager Joseph Mitchell of Newburgh, New York, under fire for cracking down on welfare recipients in his medium-sized community. "Not an overly inspiring evening, one would think," Rusher observed. "And yet 500 people turned up on a hot Friday night in mid-August and paid cash to get into that auditorium."[86]

Rusher's long memo now turned sour. The basic problem gnawing at him was this: what organization, other than YAF with its sole focus on young people, should lead the grassroots Right? Even apart from Robert Welch's views, the Birch Society wasn't the answer, because it was "simply too discredited, for one thing." Rusher had recently been delighted to hear that Clarence Manion, a broadcaster and former Notre Dame law school dean, would be organizing his nationwide radio audience into Conservative Clubs. "Manion is no particular hero of mine," he told his colleagues, and the clubs couldn't be "the ultimate repositories of conservative hopes." But they could, at least, serve as "an alternative lightning rod . . . [down which] the accumulating static electricity of conservatism might run safely to the ground, in preference (and perhaps in some artfully-contrived rivalry)" to Welch's. The Manion chapters could sign up people who might otherwise become Birchers.

The project, Rusher had recently told the editors, deserved "a pat on the back" from the magazine. They had refused, fearing Manion was too personally ambitious—or, as a leading Bircher himself, might be establishing a front group for Welch. *National Review* ignored the Conservative Clubs in its next issues, but Rusher kept trying. At one point, he now recounted, "my remonstrances became so noisy that a conference was finally convened—attended by Bill [Buckley], Jim Burnham, Frank Meyer, Marvin Liebman, Stan Evans, David Franke and myself. Unfortunately it was held during the sandwich lunch hour of an editorial Wednesday, and got practically nowhere . . . It is now adjourned *sine die*." This indefinite postponement was dangerous, Rusher thought, because time was short. Manion, Welch,

right-wing minister Billy James Hargis, and others were "organizing mer-
rily away and holding well-publicized conventions all over the South and
Midwest, at which they give the keynote addresses to each other's organizations."[87] *NR* was negligently standing by, Rusher complained, even as the
grassroots Right developed more dubiously on its own:

> As nearly as I can tell, the sentiment in the higher reaches of *National
> Review* seems to be that, when we want the conservatives of America
> to organize, we will tell them about it; and that meanwhile they can
> darned well wait. My objection to this viewpoint is that, in all likeli-
> hood, they *won't* wait; that, instead, increasingly frustrated by their
> country's desperate situation and justifiably contemptuous of both
> major parties, they will fall into the hands of men and organiza-
> tions woefully unsuited to the responsibility—and, with just a little
> further bad luck, into the hands of the first really slick demagogue
> that comes along.

From that point, he could see a downward spiral. *NR* would "righteously
denounce" the movement's irresponsible new leadership. That would result
in praise from people like Garry Wills and literary scholar Hugh Kenner,
intellectuals who were personally close to Buckley. But the magazine, Rusher
continued in his hypothetical scenario, would then be "attacked . . . by the
hard Right on grounds of deviationism, dilettantism, and moderatism."
Next, it would "break permanently with the great bulk of conservative activists." The split would disastrously leave *National Review* "where some of its
friends (e.g., Gerhart Niemeyer, but not yours truly) have always wanted
it to wind up: i.e., as a 'respected'—which is to say, harmless—spokesman
for a benign brand of conservative Republicanism." In short, the grassroots
and *NR* would be estranged from one another, a situation Rusher predicted
would cost conservatism "its only chance of really imaginative leadership."
The movement might "do better for a time than some of its contemnors
suspect; but it cannot, without *National Review*, do what needs to be done—
and there will go the ball-game."

Uncertain about his long chain of speculation, Rusher then admitted
that he hadn't described the problem as well as he would like. His goal was
really "to start your own fertile mind [presumably Bozell's—Buckley and
Meyer were copied on the memo] considering the matter." He thought the
nascent effort to build a presidential campaign for Goldwater might, with
luck, put a lot of conservative energy and money to good use. But it was "by
no means clear that even this would satisfy *National Review*'s finicky appetite." The publisher told his colleagues, in effect, that *NR* was being selfish in

its relationship to the Right as a whole. "The real problem is our own dog-in-the-manger attitude; we are unable to organize America's conservatives ourselves, and unwilling to let anybody else do it." Rusher also accused the magazine of "serene indifference to political realities."[88]

Liberals' counterattacks against the Right, in alliance with President Kennedy, soon gave Rusher another reason to stress the need for more centralized conservative leadership. In late 1961, Kennedy delivered speeches in Los Angeles and Seattle perceived as attacking the movement in addition to its extremists; both speeches were covered on the front page of the *New York Times*. The issue also received major play on the cover of *Time* and elsewhere. A White House report in this period said the true danger came from organizations allied with *NR*—including YAF—rather than the Birch Society, because these groups focused on "the winning of national elections" and "the re-education of the governing classes." Their real goals, the report speculated, might be "to replace the erratic Welch with a man whose thinking parallels that of *National Review*" and to "channel the frenzied emotional energy presently expended on futile projects to impeach [Earl] Warren and repeal the Income Tax into effective political action" instead. In this climate of establishmentarian angst, the president ordered a White House aide to prepare monthly reports on conservative groups. He also told the Internal Revenue Service to begin gathering data on those that were tax-exempt.[89]

The Seattle speech, Rusher told Buckley in March 1962, had laid the foundation for a "great pyramid of denunciation" that must be taken very seriously. It represented

> an impressive—and, in my opinion, a devastatingly effective—performance. Substantially all of the mass-based organizations through which the Right has attempted to mobilize itself for political action have been lumped together in one ball of wax and lustily smeared by everybody from Kennedy and the Liberals through the Luce publications [such as *Time*] and (now) by unassailably definitive institutions within the Catholic Church. It would, I think, be idle to pretend that this attack has not been tremendously effective.

He again pointed out that the magazine hadn't been able to "found, or at least find . . . a mass-based organization to which we can give allegiance and support." But then it seemed *National Review* couldn't run such an entity, since even YAF "has nearly proved more than we could manage." Rusher seemed close to despair. "The truth, I begin to suspect, is that the whole conservative renaissance is premature as a political movement; that we must reconcile ourselves to being tablet-keepers, and let it go at that for the moment."[90] Cautiously, however, he sent these thoughts only to Buckley, choosing not to write a general editors' memo unless he found them to be his considered views. To some extent they were not, Rusher told Buckley ten days later, because he had been a little too depressed. He was now inclined to think there would be "conservative mass organizations whether Kennedy (or Buckley!) wants them or not." Still, he saw "plenty to be gloomy about, if we cannot develop a better relationship to the action organizations of the Right than we are managing to maintain in the case of YAF."[91]

Meanwhile, the respectably sized national YAF rally in 1961 was followed by a much larger one, as more than eighteen thousand people attended the "Conservative Rally for World Liberation from Communism" at Madison Square Garden on the evening of March 7. Senator Goldwater spoke very late, after a long speech by Bozell. The *NR* writer and would-be political theorist drew explosive applause after turning away from a drawn-out philosophical analysis and demanding: "To the Joint Chiefs of Staff: *Prepare an immediate landing in Havana!* To the Commander in Berlin: *Tear down the wall!* To our chief of mission in the Congo: *Change sides!*" At the event, Rusher told the vacationing Buckley: "The name of *National Review* and everybody associated with it (most particularly including yourself) was lustily cheered."[92]

## "Favored Child"?

Although the national picture in 1962 seemed doubtful for the conservative cause, things in New York State were looking up. With the cooperation of Buckley, Meyer, and Rusher, a serious new party had been established the previous year. The prospectus for the Conservative Party, from its cofounders J. Daniel Mahoney and Kieran O'Doherty, was mailed to potential supporters along with a cover letter from Buckley, and Rusher was closely involved in its formation.

The editor had actually shown interest in a national third party as early as the spring of 1956, when he was among the signers of a statement announcing a campaign to place independent electors on the ballot as the "sole Constitutional method . . . whereby [a] conservative All American could be elected President and thereby defeat international Socialism which has captured both political parties." Buckley did so despite Burnham's warning that third-party advocacy would ally *NR* with "plain racists masquerading as conservatives" and with "all sorts of cranks and anti-Semites."[93] Little came of the independent-electors idea, but in early 1957 Buckley and *NR* staff member Mike Mooney met with Brooklyn activist Eli Zrake about the possibility of forming a third party in New York (really a fourth, following the Liberal Party). After Rusher became publisher, Buckley gave him responsibility for continuing the discussions.[94] Zrake had essentially the same vision as the Conservative Party founders a bit later—an electoral competitor to pressure the GOP from the right—and his death in 1959 delayed the attempt to establish such a party only briefly.

An emotional basis for a third party existed in self-conscious conservatives everywhere, since they understood that their beliefs and the GOP were not the same thing. As Rusher points out: "Anybody who was in the conservative movement, simply by virtue of that affiliation was testifying . . . that the Republican Party alone was not enough for him."[95] But in New York the soil was much better prepared than in most states. Many Republicans felt acutely dissatisfied with its liberal-leaning party hierarchy, and too many Republican officeholders and candidates were moderate or liberal. Right-wing third parties elsewhere "lacked the local inspiration," as Rusher later explained, of Republican leaders as liberal as Governor Rockefeller and Senator Javits.[96] New York was also the only state that permitted "fusion"—nomination by more than one party, and therefore dual identification of such candidates on the ballot. This meant that a minor party could generally align itself with a major party while remaining independent of it and able to pressure it.

Conservative Party founders saw a national angle in addition to their statewide concerns. The New York GOP, Dan Mahoney believed, had been "the single most important force" thwarting conservatives in nationwide party battles since 1940. Because of the more liberal New York party's clout, the national party tended not to offer "sharp, clear alternatives" to the Democrats.[97] The Conservative leaders also hoped to appeal beyond the Republican base. In one of the party's early statements, Kieran O'Doherty addressed "Al Smith Democrats" and "independent conservatives" along with "Robert Taft Republicans." All of these groups were disenfranchised statewide, and they all opposed the use of New York's "vast political influence for liberal causes and candidates" at national conventions.[98]

Recently arrived from Texas, Richard Viguerie sat fascinated in the back of Marvin Liebman's small conference room while Rusher and his boss met with the two cofounders as often as several times a week to work out their plans. They were "very excited about it," Viguerie recalls, approaching the meetings "with a hard agenda . . . very focused."[99] Things were coming together, Rusher told his colleagues in September 1961. Helped by his practical advice and contacts, Mahoney, O'Doherty, and several of their friends had set up a preliminary organization for the party. "I am giving them a great deal of encouragement—attending their planning sessions, suggesting

the proper sequence of steps, and introducing them to prospective financial supporters." He expected "all hell will break loose" once the Rockefeller
forces became aware of what was happening, but added: "The boys in charge
of this one are tough. It ought to be fun!"[100]

Less than a year later, the new party announced its candidates against
Rockefeller and Javits, both up for reelection in 1962. Democracy "can survive only if there is discussion and debate of the fundamental issues of our
time," noted Robert Thompson Pell, the Conservative challenger to Javits,
and such debate would be rendered impossible "if the Republican Party
becomes the craven image of the Democratic Party." Javits's voting record
was so awful, Pell said, that he had earned the nickname "Mr. A.D.A." for
close adherence to the liberalism represented by Americans for Democratic
Action. As for Rockefeller, Rusher had disliked him since before he was
elected governor in 1958—actually "from the first time I ever saw him," at
the 1956 Republican convention in San Francisco, where Rockefeller did
"formidable work" urging players in the party to back Javits for the Senate
nomination.[101]

In the fall campaign season, Rusher again found himself pressing movement advocacy with Buckley. It seemed that Rockefeller's Conservative
opponent, a business executive and distinguished community leader from
upstate named David Jaquith, would not be well served—nor would the
young party, or readers—by an upcoming pair of stories on the race. Rusher
reminded Buckley of the latter's recent commitment that *NR* would, in the
publisher's words, "continue to look favorably on the Conservative Party,
treating it as an interesting and encouraging development." The envisioned
stories were inconsistent with this.

"Instead of treating the Conservative Party as a rather specially favored
child," Rusher wrote, "the clear implication of such paired articles is that
*National Review* sees the race between Rockefeller and Jaquith as one in
which we have no particular bias one way or the other, feeling that conservatives could equally well jump in either direction." Also misguided was the
idea that these pieces should limit themselves strictly to Rockefeller's record
in office. The suggestion could only help the governor, Rusher remarked,
and he suspected it had been made for this reason. Its advantage to Rockefeller was that larger questions, especially his suitability as a future presidential nominee or president, would go unaddressed. Rusher cited no culprit
for the suggestion, but Burnham was the most logical one.

After all, Rusher argued, the idea to form the Conservative Party had
originated with Buckley, and its leaders naturally wanted far more than "a
glassy stare and an equally clinical interest" in both candidates. If *NR* now
seemed to be less than a good friend, would they look to it for guidance any-

more? "If we decide to throw dust in the eyes of our readership . . . just before the Conservative Party faces its ultimate test at the polls, we will not only inevitably hurt its showing—and hurt it badly—but will put ourselves in the worst possible position to exercise a healthy influence over it afterward."

The publisher also mentioned Rockefeller's aide for outreach to conservatives, who had become friends with the two YAF leaders a year before. He knew that Martin McKneally would like to meet with the editors of *National Review*. Obviously it was up to Buckley, but Rusher wouldn't take such an accommodation quietly: "If you do invite him to an editorial lunch, I promise to make a monkey out of him, and his employer, before we have finished the tomato juice."[102]

# 6

# The Insurgent

Rusher's hostility toward Rockefeller had a precedent in his alienation from the Eisenhower administration—and the magazine's. The moderate Republican president was often a natural foil for *National Review*, and when he won reelection by a wide margin in 1956, *NR* was not among his supporters. In foreign policy, its complaint against Eisenhower reflected hard-line anticommunist internationalism. America was barely fighting the Cold War at all, the editors thought. In addition, with the breakdown of the European colonial empires and the rise of the neutralist "nonaligned" third-world movement, a sense developed among conservatives that geopolitics were shifting in the Soviets' favor across the globe.

Even as Eisenhower was reelected, two great events were occurring that defined the fears and frustrations of the era: the brutal Soviet repression of the democratic revolt in Hungary, and the invasion of the Suez Canal by Britain, France, and Israel, intended to keep it under Western control rather than accept that of a hostile Egyptian regime. The president felt unable to prevent the Hungarian bloodbath or punish the Soviet Union for it, and he was unwilling to back the Suez action even though it was initially successful. To many conservatives, these were golden opportunities lost—and ominous Western defeats. In 1957, it was the Russians, not the Americans, who launched Sputnik, the first Earth-orbiting satellite, and thus appeared to be leading in the technology of the dawning space age. The "Communist threat," Rusher told a friend in early 1958, had "materially increased during the Eisenhower Administration."[1]

At home, little was done to reduce big government. Eisenhower proposed more of it, though on a modest scale, and barely tried to articulate a
case against statism. He didn't seem committed to either side of American
politics but rather to view things in his own mysterious way. After naming
the new chief justice in 1953, he explained that Earl Warren was "a liberal-
conservative" and therefore represented "the kind of political, economic,
and social thinking" needed on the Supreme Court.[2]

In the middle of the Eisenhower period, there was talk of a centrist
synthesis tied to the president. A main advocate was administration official Arthur Larson, who explained the idea in a book titled *A Republican
Looks at His Party.* Eisenhower's popularity and moderation, he argued, had
brought the GOP into a commanding position. "The Republicans now hold
the Center," and "in politics—as in chess—the man who holds the center
holds a position of almost unbeatable strength." Larson called this the New
Republicanism, claiming it was both "liberal in the true sense" and "conservative in the true sense."[3] Also known as Modern Republicanism, it seemed
to its adherents like a practical adjustment to the needs of society.

In direct contrast, the first issue of *NR*, in November 1955, stressed the
need for a clear ideological divide on the grounds that both parties seemed
in danger of turning into quasi-socialist forces. In a statement explaining
the magazine's main beliefs, readers were told that the "most alarming single
danger to the American political system" was the "team of Fabian operators"
who intended to control it under "such fatuous and unreasoned slogans as
'national unity,' 'middle-of-the-road,' 'progressivism,' and 'bipartisanship.'"
Genuinely democratic politics required not this but large, vigorously contested differences between Republicans and Democrats. *National Review*
would "advocate the restoration of the two-party system at all costs."[4] The
following year, Burnham was unsuccessful in urging Buckley to endorse
Eisenhower: "You are implicitly deciding here whether your objective is to
make NR a serious (whether or not minor) force in American life, or to be
content with its being essentially a literary exercise—a kind of high-grade
game."[5] To Burnham, being serious in politics meant working with what was
on the table. Buckley didn't necessarily agree.

When Eisenhower's presidency ended four years later, *National Review*
wouldn't miss him. Although "manifestly . . . a good man," he was a "miserable President." He had accepted a "strategically indefensible" settlement
of the Korean War, then "stood impotently by and let Hungary go." More
generally, communism had benefited from "the lethargy, indecision and
ignorance of the goodhearted man providence inflicted on the West." On
domestic policy, the editorial continued, Ike was no better: "The forces that
gnaw at the strength of our country grow stronger—the bureaucratic para-

sites, the labor union monopolists, the centralizers." The old soldier should "fade away in the illusion that the world responded to his goodness . . . We pray he will never realize what a total, desperate failure he was, compared with what he might have been."[6]

The Republicans also suffered terrible losses in the 1958 midterm election, which gave the Democrats margins of 283–153 in the House of Representatives and 64–34 in the Senate, their largest since the Roosevelt era. The congressional Democratic Party had many new members from the Northeast and Midwest, less southern dominance, and a more liberal orientation. In *National Review*, Washington correspondent Brent Bozell and James Kilpatrick, a writer on politics for the magazine, sought to make sense of the rout. "Big Labor's vaunted political machine at last came into its own," Bozell observed, but "the real cause of the Republican party's death was internal." Because its national leadership had adopted essentially the Democratic program and philosophy, the Republican organization lacked a reason for working in elections or even existing. The party "*made* Dwight Eisenhower its high priest, in exchange for its soul."

At the same time, Bozell denied there was a conservative majority: "The 1958 election laid to rest the myth that has comforted so many conservatives, the idea that there exists a large ready-made conservative vote awaiting only candidates to vote for." The decisive sector in politics was the "great majority" who supported Democrats or Modern Republicans without being "ideologically wedded to their programs." From this uncertain middle, a "conservative electorate has to be created." Bozell saw a daunting prospect for the movement. Turning back the growth of statism remained possible. But it was "infinitely harder . . . than conservatives had assumed."[7]

Agreeing with Bozell's explanation of the election results, Kilpatrick advised a better acquaintance with political reality: "Too many people who write about politics have never gone down to the firehouse." The movement would have little future unless its "philosophers," meaning "we critics in the grandstand," and its practitioners came together more. Kilpatrick similarly urged "a little more tolerant eye" for politicians, more acceptance of their compromises. The ones who were "generally conservative" were good enough. Conservatives should, however, "seek actively to take over control of Republican machinery" and create an "army" of supportive partisans. "If the conservative cause is to get anywhere," Kilpatrick wrote, "it must get there on a Tuesday."[8]

New York conservatives had been disappointed that year in the East Side's affluent "silk stocking" congressional district. Frederic Coudert Jr., a staunch conservative, was stepping down from his House seat, and he wouldn't be easy to replace. Coudert was "one of the most brilliant people

I have ever known," recalls Rusher's former YR comrade Wilma Sievertsen Rogalin. "He spoke beautifully." In the party, an ideologically divisive contest for the open seat resulted. Rusher's friend John Thomson attended a debate between the liberal candidate, John Lindsay, and his conservative opponent. "Lindsay got up and he said: 'When you look at me, don't ask me how many buckets of water I've carried to the elephant,' and he didn't even mention the Republican Party after that." Winning the nomination and the general election, he became a new star for the New York GOP's liberal establishment. Like other conservatives, Rusher found it hard to take a new congressman who was only a nominal Republican. He would "muse on it" with people, according to Thomson, urging that "we have to gird our loins when it comes to a primary fight."

After Rockefeller won the governorship in 1958, state party chairman Judson Morhouse purged everyone from the YR leadership who was known to be close to White and Rusher. On the national scene, Senator Jenner of the Internal Security Subcommittee had retired, despite Rusher's previous encouragement to seek a third term. He was, Washington reporter Robert Novak later remembered, "a genuine conservative who antagonized other members of the Indiana delegation by trying to limit pork for his state." Much of the reason why Jenner quit at a relatively young age, according to Novak, was that he "detested moderate Republicanism and what he perceived as the nation's leftward drift . . . which he considered himself powerless to stop."

Rusher talked a lot in these years about "the corrupting nature of politics," Thomson recalls, and knew it was crucial to find candidates who would stand up to its temptations. "The more mature in his ideology he became, the more he looked for that kind of person." He considered younger people cleaner in spirit, less blemished by power and financial gain.[9]

In 1960, Rusher's hopes were briefly raised by the Senate candidacy of Bob Morris, his old boss at the Internal Security Subcommittee, running for a second time in the Republican primary in New Jersey. Morris lost to the liberal Clifford Case, who went on to the Senate. His defeat was cited as evidence that movement conservatism held little public appeal. Most voters were "simply not having any of the far right's bill of goods," explained Rusher's once-esteemed boyhood paper the *Herald Tribune*. Columnist Joseph Alsop welcomed Morris's loss in similar terms, for showing the "total hollowness of the talk about a 'conservative groundswell.'"[10]

Shortly after the primary, Rusher told an acquaintance: "I think we had better pull in our belts and buckle down to a long period of real impotence. Hell, the catacombs were good enough for the Christians!"[11]

## Goldwater Takes the Stage

As Republican regulars prepared to nominate Vice President Nixon as Eisenhower's successor, a small faction of conservatives ran a campaign on behalf of Senator Barry Goldwater. The project began with Clarence Manion, the former dean of the University of Notre Dame law school who became a conservative writer, lecturer, and radio broadcaster. As early as 1959, Manion and an old friend of the senator's from California, Hubbard Russell, met with Goldwater to discuss the possibility of a presidential campaign. The party would be destroyed, Manion suggested, if Nixon or Governor Rockefeller won the nomination. Goldwater replied that various southerners, including Senator Strom Thurmond of South Carolina (then still a Democrat), had already approached him about a candidacy. He wasn't interested. In the meeting with Manion and Russell, the Arizonan reiterated his public support for Nixon. Asked not to repudiate their unauthorized campaign, however, he agreed.

A Goldwater for President committee was organized with the participation of many prominent figures on the Right. Manion's plan, which the committee ratified, called for Goldwater to have a book explaining his beliefs published under his name. A grassroots campaign would follow, fueled by its anticipated popularity. Manion expected Rockefeller would win the nomination. But he hoped the failure of a Goldwater candidacy might cause a conservative breakaway from the Republicans—and thereby a national third party.[12]

The book's title, *The Conscience of a Conservative*, came from Manion as well. Its real author was Bozell, who had previously written speeches for Goldwater, drew on some of the senator's addresses in writing it, and got his casual approval of the final manuscript.[13] Buckley didn't foresee a great success: "I doubt there's much money to be made by mass sale of a Goldwater manifesto," he told Manion, noting that a foreign-policy book by Robert Taft hadn't done well in 1952. In fact, *Conscience* became a milestone in conservative history. Its sales were wildly successful. Pundit and presidential candidate Pat Buchanan, speaking for many, would recall it as "our new testament . . . We read it, memorized it, quoted it."[14] Meanwhile, three separate groups promoted Goldwater at the 1960 convention: the people enlisted by Manion, a precommitted South Carolina delegation led by Greg Shorey and *NR* donor Roger Milliken, and a separate Youth for Goldwater for Vice President campaign.

Goldwater had been a rising figure in the national party since his election to the Senate in 1952, when he unseated the Democratic majority leader, Ernest McFarland. Even in the first years of his term, he went around the country speaking on behalf of the GOP. Having demonstrated popular appeal, he was chosen by colleagues as chairman of the Republicans' Senate campaign committee. During his six years in that position, 1955–56 and 1959–62, Goldwater traveled more than two hundred thousand miles to nearly every state. He gave about two thousand speeches and got to know party officials down to the district and county levels. He spoke not only for the GOP and its candidates but also for "individualism" against collectivism: "this race for the minds of men," as he said in a 1955 speech. His maverick image, his hobbies as a skilled amateur pilot and photographer along with service in the Air Force Reserve, and his candid, quotable comments drew an unusual amount of media coverage for a junior senator: frequent national exposure in the *New York Times*, the weekly magazines, and the television news shows.

Goldwater was always on the right wing of the party, although he favored Eisenhower rather than Taft for the presidency in 1952. He became especially well known as a passionate anticommunist. In 1956, Goldwater helped to produce a documentary film, *For Freedom's Sake*, warning against Soviet expansionism. In it he narrated scenes of life in communist nations, where "men and women and children disappeared in agony and terror to be regurgitated as listless, pathetic human ciphers without meaning or dignity."[15] The senator was a strong economic conservative as well, memorably blasting the Eisenhower administration on these grounds in the president's second term.

As a member of the Senate Labor and Public Welfare Committee, Goldwater took a special interest in abuses by unions, then at the height of their power. He outspokenly backed legislation that would grant labor-relations jurisdiction to states, enact the right-to-work principle nationally, curb secondary boycotts, and even forbid union political activity. In Michigan he attacked the United Auto Workers and its president, Walter Reuther, who had turned the state's Democratic Party into a union-dominated machine. Here was "something new," Goldwater warned, "and something dangerous—born of conspiracy and violence . . . This is the pattern of political conquest." In an unplanned conclusion to another speech, he claimed that Reuther, in some respects the country's most prominent labor leader, was a "more dangerous menace than the sputnik or anything Soviet Russia might do to America." Goldwater, Reuther fumed in response, was a "moral coward" and "political hypocrite," the country's "number one peddler of class hatred . . . a reactionary . . . a stooge for big business."[16] In his aggressive, well-organized 1958 reelection drive, Goldwater accurately portrayed himself as fighting a national labor movement desperate to destroy one of its strongest critics. He won his rematch against ex-Senator, now Governor

McFarland with 56 percent of the vote—even as the Republicans nationally lost thirteen Senate seats.[17] For conservatives, it was an encouraging exception to the Democratic tide.

Speaking at the national meeting of YR leaders where Rusher first saw him in 1955, Goldwater showed a provincial side when asserting his views on the long-standing water dispute between Arizona and California. He complained so loudly about it, according to Rusher, that California committeewoman Emily Pike was moved to bring him a glass of water. But in addition to liking Goldwater ideologically, Rusher was impressed by his western style—a trait conservatives were not yet identified with, and one in which "I saw a great deal of merit."[18]

Although he projected a dour image to many in the 1964 campaign, Goldwater had first become known among Republicans as an attractive leader, not just an admirable one. As Bob Novak wrote, he was "a conservative who smiled, who laughed, who was young and dynamic."[19] To Draft Goldwater committee treasurer J. William Middendorf, "he signified the last of a breed—independent, unbending, a bit unreal in the middle of the twentieth century, when most Americans had adopted 'luxury' as the standard and replaced self-reliance with convenience."[20]

Goldwater's style of patriotism and opposition to big government, mixed with calls to a higher citizenship, had a bracing quality for many who heard him. "Life was not meant to be easy," he told a Pasadena, California, audience in early 1960. "The American people are adult—eager to hear the bold, blunt truth, weary of being kept in a state of perpetual adolescence." Goldwater took intellectual conservatism seriously. Writing to Buckley the following year, Russell Kirk suggested that he might be "the only politician of note who has real respect for ideas and people with degrees—perhaps because he didn't finish college himself."[21]

He was also difficult at times. Marvin Liebman, the anticommunist publicist and fund-raiser, would remember him at the 1962 national YAF rally in New York. Late that night, as he waited to give the concluding address, Goldwater's patience was sorely tried as Bozell from *National Review* continued his "brilliant and endless" speech. The senator "strode up and down" in a holding room, Liebman recalled, "cussing out Bozell, YAF, and just about anyone else he could think of. But when he went on stage, he was terrific."[22] Despite the tense scene at the rally, Goldwater had a good relationship with *NR*. He was a devoted reader of the magazine, got along well with Buckley, and signed a solicitation letter in 1961 that brought seven thousand new subscribers.[23]

Just before being nominated for president at the 1960 Republican convention, Nixon met with Rockefeller for hours on the night of July 22. He wanted the governor as his running mate, although he didn't really expect an acceptance. Nixon's hunch proved correct, and talk turned to the meeting's main purpose, the party platform. Rockefeller had a statement of principles he believed ought to shape the document. It stressed a more hawkish defense policy—an awkward position for a man who had spent the past eight years as vice president and inevitably drew upon the outgoing president's popularity. In domestic policy, it stressed a more liberal civil-rights plank. The mere fact of a substantive platform accord with the nominee would also signify Rockefeller's bold assertion of power in the national party. But Nixon agreed to what became known, after the governor's Manhattan apartment where they met, as the "Treaty of Fifth Avenue."

Goldwater attacked the agreement as "a domestic Munich" because he, like other conservatives, found it too liberal and also because he thought the nominee shouldn't be dictated to. Nixon offered the vice-presidential nomination to a strong conservative and leading anticommunist, Congressman Judd of Minnesota, who preferred to stay in the House. He then picked United Nations ambassador and former Massachusetts senator Henry Cabot Lodge Jr., from the eastern establishment wing of the party—apparently hoping this would highlight what Nixon presumed was the Republican foreign-policy advantage. Goldwater called the choice "a disastrous blunder."[24]

The senator's name was placed in nomination, allowing him to give a speech. Goldwater was welcomed by a "tremendous demonstration," and when he promptly withdrew from consideration, in the words of White, who was working there for Nixon, "a great groan of disappointment descended from the galleries [and] swept across the convention floor." Delegates who came expecting to reluctantly back Nixon were prepared—reacting, White believed, against the Treaty of Fifth Avenue—to get behind Goldwater. They "lent their voices to the chorus that rose and swelled to a deafening 'No!'"

Goldwater spoke: "This great Republican Party is our historic house. This is our home . . . if each segment, each section . . . were to insist on the complete and unqualified acceptance of its views, if each viewpoint were to be enforced by a Russian-type veto, the Republican Party would not long survive." America was "too great for any man, be he conservative or Liberal, to stay home and not work just because he doesn't agree. Let's grow up, conservatives!" The senator added: "If we want to take this party back—and I think we can some day—let's get to work!"[25] He meant: for Nixon's election, as loyal Republicans.[26]

After the convention, Bozell shared extensive misgivings in *NR*. A major point was that the last conservative leader of such stature, Senator Taft in the 1940s and early 1950s, had "organized his power through years of legislative battle and maneuver" and in "a series of hard-fought Presidential campaigns." Goldwater had "organized nothing," simply taking the stage with his conservative positions. He was also given too much credit for being charismatic, Bozell suggested, adding that the movement "had begun to think dispiritedly and unhealthily in terms of a Messiah." Furthermore, he might really be too conventional a Republican, uncomfortable in a movement-type leadership role. Criticizing Goldwater's speech for "fuzzing over" differences about the platform and between himself and Nixon, Bozell continued: "Nor was it wise, let alone generous, for a movement's newly-crowned leader to address his followers as naughty children. Conservatives, at that moment, deserved better than a scolding." *National Review* had little connection with the Goldwater boomlet, except for the fact that Bozell had written *Conscience*. Rusher didn't take the agitation on behalf of the senator seriously. Having attended three Republican conventions in a row, he even missed this one. But in the fall, refusing to vote for Nixon, he would write in Goldwater's name.[27]

## Rusher vs. Nixon

Sounding like Rusher's college thesis, Vice President Nixon told an early biographer: "I reject and have no patience whatever with the approach of some ultraconservatives who defend the status quo and speak of going back to the 'good old days.' Conservatism at its best is progressive. The Republican Party in its greatest years has been progressive, while at the same time following conservative economic policies." Nixon looked to pragmatism, not free-market principle. "If I thought the 'let-the-government-do-it' type of programs would work, would produce more, would in the long run be best for the great majority of the people," he said, "I would probably be the most enthusiastic radical in these fields that you could possibly imagine."

He had often taken—or rather, wanted—a harder line on foreign policy than Eisenhower. In 1953, he opposed the armistice in Korea, believing the U.S. should retake the offensive it had achieved early in the war and liberate the whole peninsula. A year later, he wanted to support the French in Vietnam, while Eisenhower stayed out. In 1959, Nixon preferred higher defense spending; in 1960, he favored an invasion of communist Cuba. But in none of these cases, apparently, did he express his views to the president. To journalist Earl Mazo, he said: "We should adopt as our primary objective not the defeat of Communism but the victory of plenty over want, of health over disease, of freedom over tyranny." The implication was that defeating communism should be about one-third of a president's foreign-policy agenda.[28]

Rusher's attitude toward him was cool. "For a long time I was sort of indifferent to Nixon," and gradually that "hardened into a generalized suspicion."[29] Frank Meyer disliked him as well. Whittaker Chambers, who had known and admired him since the time of the Hiss case, told Buckley in March 1960 that he was now disappointed. Meeting Nixon for lunch and a long talk in Washington recently, "I came away with a most unhappy feeling," Chambers wrote. He sensed that the candidate was short on energy, convictions, ideas, and grasp of the world crisis. Nixon remained the best among the current presidential possibilities, Chambers thought, but the odds against any president being effective were heavy.[30]

His campaign against Senator John F. Kennedy did little to improve perceptions of Nixon among conservative critics; it was what they called "me-too" Republicanism. One of Kennedy's more specific criticisms of the administration, for what he claimed was insufficient defense spending, presumably made it especially important that his opponent stake out conservative ground. Goldwater told his friend William Rehnquist, then a Phoenix attorney, that "Dick has shown a decided tendency to drift far to the left" in recent weeks, adding that party workers across the country were upset by this. Although he hoped it would be possible to "get him back on track," Goldwater noted: "I would rather see the Republicans lose in 1960 fighting on principle, than . . . win standing on grounds we know are wrong and on which we will ultimately destroy ourselves."[31] Rusher and Meyer took essentially the same position.

The publisher was heeded on electoral politics at *National Review* partly because of his nationwide network of friends and contacts. As Bozell told Goldwater's friend Hubbard Russell in 1962: "Rusher has this special advantage, that among young men with unmovable conservative convictions who are presently active in politics, he is better acquainted than any man in the country."[32] They kept him, and thus the editors, current on things that hadn't made the news. Although not necessarily important in themselves, Priscilla Buckley notes, they were "important sources." Rusher could also explain why seemingly trivial items in politics deserved colleagues' attention. Bill Buckley "was not interested in how many votes we were going to get in Indiana in a House race, whereas Bill Rusher might say: 'Well, it is totally significant because it means these other things.'"[33]

The editors, according to Rusher, generally lacked familiarity with politics' detailed logic. "It was just that their minds didn't work in those particular ways. Things that I might instinctively know Rockefeller, or Nixon or whoever, would never do for some obviously political reason, they wouldn't realize . . . [whereas] any politician wouldn't need it spelled out for him."[34] Despite his ideological passion, he knew it was desirable to avoid unnecessary antagonism in politics. He appreciated those who got along with adversaries better than he did or chose to. In the late fifties or early sixties, Rusher remarked favorably that his friend Jack Casey, a politically active attorney in New York, had been "fooling the liberals for years" because he was good at socializing with them despite his own strongly conservative beliefs.[35]

In the debate over whether *National Review* should endorse Nixon in 1960, Meyer argued that eight years of what he called a liberal Republican president had greatly weakened opposition to liberalism. Nixon's "opportunistic" movement leftward now threatened to take the process much further, whereas a Kennedy presidency would mean a much better chance for an effective opposition to grow. Their magazine, Meyer also told the editors, had made itself the center of the conservative movement. As such, it must maintain, and keep developing, a position apart from that of the political establishment, whose views Nixon basically represented.[36]

Rusher seemed to reject not only Nixon but also the Republican Party itself. In early October, he told Buckley: "Both major parties, as presently constituted, are simply highly efficient vote-gathering machines. It is pointless to upbraid such a machine for failing to concern itself with principles—just as it would be pointless to reproach a pear tree for failing to bear plums." For principle-oriented activists, it wasn't worth it to labor within the GOP, where they would always be "forced into enervating compromises." Instead, they should work "in the field of pure opinion, through journals like National Review."

But Rusher probably meant that working in the field of opinion was preferable to efforts in the current Republican Party, not that it was necessarily preferable to political activism as such. Perhaps one of the major parties would absorb a rising conservatism, he told Buckley, but "my own hope—which is sufficiently reasonable to be called a modest expectation—is that it will be manifested in a new and more highly ideologized political party; a third party, or perhaps (like the Republicans in 1860) a new second party." Rusher continued: "A vote for Nixon, it seems to me, merely enhances the power and prestige of the present management of the Republican Party, in return for being given what would be accorded anyway: namely, a voice we may not even want, in a party it may prove desirable to oppose."[37]

He recommended that the magazine neither endorse Nixon nor ask readers to abstain. To begin with, there was no agreement on the question at *NR*. In addition, taking either stance was "the one sure way of alienating at least a part of our following." Finally, *NR* would have more leverage with a Nixon administration if it had refused to endorse him. "Politicians are characteristically most polite to people whose support they hope some day to get," Rusher observed, "not to those whose support they already have." If the magazine were to endorse Nixon, "I can tell you right now that, in

Republican circles generally, the conclusion will be that our bark is considerably worse than our bite." Rusher also saw no point in support modified by caveats, as Burnham had suggested:

> Let's stop kidding ourselves that an endorsement of Nixon would be understood by most of our readers, let alone reported elsewhere, as subject to saving qualifications . . . Within forty-eight hours, it would be known that 'National Review has endorsed Nixon'—period. Nor will it do to pretend that misconstructions of our position are irrelevant; the very quality of such an act as endorsing Nixon consists of its political relevance. St. Peter may understand what we have done, but the vast majority of Americans will misunderstand, and we will have no one but ourselves to blame.[38]

Burnham, while admitting that he might be unable to bring himself to vote for Nixon, insisted that "the public, objective conservative position" was to back him. The "Rusher Withdrawal stance," in contrast, was subjective and sectarian. The objective reality was this: Supporting Kennedy were nearly all "the forces, groups, tendencies and individuals that *NR* is not merely against, but recognizes as its primary targets." Among those adversaries were "the disintegrative leftist ideologues, including those who ruin our educational system," "the most dangerous and ruthless of the trade union bureaucracy," "the most extreme secularists," the urban "lumpenproletariat," and "the appeasers, socialists and collaborators of the entire world" and at home. "These are the things that NR is against," Burnham added, "and if it is serious, it ought to declare publicly against them." The situation required an endorsement of Nixon: "You cannot refuse to go into battle because you think the captain is lousy."[39]

Priscilla Buckley agreed, on narrower grounds. She had thought that *NR* should essentially sit out the election, but the "transcendent importance" of the worldwide struggle against communism changed her mind. Although Nixon was "hardly the champion we would choose" for this struggle, "the empirical evidence is that he and his advisers are less apt to play the appeasement game than Kennedy and his advisers." When *NR* refused to endorse in 1956, the situation had been different, the managing editor noted. Eisenhower seemed the quite probable winner anyway, and the drive toward appeasement was "far less developed."[40]

Her brother decided against endorsing Nixon, explaining to Burnham that the "gravity of the historical situation" required *National Review* to uphold an ideal of conservative politics and that a pro-Nixon position would blur it. Hedging was not an option. An endorsement must be strong, not iffy, and a strong endorsement was neither justified nor journalistically smart. To forcefully back Nixon would be to contradict "five years' analyses of events" by the magazine, analyses to which Burnham more than anyone had contributed. *NR* would "run the risk of appearing unintelligible," Buckley told his esteemed colleague. In addition, "a very good case can be made—indeed, I think Rusher has made it—for suggesting that we actually increase our leverage on events by failing to join the parade."[41]

Although Buckley wrote a no-endorsement editorial, its spirit and message were different from Rusher's. It briefly laid out two views a conservative might take on the election, denying *NR* should point readers toward either. One possibility was to admit that any party was inevitably a coalition, thus accepting conservatism's current status as merely a force within the GOP, not its rightful ruler. The other was to accept a Republican loss of the White House in 1960 as the necessary precondition for freeing the party from liberal control. Both were reasonable stances, Buckley concluded, and the magazine wouldn't choose between them.

*National Review* "was not founded to make practical politics. Our job is to think, and to write; and occasionally to mediate." In this case, it had to mediate: "Our job today is surely to remind ardent members of the conservative community that equally well instructed persons can differ on matters of political tactic, and that it is profoundly wrong for one faction to anathematize the other over such differences." Buckley concluded: "We do not intend to exhort our readers in a particular line of political action."[42]

## "A Football in Play"

Shortly after the election, Rusher told a friend he didn't feel "too excited over the defeat of a man . . . who has the nerve to contend that America's prestige today 'is at an all-time high,' when the merest glance at any newspaper's front page will demonstrate that this simply isn't true."[43] A *National Review* editorial, probably by Burnham, shared the publisher's calm reaction to the narrow Nixon loss. But it also distinguished sharply, as Rusher tended not to, between the Right's electoral success and its political success. "Winning elections, as we periodically repeat, is not the primary business of conservatives, even for the sake of practical influence; nor is losing them the ultimate defeat. Among the lessons of this election . . . it may be that this one, so hard for so impatient a people as Americans to admit, will in the longer run prove the most valuable."[44]

Rusher got several people in his political circle to meet with Clif White and deliver a heartfelt warning about conservatives' dissatisfaction. It was a stressful, unhappy time for his friend. White had been the director of organization in Volunteers for Nixon-Lodge. Afterward, through campaign manager Leonard Hall, he unsuccessfully urged Nixon to contest an election he suspected—based on "mounting evidence" in reports he was getting from four states—the Democrats had probably stolen. Among the conservatives Rusher brought to meet with White were Thomson, Jack Casey, and another New York lawyer, future *NR* board member Arthur Andersen. Their message was: "Clif, no more of this." They couldn't emotionally invest in figures like Nixon anymore. He was not a conservative, lacked defining principles, and had run a weak campaign. Furthermore, Nixon sought the presidency only for the sake of having it. They were also through with following the party leadership and its many ideological accommodations to liberalism. White was "absolutely stunned," Thomson recalls. Rusher told White he hadn't meant to blindside him but thought he should hear these sentiments.[45]

Looking ahead in *National Review*, Bozell wrote that future success for conservatives required "educating, inspiriting and capturing the Republican Party organization," rigorously concentrating on "potentially-conservative geographical areas," and what he called "Goldwater salesmanship." Frank Meyer speculated that if conservatives could capture the party, their candidate might forge a "new majority" including the South and West. Whether he won the next election or not, Meyer thought, Goldwater as nominee would go a long way toward creating such a majority. *NR* readers could also glimpse the Republican future in an interview with the senator that ran in January. What could conservative activists do "most profitably" in the next few years, Bozell asked, and would he "greatly object if some of them should conspire to secure your nomination for the Presidency?" Goldwater urged people to "work within the framework of the Republican Party [so that] delegates, precinct committeemen and so on are of the conservative mind." He left the second question unanswered.[46]

Although Rusher later pushed all of these points hard, at the moment he simply foresaw more exciting action within the party than had occurred on Eisenhower's long watch. There would be "some perfectly wonderful fights in it during the next few years," he told his friend Bill Runyeon in mid-November. "I will participate in them, merely because there is nothing much else to do at the moment, rather than because I seriously expect that it will ever turn truly conservative again (e.g., by nominating Goldwater or something like that)."[47] As Rusher later described his political mood in the first months of 1961: "The analogy that insistently forced itself upon my mind, as winter turned into spring, was that of a football in play, lying there on the field. Which player would get to it first and take control of the ball?"[48]

Yet his comments to like-minded associates also indicated strong frustration with the party and cynicism toward it, similar to what he expressed the previous October to Buckley. In March, he told Bozell: "I made up my mind years ago that salvation for America, if it is to come at all, will not take place through the medium of the Republican Party. The individual form of this dictum is embodied in what has come to be known as Rusher's Razor: 'No one, today, can be simultaneously honest, informed, and successful in the Republican Party.' That goes for everybody—from Rusher to, and including, Goldwater." In a presidential campaign, the senator "must either trim [his principles] or fail," and in trying to compromise between these possibilities, he would likely end up doing both.

But such opinions were not for the readership. The magazine, Rusher continued, shouldn't denigrate a potential Goldwater candidacy or its chances: "Because if *National Review* is to have the desired effect, it must retain a substantial following among responsible conservatives, and too precipitate a separation from Goldwater now would alienate many people that we can ill afford to lose." He illustrated the point by reminding Bozell of the first national YAF rally, held recently in New York: "As I watched and listened to it, I was profoundly glad that Bill [Buckley] was up on that stage too, and that he was identified in the minds of the audience as a friend of the cause they believe Goldwater to be championing—rather than as the editor of an impossibly perfectionist journal which had just brushed Goldwater from its sterile toga."[49]

A brief but unforgettable disappointment came on an early-1961 visit to Washington, when Rusher ran into Carroll Reece, who as RNC chairman in 1947 had urged him to start the Young Republicans at Harvard. Sitting in the lobby of the Metropolitan Club, the Tennessee congressman, elderly and ailing but still a prominent conservative, asked: "Bill, can anything be done with Nelson Rockefeller?" No, he thought not, an "appalled" Rusher said quickly, moving along to a lunch appointment. The incident would stand in his memory as "one of the conservative movement's darkest days."[50] Surprised and saddened by the experience with this ex-Taft supporter, he discussed it with White, who would recall: "We both perceived that Carroll Reece, like so many other people in the Republican Party, was grasping for a straw—*any* straw—that they thought might keep the party afloat on the storm-tossed political seas of the 1960's." It was further evidence of "what Rusher and I and several others were . . . beginning to detect: namely, that a leadership vacuum existed" within the party.[51]

White had become restless as well. For the past several years, he had made a living as a self-employed public-affairs consultant to industrial firms. Continuing his travels in the spring and summer of 1961, he perceived a growing dissatisfaction among the public. He also noticed much interest among the grassroots Right in the next presidential campaign. In addition to Goldwater, "other conservatives were being mentioned too—or men the people hoped or believed were conservatives." White was impressed by this. It was rare for people who weren't professionally political to concern themselves with an election still three years away. Many citizens were clearly anxious, especially about foreign policy. There was Kennedy's failure to back the freedom fighters at the Bay of Pigs, "men who had been trained, equipped and encouraged by our government" to liberate Cuba from tyranny. There were signs of American diplomatic weakness in Indochina. The Kennedy administration also seemed to be moving toward concessions on disarmament, suggesting a dangerously "increased faith in the Kremlin's empty promises" despite communist aggression and a long record of broken treaties.[52]

A more concrete indicator of new opportunity for the Right came in Texas. In a special election that May, the Senate seat of the new vice president, Lyndon Johnson, was captured by conservative professor John Tower, who had considerable support from Goldwater. He was the GOP's first senator from the state since Reconstruction.

Events in the Young Republicans had further interested White and Rusher in possible changes in the senior party. In 1959, the Syndicate had retained the national chairmanship with a new majority consisting of former Taft states in the Midwest, plus the South and, more than previously, the West. This showed that a conservative coalition might win a national Republican convention without friendly delegations from more liberal states.[53] But at the next YR convention, in mid-1961, the more liberal faction finally defeated the Syndicate. Rusher went to Washington in early July, thinking he would "repair a few fences after the storm" by talking with old friends. They would plan for the alliance's survival, perhaps its restoration to power, in the Young Republicans.

## "National Network"

One of his meetings was with former YR chairman John Ashbrook, now a first-term congressman from Ohio. Lunching in the House members' dining room, they "discussed the void in the GOP at some length." The established GOP leadership was out of shape; not since 1952 had it needed to engage in a struggle within the party. Rusher found himself "thinking nostalgically of that splendid national network" with which he and White had won their YR conventions. If it met again, it would likely be among the largest Republican factions.

Ashbrook agreed. He brought Rusher to his office after lunch and pulled a drawer from a filing cabinet, revealing the correspondence he maintained with much of this network. There were perhaps forty or fifty such people, nearly all with long records as YR leaders. Now they were active in the senior party in their states. Rusher knew they would gladly cooperate if invited to a reunion and asked to help build support for Goldwater. His mind was "abuzz" with speculation. Upon returning to New York, he called White, certain that his friend was the man to lead "the drive for conservative control of the GOP."[54]

When they met a few days later, Rusher explained the discussion with Ashbrook and his look at the congressman's files. White kept files too. In them were Young Republican and regular party contacts, plus people he had met through his public-affairs courses for the business community. Rusher and White discussed how the large cache of names might be used to begin a project aimed, White would recall, at "the nomination of a conservative candidate, or at the very least the drafting of a conservative platform" in 1964. They decided to think about it and meet again.[55]

White sought an opinion from Charles Barr, a "large, heavy-set" Standard Oil lobbyist based in Chicago who wasn't easily fooled (he was "considered the most knowledgeable Republican in the Midwest," according to Stephen Shadegg, the manager of Goldwater's previous Senate campaigns). Grassroots support for a conservative candidate was growing quickly, Barr agreed during their long talk in Washington. He had nothing discouraging to say and indicated he would help as much as possible. This strengthened White's confidence that the project might work.[56]

Meeting Rusher again on August 1, he was ready to start. At the moment, it seemed best to limit themselves to building conservative strength for the convention. They both had Goldwater in mind, but White cautioned Rusher that it was too soon to push a candidate. If 1964 were to become a strongly Democratic year, "it might strengthen the conservative movement more if we throw the nomination to a Liberal." Rusher responded uncomfortably to this negative strategy: a discrediting of the liberal Republicans if one of them lost to Kennedy, rather than a conservative victory in its own right. "Bill winced at that," White recalled. He accepted the idea as a valid possibility before they finished eating but probably returned to his office with "a slight case of indigestion."

Next, White met with Ashbrook. They drew up a list of people in every state on whom they hoped to rely. The list was far too long, but Rusher, who was allowed to add names for consideration, would help them shorten it. Gathering in New York on September 7, the trio found it difficult to winnow the field. They had to consider an individual's position in the Republican

Party, past and current allegiances, talent and potential. Especially important was his ability to keep the group's existence a secret. Premature public
exposure would convey the image of a plot.

In many instances Rusher, White, and Ashbrook regretted that friends
with whom they had once worked must be excluded on account of some tendency toward the party's more liberal wing. At first, they wanted to name
only people about whom all three felt certain. But with insufficient overlap
among their truly close acquaintances, this proved impractical. It would be
adequate if Rusher, White, or Ashbrook could guarantee a prospect absolutely.
By the time they finished dessert and coffee, twenty-three names remained.[57]
Rusher was pleased with the "highly selected group who . . . in fight after
fight, had demonstrated themselves absolutely dependable." They were comrades whom "we were prepared to call on again, and count on as much."[58]

As they contacted people about the Chicago meeting, Rusher, White, and
Ashbrook explained only that they were "getting a group of friends together
to talk politics" and that "the three of us felt it was important enough for
them to be there—and they came." The handful who couldn't had good
excuses and attended the later meetings.[59] The fact that White and Rusher
were leading a new political project would have surprised few or none of the
invitees. The two seemed "joined at the hip," recalls Tom Van Sickle, who
was not in the initial group but had spent the past two years as chairman
Cushing's executive assistant in the YRs. "It was only later on . . . that they
became different people in my mind."[60] To the former Young Republicans
among them, Rusher notes, that experience had been "a wonderful time in
their lives. It looked like this might be starting again, and they were all ready
for it . . . delighted to hear there was something else they could do."[61]

On Sunday, October 8, the group met at 2 P.M. in a conference room at
a somewhat disreputable motel on South Michigan Avenue. Most were relatively young; the average age was about forty. Most were World War II veterans. Although they all had the confidence of at least one of the meeting's
organizers, only a few held highly influential positions in the Republican
Party.

In some ways, the group was diverse. Gerrish Milliken, one of NR's top
contributors, was a textile manufacturer in Connecticut. Charlie Barr, the
knowledgeable Chicago lobbyist, attended. There was an "Indiana gang":
Congressman Donald Bruce, state treasurer Robert Hughes, former state
GOP chairman Robert Matthews. Three others were South Carolinians who
had backed Goldwater at the 1960 convention: state party chairman Greg
Shorey; businessman Robert Chapman, who would be state chairman the
following year; Roger Milliken, Gerrish's brother, also a textile magnate and
a top NR donor. Among the most politically professional was lawyer Charles

Thone, a former YR president in Nebraska, now on the Republican National Committee and later a congressman. Rusher's friend Roger Moore was a fellow Harvard Law alumnus, active in the Boston-area Republican Party and president of the Beacon Hill Civic Association.

In addition to White, Ashbrook, and Moore, Rusher had been close or relatively close to several others who came to the first meeting or soon joined: Bob Morris, now president of the University of Dallas; first-term congressman John Rousselot of California, also a John Birch Society official; David Nichols, state party chairman in Maine; businessman John Keith Rehmann of Iowa; Ned Cushing, the most recent conservative YR chairman and a rural bank president in Kansas; attorney Sullivan Barnes of South Dakota, elected YR chairman by the Syndicate in 1953; and steel executive John Tope, yet another previous YR chairman.[62]

White had prepared the meeting carefully. He spoke of a long road ahead, of "powerful and ruthless forces aligned against us." Those who ran the national party might be old, tired, "somewhat disorganized." But once they caught on to the project, they would "fight us tooth and nail every inch of the way." If anyone found it necessary to switch sides at some point, White said, please be honest enough to inform the group. Frank Whetstone, a small-town newspaper publisher from Montana with a long-standing taste for politics, stood for a moment "glowering" at the others, looking like "a gigantic frontiersman who had accidentally put on a business suit." Emphasizing that they would be "on the firing line in a national convention," Whetstone said he could trust White and himself but demanded to know "where the rest of you s.o.b.'s will be when we get down to that final ballot." They all pledged to stick with their comrades, whatever pressures might be brought.

White explained the plan that he, Ashbrook, and Rusher had conceived. Some wanted an immediate commitment to promote Goldwater. But White told them, as he had told Rusher, that it was premature to tie themselves to a candidate just yet. Although he was unanimously assigned the lead role in their work, White refused to pledge himself to it until both he and they could think a bit longer. A final commitment should wait until the team felt certain there was a good chance of success. They should meet again in two months to make that evaluation. But White left Chicago with a sense that "we were putting together a winning combination."[63]

## "Guerrilla Operation"

Now they would tell the man himself. White barely knew him, and this later became a problem. In January 1961, Rusher had visited Goldwater at his

Senate office and informed him that White was interested in the chairmanship or the number-two job at the Republican National Committee. The
senator was already backing Ohio state chairman Ray Bliss. But even after
Congressman William Miller of upstate New York seemed likely to become
chairman, Rusher continued to promote White—now for the second spot at
the RNC. "Measuring my words carefully," he wrote to Goldwater in May, "I
consider him the ablest practicing professional politician I have ever met."
He knew the national party "from A to Z" and was well known to most of
its leading players around the country, who liked and respected him. Having known White well for thirteen years, Rusher added, "I can vouch for his
basic conservatism."[64] But nothing came of it.

Before briefing Goldwater on the newly formed cadre in late 1961, White
had really talked with him just twice: in 1955, when the freshman senator
was invited to the New York State YR convention at Rusher's urging; and
in 1958, to explain ideas White would be trying out in Arizona that might
help the reelection campaign. On the first occasion, White was impressed by
Goldwater's forthrightness and integrity in a half-hour conversation; on the
second, the senator gave his typical "most courteous" response. This time,
he got no response when he called to ask for a meeting, perhaps because a
secretary lost his phone number.

Rusher then sent a special-delivery letter to Arizona, announcing "a
development . . . potentially of the utmost importance." Could a few people
explain the group's plan to Goldwater before its next session? Acknowledging that the senator would have a crowded schedule during the holidays,
Rusher insisted: "I would not bother you about this, as I think you know,
unless I were convinced that it represents the beginning of the most serious
*professional* effort in almost a decade to turn the Republican party into a
more conservative channel."[65]

Goldwater quickly authorized the meeting, which Rusher didn't attend
because White settled on a date when only he and Charley Thone, of the several people they had in mind, could be in Washington. The senator listened
attentively, "cheerful and relaxed." This wasn't about a particular candidacy,
White said; such a decision should come after the 1962 midterm election.
For now, the group would be linking up with others who wanted the party
to go conservative. Goldwater said it sounded like "the best thing I've heard
of" since becoming a national Republican figure in the early fifties. White
requested occasional thoughts on how to develop the group's program. He
also asked Goldwater to meet with members during his travels, and to point
the cadre toward new allies. Goldwater agreed. But when talk turned to the
presidential picture, he seemed to think Rockefeller had practically won
the 1964 nomination already, with no potential candidate who could beat

him. White found that a bit surprising. The senator showed more interest when they discussed the Republican platform. Still, their meeting had been friendly and constructive.

At the group's next gathering on December 10 in Chicago, it was clear the members were determined to proceed. White presented a $65,000 budget for operations in the first year, to consist mainly of "a nationwide search for conservative Republicans we could recruit to help win control of the 1964 convention." Explaining his plan for nine part-time regional directors in charge of finding and activating helpful individuals, White named the people he had in mind for each region.[66] "Somebody said: 'Well, what about Rusher?' I hadn't gotten an assignment. Somebody else said: 'Oh, Rusher's in charge of the kooks.' Which was a politician's way of saying: 'Rusher is our contact with the intellectuals.'" Most in the group probably weren't *National Review* subscribers at the time, according to Rusher, and there was a highly appreciative but independent attitude toward the magazine: "We're glad to have it, and we even have a representative of it here. But on the other hand, they don't lead us around, and we don't pray to it or anything like that."[67]

White outlined "a long-term political guerrilla operation," as he would later describe it. "Although I did not express it at the time, I had never been so fired up in my life." After the meeting, about a dozen members of the team, their departures delayed by the weather, sat down at a restaurant for a cheerful dinner: "Politicians are rarely so happy," Rusher would reflect, "as when they have embarked on a course they believe in and which they are convinced has a real chance of succeeding."[68] Meanwhile, some enthusiasm was already brewing independently. By the end of 1961, a Californians for Goldwater organization had eleven chapters with six hundred members.[69]

Back in Manhattan, White found a two-room office in the Chanin Building at 42nd Street and Lexington Avenue, several blocks north of *National Review*. When Rusher dropped by within a day or two, he asked what it would be called. "Just Suite 3505," White said. Rusher laughed: "I think that's a great no-name. It'll be a while before anyone penetrates that cover." The publisher persuaded a successful career woman, also a former chairman of the Young Women's Republican Club in New York, to consider helping out. White considered her a lucky find. As his "all-around girl Friday and coordinator of women's activities," Rita Bree was an "invaluable asset" who worked away and never complained, her strong example a boost to everyone's morale.[70]

White and Rusher, who communicated in person and by phone, producing very little mutual correspondence for the record, had a lot in common: their political beliefs and idealism, a fascination with electoral politics, much Republican organizational experience. But while Rusher liked to express his thoughts on paper, White generally wouldn't, preferring to follow "a politician's rule: Never sign anything you write, and never write anything you sign." He simply "didn't like to be committed" in that sense, Rusher explains, and was "superstitious about it, maybe too much so."[71]

The leader of the early Goldwater forces would have a "curiously unsatisfactory chemistry" with Goldwater, Rusher later observed regretfully. His strengths included "absolutely spotless personal honor" along with "great tact and restraint." But Rusher sensed, having perceived this even in his friend's previous distant relationship with Governor Dewey, that he might have trouble getting comfortable with a superior. As a "shy, warm human being who found it difficult to express easily his deep affection for those for whom he worked," White may have been too deferential with candidates. While he tried to "act out his sentiments by truly selfless devotion," his over-modest attitude could inhibit personal communication, and politicians couldn't easily understand such a man. For his part, Goldwater had certain insecurities—being from a small state, also doubting his ability to be a good president. "Perhaps as a cover for his own political nakedness," Rusher suggested in *Rise of the Right*, he had "developed . . . a profound admiration for the Republican party's pros." White and his group seemed to fall short of that status.[72]

In the opinion of Lee Edwards, director of information for the Goldwater primary campaign, press aide in the general-election campaign, and author of a major biography of the senator: "The fact that Rusher could always get in to talk to Goldwater . . . is a sign that he respected him, or at least thought he was someone who knew politics and was something of an operative. I think he made, in that sense, probably a better connection with Rusher than with Clif White." The senator "always thought of Clif as a New Yorker type—and also a pro who was trying to use him, Goldwater, to advance his, Clif White's, career." In contrast, Edwards "never heard or felt anything like that with Rusher. I think he saw Rusher as somebody who was more truly interested in the movement, in the party; who was smart, a good analyst, and . . . whom he, as I say, respected."[73]

Following the December 1961 meeting where he was said to be "in charge of the kooks," the publisher decided to tell his colleagues what was up. Buckley and others at the magazine knew he made occasional trips to meet with former Young Republican "cronies," but not their purpose. After the senior editors' weekly dinner in the first days of 1962, Rusher got Burnham and Bill Rickenbacker to stay for a nightcap so he could brief them. He was disappointed:

> I am not sure precisely what reaction I expected from these two old
> friends . . . But I was certainly not prepared for the reception I did

encounter, especially from Burnham, which rather reminded me of the pleasure expressed by a parent when a retarded child does exceptionally well in school. He and Rickenbacker heard me out, expressed their gratification, and praised the initiative of my political colleagues, but it was clear that they didn't take my report seriously . . . Brooding over the discussion afterward, I hit on an explanation which I later formulated mordantly as one of Rusher's Laws: *No* National Review *editor ever believes anything until he has read it in the* New York Times.[74]

It also became a pattern. When Rusher reported on the group's progress, his colleagues "nodded amiably and took care to understate the story in their editorials."[75]

The blasé response from Burnham and Rickenbacker was an unpleasant opening to a tough year for the Goldwater cadre, which Rusher would compare to Valley Forge in the Revolutionary War. "It was a period," one member noted, "when we had to feed on each other's enthusiasm and confidence."[76] In the fall of 1962, money grew so short that White was ready to give up when he met Rusher and Rita Bree one day for lunch at the Commodore Hotel's Tudor Room, where the project was first discussed the previous year. It was time to quit, he told his friend, but "Rusher argued against the decision so persuasively that I finally agreed to hang on just a little longer if Rita would stick it out too." Soon enough, more sizable contributions were rounded up.

White's feelings of discouragement were not infrequent during the drive to nominate Goldwater, according to Rusher. "I remember plenty of conversations . . . in which I was trying to pep him up, and be a cheerleader for the idea of going on." White felt burdened, Edwards explains, not just by the financial troubles and the stress of dealing with Goldwater, but also by having to travel around the country all the time, with the "frustrations of keeping all these various people together." Without Rusher's unfailing optimism, Bree later said, the draft campaign would have disintegrated.[77]

For all his new determination to fight within the party, Rusher knew the ultimate success of a Goldwater candidacy depended on what the general public believed and how strongly they believed it. In his interview for Jeff Bell's short-lived college journal *Foundation* in late 1962, he predicted: "There will inevitably come a time when the American people determine that world Communism must be destroyed. If that time comes before November of 1964, Goldwater will be elected. If it comes after 1964, he will be defeated."[78]

## Crossroads

In this difficult season for the Goldwater project, the midterm election produced results a Republican could interpret in different ways. The party made a tiny gain in the House and actually lost a bit in the Senate. For possible presidential candidates, the outcomes were mixed. Rockefeller was reelected but only by a modest margin despite substantial advantages. Nixon lost his race for governor in California. At his legendary "last press conference" the next morning, the former vice president said the midterm's most significant result—amounting to a "revitalization" of the party—was the election or reelection of Republican governors in other large states, including Rockefeller, William Scranton in Pennsylvania, and George Romney in Michigan.[79] All three were moderate or liberal and would be Goldwater opponents at some point in the 1964 cycle.

Rusher had long been wary of Rockefeller's ambitions. At the height of the 1958 campaign in New York, he passed along the assessment of a highly placed source: the then gubernatorial candidate apparently planned to challenge Nixon for the 1960 nomination. Rusher urged *NR* to "consider making a big hue and cry about this" in hopes that "Rockefeller may be forced to deny it, or even to hedge a denial—in which case he may [in the race for governor] lose a good many votes of Republicans who want Nixon in 1960."[80] Now, in late 1962, White became concerned about a surprisingly friendly personal relationship between Rockefeller and Goldwater. Believing the governor already had the 1964 nomination won, and that he could be influenced ideologically, Goldwater was telling people: "Rocky's not such a bad guy. He's a lot more conservative than you think." Rockefeller was calling Goldwater "a great Republican."[81]

In the dual context of Rockefeller's behind-the-scenes campaign and the growing interest in Goldwater among southern conservatives, Rusher stressed the latter point in "Crossroads for the GOP," which ran in the February 12, 1963, issue of *National Review* and became one of his claims to fame.

The long essay began with a denial that Rockefeller would be a good presidential candidate for the Republicans. He had been reelected by an unimpressive margin, Rusher emphasized—against an opponent, Robert Morgenthau, with a wooden personality who ran a passive, poorly financed campaign. Rusher contended that the governor's relatively weak showing in New York, plus the Nixon defeat in California, virtually proved the liberal favorite would lose both megastates in 1964. Since this seemed to erase the main argument for a Rockefeller candidacy, the best chance to beat Kennedy lay elsewhere. Special-interest and ethnic politics in large northern states were unhealthy for the GOP, and they didn't or wouldn't work. "The Republican Party, like it or not, has a rendezvous with a brand new idea."

This was among the first articulations of what became known as the "southern strategy" and was perhaps the most consequential, for it may have nudged Goldwater closer to a candidacy. As Rusher described it, the idea was to nominate a conservative presidential candidate—presumably also a candidate with good personal appeal, although he didn't discuss this—who would have, simply by being conservative and by strongly contesting the southern states, the best chance to carry a large region that had been Democratic for over a century but seemed increasingly open to voting Republican. Should this happen, it would radically upset the traditional balance in the Electoral College. Provided the candidate's losses, if any, in historically Republican states were small, a conservative could—probably would—become president.

The analysis was based to a considerable extent on Rusher's point that the region was becoming less southern. He called special attention to the new white collar and professional people in many southern cities. They were much like white-collars and professionals in the North and West, and they were already voting Republican. The party's total vote for the House of Representatives in the eleven ex-Confederate states had nearly doubled between the midterm elections of 1958 and 1962, reaching 31 percent; and it would have been higher but for the fact that many southern districts still had no GOP candidate.

Rusher then argued that Republicans in these states wanted a conservative nominee. Texas state chairman Peter O'Donnell, his party already benefiting from "resignation rallies" at which lifelong Democrats publicly defected to the Republicans, reported that converts were insisting on a candidate from the Right and saying that they wouldn't vote for Rockefeller or any other liberal. Leading Republicans across the South were telling the same story, Rusher added.

Could a Republican capture the region? Several states had backed the party's candidate at least twice in the three elections from 1952 through 1960, while Louisiana went Republican once. In heavily Democratic Alabama and Mississippi, the party's "vigorous young" chairmen believed a conservative Republican would win their states in 1964. Rusher quoted John Grenier of Alabama: "It'd be the easiest campaign I ever ran."

Might it be too easy, in a moral sense? Rusher acknowledged the question but rejected its implication, the charge that "*any Republican concession to Southern sentiment is a venture in sheer racism.*" He pointed out that the Democrats, while endorsing segregation, had been "calmly raking in" a near-monopoly of elective offices in the region for decades. Republicans "would have to drink deep indeed at the racist trough" before they equaled the Democratic record on behalf of Jim Crow. But there was a better response, Rusher continued. The GOP in the South was generally "far less committed to all-out segregation" than the Democrats. This had a practical basis: the main Republican strength lay in the cities and suburbs, areas "where the tides of social change are tending to run fastest." In state after state, the really hard segregationists were the "primitive wool-hats"—rural poor whites, not the demographic he was talking about. Also, southern Republicans accepted their inability to "dictate a national Republican platform or candidate committed to segregation."

To the objection that northerners and southerners in the GOP nonetheless felt differently about the issue, Rusher responded that American society "is deeply riven on the subject" and therefore "no party that pretends to national scope can, by definition, do other than reflect—as the Democratic Party has for 80 years reflected—this division itself." He quoted the Republican National Committee chairman, Congressman Miller of New York, who had told the RNC at its recent meeting: "Don't let them give you a sense of guilt" about seeking southern votes.

Rusher did not guarantee that Goldwater would be elected. But he asked: Even if 1964 ended up as a Democratic year, how should the GOP build for its future? "By turning its back on the new, conservative and increasingly Republican South and gumming blintzes with Nelson Rockefeller? Or by nominating a candidate who—win or lose—will galvanize the party in a vast new area, carry fresh scores and perhaps hundreds of Southern Republicans to unprecedented local victories, and lay the foundations for a truly national Republican Party, ready to fight and win in 1968 and all the years beyond?"[82]

The southern strategy as a Republican doctrine, beginning with the Goldwater candidacy and continuing ever since, is typically alleged to have been racist or racially exploitative. The ubiquitous charge tends to blame strategists and candidates for the racist and segregationist intentions of some voters. The latter undoubtedly helped Goldwater, for instance, to win much of the South in the general election. What would have happened if the senator had voted for, not against, the Civil Rights Act of 1964 is unclear. While Rusher admitted in his article that the Democratic Party's increasing liberalism on civil rights gave Republicans part of their southern opportunity, he did not advocate that the GOP take a segregationist or anti-civil-rights line. He also stressed the New South—educated people in the modern industrial economy, less committed to segregation and in some cases against it—as the region's main source of Republican growth.

Rusher had, in any case, pointed conservative readers toward a fundamental opportunity whose rewards would pile up for decades. "Flipping the

South . . . was the key to everything," Stan Evans notes. "The key to the presidency, the key to the Congress. You had to have those votes, and when we got 'em, we won—and Bill saw that."[83]

At the moment it was far from clear, however, that the 1964 campaign would give Rusher's new southern Republicans much to excite them. White's group, Rusher included, had viewed Goldwater throughout the process as a potentially willing candidate, although a wary and unenthusiastic one for the time being. By early January 1963, White sensed more negativity. Because its most recent meeting had been infiltrated, the project was now public knowledge. "The conservatives are guilty of bad timing, narrow motives and poor politics," complained the *Herald Tribune*. "The luxury of partisan bickering of the kind we have just seen in Chicago is political nonsense."[84] Goldwater's immediate comment when the story broke was hard to interpret. But he said shortly after New Year's: "I hope they won't go ahead on this timetable. I'd rather stay in a fluid position for the rest of this year."[85]

Still, a fluid position was not a refusal. A few days before White's next meeting with the senator, set for January 14, Rusher wrote up a stack of advice. Most or all of it must have occurred to White, he noted, "but two heads allegedly are better than one." First, Rusher urged: "Difficult and delicate as it may be, I think you should press Goldwater into privately assuring you that he *will* run for the nomination if an adequate war chest and organization can be put together." This basic point "should not be fudged or left implicit any longer"—although if White ran into serious resistance, he shouldn't "break any bones." A national finance committee "with a good clear name [and] as many prestigious millionaires as possible" should be started, and "put to work very quickly indeed." A good public-relations firm should be hired promptly.

It was also time, Rusher added, to form the beginnings of a campaign staff and the nucleus of a "brain trust." Goldwater the senator was relying on Buckley and Kirk as intellectuals, and rightly so. But neither would work full-time, as a presidential race required. Bozell had previously done "most of Goldwater's heavy thinking for years," and he might be just right for this. The two did have something of a falling-out when the senator told his admirers at the 1960 convention to get behind Nixon. White might raise the possibility of bringing back Bozell—but "venture gingerly," Rusher advised, "without getting wet above your ankles." In addition, the campaign's top leadership should be chosen or at least discussed. And finally, a target date for an announcement should be set. Rusher hoped the kickoff would occur as soon as possible. It was "getting harder all the time to persuade people to hold their horses."[86]

What followed next astounded both of them. The week before talking with Goldwater, White spent three days in Washington meeting people at a conference sponsored by *Human Events*. Explaining his organizational strategy to conservatives from around the country, he felt strongly encouraged by their responses and found many new allies. By Monday morning, word of their reaction had presumably gotten back to the senator. In their meeting, White gave Goldwater an advance copy of Rusher's "Crossroads" essay, suggesting he read it carefully. He started to give a promised report on the December meeting's decisions, among them a schedule for further organizing—and a March 15 announcement, subject to the senator's permission, of a public Goldwater committee.

About five minutes into the presentation, Goldwater held up his hand. "Clif," he said, "I'm not a candidate. And I'm not going to be. I have no intention of running for the presidency." White tried to smile: "Well, we thought we would have to draft you." Goldwater was unmoved: "Draft, nothin.' I told you I'm not going to run. And I'm telling you now, don't paint me into a corner. It's my political neck and I intend to have something to say about what happens to it." White responded: "Senator, I'm not painting you into a corner. You painted yourself there by opening your mouth for the last eight years. You're the leader of the conservative cause in the United States of America, and thousands—millions—of people want you to be their nominee for President. I can't do anything about that and neither can you." Goldwater: "Well, I'm just not going to run. My wife loves me, but she'd leave me if I ran for this thing."

White walked out of the Senate Office Building into a cold wind, taking a cab straight to the airport despite plans to see several others in Washington that day. Back in Manhattan, he went up to the secret command post in Suite 3505. "We were like mourners sitting around a corpse," Rita Bree would recall. Rusher came in and asked how the meeting went. "I'm going to give up politics and go back into business," White answered. It was a rare moment: "Rusher, who seldom shows that he is surprised at anything, looked as though he was about to lapse into a state of shock." Goldwater wouldn't even permit a draft, White explained. "This was one of the few times I've ever seen Bill Rusher really discouraged. He kept pecking away at possible alternative courses of action, but in the end he came to see that you just couldn't take a grown man by the scruff of the neck and force him to run for President of the United States."[87]

On the same day, Rusher shared his reaction with Buckley. Noting that he still thought Goldwater might eventually change his mind and run, he also feared that the best chance of a successful bid for the nomination was probably lost. Such a large, complicated project required a lot of time and money. The White operation "was ready and willing to devote both, in ample measure, to Goldwater's cause." Now it would have to close down.

Even if Goldwater should later decide to run, Rusher told Buckley, his refusal to let the draft organization proceed would end up costing him the nomination. That failure, in turn, would "delay the reorientation of the Republican Party . . . along more conservative lines for four crucial years."[88]

The situation was actually more complex. Goldwater's ambivalence is not in doubt. When people close to the senator—a circle that did not include White and Rusher—tried in the early 1960s to discuss a possible campaign for president, he often "became irritable and short-tempered," according to Steve Shadegg, his old campaign manager.[89] Yet he had told the *Arizona Republic* newspaper, just a few days before disappointing White, that if he *were* interested in running, it "still makes more sense for me to delay. I've done my backroom work already. Nobody's been around the country more in the last ten years than I have . . . Another thing, I am the only conservative in the presidential picture. The others are . . . liberals. You might say, 'Let them fight it out for a while.'"

In his memoirs, Goldwater would cite strong personal reasons for his reluctance to run: "The possibility of being a prisoner in the White House, my every move attended by the Secret Service, surrounded by a corps of sycophantic advisers, with every move I made, every word I spoke interpreted and analyzed by the national press, was repulsive to me." Furthermore, he was "overawed by the presidency" and had "no lust for the power of the office." In addition, he saw heavy odds against an "outsider" from a small western state.[90] In 1984, Goldwater told Rusher that he "was probably not mentally equipped" to be president: "It's really the major reason why I didn't immediately embrace your efforts. It's like old [Senator] Dirksen once said, 'The only trouble with Goldwater is he doesn't think he can get the job done.' And, while I've had plenty of examples in my long life of getting the job done . . . I still am haunted by the idea that I might not succeed in an effort that was of great importance to my country and the American people."[91]

Yet Goldwater had chosen politics and stayed there. A private comment on his successful first try for elective office in 1949, a Phoenix city council campaign, was half prophetic: "It ain't for life, and it may be fun."[92] It was more or less for life, as it turned out, but also mostly fun. Goldwater loved serving in the Senate. He also had, Rusher says, "a politician's general enjoyment of seeing people running around talking about him for president."[93] The publisher's sense that a campaign might happen anyway, despite White's bad news that January afternoon, ultimately proved correct.

Four days after Goldwater flatly refused to run or permit a draft, Rusher wrote him a long letter. It completely ignored his refusal, focusing instead on his relationship with the White team. Rusher understood "perfectly well, or think I do, the whole myriad of considerations" Goldwater had against allowing an organization to seek money and delegates on any assumption that he would definitely run. It was "strategically too early for you to make such a decision, and certainly tactically far too early to announce it." About a year later—"your view, as quoted in the press in recent weeks"—would be soon enough to announce a decision for or against.

Rusher added: "I am extremely anxious that the time and effort which Clif and I and all the others have expended on our project over the past 15 months or more shall not go to waste—as it inexorably will if we are not allowed to launch, on our own, a national draft-Goldwater organization in the near future." The senator might not fully realize how far along their plans were, and "how large and influential a portion" of the party's leaders were involved. He might not fully understand, either, "what a deadly blow to the morale of everyone concerned—[and] to the organizational framework itself—a seeming repudiation of this project by you would be." Were this to happen, "all that would remain would be a few files of names, in mothballs."

It was therefore essential, "I earnestly submit," that the group "be allowed to go ahead on our own." Goldwater could still keep a distance. "It would be both natural and seemly for you to be able to say that you have heard, in a general way, of our activities; that you are of course flattered; and that—not having started the organization—you do not feel that you are in a position to order it to stop." This seemed fully consistent with allowing himself a year before making up his mind. Rusher concluded his plea with a characteristic blend of deference and zeal: "I hope you won't consider that I have been presumptuous in talking so frankly and so urgently about a matter that, after all, touches you personally and very deeply indeed. But I am profoundly convinced that the organization we have built in the past year is very probably the last one that will ever seek, in a serious and systematic way, to turn the GOP into more conservative channels, and I know that you would deplore as sincerely as I would anything that might prevent that from happening."[94]

Goldwater responded by suggesting that the work of rounding up conservatives and promoting their role in the nominating process remained welcome, but that the organizers should not promote *him*. He had never committed to anyone that he would run, nor had he "indicated that I would stand still for a draft," and thus he saw no need to repudiate the project publicly. He added: "I do think that there has been a good job in the general field in which I thought work was progressing," namely "conservative strength at the 1964 Convention for any purposes later to be decided upon." But he concluded by saying, in effect, that he preferred his current job to a presidential race: "Any overt action at this time could do me irreparable damage, because I plan to run [again] for the Senate in 1964 and do not want anything like this to happen."[95]

Unwilling to quit, Rusher answered carefully the next day. With a hint of defiance, he referred to Goldwater's rejection of a draft as "your present viewpoint." Then, accepting that the senator opposed the idea "at this point," he added: "We will loyally cooperate in whatever course you personally wish to pursue." But he went on: "There remains the matter—in which I believe we still see eye to eye—of not permitting all the good work that has been done to go to waste. If a candidacy or a draft movement is out of the question for the time being, then we must think of something else. To that end, I do hope that you will talk further with Clif, and perhaps with others in the group." Over the past year, Rusher noted, his work with the cadre had led him to believe there was "far more opposition to Rockefeller—or any other Liberal candidate—in Republican leadership circles around this country than is generally supposed."[96] For the next three months, the White team waited and worried, once nearly giving up.

# 7

# Goldwater Feels a Draft

White and Charlie Barr met with Goldwater on February 5, but his lack of interest in a draft remained unchanged. Rusher relayed mixed news to Buckley that day, once again wasting no time in keeping him posted. On the negative side: Goldwater seemed to think that because Kennedy would beat any opponent, a candidacy would necessarily fail. This would give "Republican conservatism a further black eye." It would also cost him his Senate seat, up in 1964. On the brighter side, Goldwater "seemed much more persuaded, this time, as to the importance of maintaining the conservative nucleus we have built up around the country among professional Republicans."[1]

Two weeks after this meeting, the group's de facto executive committee gathered near the Chicago airport at the O'Hare Inn. With the drapes drawn not just for secrecy but also to block out a wintry gray sky, they ate breakfast and drank gallons of coffee in the conference room. White would remember it as "one of the gloomiest" political meetings he had ever attended, Rusher as "one of the strangest." White described his fruitless talks with Goldwater. The activists knew the gravity of the problem. A minimal amount of cooperation from their intended candidate, something better than a clear repudiation, was necessary. But it seemed "too cruel a fate," according to Rusher, "to be deprived of such a historic triumph merely because the candidate was, for the moment, not willing to run . . . Disconsolately we picked at the problem. The argument was dismally circular."[2]

After about an hour, the meeting lapsed into several minutes of silence. "There's only one thing we *can* do," growled a midwestern voice. "Let's draft

168

the son of a bitch." "What if he won't let us draft him?" someone asked. "We'll draft him anyway. I mean *really* draft him." As White would recount: "Something in Bob Hughes' determined voice, and the earthy way he expressed his solution, suddenly made us all sit up and ask ourselves if we hadn't been rejecting what was obviously the only way out of our dilemma."[3]

The idea caught on at once, winning unanimous approval. They would launch the National Draft Goldwater Committee after all. Chosen to lead it, by friendly draft, was one of the attendees. The new GOP chairman in Texas, Peter O'Donnell, then just thirty-eight, already had an impressive party-building record in previous positions in his state. As a committed, independently wealthy conservative, he was a man "nobody could order around." White, however, was to continue as essentially the executive direc-tor.[4] Because of his duties in Texas, O'Donnell accepted the full chairman-ship only after White "readily" agreed to actually run the committee.[5]

Rusher reported to Buckley that the group was now moving on plans to raise money for and establish a national Goldwater organization. They didn't think the senator wished to "repudiate us totally," he wrote, also sug-gesting that the hoped-for candidate was confused. "Goldwater's recent pri-vate remarks on his intentions seem to have varied from the merely incon-sistent to the positively incoherent. Steve Shadegg recently told one of our people that he has never seen Goldwater (who is usually quite decisive) so torn with uncertainty about anything." Apparently, Rusher continued, he had complained that those urging him to run were almost all amateurs. The group's "tentative plan . . . is simply to ignore the good Senator for the time being, and try to set up a really formidable public organization with some heavyweights as its nominal leaders."[6]

As the campaign season drew closer, Rusher increasingly served as a Goldwater advocate at *National Review*. He had good support from Meyer, who told Buckley in late February, for example, that it was essential "to find a center around which to consolidate political conservatism" and that Gold-water was "the only man we've got."[7] Rusher thought it was also important to build confidence among the editors about Goldwater's chances. He assured Buckley that some recent bad poll numbers didn't worry him. A Gallup sur-vey a few months earlier had Rockefeller leading Goldwater among south-ern Republicans by 41 to 17 percent. That was nonsense. O'Donnell called Rusher about it and "began laughing . . . in sheer irresistible amusement at its inaccuracy." The polls might simply reflect voters' expectations about who *would* be nominated, Rusher suggested to Buckley. In any case, he had carefully sampled the views of professional Republicans with "no reason to lie about the matter." They told him the attitude in the party toward Rock-efeller was tepid at best.[8]

The formation of the official Draft Goldwater Committee was announced at a press conference on April 8. "By the grace of God," Rusher reflected in later years, Goldwater's reaction was "grumpy" but bearable. The senator said he would take no position "on this draft movement. It's their time and their money. But they're going to have to get along without any help from me."[9]

Meanwhile, the "Crossroads" article, which NR offered in pamphlet form after it ran, became the magazine's best-selling reprint up to that time. Dozens of conservatives sent copies to Goldwater. There were rumors that he had read the essay and been impressed by the argument.[10] By March, according to Rusher, Goldwater was telling friends he could carry southern states that were previously considered impossible for a Republican.[11]

The occasional NR political writer James Kilpatrick, himself a southerner and lead editorialist of the Richmond Times-Dispatch, best known at the time as a defender of segregation, corroborated Rusher's description of a pro-Goldwater region, estimating the senator would win nine of the thirteen southern and border states in a general election. The essence of Goldwater's appeal in the South, Kilpatrick wrote, was that he had "nothing in common with Jack Kennedy."[12] Bozell agreed with Rusher's southern concept even more explicitly. In the long term, he told readers, it was the party's "only realistic hope of escaping" from the two undesirable alternatives: "throwing itself on the mercy of an Eisenhower-type personality cult, or accepting national minority status."[13]

## Advice and Advocacy

Rusher was among about a dozen people who met regularly to guide the Draft Goldwater organization. "His advice was excellent," Peter O'Donnell recalls. Among other things, he continued to take Young Republicans seriously in senior party politics, both as allies and as enemies. "Some of 'em are just like baby adders," O'Donnell remembers Rusher saying. "If one of 'em bites you, they can kill you just as dead as an atomic bomb." Ned Cushing recalls: "When he did talk, you listened, because you knew it was something generally of importance; and you always learned something when you listened to Bill, I felt."[14]

In June, Rusher offered the Draft Goldwater chairman several pieces of counsel. One involved the man emerging as their main opponent. Rockefeller's divorce of his wife of more than thirty years in 1962, followed in May 1963 by remarriage to a much younger woman, didn't immediately strike most politicians as a great problem for him, even though his new wife was the mother of four young children and divorced her husband in order to marry the governor. These political leaders were surprised when it became clear they were wrong.[15] Or perhaps, as Rusher would later maintain, Rockefeller's remarriage "simply provided a golden excuse for the party to reject a man it disliked anyway; it has never nominated a gung-ho Liberal and wasn't about to do so in 1964."[16] At the time, he argued it could be a significant factor for many voters, telling O'Donnell that women wouldn't like "seeing one of their number divorce her husband, marry a presidential candidate and in due course become First Lady of the Land."[17]

Rusher offered the chairman two reasons why the Goldwater leaders should publicly "dismiss Rockefeller . . . as any longer a serious possibility." First, "I honestly think he's through." Second, attacks on him would play into the strategy of Governor Romney's people, which was to offer their candidate "as a last-minute compromise." It was preferable to concentrate on driving Romney "further out into the open, discussing his weak points," and making him controversial. Rusher also raised a deeper concern than the immediate competition. Its significance would become apparent before, and even more apparent after, the convention a year later. "I wonder if we shouldn't be giving some thought to winning some Eastern business support for Goldwater," Rusher wrote, "or at least reassuring that influential community that Goldwater's election need not alarm them." With permission from O'Donnell, he would come up with a proposal or two for this purpose.[18]

The southern aspect of the Goldwater campaign angered eastern GOP leaders even in mid-1963, and the *Herald Tribune* ran a strong editorial alleging a turn toward racism within the party. Rusher hit back hard against "the latest in a series of articles, columns, and editorials" that had "this long-time reader . . . seriously wondering whether you have taken leave of your senses." The *Trib* had cited nothing "ever said by Senator Goldwater or by his responsible supporters to suggest that the Republican Party, under their leadership, contemplates an essentially anti-Negro policy." Rusher defended the candidate on a personal level, also noting a difference between integration as such and federally mandated integration. "Senator Goldwater's appeal to the South is primarily as a conservative," Rusher wrote. "He is himself in favor of integration, but opposed to the kind of coercive integration which President Eisenhower and President Truman also rejected. Does this make him or his backers racists?"

Rusher perceived the controversy as a major element in the intra-Republican power struggle. Behind the paper's charges of racism, he saw not moral motives but selfishness—a growing concern that the Republicans might build a new political coalition, one that could succeed without the Northeast and was "far less dependent . . . on the interests, the personalities, and the institutions which make up the Tribune's diminishing world."[19]

By this time, with the eruption of violence in Birmingham, Alabama, civil rights became not only an issue but a political focus for many Americans who hadn't taken either side. Unlike Goldwater, Rockefeller clearly favored the civil-rights movement. In what became known as his "Bastille Day Declaration" of July 14, 1963, he argued that the GOP "is in real danger of subversion by a radical, well-financed, and highly disciplined minority." The radical minority offered "no program for the Republican party or the American people," Rockefeller claimed, "except distrust, disunity, and the ultimate destruction of the confidence of the people in themselves. They are purveyors of hate and distrust in a time when, as never before, the need of the world is for love and understanding." The southern strategy's purpose was "to erect political power on the outlawed and immoral base of segregation and to transform the Republican party from a national party of all the people to a sectional party for some of the people."

Conservatives, including Goldwater, viewed this as a broadly targeted attack on themselves. A few weeks later, Rockefeller said he wouldn't support Goldwater against Kennedy "if he were a captive of the radical right," meaning both segregationists and conspiracy believers such as John Birchers.[20]

At *NR*, Buckley sought Rusher's counsel: what kind of editorial should be written on the dilemma set for Goldwater by the insistence, among liberals in both parties, that the senator and his backers denounce what they called the far right? The publisher urged: "*National Review*, as the tablet-keeper of conservatism, should nail this demand for the intellectually dishonest trick it is." Rockefeller and the others tended to be vague—deliberately, Rusher added—about who exactly should be spurned. "The truth of the matter is that Goldwater not only has repudiated, but has already been repudiated by, all of the really malodorous extremists on the right. He has refused to condemn the John Birch Society *en masse*, for the very good reason that to do so would unfairly injure many good people. I repeat: this is essentially a job for the tablet-keepers. And that's us."[21]

Late that summer, Rusher gave advice to *National Review* readers in an article titled "The Draft Goldwater Drive: A Progress Report." He told them it would be foolish to worry that the Goldwater effort might peak too soon. The danger was the opposite, too much delay. The media and eastern big business, being opposed to Goldwater, would exert "intangible but very real pressures" against him. If pressured conservatives were to stand by their candidate, a "massive wave of public sentiment" would be necessary. The work needed to produce it must begin now.

Rusher also confronted the recent charge from Rockefeller and Rockefeller-type Republicans that a special emphasis on southern votes would be racist. "To say that any Republican courtship of the South necessarily entails a segregationist policy is flatly untrue," he told readers. "Every newspaper story to that effect should be nailed by a letter to the editor." Goldwater's "personal record of friendliness toward Negro aspirations can be traced far back in his career, and long before his entry into politics," Rusher pointed out. "But the South must choose, in the long run, between the two existing parties, and there is no question whose view is closer to the Southern view on *almost* every issue."

Stressing the high stakes in the campaign, Rusher also implied that the candidate would make it to the White House: "In Barry Goldwater," he told readers, "America has found a pivot strong enough to bear the crushing weight of the turn our country must make. Nothing can stop that turn from occurring, late or soon; and it seems clearer every day that the year of destiny will be 1964."[22] Now forty years old, Rusher had lost the cynicism about Republican politics that he was expressing just two years earlier. He was "incredibly happy and optimistic," according to Jeff Bell, who saw a fair amount of him in New York: "'My God . . . we got the key guys in Wyoming,' or 'We got the key guys in Colorado,' and: 'Nobody knows this, nobody's writing it, but we're winning.'"[23]

Although 1963 was the springtime of the Goldwater movement and in that sense satisfying to the "tablet-keepers" at *NR*, the magazine also ran into serious disappointments in its relationship with the presumed candidate. After living and writing in Spain for a period, Bozell returned to the United States in the first half of that year and was interested in working for Goldwater again, but the senator wasn't responsive. In September, Buckley and Bozell set up a meeting in Washington with a Goldwater adviser, Dr. Charles Kelley, to see how they might help the campaign. Unexpectedly, Goldwater's close associates Denison Kitchel, a labor lawyer in Phoenix, and William Baroody, president of the American Enterprise Institute, were present as well. When Buckley and Bozell volunteered to set up an organization of pro-Goldwater academics, they were turned down.

The embarrassing incident leaked immediately to the press, and the next day's *Times* described an aggressive move by *NR*: "a boarding party" from the forces to the senator's right. When Buckley and Bozell "cornered some Goldwater aides" and sought to "join the campaign organization on a policy planning level," the advisers refused, believing "what their candidate needs least is more support from the far right." The distortions angered Buckley and Bozell. Goldwater aides have named Baroody as the likely source of the leak.

But from *NR*'s standpoint, the problem went beyond one hostile maneuver and article. Kitchel, who would become the campaign manager when Goldwater actually ran, also opposed any association between the campaign and the magazine. Its readers, he assumed, would back Goldwater in any case, and "by keeping away from Buckley and Bozell and that crowd, we thought we could appeal to a lot of people who don't like *National Review*."[24] An unidentified source, presumably from the campaign's high command, told campaign journalist Theodore White, author of the *Making of the President* series, that Buckley, Burnham, and other conservative intellectuals were "too arrogant, too cold, too intolerant" and that they "couldn't talk to people."[25]

After the boarding-party story, according to Draft Goldwater treasurer Bill Middendorf, who took notes at the time on the committee's work, Rusher "continued to attend some of our meetings, but without much enthusiasm."[26] The Goldwater managers' general distancing from the *NR* figures may have been a serious mistake. The latter weren't able to play "the role they should have played, and could have played," according to Lee Edwards. "It would not have helped win the election for us, but I think certain mistakes would not have been made. Because Baroody and Kitchel, and all the people at the top, had nothing like the political expertise, or knowledge or ability, that Rusher and others had." Goldwater himself later expressed regret that Buckley, Bozell, and Rusher were not on board, writing in his 1988 memoir that shutting them out of the campaign was an "undeserved, unconscionable act on our part."[27]

But for Goldwater's prospects, things continued favorably well into the fall. A major poll now had him leading Rockefeller among Republicans by 59 to 41 percent. In addition, it lent further credence to Rusher's contention that Goldwater would be the strongest nominee in the South. There, he led JFK by a whopping 54 to 34 percent, while Romney had a much smaller lead of 47–40. Rockefeller looked notably weak in the South, losing to Kennedy by 39–44.[28]

At *NR*, Rusher continued to be a sounding board in lesser political matters as well. When University of Chicago political scientist Robert Goldwin urged the magazine to back a moderate Republican in a gubernatorial primary, explaining that he would help the presidential nominee to carry Illinois, Buckley asked Rusher for a comment. Free as usual with his detailed political knowledge, the publisher wrote an ample response.

Rusher quickly identified the recommended candidate, Charles Percy, by explaining that he had been "President Eisenhower's fair-haired boy . . . carving out those platitudes which characterized" the administration. Percy was also the individual most responsible for crafting the 1960 Republican platform, which conservatives had disliked. Now running for governor, he claimed to have "shifted sharply to the right in his thinking," Rusher wrote. "At the same time, though not suffering from any known speech defect, he has avoided endorsing Goldwater." Furthermore, "some of Percy's tactics in luring the support of Goldwater backers are open to the charge of sharp practice."

The publisher then offered an admitted guess that he knew he couldn't win the primary and probably was setting up for a Senate race. If Percy continued to "develop along conservative lines," the magazine might reasonably back him. But solicitations for candidates should be eyed critically. It was not enough for them to be "kind enough to express an interest in our support."[29] Percy won the primary and lost the general election. He ran for the Senate at his first opportunity in 1966, won, served three terms—and compiled a relatively liberal voting record, representing to Rusher a classic case of establishment Republicanism, much as he had in 1963.

The assassination on November 22 changed things. No longer running against Kennedy, a polished northeasterner with whom he seemed in such contrast, Goldwater now faced not only a new president who started out with the public's goodwill, but a folksy, self-made Texan who was somewhat identified with the southern wing of the Democratic Party. Goldwater's campaign, Rusher later explained, "would never be able to persuade most American voters that Lyndon Johnson represented any of the new tendencies . . . which so many of them feared and opposed."

Goldwater had envisioned a high-minded, civil campaign in which he and Kennedy, with whom he was on good personal terms, might even share plane rides to joint appearances. He took the assassination hard, and he initially decided against a run. According to Edwards, the foremost reason was "his cold contempt for Lyndon Johnson, who would not engage, he was certain, in the issue-oriented campaign that he and Kennedy had envisaged." Even late in life, in his memoirs, Goldwater considered LBJ "the epitome of the unprincipled politician," both "treacherous" and a "hypocrite." He also thought Johnson was unbeatable, since the people didn't want three presidents in just over a year and therefore would not elect a challenger.[30]

On December 12, Goldwater met at his Washington apartment with a group he took more seriously than the draft committee. Among them were Senators Norris Cotton of New Hampshire and Carl Curtis of Nebraska, former Senate minority leader William Knowland of California, and Congressman John Rhodes of Arizona. Also present were three Goldwater associates who would run much of the general-election campaign: Kitchel and Dean Burch, political lieutenants from Arizona, plus Baroody of the American Enterprise Institute.

"Our cause is lost," Goldwater said. Kennedy's death had ruined the strategy behind the campaign. Voters wouldn't throw out a new president under the circumstances. Goldwater did not wish to run against a man as contemptible, in his view, as Johnson. The group tried to persuade him. The issues and the cause remained the same, they argued. The conservative movement must continue, not stall. Goldwater owed his supporters leadership. America, Senator Cotton emphasized, was getting soft and needed a new president.

The meeting ended inconclusively. Goldwater sat alone with Denison Kitchel, sipping bourbon, and asked for his advice. "Barry, I don't think you can back down," Kitchel answered. One man's wishes, he explained—much as White had done back in January—were less important than the millions of conservatives who were already standing for him. "Alright," Goldwater said, "God damn it, I'll go."[31] According to draft treasurer Middendorf, the senator "told his wife that he really didn't want to run, he didn't want to be president, but that he did want to give conservatives a cause and a voice. 'Lose the election,' he said, 'but win the Party.'"[32]

Goldwater announced on January 3, 1964, at his home outside Phoenix. Like many politicians, he chose his top campaign aides with an eye toward personal history and confidence, not preparation for the job. Kitchel and Dean Burch knew almost nothing of politics outside Arizona, but the candidate knew and trusted them.[33]

In his discomfort with White, Goldwater may have overlooked or undervalued many helpful qualities. Tom Van Sickle, his administrative assistant in Draft Goldwater, found him disorganized and inattentive in some respects but also able to "filter through all the chaff . . . come down to what was really important." In addition, admirers in the press considered him credible because "everything he told them happened the way he told them." White was "slow-spoken, methodical, point for point," according to Bob Bauman, who assisted him in organizing a national Goldwater rally in Washington in 1963. "You had the impression of a very thoughtful guy." Judy Fernald, who knew White in the draft campaign as well as older YR politics, remembers him as a "Christian politician" in the sense that he could work with anybody, including Democrats.[34]

Goldwater admitted in his memoirs that it was "a serious error on my part" not to name any leaders from the draft committee to his top team. But Richard Kleindienst soon asked White, who was supposed to be merely his assistant, to share the job of field director with him.[35]

With its candidate now officially running and therefore in ultimate charge, Draft Goldwater closed up shop in January, although White's army continued its labors throughout the country. Thanking Rusher, draft committee chairman O'Donnell wrote: "Your considerable knowledge of the political situation in most states was a contributing factor to many of our decisions." Rusher's advice "was highly valued by me and the other members of the committee . . . [and] as you suffered through our 'ups and downs' you were always able to maintain your sense of humor."[36]

At the end of February, Rusher told Buckley about the recent national meeting he had attended in Chicago, called for the purpose of introducing Goldwater and his staff to various state leaders of the draft organization. The mood was one of "well-grounded optimism," and the Arizona group made an impressive presentation of its campaign plans. Although White's feeling that he had been organizationally downgraded was largely justified, and others felt hurt by this too, "I would be the last man on earth," Rusher wrote, "to turn sour on the campaign as a whole for such a petty reason."[37]

The memo to Buckley was less informative than it might have been. White later recalled that although many Goldwater state chairmen were hostile toward the Kitchel team, "loaded for bear" going into the meeting, they withheld any heavy criticism because the briefing went so well, which led them to think the Arizona people were "developing into real professionals." But actually it was White who had prepared the presentation and expected to give it. He was told only the night before that Kitchel would run the briefing. The Arizonans were just "following a script."[38]

As the primary season got under way, Rusher grappled with Burnham's relative lack of respect for Goldwater and with Buckley's uncertainty about him as a presidential candidate. Burnham, inclined toward Rockefeller, had told the editor in mid-February: "The fact is, as we know, that Goldwater is a second-rate person; and he seems to be surrounded by third- and fourth-rate persons."[39] Although Rusher thought long before the first primary that Rockefeller was in a very weak position, the governor remained a high-profile candidate and a worry for the Goldwater campaign in part because of his money. He also had "a delight in meeting people," according to Teddy White, and was "one of the sunniest, most expansive and outgoing personalities" in American politics.[40]

Rockefeller had great ambition and drive as well. Rusher opposed most of his political positions, disliked what he saw as his incessant personal efforts to buy support among party figures around the country, and wanted to destroy his prospects as a national Republican leader. But in retrospect, he admires the ambition and energy: "Here's a guy born with umpteen million dollars—and as collateral to that, all women fell over backwards at his approach. What the hell do you do to prove yourself, if you want to accomplish something, if you want to test yourself against the world? . . . I think it's greatly to Rockefeller's credit that he didn't just spend his money and go after his women. That he really went after the governorship, and the presidency of the United States."[41]

Along with Meyer, Rusher now had the voice of senior editor Bill Rickenbacker, who seemed uninterested in the early Goldwater project two years before. He now agreed vigorously with Rusher on this issue, as he had generally supported the Rusher-Meyer positions in regard to the magazine. But in addition to serious doubts about Goldwater, Burnham kept continuing hopes for the governor and for *NR* conservatives' ability to influence him. He thought Rockefeller was both a good public servant and more electable as a national candidate. Burnham's ongoing interest in Rockefeller, *NR*'s Jeffrey Hart would later suggest, may ultimately have arisen from a sense that "the passing of the older Eastern elite, with its manners and manifest attractions, [was] a tragedy and perhaps unnecessary."[42] A young aide to Buckley later recalled meetings in which, as Burnham "subtly but persistently" spoke favorably of the governor, "Rickenbacker and Rusher would clutch their chests." Only Burnham and Buckley, though, were skeptical of the Goldwater candidacy. "The rest of us were cheerleaders, led by Bill Rusher."[43]

To the candidate's enthusiasts at *NR*, an enormous amount was at stake. Rickenbacker told the editors: "We are willing, I take it, ultimately to sacrifice our lives in the cause of Christian civilization; we should be no less willing to dedicate our magazine to the only major public figure who proclaims our beliefs."[44] Rusher did not speak or at least write of "dedicating" the magazine, but he kept a close watch on what it reported about the race. A few days before Goldwater's announcement, he signaled colleagues that he expected them to use political, not only journalistic, judgment. "I assume—correct me if I am wrong—that *National Review* is for Goldwater," he began sarcastically. *NR* should report "all of the relevant news, including the bad news," but should also present the response "of the intelligent Goldwater forces" to it. Rusher admonished: "I can scarcely imagine the 'New Republic' relentlessly vacuuming the opposition press for items unfavorable to its candidate, then printing these without the slightest qualification, explanation or mitigation."[45]

A month later, in early February, the publisher informed Buckley that Burnham seemed to wish the magazine would take a largely self-interested approach toward the campaign. He liked the "excellent" editorial Burnham had recently written on Goldwater, which mattered far more than the attitude taken in a previous discussion in Rusher's office. But it was still important to describe the gist of that conversation:

> He began by saying that he thought our posture in respect of Goldwater is wrong—"he doesn't acknowledge us, yet we have been servile to him." (As you know, I have tended to expect far less of Senator Goldwater than certain of the editors, in this matter of dancing attendance on *National Review*.) Jim went on to point out that for

*National Review* to be critical of Goldwater is "more newsworthy" than for it to support him. (I leave it to you to imagine what I think of this as an argument for criticizing him!) Finally, Jim considered that Goldwater was doing badly and that *National Review* "should avoid going down to defeat with him." (Even granted his premise, I do not consider that there is anything the least dishonorable about losing in a good cause.)[46]

In response, Buckley briefly expressed his concern about the relationship between Rusher and Burnham, about "peace in the kingdom," while noting his gratitude for "the job you are doing to maintain that peace."[47]

At the beginning of March, Buckley told the editors he had a "sinking feeling" about the campaign. It would be wrong to "let Goldwater down in any way." But *NR* must be prepared, at some point, to tell readers they should maintain hope for the eventual election of a conservative president despite the discouraging "experience of Barry Goldwater . . . *who, after all, did not really have his heart in the campaign, and was not as well qualified to run, or serve, as* (fill in the New Hero)."[48]

Rusher was less interested in what the magazine might say if the primary campaign failed than in coverage and commentary while it remained viable. He also worried about the morale among people who either supported Goldwater or ought to. Media attacks had already affected some of them significantly, he told Buckley. *NR* could "do Senator Goldwater profound and irreparable damage by ill-considered and allegedly 'objective' comments about what may befall him in this campaign . . . The stream of abuse and contempt for Goldwater, from the expected Liberal sources, has been utterly merciless, and has had a wilting effect upon loyal conservatives that I confess both surprises and sickens me. If *National Review* appears—I repeat, even appears—to join the barrage of criticism, the reaction will be far deadlier than you may realize."[49]

In late February, shortly before the first primary in New Hampshire, Rusher advised the editors to neither panic nor exult about the outcome. Nobody would get close to a majority, not with the flood of Rockefeller money plus the well-organized write-in drives for Nixon and Henry Cabot Lodge (the former Massachusetts senator, former UN ambassador, and former Nixon running mate, now ambassador to South Vietnam). In addition, New Hampshire wasn't naturally favorable to Goldwater, since it was so geographically and culturally distant from Arizona. Simply getting the most votes would be impressive.

Whatever happened, a hopeful attitude was called for. If Goldwater finished a close second, Rusher wrote, "I would expect *National Review* to point out the smallness of the margin," thus trying "to correct what will undoubt-edly be a major press effort to depict such a result as a Goldwater 'disaster.'" Should it be a distant second or worse, *NR* ought to admit that. It should not "compete with" anti-Goldwater reporters in predicting a dire effect on the campaign. That early in the process, "it would be ignoble . . . to attempt, by what we say or the tone in which we say it, to desert a candidate [whom] we have endorsed for reasons of the highest principle." If New Hampshire was bad, "life will go on . . . and I suggest again that we all get a grip on ourselves and prepare to go on with life—yea, even conservative life."[50]

Rusher had urged Buckley to write New Hampshire voters. Agreeing at first, the editor noted: "I must have your help. What length should it be? How should I more or less introduce myself, i.e., as an interested out-of-stater? To whom should I mail it, and when? Can you bring me up to date a little bit on the points that ought to be stressed? I feel rather out of the swing of things now."[51] Responding by telegram to Switzerland, Rusher urged speed and simplicity: "TIME SHORT SUGGEST OPEN LETTER TO NEW HAMPSHIRE VOTERS IN YOUR COLUMN NO SPECIFIC ADDRESSEE NOT TOO DETAILED JUST LET EAGLE SCREAM."[52]

Two weeks later, a week before the March 10 primary, Buckley told Rusher he had decided against making the appeal. As a message specially directed to one state and "fairly emotional in content," it would likely have annoyed editors elsewhere. Buckley added: "I devote roughly 75% of my col-umns to running interference for BG, and cleaning up after him. A sharp, direct, emotional letter might raise the eyebrows of editors who would then clamp down on those columns in which I labor mightily for Our Hero."[53]

The day before Buckley sent this disappointing update, Rusher made a subtle dig at him when he thanked Jerry Harkins, a Missouri state legisla-tor and Draft Goldwater leader (also personally close to Buckley), who was initially unhappy with the top-level conduct of the campaign, for updating Buckley about his new confidence in the candidate. This "should certainly go far toward straightening him out," Rusher told Harkins. "Remember that, sitting over there in Switzerland, with nothing to read except the Paris edi-tion of the 'New York Times' and 'Herald Tribune,' he is particularly vulner-able to any straw that may blow his way in a wind from the United States."[54]

Goldwater got 23 percent in New Hampshire, a fairly distant second, and Rockefeller was just 1,200 votes behind him. Looking back, White called the result "a thoroughgoing rout" for his candidate. Lodge had won the pri-mary not only as a write-in but also with a delegate slate of unknowns rather than prominent figures.[55]

At *National Review*, Rusher maintained the results weren't so bad. Writ-ing to Buckley, then staying in Paris toward the end of his winter vacation, "for your background information and guidance," he noted that Goldwater had lost to a candidate who was unlikely to go the distance: "All of us here concur in being profoundly grateful that his vanquisher was Henry Sabotage. However puissant his name may be in New Hampshire, it is almost certainly not salable to the American public at large, thanks to his messy involvement in the [November 1963] overthrow of the Diem regime and in the Vietnam debacle in general."

Rusher agreed with a point Burnham made in an editorial, that the Lodge vote really meant Undecided. The picture, he told Buckley, would be much worse if Rockefeller—or especially Nixon, or Pennsylvania governor William Scranton—had won. Rockefeller's impressive campaign in the state ended in third place, and he now seemed "well on his way to the showers." Also, the inexperience of Goldwater and his staff had gotten things off to a poor start, despite improvements later there.[56]

On the same day, Rusher sent campaign manager Kitchel a few recommendations. It was a mistake, he thought, for Goldwater or prominent backers to predict large victories in primaries; better just to say the candidate expected to win. Friends in California had told Rusher that former senator William Knowland was predicting Goldwater would beat Rockefeller there by half a million votes. This, he warned Kitchel, would let the media categorize a one hundred thousand-vote margin as a moral defeat. He also suggested, although surely this was "obvious," that Social Security would be a major problem even in the primaries. On this point, he cited Bob Morris's loss of elderly Republicans by nearly a nine-to-one margin in the 1960 New Jersey Senate primary. Admitting he had no "breezy solution" for how to discuss the entitlement program, Rusher stressed that the Goldwater campaign "must avoid the defensive if at all possible. How about claiming, loudly and affirmatively, that 'the first obligation of the Social Security system must be to protect the investment of those who have contributed to it, and to repay that investment to them in honest dollars,' or something like that?"[57]

Rusher didn't lose sight of the unforced errors in the campaign, or of the larger reality that it would be hard for a Republican to beat Johnson. But he remained excited about Goldwater's significance. Shortly after New Hampshire, he told his friend Runyeon:

On the national scene, the Goldwater effort strikes me as resembling a nest of Chinese boxes: a somber outer box representing my gloomy conviction that America simply can no longer be saved by the normal political processes; inside that, a cheerful-colored box representing the stunningly candid and courageously hard-line campaign the Senator is waging; and, inside that again, a black box representing the really deplorable mismanagement, inefficiency and amateurism of his jerry-built, Arizona-bred campaign staff (and, to be entirely fair about it, Goldwater's own rather amateurish under-estimation of the problems and perils of a Presidential candidate).

As to the negative factors, Rusher added, "we must walk before we can run." For the first time since 1952, conservatives had "a serious spokes-man in the field. That, to coin a phrase, ain't hay."[58] Buckley, in contrast to Rusher's disappointment in this respect, obliquely linked the tactical and executive weaknesses to the straightforward message he and Rusher both admired. "There is a sense in which Goldwater's campaign is almost neces-sarily amateurish," Buckley had written in his February 26 newspaper col-umn. This "altogether uncynical" candidacy was "seeking first and foremost the popular acceptance of a fresh series of attitudes towards the world and its problems; not, first and foremost, his nomination and election."[59]

During the primary season, Rusher's sources included various YAF and Young Republican members, who sometimes sought advice while shar-ing what they knew or heard. In January, Robert Sprinkel of the Califor-nia Young Republicans told him a Rockefeller victory seemed probable on June 2 for three reasons: the competence of the Rockefeller team in the state, the likelihood that few newspapers would endorse Goldwater, and a "lack of vigor" in the senator's California organization. Many apparent support-ers "simply do not care about Barry Goldwater," Sprinkel warned. Worried about his half-Jewish ancestry, membership in the Urban League, and for-mer membership in the National Association for the Advancement of Col-ored People (NAACP), they considered him "some sort of a Zionist threat."[60]

All was not well in California, a YAF official there agreed three months later. Many in the state's Goldwater campaign complained it was being sabo-taged, according to Ted Hicks. There had been "one complete foulup after another." In Los Angeles, nearly every conservative had been taken off the Goldwater committee. In Santa Clara, "the most effective precinct organizer was removed from his job—his sin—he wrote a letter to Denison Kitchel!!!!" Naming two "fishy" individuals and one "boob," Hicks suggested a full investigation of all this.[61]

Answering right away as he generally did with correspondents, Rusher struck a balance between respect and mild rebuke. "I hope you won't feel," he told Hicks, "that this short acknowledgement means that I didn't pay much attention to it—I certainly did, and will pass along your comments to the appropriate authorities." But he added: "Let me warn you against getting into the kind of Florentine intrigues which end up supposing that there is a Great Communist Conspiracy within the Goldwater camp . . . Seriously,

I would counsel you against spending too much of your time and energy on these matters of internal politics. Just put forth the very best effort you possibly can in the primary itself, and there will be glory and reward for us all."[62]

The advice was in keeping with Rusher's encouragement of conservatives elsewhere. Stan Evans remembers that he was "always trying to calm me down" about Young Republican conventions in the 1960s, where bloody ideological warfare could take place. "The thing about Bill, which is one of his great strengths, is that he . . . has a much more optimistic view of things than I . . . We're temperamentally different, even though philosophically the same. I would always [say]: 'This is really bad.' He would look on the bright side and try to cheer me up, or get me to be more supportive of whatever was going on."[63]

## Burnham and Buckley on the Campaign

In his own more solitary manner, James Burnham too enjoyed collecting information and opinions. As Buckley points out, he "was very much concerned" with the views of the public and sometimes "traveled conscientiously to familiarize himself with grassroots opinion—much more so than I was ever disposed to do."[64] In early 1964, Burnham took a long car trip, paying special attention to talk of the presidential race. He found there wasn't much. Breakfasting at a large restaurant in the Midwest, he noticed that every newspaper reader was looking at the sports section except for one man reading the business news. In Denver, describing his experience across more than half the continent to *NR* readers, Burnham reported a thriving economy and a prevailing sense that "bad public troubles are far away or postponable." He noticed little interest in the campaign except among "the pre-committed" and political professionals. The public mood was largely "cheerful, the outlook optimistic . . . There is no strong feeling, even in these Goldwater prairies, for a White House change. I have heard—how extraordinary a contrast to his predecessor's case!—no bitterness against the President or his policies from anyone."[65]

From Arizona, Burnham wrote that people in the West did feel dissatisfied with the country's establishment. But it seemed less a matter of politics than of culture and regional pride. "The Easterners have been running the country a long time, in their own way, and with their own ideas—drawn of late from their teeming mongrel cities and cosmopolitanized universities—that they try to impose everywhere," he wrote. "The outlanders, their regional bases filling now with the bodies, machines and new wealth that are the stuff of power, feel ready to take their turn. The program is obscure, confused; but they want *our kind of people* on top." It was this feeling that "fueled the Barry Goldwater boom, and got verbalized in the 'Southern (and Western) strategy' that was going to carry him to the White House."

Writing later from Tennessee, Burnham explained that the pragmatic mind-set of Americans, as seen in the focus on economics he had noted throughout his journey, worked—absent "actual catastrophe"—against any message from the Right. It inclined voters toward "buttered bread" from government.[66]

Meanwhile, Rusher upbraided his counterpart in a memo to the editors—apparently not distributed. In a recent column, Burnham had predicted Goldwater "would almost surely lose Texas to Johnson" and made what Rusher called an outdated complaint about too many "home-state cronies" on the Goldwater staff. Also unimpressive was his suggestion that the candidate, in Rusher's words, "go barnstorming through four Liberal-dominated capitals of Western Europe at this stage of the campaign" in order to strengthen his foreign-policy credentials. Worst of all was Burnham's contention that Goldwater hadn't yet "made good a claim to the Presidency." If that "most serious possible charge" was true, why had the magazine gotten behind him? Goldwater supporters would inevitably ask: "What on earth is *National Review* trying to do to us?"

Burnham was conducting a "broad-gauged and sustained" assault on the candidate, Rusher alleged. This kind of thing should run in the magazine's Open Question box, where people knew they were reading something controversial among the author's colleagues, and "where it can (I assure you) be speedily and effectively answered."[67]

At the height of the California campaign, Goldwater had already come close to winning the nomination largely because of victories in the caucus and convention states, which were White's responsibility. In these states— still a substantial majority at the time—a motivated, well-run grassroots campaign could take over the delegate selection process even if Goldwater had only modest popularity among their Republican electorates. Ned Cushing recalls with amusement the liberal Republican governor of Kansas "going up and down the halls, trying to corner these midwestern farm boys that we'd recruited to go as delegates." Suddenly, outsiders to the power structure mattered more than political professionals were used to seeing. "No one ever heard of a governor coming . . . to talk to these people one-on-one."[68]

California was another story. As a primary state, now the most populous state, a state with a large and aggressive conservative movement (some of it ultraconservative), and the last major state to vote, it was the place where the Goldwater and Rockefeller campaigns most truly gave it their all. The Rockefeller approach was scorched earth. "We had to destroy Barry Goldwater as a member of the human race," according to Stuart Spencer, the campaign's consultant in California. WHO DO YOU WANT IN THE ROOM WITH THE H-BOMB BUTTON? one flier asked. Spencer's firm had more than two million dollars from Rockefeller, "a dream campaign with all the money they need."

The Goldwater campaign, though also well funded, countered with a grassroots army catalyzed by YAFers, Young Republicans, and John Birch Society members. In a special push on May 23, eight thousand Goldwater volunteers went to six hundred thousand homes. Supporters elsewhere were asked to write Californians they knew, even "school chums" and "old army buddies," on Goldwater's behalf.[69] In many towns in these other states, "volunteers organized letter-writing bees. People assembled in homes, church basements, firehouses—anywhere they could set up tables and chairs." Goldwater struck a careful balance. He reaffirmed his support for the UN and Social Security, but also refused to disavow the Birchers who were helping him, saying he welcomed their votes.[70]

Whether it was essential to win the state was unclear. Goldwater and Kitchel said it was. White said he didn't believe this, either then or later. The idea that many delegates would have "melted away" if Goldwater lost California was outdated, White explained. These were not "old-fashioned delegates . . . often easily swayed by the promise of a job or a fat business contract. Our delegates were a brand-new breed. Nothing could shake them. I cannot conceive of any large-scale desertions we could have suffered."[71] But decades later, Goldwater said in his second volume of memoirs that he "leaned toward dropping out" if he were defeated in California. According to Edwards, the candidate "would probably have convinced himself" he didn't deserve the nomination.[72]

In any case, the June 2 primary was important as an especially large test of the campaign and for perceptions about Goldwater's real strength in the party. Buckley thought that if Goldwater came up short in California, *National Review* should urge him to quit the race, thus sparing himself an even more embarrassing defeat at the convention. He announced this in a late-May editorial meeting. Rusher prepared to resign if the magazine ran such an editorial.[73] Had *NR* actually done so, Buckley recalls, it would have "violated all of his canons and all of his commitments." The editor learned only later of Rusher's intention. Should a similar situation arise in the future, he ought to tell him, Buckley urged. "I am medium-good at finding compromises on these things."[74]

Goldwater won California with 51.3 percent, beating Rockefeller by fifty-nine thousand votes—not the five hundred thousand Bill Knowland, inadvisably Rusher thought, had once forecast. The moderates and liberals so widespread among the party leadership—thirteen of the sixteen Republican governors, for example, were nonconservatives—made final attempts to build momentum for a fresher alternative than Rockefeller. One illustration of the Goldwater triumph came after their late-stage choice, Pennsylvania governor Scranton, asked Tom Dewey, erstwhile leader of the Republican establishment, for help. Dewey gathered nine high-level establishmentarians of the type who had served Wendell Willkie and Eisenhower so effectively in the 1940 and 1952 nomination battles. What followed was "just incredible," a source told Teddy White. "We called all the old names; but they weren't there any longer, or they weren't in politics any longer. It was as if the Goldwater people had rewired the switchboard of the Party and the numbers we had were all dead." Dewey wouldn't even attend the convention.[75]

Buckley was thrilled by the California victory, and *NR* ran an editorial emphasizing the same delight Rusher felt at the changing regional alignment in the party. It celebrated the "Californians' refusal to repudiate Goldwater" as a "sectional self-assertion of enormous and enduring political and cultural significance." Despite the near certainty of resentment by eastern forces, which could well prove heavily damaging in the fall, "the Republican party will never again be dominated by the editorial writers for the *New York Herald Tribune*. Free at last."

At the same time, the editor was writing freely about what he considered Goldwater's slim chances. In his June 16 syndicated column, Buckley remarked that "the Archangel Gabriel running on the Republican ticket probably could not win." His column two days later gave five-to-one odds against Goldwater.[76] Rusher accused him of developing "a compulsion to proclaim" the candidate would lose badly. "What concerns me is that what you say about Goldwater's chances . . . can have a measurable effect on those chances." He urged Buckley "above all to avoid doing unnecessary harm to a cause that, win or lose, must of course get the largest vote possible."[77]

Buckley answered these points in his July 2 column. His estimate of heavy odds against Goldwater had caused "some of the faithful, including some of my dearest friends and mentors," to react as if he were a traitor. Buckley thought, however, it was "not helpful to Goldwater or to the conservative cause to assert apodictically, and pridefully, that he *will* win. Goldwater's supporters have a less theatrical, but ultimately more alluring standard: that he *should* win" and that his showing would be better than any other possible Republican candidate's.[78]

Meyer was more optimistic, telling readers: "Johnson can be beaten . . . because Goldwater, running on a Goldwater platform, will give form and substance to the native beliefs of the American people, beliefs which have had no champion in the last seven Presidential elections. Those beliefs, not Rockefeller's Establishment ideology, are in the true 'mainstream' of America."[79] Much as Rusher had warned Buckley about the dangers of negativity, Meyer told the editors such predictions could affect the outcome by affecting the "enthusiasm, capability and skill" of Goldwater supporters. Alternatively, *NR* could "play an enormous role in maintaining and developing" these assets.[80] Here again, "our purists," as Brent Bozell had once called them, saw the magazine's obligations in much the same way.

## "What in God's Name Has Happened . . ."

Rusher considered a possible problem at the convention that would prove to be a quite real one. In mid-June, he told White he could see the spectators' galleries "seriously hurting our man's chances and the cause of party unity by disrespectfully booing" such figures as Rockefeller, Scranton, and even Eisenhower. Rusher suggested there be "well-trained cheerleaders (probably Youth for Goldwater types), duly designated by some sort of badge, to ride herd on our claque." It might also make sense to distribute a handbill with Kitchel's signature, "requesting courtesy for other candidates and speakers and urging our crowd to blow off their steam with enthusiastic approval for our friends rather than boos for our enemies." Appealing to their mutual YR background, Rusher reminded White this was "the sort of thing that can make or break a tight vote sometimes—as you well know."[81]

Rusher's thoughts when looking back on the nomination contest were written up in *National Review*. Five lessons, he ventured, had historic importance. He offered them "for the benefit of a forgetful future."

1. A conservative could win the Republican nomination. This simple fact should be "burned into the brains of chronic pessimists—of whom conservatism seems to have more than its share." For the past quarter-century, one of the more liberal candidates had taken the nomination every time, and the "bipartisan Liberal movement had come to regard this agreeable treat as its due." It therefore reacted to Goldwater's nomination "as though it were something totally outside the order of nature, like a sunrise in the west."

2. Money alone couldn't buy the nomination. Rockefeller had enjoyed a "matchless financial advantage." For more than five years, "he caromed tirelessly around the country in one or another of his family's private planes, hiring every worthwhile Republican politician whose services could be bought, and sorely tempting the rest." It wasn't enough.

3. Don't believe the polls—not new wisdom, Rusher admitted, but the lesson seemed especially clear in 1964. That spring, Gallup found only 15

percent Republican support for Goldwater even though he was winning half the votes cast in the primaries. Although often wrong, polls could be dangerous, because some voters in this "increasingly other-directed society" would line up with the apparently probable winner. It was best to ignore them. Pollsters now expected a severe loss for Goldwater in the fall. Conservatives should "remember their ignorance, their ineptitude, their sublime wrongheadedness" in the spring "and not be dismayed."

4. The Goldwater experience taught something new about the limited effect of media hostility. Rusher ridiculed the media elite as "mighty dinosaurs," playing his prehistoric metaphor to the hilt. Being dinosaurs and therefore sluggish, nearly all of these "Liberal masterminds" ignored a growing conservative movement that had been obvious to more objective people at least since 1959. Prompted by Kennedy's public attack on the far Right in 1961, the "slumbrous press was wide awake, gnashing its formidable teeth" at the Birch Society and others, but it missed the Goldwater activism. Viewing the Right as "a visitor from some alien planet," the media considered talk about Goldwater a joke.

By the spring of 1963, the grassroots campaign was too large, and the southern strategy too plausible, to deny. "Once more the dinosaurs thrashed." But after Kennedy's death, the media lazily assumed the loss of JFK as an opponent would badly weaken Goldwater's appeal in the South. In the primary season, the press fought him with "petty distortions and cheapjack lies," which failed, thanks to the good sense of Republican voters. Rusher suggested media hostility might help even Goldwater, by reinforcing his "underdog" image, as he thought had already occurred in the primaries.

5. After these encouraging lessons, Rusher added a strong note of caution: *Conservatives are a timorous lot.* His deepest disappointment in the campaign was the "faint-heartedness of many conservatives who should have known better." Too many Goldwater backers quickly believed negative polls during the primaries and "sank into" despair. Likewise, they often bought into media distortions despite having complained about them for years: "When the campaign was at its height, any ragged figment of a Liberal reporter's perverted imagination was swallowed by many conservatives as a Boswellian account of what Senator Goldwater had actually said or done— and was even put forward as a solid reason for ditching him altogether and switching to Nixon." That was a poor show. "Conservatives," Rusher preached, "should be made of sterner stuff."[82]

In regard to 1964's final outcome, he conceded only that Johnson was the favorite at the moment, remaining silent about Goldwater's chances while briefly noting the difficulty of the challenge. He implicitly asked *NR* readers to focus on a larger picture. Voters had been "subjected to 30 years of unremitting Liberal propaganda, most of it from the heights of power." A single campaign could hardly make up for it all. But Goldwater's candidacy was, at least, "an indispensable first step toward righting the dangerously distorted balance of American politics." The Goldwater movement had brought "the most drastic change on the American political scene in more than a quarter of a century." Its consequences would "stretch far into the future . . . Win or lose in November, we are here to stay."[83]

The convention in San Francisco mirrored and heightened the deep divisions that had grown in the party over the last few years, largely but not wholly as a result of the Goldwater campaign. Except for the fact that the winner was known in advance, it was nearly the opposite of the canned, almost news-free conventions of the 1980s and later. For the right-wingers present, it was and would remain a once-in-a-lifetime experience.

On the first night, Young Americans for Freedom sponsored a two-hour San Francisco Bay cruise on the "SS Young Conservative." Rusher, his protégé Bob Bauman, and others gave speeches on the occasion, and a group of YAF folk singers, The Goldwaters, performed.[84] Rockefeller, Henry Cabot Lodge, Jacob Javits, and New York's other Republican senator, Kenneth Keating, spoke at a civil-rights rally sponsored by labor and church groups in the city just before the convention. At the airport, hundreds of friendly demonstrators from YAF welcomed Buckley when he arrived. From a flatbed truck outside the Cow Palace, where the convention was held, Bauman as national YAF chairman introduced the conservative actor Ronald Reagan— a registered Republican for two years now—to an audience of several hundred.[85] Bauman had become a delegate in Maryland by defeating his Republican district chairman by one vote. The state's former governor Theodore Roosevelt McKeldin, a liberal and among the great orators in the party, had given a stemwinder of a nominating speech for Eisenhower in 1952 but had no such role to play this time. "He was constantly on my back during the convention," Bauman remembers, "calling me 'Mr. Goldwater.'"[86]

In his suite at the Mark Hopkins Hotel, looking through the roster of delegates, Lodge cried out: "What in God's name has happened to the Republican Party! I hardly know any of these people!" Novelist John Dos Passos, a man of the 1930s Left who had turned rightward in the postwar period, covered the convention for *National Review*. "Caught in a sort of nightmare horror," he wrote, "the Liberal journalists see the comfortable certainties they helped construct crumbling all around them." It was "the mightiest conflict in a generation."[87]

The point of fascination for Rusher was a trailer outside the convention hall just south of the city. Inside, Clif White was at the peak of his career, directing by remote audio the leaders of the Goldwater delegations on the floor of the Cow Palace as they placed their hero at the apex of the Republican Party. Rusher had trouble getting into the "fascinating" secure trailer. When Clif finally let him enter, he "shrank against a wall to watch my old YR cronies win a Republican national convention at last."[88]

Losing candidates, though, were outside Clif's control, as were the galleries Rusher had worried about. When Rockefeller spoke on behalf of a proposed platform amendment urging the GOP to denounce extremism—defined as including the Birch Society along with the Ku Klux Klan and the Communist Party—the convention floor remained "comparatively quiet," Teddy White later wrote, "Goldwater discipline holding firm . . . But the 'kooks' dominated the galleries, hating and screaming and reveling in their own frenzy." It had built up as Rockefeller's "tone alternated between defiance and mockery," and he was, after all, "the man who had savaged Barry . . . all through the spring . . . who called them kooks." With "a passion that he had rarely achieved" in his campaign, "he was reaching emotion—and delighting in it. And as he taunted them, they raged."[89]

"*Cut it,*" Clif White signaled upon hearing the first jeer. As the "booing and catcalls continued," he told his regional directors in the trailer to check on what was happening and where. The noise came only from the galleries, it turned out. Their workers came back to say: "These are not our people." The strangers "kept right on . . . In defying our orders, they were obviously carrying out someone else's."[90]

White was also keenly disappointed by the enduringly famous couplet in the acceptance speech on the final night. Despite a flat, somewhat hoarse, "almost harsh" voice that evening, Goldwater began well. He noted his "deep sense of humility" upon receiving the nomination, then issued a warning against those "who seek to live your lives for you, to take your liberties in return for relieving you of your responsibilities—those who elevate the state and downgrade the citizen." He predicted communism wouldn't win but would "give way to the forces of freedom." Only once, in White's opinion, did Goldwater really try to welcome support from the sectors of the party that had opposed him, but at least he did so: "Balance, diversity, creative differences—these are the elements of the Republican equation . . . This is, this Republican Party, a party for free men—not for blind followers and not for conformists."

Then Goldwater edged toward the fatal words. "Any who join us in all sincerity, we welcome," he said. "Those who do not care for our cause we do not expect to enter our ranks in any case. And let our Republicanism, so focused and so dedicated, not be made fuzzy and futile by unthinking and stupid labels." The candidate liked the next sentences so much he had double-underlined them in the text. "I would remind you," Goldwater called out to the convention, "that extremism in the defense of liberty is no vice! And let me remind you also that moderation in the pursuit of justice is no virtue!" The crowd cheered enthusiastically—"insanely," thought White, who sat stunned in the trailer. Bob Bauman was among the enthusiasts. "I just stood up and cheered. I looked over, and McKeldin was sitting there crying."[91]

Neither White nor his immediate team had expected this kind of seemingly deliberate rebuff to moderates and liberals in the party "and to the millions we had hoped to draw to our cause." This was "the time for magnanimity," he explained in his 1967 campaign chronicle, "the time for building bridges across the gulfs that separated Republicans from one another and from countless thousands who were not Republicans and probably never would be." The "magic moment" of an acceptance speech had passed. "Never again would Barry Goldwater have this opportunity." After the speech, White's regional directors and their assistants got up to leave the trailer, their work done. With one exception, each "was shaking his head in sorrow."[92]

Rusher was not. "I have read the famous remarks on 'extremism' drunk and read it sober," he told *National Review* contributor Donald Coxe, who considered them unwise, "and by the living God I can not see . . . the offensive qualities attributed to it by Goldwater's Liberal critics. Look at it in its context. The immediately preceding sentence was a warning against being misled by fuzzy labels . . . Goldwater merely pointed out that the terms themselves are meaningless until we know the content to which they apply—and all hell broke loose."[93] Politically he was proved wrong: "Within days," he noted in *Rise of the Right*, "millions of people who couldn't have quoted Goldwater's statement correctly if their lives depended on it were sure that it revealed his essential kookiness." Looking back now, Rusher says: "I was more of an ideologue than White, and he was a pragmatic politician. He would know quicker than I, in any case, whether a thing pragmatically was good or bad."[94]

The morning after Goldwater's nomination and before his speech, a member of the campaign's finance committee inadvertently revealed to White that Dean Burch would become party chairman. The position was especially important that year because Goldwater and his top aides had decided that the RNC chairman would really be in charge of the campaign. White had hoped for the job but was most disappointed that "the Senator hadn't chosen to discuss it with me" before announcing his decision. The news, also a surprise to Rusher, had a ripple effect. Some of the draft committee's state and regional directors, "heartsick and angry, didn't bother to try" for positions with the general-election campaign.[95]

At the Fairmont Hotel on Nob Hill shortly after the acceptance speech, the White cadre met for a planned celebration of its victory three years in the making.[96] Rusher, their "unofficial historian" according to treasurer Middendorf, now made "an eloquent little speech, reminding us of where we had started and how far we had come." Talking with and listening to his comrades individually, he didn't quite understand the gloom. "I wasn't on the same wavelength as most people," Rusher recalls. "They were all downhearted, and I was still Mr. Optimist. *Goldwater had been nominated, hadn't he, and we'd won.* 'Yeah, he'd won—but Clif wasn't going to be chairman, you know.'"[97] At first, Rusher couldn't believe White and some of the others would be largely sidelined. "For a day or so my mind simply refused to accept the significance of what had occurred. Nonsense, I told worried friends; everything would work out all right. Goldwater naturally wanted his Arizona pals around him, but he wouldn't, he couldn't totally overlook what White and his team had accomplished . . . could he?"[98]

Don Coxe, observing Goldwater's nomination happily from his home in Toronto, told Rusher he could take great satisfaction in such an achievement: "Your efforts are, to an enormous degree, responsible for the astounding fact that 'The Making of the President, 1964' will be telling a much more exciting story than the first in the series."[99]

## No Pale Pastels

Liberals lost no time in pouncing on the excesses at San Francisco and linking them to a far-Right ideology. Just after the convention, a *New York Times* editorial lamented that Goldwater had reduced "a once great party to the status of an ugly, angry, frustrated faction." Leading Democrats produced two of the colorful year's most memorable quotes as California governor Pat Brown claimed that "the stench of fascism is in the air" and Senator J. William Fulbright of Arkansas, on the Senate floor, called the Goldwater movement "the closest thing in American politics to an equivalent of Russian Stalinism."[100]

Rusher moved on from the bad news about White. A week after the convention, he wrote Kitchel to remind him of their discussions and correspondence about setting up committees of pro-Goldwater intellectuals and of black or minority supporters. Regarding the academic project, he stressed: "All of us here at *National Review* stand ready to help." He also passed along some recent intelligence. A source "extremely close" to Doyle Dane Bernbach, the agency handling the Democratic advertising campaign, said "they are preparing a series of 'unbelievably devastating and superlatively executed' ads attacking Goldwater . . . I have no doubt the report is accurate."[101] On September 1, Rusher sent Burch, the newly appointed Republican national chairman, four pages of material he should have immediately—radio and television scripts, under preparation by the Democrats' firm, that came from "one of my most deeply buried agents."[102]

The postconvention campaign generally didn't go well. Decades later, Middendorf remembered the situation: "They called, they wrote, they affirmed their readiness to launch the charge. But calls were not returned and letters went unanswered because the national staff was not yet in place; the designated leaders of the campaign were not ready to lead. Clif White's legions, carefully assembled precinct-by-precinct, were in limbo, and no one at the top seemed to notice or care. And things went on this way not just until Labor Day, but for much of the campaign."[103]

Goldwater himself was not at his best. Middendorf would note: "He was often an inept campaigner, irritable and impatient. Because he so much wanted to get his message across in an unvarnished way, 'shooting from the lip' was practically a campaign theme."[104] Rusher, for his part, "knew what was happening, and I was sorry. But I tended always to make excuses for Goldwater—as long as it could be done, at any rate."[105]

There were indeed devastating Democratic attack ads, as Rusher had warned Kitchel. Although Goldwater backers saw them as outrageously twisting the truth, great differences between the candidates were clear in their own words. As Goldwater told an Illinois audience, he didn't want votes from "the lazy, dole-happy people who want to feed on the fruits of somebody else's labor." Or those "who don't care if the Social Security system goes bankrupt as long as it keeps making more and more unkeepable promises." Or those "who are willing to believe that communism can be accommodated." President Johnson liked to say in campaign appearances: "We're in favor of a lot of things, and we're against mighty few!"[106]

White was made director of the "Citizens" organization. With only 12 percent of the campaign's budget and a comparable share of the staff, it did much of the work—producing, for example, nearly thirty million pieces of literature. It was also partly responsible for the campaign's use of the moral themes already troubling the social conservatives of the day.[107] Goldwater gave only a single speech about what was, in fact, one of his major concerns: that "the moral fiber of the American people is beset by rot and decay." Delivered at the Mormon Tabernacle in Salt Lake City, it got the largest viewership of any political address up to that time except ones delivered by a president "Agree completely with you on morality issue. Believe it is the most effective we have come up with," Goldwater told White.[108]

Working under White, Rus Walton gave his staff the motto Reagan later made famous: "No pale pastels." As one flier said, Goldwater would help to "restore law and order . . . protect your home, your family, your job—and bring moral leadership back to the White House." White, Walton, and their administrative assistant Van Sickle, who was also a state senator in Kansas, came up with the idea for a television film. It would dramatize Goldwater's stand against violence in the streets, White explained to the candidate in a memo. Goldwater approved.

*Choice*, intended for showing on NBC and local television, and in auditoriums and women's clubs across the country, did more than this. In addition to footage suggesting juvenile delinquency and reminding viewers of recent urban riots, it referred to the recent rise of pornography. The serious material was interspersed with shots of a big black car speeding on a country road as empty beer cans flew out the window, generally understood to signify Johnson at his ranch. The film also featured the Statue of Liberty and a crowd reciting the Pledge of Allegiance. "Now there are two Americas," warned actor Raymond Massey. "One is words like 'allegiance' and 'Republic' . . . the other America is no longer a dream but a nightmare."[109]

It was a no-go. "Walton did not underscore the race issue," according to White, and "there were very few scenes in which Negroes figured at all. We showed 'Choice' to a cross-section of the Republican National Committee. They were unanimous in their praise." But liberal columnist Drew Pearson viewed a copy purchased by the Democratic Party and branded the film as "racist." At White's request, Goldwater watched it at his hotel the next day. When White and Walton came to visit, the candidate said: "I'm not going to be made out as a racist. You can't show it." White stood up for the film, citing the responses of other Republicans who had seen it and never "raised any question about its being anti-Negro." It would also "lose Lyndon Johnson votes." Goldwater replied: "I don't care." White didn't argue.[110]

Rusher later remembered the episode as a substantial opportunity lost, even a poor reflection on Goldwater as a leader. The film had "squarely" fingered the key issues upsetting social conservatives, including the riots, pornography, and the Supreme Court's ban on official school prayer. In his decision to veto it, as in his "impatience with conservative ideologues who weren't pros," Rusher observed, "we see Goldwater shying away from the very insight that made his candidacy different from any other."[111]

A greater source of distress in 1964 was the split in the party. Defections among the Republican elite were massive, and Goldwater's former opponents, Rockefeller above all, could be grudging. More than eighty officials from the Eisenhower administration, including seven former cabinet secretaries, issued a statement attacking the nominee. Senator John Sherman Cooper of Kentucky contacted Johnson with advice on how to win his state. Romney, scheduled to introduce Goldwater at a Michigan county fair, stood him up, fearing for his own survival in the governor's race. Scranton, campaigning with Goldwater in Pennsylvania, noted his disagreements with the nominee several times in every speech. Rockefeller, when offered Goldwater buttons at a rally for the candidate, simply pocketed them.[112] Even late in life, Goldwater would blame the campaign's "major distortions" on such Republicans, who provided the opportunity the Democrats exploited. He believed it was Rockefeller, Scranton, Romney, Lodge, and other significant people in the party who made Johnson's victory "such a runaway."[113]

Goldwater also had trouble, to say the least, with the media. The coverage was biased enough, the candidate and his supporters thought. But in a time when even large papers tended to endorse Republicans for president, many of the editorials and Johnson endorsements also stung. The normally Republican *Herald Tribune* came out for the incumbent. Goldwater, wrote the usually Republican *Saturday Evening Post*, was "manifestly unqualified to be President . . . a grotesque burlesque of the conservative he pretends to be." The editorial concluded: "For the good of the Republican Party, which his candidacy disgraces, we hope that Goldwater is crushingly defeated." The paper also hoped such an outcome would "drive the fanatic saboteurs of the Republican Party back into the woodwork whence they came."[114]

At *National Review*, the professorial Burnham tried to do his part. Apparently in response to a contemplated Democratic attack, he proposed and wrote a Goldwater ad on what would later be called "law and order." It was both artful and hard hitting. Rusher sent Burnham's text to the Republican National Committee, with a noncommittal note: "He tells me that he has also formulated several others in his mind, in case you can use this sort of thing." The spot was "very possible," the RNC public-relations director answered blandly. "I am passing this along to the creative people at our agency for their consideration."[115]

Although he sought to help the campaign, Burnham still expressed his thoughts about where conservatism really was in 1964. The movement remained "immature" despite its "astonishingly quick growth," he wrote in a freelance piece for the London *Sunday Telegraph* sent at the end of August. It hadn't "produced a meaningful and coherent program. There is at present a medley of conflicting, sometimes unrealistic or absurd, scraps of program, much of which cannot be taken too seriously." In addition, a conservative president probably couldn't form an administration that was both like-minded and competent, since there were not enough "trained men capable of filling leading roles on a national scale." For these reasons, Burnham thought it "would probably be unfortunate for the conservative movement if Goldwater should, on the off chance, be elected."[116]

Buckley also remained something of an independent analyst as he backed Goldwater. At the YAF convention in September, he conceded frankly that the candidate would lose. It was unrealistic to expect otherwise this year, he told the young idealists: "A great rainfall has deluged a thirsty earth, but before we had time properly to prepare it." The election of Goldwater "would presuppose a sea change in American public opinion"—a sudden awakening to the meaning of freedom among a people long misled by "thousands of scholars, tens of thousands of books, a million miles of newsprint." Buckley wanted to look ahead. The point of the 1964 campaign, he said, "is to win recruits whose attention we might never have attracted but for Barry Goldwater." It could "infuse the conservative spirit" into enough people that the movement might realistically hope for victory "on a great November day in the future, if there is a future."[117]

## "Baptism of Fire"

Rusher was proud to be one of the Republican Party's fanatic saboteurs, as the *Saturday Evening Post* called them, and as publisher of a major national magazine, he couldn't be driven back into the woodwork. But he scheduled a lengthy overseas trip, something he took most years, for much of the fall: "about the only time I could possibly take six weeks off," he told a young friend. The odds were against Goldwater, "but I am certainly not running away on that account. I will be in Istanbul on Election Day, and if he loses I intend to take a boatride on the Bosphorus and meditate on the fall of the eastern Roman Empire."[118] Before leaving on October 19, Rusher appeared as a Goldwater advocate on every radio and TV panel that invited him: "nominal campaigning" but done "cheerfully enough." Like others from the original Goldwater group, who also continued helping from the sidelines, he hoped the candidate would do as well as possible even though they all knew by now that he would lose.

Rusher cast an absentee ballot for Goldwater and for the Conservative Party nominees (or Republicans also nominated by the third party) seeking lesser offices in New York. The world tour took him to Europe, the Middle East, and Asia. On schedule, Rusher heard the news in Istanbul. From Beirut the next day, he called his office at *NR* for the details and other results.[119] The other results were rarely good, especially in the House of Representatives, where the Republicans lost thirty-seven seats, and the state legislatures, where they lost well over five hundred. Of the fifty-four House Republicans who endorsed Goldwater before the convention and also sought reelection, twenty were beaten. Although the Republican did win most of the Deep South, Johnson defeated him nationwide by 61 to 38 percent in the only comparable landslide since 1936, the first election Rusher followed.[120]

Most saddening personally was the loss of New York State senator Walter Mahoney, who had brought Rusher on board for the Isador Lubin investigation a decade before, then run against Rockefeller for the gubernatorial nomination in 1958. He had waged a "long and often lonely battle for economy, common sense and simple patriotism" in the legislature that was an inspiring thing to watch. "It is of course ironic that this should happen to you in, and perhaps as a consequence of, a national campaign that was unique in our time for the candor and essential integrity of the Republican effort," Rusher told Mahoney. "But, in another sense, if one must lose, then surely that is the way and the time to lose—fighting the good fight for truths which may not always be popular but are nonetheless truths for all that."[121]

In a column just after the election, Buckley again affirmed that the campaign was well worthwhile, writing of Goldwater: "The course he set is the only profitable one for the Republican party in the future—because the Republican party was getting awfully tedious and parasitic in its role as the voice of the moderate Democratic party."[122]

Reviewing two campaign books a few months later, Rusher exulted that the very different year initially "planned" by the liberals had been thoroughly ruined: "That script called for the nomination of Nelson Rockefeller, to be followed by a taffy-pull between the rival candidates over how best to expand the welfare state and civilize the Russians. Instead, America's growing conservative movement knocked over the Louis Quinze vase, seized control of the Republican Party, fielded a candidate who called a spade (imagine!) a spade, and forced the Liberals to exert their full—and formidable—strength to persuade 3 out of every 5 American voters to ratify their dominance. The other 2 out of every 5 remain, to this day, unconvinced; and that disagreeable fact obviously Needs Explaining."[123]

In the middle of the campaign, Rusher had enjoyed an "extremely thoughtful" memo Jack Casey wrote for friends. Johnson would almost certainly win, Casey suggested, but much more was going on. The Goldwater campaign represented a shift in the party toward the conservatism expressed by Buckley and *National Review,* conservatism that fully challenged "the mores and assumptions of the prevailing power and communications structure." This insurgency "purports to represent the intellectual hard point of an arrow of the future," Casey explained, "much as the NEW REPUBLIC and THE NATION did prior to the New Deal. To that extent, it is out of the current mainstream in order to dig a new channel which will attract the mainstream in the future."[124]

At the *New York Times,* James Reston contended that Goldwater had "wrecked his party for a long time to come." He turned out to be quite wrong. Senator John Tower said more accurately that 1964 was "the Alamo before San Jacinto, to put it in Texas terms."[125] The grassroots conservatives, decided Bob Novak, then a Johnson supporter, were "the real heroes and the real winners of the Republican fight of 1964."[126] White's cadre and those they mobilized, Rusher says, "recruited to politics a lot of people who had never been interested in it before—and had never known they could be interested in it, didn't see any point to it." With the Goldwater candidacy, "they saw a point, and got interested, and saw that they had an effect."[127]

Rusher also reflects: "Goldwater's role in relation to the conservative movement was never totally satisfactory to him, nor perhaps to the movement. Goldwater was a Republican politician. He was a sincere man, a sincere conservative, but not a 'movement' conservative in the sense of working together on some great combined operation." But it was he who "stood up and took the bullets."[128]

There was a layer of truth, Rusher acknowledged in *Rise of the Right*, to "Goldwater's resentful feeling that he had, in a way, been *used* by the conservative movement." But there was "nothing invidious in this: Movements and individuals come together, and serve each other's purposes, all the time." Without explaining how it benefited the senator, Rusher added: "The Goldwater candidacy had given the conservative cause its political baptism of fire. It had blooded enormous numbers of conservative troops. It had certainly 'put conservatism on the map.' Finally, it had given the conservative movement control of the Republican party and—through Goldwater—of its machinery, at least for a time. These were not negligible achievements."[129]

# 8

# The Conservative Message

The short-term failure of the Goldwater campaign made conservatives ponder their relationship to the public, which had roundly rejected their hero. Could a conservative message win under better circumstances? Rusher thought so. He disagreed with a scholar who had written disparagingly of the very concept of a Goldwater campaign, suggesting instead that the Right should try to win converts rather than elections. America probably wasn't ready, Rusher admitted, to adopt conservatism as public policy; and yes, it had been foreseeable that Goldwater was unlikely to win. But before 1963, he noted in a letter to the libertarian *New Individualist Review*, conservatives were less aware of "each other's existence" and their combined strength. With the Goldwater campaign, they became "infinitely more experienced" in politics and "vastly better organized." No Republican national convention could ever ignore their wishes again. Privately, Rusher told a Draft Goldwater comrade much the same thing.[1]

Dedicated conservatives, Meyer wrote in *NR*, had become the party's key campaign workers because of the Goldwater candidacy, and the GOP would largely "function as a conservative party" if it functioned. The Right actually stood "nearer to victory than they ever have since Franklin Roosevelt." The essential goal, Meyer thought, was to shift 12 percent of the electorate by 1968. Ronald Reagan wanted to keep fighting as well, believing the voters hadn't repudiated conservatism. He urged that the GOP continue to reject its prominent liberals, as it had in 1964. "We don't intend to turn the Republican Party over to the traitors in the battle just ended," he told the

Los Angeles County YRs. "We will have no more of those candidates who are pledged to the same socialist philosophy of our opposition."[2]

Shortly after the election, leading conservatives met in New York with Buckley's assistance to discuss the possibility of starting an organization that might continue the Goldwater momentum. Because of his long overseas vacation, Rusher missed the preliminary discussions among former YAF chairman Bob Bauman, Congressman Ashbrook, political maestro Marvin Liebman, and others. But he attended the Washington meeting on December 18 and 19 at which the American Conservative Union was born, also helping to structure and staff it.[3]

Goldwater's attitude toward the new group and even some of its leaders was unsupportive at first. In February 1965, Rusher passed along a comment the now ex-senator had made to Clif White. "You know, I tried to stop that," Goldwater reportedly said when White mentioned the founding of the ACU. "But it won't get far. That's the *National Review* crowd—you know: Frank Meyer, Bill Rusher. When I listen to those guys I start looking under the bed." Meyer suspected, Rusher told Buckley, that the harsh remark probably resulted from "indoctrination" by the campaign's chief brain truster, Bill Baroody.[4] But the connection between the ACU and the Goldwater movement was obvious. Two early veterans of the cause, Ashbrook and former Indiana congressman Donald Bruce, were elected vice chairman and chairman. Rusher became head of its political action committee, whose purpose was to help revive grassroots activity. Meyer served on the board, as did Buckley for a few months while things got running.

The ACU's founding statement cited several ambitious goals. It aimed to provide "leadership and material for existing conservative-oriented organizations, periodicals and political leaders." It wanted to build support for such candidates and to "stimulate and direct responsible citizen action." It also hoped to influence public opinion in the direction of conservative principles. In some respects, its model was Americans for Democratic Action, which the ACU founders generally regarded as the liberal movement's leadership.[5] But achieving such a status could prove difficult and drain money from *National Review*. Rusher told Buckley he worried about a "truly alarming proliferation" of fund-raising for conservative causes: "For several years we had this sort of thing virtually to ourselves; but no more." There was now an environment of "unwelcome competition" for *NR*, and that competition would almost certainly be "emptying the conservative purse." Rusher asked Buckley to think about the point and perhaps schedule a discussion for the editors' next quarterly Agony conference.[6]

By mid-1965, ex-congressman Bruce could report that the new organization was "off to a good solid start." But Rusher had already confided, some months before, that he remained "distinctly unimpressed" by the chairman and considered Bruce "a small man . . . determined not to let anyone who is conceivably brighter or abler than he come within a mile of ACU." He told Buckley that other board members including Meyer, Liebman, and Brent Bozell agreed with this assessment of Bruce. At the next board meeting, Bob Bauman would therefore be "shoved down his throat" as executive secretary.[7] In August, Rusher wrote that as ACU activity grew, it would be "extremely helpful" if *NR* called attention to the group and implicitly encouraged people to join. Among other things, he saw a good chance it could offer a better form of activism to the more "salvageable" members of the Birch Society—the same hope he had strongly expressed back in 1961.[8]

Although Buckley's official involvement was brief, Rusher's continued for many years. When Ashbrook took over as ACU chairman in late 1965, Rusher became vice chairman while remaining in charge of the political action committee. Early the following year, Ashbrook considered resigning because of technical disagreements other board members raised over some recent decisions. "Our boys, and especially Bauman, are forever pressing too hard," Rusher told Buckley. To his friend Ashbrook, he wrote that while sharing the congressman's disgust at recent "childish behavior" among ACU leaders, he wouldn't give up on the organization. Ashbrook shouldn't resign, Rusher urged, because "we are too tantalizingly close to insuring a really worthwhile future" for the organization.

In 1967, he reported continued progress. Under Ashbrook's smooth and competent leadership, the ACU had been steered into "more peaceful waters." Although it was deeply in debt and showing little ability to raise money in 1966, he told *National Review* colleagues, former YAF executive director Dave Jones "cut expenses to the bone, placated our creditors," and turned things around. The American Conservative Union was doing much better than the Right's other activist groups, Rusher believed. He also noted happily that it relied to a substantial degree on ex-YAFers—who were "a valuable, NR-oriented reservoir of talent." Meanwhile, YAF was doing pretty well itself. As former Eisenhower aide Stephen Hess and reporter David Broder noted respectfully in a book on the Republican Party, the youth organization had eighteen full-time employees at a "posh" headquarters in Washington.[9]

## Buckley's New Celebrity

While Rusher worked with the fledgling ACU, the development catching many conservatives' attention in 1965 was the Buckley campaign for mayor of New York. Running on the Conservative Party line, Buckley would have been pegged as a minor candidate were it not for his prestige and his impressive performance. His goal wasn't to win but rather to highlight the inadequacy and stop the political ascent of the Republican and Liberal Party nominee, Congressman John Lindsay. Buckley's opponent—not just a liberal but an upper-class type and a fresh face, no Goldwater or Nixon—was already considered a possible presidential candidate.[10]

While it seemed clear that Buckley couldn't beat Lindsay, tipping the election to the Democrat would be "a moral victory," Rusher explained later, by making it much harder for the nominal Republican to run for president with any success. More generally, recalls Neal Freeman, Buckley's top aide in the campaign, the publisher also saw it "as a tonic to the national conservative enterprise, which had been deeply disheartened by the Goldwater defeat a year earlier."[11]

Rusher and Lindsay had disliked each other when they served together on the board of the New York Young Republican Club in the early 1950s, "and it went downhill from there." Lindsay had been "enough of an opportunist to play the liberal-Republican card," according to Rusher, and once told him "in a way sort of giving advice, speaking of the party generally . . . and of the conservatives in particular: 'Kick 'em in the ass. Kick 'em in the ass.' He thought that was a plus maneuver."[12]

To Rusher, Lindsay represented liberal Republicanism at its worst. After the campaign, he explained some of these sins to a Californian who questioned Buckley's choice to run against a GOP nominee. Lindsay had expressed his intention to "get as far away from the Republican Party as possible." He had chosen the Liberal Party's state chair as the nominee for City Council president, in effect as his running mate. Then there was his flat rejection of Goldwater in the 1964 election.[13] Rusher also told a friend, in late 1966, that Lindsay had a bad combination of arrogance and limited talent: "His superficial appearance is much the nicest thing about him. Basically he is a glossy opportunist, of a type that is not at all hard to find among the Wall Street law firms. His particular species is not noted for its sense of humor, but . . . he has a great deal less of this precious commodity than most. Also, and interestingly, he is not really terribly bright—or at any rate not at all quick."[14]

Knowing the youngish congressman would be the Republican nominee in the mayoral race, Conservative Party leaders wanted a good opponent for him. Before Buckley's interest in running had developed or become clear, they looked to Rusher as a possibility. Over dinner with Buckley, he "firmly closed the door" on the idea."[15] Jeff Bell, a writer at NR during the campaign, suggests that Rusher's lack of interest in seeking office may have been due especially to his strong sense of privacy. Unlike Buckley, he "didn't want to become an open book to the rest of the world." Rusher was also single. "Politicians were supposed to be married and have a presentable wife," Bell notes. "There's still some of that, but it was a big deal then."[16]

Buckley launched his race in conspicuously uncandidatorial terms, explaining at his first meeting with his campaign committee, held in Marvin Liebman's office: "I don't want any of these bumper stickers, balloons, and straw hats . . . We'll just do it on the ideas." Responding to a question at his first press conference, Buckley said he didn't see a chance of winning. He was simply seeking "as many votes as I can get, consistent with maintaining the excellence of my position." He wouldn't change his positions even minimally in order to gain support. Indeed, he hadn't given any thought to actually being mayor. Although otherwise-enthusiastic Conservative Party backers were displeased, Buckley continued in this vein a week later at a press conference held to introduce his running mates, saying he would "demand a recount" if elected.[17] "There was an existential truth in that answer," Bell recalls. "It wasn't just a funny line. Buckley was afraid of real power . . . He really didn't know what he was going to do, if he had won."[18] Rusher would now get to see an inspired amateur take his—their—politics to the people.

At first, although Buckley had written a newspaper column laying out a ten-point platform on which a hypothetical candidate for mayor might run, he didn't fully understand what the key conservative issues were in New Yorkin 1965. He thought he could win the votes of wealthy Manhattan Republicans concerned about the municipal deficit, but a month into the campaign he had drawn little interest among them. Buckley's support was coming from middle-class ethnic voters in the boroughs—Brooklyn, Queens, the Bronx, Staten Island—who were concerned about taxes and spending but also about growing crime and declining schools.[19] Many of them responded well to his style, Bell remembers. "Nobody they knew talked like that. But they enjoyed his effrontery toward the liberals, and his contempt for the *New York Times* and Lindsay and the fashionable side . . . They could sense that although Buckley was as well-educated as any of the liberals, he had their number."[20]

Because of a three-week strike at the city's newspapers, television dominated election coverage for much of the campaign. Three televised debates, plus many interviews in the broadcast media, spread and strengthened Buckley's reputation as a compelling character. "Love him or hate him," a media observer wrote after the second debate, "TV fans found it difficult to turn off a master political showman." His campaign drew coverage as a national story. The local conservative base responded vigorously to Buckley, providing almost one thousand volunteers by October. The candidate of ideas who had rejected campaign hoopla now complained to Liebman, his fund-raiser and publicity consultant, that there were plenty of Lindsay posters while he had none. He also began to campaign every day. "Bill did go into the thing for a lark," his brother James Buckley later recalled. "But I think any sense of its being a lark rapidly disappeared."[21]

Knowing New York politics well through connections going back to his Young Republican years, Rusher gave both strategic and tactical advice. "The attention span of a radio audience is brief," he advised Buckley after the candidate appeared on the Barry Gray program in late September. "Moreover, the very complexity of your sentences repeatedly led you into slips of the tongue which were perfectly understandable under the circumstances but must surely have been upsetting to voters looking seriously for enlightenment." Rusher had jotted down bloopers as he listened, including a compassionately inaccurate reference to "grocery clerks who earn $85, $95, $100 a year." He reminded Buckley not to overlook "crime, police review, neighborhood schools, and other tried and true issues. I know you have no intention of overlooking them, but that was the unintentional effect last night . . . Also, I doubt that the average listener, having heard you deplore the newspaper strike, could have said confidently what you proposed to do about ending it." In contrast, Buckley's "finest moment" was a direct attack on Lindsay. "Frequent allusions to his incredibly well-financed campaign won't harm a bit."[22]

The race's national implications were important enough to Rusher that he also recommended asking Lindsay whether he would support Nixon or Reagan, should one of them be nominated for president in 1968. If Lindsay said yes, it would clearly hurt him in the mayor's race. But if he said the locally popular thing and wouldn't support them, Rusher pointed out, such an answer would widen his "already-damaging apostasy" from the party.[23] Rusher's detailed political knowledge also helped in the formation of a group called Republicans for Buckley. On a list of sympathizers, he indicated for the campaign's convenience which ones he was confident were still registered Republicans rather than Conservatives, and which others "would be fine if they are."[24] Rusher was a "booster" of the campaign but always a realist, according to Neal Freeman. "When Buckley began to move in the polls, some of us, including WFB on one occasion, began to muse about the possibilities of victory. WAR never gave way to such fanciful thinking."[25]

The third-party attempt to spoil Lindsay's election failed as he narrowly defeated moderate Democrat Abe Beame. Buckley, however, had outshone Lindsay as a personality even while receiving just 13.4 percent of the vote. Rusher thought the winner's chances as a national candidate were badly damaged because, in particular, he was "slaughtered by Buckley" in the TV debates. The new mayor would be "extremely hard" to beat for reelection and might succeed in winning a statewide office, he told a friend a year later, but was unlikely to do well running for president.[26]

Although it fell short in immediate terms, the Buckley campaign would be remembered as a triumph of *NR* conservatism, a classic case of political audacity executed with elegance. Rusher recalls assuming that Buckley's main intention was to write a book, and he doubts the candidacy "really got much above that in his own mind."[27] Buckley did write an entertaining and provocative book, *The Unmaking of a Mayor*, and the campaign did help to make him a major celebrity, increasing his already great value to the conservative movement. "In 1964," Freeman later noted, "you would travel anywhere in the country with Bill Buckley and both of you were anonymous. By 1965, you couldn't walk twenty-five feet in an airport without the autograph hunters."[28] Having grown more experienced in the public spotlight and less dependent on *NR* for his reputation, Buckley now became a regular television presence with his new program *Firing Line*, which resembled a prizefight featuring him against a liberal opponent. It debuted in the spring of 1966 and proved to be an immediate success. A liberal TV critic in San Francisco called Buckley "one of the few live personalities on a dead medium . . . the best thing on the air."

Not long before, a *Harvard Crimson* profile had said much less of Rusher: "a nondescript sort of man, neither stilted nor folksy, laconic nor rambling, soft-spoken nor raucous. But perched on a table in a conference room or leaning over a coffee cup in the Yard of Ale, he makes a glib, effective speaker. Rusher has a quieter kind of charm than the flamboyant Buckley. He punctuates his remarks with precise gestures, and smiles often. But his eyes are hard, his lips thin, and he smiles with his mouth alone." Rusher jokes that he might as well have responded: "I can also wiggle my ears."[29]

Regardless of the gap in their public profiles, Buckley had been eager for Rusher's advice and dissent. Thanking the publisher for a long letter in early 1965, he added: "Please don't consider that you are being over-critical. I like it that way, believe me."[30] It helped that Rusher usually tried to make his point in a certain manner. He

*With Buckley and Goldwater*

Photo by Thomas Bolan, courtesy Thomas Bolan

would combine criticism and deference—sometimes walking a fine line, often keenly expressing both. In 1963, Rusher was "faintly uneasy" about Buckley's new syndicated column, On the Right. But in saying that, he separated himself a bit from the criticism of two colleagues. Passing along their comments, he added praise that might nudge the recipient. The column was not Buckley's best work, *NR* correspondent Donald Coxe and Rusher's assistant Jim McFadden had told him: "not nearly as good, for example, as the typical editorial you write for *National Review*." It could seem shallow and unfocused. "The impression that is left, I guess, is that you do the column in a hurry—in a rather slapdash manner, starting from a sound and provocative position and then rapidly extrapolating to conjectures, wisecracks and peripheral matters that are sustained by their cleverness rather than by their intrinsic weight or merit." Despite his "grave reservations about my own judgment" in such things, Rusher added, he wished Buckley would "solicit the opinions of journalists you respect"—perhaps Burnham, John Chamberlain, and James Kilpatrick. The column was too important and "downright good" to be less than the best it could be.[31]

In mid-1965, Rusher wrote Buckley twice to criticize flaws in his prose. Buckley had begun to modify his frequent reliance on long, involved sentences by trying ones that could be ungrammatically short, and Rusher called him on it: "I am a little distressed. By your newly-developing stylistic tendency to break up uncomfortably long sentences. Not by the normal processes of punctuation, let alone . . . reorganizing the sentence structure. But by simply amputating the various dependent clauses. And leaving them lying around on the syntactical battlefield. Like arms and legs severed in some ghastly explosion." Buckley should be "a little more (shall we say?) conservative" about this. A few weeks later, Rusher cited two overlong sentences, suggesting that they probably resulted from writing too fast. When he read them closely, he could understand them. "But I cannot say that the process of acquiring understanding was a particularly agreeable or relaxing one, or that I experienced any pleasurable intake of breath when, after careful study, the essential structure . . . was at last revealed to me." After elaborating on his point, Rusher concluded: "I hope you don't mind these suggestions from one who, in the matter of style, cheerfully sits at your feet . . . But you have led us to expect great things, so you have only yourself to blame!"[32]

The stream of advice also extended to Buckley's friendship with celebrity novelist Norman Mailer, an emerging spokesman for the sixties counterculture. It was understandable "why Mailer would appeal to you," Rusher wrote in 1964, since the writer had "a kind of shaggy-dog earnestness that you tend to find irresistible." But public controversy with him was best avoided. Following some "obscure self-destructive urge," Mailer had "worked long and hard . . . to impress an extremely unfavorable image of himself on the collective mind of the American people." He therefore seemed an unworthy opponent for Buckley. "When you debate him, in print or otherwise, it is that image, and not the real Mailer, with whom you are necessarily identifying yourself . . . If Lincoln had preferred to debate Simon Legree rather than Stephen Douglas, he would to some degree have 'typed' himself. Do you see what I mean?"[33]

Having known Buckley for a fairly long time now, and in a close professional capacity as publisher, Rusher could bring pointed comments about him even into internal policy issues. In 1965, he warned against spending money from *NR*'s emergency fund-raising for the purpose of speculative investment. Although modest amounts might acceptably be used in this way, more shouldn't. "Once we have established that I am, by temperament, not nearly venturesome enough," Rusher told Buckley, "please note that we have not established anything affirmative about your own qualifications as an entrepreneur. Quite frankly, you scare the daylights out of me. Your whole life-pattern (piloting, gliding, skiing, gambling; jousting with the Liberals, the anti-McCarthyites, the Yale faculty, Robert Welch, Pope John XXIII) is not that of an entrepreneur at all, but rather that of a compulsive gambler. There is nothing in the least wrong with all this, but I counsel you against misconceiving your own strong points."

Buckley, Rusher added, returning to the immediate question, hadn't seemed to learn much from *NR*'s disappointing investments in two radio stations some years before. "After all, we have spent nearly a million of American conservatives' hard-earned dollars on those two 'dry wells'—and it is by no means clear that we are finished yet." He added: "One might think that our particular mixture of over-caution and pure recklessness would result in a nicely balanced discretion, but that is not necessarily the case." The publisher's "more or less chronic state of alarm" over Buckley's financial risk taking now led him to recommend that an investment advisory committee be created, using the "best business brains" on the *NR* board.[34]

Early in the 1965 mayoral race, Rusher advised colleagues that the magazine shouldn't become too thoroughly identified with its leading figure. Was it giving too much attention to the editor's campaign, to his other public controversies? "I am fully aware of the intimate and *necessary* connection between the activities of Bill Buckley and the fortunes of *National Review*," Rusher wrote, "but I know he would be the very first to deplore the inadvertent development of a cult of personality and that is why I made so bold as to raise the point."

For his part, Buckley knew he had learned much from Rusher, but thought his colleague too often leapt to conclusions. The publisher had "a rather general jumpiness against which, as a friend and pupil, I urgently counsel you," he confided during the 1964 primaries. Buckley also disputed Rusher's belief that he was prone to poor political judgments: "For a poet, I have a not unsteady record in the field of politics."[35]

## Rusher's New Concerns

By the end of 1965, *NR* had been around for a full decade. At the magazine's tenth-anniversary dinner, Jim Burnham suggested to its large extended family that a more conciliatory presentation of conservatism was now called for. Conservatives, he said, should aim to win over "fellow citizens now trying to liberate themselves" from liberalism—and whatever young people were "not yet corrupted" by it. Therefore, it was necessary to "break out of the sectarian and doctrinaire clannishness that is natural enough in the early stages of every political movement." The Right must "become more flexible, more generous, more intelligent and more humane."[36]

A few months earlier, Burnham had taken umbrage at an editorial on the enactment of Medicare by the especially liberal Congress elected in 1964. In the Open Question space for dissents by senior people at the magazine, he wrote that he was saddened by such sarcastic and knee-jerk ("Pavlovian") commentary. "The problem of Medicare for the elderly," Burnham continued, "is not a plot by Communists, Socialists, Fabians, Liberals or Supreme Court Justices." Rather, it

> arises ineluctably out of 1) the conditions of industrialized, mobile mass society, 2) the population explosion, 3) the progress of medical science in prolonging human life, thus creating a sharply higher proportion of elderly persons, and 4) the high cost of prolonged medical care. The urbanization and mobility of our population . . . make it difficult to handle the problems of the elderly either within individual families or on a local community basis. These problems were not being well handled, while the macrocosmic affluence of our society has seemed to indicate that they could be much better handled. It is ridiculous to play with statistics pretending to prove that they *were* being adequately handled: if so, there would not have been the rising mass pressure that finally produced the bill.

Ideally, Burnham noted, conservative proposals based on private and local initiative would have been made. But these "potentially better answers" weren't given. Now conservatives must do what they could to make Medicare "work as well as possible."[37]

The following year, in the aftermath of *NR*'s full denunciation of the Birch Society, the libertarian-minded activist Meyer perceived that the movement's "populist and know-nothing elements" had increasingly split from its responsible leadership. He therefore saw little prospect of another cause with the unifying potential of the Goldwater campaign. It would be better for "opportunist politicians," rather than either liberals or irresponsible conservatives, to take the lead in the Republican Party. In view of this necessarily passive situation, Meyer continued, *NR* couldn't "give the same commitment to party politics" that it had earlier in the decade. Instead, it should examine "profound changes" in American society, as the editors had discussed at previous conferences.[38]

Rusher was more attached to the small-government philosophy than Burnham, and Meyer's new recommendation that *National Review* implicitly accept opportunist leaders wasn't one he could agree with. But he did agree with Burnham's point that the movement needed to grow, and with Meyer's that *NR* must seriously consider major developments occurring outside of politics. He continued to serve as an in-house critic and Buckley critic. As he played this role, Rusher's general theme was the constant responsibility they all had to the conservative cause. His effort to influence the conservative message, as Burnham had attempted in his address at the anniversary banquet, came only a decade later.

As early as 1965, Rusher noticed the New Left enough to find it quite troubling. At an editorial conference, he urged "more attention to these newsy little creeps . . . as a means of explicating and fortifying *National Review*'s world-view." At the same meeting, Rusher added archly, he had strengthened "my already formidable reputation as a philistine" by telling colleagues they shouldn't approach the question "with undue reverence, or in any spirit of assuming that these peyote-inflamed *barbudos* [bearded ones] have scored some sort of cosmic breakthrough on the insight front." Rusher soon followed up with a memo in which he stressed that they were being written about perceptively elsewhere. He cited a densely written article, "The New Mutants," recently published in the liberal intellectual journal *Partisan Review*, that confirmed his anxieties about the rising counterculture. It also made him wonder why his own magazine wasn't expressing them. The author had dealt "so penetratingly and—above all—so *brusquely* with these people, while *National Review* is still casting about to discover what it really thinks of them." At bottom, it seemed like such a straightforward issue.

"Why the hell," Rusher demanded, "should it be so hard for us to decide what we think of them? Isn't it obvious that they are precisely the end-products (though, to be sure—and very humanly—the *rebellious* end-products) of the great Liberal critique of the Western dispensation?" As he often did over the years, the publisher showed impatience when seeking action on an editorial question. "The New Student Left—the Beatniks—the Vietniks— the alienated—the drop-outs: they are here," he wrote. "And, as Emerson remarked in another context, 'That obscene bird is not here for nothing.' Let us get busy saying *why* they are here—and let us stop supposing there is any very instructive mystery about it."[39] Buckley concurred. "I approve strongly of your memo on the new left," he told Rusher, "although I think that any discussion of the nature of these chappies should be careful. I'll try to get someone to write on them."[40]

Despite this agreement on the sinister potential in one recent trend, Buckley enjoyed the general ferment of the 1960s while Rusher, just two years older, did not. "I thought it was an exhilarating time," Buckley later recalled, "even though more clearly than at any other time I can think of, the country was really coming apart."[41] To a young *NR* editor who liked rock music, it seemed that Buckley developed an interest in the "nonpolitical life-style manifestations" of the counterculture "because Bill is fascinated by new things." In addition, a modest sixties rebellion eventually arose in his own family. By the time he graduated from prep school, Christopher Buck-ley was "chiding his father about his intolerance toward Martin Luther King, drugs, and rock 'n' roll." Buckley, according to a nephew, "became tolerant because of Chris."[42]

In addition to a fascination with new things and a difficult relationship with his only child, the editor had some tendency—Burnham-influenced, perhaps—to accept powerful trends even if they violated his own politics or taste. In 1964, Buckley denounced the Beatles as "so unbelievably horrible, so appallingly unmusical, so dogmatically insensitive to the magic of the art . . . the crowned heads of anti-music." In 1968, he would admit to a kind of genial defeat. "I mean how can one prevail against them? The answer is: One cannot. And even if they are hard to listen to, there is an exuberance there that is quite unmatched anywhere in the world." That year, in partial defense of the rock musical *Hair*, Buckley also noted that the French novelist and critic Andre Malraux (a friend of Burnham's, quoted by Burnham on the point) "once put an end to a hectic discussion about the shortcomings of modern art by saying simply, 'But that's the way our painters paint.' In a sense Malraux was quite right: if this is the way a creative section of our youth writes musicals, then we must necessarily take them seriously."[43]

Rusher was particularly frustrated when he believed he had been shrug-ged off, as in late 1965 when *National Review* was preparing a fourteen-page special section to thoroughly denounce the John Birch Society. The attack had been prompted especially by the group's opposition to the Vietnam War as serving the interest of world communism because it weakened America. At an Agony meeting, it was agreed that *NR* would tell readers the Birch Society was ruined by the absurd contentions of its leadership over the years and by the membership's unwillingness to challenge these. But the editors had also agreed, according to Rusher, that the membership, as distinct from the leaders, wouldn't be attacked. They would be criticized only in this limited sense. As he sought to enforce that understanding, he felt deliberately ignored.

The substance of *NR*'s forthcoming special section was carefully and mutually defined in their meeting several nights before, Rusher told the editors on September 1, adding: "Bear in mind that all of us are going to be called upon to defend what is said in this projected issue . . . The fair and proper course is to give the prospective defenders at least a preliminary crack at what they are going to be expected to defend." Rusher also disliked the tenor of three recent Buckley columns that might be reprinted in the special edition. They were "a sort of running gun-battle" with angry readers, not political analysis. Buckley went too far by using terms like "mania," "zanier findings," and "advanced Birchitis." Repeating an argument he had made about the Birch question a few years before, Rusher told colleagues: "If we hope to have the slightest effect on any present member of the JBS, surely we will improve our chances by avoiding this kind of language and concentrating on sober persuasion. Moreover I must counsel you that, far beyond the borders of the Society, among friends of ours who agree with our basic position and will fight beside us to defend it, I have already heard expressions of reserve concerning precisely . . . the *tone* of Bill's three columns."[44]

His request to review drafts for the anti-Birch package and suggest changes to them, Rusher complained three weeks later, was followed by an "impressive silence." He warned of the attack's possible effect on the relationship between *NR* and the conservative movement. He admitted there would be an uptick in the magazine's prestige among "professional Republicans," who were always demanding "open warfare on the kook right." In addition, the impact on subscriptions and on new subscriptions would be "endurable." More worrisome was the likely response among conservatives who would say "they approve of our objectives but disapprove of our methods. They will have on their side the tremendously appealing human argument that, 'After all, *National Review* started it.'" Rusher seemed resigned to a lasting estrangement between *NR* and many non-Birch conservatives— and to the magazine's losing, therefore, much of its ability as "a vehicle for political leadership." Perhaps, though, the ACU and YAF might take more of that role. Less involvement in political leadership, Rusher suggested tentatively, "may not be altogether a bad thing." Such a role was indeed quite different from putting out a lively and educative opinion journal.[45]

But still, he sought to influence the special section. Writing a week later, on September 30, Rusher felt angered by "the apparently permanent absence of any reply to my memo of September 1st (although WFB certainly seemed to call for such a memo . . . and I devoted a great deal of time and care to the comments I made therein)." Trying again with the editors, he noted Clif White's advice that the magazine, in Rusher's words, should avoid implying "that the individual members of the JBS were all foolish to have joined . . . whether we in fact believe that to have been the case or not."

In a "generally excellent" draft of a Burnham column that would go into the special issue, he disliked a reference to "Birchites," wishing Burnham would stick to the JBS as an institution. He thought it was obnoxious to call its president "General Welch" and excessively smug to write "the grownups among us." He hoped all of this would be removed. Burnham had also criticized some "populist animosities," as Rusher put it, of the Birch Society. "I recognize that Jim and I may differ on this," he reminded the editors, "but I am rather anti–New York and anti–Eastern Establishment myself; and so, I think, is *National Review*. Certainly a great many of the tendencies we have encouraged in the Republican Party could be so characterized—and are . . . Let us not give Welch a golden opportunity to say that we are pro–New York and pro–Eastern Establishment in this well-understood sense."

Rusher also made one criticism of Meyer's draft, which claimed "the John Birch Society has nothing in common with patriotism or conservatism." If that were true, the publisher pointed out, "we would have much less to fear" from the group. A more "judicious" sentence should be written. And it offended Rusher that the three newspaper columns of Buckley's, to which he had strongly objected a full month ago, would be running in the special issue: "That they were not the subject of a collegial debate *a priori* was perhaps accidental. That they were denied [a debate] *a posteriori* unfortunately cannot be."[46]

Several months after the anti-Birch package was published, Rusher stood by it with more than perfunctory loyalty. "We think the time will come," he told a man who canceled his subscription or donations, "when responsible Americans will thank *National Review* for repudiating the utterly untenable contentions that Mr. Welch has imposed on the John Birch Society. Only a responsible conservatism can possibly win broad support in the country—and indeed only a responsible conservatism deserves to." The magazine's "all-out attack" on the JBS, Rusher noted to the editors in late 1966, had been "richly justified" editorially speaking.

Although his strenuous challenges on the details of that attack had nothing to do with affinity for the Birch Society, he very much wanted *NR* to maintain its old militance. In early 1966, Rusher criticized what he considered weak reactions to some news stories involving American communists and leftists. Each, he believed, called for a more ideological response. "As I have said at several recent editorial conferences, I think we are beginning to sound irresolute, Hamlet-like and old-maidish about various topics in the news." About a visit to Hanoi by left-wing professor Staughton Lynd and "his Communist buddy" Herbert Aptheker, the magazine was "unable to clear our throat and say anything very forceful."

In this instance and two others, Rusher had suggested that "our general *tone* should be one of robust, no-nonsense contempt." All three times, he was met "by a sepia-like cloud of second thoughts." The editors' reaction was disappointing because, it appeared to Rusher, the situations were "classic cases of Liberal or Communist psywar against the body politic—each involving the old ju-jitsu trick of using our own concern for freedom and its traditional forms against us." When this occurred, it was best to tell readers "what America's foes are up to, and how to circumvent them." He suspected his colleagues probably felt some "misplaced fear" that a strong response to these stories would make *National Review* seem far right.[47]

At least on the broader question at issue, Rusher had some outside support. A prominent member of the *NR* family, Neil McCaffrey of the conservative publisher Arlington House, also advocated a sharper edge. Although the magazine "performed superbly on the political level from 1960 through 1964," he told Buckley, Rusher, and McFadden in a memo, it had now entered a quiescent period. He passed along a comment McFadden had made at a recent luncheon: "*NR* is no longer sore at anyone." It was therefore "losing its main thrust," McCaffrey added. "We have always reached new plateaus on wings of indignation. But lately the magazine has been suffering from creeping moderation—this at a time when indignation was never more appropriate. The history of *NR* has proved that it is possible to be indignant yet responsible. It is also good business."

The commentary on the Vietnam War was "entirely too judicious," McCaffrey continued. "It's all very well to give Lyndon points where he deserves them, but for balance you should go after him even harder for temporizing" in his prosecution of the war. "For the first time, the indecision and malaise of the Republican leaders seems to be affecting *NR* as well." McCaffrey also thought the denunciation of the Birch Society should have been accompanied by "vigorous new attacks on the Liberals. Unless the magazine does both, it risks its leadership position in the conservative movement. Or rather, it threatens to become a leader without followers."[48]

Having perceived too many cases of editorial irresolution in early 1966, Rusher similarly suggested at the end of the year that *National Review* was showing little sense of direction. Although hopeful, even somewhat excited about the current state of politics—the strong Republican rebound in the midterm congressional election, and Reagan's million-vote victory in the California governor's race—the publisher voiced doubts about the magazine. He asked the editors to spend much of the next Agony conference on an "extremely important question, Where is *National Review* going?"

In making this request, Rusher expressed acute concern from a business standpoint as well as a political and journalistic one. It had been a financially tough year for *NR*. One reason was an ultimately unsuccessful libel lawsuit brought by scientist and peace activist Linus Pauling. The suit stemmed from a 1962 Burnham editorial that accused Pauling and other leftist figures of giving "aid and comfort" to the Soviet enemy and called the scientist a perennial "megaphone for Soviet policy."[49] Citing the substantial legal costs of the Pauling case, Rusher added that the larger drain was declining subscription income. He attributed it to two things. Certain promotional mistakes had been made, for which he took some responsibility. There was also the magazine's anti-Birch package in the fall of 1965—which, although justified, had caused a "powerful and long-lasting depressant effect" on renewals. Likewise, it reduced the yield from the "conservative lists that have historically worked for us" in finding new subscribers.

At the same time, Rusher worried about the quality of *NR*. "When all is said and done . . . no amount of promotional ingenuity could long protect any magazine from the consequences of its editorial inadequacies." He was unimpressed by various changes that were recently "indulged in," including the introduction of photos. He was tempted, actually, to call this "our frantic eclecticism." But his main concern was that *NR* might lose its "sense of purpose, and of direction." As he so often did in controversial memos, Rusher briefly noted a milder possibility. Maybe the editorial slump he now saw would prove to be temporary; maybe the magazine would enter a better-defined stage, like a teenager becoming an adult. But in any case, he feared that *NR* had "pretty thoroughly lost our function, definition and identity as the house organ of the hard right *without* yet discovering a new one." Because of its "wit and intelligence," it would remain the most respected conservative publication indefinitely, but being respected wasn't enough.

It troubled Rusher that "we are no longer even pretending to do—quite frankly, are just not interested in doing—the journalistic housekeeping chores for conservatism." In the past year, it was mainly *Human Events* that had done so, and the editors ought to stop "looking down our noses" at the Washington-based weekly. *National Review* could not "sustain ourselves indefinitely by sharing our secret joys with a few rare friends—those who know German, or Spanish, or French, or who are aware of [British public intellectual] C. P. Snow's 'Disappearance,' etc." It was, Rusher continued, "sliding into the bad habit . . . of getting along on its personality without actually shouldering any particular job." He chose to leave his argument there, however, because these questions were "subtle and intractable."[50]

Buckley apparently rejected the memo's basic thrust, answering with what Rusher called "a spirited defense of the status quo." In reply, the publisher noted that his intentionally "hard-hitting" remarks seemed to have damaged his argument. But he suggested, in a collegial tone, that he would stoutly maintain his critic's role: "I do heartily endorse your point that we must seek to communicate. Actually, I think we do remarkably well, considering the little time we have for that sort of thing. But I am always ready for more—precisely because I believe that I do know what *National Review* is about, and admire it intensely, as I always have."[51]

## Nixon or Reagan?

In Republican politics, meanwhile, Richard Nixon awaited his second chance and Ronald Reagan came under consideration as a national figure. Although Reagan's inspiring "A Time for Choosing" speech on behalf of Goldwater in late October 1964 had allowed a bungled campaign to end on something of a high note, the defeated candidate was impressed by Nixon—not only as a seasoned figure but especially because he had campaigned energetically for Goldwater when many others hadn't. In early 1965, the now ex-senator promptly endorsed Nixon, should he seek the nomination three years hence. But the conservative base was already showing interest in Reagan. YAF leaders, polled at their 1966 summer conference, were 53 percent for Reagan and 30 percent, defiantly, for Goldwater. Only 15 percent wanted the former vice president.[52]

In mid-1966, the *Ripon Forum*, a liberal Republican journal, reported that Rusher had already "spoken of Reagan for President plans" and that he saw Reagan "as the possible nominee of a third conservative party" were the GOP to choose a perceived liberal. The statements, he protested, "inaccurately reflect my views." Although Reagan would undoubtedly be eyed as a potential 1968 or 1972 candidate, Rusher had never considered him a possible third-party nominee. "As I have taken care to point out repeatedly, *National Review* opposes the organization of such a party under any circumstances that might be legitimately described as foreseeable. And so, I am sure, does Mr. Reagan."[53] But Rusher's hopes or speculations about the then gubernatorial candidate were clear when he wrote his lifelong Democratic friend Tom Farmer, now general counsel at the Agency for International Development, to seek help in setting up a briefing he wished to have in London on an upcoming trip. "I will be grateful for anything you can do," Rusher wrote. "And some day, when Ronald Reagan is president and [Conservative member of Parliament] Enoch Powell is prime minister, I will be glad to reciprocate the favor!"[54]

Rusher had tangled with Nixon in 1965 after the former vice president was quoted, in the Rowland Evans and Robert Novak column, as condemning *National Review*–type conservatives. He wrote Nixon to ask whether it was true. With no response after two weeks, he tried again, pressing for an explanation: "In the interests of simple justice, and more particularly in the interests of a sound future for the Republican Party, it is important to know whether you in fact described 'the Buckleyites as a threat to the Republican party even more menacing than the Birchers.'" Rusher added: "Quite frankly, I cannot believe that you uttered those words." It was presumably well recognized by now "that there are responsible Republicans considerably to the right of the last identified position of General Eisenhower."[55]

Nixon didn't reply to this letter either, and Rusher tried yet again. Finally, after *NR* in a March 1966 editorial gently but clearly urged the former vice president to address the question, his new conservative aide Patrick Buchanan answered with a letter to the magazine. Rusher later called it "a masterpiece of broken-field running." It explained that Nixon had merely observed, at several press conferences, that Buckley became a stronger candidate in the mayor's race by repudiating the Birch Society in his magazine and column. The confusion, Buchanan implied, was caused by "contradictory press reports of that statement." (The Evans and Novak column, however, had said Nixon made his anti-Buckleyite remark in a "conversation" with reporters.) Acknowledging and quoting from Buchanan's account, *National Review* "gladly" accepted it and said "we believe it is" correct. The editorial also hinted that it was evasive of Nixon to respond through an aide, then stated directly that the previous nonresponses to Rusher's question represented a "calculating caution," all too typical of his public style. But it added that if Nixon were "willing to give personal leadership to the Republican conservatives, he will find them ready to follow him."[56]

Rusher had told an *NR* supporter that Nixon himself "stood mute, through three letters and a television program in which I have tried to get him either to affirm or deny making the quoted remark." He added: "It is a rather pathetic thing to see a man of Nixon's stature . . . so tangled up in the complexities of his cork-screw course toward the Presidency that he doesn't dare risk answering a simple question for fear of spilling some of the water he is forever carrying on both shoulders." Continuing with his scornful dismissal, Rusher explained that his repeated challenges over the alleged comment were not about bringing Nixon into harmony with the magazine

or its readers. "I couldn't care less what hole Mr. Nixon finally comes out of
. . . Certainly I am not repining over his unkindness to the Buckleyites; we
can take care of ourselves. Meanwhile, the world has another chance to see
for itself with [*sic*] a devious mess Richard Nixon has made out of a once
honorable career."[57]

Nixon built more goodwill among conservatives, as he had in 1964, by
campaigning assiduously for the party in that year's elections. Rusher's attitude mellowed for a time. After Reagan won a landslide victory over Governor Pat Brown in California, the publisher told Buckley that he would be
worthy of conservatives' support for president if he proved himself in office.
But the same might be true of Nixon, "if he keeps on behaving." In the 1964
cycle, Rusher added, the Right had simply favored Goldwater. No candidate
was the obvious and sole choice of conservative Republicans for 1968.[58]

Around New Year's, Rusher sent a campaign prognosis to *NR* editors
and others. It began by negatively assessing George Romney. The Michigan governor, a former CEO of American Motors, got substantial media
play and looked strong in the polls. Apparently the party's eastern liberals
had decided to back him, or at least "give him the first crack at the brass
ring." But Rusher pointed, many months before Romney's damaging "greatest brainwashing" gaffe, to his "essentially vapid" comments on Vietnam
and other subjects. "Moreover, there are certain qualities inherent in the
man—in a way, almost the most appealing things about him, since they are
the most authentic—which make him an unlikely winner in the long run:
an idiosyncratic stubbornness, a noisy religiosity and a businessman's contempt for politics and politicians." Romney was quite unlikely to "maintain
a firm grip on his indispensable Eastern Liberal support" or do well in the
primaries.

Rusher then noted that Nixon was deservedly getting credit for all his
campaigning on behalf of the ticket in 1966. Although the many appealing,
just-elected Republican senators and governors were a serious problem for
him, politically outweighing the party's gratitude toward Nixon, Rusher also
thought he had "great residual strength" and would be a major contender.
He would likely benefit from at least two advantages: a long-standing friendship with leading Republicans in many states, and a weak opponent in Governor Romney. The smarter liberal Republicans, as they tried to stop Nixon,
might try to find a substitute for Romney. It could be the recently elected
senator Charles Percy of Illinois, who might win Democratic in addition to
liberal-Republican support. The distaste for President Johnson among the
general liberal establishment, Rusher explained, was already obvious and
would probably grow. If he sought reelection, liberal Democrats might prefer
a politically congenial Republican. After all, they had favored John Lindsay

in the 1965 mayor's race and repeatedly backed Governor Rockefeller and Senator Javits in New York.

Meanwhile, nonideological Republican leaders would fear, rightly, that Nixon seemed "too old and familiar . . . too tired" for the general election. Although he was, in fact, a bit younger than Romney and Reagan, voters in 1968 would think Nixon had been around "since God was a child." This sense of staleness was enough to make him a questionable rallying point for the Right as well. "Johnson is the quintessential pro," Rusher cautioned, and such a shrewd politician "should be opposed by a fresh, comparatively young-looking face." Therefore, party leaders interested simply in winning the White House might join the liberal Republicans in backing Senator Percy. To successfully counter these forces, conservatives would need their own fresh candidate. It seemed "perfectly obvious that there can only be one possible choice." That was the just-elected Governor Reagan, if he did well in his new job.[59]

Rusher had not, in this detailed analysis, said much about his interest in Reagan. He said more in a letter to his friend John Thomson several weeks later. In it, he first predicted that Percy would probably be stronger than Reagan in the general election, since the liberals were "ready to cut Johnson's throat" if the Republican alternative seemed liberal enough. Nor was Percy "unbearably liberal, at least as far as I know," Rusher added. He actually "reminds me more of Dewey than of anybody else. But circumstances will make him the liberal choice for the Republican nomination, and his native opportunism will do the rest." Then Rusher turned to the possible conservative standard-bearer.

"As for Reagan," he told Thomson, "I think that you are underrating the man. Essentially, there is no really good preparation for the Presidency, save perhaps being born into a family that somehow manages to endow its children with character." His performance since taking office on January 1 was "impressive, and if it continues impressive I see no reason why he should not be the Republican candidate in 1968." Although Percy would still be easier to elect, "I did not say . . . that Reagan would be impossible"—and he was "infinitely more adroit than Goldwater."[60] Thomson remembers being concerned that "the political process will chew up the neophyte." A strongly favorable point for Rusher, he says, was that the new governor, then in his midfifties, "was mature but was not sullied by the political process." Starting out in public office at such a high level, Reagan hadn't made "127,000 deals to get there."[61]

Aware of the possibility Reagan could be dismissed as a lightweight, Rusher suggested to Thomson that he might be mocked while living but deeply honored later: "Do you remember what the great 'Punch' cartoonist

Sir James [*sic*] Tenniel, who had regularly portrayed Lincoln as an ape, etc., wrote after Lincoln's assassination?—'Yea, he had lived to shame me from my sneer: / To lame my pencil, and confute my pen; / To make me own this kind of prince's peer— / This rail-splitter a true-born king of men.'" Rusher added: "It may be that, some day, a Ronald Reagan will exact a comparable posthumous tribute from the perfectionists of America."[62]

In a column on the question two months before, Buckley had said that Reagan certainly wasn't a viable candidate. "No one has been clearer on the subject than Mr. Reagan himself, but unfortunately, such is the tradition of political double-talk that few people tend to take seriously a politician who goes about minimizing his ambitions . . . And Mr. Reagan's dilemma, of course, is that the ['Shermanesque'] statement which would serve to eliminate him from the field [is one that] he cannot for political reasons utter." Buckley thought it was unlikely, "to say the least," that Reagan would become a candidate. He didn't have "obsessive personal ambition" or use "egomaniacal" reasoning. Given his "background spent out of politics, he cannot emerge as a credible candidate until his contributions to the art and/ or practice of government become incandescent, and it is unlikely that even if he were Cato the Elder he'd have much of a chance to pile up that kind of a record in 18 months." Reagan would, Buckley concluded, "influence" but not "direct" things in the Republican Party.[63]

The new governor arguably got off to a strong political start. Weeks into his term, he was becoming known as a governor, not just a former actor and a right-wing speaker. He appeared on the national newscasts for eight consecutive nights, "facing down angry student pickets, coolly answering questions from hostile reporters."[64] Essentially agreeing with Reagan about the budget issue in California's public-university system, Buckley told readers he had also "acted rather too brusquely, and without paying sufficient attention to some of the immediate consequences of his proposals." The column blamed this on what was, Buckley noted, an almost necessarily inexperienced Reagan staff. It also suggested that in attempting his 10 percent spending cut, the governor should be framing his case more effectively and be more aware of academic logistics. "But this awkwardness will pass," Buckley added. He assumed Reagan would "make . . . the necessary modifications," and the firmness he had shown was "heartening."[65]

A young aide named Thomas Reed had already begun some preparations for a Reagan campaign. An engineer by training who had worked on nuclear weapons at the Lawrence Livermore Laboratory and made money in land development, Reed was also an advance man for Goldwater in 1964 and two years later became Reagan's Northern California campaign chairman. He served as the appointments secretary for the incoming Reagan administration, helping to choose its major officials. Reed considered Reagan the party's obvious new leader and therefore believed he should, whether he ran for president or not, use the governorship as a national platform. Nixon, in contrast, had lost both the presidency and the 1962 gubernatorial race; it was clear he "couldn't win anything."

On November 17, having discussed a possible presidential campaign with the Reagans that same day, he met in the evening with Rusher in San Francisco, where the publisher was passing through on a speaking tour. Rusher was already in direct touch with Reagan himself—"my position as publisher of *National Review*," he later explained, "opened that door without the slightest difficulty."[66] Reed had just been authorized to contact Clif White. Rusher strongly encouraged this, urging that he try to recruit him as a national prospector for Reagan support.

Within days, over lunch at a country club in suburban Rye, New York, White showed interest, thinking the governor-elect was the strongest challenger to Johnson while also believing, like Rusher, that he needed a track record in office. He discussed the possible race with Reed, who soon discussed it with Reagan, who approved bringing White on as a consultant.[67] In addition, there was a potential team of people White could activate. Members of his early Goldwater cadre, and others who joined them in the draft campaign, had remained in touch over the years, calling themselves the "Hard Core." In March 1967, they met in Chicago. Most of them agreed that Reagan was their preferred candidate.[68]

What followed was a highly preliminary campaign. Although fully aware of Reed's activities, Reagan had much else on his mind: "Once he got caught up in the problems of being governor, he really turned his attention to other things. I think he was moderately interested until the summer of '67, when a lot of other distractions came across his plate." According to Reed, the scandal involving homosexual aide Philip Battaglia caused a "mental retrenchment" on Reagan's part, a mood of "who can you trust?" Biographer Lou Cannon describes the governor as approaching the national-candidacy process from the beginning with his typical "combination of caution and ambition."

Reed also recalls that among major political backers such as Henry Salvatori, Holmes Tuttle, Ed Mills, William French Smith, and his old Hollywood ally Taft Schreiber, people were asking Reagan what he was up to, why he hadn't told them of the presidential activity. They were "interested in the process," Reed says, but in a "not particularly professional fashion." Reagan's Southern California circle viewed "tinkering with the presidency as sort of a hobby" and didn't understand delegate hunting. In addition, their opinions on a national candidacy differed, and some were Nixon supporters, and at least one favored Rockefeller. As a result, Reagan had many people "lobbying him in different directions," especially at group dinners in Los Angeles on weekends. Although aide Lyn Nofziger, in addition to Reed, was promoting a Reagan candidacy, the governor's chief of staff, William Clark, wanted him to focus on his job.[69]

Reagan told both Nixon and Buckley that any candidacy would be of the favorite-son type, not a true presidential race. He traveled around the country in a politically ambiguous mode. Reed remembers him as somewhat "distracted and not focused" on these trips, while doing very well with audiences. In late 1967, in Illinois, South Carolina, and Texas, home states of his most important potential backers in the Senate, the governor didn't express clear intentions. "We'd go to those places, and he gives a great performance, and then he meets with them and he doesn't close . . . They got in a room—I was there—and they wanted to talk turkey, and Reagan would not talk turkey." With Everett Dirksen, Strom Thurmond, and John Tower in their respective meetings all "basically saying: 'Are you going to be a candidate?' . . . he waffled, and danced around, and talked about the favorite-son." Unwilling to attach themselves to a prospect who remained less than a candidate, the key senators "drifted off into Nixon support" (though Thurmond was tempted to back Reagan in the spring of 1968), and therefore, Reed believes, Reagan lost the nomination.[70]

Rusher, meanwhile, had evidence upon which to advocate. On November 8, for example, Reed sent him a summary of Reagan's recent travels. From late September through late October of 1967, the governor had spoken at events around the country that produced, he told Rusher, well over a million dollars for the GOP and its candidates. Counting both party events and a few nonpolitical ones, Reagan had eleven out-of-state appearances, with crowd sizes up to twenty thousand. At the National Governors Conference, *Newsweek* reported, "there was little doubt" that Reagan rather than Romney or Rockefeller "had shown off to best advantage." In Cincinnati, the GOP county chairman attributed a sweep in the city's local races, "beyond our wildest dreams," to a huge rally-fund-raiser. He referred to it as the "Reagan rally."[71]

But Nixon had reached out effectively to leading conservatives. In August 1966, he and his young aide Pat Buchanan met in Washington with a large number of movement figures including Rusher, Congressman Ashbrook, Marvin Liebman, editor Tom Winter of *Human Events*, and three YAF leaders. At this session, he predicted that by 1968 conservatism would become economically respectable because of a major recession. Nixon therefore advised the Right to stress economic issues. Without mentioning a candidacy, he had opened a line of communication.[72]

Nixon also pursued Buckley, successfully. In January 1967 the former vice president, who had moved to New York earlier in the decade and was practicing law there, invited Buckley, Rusher, and a few other conservatives to spend a Sunday afternoon at his Manhattan apartment. For three hours, Nixon talked about politics and international events. "He gave us all the time in the world," Rusher recalls. "He seemed quite open and ready to discuss his views." Rusher didn't change his general opinion of Nixon but felt, "if anything, more impressed that he had put the whole meeting together and was trying [so intensively] to sell himself to conservatives. That was interesting."[73] Neal Freeman, who also attended the meeting, would remember: "I knew when we went down the elevator . . . that Bill Buckley was going to find some reason to support Richard Nixon. Bill was *very* impressed with how wide-ranging and thoughtful Nixon's conversation had been."[74]

The editor already had a good opinion of him, shaped partly by the fact that Nixon had been quite close to Ralph de Toledano. The conservative writer-journalist, also a good friend of the late Whittaker Chambers, was "such a profound anticommunist," Buckley notes, and "always swore by Nixon's 'great faiths,' and always very satisfactorily so." For years "he was the reliable voice advising [us] of what was going on that Nixon was involved in." Although Buckley recalls that Rusher "hated Nixon," the publisher respected him in a narrow but important sense. He was "eminently" qualified to be secretary of state in a Reagan administration, Rusher noted to colleagues in late 1967. In that position, Nixon would probably "distinguish himself."[75]

Promoting Reagan at the magazine, Rusher told the editors in July that there was "a tremendous upsurge in interest" in him, adding: "I again implore you not to underrate the governor of California." But he cited no specifics in this case, instead passing along what he admitted were secondary developments—growing support for Nelson Rockefeller among other liberal Republican governors, growing interest in Romney among certain liberal reporters whom Rusher spoke of as participants in the process, and the fact that Nixon apparently had started placing himself slightly to Reagan's left on foreign policy.[76]

In mid-October, the Hard Core of ex-Goldwaterites gathered for three days at a Miami hotel. The meeting was deliberately located near the 1968 convention site, according to Rusher, so that White could show "his regimental commanders . . . where they would wage their next battle." They "authorized" White to make a formal agreement with Reagan's representatives, who soon let him begin an exploratory operation. He was given only a limited ability to schedule the governor for trips outside California. But despite this difficult restriction from Sacramento, the onetime Goldwater cadre and its marshal had stepped forward as a serious, experienced resource for Reagan.[77]

While Tom Reed was finding the governor's indecision frustrating, Rusher told *NR* editors a few days after the White group's Miami meeting that an ambiguous stance made sense: "Of course he will seek the presidency in 1968, and we may confidently assume that his present posture in the background is carefully chosen. He must be understandably reluctant to plunge into the primaries, with all their perils and their evanescent rewards. For him, the great strategic problem is to make sure that Nixon does not somehow obtain an unsurpassably long lead—and to do this without, in the process, so antagonizing the Nixon supporters (and especially the conservatives among them) that they grow unmanageably vindictive." In this context, a favorite-son strategy made sense, and Reagan would, Rusher predicted, be discreetly encouraging it among other political players.[78]

The governor's supporters faced natural concerns about his unusually brief experience in public office and elective politics. In the early-1967 meeting with Rusher and others, Buckley had told Nixon it was "preposterous even to consider Reagan as an alternative . . . an ex-actor, who has been in office now for a month." Nixon disagreed. "It isn't preposterous," he said, because Reagan was nonetheless the governor of California. With his colleagues at *National Review*, according to Rusher, Buckley similarly ruled out Reagan on the merits, not only in political terms. But he also doubts the editor's depth of conviction on the point, suspecting he did this "because he was already practically committed to Nixon, and the apparition of Ronald Reagan suddenly was a great inconvenience."[79]

When Rusher briefly visited Vietnam on a tour of the Orient in late 1967, Jeff Bell, serving in the Army there, got a short leave in Saigon to meet up with him. They disagreed at length over the Nixon-or-Reagan choice. The younger man thought the front-runner was the best they could get that year, a "50 to 60 percent" conservative. Although they enjoyed debating the question over their meal, Bell recalls, Rusher didn't consider his resigned preference for Nixon a matter of trivial disagreement. "On one level he was amused, but on another level he was miffed." After completing his Army duty, Bell went to work with the Nixon campaign.[80]

# 9

# Reagan vs. Nixon

Buckley had become more pragmatic about presidential politics than in 1960, when he sided with Rusher, not Burnham, and chose against giving Nixon *National Review*'s endorsement. Rusher's thinking had remained about the same. In early 1966, he observed in a letter of which he sent a copy to Buckley: "I think Nixon's defeat . . . was absolutely essential to the cause of conservatism generally, and obviously there never could have been a Goldwater campaign without it."[1] Buckley responded by noting the heavily liberal character of the current Congress, which owed much to Goldwater's landslide defeat, and the fact that a Democratic president who strongly shared its domestic-policy liberalism was in office.

"I think you risk losing something of your reputation as a political seer by at this point saying you are glad Kennedy was elected rather than Nixon," he told Rusher, after much of President Johnson's expansionist and expensive social-welfare agenda had been enacted. "Nobody will wring anything out of that," Buckley added sharply, "other than petulance and a sort of historical indifference to what actually is the result of ADA government. At least, that is my opinion."[2]

By the fall of 1967, Buckley took Reagan more seriously as a possible presidential candidate, writing that he seemed the likely alternative to Romney "if Nixon fails in the primaries." Reagan, he wrote, had risen in "the public esteem" that year about as quickly as Romney had fallen. "The perspectives are very good, the mind very quick," Buckley added in a substantial *National Review* article about Reagan's governorship.[3] But although *NR* did not endorse a candidate in the 1968 primary season, the editor made his sympathies with the former vice president clear in public appearances.[4] "Nixon was going to get it," Buckley recalls, "and nobody was going to think of us as ideological derelicts for failing to back him [Reagan], since this one belonged to Nixon in the judgment of people like Strom Thurmond." The governor's campaign was "irrelevant."[5]

## Season of Frustration

As a Reagan advocate at the magazine, Rusher also had to contend with fears about a possible Rockefeller nomination after Romney quit at the end of February 1968. Two weeks later, Meyer told Buckley of second thoughts he was having. He asked that they be kept confidential for now—"at least as far as Bill Rusher is concerned, since I have had a number of arguments with him and I want to tell him myself." With Romney out, conservatives' "first concern" was the possibility that Rockefeller might somehow be nominated. Meyer found him unacceptable for three reasons: "my fundamental objection to him as a liberal," the likelihood that he would have "a much worse position on Vietnam than Johnson," and the fact—not just possibility—that "his nomination would shatter the conservative movement." In the fall, Meyer predicted, many in the movement would support the populist former Alabama governor George Wallace as a third-party candidate, some would vote for Johnson, and some would vote for Rockefeller. Such a drastic split would "create a bitterness among conservatives that would be very hard to overcome" in the future.

Meyer also warned Buckley that he perceived, "at least in Bill Rusher and with some signs elsewhere" among Reagan backers, "a bad tendency . . . to be so concerned with eliminating Nixon that their opposition to Rockefeller tends to disappear. Their hope is that Rockefeller could knock out Nixon and then that they could knock out Rockefeller." Meyer, though, believed it was quite possible Rockefeller might ultimately win in a straight contest with Reagan. In addition, Nixon was looking better from a conservative standpoint than previously. His comments on the liberal Kerner Commission report dealing with the causes of black riots, Meyer noted, were "courageous and sharp." Nixon also seemed to have a firm position on Vietnam. Furthermore, "I have been a little disappointed in Reagan," Meyer told Buckley. "When Goldwater said that he would [in the general election] have to seriously consider whether he would support Rockefeller, Reagan rushed into print the next day to say that he definitely would." In general, "I still probably would prefer Reagan. But the issue is not drawn that way." The fundamental thing, Meyer concluded, now seemed to be "the

urgent necessity of stopping Rockefeller." The magazine should direct all its
energies that way. That didn't necessarily mean endorsing Nixon. But the
editors should consider it.[6]

Rusher thought a partial campaign probably wouldn't win Reagan the
nomination or even build him much clout. In late March, he told White,
Reed, and other Reagan supporters that "slow and silent methods" were
probably inadequate for "maximizing Reagan's influence" at what was likely,
Rusher thought, to be a brokered convention. Without calling for a declaration of candidacy, he urged that the governor make it clear he was "available for the nomination if he is wanted." Reagan should announce—Rusher
wrote a statement to illustrate the point—that "I have decided to devote as
much as possible of the days and months ahead to an active participation
in the many-sided dialogue" whereby the party would make its choice. He
should point out that Rockefeller—who wasn't a candidate but called himself
available for the nomination—had said he would spend the preconvention
months discussing issues for the sake of influencing the Republican platform.
Reagan would therefore do the same, Rusher's statement for him continued,
in a "series of policy talks" starting April 10 "right here in Sacramento."

It didn't happen, but Reagan began to openly pursue delegate support
while still defining himself as a favorite-son candidate. Rusher, in keeping with Reed's recollection, would later attribute the increased activity
to Senator Bobby Kennedy's entry into the race and to President Johnson's
withdrawal at the end of March, which made the new candidate a stronger competitor for the Democratic nomination. According to Reed, Reagan
considered Kennedy a "really appalling" prospective president.[7] Although
he declared a candidacy only in August, at the start of the Republican convention, Reagan explained to a Southern California backer that he was now
campaigning because it was his duty to "enunciate my principles" and to
influence the party's course.[8]

Rusher thought highly of Reagan's ability as a communicator, telling
reporters on a California campus visit in January that he stood the best chance
of beating Johnson. The governor was both "new" and "attuned to . . . TV,"
Rusher explained, presenting "the best contrast to the image of LBJ. I don't
think he would posture himself as 'Fangs Reagan—the '68 Goldwater' but
would run the type of campaign that he did in '66 for governor, unifying the
Party, with Percy as his running mate."[9] But Rusher became concerned that
Reagan was, in fact, sounding too ideological. He sent along a page of material
he had written, hoping something similar might go into a speech the governor
would be making on April 5 at the National Press Club in Washington.

With an unusually elaborate protestation of deference, Rusher began:
"Please let me emphasize, with all the power at my command, that I hold no

particular brief for these paragraphs—I have never written a speech for anybody in my life, and have probably fumbled the ball [here] in half a dozen ways." He intended the remarks as an example of a message Reagan would help himself by using in the campaign. "Nobody knows better than I do that this kind of stuff is basically gooey sentimentality," Rusher added, "but, at least when it is well done (and I repeat I am not for a moment saying that this specimen is well done), it brings tears to the eyes of liberal reporters and voters." In a word, it was about Reagan sounding more mainstream: "As I have indicated before, I think a strenuous effort must be made to broaden Governor Reagan's image; we dare not depict him as the 1968 version of Barry Goldwater." Rusher proposed that he say, in part:

And now let me say a word to my fellow Republicans. You know, and I know, how deep is our concern for *all* the people of this country. It is simply not true that we place property rights ahead of human rights, or whatever the fashionable cliché may be. But I think our critics have a point when they accuse us of tending to think only with our heads and not with our hearts. Precisely because we know so well that 2 and 2 make 4, we have tended to state our case in terms too coldly mathematical . . . The heart goes out, and will almost always go out, to that man, that cause, that party which knows how to reach beyond the statistics to the hope and the terror of the human condition. And if we Republicans hope to propose real solutions to the crisis in our cities and in the relations between the races, it must, in both act and imagination, place itself in the minds and hearts of the oppressed, the defenseless and the poor . . . That is the spirit that must animate our party if it is to escape the criticism that it has upheld the substance but forgotten the spirit of the American dream.[10]

In April, Rusher heard that Clif White had said—to Buckley—that he didn't think Reagan could be nominated. Hearing this from the editor, Rusher complained to his old friend. Such a prediction reinforced Buckley's pro-Nixon stance and expectations. It also seemed to contradict everything Rusher had ever heard from White, "and everything I know about the situation."[11] The publisher thought media accounts of Nixon delegate strength were very unreliable. As he told his *National Review* colleagues in early May: "Again and again, the press has reported delegates as being 'for Nixon' when even the most cursory investigation would indicate that their first preference is for Reagan."[12] Three days later, Rusher urged White to consider unleashing the grassroots activists. ACU members, YAFers, and other conservatives, he suggested, were eager to start working for Reagan. Without "exaggerating what these people can do" in the circumstances, Rusher warned that some kind of organization was needed. Otherwise the campaign might collapse.[13]

By late May, Meyer was aligned with Rusher in favoring Reagan. He told the editors he was offended to learn only accidentally that an upcoming meeting would consider a Nixon endorsement. The magazine's current position was to "implacably oppose Rockefeller," in Meyer's words, and "treat Nixon and Reagan with complete even-handedness." There seemed to be two reasons justifying a possible endorsement of Nixon. Journalistically it would be best, it was thought, to support one candidate rather than stay ambiguous. In addition, there was the view that Reagan should be ruled out. "I insist that Reagan is a serious candidate," Meyer wrote. And if it were deemed journalistically necessary to back a candidate—a point he still didn't concede—then "it would unquestionably be our duty to make Reagan our choice." NR should also attack Rockefeller more strongly than it had. He was, Meyer wrote, "a greater evil" than Vice President Hubert Humphrey, the Democrats' ultimate nominee after Johnson chose not to run again. Should "any softening on Rockefeller" or a tilt toward Nixon occur, Meyer might write an Open Question dissent. It would be "a full endorsement of Reagan," and he would ask that it run in the same issue.[14]

Along with his regret over Buckley's pro-Nixon perspective, the publisher continued to find the editor's lighter penchants irritating at times. In January, Rusher had suggested that Buckley commit to writing one piece for each edition. His new miscellaneous feature "Notes & Asides" was agreeably light, but not "Buckley at his best"—which readers would appreciate and were entitled to. The three Buckley columns that would soon run in each issue didn't belong in the magazine, the publisher thought. Readers would have seen them in the newspapers already and would feel shortchanged.

On February 1, the day after Buckley had left for his annual vacation in Switzerland, Rusher sent him a short but wholly negative memo with multiple criticisms of the Notes & Asides he had just written. He began by mocking Buckley for opening with a trivial item that even the "three readers" who understood it probably wouldn't find amusing. Next, he complained that Buckley wasn't clearing references to the Linus Pauling lawsuit against NR with their lawyer. He had also misstated the title of an article, "A Nervous View of Ronald Reagan," as "An Uneasy View of Ronald Reagan." Finally—implying that Buckley's lifestyle wasn't something smaller contributors should be reminded of when another request for money was pending—Rusher wrote that he despaired at the editor's "breezy tendency to announce your departure for two months in Switzerland, less than a month prior to the mailing of your annual personalized fund appeal letter to a list whose backbone consists of $100 donors." Rusher suggested this was early evidence that Notes & Asides was in danger of being sloppily written. If so, his concern should be dealt with in an upcoming Agony conference.[15]

Buckley responded with contempt. "If I may say so," he began, "it seems to me that all that is proved is that you do not like badinage. Well, I do. And my guess is that others do too. Those who don't, needn't read it . . . I hate to think what a magazine you edited would have had to say on the appearance of Alice and Wonderland." As for Rusher's concerns about the Pauling suit, Buckley wrote: "Somewhere along the line, I am going to be constrained to comment that the law is not written in Chinese, and that mentions of it by me will henceforward not be treated as a capital offense." Buckley noted that he always worried about the annual fund appeal himself. "But my movements are not all that easy to conceal," he added, in reference to his vacations, "and I doubt very much if it would occur to the fund supporters that I am using Company Funds to wax my skis." Buckley concluded: "What does bother me, which inexplicably you did not raise, is the hair-raising typographicAL maelstrom in the penultimate paragraph. Perhaps you would address your next complaint to the printers?"[16]

## Young People

Public speaking was in some ways a better outlet for Rusher than *National Review*, as well as an income supplement. It also helped him to stay in touch with the younger generation on the Right, a connection that mattered greatly to him. By 1966, he had "worked the college vein" on the West Coast "nearly to death."[17] At the beginning of 1968, Shawn Steel, as California YAF chairman, organized a series of appearances on the state's campuses after the national chairman called and asked if he would like to have Rusher out. Familiar with him from the 1965 and 1967 YAF conventions, Steel enthusiastically agreed. Rusher was "our best guy, our heaviest machinery."[18]

Among his engagements were debates at the University of California-Berkeley and UCLA, a speech at UC-Irvine in Orange County, and a speech at Occidental College in Los Angeles. Debating philosophy professor Donald Kalish, he told a UCLA audience of more than eight hundred that Americans were "not in Vietnam to imperialize; to spread Coca-Cola," and explained: "The U.S. is obliged to keep alive the possibility of not living under a communist regime for those countries who don't want to. But this doesn't mean we're committed to defend every square yard of land not dominated by communism . . . we must make the strategic decision as to where to draw the line."[19]

Speaking at Irvine, Rusher said South Vietnam's freedom was not, in itself, a sufficient reason to commit American lives. What justified the war was the need to fight communist aggression in general. Rusher concluded by saying that the military, economic, and political situation in the country had "greatly improved in recent months" and that the tide was turning in America's favor.[20] At Occidental, he said that although Vietnam might be strategically the wrong place to "make our stand," one must be made somewhere. America shouldn't serve as "an international policeman," Rusher continued, but "we are nevertheless obliged as the 'responsible first nation' of the free world to grant assistance to those countries who choose to oppose a 'communist take-over.'"[21] Asked about the draft by a journalist or student journalist at UCLA, he answered sourly: "I would like to think we had a country where we could expect everyone to participate according to established norms, but most of those glue-sniffing creeps wouldn't make good soldiers anyway—so let them stay out."[22]

In what proved to be the last civil debate tour in his YAF experience, Steel recalls, the atmosphere was one of "honest listening." There was already a sharp contrast between the audiences and "Bill Rusher, man of the '50s and early '60s" in his "nice thin tie . . . great shoes." He stood out as "virtually the only person in the auditorium who was dressed that way at all, including the YAFers. Everybody had learned to dress down by '68." The crowds respected Rusher, according to Steel, because he dealt with the issue so rationally and because people could also tell he was "absolutely sincere." The YAF members were additionally pleased that he wasn't the kind of speaker who felt too important. Before or after each debate, Rusher visited comfortably with them, considering it a fine use of his time. He talked about NR, international communism, and the war, stressing that "the essential reason for Vietnam was freedom—our freedom, and freedom for the Vietnamese. It was a really clean and elegant and lofty approach." In personal terms, Steel most enjoyed his "wry wit . . . part of the National Review mystique."[23]

The previous academic year, Rusher had a speaking engagement at the University of Florida, which he kept despite having a bad flu. Frank Shepherd, a junior active in the speakers program, was assigned to bring him to the auditorium. As they waited in the student union after his arrival, Rusher asked Shepherd about himself. He was a political-science major and a Johnson Democrat. What was his favorite city? "I said Los Angeles, and he couldn't accept that," Shepherd recalls. "I think I was demonstrating . . . that I was very unsophisticated, which I was." Rusher started a correspondence.

After they became better acquainted in this way, he asked if Shepherd wanted to come to New York for the summer. The young man was glad to, having been outside Florida just once in his life. Rusher called a friend at *Newsweek* and got an internship for him. They ate dinner at a restaurant or the University Club, once a week "like clockwork." It was partly an education in fine food and wine, as Rusher had done with other young people in the city. But the conversation didn't, as with Anne Edwards, have much of a practical element. Frank wasn't yet a Republican or an active partisan. Rusher spoke of politics, Shakespeare, the opera. He provided books, including *Witness*, which Shepherd read and loved. He suggested that Frank see certain sites, like the city's museums and cathedrals. "I learned New York through him."

Rusher was always quoting Shakespeare, and sometimes at his apartment would open a book and read aloud. A favorite was Ralph Waldo Emerson's essay "Self-Reliance." Alternatively, they might listen to a classical music or opera record for a while. There might be a call, perhaps from Frank Meyer, but it would last only a few minutes. Rusher, Shepherd notes, wouldn't use ten words where one would do. The routine was repeated in the summer of 1968, when the young man worked at *Reader's Digest*. By then a recent graduate, Shepherd subscribed to *National Review* and had begun, through Rusher's tutelage, to appreciate conservative principles: He was "usually talking over my head, but that's the way to learn." He didn't expect his young friend to run for Congress but was simply "enculturating from a classical standpoint, as best he could, somebody who grew up in Lantana, Florida . . . whose father was a grocer and mother a homemaker."

The close friendship continued over the decades, although anxiously unequal on Shepherd's part for a long time. He would prepare for a visit by thinking of conversation topics, collecting his thoughts about them, reading the latest *NR*. "I didn't want him to think that I was stupid; or worse yet . . . wasn't interested in the cause, and trying to keep up with it and do what I could." Because Rusher had an "intellectually intimidating" effect on him, Shepherd wouldn't feel truly comfortable on their visits until he was well over forty. But he remains deeply grateful for his entire friendship with the man who was "my father in almost all respects, or all respects, except in a biological sense."[24]

In these years, Rusher was also writing his first book, *Special Counsel*, a memoir of his time at the Internal Security Subcommittee. The publisher, conservative Arlington House, billed it on the dust jacket as "an inside report" on the Senate's anticommunist investigations. Against a black background was a drawing of the Capitol, with a huge magnifying class over the dome. The title and the author's name appeared in modish lowercase letters: "special counsel" by "william a. rusher," perhaps reflecting Arlington House president Neil McCaffrey's wish to convey a sense of excitement in the story and to achieve a colloquial prose style.

The author, who thought the book had its share of excitement anyway, largely rejected what he considered McCaffrey's attempt to push a breezy, less-dignified mood and language on him. *Special Counsel* was written mainly with young readers in mind. They were an audience he "earnestly" hoped to reach on the vexed subject of internal-security investigations, sometimes known indiscriminately as McCarthyism. As Rusher told Ruth Matthews, widow of the prominent anticommunist investigator J. B. Matthews, many young people were ready to hear the conservative side of that story but wouldn't be likely to appreciate an account that seemed "flippant or even unduly polemical."[25] He ran his draft by Mrs. Matthews and his former chief, Bob Morris. In addition, Rusher told readers in the foreword, Buckley gave "long hours of his time" to a "gentle yet penetrating criticism, both substantive and stylistic . . . so much better than mere praise."

The idea for the book had occurred to him one spring evening in 1965 as he chatted amiably with two young people who, bright though they were, didn't remember the period. The subject retained an "intrinsic fascination," Rusher believed. He wanted to reach both their generation and anyone else who was "sufficiently detached, now, from the controversies of that era to view it with modest objectivity." He had chosen, for the most part, to "simply let the story tell itself."[26]

*Special Counsel* drew upon a combination of personal recollections and the subcommittee's transcripts and reports. In the interest of precision, legal prudence, and occasional drama, Rusher often quoted at length from ISSC testimony. But his skill as a writer—Buckley would later recall him as a "good wordsmith"—was fully visible to the public for the first time. Rusher's relatively few *NR* articles and reviews, mostly political and not needing much of a personal quality, had nicely reflected his verbal wit but tended to lack color and warmth.

"The really supreme accomplishment of the Senate's talented chefs is Senate rum pie," he now wrote in an extended camera-eye description of the upper house's characters and culture, which took up most of his first chapter. "If I am ever sentenced to be executed, I plan to ask for it as the dessert of my final meal. Unfortunately the execution will have to be scheduled rather carefully, for Senate rum pie is prepared and served only on Wednesdays . . . To paraphrase Izaak Walton's Dr. Boteler, doubtless God could have made a better pie, but doubtless God never did." Writing of Senator McCarthy's aversion to cats, Rusher seamlessly led readers to a surprising illustration of his point that much about him was not as they were told: "He clearly wanted nothing to do with Brent Bozell's handsome collection of Siamese cats, which regally roamed the house . . . I asked McCarthy how he explained this odd revulsion, and he said he thought he could trace it to an episode when he was a boy on the farm, back in Wisconsin. He had watched a cat corner a rat in a barn, play with it, and finally tear it to bloody pieces, and the sight had left an indelible impression on him."[27]

In his conclusion, Rusher wrote that communism was "based on a fundamentally inadequate and mistaken concept of man's nature" and that he therefore believed it was "doomed to final failure." But this was different, he added, from "the free world as we know it" winning its "mortal struggle" with communism. That struggle might well be lost. Free men were "divided among themselves, and profoundly unsure of their course." Rusher lamented that "God is 'dead' in the hearts of many good men, and Science is our king." It was, really, "impossible to feel that the prospects for victory of free men are very bright, still less that their victory is inevitable." But Rusher's frequent technique of writing through to the depths of his fears or worries, then adding a more hopeful possibility, was at work: "Since the real problem is . . . our own weakness and irresolution, the remedy lies within us. Communism's absurd and primitive scientism could not possibly prevail against a free world sure of its own meaning and destiny."[28]

Despite Rusher's wish that he might influence the younger generation's perception of the "McCarthy era" and of domestic communism, he never saw or heard evidence that *Special Counsel* had any such impact. As for the scholarly revelations, after the opening of Soviet archives in the 1990s, about the extent of domestic communist espionage in the U.S., Rusher reflected sadly in 2006 that although the research was certainly worth doing, he did not think it would affect the public's or even many younger conservatives' understanding of the issues involved. Too much time had passed. In that time, too many distorted lessons were taught, going almost unchallenged: "We had been licked by the liberals, and now it was too late."[29]

## A Handful of Votes

As *Special Counsel* rolled off the press, Rusher's hopes for a stronger Reagan campaign went unfulfilled. Biographer Cannon would attribute the reluctance mainly to "Reagan's cautious nature, compounded by inner doubts about whether he was ready to be president." In January, journalist David Broder had written that Reagan was "described by his associates as fatalistic almost to the point of naivete in his belief that events will order themselves. 'Ron honestly believes that God will arrange things for the best,' says one Republican colleague."[30] Rusher stresses the political context, including possible home-state reaction to an extensive campaign by the new governor: "I think in 1968, Reagan was not worried about his own inadequacy as much as he was concerned that the people of California, and the people of the country generally, might feel that two years as governor of a state was not enough to qualify him thoroughly for the presidency. He was afraid people wouldn't like that. I don't think he doubted himself, particularly."[31]

Reagan campaigned openly at the Miami Beach convention. His official delegate count was rather low. But the hope of the Reagan forces, led by White, was that various candidates would have enough delegates, all told, to prevent Nixon from winning his necessary simple majority on the first ballot. Reagan might win a majority on the third ballot. To deny Nixon an early victory, it was essential to pry away lukewarm southern delegates whose hearts might be with Reagan but whose delegation leaders had committed to Nixon. Rusher believes the governor would have been nominated in that case, might well have been elected, and would have done well as president despite his limited experience. The near miss, he says, was a "tragedy."[32]

The very large conservative support for Nixon, after disappointing him throughout 1968, was closer and more personal here. With a "nod and a rueful grin," Rusher walked by former Draft Goldwater chairman Peter O'Donnell of Texas, who wore a saucer-sized Nixon button. Congressional aide William Timmons of Tennessee, formerly one of his staunchest Young Republican allies and a Goldwater man, leaned against a railing as he held one of the Nixon team's walkie-talkies, smiling tolerantly as Rusher had a "frantic conversation . . . on the fatal night" with ex-congressman James Martin of Alabama.

At least many of the young conservatives had a good time. Shawn Steel of California—later the state Republican chairman and a national committeeman for the party—was busy with YAF-type activity, spying on the Rockefeller and Nixon forces and making trouble for them, "probably with or without orders." In his "first major public good for journalism," he swiped an all-events pass from the pocket of a *New York Times* reporter and could now go anywhere.[33] Ronald Docksai of New York had graduated from setting up outdoor card tables for Goldwater in 1964, and helping organize high-school students for Buckley in 1965, to a role at the convention. To Docksai, now an entering college freshman, *National Review* and the people associated with it were "the war room of New York conservatives" and Rusher had been "the avuncular, serious presence to those of us who were in the peanut gallery." Although Docksai and others were told before going to Miami that Reagan didn't want them working for him at the convention, Rusher advised the young Reagan supporters to proceed—as long as they didn't claim the candidate endorsed their activity. They met Reagan everywhere with supportive demonstrations, and Docksai also gave out copies of Clif White's painstakingly detailed inside account of the Goldwater campaign, *Suite 3505*, published the previous year. Mr. Rusher provided the shipment.[34]

Rusher was ready to help too. He called White, hoping for access to his friend's and Reagan's adjoining suites. "What the devil do I have to do to get up there?" he asked. "Work," White said. Rusher and others did their best to explain to visiting delegations why Reagan would be a better nominee than Nixon. Senator Thurmond told White that Rockefeller would end up as the candidate if the southern delegations broke away from Nixon and thereby caused more balloting. "That's not true, not true at all," White objected. Thurmond answered: "Well, you may be right, son, but we just cain't take that chance."[35]

The Oregon delegation, including Rusher's friend Donald Hodel, a former Harvard YR, was seated in front of the South Carolinians. "In conversations with them," he remembers, "it became apparent that their hearts were substantially with Reagan." A newspaper reported that Nixon would name Mark Hatfield, a liberal new senator from Oregon, as his running mate. Hodel saw Rusher take the paper to Thurmond and tell him, in effect, that he was about to be "the victim of the biggest double cross in the history of American politics." It had "an immediate and profound impact," Hodel recalls. Thurmond picked up his special phone, a direct line to Nixon, and warned that if the story was true, he would instruct the South Carolina delegation to withhold its support.

It was one of the Republican Party's last truly dramatic conventions. "If Nixon didn't get it on the first vote," Tom Reed believes, "he was dead." Absent a first-ballot majority, the states in question "would have come flocking to Reagan."[36] According to White, his Reagan forces "came within a handful of votes" in four southern delegations of breaking the unit rule— some delegations had a requirement, which they could waive, to vote unanimously on the first ballot—and thus denying Nixon an immediate nomination by freeing many pro-Reagan delegates. He had secret pledges from many that they would vote for Reagan if Nixon fell short on the first ballot. But they feared political retribution if they aligned prematurely with the governor and their votes then proved insufficient.[37]

After Nixon won, Rusher addressed the young Reaganites in what Ron Docksai would recall as a combined "pep talk" and political analysis: "explaining everything, putting it all together, and saying why . . . this would mean great things in the future."[38] In the ensuing weeks, Rusher did a lot of consoling and congratulating. To Don Hodel, Diarmuid O'Scannlain, and Don Pearlman of Oregon he expressed thanks for "fighting the good fight . . . straight through the disappointing climax." He noted the election of Eisenhower in 1952 and the Goldwater nomination as examples of "how illusory" political triumphs could be, adding: "It is well to remind ourselves that defeat, too, is deceptive."

To Reagan, Rusher wrote that he knew how free the governor's actions in 1968 had been "of the typical motivations of politics." He added: "I know you . . . are well aware of the equally selfless efforts made by hundreds and even thousands of dedicated men and women on behalf of your cause and all that it represented." Reagan had been important "as a rallying-point for the idealistic young conservatives" who backed him; and they would, Rusher predicted, eventually "be running our party and our country." He had also "profoundly" influenced "the whole power structure of the party . . . the tone of the platform, the general attitude and position of the successful candidate, and his choice of a running-mate."

Noting that he was happy to have met Mrs. Reagan for the first time, Rusher gladly accepted her invitation to visit them in California, then told the governor: "You continue to have my entire political loyalty." Reagan replied, "Dear Bill: I have no words to express my appreciation for your kind letter. You give me more credit than I deserve and make me very proud indeed." He assured Rusher: "We think alike with regard to the young people. I can never forget their faces that last late night after the balloting . . . I will never betray their faith and trust."[39]

Reaching out to the other side, Rusher told Pat Buchanan: "If Nixon made any mistakes during the pre-convention campaign, I can't imagine what they were." There was "no doubt that you are entitled to a large share of the credit for the things . . . that went right." Assuring the conservative aide he would support the ticket, Rusher added: "I hope very much indeed that your own personal influence, at the policy level, will broaden and deepen during the campaign" and in the administration if Nixon won. Buchanan responded promptly. The note was "gracious." If Reagan had won, Buchanan in contrast "would have become an immediate problem for his Secret Service escort," given that he had gone through thirty months of work to nominate Nixon. Buchanan claimed he was "a bit surprised that William Rusher has given an unconditional endorsement two and a half months prior to an election," adding: "I trust we shall do or say nothing to make you wish you had a string on it." Buchanan wanted to meet with Rusher as soon as possible and get his thoughts on various things. For now, though, he had temporary duty at the Democratic convention in Chicago, where his job was "to watch—and perhaps to assist—the disintegration of the old Roosevelt coalition."[40]

Rusher also wrote his fellow Harvard Law student and Young Republican leader Charlie McWhorter, later a Nixon aide in the second Eisenhower term and now on the campaign team. They hadn't been political soulmates for well over a decade, since Rusher began to consider himself a serious con-

servative in the midfifties. It was McWhorter whom he had tried, unsuccessfully, to persuade into the conservative movement back in 1957. At some
point, Rusher had come to think of the belief in getting elected at all costs as
"the McWhorter Fallacy."[41] He now told his friend that because he saw the
circumstances of 1968 quite differently from those of 1960, "I expect to have
no difficulty in supporting the Nixon-Agnew ticket . . . Now that we are on
the same side again for a change, let's keep in closer touch."[42]

While friendly with recent adversaries in the party, Rusher told colleagues at *NR* immediately after the convention that he was offended by
many of the reactions he had gotten to his Reagan advocacy and analysis.
He didn't name names, even Burnham's. But his complaint was among the
strongest he ever put in writing at the magazine. Recalling to the editors
that he had been wrongly accused of giving them biased evaluations of Reagan's chances, Rusher noted that he was prepared to hear this again in 1972,
should there be a contested Republican nomination. "But I would like to
think," he added, "that the relevant parties might abjure, next time, those
relentless declarations many months in advance, that Candidate X had it 'all
locked up'—declarations fortified, this year, with displays of mathematical
logic and quotations from Cosimo de Medici, and buttressed by reiterated
offers of cash wagers, all at a time when the merest YR in south Jersey knew
that the outcome was still very uncertain indeed."

He wasn't finished. In addition to false political wisdom, Rusher went
on to speak of intellectual dishonesty and self-fulfilling prophecy:

> The sort of thing I am talking about is not an attempt at a legitimate
> forecast but simply a human (though immature) effort to immedia-
> tize the future . . . so that restless minds can sleep o' nights. Politi-
> cians, being realists, know better; I am sure that Cosimo de Medici
> knew better. The events of this August happened only in August,
> and were not foreordained, nor even predictable by intelligent men
> in possession of the available facts, despite all the blare and certi-
> tude that resounded in our editorial conferences. Moreover, these
> gratuitous, hard-breathing *pronunciamenti*, appearing (as they did
> this year, on more than one occasion) in the pages of NR, do con-
> tribute in some small measure to the very outcome they predict . . .
> And this, I think, trenches unfairly upon the collective prerogatives
> of the editorial board, which alone, under Bill Buckley, determines
> whom we shall support.[43]

Decades later, Buckley would cite Rusher as a "politician *manqué*," a
would-be politician who hadn't quite made it, for his persistent backing of

Reagan that year. But he may have helped more people to see the governor as a national leader. Rusher played an "indispensable role," according to Freeman, by "making Reagan credible to Eastern 'intellectual conservatives,' including WFB and much of the NR circle, which still regarded Reagan as a second-tier Hollywood type."[44]

In the same August memo in which he commented on attitudes toward the primary campaign and the nomination at *National Review*, Rusher emphasized how much the nominee owed to conservative politicians, donors, and delegates. Nixon had benefited enormously from the early endorsement by Goldwater, fund-raising by New York financier and major Goldwater donor Jeremiah Milbank, Buckley's support, and the "literally indispensable" backing of Thurmond. Rusher wrote as if a largely conservative administration would be almost a given if Nixon were elected: "When you put a chameleon on blue, he doesn't normally turn pink. We have every right, logical as well as moral, to assume that on the big issues that really matter Nixon will be (within the limits of his inherently ambiguous personality) essentially conservative—indeed, that he is to an almost frightening degree the creation and prisoner of one bloc of conservatives. And the countervailing exterior pressures will not be exclusively liberal, for there is still the Reagan bloc—and, out there in the darkness, Wallace." In addition, the Republican Party of 1968 bore "gratifyingly little resemblance" to the one whose nomination Nixon received in 1960. "On that occasion, you will recall, he crawled all the way to New York and licked the polish off Rockefeller's shoes. This time he displayed an even greater appetite for the Kiwi on Senator Thurmond's."[45]

Gratifying though such points may have been to conservatives, Rusher's perception of Nixon as the virtual "creation and prisoner" of those on the Right who had importantly backed him was proved largely irrelevant in the first case, and wrong in the second. In October, Lee Edwards warned him that *National Review* was far too "myopic" about the Republican candidate: "You, he and I all know that Dick Nixon is not a conservative. I am puzzled by N.R.'s insistence that he is."[46]

Nixon's fall campaign didn't impress Rusher; he told a friend he had found it "rather static" in comparison with Vice President Humphrey's hard-fought comeback, which made the result a squeaker. But he was impressed by the total vote for Nixon and George Wallace of Alabama, the third-party candidate on the social right, previously known as a champion of southern resistance to integration. In a runoff, he thought, Nixon almost certainly would have won a large majority of the Wallace supporters. In addition, Humphrey had received less than 43 percent of the vote, not a great deal better than Goldwater in 1964.[47]

Satisfaction with the election results and with conservative power in the party was one thing, but identifying with the new administration was another. During the last inauguration of a Republican president, Eisenhower's second in 1957, Rusher had gone to work as usual at the Internal Security Subcommittee just a few blocks away, then headed to Joe McCarthy's house with Bob Morris. On January 20, 1969, he would be at the Hotel Pierre in Manhattan—where the Confrerie des Chevaliers du Tastevin, a wine-importing society, would "knight" him as a full member at its annual initiation dinner (white tie preferred, ladies welcome).[48]

# 10

# Neither Nixon nor Woodstock

Just after the election, Buckley wrote a column endorsing two liberal Republicans who were considered possible cabinet appointees, describing them as good choices for the Defense and State departments. Nelson Rockefeller had "flogged the right wing mercilessly" in previous years and was addicted to "liberal . . . clichés" in domestic policy, but he was an "expert administrator" who would do well as defense secretary. He also had a firm, decades-long commitment to anticommunism and "would be the last man in America to be fooled by phony disarmament drives." Buckley noted further that eastern establishmentarians, "Rockefeller's clientele," were "greatly needed in support of tough defense policies." Less strongly, he suggested that former Pennsylvania governor William Scranton would be a good secretary of state. Highly competent and diplomatic, he would be the cooperative surrogate Nixon wanted in that job. Buckley balanced these recommendations only by suggesting that two other liberal Republicans, Mayor Lindsay and the lame-duck senator Thomas Kuchel of California, would be unacceptable cabinet choices.[1]

Rusher reported that conservatives on the Nixon team seemed "badly upset" by the column—adding that he had, nonetheless, told the complaining aide that Buckley possessed a keen eye for political truths. The day before, Rusher starkly admonished Buckley, who was about to meet with the president-elect's campaign manager, John Mitchell: "I hope you will try to consider yourself a spokesman for conservatives, bent on increasing their influence in the Nixon administration."[2]

As it turned out, the secretary of state was New York lawyer William Rogers, a former associate of Dewey's and an attorney general in the Eisenhower

administration. The secretary of defense was Melvin Laird, a moderately conservative congressman who would become a tenacious, bureaucratically adept
advocate for winding down the American presence in Vietnam. The appointment of Harvard political scientist and Rockefeller associate Henry Kissinger
as national security adviser gave Buckley a special link to the White House.
He had known Kissinger since 1954, was instrumental in introducing him to
Nixon in 1968, and considered him "one of us" ideologically. During Kissinger's White House tenure, Buckley would visit Washington many times to see
him and they would talk frequently on the phone.[3] Rusher got along with the
new national security adviser, having been repeatedly invited to his International Seminar to explain American conservatism to up-and-coming young
professionals from abroad. Telling a friend he considered the appointment a
notably positive one, Rusher called Kissinger "a solid citizen," adding: "The liberal praise for him is (I suspect) mostly whistling to keep up their courage."[4]

In February 1969, White House aide Tom Charles Huston, a former YAF
chairman, called Rusher to request pressure on Nixon. Huston and other
conservatives among the presidential staff were upset by what they viewed as
a "disastrous series of liberal appointments," Rusher told Buckley, reporting
on their talk. When the publisher noted that *Human Events* had made some
complaints, Huston said the only conservative writers Nixon respected were
Buckley and *NR*'s James Kilpatrick, that the message would best come from
them. He also said: "We need it bad." Rusher therefore urged the editor to
respond with "all the help you can." Answering eight days later, Buckley said
he would certainly write a column if Rusher provided "a list of Nixon's most
objectionable appointments and . . . his most conspicuous delinquencies."[5]

Twelve days after that, Rusher pushed him again. "I had rather expected,
after our business conference at Stamford during which I gave you various
documentary summaries of Nixon's growing neglect of the conservatives,
that we might be getting a critical column from you on the subject. It hasn't
arrived, and I wonder whether you have changed your mind or are perhaps
marking time?" In another two weeks, Buckley could report that he had
now written two "slightly anti-Nixon" columns. One warned of signs that
the administration would aggressively pursue "forced integration" of public
schools—especially given the appointment of Robert Finch, a liberal, as secretary of Health, Education, and Welfare (HEW). The other raised the possibility that "ideological spite" stood in the way of recruiting conservatives
to administration posts.[6]

Although the differences between Rusher and Buckley had sometimes
been acute in the past half-decade, the editor scheduled a dinner in Rusher's
honor at the Plaza Hotel on April 10. The idea, Buckley told the audience,
was to "celebrate his achievements and his person." In a quirkily appreciative

speech, he called it a miracle that the publisher had endured the "disorderly habits of his colleagues" for so long. He was "the quintessential Republican" in his willingness—which Buckley called "thorough . . . unrelenting" but not "tiresome"—to question spending at the magazine. As part of his mission to impose order there, Rusher had long presented graphs measuring everything from its promotional expenses to its political influence to the conservatism or nonconservatism of public figures. At the weekly editorial conferences, Buckley confided, the publisher expressed scorn toward politicians and others he thought were doing something "contemptible"—and toward *NR* colleagues when they were less upset about it than himself. These performances ranked among "the great running acts on the ideological stage." But Rusher had also won the affection of his colleagues: "The most exasperating people in the world are so often the most beloved, and he is no exception."[7]

Rusher told friends later that the evening had been "a thoroughly lovely occasion." Closing his own talk at the dinner with a short poem, he promised lifelong loyalty to those in attendance:

> Some friends are meant to share the smiles or tears
> Of one brief moment, and be on their way;
> And some are sent to brighten many years,
> And others are to savor for a day—
> And cast away.
> But I have found in you a friend whose ways
> So blend with mine that, fusing all their parts,
> We shall become, in old Ulysses' phrase,
> "One equal temper of heroic hearts"
> Till life departs.
> So here's my hand; and here my guarantee
> Against whatever tempests Fate may send:
> All foes of yours shall find a foe in me,
> And I will honor you, and be your friend
> Until the end.[8]

## Emerging Majority?

Despite his early concerns about the administration, Rusher found two political events in 1969 highly encouraging: the publication of *The Emerging Republican Majority* by Kevin Phillips, a self-taught election expert, and the tough speeches by Vice President Spiro Agnew, especially against liberal bias in the news media.

*The Emerging Republican Majority* argued that the GOP could attain the political predominance that had long eluded it, and could do it soon, for three reasons: a trend toward the party in the South, which had been the focus of Rusher's 1963 "Crossroads" article; growing electoral votes and conservatism in the prosperous Sunbelt states; and discontent with liberal policies among Democratic working and lower-middle-class voters, often white ethnics, in the Northeast and Midwest. Anxiety about issues like crime, welfare, and forced busing for the purpose of integrating schools, Phillips noted, could help the Republicans greatly.[9]

"I trust you are planning . . . a 21-gun salute," a delighted Rusher told Meyer, who ran the magazine's book-review section. "As the nearest thing we have to a House Pol," he told the editors as a whole, "I would be derelict in my duty if I did not call [the book] most forcefully to your attention." Its thesis amounted roughly to what Rusher and others had maintained for six or seven years—but they had "merely *said* this." Here, in contrast, was a treasure of hard data squeezed from election results. In a "fascinating and wholly convincing demonstration," Phillips nailed down the new-majority argument with evidence illustrated on "143 charts and 47 maps." And he wasn't just some marginal observer. Rusher found Phillips's educational credentials impressive and happily noted his strategic place in the new administration as a special assistant to Attorney General Mitchell, more relevantly Nixon's recent campaign manager.[10]

The conservative southern liaison for the White House, Harry Dent, advised the president that the Republican Party should "follow Phillips' plan" while publicly disavowing it. After reading the book over the holidays, Nixon in January 1970 instructed his chief of staff, H. R. Haldeman, to use its author as an analyst and "study his strategy." The White House, he added in his note, "must learn to understand Silent Majority."[11] Two months before, the president had used the phrase in a speech about Vietnam, asking "the great silent majority of my fellow Americans" to be "united for peace" and "united against defeat."[12] His address was well received by the public— and about three-quarters of voters, in polls taken for the White House over the next year, said they identified with the "silent majority."[13]

Vice President Agnew had already used the term repeatedly in one of his own speeches. Speaking at Ohio State University in June 1969, Agnew also attacked the "sniveling hand-wringing power structure" and "the effete corps of impudent snobs who characterize themselves as intellectuals," meaning, in the latter case, antiwar demonstrators and those in the Democratic Party who sympathized with them. That fall, he began to go after the media by rebuking television's "instant analysis" commentary as presumptuous and its tendencies in reporting the news as too adversarial.

The passionate Des Moines speech—written by Buchanan but read closely, approved, and actually toughened by Nixon—was followed a week later by a hard-hitting speech in the South that strongly criticized the *Washington Post* and the *New York Times*. The vice president also spoke out on drugs, sexual mores, and rising violent crime.[14]

Rusher hadn't been impressed when Nixon ended up picking Agnew, the little-known governor of Maryland whose conservative credentials consisted mainly of a clash with black community leaders after the Baltimore riot that year, as his running mate. Given the complicated situation at the convention, he told colleagues, it had been necessary to name "the Hon. Agnew T. Whoever of the great state of Catalepsy" rather than a figure with a clear political identity. Nixon did what was probably "most congenial to him anyway, and what I predicted way back in October 1967 he would have to do: namely, select 'another centrist as faceless as himself.' What price he, his backers, the party and the country will ultimately have to pay for this lackluster solution to the problem remains, perhaps mercifully, hidden by the veils of the future."[15]

It wasn't long before many conservatives had much higher hopes for Agnew. "I was quite close to him and liked him a lot," Rusher recalls. "He was a true convert to *National Review* . . . He became a real big fan of the magazine, and it wasn't phony." The vice president was "a thoughtful, decent man . . . very sincere. Conservative, becoming more so as time went along." In a matter of months, he seemed to grow "almost visibly" in his understanding of the movement and in his identification with it. Agnew, whom Rusher would visit at the Old Executive Office Building next to the White House, requested half a dozen copies of each *NR* so he could share them with friends. The publisher was soon pleased to hear that he had actually done this.[16]

The vice president's staff came to include former YAF chairman David Keene and former *NR* writer John Coyne. Although not "overly educated," Keene recalls, Agnew was "very, very smart . . . completely enamored of ideas" and took an interest in conservative and center-right intellectuals. "He'd read an article, say by Jeane Kirkpatrick, and he'd say: 'Let's get her up here for lunch; let's have some people up here and talk about this.'" Guests at the sessions in Agnew's executive dining room would include neoconservatives Irving Kristol and James Q. Wilson, Buckley, Rusher, and representatives from other conservative publications.[17]

Buckley felt ambivalent about Agnew, saying the vice president was "not skilled in polemics" and had some "rhetorical misfires," but he also defended the Des Moines speech as "balanced" and "very good." Here and elsewhere, Agnew had "done an extremely useful service" by stating obvious yet forbidden truths.[18] Burnham too reacted favorably, telling Buckley he had obtained the full text of many of the vice president's speeches and "must say I thought them pretty good: including the rhetoric; some of his aphoristic sentences are at a pretty high intellectual level for a speech. In fact, I think that Agnew's speeches are intellectually superior to those delivered by any other U.S. political big shots for many years . . . They really do say something about serious subjects."[19]

In his perception of the president, on the other hand, Buckley differed more substantially with Rusher, who found him "too Machiavellian." Asked in a 1970 *Playboy* interview: "Is Nixon conservative enough for you?" Buckley replied that his "ideal conservative president" would attempt "certain radical reforms that . . . would greatly benefit America and augment human freedom." But such a person couldn't be elected at this time or move his agenda through Congress. Because the "paramount need of this highly divided society at this particular moment is for conciliation," Nixon, by attempting that, was "a good President from a conservative point of view." The fact they had met privately once or twice at the White House, Buckley conceded, might inhibit his criticisms. "I have discovered a new sensual treat, which, appropriately, the readers of *Playboy* should be the first to know about. It is to have the President of the United States take notes while you are speaking to him, even though you run the risk that he is scribbling, 'Get this bore out of here.' It's always a little bit more difficult to be rhetorically ruthless with somebody with whom you spend time."[20]

What such contacts meant for the Right or even the editor of *National Review* was unclear. "He liked him," Kissinger later said of Nixon's attitude, "but Buckley would make him uneasy, and he thought he was not really relevant to the decisions that he had to make."[21] In Rusher's opinion, the president "had every opportunity to become the leader of the conservative movement" but couldn't fill that role because he viewed the Right as simply an interest group. Nixon was, however, "very adroit in handling the conservatives. He may have convinced them they were getting more than they were getting, and persuaded them to be satisfied with what they got. He didn't persuade me."[22]

One thing already troubling Rusher was the uncertainty of Nixon's commitment in Vietnam. He had shown an early gut-level engagement with the issue in 1965, angrily calling attention to a CBS report that showed American troops setting fire to a village and portrayed this as an overreaction to a few shots fired at them. "The score: two women and three babies killed," the broadcast concluded tendentiously, "and captured—four old men." Rusher had seen plenty of "anti-American propaganda" in his day, he told Burnham and Buckley, but here was one of the worst examples. If the event was reported fairly, as he certainly didn't believe, that would mean the American troops were bloodthirsty killers. If it was distorted, as seemed very likely, "priceless aid and comfort" had been given to the enemy. "In either case, it is utterly inconceivable to me that our armed forces should permit this kind of reportage."[23]

Two years later, Rusher suggested that if the magazine's pro-Vietnam War stance was to be maintained effectively, it was probably best to urge "all-out escalation"—meaning "the obliteration of the military power of North Vietnam, even if this entails a further risk of war with Red China." If, on the other hand, the editors wanted to propose American withdrawal, they must first decide: "Do we abandon the Domino Theory altogether or do we have in mind some domino which will *not* topple? . . . Personally, I think there is a great deal to be said for the Domino Theory, but I am open to suggestions if somebody really thinks we can hold the line less expensively" in another country. If *National Review* were to show the "slightest hint" of supporting an end to American involvement without adding "major and well-emphasized qualifiers," the Left would seize upon that to propagandize further against the war effort.[24]

Rusher repeated his insistence on the war's importance in a 1968 memo about the presidential campaign. Talk had arisen among conservative anti-communists, about a year earlier, of actively supporting President Johnson should the Republicans end up nominating an antiwar candidate—and such sentiment still existed, Rusher told Buckley on March 26, five days before the president announced he would not seek reelection. "Johnson's conduct of the war may be deplorable, but these things are relative, and it is by no means as deplorable (at least to me) as the 'dove' position. If the Republicans were to nominate a dove (unlikely as that is), I personally would support Johnson. And so would a lot of other Republican hawks."[25] Now, in mid-1969, Rusher sought a discussion of the war's ultimate significance at the next Agony meeting, asking the editors to consider his suspicion "that America's determination . . . to prevail in Vietnam is very probably *the* crucial test for the future of American society." If the country passed it, "we will have validated our national right (and will) to survive; if we fail it, we are probably through—though our fall may take a while, considering the distance to be traversed."[26]

In a letter to Nancy Reagan a month later, Rusher made his point less drastically but with the same anxiety. Having been at the governor's birthday dinner in February and enjoyed a private talk with him that day or evening, he now took the opportunity of his growing relationship with the Reagans to send them some observations on the state of things, mainly on Vietnam. It seemed "about time" to make them. Citing the British historian Arnold Toynbee on the nature of civilizational decline, and noting that the insight in his opinion applied equally to nations, Rusher told Mrs. Reagan he suspected Vietnam was "an absolutely basic challenge" to the United States: "Either we prevail there, or we take the low road and fall back into the ruck of history—just another big-shot that tried and failed. At any rate, I cannot see any point at which one could rationally hope that America, having deserted Vietnam, would stand and fight"—unless there were, as there might well be, "a convulsive mass reaction" to such a defeat, "leading directly to a major conflict between the Great Powers."

Rusher also saw a "very good chance" of withdrawal from Vietnam in the not-too-distant future. "If that happens, certainly a major segment of the American right will break inevitably with Nixon." Those conservatives, himself included, "simply will not remain on friendly terms with any administration . . . that betrays the Americans who have already died in Vietnam, surrenders the people who live there and all their neighbors to Communism, and sets America on the downward path forever." Rusher's thoughts were intended for the governor as well "if you feel he would be interested in them." In response, Mrs. Reagan wrote that "Ronnie and I were fascinated" by the analysis, "although at the same time disturbed and frightened. I suppose mainly because we agree with you."[27]

In general, Rusher remained mildly favorable toward the president, telling the Reagans that most conservatives were "reasonably well satisfied with most of his actions and appointments to date—barring, of course, the obvious exceptions like [Secretary] Finch and the HEW staff."[28] But several months later, a year into Nixon's term, he asked that *NR* educate readers on three major policy developments, all of which he deplored.

The administration had recently proposed its Philadelphia Plan, which Rusher described as "black quotas on Federal construction projects" and which in fact included federally funded construction as well. To managing editor Priscilla Buckley, he relayed his understanding that it was being presented as a political scheme of Nixon's. White House representatives on Capitol Hill were "pleading with appalled Republican congressmen to at least let the Philadelphia Plan be tested in the courts—apparently on the theory that it will ultimately be thrown out there, and meanwhile embarrasses the hell out of the Democrats, who are forced to do the splits between their Negro and labor backing." Rusher also warned that quotas might well run out of control. Even though "Nixon doesn't plan to go that far," he explained, "if the liberals get away with this one, there is no earthly reason—certainly no Constitutional one—why they cannot impose racial quotas on any business involved in interstate commerce, including the Board of Editors of *National Review*."

Also needing coverage from the magazine's standpoint was the increasingly powerful environmental issue. Rusher thought the public was responding uncritically to it. "We are all, as a nation, going certifiably crazy on the subject of pollution—and the pity is all the greater because there really *is* a pollution problem, buried far down under all the hysteria," he wrote. "My own guess is that the real big winners are going to be (as usual) the politicians and their business friends who make off with the untold millions and billions America is now predictably going to spend on this problem." Another important topic was Democratic senator Birch Bayh's constitutional amendment to abolish the Electoral College, a threat *NR* hadn't taken "nearly seriously enough." The publisher asked for close attention to material he was providing on the question.[29]

Rusher's reference to Nixon's alleged cynicism in proposing the Philadelphia Plan reflected his interest in keeping close tabs on Washington developments. Former YAF leader Bill Cotter, then a junior official in the administration, recalls his onetime antagonist's friendliness when they occasionally met for lunch. Their visits were "all amiable and good," with no rehashing of past troubles in the organization. Rusher was "always a fountainhead of knowledge, of information about what the hell was really going on."[30] To what extent that could be said of *National Review* was unclear not only to Rusher but also to many in Washington—who also questioned the magazine's influence.

In early 1970, Neal Freeman, now executive editor of King Features, told Buckley and Rusher that *NR* had a "very low profile" in the capital, while *Human Events* had "significantly more clout among the Nixon people." He thought this was partly *NR*'s fault and partly a result of the weekly paper's industriousness: "They hold monthly luncheons with top conservative figures in the Administration; they exploit their contacts on the Hill by playing them off against White House sources; they are hiring a top-flight investigative reporter to keep everybody alert; they are cultivating the non-Establishment conservatives." *Human Events* editor Tom Winter knew perhaps one hundred congressmen on a first-name basis, and he lobbied for legislation and appointments conservatives favored. *National Review* had "vastly greater resources" than *Human Events* and should "become a factor in this Administration," Freeman continued. "I cannot fathom why *NR* is increasing its lit-set material and phasing out its political activism at the same time as a conservative Administration is trying to take hold in Washington. The perfect statement of *NR*'s approach seems to be the elimination of the Washington column followed a few months later by the introduction of a 'Delectations' [food and wine] feature: we are withdrawing to the parlor, where the action isn't."[31]

Rusher sent Freeman's memo to the senior editors, asking them to look it over. Without suggesting an agenda for a heightened presence in Washington, he seconded the observation that *National Review* tended to neglect it. "Of course, we can never (and probably should not try to) compete with 'Human Events' at the game of Capitol Hill checkers," he told Buckley. "But it doesn't hurt to remind ourselves from time to time that there *is* a Washington and that we might give it a fairer share of our attention."[32] Freeman may have touched a sore point when he questioned the food-and-wine column. "Delectations" was sacred. As Priscilla Buckley noted to readers in her next light roundup piece about the magazine, it was the only feature the staff never sacrificed to make space in a crowded edition—"no matter what the pressures."[33]

In continuing to urge close coverage of political developments, Rusher too continued to find himself in conflict with *NR* culture at times. When John Lindsay finally left the GOP and became a Democrat in 1971, he agreed it wasn't earth-shattering news but criticized his colleagues for not giving it more notice. Rusher cited what he considered an absurd contrast to the minimization of the Lindsay story. In playful response to the *Times*'s publication of the Vietnam-policy archive known as the Pentagon Papers, the editors "found plenty of room to publish 14 pages of nonexistent 'Secret Papers'" and followed up with seven more pages "over two more issues, explaining and defending" their hoax. "Surely our priorities are a little out of kilter here?"[34]

Still, Rusher usually tolerated the magazine's fun-loving propensities. "He had, and has, a sense of humor," Buckley recalls, "but it's one that exercises itself within an orthodoxy. For instance, when I decided to have the special issue of *National Review* in which we made up stories, the idea being to tease the establishment—in our fake headline, 'The Pope confesses that he's not . . .' and 'Whoever made the typewriter for Alger Hiss confesses,' all that kind of stuff—Bill took a sort of professional interest in the event, but it was not the kind of thing that he originated." In differing on editorial taste, "he was never aggressive about it," Buckley says. "He wouldn't call me up and say: 'That paragraph shouldn't have been run because it's too iconoclastic' or whatever. So there was never a working problem."[35] Rusher's relationship with Buckley was "friendly, always very positive, and yet a little bit detached," according to Joseph Sobran, who began as a writer at the magazine in 1972. The editor "liked to provoke him a little bit," often needling him at meetings, but Rusher took it well.[36]

He did object to four-letter words in *NR*. In 1968, Rusher had asked Buckley to schedule an Agony deliberation on the question. "I use these words all the time in my own private conversation," he noted, "so my position is not precisely that of (say) Dan Mahoney or Mrs. Bonbrake or some other real bluenose." But upon seeing a newspaper story about a student editor who was fired after printing "the worst of these words" in his college paper, "it suddenly occurred to me that he might [conceivably] . . . be a

*National Review* fan who has been watching our progress." Rusher explained:
"I desperately want *National Review* to be up-to-date; but I also think that
somebody must maintain standards in these matters, if only for the benefit
of the young, and if *National Review* doesn't, who the ——— will?"[37]


## YAF Revisited

Rusher still paid a good deal of attention to YAF, which emerged as the
main organized resistance to the radical student Left. In 1968, members led
by Ron Docksai held a sit-in at the headquarters of the antiwar National
Mobilization Committee in New York; he also led a group, including Frank
Meyer's activist son John, in temporarily "liberating" a Greenwich Village
office of the radical Students for a Democratic Society. A large Veterans Day
rally at the Washington Monument in 1969, put together by former YAF
leader Edwards, supported the troops in Vietnam and served as counter-
publicity to the massive National Mobilization rally held less than a week
later. In addition to running or backing candidates for student-government
positions, YAF members filed lawsuits demanding that officials at their universities maintain order. They organized refusals to pay student-activity fees
until speakers' programs were ideologically balanced and the like. They pro-
tected military and corporate recruiters on campuses. At one point, more
than sixty student-body presidents, and hundreds of thousands of others,
signed petitions to "Tell it to Hanoi." YAF was also, mainly in 1969, wracked
by internal ideological conflict. And many members of the now-booming
organization were looking more like products of the decade.
     Docksai, a student at St. John's University, had joined the national board
in 1968 and became vice chairman at YAF's legendary August 1969 convention in St. Louis. At that convention, fusionist and mainstream traditionalist
conservatives, or "Trads," like himself, defeated the minority of doctrinaire
libertarians, or "Libs," many of whom advocated an antiwar alliance with
the New Left, active draft resistance, and marijuana legalization. Buckley,
Rusher, and Meyer—all of whom opposed the libertarian revolt in YAF—
spoke at the convention. Citing his pressing schedule, Buckley declined
an offer by Karl Hess (a 1964 Goldwater speechwriter who had recently
cofounded the dissenting Radical Libertarian Alliance) to debate at the
city's Gateway Arch. Radical libertarians booed Buckley's opening address;
as they did so, Buckley said critics like Hess were "cankerous." One slogan
chanted at the convention was "No More Vietnams." Another was "Fuck
the Draft." A Lib burned his draft card on the convention floor, setting off
a half-hour melee in which enraged Trads yelled: "Kill the commies." In

response to a flag-burning, according to Docksai, Rusher advised his side to keep its cool, and it did.

The mainstream conservatives easily won the national-board election, and the delegates rejected immediate withdrawal from Vietnam. But according to libertarian writer Jerome Tuccille, so many radical Libs were denied credentials that they were unable to put up an effective fight for their positions and candidates. More than three hundred radicals left YAF and formed the Society for Individual Liberty. Many YAFers from various states joined the splinter group or other libertarian organizations. In the months after the 1969 convention, new national chairman David Keene came under fire for removing the Lib chairman of the California YAF. When Keene left to work for Vice President Agnew, Docksai became national chairman.[38]

After talking for two hours in Washington with much of the YAF board four months after the wild convention, Rusher reported his tentative conclusions to Buckley. The board was largely sound. "In supporting it, we are backing the right horse." But in the last three years, the "nutty season" at many schools had caused YAF real problems. A chapter chairman, for example, might be "seriously torn between a perfectly human desire to accommodate himself to the prevailing behavioral patterns on his campus, and a perfectly sincere loyalty to the higher principles and more profound commitments of YAF. Shall he wear his hair long and smoke pot, or wear a vest and read *National Review,* or both?"

The board and other YAF leaders took the problem seriously, Rusher indicated. But adjustments to the new college culture might nonetheless be weakening the group's identity. Although its opposition to the draft, stated back in 1967, was an "early attempt to build a bridge between sound conservative-libertarian philosophy and the modern campus," unfortunately "this sort of thing has tended to exacerbate the very problem it was devised to solve." As a result of such flexibility, YAF now included people who were "not, in the broader perspective, really very conservative at all." As he warned against a diluted message and membership, Rusher also sympathized with the rights of local units to an extent. The national leaders, he told Buckley, may have handled conflicts more by withdrawing their charters and by expelling people than by negotiation or compromise. Now, it seemed they were trying to "meet their critics half-way." Rusher added that he had strongly advised the national board to "rely more on diplomacy and less on sheer clout, and above all to get going on the rectification of their image" as too arbitrary. He expected the advice would have an effect. Generally speaking, YAF was on course.[39]

A year later it was broke, although the conflicts had diminished considerably. Writing to Senator Goldwater about the financial crisis, Buckley said he had looked into the situation and also asked Rusher to investigate. Rusher had identified three reasons why YAF fund-raising appeals were falling so short. There had been much competition from other conservative fund-raising, including that for the James Buckley Senate race in 1970. In addition, the campuses had largely calmed down. This meant, Buckley explained, that "the usefulness of YAF is, though as real as ever, less apparent than usual." Rusher had also concluded that future operations must be carefully budgeted and more modest.[40] Disaster was averted by a combination of substantial spending cuts, which had already occurred, and a highly successful direct-mail solicitation. There was soon a surplus—but by early 1972, YAF faced a large deficit again.[41]

Years of continued contact had maintained Rusher's credibility and clout. His ability to advise YAF and look into its problems owed much to a willingness to spend time with activists who were now a quarter-century younger than himself. As national chairman from 1970 to 1975, Ron Docksai called upon Rusher and Buckley, but especially the more easily reachable Rusher, for advice. Docksai had been one of the young people he introduced to good wine and other niceties, bringing "an element of style, just like Bill Buckley, to those of us who were lower-middle class kids from Queens and Brooklyn." At the same time, such disciplines as drill and chain of command were instinctive with Rusher, partly exemplified by his brevity on the phone. Docksai, who would later serve in the Army's Eighty-second Airborne, found him dependable and notably clear in his guidance, "much more military than Bill Buckley."

Rusher placed a lot of emphasis on simple prudence. Count to ten, he would tell YAF leaders, before taking action in a difficult circumstance. Similarly, as Docksai debated leftists around the country and thus risked violent confrontations at times, he urged: "Never debate alone. Have a flotilla with you."[42] Docksai thanked him for speaking at a convention banquet session in 1971, where YAF leaders had hoped to "impress certain harsh realities" upon the delegates. Rusher taught the most important of these lessons perfectly, in a "conversational manner which I later learned converted your whole audience." Even more, they liked his willingness to socialize with them afterward. That discussion would "live in history," the chairman wrote, for all the YAFers "who never dreamed of *personally* spending time with William A. Rusher."[43]

## Reactions to the Counterculture

Despite his ability to mix well with many young conservatives, Rusher remained mostly a creature of habit. He was "born a Tory," as a Princeton classmate later recalled, and always preferred dignified surroundings. In 1965, Rusher had protested television's encroachment at his University Club. "Thanks most sincerely for your letter of June 4th, containing the good news that Seasoned Ry-Krisp will soon be available again," he wrote the manager. Would it also be possible to separate the main bar, formerly "one of the most civilized places in town" but now an unlikely spot for quiet conversation, from "that dratted" television and the few who insisted on watching it? The backgammon room, Rusher suggested, could be partitioned off for either the traditionalists or the TV watchers.[44] The next decade would be a trying one indeed.

Rusher continued to urge that the magazine pay serious attention to the younger generation's growing radicalism and what it might mean. In early 1968, he had asked the editors to finally commission, assign, or write a thorough analysis of the large intellectual differences between the New Left and the old economically oriented socialist or communist Left. At the time, Rusher was less hostile than he had been two years before, when praising the "New Mutants" article in *Partisan Review*. He now thought conservatives might use the differences between the two Lefts to their own advantage—and that the newer Left was right on some points. Alternatively, he wondered: "Surely we can at least have some fun with all this?" These possibilities had become especially clear to him when debating Carl Oglesby, a former president of Students for a Democratic Society, a month earlier. To the editors, Rusher praised his opponent for condemning the "utilitarianism, positivism, and pragmatism which are the identifying characteristics of the dominant rationalist materialism in America." Similarly, his debates with radical journalist Robert Scheer and with Ted Keating had "turned out to be joint bombardments of liberal audiences."[45]

As the New Left's sensibilities spread and its actions grew more extreme, Rusher focused on denouncing the movement rather than on finding common ground in antiliberalism. In a 1969 lecture titled "The New Barbarians," he denied several explanations for the violent campus protests the previous year: youthful exuberance, lost parental influence, genuine educational grievances, idealistic insistence that America live up to its values. "Baloney! . . . They are inadequate rationalizations." The truth was much uglier. Rusher noted that Oglesby "made a brilliant attack on the 'liberal establishment'" when they debated, but "had no program, and he made no bones about it. I commented to him, 'My friend, you haven't got program enough to keep a flea circus alive for an hour, let alone American society.'"

Behind the student radicals, Rusher argued, was a total and purposeless "nihilism." Acting merely from "primitive instincts," they were "bent on one thing only: the destruction of the society that gave them birth." The blame for this stretched back to the relativism among a previous generation in the 1920s through 1940s—not communists, but people who had been swept by the "liberal interpretation of ethics." In the raucous occupation of the Columbia University administration building in 1968, president Grayson Kirk straddled "both sides of the barricade," Rusher said. "Part of him was in that office fending them off, and the other part was out there banging on the door . . . In a way, he sensed he was boxing with himself and he had lost."[46]

Seeking a guest appearance on *The Merv Griffin Show* in 1970, Rusher noted that in the last two years he had debated not only mainstream liberals such as journalist David Halberstam and some congressmen but also countercultural figures like former SDS leader Tom Hayden, Youth International Party (Yippie) cofounder and Hayden's fellow 1968 Chicago Democratic convention militant Abbie Hoffman, and prizefighter-turned-draft-resister Muhammad Ali, a convert to the black Muslims. Among his lectures in the past year, the topic most in demand was "Have Students Gone Crazy?" It was, he told the *Merv Griffin* producers, a "basically negative analysis" of the current college generation.[47]

Having voiced his contempt for bearded and peyote-inflamed youngsters as early as 1965, Rusher now tried to keep *National Review* itself from becoming infected with any such sympathies. In 1970, a young reader complained that it took an excessively negative attitude toward the youth culture and gave only one-sided commentary on the student revolt. Its tone was gratuitously hostile, according to Tom McSloy, who had previously edited a college conservative magazine. *NR* bristled with jibes that "place you pretty far into the Pig Camp," and he was "damned tired of those little innuendoes" against things young people liked. Although it did run occasional pieces on rock music, there was no regular column on it. There had been a feature on marijuana but no follow-up. The magazine hadn't "come to grips with . . . whether cops beat up on kids or not." McSloy also suggested an article on long hair. Thanks to *NR*'s uptight attitude, he had a hard time reaching his peers with a conservative message; its "put-downs" made the task even harder. Upon reading one of the editor's columns, a young man whom McSloy had worked to influence complained: "'You told me this Buckley guy was so groovy—why he's just an old fart like the rest of them!' Well, of course you're not, Mr. Buckley. But the magazine does have its moments."

The editor found these observations significant enough to run four pages in response. Burnham, Priscilla Buckley, and Jeffrey Hart (seven years younger than Rusher and recently made a senior editor) were conciliatory: McSloy wasn't right about everything, but what he was right about was important. Rusher and Meyer disagreed, insisting the young man was almost completely wrong.

Hart disliked McSloy's partial identification with radical protest against college administrations but sympathized with his points about rock music, in which he saw interesting developments worth serious attention—despite the "repulsive cultural circumstances in which it is often encountered." Managing editor Priscilla Buckley assumed that *National Review* wouldn't "abandon any of its basic beliefs" in order to attract the people McSloy represented, but called for an attempt to "make a teen-ager or college student eager to pick up and read" the magazine. There should be "a major effort," she wrote, "to explore and answer the questions these young people are raising." Burnham agreed with McSloy that for young readers *NR* was, in Burnham's words, "too often irrelevant, undiscerning, philistine and stuffy." He urged that the magazine show a "humane appreciation of the causes" underlying their concerns about Vietnam, race relations, wasteful consumerism, and pollution. It should run serious analyses of major New Left intellectuals. It went "too easy on business and businessmen, bureaucrats, pompous conservatives," and the Nixon administration. And it could be "too solemn about the youth antics," Burnham added, some of which were "largely put-ons that can be laughed at."

Meyer, Rusher's ally here as elsewhere, wasn't laughing at all. He gladly accepted placement in what McSloy called the Pig Camp, telling readers: "All I can say—and with enthusiasm—is 'oink.'" He condemned the student revolt as a rebellion "against the standards of Western civilization" and a "radical speeding up of the glacierlike erosion of those standards by liberalism over the past decades." Rock, marijuana, and loose sex might be mere issues when viewed individually. But in fact, they converged as "the sacred symbolism of the revolt against the West . . . as clearly as long hair (per se only a matter of taste) is the uniform of its armies."

Rusher too rejected McSloy's challenge, arguing that his letter sought approval of the trends it was citing. *NR* should concede whatever merit some aspect of the cultural revolution might have, but seeing the general situation was more important. The youth rebellion signified what the magazine was "founded to expose, denounce and resist," Rusher argued, "the disintegration of those normative standards which are the fundamental precondition of any viable society whatever." He gave McSloy credit for wanting to respect *National Review*; goodwill of that type was "not lightly to be thrown away." But fortunately, student riots had reached the point of exhaustion, drugs were becoming less glamorous, and society was regaining "its equilibrium on the whole subject of youth."

The publisher also saw a latent conservative impulse beneath the revolt. He suggested that McSloy and most of his generation really craved "the sense of solid ground beneath their feet—of a moral horizon that remains fixed—of a known and dependable and *therefore* valuable relationship to their society and to the world." Certainly that was all *National Review* could offer them. It could only "preserve and hold forth a respect for truth and logical processes to which they can repair with confidence, and perhaps with relief, when the passion for novelty and mere sensation has subsided a bit in their young and hungry hearts."[48]

Several months before, Rusher had proposed a different connection with this generation. In 1967, a young man at Indiana University named R. Emmett Tyrrell Jr. started a magazine called the *Alternative*, eventually renamed the *American Spectator*. Tyrrell and perhaps one or more of his staff, Rusher now suggested, might be made correspondents of some kind. It might be worth giving them a page in each issue or every other one to "sound off (with appropriate editing) from the standpoint of conservative students." On a recent trip, he was "powerfully impressed with the flair and cleverness of their publication, the general quality of their writing . . . and their devotion to the general viewpoint of *National Review*." Rusher urged: "If we really want to be 'relevant' to the present student generation, this strikes me as a far better way to do it than by publishing effusions about the Woodstock Festival. As a matter of fact, I think it would give our publication quite a dose of monkey glands!"[49]

Monkey glands or not, Rusher made his virtual despair about most young people clear in a 1970 criticism of Goldwater's new book, *The Conscience of a Majority*. As he noted in his review, unlike *Conscience of a Conservative* it was the senator's own product, based on oral dictation. Goldwater, he told readers, showed "a confidence in the general run of present-day youth" for which there seemed little basis. The senator (now sixty-one; Rusher was forty-seven) cited the admittedly "impressive fact that he speaks on perhaps a hundred college campuses every year." But Rusher spoke at roughly one-third as many, "and I totally lack his optimism." Although his negative feelings didn't apply to conservative young people, most of the generation looked dismal. Without perceiving their low caliber, one misunderstood the times:

> It is true, as Goldwater doggedly insists, that the real troublemakers are in a minority; but they are, almost everywhere, a dominant minority, leading a bemused and plastic majority. When Goldwater calls for the eighteen-year-old vote and abolition of the draft, he is betting on strengths that simply aren't there. But here we have come to the edge—and end—of Barry Goldwater's world. To speculate on what it takes to keep a society going, and whether America today has whatever that may be, is to step through the looking-glass that bounds his universe. To Goldwater, America is quite simply the greatest country in the world, and its people the greatest people; the

rest is detail . . . His vision is limited to what a conservative twenti-eth-century American might safely be expected to see.[50]

## Enforcer, Gourmet, World Traveler

Despite his alienation from much of the youth generation, Rusher got along well with some of the junior talent at *NR*, including John Coyne and a bit later Joe Sobran. Coyne had as his first assignment a cover story on Mayor Lindsay, running successfully for his second term in 1969. Rusher tutored him in New York politics. "The door was always open," Coyne recalls, "and he was generous with his time." Sobran remembers the publisher as "kind and gentle" in their many talks over the years. Coming to *National Review* in 1972, he initially considered Rusher a somewhat "forbidding man, but the better I got to know him, the more lovable I found him to be. He was very fatherly to me." As the most devoted Shakespeare expert and enthusiast at the magazine, Sobran also found that Rusher had a substantial knowledge of the playwright's work and "knew his stuff" when it came to poetry.[51]

What he disliked wasn't new or young colleagues, but rather the possi-bility that some might either weaken *NR*'s character or dilute his own influ-ence. Already in 1968, Rusher had criticized the role a few youngsters were playing in the weekly editorial meetings. Chris Simonds, Phil Ardery, and Lawrence Chickering—"none of whom may, as it happens, accurately be described as a conservative"—had enthusiastically intruded into a debate on the side of Burnham. "I don't suggest that their contribution influenced Jim in the least," he told the editors, "but they do most definitely serve to distort what might be called the median line, or consensus, of these confer-ences, and that is, or ought to be, important." The meeting hadn't really been typical, he added scrupulously, because Buckley and others weren't present. But it was indicative of how editorial decisions and "tendencies" were now being shaped. "I would be the last person on earth to minimize in any way the importance of Jim Burnham's contribution to the editorial policies (let alone quality) of *National Review*," the publisher explained. "But I think even he might concur that we are falling somewhat short of a salu-tary collegiality if the position of this magazine on important questions is to be determined by him alone, after I have shot my bolt and departed [for my office work], leaving him restrained only by the exiguous conservative impulses (if any) of Messrs. Simonds, Ardery and Chickering."[52]

Rusher continued his long-standing office strictness at *NR*, and behind the exacting words was a man who matched them. His trim pronunciation and always-short hair seemed "almost severe," Richard Brookhiser noticed after starting there in 1976. Rusher stood in stark contrast even to the physical environment: messy and dirty offices, Priscilla Buckley later wrote, "became almost an Olympic sport" at the magazine.[53] "He was the enforcer," notes Linda Bridges, who was hired at *NR* after graduating from college in 1970 and would eventually become managing editor. "New people who came into the office were quickly told, by the ones who'd been around a while, that he was the bad cop. He was the one that Bill Buckley had brought in because he, Bill, couldn't bear to fire people—or discipline them, really." Rusher was "always being very stern" about things, "so we kind of got a kick out of it when Jim Burnham would tease him, as he would at every editorial conference." One example of the publisher's attitude was his seriousness about working a truly full day and week. On Friday afternoons, he would make the rounds at about 4:45 to see who was still there. But even in that, he could have a light touch, once asking Bridges: "Are you left alone to tell the tale?"[54]

Rusher had trouble with secretaries, or at least many of his own. Although "basically a nice, kind man . . . he didn't know how to treat a secretary or a clerk or a mail boy who was sensitive," according to Priscilla. One problem was "the nitpicking aspects . . . If he told a secretary to take a paper to Frances [Bronson, Buckley's secretary beginning in 1968] for Bill, and she wasn't back at her desk in four minutes, he would call around to find out where she was—that kind of thing, which drives intelligent people nuts." They also "couldn't stand the fact that he wouldn't say 'good morning' when they came in," Priscilla recalls. "Bill, especially in the early years, had a different attitude towards people who were inferior in rank than the rest of us did. We were all informal, and the mail boy was calling [Buckley] 'Bill,' but he was always calling Mr. Rusher: 'Mr. Rusher.'" Once, after several secretaries had quit, Rusher asked her and Buckley to explain what he was doing wrong. Buckley "finally said: 'Bill, it's something like saying: Good morning, Mary. Did you have a nice weekend? Or: Mary, I heard your mother was sick. How is she?' Bill [Rusher] wouldn't think, ever, of being personal that way." But he changed over the years. "I think he learned to be better with his secretaries—and he ended up having some absolutely devoted ones, who would do anything in the world for him."[55]

Even before moderating in this respect, Rusher got along very well with Ann Turner, his secretary for much of the 1960s. He also showed a sense of humor about his tendency to fire secretaries or not keep them. In the early 1970s, he once called Priscilla, needing a new one yet again. She shared the experience in the next anniversary issue. He felt, Rusher had said, "a little like the Roman impresario who calls a talent scout and tells him, 'One of my Christians just died. Do you know anyone who would like a big night in the Colosseum—one night only!'"[56]

His toughness at work and disapproval of the new times hardly kept Rusher from enjoying his leisure. For more than a decade now, he had been accustomed to lengthy overseas vacations owing to Buckley's "very nice" rule that both he and the publisher could take an indefinite amount of time off whenever they wished. To an extent, these vacations mixed business and pleasure. In late 1967, Rusher had initially planned only another trip to Taiwan. Buckley either told him to visit or reinforced his interest in visiting ("I would certainly include") South Vietnam and most of the other countries that ended up on his itinerary, subsidized by *NR* and the anticommunist Asian American Educational Association. Rusher should please learn what he could in the way of "news, contacts, local color and travel data" about the Far East and the Southwest Pacific.[57]

Rusher's pride in his sophistication remained hard to conceal. "As for my wine," he joked to a traveling companion, businessman Tom Stalker, after their South American tour at the end of 1965: "I think you are probably right—you have nothing to offer that would entitle you to a single drop. I doubt you could appreciate it anyway; you are an Inca Cola man if I ever saw one."[58] But although he enjoyed the best accommodations when he could— the Grand Hotel in Taipei, the Raffles in Singapore—his sense of adventure didn't always require comfort. After Buckley traveled to Antarctica in January 1972, Rusher asked for a paragraph or two of impressions: "It is a place I have always wanted to visit." Describing a trip to Easter Island later in the decade, he told readers he had "bounced over the dirt tracks and lava-strewn fields . . . from one end to the other" in a truck with its museum curator and resident archaeologist. They climbed up three volcanoes and descended into a cave that was "carved in a lava cliff by eons of pounding surf." Rusher had decided to see Easter Island at the end of a visit to Chile. "Thor Heyerdahl, the intrepid explorer . . . called it 'the loneliest inhabited place in the world.' Loving superlatives, I couldn't resist."[59]

The frequent world travel, according to his friend Daniel McGrath, "probably had to do with his insatiable curiosity." In the late sixties and early seventies, the publisher often took his trips with McGrath, an admirer of *National Review* who became, on Rusher's recommendation, a member of its board. He was in the advertising business and did most of the media planning and ad-buying for the Jim Buckley campaign in 1970. Six years later, he was similarly involved in the senator's unsuccessful reelection race against Daniel Patrick Moynihan. McGrath had many qualifications for extensive travel with Rusher. He was still single and thus could find the time, he could afford it, and he could drive—a skill that Rusher, a virtually lifelong urban resident who lived just a few blocks from work, never learned. And his political views were nearly identical to the publisher's.

The only unfortunate thing about getting married in 1976, McGrath recalls, was having to give up the trips. They were "almost like a Ph.D. in the world. Bill was just so knowledgeable about everything, and of course he was well-connected." Often they met with high-level government officials—especially in Taiwan, where Rusher "was a legend," and South Africa, whose government he sympathized with and generally defended in the newspaper column he began writing in 1973. Among their vacations was one of the four round-the-world trips (five, counting the wartime sea voyage to Bombay) that Rusher would take in his life. "Bill said it was 'the right-winger's ultimate fantasy tour. We only went to countries run by colonels and generals.'" [60]

In 1971, Rusher wrote in a piece for *NR* readers that although he had visited "almost every country and city on earth for which a kind word could be said," he expected to stay in New York. At one point he "fell hopelessly in love with San Francisco, and often wished I could start my life all over again beside that beautiful Bay—until, I grieve to say, San Francisco became so infested with beatniks, acid-heads, bums and weirdos, and so placarded with leering invitations to Topless this and Bottomless that." Rusher had also speculated about moving to London, with its "ambience of an older society that has learned how to combine discipline with grace."

New York, his original choice, was still right for him even though his initial reasons for living there, early ambitions in the law and elective politics, proved wrong. Even though the prevailing attitude among the city's residents was "a kind of smart-aleck nastiness," the streets were filthy, and the traffic was awful. Even though one-eighth of New Yorkers ("largely blacks and Puerto Ricans, imported by cynical politicians for their votes and herded into fetid ghettoes") were on welfare—living in such "misery and monotony" that they often resorted to crime or unconsciously attempted the "slow suicide" of drugs. Manhattan remained "indisputably the white-hot nucleus of mankind's whole effort, the cultural and intellectual capital of the world." She was "a barbaric beauty," thrusting "blazing spires into the black night sky."

In cuisine, the city reigned "absolutely supreme." As a bachelor, Rusher ate only breakfast at home, otherwise relying on restaurants. He had, by this point in life, compiled a list of around eighty in New York that would justify a visitor's attention. Café Nicholson on East 58th Street served an "inexcusably rich" chocolate soufflé and as much house wine as you could reasonably hold. It must have been some classy "turn-of-the-century Cairo brothel" that inspired the decor: a huge Tiffany glass chandelier, marble tables and alabaster statuary, Dutch tiles on the walls, a green parrot "dozing . . . atop his ornate cage." Then there were the two Le Perigords on East 63rd and 52nd with their exceptionally courteous staffs. The Four Seasons in the Sea-gram Building, featuring one of the world's most elegant dining rooms, had invented dozens of deliciously ingenious dishes. Nicola Paone, the *NR* hangout since the late 1950s, was a personal favorite as well. Its namesake owner was, "in a quiet, wholly commendable way, a fanatic . . . sampling every sauce, watching every order, greeting every customer, brooding, as only a Sicilian can brood, over whether he dare leave the actual cooking to anyone else, even for an hour. Try his baked clams *origanati*, followed by his veal *pizzaiuola*, and then drop me a note of thanks."[61]

Accordingly, Rusher and Dan McGrath ate out together often. Rusher shared maxims rooted in his mordant wit. "Ride the decline," he would say, meaning: If society is going to hell, enjoy life while you can. "When you find a good thing, run it into the ground." He inspired his younger friend to join a costly association of wine connoisseurs for a year. On one occasion, McGrath recalls, "we had dined at some very upscale restaurant on the East Side . . . and we came out of the restaurant, and Bill said: 'Dan, tell me—what does Nelson Rockefeller have that we don't have? You only eat one good meal at a time.'"[62]

There was a large, adamantly held exception to his appetite for international travel. He refused to visit a communist country, "because in theory you had to ask their permission to set foot there, and I didn't think they had the right to grant permission. So I would just wait until they were thrown out, and then I would go." His friends "knew my rule," Rusher recalls, "and in some cases didn't particularly approve of it. I remember saying to Buckley, at one point, that I would no more go to the Soviet Union on vacation than I would, if Hitler had permitted it, have skied in the Austrian Alps during World War II. He took exception to that, for some reason . . . It's a rather specialized point of view, I think. It handicapped me a little bit, but I stuck with it."[63]

## Fame on Television

Rusher the sophisticate hadn't lost his taste for confrontation with political opponents on the air. In early 1970, *National Review* proudly ran a long exchange with Theodore Sorensen on Barry Farber's radio talk show. The former speechwriter for President Kennedy was expected to announce a run for the Senate. Rusher immediately went on the attack, reading from a three-year-old article in which, the magazine's note explained, Sorensen said "he could not possibly be a viable candidate for the Senate from New York." Annoyed, he began "referring to Rusher, apparently in a spirit of contempt, as 'Mr. Busher.' Finally, as Rusher continued to read from

Sorensen's own 1967 description of his various disabilities as a senatorial candidate, Sorensen . . . had his finest hour since helping to write Teddy's TV statement on Chappaquiddick." The Camelot wordsmith overreacted, and Rusher nailed him:

> *Sorensen:* Mr. Busher, you're frustrated, you're bitter, because you represent a point of view that has never succeeded in getting the people of this state behind it. George Wallace represented it, fine. The local Nazi Party represented it, fine. But you have never been able to get either the Democratic Party or the Republican Party to accept the kind of racism and militarism that is preached by your publication. And I fully understand why you are bitter and frustrated and angry and resentful at any moderate politician who may come along. So go right ahead and vent your spleen on me. I understand completely.

> *Rusher (to Farber, who is groaning):* Let me have this, if I may. Just stand back for a moment.

> *F:* Will somebody first explain the "Busher" reference? I don't know who "Busher" is. I know who Hitler is.

> *R:* I take it that Mr. Sorensen is making this mistake intentionally. (*To Sorensen*) Is that right?

> *S:* No, I'm sorry; I'm sorry. "Bill Rusher." I thought it was "Rill Busher."

> *F:* Well, who is "Busher"? Why should I be the only illiterate in the house?

> *S:* "Rusher"; I've got it, okay.

> *R:* Well, now that we've got that cleared up, where in my publication, Mr. Sorensen, *National Review*, is racism advocated?

> *S:* I will be glad to get that out for you and send it to you after I've had my librarian check it.

> *R:* You'll be glad to get it out for me and send it to me?

*S:* I will indeed.

*R:* Well I'll make a little date with you, Mr. Sorensen—and Barry knows I keep these things—we'll come back on this program and hear where and when *National Review* advocated racism, and perhaps you can show it to me; and if you can't, at that point I'll call you a liar . . . You may think you've been in New York long enough to be a viable candidate for the United States Senate, but on the basis of your hysterical showing this evening you wouldn't make a viable candidate for dog catcher of New York City.

*S:* Now it seems to me, Mr. Rusher, *you're* being rather hysterical.

*R:* Yeah, but I'm not running for the Senate . . . You do want to stick to the charge? You wouldn't want just to withdraw it, would you, by chance? Because you're going to be required to, if you stick to it. (*Long pause*) Take your time and make up your mind.

*S:* About what?

*R:* Do you want to charge that *National Review* has advocated racism?

*S:* I think the policies supported by *National Review*, and the candidates supported by *National Review*, have not advanced race relations in this country.

*R:* But that's not quite the same thing. Are we advocating racism, or have we?

*S:* I just stated my statement . . . Well, let me ask you: Do you support the Kerner Commission report [on the causes of black riots]?

*R:* No, I think it's wrong.

*S:* Well the Kerner Commission report, I think, pointed out very clearly what white racism is in America.

*R:* Yes, I know perfectly well that it blamed the troubles of America in the race area on white racism, and I think it was wrong to make that particular emphasis at that time. But you have made a specific charge, Mr. Sorensen, and you might as well inaugurate your campaign by either backing it up or withdrawing it. Does *National Review* advocate racism or not?

*S: National Review,* in the sense of the Kerner Commission report, has contributed to this result. That's exactly right.

*R:* In what sense is that? (*Pause*) What kind of a weaselly statement is that?

*S:* That's not a weaselly statement. As you've just pointed out, you don't agree with the Kerner Commission report.

*R:* And therefore I'm a racist? Anybody who disagrees with it is a racist?

*S:* No, of course not.

*R:* Well then, what?

*S:* What what?

*R:* Well then, what is the point of bringing it up? . . .

*S:* [*NR*] has contributed to the atmosphere of racism that has unfortunately set back race relations in this country.

*R:* And it has done this in what way?

*S:* In its articles.

*R:* Which articles?

*S:* And in the candidates it has espoused.

*R:* Which candidates?

*S:* And in the policies that it has backed.

*R:* Which candidates?

*S:* And I intend to send you the documentation.

*R:* You're aware that we opposed Wallace, are you not? Maybe you're not. It occurs to me that you probably aren't.

*S:* Well, you opposed Wallace because you had Mr. Nixon, who was equally close to your point of view.

*R:* And you think that supporting Richard Nixon makes us racists, indirectly or directly?

*S:* No.

*R:* Well then, what does?

*S:* Why don't you wait for the documentation?

*R:* All right, that's what we'll do.

Sorensen failed to provide documentation, sending a retraction to Farber instead: "I very much regret having used the words 'racist' and 'American Nazi Party' in connection with the *National Review* during your radio show of February 9. My apologies to you and Mr. William Rusher for this unfortunate error."[64]

Later that year, Rusher began regularly appearing in living rooms as the conservative mainstay on *The Advocates*, a national show on PBS. The program featured two debaters, acting as lawyers, who argued cases for and against policy positions. In addition to making direct arguments, they called expert witnesses to question and cross-examine. A live audience surrounded the stage. Viewers at home, the jury, mailed in their votes.

Rusher, a traditionalist who disliked blurring lines of distinction, may have been slightly embarrassed at first. As he wrote apologetically to *NR* attorney C. Dickerman Williams, a former law clerk to Chief Justice William Howard Taft: "I am afraid that the 'court procedure format' . . . bears painfully little resemblance to anything you, or any other practicing lawyer, might be familiar with. Considerations of competence, relevance, materiality, etc. are wholly (and probably necessarily) disregarded; hearsay is welcome; cross-examination is not limited to the scope of the direct; etc., etc." Rusher added cheerfully that he and his liberal adversary Howard Miller agreed the show was "probably ruining both of us permanently" for real legal practice.[65] But even his first season was a success. "You have every reason to be extremely proud of the record you have turned in on *The Advocates*," wrote Buckley, himself a highly experienced debater.[66]

In its first year, before Rusher joined the program, the advocates weren't politically identified for the audience, and it was more a discussion than an ideological combat. But a liberal-versus-conservative theme was adopted starting in the fall of 1970. Miller, a young University of Southern California law professor and Rusher's opponent most of the time, was a "pure and unpolluted" liberal, as Rusher later described him, who might have "spent his nights sleeping under a bell jar in the National Bureau of Standards."[67]

The tapings were in Boston, where the producing station WGBH was located, and in Los Angeles, where Miller lived. On each show, the advocates took opposite sides of a specific policy question whose exact form required lengthy discussion. Despite the high quality of the *Advocates* staff, the two principals wanted to do this themselves. "People sat open-mouthed," Miller recalls, "as Bill and I would negotiate for a couple of hours or more over the precise wording." Despite the intensely competitive format, they got along well. "We became very fond of each other" and there was "never any personal animosity . . . I think we both respected each other's skills, just like good lawyers always want to be up against the best lawyers on the other side." Rusher never tried to land a low blow, "never crossed the line of antagonizing people because of his assertiveness."

His contacts among prominent conservatives made them more available as witnesses. Because the cross-examination—"the heart of the show"—was unrehearsed, Miller explains, "you really had to feel that the person who'd asked you to be on was straightforward" and was somebody whom "you could trust and would protect you. I think that was an important part of Bill's ability to get very high-profile people." The quality of the conservative witnesses Rusher could obtain, according to Miller, leveled what might otherwise have been an uneven field. "There were people who had been very suspicious of appearing on a PBS show, and this way they really felt great comfort . . . Bill overcoming that suspicion was a major, major advantage for the show." Rusher's presence was probably one reason why Governor Reagan appeared on *The Advocates* three times. When President Nixon imposed wage-price controls in 1971, a program was promptly taped with Buckley and free-market economist Milton Friedman as Rusher's witnesses and a major left-leaning economist, John Kenneth Galbraith, as Miller's main one.[68]

Defending FBI director J. Edgar Hoover against the proposition that he should be replaced, Rusher was, according to a Bureau report, "a tough-minded able advocate . . . for the Director and certainly was far more effective than anyone on the opposition . . . [investigative reporter] Jack Anderson, who appeared pretty sure of himself on direct examination, began to come apart under Rusher's cross-examination." Hoover immediately sent a thank-you note to Rusher, who acknowledged his "very kind comments."[69]

Debating a guest opponent, law professor Alan Dershowitz, on the death penalty, Rusher cross-examined a psychiatrist. "I participated in an execution in Iowa," testified Dr. Louis West. "We hanged a fellow there for murder. And as medical examiner, I stood at the end of a rope and listened to his heart slow down and stop. It took about twelve and a half minutes . . . I've studied it carefully for twenty years, and I'm now absolutely opposed to the death penalty for any reason." Unfazed by emotional points in debate, Rusher moved quickly to neutralize this one:

*Rusher:* I can sympathize with your feelings as you watched an execution. Were you, by any chance, the medical examiner who examined the bodies of Sharon Tate and Charlie Manson's four other victims?

*West:* No, sir.

*R:* You will recall that Sharon Tate was pregnant and that, I think, all of the victims had some thirty or forty stab wounds in them?

*W:* Gruesome murders, indeed.

*R:* Would you consider the gruesomeness of that spectacle a logical argument in favor of the death penalty?

*W:* No, not a bit.

*R (angrily):* Well, then, why do you consider the difficulties that you observed when a man was hanging as a logical argument *against* it?

*W:* I didn't say it was a logical argument.

*R:* Why did you use it?

*W:* I used it as a description of the onset of my study of this, which was based upon me as a physician participating in a procedure when a helpless captive was exterminated.

*R:* I suggest to you that you used it as an emotional device. Or perhaps Professor Dershowitz suggested that you do so.

*W:* Until you've been at a hanging, sir, don't put down the emotionality of it.

*R:* I'm not putting down the emotionality of it—nor the crimes that
were committed by Mr. Manson.

Rusher was proud that he won the viewers' vote thirty-three times in
fifty-eight programs. Given the home audience's political makeup, Miller
says, "even 50–50 . . . would have represented a triumph for him."[70] "Buckley,
rightly so, was known as a great debater," recalls Lee Edwards, who often saw
*The Advocates* with his wife, Anne. "But I think in a sense that Bill Rusher,
you could say, was even a better debater than Bill Buckley . . . I think he very
often would have a better command of facts, of figures: the lawyer preparing
himself for a particular presentation." The combination on their respective
shows was a "one-two punch," with Buckley on *Firing Line* more of "a jab-
ber," Rusher on *The Advocates* like "the knockout guy . . . coming at you and
swinging hard."[71]

Miller, who cross-examined Buckley on two or three *Advocates* shows, saw
one quality Rusher lacked: an ability to parry with humor, at which Buckley
was "matchless . . . It took maybe four of the six minutes just to get through
the humorous comments, to get to the substance of the question dealt with."

*Wagner International Photos*

Rusher was "much more the
rational debater on the merits. He didn't use diversions,
he didn't use humor to deflect.
He just came right at it, in
terms of the substance. He
never ran away from dealing
with the substance."[72]

*The Advocates* left a legacy
in the movement, according
to Edwards, by making many
younger conservatives want
to be as prepared, organized,
and aggressive as Rusher. It
was also part of "a growing
self-confidence that 'we can
stand up for what we believe
in.'"[73] As Miller points out,
it had a "much wider impact
than     an     equivalent     show

*Debating on* The Advocates

would have today, with the hundreds of choices" on cable television. Many members of Congress watched it, and both sides often talked with legislators and congressional aides in preparing their cases. It therefore made Rusher better known among politicians in addition to the audience. "A number of political figures got to know me at that time—a lot of them," he recalls. The memory often stuck: Rusher was that conservative debater on TV. "I remember once calling Newt Gingrich, before he was Speaker, about something that was happening in the Reagan administration that I was worried about . . . He gave me the names of six congressmen to get in touch with, and I said: 'Well, I don't know any of those people.' He said: 'No—but they know you.'"[74]

It was all a heavy commitment for Rusher, and he told Buckley in the middle of his first year that *The Advocates* had been taking too much of his time. He found himself "trying to desperately round up witnesses, flying hither and thither for tapings, and enjoying life rather less than I did back in the good old days."[75] But the executive editor at WGBH pressed him to reconsider his intended cutback in appearances. The show's improvement in its second year was due entirely to Rusher, according to Peter McGhee, who hadn't always agreed with him but especially liked "the sign of caring that invigorates every word you say on the air." Probably for this reason, the program was no longer "a dignified, gentlemanly, and largely irrelevant debate." It was now "a fight; well argued, well expressed, but a fight nonetheless. Some people are offended by that . . . but being offended may be one of the first steps on the road to thinking about things a little more."

Rusher said the compliments meant a great deal to him. But continuing to feature the same debaters all the time would tend toward monotony, and the show had drained his energy. He needed more time for his *NR* duties—and perhaps especially to "build up a little fresh physical, emotional and intellectual capital." On the other hand, *The Advocates* had "transformed" his life. WGBH could "depend on this old war-horse to come charging out of the tent again whenever you really need him." Rusher could do up to one-third of the debates, maybe more if that wasn't enough.[76]

His frequent appearances continued until 1973. The regular *Advocates* program ended the following year because funding dried up, although specials were occasionally produced later. Priscilla Buckley attributes Rusher's gradual mellowing partly to the PBS show by which "he suddenly became a national figure . . . I think that made him a little less nitpicking around *National Review* itself."[77]

In addition to arguing unyieldingly for conservative positions to the public-television audience, Rusher was intentionally symbolizing those in his generation who refused to make cultural concessions to the era. After taping an *Advocates* show with him in late 1970, Ernest van den Haag, a social scientist who taught in New York–area universities and also wrote for *NR*, politely offered a few suggestions. Rusher had done well, van den Haag explained, but "your image comes through as too combattive [*sic*] and up tight." Without changing his general style, he could make smaller adjustments by getting horn-rimmed glasses (preferably with a heavy black frame), growing his hair a little longer, and wearing tweed instead of a smooth fabric.

Rusher was sufficiently interested in the question to write a two-page response. He knew he came on strong, having understood this at least since he got heavily into radio debating a decade before. Over that time, he had given much thought to his public personality and firmly decided that "probably nothing can, and in any case nothing should, be done about it." Furthermore, Rusher felt a long-standing "resistance to the idea that I must 'appeal' to other people, 'win their approval,' or anything of the sort." In 1956, he had decided that politics, in the sense of either seeking office or "trying to be 'appealing' or 'persuasive,' was just not for me." Ever since then, he had enjoyed the freedom this insight allowed him. Rusher also told van den Haag that he had become steadily more "influential, and probably in the crass sense 'better liked' by more people," after abandoning any worries about popularity. Besides, if he was already winning most of the audience ballots, he must be doing something right.[78]

Van den Haag tried again, repeating that his concern was immediate impressions, not Rusher's basic "personality or manner," which shouldn't be changed. It seemed "part of the image you create is not intentional; that it actually does not do justice to your intent; and that it makes it harder for viewers to understand what you actually want them to understand." Conceding his advice was well intentioned, Rusher set van den Haag straight: "Let me assure you, my friend: There is nothing in the slightest accidental about the image I project. It is precisely the image I *want* to project—right down to the flag lapel pin and all of the other obnoxious parts of it. The fact that these attributes or characteristics are adjudged offensive by certain members of the younger American generation not only does not bother me; it positively gratifies me." Van den Haag answered simply: "I surrender."[79]

Rusher's distinctive features—natty dress, alert gray eyes, thick glasses, high forehead, tight mouth, thin light-brown hair—were evident and memorable on his compact 5'8" frame. A young *NR* writer, Keith Mano, noted that his voice could sound like an engine when they talked, idling audibly at a half-suppressed growl between sentences. His small apartment, neatly lined with books and *objets d'art*, had a living room that would "make a four-year-old whisper." Rusher saw a significance in his self-presentation at the magazine and elsewhere. "He was defiantly square, proudly square—

whatever he could do," recalls Kevin Lynch, a *NR* staff member and writer in the 1970s. "I mean, he was the real revolutionary in New York at that time, because he was just going completely against what everybody was doing, and perfectly confidently . . . He just relished that role."[80]

In contrast, the aggressiveness in debate and public speaking that Buckley and many others liked in him had a philosophical or strategic grounding. Rusher continued to believe, much as he had suggested in his 1958 memo to Buckley dismissing criticism of the editor's talk at the National War College, that a properly managed aggressiveness could get results.

# 11

# Running Right

Like Rusher, President Nixon wore an American-flag lapel pin. Like most *NR* conservatives and especially Rusher, he believed the major news media were deeply unfair, biased against conservative positions and against him. He spent large amounts of time trying to respond tactically to the problem.[1] The president saw several "thems" in American society, including the academic elite and the counterculture. But he perceived the media as the truly "formidable and infuriating" opponent, a "magnifying glass and public address system" for the others. According to speechwriter William Safire, Nixon's attitude was that they were "to be hated and beaten."[2] In addition, he was somewhat socially conservative, strongly opposed in private to forced busing for the purpose of racially balancing schools and against abortion on demand. He viewed both abortion and pornography as ugly signs of the times, associated with a decline of Western civilization.[3]

Nixon was long considered a hard-line anticommunist as well. Leftists and many liberals had hated him at least since 1950, when he defeated Helen Gahagan Douglas—"the Pink Lady," as her Democratic primary opponent had called her—for a Senate seat after a rough campaign on both sides. He had served on the House Committee on Un-American Activities, where charges of communism were first publicly made against Alger Hiss in 1948. Nixon played a significant role in the case and developed something of a friendship with the accuser. Among knowledgeable conservatives, such history could still matter. Buckley now told a friend: "Remember, a phony would not have got by Whittaker Chambers."[4]

Upon taking office, however, Nixon wanted to pull back from the Cold War, seeing a new age of multipolarity and a need for American retrenchment. He spoke of and seemed to endorse a new international order with five great power centers—communist China among them. While strengthening South Vietnam's ability to defend itself and continuing to fight there with substantial success, Nixon also made clear that he would bring the troops home without military victory, provided the country's government could be maintained. An early analyst of his administration's policies would conclude that although he opposed communism as an expansionist force, understanding it to be trouble for the United States, "anticommunism was not itself a basic value for Nixon." To him, the problem was the geopolitical behavior, not the thing as such.[5] But his anticommunist credentials remained useful in politics. According to Garry Wills, who covered and intensively reported both parties' 1968 conventions, Nixon promised southern delegations he would maintain military superiority over the Russians.[6]

Nixon was tacitly allied with *National Review* conservatives when they helped elect Buckley's brother to the Senate as a third-party candidate against an appointed Republican in 1970. Rusher was in the thick of it. Jim Buckley, who had challenged Senator Javits as a Conservative in 1968 and received an impressive 17 percent of the vote, initially refused when the party's leaders, Dan Mahoney and Kieran O'Doherty, asked him to run for the other New York seat. Later he approached Rusher for advice, saying he would run if he really had a chance. Rusher was glad to hear it. But rather than guess about such a race, he turned to Clif White, who then hired pollster Arthur Finkelstein to run a survey. It appeared that Buckley, a business lawyer who had never held public office and wasn't a natural politician, would start with a base of 25 percent whoever his opponent might be. Finkelstein told him victory was possible in a three-way race, Buckley decided to run, and White was brought on as campaign manager.[7]

Rusher found the campaign a finance chairman. He called his friend Lee Weil, formerly of the New York Young Republicans, and asked him to meet with White. Then a "struggling" stock broker at a small-to-medium-sized firm, Weil felt somewhat surprised when asked to take the position as they talked in a hotel bar. "I was joking with Clif and Bill," he recalls. "I said: 'Gee, my name begins with a W. You guys must have gone down the list until you got to the bottom. I mean, why didn't you pick somebody who was really well-known and more experienced?'" When the candidate and his campaign aide Dave Jones, a former YAF executive director, sought editor Buckley's recommendations about who should serve on their state committee, Buckley forwarded the request to Rusher: "WAR—Would you please reply for both of us?" The publisher provided a list of sixty-four names and addresses. He also met in Washington, on July 9, with White House speech-writer Buchanan to seek assistance or advice for the Buckley campaign.[8]

Photo by Henry Krupka of D'Arlene Studios, copyright Christina Krupka. Courtesy Ashbrook Center Archival Collections, Ashland University, Ashland, OH.

*With F. Clifton White*

The meeting was a natural one from a White House as well as a *National Review* perspective. Rockefeller-appointed incumbent Charles Goodell, who had succeeded Bobby Kennedy in 1968, proved to be a liberal Republican in the Senate, among other things greatly upsetting Nixon by advocating complete withdrawal from Vietnam. The Buckley campaign, under White's direction, used carefully chosen appeals to the Right and its sympathizers while avoiding hard-line economic conservatism. Nixon allowed or told Agnew to signal negativity about Goodell and sympathy for Buckley, and the vice president did so. The president also helped the Conservative candidate by helping to cut off Goodell's financial support.[9]

Meanwhile, Barry Farber, long an admirer of Rusher, was running against Bella Abzug, a virulent leftist who had defeated a Democratic congressman in a primary on the Lower East Side. Because of Abzug's extremism, the talk-radio host had an unusual set of endorsements, winning not only the Republican but also the Liberal nomination and the backing of the old Socialist Party. His supporters included anticommunist social democrats such as Albert Shanker, president of the main New York City teachers' union, and civil-rights activist Bayard Rustin. The Conservative candidate, who had not anticipated Farber's Republican nomination, also wanted to endorse him but couldn't get off the ballot. Some conservatives were reluc-

tant to help a candidate who had the Liberal but not the Conservative des-
ignation. Rusher was "smart enough to know," Farber recalls, "that the best
anticommunists in America were the founders of the New York Liberal
Party."

Attending campaign meetings and giving advice on dealing with the
media, Rusher put significant effort into the congressional race. The complexity of the Senate campaign—Goodell the liberal Republican, Congressman Richard Ottinger the Democrat, and Buckley the Conservative—posed
a problem to a House candidate with diverse ideological support. Rusher
took him through "that minefield," Farber recalls. "I remember him smiling, as time after time he would say: 'Barry, your answer is: New York is fortunate in having more than one good candidate.'" Farber was delighted with
the help. "I couldn't have asked for a better supporter, or for better answers."
Able now to handle questions effectively in front of the camera, he became
"a mini–Bill Rusher on more than one occasion."[10] Farber lost by only about
eight thousand votes.

Rusher grew confident of Buckley's prospects in the Senate race. Judy
Fernald, hospitalized after surgery, could see no hope for the campaign, but
on a visit to his friend well before the election, Rusher predicted their man
would win. "Bill told me what was going to happen and the way it was going
to happen," she recalls, "and as I lay there watching TV, I could see exactly
what Bill said coming to pass—and Jim Buckley won." *National Review* and
the movement were gratified by the unusual victory, achieved without a
Republican nomination. Nixon even invited Bill and Pat Buckley, plus the
two Conservative Party founders and their wives, to his retreat in the Baha-
mas after the election.[11]

## Suspension of Support

Events in 1971 placed the president's relationship with conservatives under
great stress. They were already disappointed by extensions of big government: high domestic spending, the enactment of vast new environmental
laws to be enforced by the newly created Environmental Protection Agency,
and the Family Assistance Plan, or FAP. The proposed welfare policy, which
included a guaranteed annual income for the poor, was sold to the president
as a means of reducing bureaucracy.

The White House had welcomed the public's conservative mood or reaction against liberal excesses, attempting to use it in the 1970 elections with
meager results, Jim Buckley's upset in New York notwithstanding. But Pat
Buchanan, a strongly conservative voice among the White House staff, had

plenty to complain about in a January 1971 internal memo. He cited the
proposed new federal budget aimed ambitiously at full employment; Nixon's
related remark that "I am a Keynesian now," meaning he thought deficits
and higher government spending were sometimes good economics; and the
fact that the president had not only proposed the FAP welfare plan but even
regarded the failure to enact it thus far as one of his greatest disappointments. Indeed, when the White House congratulated itself, it did so for liberal things. Nixon was "no longer a credible custodian of conservatism,"
Buchanan wrote.

Bill Safire, a moderate speechwriter on the staff, responded by questioning how strongly average conservatives really felt about their ideology.
Buchanan's standpoint reflected the "spoken opinions *but not the attitudes*
of most people who identify themselves as conservatives." Most of them,
for example, worried more about unemployment than "the intellectual ideal
of a balanced budget." Bill Buckley and his following, Safire argued, didn't
"represent the gut feelings of the majority of people who accept the label
'conservative' in their voting patterns." Belief systems among the public had
grown less clear and stable. The political center was the place to be.[12]

On July 15, 1971, Nixon announced a visit to the People's Republic of
China in which he would explore the possibility of a normalized relationship
with its communist government. The United States had yet to diplomatically recognize the twenty-two-year-old regime in Peking—owing partly to
pressure from the so-called China Lobby, a mostly conservative alliance that
favored "Free China," the independent and increasingly prosperous island
of Taiwan. Rusher, who had already made numerous visits to the country as
a guest of its government, admired it greatly. He was far from alone in this.
For strong anticommunists on the Right, Taiwan was both an ally of America and an inspirational symbol of freedom. "Red China" was the product of
mass murderer Mao Tse-tung and was still ruled by him.

Simultaneously, Nixon pursued the lessening of tensions with the Soviet
Union, known by the new term *détente*, and began to reduce the defense
budget. The Russians, conservatives feared, had caught up with the U.S. in
strategic nuclear weapons or were getting close—and this in addition to
their dangerous conventional military superiority in Europe. The administration was risking further slippage, many conservatives thought, by the way
it had been dealing with nuclear weaponry in the Strategic Arms Limitation
Talks. In a column in May, Buckley wrote of its "public nonchalance" about
how an effective American strategic deterrent would be maintained. Under
pressure from the spirit of the times, which encouraged "the superstition of
détente," Nixon was "fiddling . . . while Rome burns . . . sitting in the White
House while the Soviet Union is accumulating a first strike capability."[13]

On August 15, perhaps motivated by the political angst of facing reelection in a year, Nixon announced a "New Economic Policy" that included a three-month period of wage and price controls. According to a key aide, economist Herbert Stein, the president didn't actually think wage-price controls were a good idea but believed public opinion was demanding immediate relief from inflation and that he must go along with the idea. According to another high-level aide, Arthur Burns, he was convinced on the merits.[14]

Most of the Washington-based movement conservatives were "furious at Nixon" in these months, recalls Jeff Bell, then a staff member at the American Conservative Union. Knowing firsthand how seriously he had betrayed their principles, they believed "we had to fight Nixon or . . . lose our soul as a movement." In January, leaders of the ACU, YAF, *Human Events,* and *National Review* had already begun holding meetings at which they expressed policy concerns; in May, they met to discuss possible responses.[15] On an afternoon in late July, leading conservatives met again, this time at Buckley's Manhattan townhouse. Deciding to issue a public statement criticizing the administration, they debated how strongly to word it. Burnham suggested the idea of "suspending support" for Nixon—rather than repudiating him, as some wanted to. Uncomfortable opposing the president so directly, Buckley agreed with Burnham. The group, known to itself as the Manhattan Twelve, carefully negotiated a statement, as Bell later remembered, that would "keep Bill on board."[16]

Its signers included Buckley, Burnham, Meyer, Rusher, Conservative Party chairman Mahoney, and leaders from the ACU, YAF, and *Human Events.* Because Buckley vetoed several specific complaints about domestic issues, ACU chairman Stan Evans refused to add his name. Published in *NR* on August 10, the manifesto complained briefly of "excessive taxation," "inordinate welfarism," and other domestic-policy disappointments. But these were presented as far less important than Nixon administration "tendencies" in foreign policy. While applauding the president's refusal to pull out of Vietnam, the statement complained of his "overtures to Red China" and "*above all,* his failure to call public attention to the deteriorated American military position, in conventional and strategic arms."[17]

In the *Times* several weeks later, the popular conservative political novelist Allen Drury dismissed the statement from "the pouting panjandrums of the Righteous Right . . . the Moody Elves of the Miffed Minority" as ineffectual "hysteria." Conceding that Nixon was taking risks in foreign policy, he argued that the president was "perfectly capable of shifting strategies overnight if he decides his course is wrong or really dangerous." There were, Drury agreed, "many disturbing trends that appear to be adding up to a steady and perhaps irreversible increase in Soviet advantage." But in the case of both Russia and China, the president might well have good reasons for his policies. Nixon's patriotism, intelligence, and diligence could be presumed; without proof to the contrary, it seemed "a little ridiculous to abandon him."

In response, Rusher began by accusing Drury—who noted in his piece that he had been "around the White House for a while in connection with a book"—of being "coopted to defend the President." The Manhattan Twelve statement, he told *Times* readers, had been personally kind to Nixon and had given him credit for some "solid achievements." Rusher added that he didn't question the president's good intentions or expertise but rather his judgment. Both before and after the statement was published, he had heard "some of the very highest officials in the country" admit the "shocking facts" about America's current defense situation. How could Drury suggest that administration decisions be accepted on faith? A president wasn't "an omniscient mastermind."[18]

Rusher strongly opposed the moves toward Red China and further détente with the Soviets. But in regard to pocketbook issues, he wondered whether it was realistic to expect a president to uphold principle firmly. He wasn't sure Americans wanted to insist on self-reliance anymore. Commenting the previous year on decadence among the 1960s generation, he had asked: "And what is to become, in the long run, of these young people . . . I have a hunch that this is what the [proposed] guaranteed annual income is all about: a subliminal decision, on the part of the American society, that it is going to have to carry about 7% of the population on its back, permanently."[19]

Conservatives "are right about economics—in theory," Rusher now told the editors, shortly after the wage-price controls were announced in August. For two and a half years, Nixon had done his best to follow such principles. "He precipitated a small but necessary recession, and deliberately threw a substantial number of people out of work—all at very considerable peril to his skin, which he deliberately risked in the name of sane long-range economics." Now, seeing that "this would simply lose him reelection," he had done "what *almost* any President would do: scrapped the game plan and adopted a new one designed to produce short-term economic and political gains at the cost of longer-range misfortunes impossible to measure." One could imagine a president, Reagan or perhaps Goldwater, who would be so principled as to accept defeat "rather than engage in demagogy." But Rusher waved away the possibility. "I don't think conservatives can reasonably expect to elect many (if any) such Presidents in a world as wicked as this one." In a previous column, Buckley had tolerated the possibility of wage-price controls on different grounds, describing such a decision by Nixon as a good way to discredit an unwise policy liberals had been calling for.[20]

At the initial Manhattan Twelve meeting toward the end of July, Rusher later reminded Buckley, he had been willing to state a case for Nixon. But the departures from conservative principle had piled up ever since. Rusher would later write that his "personal and final" break with the administration came over Taiwan, officially the Republic of China. In the years since its founding in 1949 by the mainland's defeated Nationalists under Chiang Kai-shek, the country had, he agreed, a staunch friend in Nixon.[21] Now that long-standing friendship seemed to be gone, and especially outrageous to some conservatives was the expulsion of Taiwan from the United Nations in late October 1971, while Red China was admitted. The U.S. nominally opposed the expulsion, but arguably Nixon's moves toward rapprochement with Peking had paved the way.

The next morning, Rusher called Buchanan at the White House, explaining in what he would recall as his "iciest tone" that he wished to say goodbye to the administration. He invited the speechwriter to come along. "'Yeah?' Pat croaked, nervously but noncommittally. 'Where're we going?'"[22] It was a difficult question. Most Republican officeholders didn't speak out publicly on either the policy toward China or the wage-price controls. Senator Goldwater agreed with the decision to approach Peking, although he opposed the UN admission. Governor Reagan favored the trip, calling Nixon's attempt to engage the regime a "bold and decisive move." When the disgruntled conservative leaders decided, toward the end of the year, where they were going, conservatives in office didn't follow. Of the Manhattan Twelve statement, Rusher would later admit: "I don't think it had a particular impact in the party."[23]

But the signers also decided a statement wasn't enough. At a September 20 meeting of a portion of the group, Rusher was instructed to contact a consultant who would be asked to prepare a report on political action that those in the conservative movement who agreed with the Manhattan Twelve might take against Nixon. On October 12, Jerry Harkins, who had been in charge of the 1964 Goldwater campaign in Missouri, was hired to look into the possibility of running a primary candidate against Nixon. On October 21, the group decided to draw up a list of demands that would be given to White House counselor Charles Colson.[24]

To Rusher, a centrist or liberal-leaning Republican administration was a dangerous disappointment, and conservative politicians who didn't attack one for such failings were shirking their responsibilities to the cause. "I cannot recall when American conservatism has been in greater disarray," he would tell Buckley in March 1972. "Not even under the early Eisenhower: for he not only presided over nothing so ruthlessly violative of conservative principles as a $40 billion deficit, or wage and price controls, or the present

defense posture, or the Peking communiqué, or FAP, but such conservative
spokesmen as there were . . . had fewer compunctions about opposing him
publicly. As a matter of fact, modern American conservatism largely organized itself during, and in explicit opposition to, the Eisenhower Administration. Under your leadership."[25]

As the Manhattan Twelve considered whether to back an anti-Nixon
candidate in the 1972 primaries, however, there was some dissent against the
idea. Meyer told them he didn't think "we have either the candidate or the
potential money to make a primary threat realistic."[26] Another signer of the
manifesto, Anthony Harrigan, a vice president of the Southern States Industrial Council and a sometime conservative journalist, suggested the group
could be politically credible only by helping a third-party campaign—a tactic that might prove effective by tipping electoral votes away from Nixon.
A New Hampshire primary challenge would only make their faction look
impotent and isolated. Harrigan also questioned the emphasis on foreign
policy and defense. They weren't "gut issues" to average Americans, who disliked the liberals but didn't read the conservative press and commentators
much. Ordinary people worried more about welfarism, crime, and school
busing. To have a stronger impact on politics, the Right's intellectuals must
stress domestic issues with "high emotional content." All these points were
"well taken," Rusher replied.[27] His interest in social issues as conservative
issues would increase in the coming decade.

## Protest Candidate

The Manhattan Twelve met again in late November and decided, having
heard Meyer's and Harrigan's objections, to encourage a conservative candidacy against Nixon in the primaries. Jerry Harkins had looked into New
Hampshire and concluded that a candidate from the Right might do well
there.[28] Rusher, *Human Events* editor Tom Winter, and YAF chairman Ron
Docksai approached John Ashbrook. A national Young Republican chairman in the 1950s, Rusher's old ally in the YRs, and a congressman from
Ohio since 1961, the potential candidate had also been a cofounder of the
Goldwater drive and the ACU chairman. In the House, he had an essentially
perfect conservative voting record.[29]

Rusher hoped for a best showing of 15 percent or more, and the White
House took the situation seriously at first. In December, Buchanan offered
three pledges on the president's behalf if Ashbrook didn't run. There would
be a clear signal that Nixon would choose Agnew for a second term, another
clear signal that the FAP welfare proposal would be dropped, and certain

increases in the defense budget. Ashbrook and his advisers shrugged off the proposed deal.[30] Rusher, meanwhile, continued to encourage the emerging candidacy, attending a dinner on December 13 at the National Press Club in Washington, where the congressman was urged to enter the race, and giving him a personal contribution of $1,000 at the event.[31]

Two days later, the vice president met Buckley and Rusher for breakfast in New York. He wanted to convince them that the administration was moving rightward and that an Ashbrook candidacy was a bad idea. Following his lawyerly instincts, Rusher wrote a detailed recollection of the meeting for himself. Agnew, he recorded, told them the administration planned to boost the next defense budget by 4 to 5 percent. Rusher responded by citing what he heard from a Washington journalist: that the administration wanted the new Pentagon budget to *look* as large as possible and that the few billion dollars would never be spent. Agnew and his aide David Keene, "deeply distressed" by Rusher's reaction, insisted "we should not believe such obviously trouble-making reports from an inimical reporter."

The vice president then told Buckley and Rusher that he believed the White House liberals were losing their clout but didn't explain how or why. He also said he was prepared to insist that the president's chief domestic-affairs adviser, John Ehrlichman, be replaced. But if Ashbrook should run, "I'll be through in any case," Agnew warned. Nixon would either choose the insurgent as his running mate to calm the conservatives or pick a liberal like Rockefeller if he felt resigned to losing them. Rusher recorded in his recollection: "Mr. Buckley and I both tried to assure him that, unless he alienates the Ashbrook backers totally, his leverage with Mr. Nixon will actually be increased by an Ashbrook candidacy in the New Hampshire Primary; but he was not to be consoled."

Buckley and Rusher stood their ground with Agnew, making it as clear as they could that Nixon needed to "make much more persuasive and effective concessions to the right than have recently been forthcoming, if fatal trouble is to be avoided." Rusher "specifically told the Vice President that, if a bright young Ph.D. had been selected on July 26th [when the Manhattan Twelve began meeting] . . . and told to devise the most offensive possible series of gestures toward conservatives . . . he could not possibly have done a better job than had been done by the President himself in the ensuing months." The memo said nothing of Agnew's reaction.[32]

According to an extensive analysis of the 1972 campaign by the liberal-Republican Ripon Society, the Committee to Re-Elect the President leaned heavily on Goldwater, Reagan, and their supporters, as well as young congressmen associated with the conservative movement, not to endorse Ashbrook. It also successfully pressured potential large donors not to back him.[33]

At the same time, a more principled argument could be made that Nixon was constrained by the Democratic Congress and shouldn't be blamed unfairly. In a statement at the end of December, Goldwater said he could understand Ashbrook's objections to certain administration policies but denied the president was "in any way at fault for our present defense posture." The man responsible was Robert McNamara, defense secretary under Kennedy and Johnson from 1961 through 1967, who "cut back so far on research and development that serious gaps now exist." Each year, Nixon sought more money for national security, and Congress turned him down. Goldwater, a member of the Senate Armed Services Committee, added that the president had led the battle for the antiballistic missile system (ABM) and that the administration had "time and again . . . taken the lead in fighting for new items of defense." Reagan, also precommitted to Nixon, said during the campaign that he was in "complete disagreement" with the congressman's challenge.[34]

Like Rusher, Ashbrook didn't habitually defer to objections by major figures or to predictions that he would not succeed. Keene fondly remembers his stubborn rationale for the campaign. "I said: 'John, why are you doing this? You're not going to get more than 10 percent of the vote,' and he said: 'Someday, we're going to want to be able to say—We weren't there.' I often quote that now." Conservatives, Ashbrook meant, would be better off challenging Nixon than tacitly accepting policies they disagreed with, because such an acceptance would associate them with those policies and their results.[35] But even so, a primary campaign against the president under the circumstances probably required an individualistic sort.

Rusher remembers Ashbrook as personally "affable and gregarious" and as a "well-versed politician" with a sharp mind. But he was "not a team player," tending toward political solitude. "He didn't join any of the caucus factions in the party in the House—or if he did, he didn't pay much attention. He went his own way, did his own thing." Although this limited Ashbrook's effectiveness among congressional Republicans, Rusher still thought quite highly of his fellow Harvard graduate. After serving for twenty-one years, the congressman would die at a tragically early age of an abdominal hemorrhage in 1982 while running in a Senate primary. At a meeting not long thereafter, "I told a group of conservatives in Washington that his memory was so vivid we could almost expect that the door might open . . . John would come in, with his coat over his shoulder, and say: 'Hi, how are you all? How is everybody?' You just expected geniality of him."[36] Buckley held a high opinion of Ashbrook as well, writing immediately after his declaration of candidacy that he was "among the world's most charming, intelligent and natural men." After the campaign had run its modest course,

Buckley noted that the congressman was "articulate . . . patently sincere, moderate in his rhetoric, compassionate in tone."[37]

Announcing on December 29, Ashbrook noted that Nixon in 1968 had spoken of the need to end large federal deficits and to avoid economic regimentation, also saying he would oppose the guaranteed annual income plans already being discussed. Similarly, the president had now walked away from his 1968 position on defense—that America needed superiority to the Russians, not mere "sufficiency" or parity.[38] Ashbrook's backers, including Rusher, hoped he would do well enough in early primaries to enable fundraising for strong efforts in later ones—especially California, where many conservatives reportedly were ready to vote against Nixon. Rusher kept his promise to campaign a bit for the congressman, speaking over the course of two days in late February at Dartmouth and St. Anselm colleges and also in three New Hampshire towns; he campaigned for a day in Florida as well.[39]

Just before the primary season, a *National Review* editorial explained supportively to readers that the candidacy was intended to prove the existence of a strong conservative element in the Republican Party and to show Nixon clearly that this element rejected some of his policies.[40] Buckley, however, although he had joined in Rusher's insistence at the recent meeting with Agnew that the president tack strongly to the right, opposed an actual race by Ashbrook. And as he noted impatiently to a White House friend who criticized *NR*'s friendliness toward the campaign, his own preference that the congressman not run quickly became common knowledge in Washington. But since Ashbrook was running anyway, there was now a competition between him and another insurgent, antiwar Republican congressman Pete McCloskey of California, to win the largest protest vote in New Hampshire. In this context, the editor explained to Nixon aide Peter Flanigan, *NR* naturally backed the conservative.[41]

In his column, Buckley wrote that Ashbrook's candidacy might prove to be counterproductive but was at least expressing "an élan vital in the conservative movement" and a return to the lapsed tradition of conservative "soldiers" in Congress doing "round-the-clock-duty." In the spirit of 1964, and "agreeing with him [Goldwater] that the world threat is apocalyptic," Buckley added, the Right could not "accept with continuing docility the policies responsible for leading us to the brink."[42] He also publicly urged Ashbrook to promise he would endorse Nixon for reelection. This assurance would probably bring him more votes, Buckley wrote, given that many people wanted to send a message but didn't "want to associate themselves with someone who is dallying with Republican mutiny." Rusher, in contrast, saw the Ashbrook challenge as the possible beginning of a third-party campaign. After their December meeting, Agnew wrote to Buckley that although he had "great respect" for Rusher's ability and integrity, he hoped the publisher could be "dissuaded" from such an intention. In response, Buckley appeared to distance himself from Rusher's political judgments: "My colleague is a very passionate gentleman and that's OK. But it doesn't make for the most purposive discussions."[43]

*National Review* strongly endorsed Ashbrook on January 21. Dissatisfied with the editor's own limited support, however, Rusher told him at the end of the month that his personal involvement mattered considerably. Right-wing publisher William Loeb, through his paper the *Manchester Union Leader*, would deliver the votes of the most ideological conservatives. But he was "cordially detested by just about everybody else in New Hampshire," Rusher warned, "and it would be fatal for Ashbrook to become known as 'the Loeb candidate' or anything like that." Buckley would be of more help. "Your name . . . strikes favorable chords in the minds and hearts of about a third of Republicans and independents up there—which means that you are much the most important endorser Ashbrook has, as far as New Hampshire is concerned."[44]

Despite the campaign's poor funding and inability to air the television ads that were produced, its lack of support from elected officials, and its association with hard-core movement types, Jim Burnham—longtime Rockefeller admirer, advocate of a Nixon endorsement in 1960 even if "you think the captain is lousy"—thought Ashbrook was on a worthwhile mission. "However things turn out in percentage terms," he told Buckley in early February, "I continue to believe that his running is a necessary operation, both from the point of view of an honorable portion of the conservative constituency and for the historical-moral record." Burnham might vote for the president anyway, but not because Nixon was "my leader." Rather, he would be "(or would like to think myself) in an autonomous section of a pragmatic united front." The Ashbrook campaign was the only way to symbolize the independent kind of relationship many conservatives, including Burnham, preferred to have with less-principled figures such as the current president.[45]

The primary challenge, Rusher now told Buckley in similar terms, had "preserved the conservative position—not in good health, to be sure, but at least alive and capable of being fought for." The *New York Times* was "obviously trying to . . . pin the new Nixon positions to the wall as the limiting definition of responsible conservatism," he added, suspicious as always of the liberal media. "Anything to the right of these is henceforth to be regarded as mere kookery . . . This, I trust I need not say, simply cannot be permitted. If we accept this for an instant, conservatism—at least, conservatism regarded as anything other than a vagrant impulse on the part of certain members of the Nixon Administration, to be consulted by the President when and if he pleases—is simply out of business . . . [and the] fight that *National Review* has waged—that you have waged, and I have waged—is, quite simply, over."[46]

Two weeks later, when Ashbrook seemed in danger of a third-place finish behind Pete McCloskey in New Hampshire, Rusher downplayed the state's primary as he had in 1964. When the campaign was being planned, he hadn't expected such a situation. Later he was "taken considerably aback" by the observation of an Ashbrook supporter in the state that any liberal could expect about 20 percent in its Republican primary. In 1968, Rusher told Buckley, write-ins for Rockefeller and liberal Democrat Eugene McCarthy, plus a small vote for George Romney, had totaled 18.5 percent in the GOP contest. But Rusher urged the editor not to worry too much about New Hampshire. A week later in Florida, Ashbrook would probably do much better. Its Republican voters, mostly "solid middle-class people," often had a Midwestern background and were far more representative of the party than "the introverted burghers of New Hampshire." And the next serious test after Florida wouldn't be until California in June.

The intervening period, as Rusher pointed out, would coincide roughly with *NR*'s annual fund appeal. He applauded the "cautious" stance the magazine had taken on the Ashbrook campaign and wouldn't object to columns and editorials that were "relatively objective, largely reportorial" in their treatment of it. Still, Rusher strongly opposed "any public change" that would make it sound like Buckley was actually dropping Ashbrook. The *NR* fund appeal might suffer in that case. Furthermore, Ashbrook would be around long after the 1972 election. He would, Rusher predicted, become an increasingly prominent spokesman for conservatives dissatisfied with Nixon. Any "well-publicized departure" by Buckley would leave a bad taste with the candidate.

Rusher would accept a "gradual diminuendo in your . . . degree of warmth" toward the campaign, especially given the editor's closeness to the Nixon administration and some of its major personnel and supporters. But an obvious abandonment by Buckley would, in addition to the other problems Rusher cited, lead to a "public difference of opinion among major blocs of responsible conservatives" about the Ashbrook challenge. Yet another negative result was that any kind of clear change in his position would be so widely overinterpreted: "treated by the national press as an out-and-out bolt from the Ashbrook candidacy, a master-stroke for the administration, a gratuitous stab in the back (by many conservatives) and, generally, a major contribution to the growing fissure" in the movement. In a tone of elegant desperation, Rusher added: "I urge you most humbly to consider whether any purpose you aim to serve by such an action will bring rewards commensurate with these desperately disagreeable consequences."[47]

Four days later, a week before the New Hampshire primary, Buckley appeared with Ashbrook at a press conference in the state and personally endorsed him—although he talked more about Nixon's China trip, from which he had just returned. Before leaving for Peking, he had also recorded radio spots for Ashbrook.[48]

Buckley, who participated in the trip as a journalist, grew increasingly angry about the president's dealings and conduct with the communist Chinese leaders. The joint diplomatic communiqué adopted before Nixon returned to the U.S. had "substantially altered" the American position on Taiwan in three ways: by making no reference to the security treaty between the two countries, by pledging to remove American forces and military installations, and by stating that the U.S. did not challenge mainland China's claim to the island. The communiqué was a "staggering capitulation," Buckley wrote in a column at the end of February. It lacked even "one word on the applicability of our principles of self-government and independence to the people of Taiwan." America had "lost—irretrievably—any remaining sense of moral mission in the world."[49]

Agnew's aide Keene was right in his prediction. Ashbrook approached but didn't break 10 percent even in California, his best state; nor had he improved upon his comparable New Hampshire showing in Florida, Rusher to the contrary. In addition, Buckley went against Rusher's and the candidate's wishes by describing the California campaign as "implausible."[50] But Ashbrook had an impact nonetheless. His race drew substantial enthusiasm from YAF volunteers, while Richard Viguerie's professional fund-raising for it expanded the pool of potential direct-mail donors to conservative causes. The insurgency may also have turned Nixon to the right on some domestic issues and helped to keep Agnew on the ticket.[51] Both the visit to Peking and the later Russian trip in mid-1972, on the other hand, boosted Nixon's popularity. During the Moscow summit with Soviet leaders, the president told chief of staff Bob Haldeman the reelection campaign should focus on foreign policy, since that was where he would gain the most new votes.[52] Outside the movement, denunciations of Nixon's leftward drift on defense and communism from conservative spokesmen like Buckley had fallen on deaf ears.

The next decision was whether to back the president against an especially liberal Democrat. An increasing number of people on the Right had come to think a Nixon defeat in 1972 might be acceptable, that a Democratic president might be better for conservatism than such ideological confusion. Rusher had written to Buckley early in the year that whatever limited ideological satisfactions conservatives would get from a second Nixon term might be outweighed by the advantages of standing in opposition to a Democratic administration.[53]

But the general election, it turned out, was between Nixon and George McGovern. The South Dakota senator, who defeated Hubert Humphrey and other more traditional Democrats for his party's nomination with a powerful grassroots campaign, was the favorite of the antiwar and countercultural Left that year. Undeterred by the prospect of such a presidency, Rusher wrote a piece that argued against voting for Nixon. Since he held the rank although not the title of a senior editor, it had always been his privilege to write in opposition, under the magazine's Open Question heading, to any editorial with which he disagreed. This time Buckley was reluctant to allow it. "I felt that his position was eccentric," he later explained. "And that to have the publisher attached to that position would hurt *National Review*. It would make it sound flaky."[54]

Rusher got the piece into the *Los Angeles Times* instead—hoping Nixon would read it over breakfast at his San Clemente getaway. "For conservatives," he began, "the presidential election of 1972 is truly the winter of our discontent." Conservatism had "all but vanished as a force in American politics." Nixon had made a mockery of "almost all of conservatism's basic principles . . . largely silenced its leaders, confused or seduced a good part of its following and effectively paralyzed the whole conservative movement." As to whether McGovern was really preferable as president, Rusher called it a "hard question." Opposition from the Right to liberal proposals "would be vehement and frequently successful (many would never become law), whereas under Mr. Nixon such opposition is for all practical purposes nonexistent."

Recent history confirmed his perspective, Rusher added. During the Kennedy administration, the movement "grew from the fancy of a coterie to a national force." In the Johnson years, it captured the nomination for Goldwater; it also kept control of the Republican Party thereafter. Furthermore, pressure from the Right prevented Kennedy and Johnson from adopting certain policies Nixon later got away with. Both the conservative cause and the nation "would on balance . . . actually do better, in raw policy terms—under, and in spite of, a President McGovern." Rusher tempered his prediction by adding: "At a minimum, we would be compelled to watch the steady disintegration of the American society and either resist it or confess our acquiescence in it, rather than have it shielded from our sight by the comforting but wholly meretricious notion that a vote for Mr. Nixon is somehow a vote against it." Meanwhile, he would sit out the presidential race and concentrate on down-ballot elections.[55]

*National Review* endorsed Nixon early in the general-election season, saying a campaign with such a challenger was no time to "assign blame for the failures" of the last few years and that the possibility of his winning was "not something with which a grown-up superpower can play." While acknowledging the argument that a McGovern administration might serve to strengthen the conservative movement, the editorial denied "that the chance is worth taking . . . Too much hangs on the possible consequence of George McGovern's exercise of the power that has attached to the Presidency." Under the circumstances, any other arguments were "frivolous."[56] A previous editorial by Burnham had called the senator's campaign an "enemy," not merely an opponent. Rusher's ally Meyer had passed away earlier that year, but according to his elder son, he undoubtedly would have voted for Nixon against McGovern.[57]

Although Rusher had come to reject Nixon as a leader of the Silent Majority and as a president, he felt pleased by the size of his reelection margin, close to Johnson's over Goldwater. The antiliberal vote had been nearly as large in 1968, but it split because many social conservatives and southerners went with George Wallace. The major new development in 1972 was that the economic and social conservatives backed the same candidate. McGovern's massive defeat was the "clearest possible" demonstration, Rusher later recalled, that "liberalism in 1972 commanded the allegiance of far less than a majority of American voters." It seemed that a "precarious but powerful antiliberal coalition . . . was now the dominant fact in American politics."[58]

# 12

# Years of Doubt

nxious about ineffective leadership among conservatives, Rusher prodded Buckley to strengthen the identity of *National Review* so it would reclaim what he saw as its lapsed political role. In making similar complaints previously, he had done so with more allies. Now *NR* was a lonelier place for its brooding publisher. The previous Easter weekend, comrade Meyer had died of lung cancer. When Rusher remarked to a friend at the open-casket visitation: "First time I've ever seen Frank Meyer without a cigarette in his hand," it was a nod to the stubborn intensity he admired in his late colleague and elsewhere. Another ally, Bill Rickenbacker, had left the editors' roster after the 1968 election. The main interests of Dartmouth professor Jeffrey Hart, for the last few years a senior editor, were "literary, philosophical, and cultural rather than political."[1]

Brent Bozell, once an instinctive activist like Meyer, was a lost internal ally and perhaps a lost opportunity: "a brilliant man and a wonderful speaker," Rusher recalls, "and in many ways much closer to the political arena than Bill Buckley ever got. I thought myself—many people did—that he had a brilliant future ahead of him in Republican and conservative politics."[2] Instead Bozell drifted away from the conservative movement, becoming one of its first famous exiles. For the past several years, he had edited a traditionalist Catholic journal called *Triumph*. In 1969, Bozell wrote that the movement was now dead because it was based on false, secular principles.[3]

## "Less *Something*"

The magazine, Rusher warned his colleagues more empirically in January 1973, had lost much of its old distinctiveness, and complacency and snobbery in its higher councils were preventing it from recovering its true style. Among those who had known it longest and best, perceptions that *NR* had mellowed excessively were now typical. It was wrong to assume certain people's opinions ("Who cares what Mrs. Bonbrake thinks?—what Neil McCaffrey thinks?—what Dan Mahoney thinks?") didn't matter. It wasn't just "right-wing Catholics, nostalgic for Willi Schlamm" who were criticizing the magazine, Rusher added, and the editors shouldn't ignore complaints "on the comfortable assumption that *National Review* clearly occupies higher social or intellectual ground" than its critics.

Everyone there had grown older, so they naturally tended to see the world differently. Rusher himself did. But the fact, or certainly the perception, was that the magazine had become "less *something*." He listed several possibilities for what the missing element might be: "conservative," "pungent," "rabid," "effective," "brash," "vigorous," "youthful," "shrill." Not all of those qualities should be encouraged, but Rusher couldn't believe "we are gaining as much as we are losing." Adding to his warning, he noted that paid circulation, which had peaked several years earlier at more than 135,000, had now sunk to between 105,000 and 110,000. The editors seemed to be faced with two alternatives: "Can we recapture our old ability to criticize—constructively . . . but also sharply, vividly and brilliantly—the tendencies and directions of the American government and society? Or are they, in our present collective opinion, beyond all but muted criticism?" If the magazine felt "basically satisfied with those tendencies, and with the men who direct them . . . how can we best put out a *gruntled* journal of opinion?"

Perhaps conservatives' current weakness offered *NR* a good opportunity. Events in the last decade had rendered the movement almost unable to "define, let alone organize" itself, and nearly all of its leaders were "badly compromised by their own faltering performances." Rusher proposed that this arid situation might be a sort of kindling, ignitable by a "new spark." He wondered: "Have we really tried hard enough?" The question was rhetorical. He believed the editors hadn't.

> I asked, at an editorial conference not long ago, and I ask again: When was the last time *National Review* became condignly *indignant* about something? We can hardly expect the American society to get very upset about anything, at least in a conservative direction, unless we do it first; yet our general tone, even when we choose to disapprove of

something, tends to be rather languid and soigné. We get our kicks, and give our readers many of *their* kicks, by freakish capers along the lines of the Hoax Papers, or by publishing articles in support of marijuana, abortion, the "New York Times," etc. But "Man Bites Dog," while a notoriously good headline, can hardly serve as a policy—and would cease, even if it were one, to be much of a headline.

To illustrate this mentality, Rusher cited the facile dismissal of two suggestions he had recently made. In labor disputes where a work stoppage would be "clearly aimed at the public convenience" rather than at economic pressure on the employer, he thought *NR* might endorse a ban on strikes as well as compulsory arbitration. That, he was told, was "fascism pure and simple." Rusher also urged that *NR* pay attention to the media's growing claims to political power—evidence of which was their "savage counterattack" under way against the Nixon administration. No, he was told, Agnew had said essentially that back in 1969.[4] For use in future meetings or correspondence, Rusher began to set down more such examples. Among eleven ideas and policies brought up were a proposal to make Social Security voluntary for people with an adequate private retirement plan, Governor Reagan's proposal to constitutionally limit taxes in California, and a possible editorial attack on environmentalists for having made further energy development next to impossible in America. Nothing was done about nine of the eleven ideas. Burnham had deflected several: "this did not seem to be precisely the appropriate time"; "questioned whether anything was wrong with Social Security, beyond the philosophical point"; "the desirable course would be to blur the issue"; "conservatives are really of two minds on the question."[5]

Writing to Buckley, the publisher got more specific. "Briefly," he explained in a long memo sent to Switzerland that winter, "I have come to the conclusion that the problem is Jim Burnham. More precisely, it is the problem of your all-too-frequent absence, together with Jim's presence (and editorial dominance)." Rusher added: "Nobody appreciates more than I do the strengths that Jim Burnham brings to *National Review*." But he reminded Buckley that things had changed. "In the old days, there were any number of proud, powerful, independent spirits around the office, boiling with new ideas, good and bad, big and small. Nowadays there are pitifully few of us willing or able to put a fresh, challenging and specifically *conservative* idea before Jim with any serious hope that it will receive his approval."

Rusher continued:

I know whereof I speak, because I have tried—and tried, and tried. I don't suppose you are deeply familiar with the way the editorial conferences are run in your absence, but Priscilla can fill you in. I almost always manage to have some suggestion for a hard-hitting editorial with a relatively fresh conservative proposal or angle. They are not, by a long shot, always good ideas; but some of them are. At least, they are if I am able to judge from the fact that I have no difficulty finding them subsequently in Jeff Hart's syndicated column, or in passing them to you for consideration and use in [your column] "On the Right." But the rule so far as *National Review* is concerned when Jim Burnham is presiding seems to be: *ils ne passeront pas.*

It was Burnham who had claimed that compulsory arbitration to settle public strikes was fascist—and in a recent column, Rusher was "delighted" to see, Buckley had called for consideration of it himself. In that column, Buckley briefly mentioned New York City's disastrous strikes, ranging from public transit to garbage collection to the schools, in recent years. The laws against strikes by public employees had simply been ignored. With more of these expected in the near future, "we should look again into the concept of compulsory arbitration." Buckley also cautioned that it "smacks unpleasantly of the syndicalism of the proto-fascists" in Europe and therefore should, as Rusher too had said, be limited to fields in which a strike would substantially affect the public.[6]

As for the publisher's idea of paying attention to "the major counterattack that the media have finally launched against the Nixon administration" and their related demand for a comprehensive shield law to protect reporters from testifying when confidential sources were relevant to a criminal case, Burnham had responded incorrectly that Agnew had said all this before. At the next editorial meeting, therefore, Rusher had stressed the difference between what he was saying about the media and what the vice president had said. At that point, he recounted to Buckley, Burnham allowed his "tremendous animus against Nixon to boil over . . . and said at last what was really on his mind: namely, that he thinks the present Nixon Administration is the most outrageously secretive and Byzantine in American history," implying that the press's aggressiveness against it was wholly justified. Hart had remained silent at this point—and understandably so, since "he is no match for Burnham." Rusher also warned that "Jim's frequently unstated, but apparently growing, hatred of Nixon is becoming a problem in and of itself." Although Rusher's own general attitude toward the president hadn't changed, he told Buckley, he was "guardedly pleased" by the recent peace settlement in Vietnam and by indications that Nixon's domestic policy was becoming more conservative.

The main point was that *NR* needed "a vigorous, innovation-minded top editor, and that we have not got," Rusher wrote. "You yourself could, and no doubt would, do the job if you were here week after week. But I am afraid that when you do turn your attention fully to the problems of the magazine, your own sense that 'it has been a long time between drinks' may impel you do to something zany . . . or simply shocking and dependably news-worthy . . . rather than emitting a laser-like beam of high-grade conservative ideas. That job devolves inevitably, upon Jim Burnham. His competence and his judgment are legendary, and deservedly so. But as Jeff Hart remarked to me the other day when I was turning over the problem with him, Jim basically wants *National Review* to be a sort of American version of the 'Economist'— analytical, respected, rather remote. That is where we are heading (if we are lucky), and it most certainly is a world away from what *National Review* started out to be."[7]

Buckley conceded that Rusher had made his case "eloquently." He asked the publisher to keep track of further rejections by Burnham so he could address the issue. But it seems there was no further correspondence about it.[8]

In his capacity as publisher, Rusher told the editors in April that subscriptions and sales remained weak. This probably had many causes, he noted. But a market analysis by the *Gallagher Report* confirmed his belief that the magazine could solve much of the problem by becoming more obviously political. "Special-audience" publications like *National Review* should emphasize special-interest material, the trade journal's recent study had concluded. If they didn't, advertisers weren't likely to stay with them. For *NR*, Rusher wrote, this lesson would require a stronger focus upon its readers' distinctive interest—mainly politics with a "conservative twist or angle." He and his assistant Jim McFadden agreed, for example, that readers would take great interest in "matching articles for and against abortion, both written by noted conservatives." Another pair of articles should promote Agnew and Reagan, respectively, for the 1976 nomination. Agreeing with Rusher that *National Review* tended toward general rather than special content, Burnham left his own position unresolved. The "exceedingly convincing" analysis from the *Gallagher Report* was basically what he had been thinking himself. While repeating his ongoing concern for standards and his continued belief that *NR* should aim mostly at relative sophisticates, Burnham acknowledged the tension between this approach and the market.[9]

Rusher continued to press his case. When *National Review* was founded and for many years thereafter, it was conservatism's "leading spokesman" and even now it remained "unquestionably the class of the array," he told the editors in April. "But, as Satchel Paige might have remarked, don't look over your shoulder—somebody is gaining on you." Except for *NR*, almost everything else on the "responsible" Right was located in Washington. Back when the ACU and YAF were "umbilically linked to *National Review*" even though headquartered in the capital, the distance from New York wasn't such a problem. But now, Rusher added, a broader "Washington Conservative Establishment" had developed, and *Human Events* was slowly, although not always "very adroitly or very effectively," taking on certain journalistic roles that previously belonged to *NR*.

He seemed to expect a tepid response from his colleagues: "Does all this matter? I rather think it does, unfortunately." The editors should ask themselves where the average conservative now learned what conservative leaders were "thinking and saying and worrying about." In recent years, there had been a tendency "to make news by coming out *in favor of* decriminalizing pot—or for Bill personally to call for a Black President in 1980, or for the admission of Israel as the 51st state, or something like that. We find ourselves increasingly in the position of a man looking for a dog to bite. Meanwhile, the conservative troops increasingly march off to tunes drummed out by latecomers."[10]

It was partly from such concerns, partly as a matter of Republican politics that Rusher began aggressively criticizing the magazine's new Washington editor. George Will, then in his early thirties, was a Ph.D. in politics whose interests had turned toward public commentary. His main political background had been as a Senate staff member, notes John Coyne, who was then a speechwriter for Agnew and later returned to *NR*. Will took "a somewhat typical High Church/Senate view of policy and politics."[11] Even on that basis, the potential for Rusher to dislike him was already there. Some conservatives were also suspicious because Will had reached an agreement to write a weekly column for the *Washington Post*, thinking he might accordingly take more interest in pleasing people there than in pleasing the Right.[12] And in addition to his Washington duties for *NR*, Will became the magazine's book editor. Leading activists, according to David Keene, were disappointed by this because they viewed Stan Evans as Meyer's heir in certain ways, thinking it best that he inherit Meyer's "incredibly important" job.

On the other hand, Will's sophistication made him a real find. "Disdain, or lack of concern or respect, for conservatives was so widespread," Keene recalls. "Buckley was the one person who sort of broke through that. People took Buckley seriously because he was Buckley, and because he had traveled in a whole bunch of different worlds." The editor admired others whom "he thought could do that. George Will was one of them."[13]

Before being hired as Washington correspondent, Will had written the magazine's anonymous "Letter from Washington." In mid-1972, one of these columns urged that Nixon drop Agnew and choose another running mate. This position sharply contradicted *NR*'s policy toward the vice president, Buckley told Will, and therefore could be published only under a byline. But Will continued his negative comments, which led to complaints from Agnew's office. At an editorial meeting in December, he later recalled, Rusher told him he must get along with Agnew; in addition, someone said *NR* had already chosen Agnew as its preferred presidential candidate for 1976.[14]

In March, Rusher attacked a column Will had written about John Connally, who was also being discussed as a Republican presidential prospect in 1973. The former Democratic governor of Texas had been treasury secretary under Nixon, who considered him his worthiest potential successor.[15] In addition to disliking the fact that Will's column in the upcoming *NR* seemed to state a case for Connally, Rusher feared he might not write such a piece on any other possible candidate "let alone Agnew." That, he told the editors, would be "a bias we can ill afford to show at this stage of the game." Rusher saw a growing likelihood conservatives would focus on Agnew "and/or" Reagan for the presidency. He also thought Will was seriously overstating Connally's desirability as a candidate: "Moreover, how glamorous is this man anyway? Am I missing something? He looks and sounds like a younger Lyndon Johnson to me—and that is hardly a recommendation in American politics, at least as of the moment."[16]

Six weeks later, Rusher stressed to his colleagues that most leading conservatives in the capital disliked Will. *NR*'s modest presence there hadn't been helped by naming him as Washington editor—"and thus, in effect, as its ambassador to the Washington Conservative Establishment." Anxiety about the writer's frequent references to his disagreements with other conservatives, and a sense that Will was too concerned about what certain liberals thought, were in fact "widespread," according to Keene. "George's relationship to the Washington organized conservative-activist community was virtually nonexistent."[17] In April, Stan Evans quit his column for the *NR Bulletin* mainly because of Will's writings, telling Buckley he felt "increasingly out of phase with the drift of things at *National Review*, particularly the book section and the political coverage." Buckley replied that some of the opposition "frankly mystifies me, knowing his views as I do, and reading his opinions as I do."[18]

In June, Will's column angered Rusher by describing Agnew as "Mr. Nixon's Nixon, the spear-point of Republican partisanship . . . not the ideal instrument for healing a troubled nation," and continuing: "In addition, there are those who believe that Mr. Agnew has certain of the same character traits that have brought Mr. Nixon low . . . a certain morbid hypersensitivity, feelings of insecurity and inferiority regarding the press, the academic community and the establishment generally." That, Rusher told Buckley, was yet more propaganda from the "fast-dwindling Connally clique" and its tireless spokesman. Will must not be allowed to "open an unbridgeable gap" between *NR* and the vice president. Shortly thereafter, at the next Agony meeting, Hart backed Rusher on the point. Buckley, too, disapproved of the deprecatory remarks about Agnew, telling Will in mid-1973 that he hadn't lived up to his earlier understanding with the editors that his commentary on the vice president would be restrained. In addition, Buckley decided, he would need to begin attending editorial meetings in New York—for better general communication, but also to "hear from us . . . the meaning of the enterprise to which several of us have dedicated our lives." Will replied that he thought his "reasoned" criticisms were, in fact, permitted. It now seemed that *National Review* was becoming a political instrument. As a writer, Will added, he increasingly felt obligated only to "defend liberty and good taste." He believed a political movement was a far less important concern.[19]

With many readers also complaining about Will, Rusher attacked again at the beginning of August. This time he argued that the Washington editor had a "stonewall resistance to constructive criticism" and seemed to want only a loose relationship with the magazine—a concept irreconcilable with that position, Rusher thought. He had praised some of Will's columns, and he considered much of the writing "sinewy and provocative" despite an often "rather bitchy" tone. But Rusher emphasized that Will "does not have, and . . . has no intention of acquiring, the general cast of mind" appropriate to the Washington editorship. "At best, we might hope to badger him into near-total silence on the subject of (say) Agnew, continue dropping those of his columns that reach the heights of fustian approached by yesterday's, and maintain a cherry-picking operation to eliminate gratuitous slaps at [the late] J. Edgar Hoover, etc. But if that is the 'best' we can hope, it is not nearly good enough." Rusher concluded: "As an occasional writer of article-length pieces on the Washington scene, George Will would have a great deal to recommend him. As the Washington Editor of *National Review*, he is little short of a disaster."[20]

Two years later, in 1975—accusing Will of "consistent shilling for established liberal positions" and continuing to stress that he was not "a competent Washington correspondent"—Rusher predicted that Burnham's high opinion of him would prevail over these criticisms. "The pressure on Bill Buckley came from nearly every segment of Washington's conservative movement," Coyne recalls, but Buckley wanted to keep Will "because he thought he had a great talent."[21] To the editor of the Republican National Committee magazine, who regretted that the writer had become "a national spokesman for conservatism" and wished *National Review* hadn't helped make it happen, Buckley made exactly that point in 1974. Will's "anti-liberal polemics," he added, "are as effective as anybody's." The following year, Priscilla Buckley sounded a quiet note of praise in the piece she traditionally wrote for anniversary editions. Acknowledging the suspicions still heard from many readers that he was a liberal given his previous anti-Agnew and anti-Nixon writings, she wrote that Will had provided the magazine with its first "analytical" Washington column since Bozell's in the early sixties.[22]

The controversy seemed to be an especially clear case of Rusher's limited clout, although Buckley reluctantly removed Will as Washington editor in late 1974 after the publisher showed him a column in which the writer disparaged Reagan for his age. Buckley was disappointed a year later when Will left *NR* for *Newsweek*. Despite Rusher's continued "very active" participation in editorial conferences and quarterly meetings, the publisher had little influence on broad editorial policy in the 1970s, according to Hart. "Burnham was absolutely dominant, although I think on information about Republican politics, Rusher was authoritative and listened to."[23]

## Columnist and Nixon Defender

Rusher made up for his limited role at the magazine partly by starting his own newspaper column, The Conservative Advocate, whose title was inspired by his television identity. "It is not always easy to get my own ideas expressed in *National Review*," he told his aunt Mary Louise, shortly before the first column appeared on August 1, 1973. In addition, many conservatives had columns now, and he began to notice that they were "picking my brains" for them. "I decided I might as well write my own."[24] Rusher believed Agnew's criticisms of the media had helped to make his *Advocates* gig—and now his column—possible. In television and on op-ed pages, demand for conservatives had burgeoned; so had demand for conservative public speakers. The 1969 Des Moines speech in particular, Rusher thought, "gave conservatism a handy boost at just the right moment."[25]

Closely tied to the news, occasionally reflecting on larger historical or human themes, his Conservative Advocate column argued across the whole range of issues. It also gave significant attention to strategy for conservatives. As an activist at heart, Rusher didn't hesitate to uncritically publicize promising leaders and causes on the Right, otherwise perhaps unfamiliar. He wrote in a precise, polished manner but more simply than to *National Review* editors. He would usually include at least one quotable witticism, frequently his own and sometimes quite funny. While often contemplative, Rusher was more often the aggressive debater. Toward liberal positions and usually toward liberals, he wrote not just as a critic but as a hard opponent, determined to win the argument and the cause. He was tough on liberals' motives, especially in the media and elective politics. But toward readers, he wrote as a patient, respectful teacher.

By the end of the year, almost one hundred papers around the country carried Rusher's column. It represented "authentic conservative opinion . . . clearly and forcefully," his friend Evans told a fellow activist. Joe Sobran, who became one of *NR*'s most highly regarded writers, found it impressively logical and "loved his very crisp style."[26] People who "wanted their conservative movement plain-vanilla," Rusher recalls, "were able to turn to me." He was aiming at "a reasonably well-educated conservative audience that . . . wanted to hear its own views expressed, and perhaps be told some things about the politics of the matter that they were not familiar with."[27]

During the Watergate saga, Rusher played a new role as a partial defender of Nixon. With his legal training and experience, he tended to consider developments in the scandal from the perspective of courtroom evidence. In addition, as a partisan despite his underlying contempt for Nixon, he viewed Watergate as a power struggle waged by vindictive Democrats and their media allies—or the vindictive media and their Democratic allies. In one of his earliest columns, written after a summer of televised Senate Watergate hearings, Rusher nominated "the Leaker" as Man of the Year. Such people, typically mid- or lower-level bureaucrats, had come to play a crucial role in politics. Their anonymity gave them an unchecked "power to destroy." Most leakers had a liberal agenda. The Leaker wasn't impartial but really "a political spy on point duty, and his employers are The Enemy."[28]

At the beginning of 1974, after the president had begun to lose some conservative and Republican support but before the strongest evidence against him emerged, Rusher indicated discomfort in defending Nixon along with his continued unwillingness to presume guilt. Some weeks after appearing on an *Advocates* show on the impeachment question, he thanked Ernest van den Haag, who also worked as a trained psychoanalyst, for complimenting his performance: "You are the psychiatrist—tell me why I do this kind of thing? I don't like the guy, never have. Yet some lawyerly impulse keeps telling me that the proof should precede the penalty. Doctor, am I crazy?"[29]

A quite different conservative analysis of Watergate came from Burnham—who now argued on the basis of *National Review*'s responsibilities, as Rusher had so often done elsewhere. As early as July 1973, he told his colleagues Watergate was already a "staggering and potentially decisive" defeat for advocates of a hard-line foreign policy. As evidence, Burnham cited an upcoming cutoff of bombing in Cambodia, the postponement of the Trident strategic nuclear submarine and other advanced weapons programs, indications of possible troop withdrawals from Western Europe, Nixon's recent weakness with Soviet leader Leonid Brezhnev in disarmament talks, and the international collapse of the dollar. These developments were early results of the weakening of Nixon by the scandal, and with a "politically crippled and irrevocably compromised" president in office, the "appeasement trend will continue and deepen. In the next three years it might well pass the point of no return." America could leave Watergate behind only by a "purge of the central figure."

In language hinting at his Marxist past, Burnham suggested a *National Review* editorial could make a real difference, serving the Right's interests as well as the country's: "A relatively small push might get history moving toward the indicated objective of resignation," he wrote, and that was also best for the Republican Party and "the conservative tendency." Burnham explained: "If the conservatives allow themselves to be saddled with Nixon and therefore with the Watergate millstone, they will be left decimated and isolated, somewhat as the last ditch McCarthyites were two decades ago." Furthermore, no political "contradiction" was involved. Because Agnew would become president in the event of resignation, "we can repudiate Nixon as an individual without repudiating conservative policy; indeed, our repudiation becomes an affirmation of conservatism." Burnham concluded: "Apart from practical political considerations, I find it difficult to see how we can avoid the moral and intellectual duty to repudiate the quality of mind, feeling, and conduct that have been revealed by Watergate."[30]

In November, after the "Saturday Night Massacre," in which special prosecutor Archibald Cox was fired and Attorney General Elliot Richardson resigned, *National Review* accordingly made a contingent call for resignation. As Burnham had, the editorial cited both the general "quality" of the Nixon administration and the president's ability or inability to govern with popular acceptance. He should quit if, as seemed likely, "the public distrust and rejection . . . persists, deepens further, and hardens."[31]

The differences between Burnham and Rusher on Watergate were far from total. Burnham agreed that it was becoming a liberal coup against the president, while Rusher felt troubled by the overall attitude in the White House. Dismayed and slightly puzzled, he wrote a column called "The Managers Around Nixon" in which he observed that the scandal seemed to have a new type of political operative at its core, perhaps foreshadowed slightly by some of the Dewey team two decades earlier. Such people seemed heartless in a sense—dedicated only to the success of their boss, not to the public or party or principle. Rusher had realized "how far gone these men were" only when he saw Chuck Colson's remark about running over his own grand-mother if necessary.[32]

In contrast to his lawyerly and political reactions to Watergate, Rusher sympathized on a personal level with Agnew, who was under investigation for alleged kickbacks from contractors in Maryland and in October 1973 pleaded no-contest to a related charge of tax evasion, resigning his office immediately. Rusher had liked him from early in the first Nixon term, appreciating the interest the vice president showed in conservatism and *NR* as well as his denunciations of media bias, while Agnew, according to his for-mer speechwriter Coyne, "valued Rusher's insights into and influence with movement conservatives."[33] Buckley later repudiated Agnew, and Rusher did not. But shortly before the vice president stepped down, Buckley wrote a column criticizing the leaks of the evidence against him when there hadn't yet been an indictment, noting that it was therefore "too late to repair" his reputation before a trial or in the absence of one. He also held out the pos-sibility of "the wildest exoneration in recent history."[34]

The publisher met the vice president for an hour-long talk on October 8, 1973. It was two days before Agnew both made and announced, according to Rusher, his decision to quit. Alone over cocktails early that evening, they spoke almost entirely about Agnew's legal and political position. The vice president began by agreeing with Rusher that "he simply could not hope for a fair shake from the U.S. Attorney in Baltimore and his superiors in the Justice Department," who were too committed to an indictment and con-viction. Agnew believed all four of the immunized witnesses against him "were lying to save their own skins." Rusher asked whether he might have a better chance of fair treatment in House impeachment proceedings. For three reasons, Agnew thought not. The witnesses' testimony would be made available to Congress. If the House took up impeachment, Nixon—"This guy is devious, Bill"—would carefully "circulate the word among certain Republicans to vote against him." And most important in Agnew's opinion, the House Democrats "could not refuse to impeach him without appearing to give him a clean bill of health, which as politicians and Democrats they would naturally be very reluctant to do."

The vice president indicated his political career was over, adding: "Bill, my family is cracking." His wife had recently fainted and hit her head while he was reading a hostile article to her. A sympathetic Rusher got up to leave: "I gave him my own advice, which was to 'hang in there,' pointing out that Americans respect a fighter, and that he would in the long run respect him-self more if he refused to quit. He nodded in acknowledgement of my point, without implying that he necessarily agreed with it."[35]

Rusher and his colleagues were increasingly at odds over Watergate. The editors hadn't actually voted to urge impeachment, but that was the dominant view in their conferences, he told them in April 1974. He chided them for naively perceiving the House Judiciary Committee now considering possible charges against the president as "good guys wearing white hats" while regarding Nixon and his aides as "swinish criminals dragging their feet." In Rusher's view, the panel issued excessive demands for documents in order to make full White House compliance as difficult as possible. Since the other charges against Nixon would probably look "so anemic," noncompliance would be a useful article of impeachment for the Democrats. Rusher concluded by urging a more politically hardheaded approach to the situation. The Judiciary Committee was "scrambling with net and trident to entangle and bring down the President. He may (or may not) deserve it; but whether he deserves it or not, why not employ a little of our vaunted realism and say so?"[36]

Buckley, as he had in discussing the Agnew investigation, denounced hostility toward the accused. Some liberals, he wrote, "want the satisfaction of a public trial followed by a public execution . . . They like the idea of 'proving' their case; and they like the idea of inflicting humiliations and torture." At the same time, though, many conservatives wanted an impeachment on selfish grounds of their own, politically calculating that a Senate trial would be Nixon's best chance for an acquittal. A trial would cause the country to suffer, Buckley concluded, and that was one of the good arguments for resignation if Nixon were impeached.[37]

Commenting on the White House tapes in May, Rusher was unimpressed so far by their substance but acknowledged that they were understandably hurting the president. Nixon's opponents, he wrote, "are reduced to leaking stories about 'racial slurs' in the transcripts and speculating about precisely which '[expletive]' was '[deleted].' No critic would waste two seconds on such side issues if he had any better shots in his locker." Rusher dismissed "as pious hypocrisy much of the shock . . . at the low moral tone of conversations in the Oval Office. The talk of politicians when they let their hair down bears very little resemblance to dinner-table chatter in a well-run vicarage, and Mr. Nixon, as revealed in the transcripts, is no worse in this respect than many of his predecessors in the White House—or than most of the members of the House and Senate, who may soon be called upon to judge him." But the revelations of "the flawed and sometimes disagreeable human being behind the presidential mask," Rusher added, had cost the president part of a chief executive's "essential equipment." While that was no ground for impeachment, it did raise "a serious question whether, once the legal charges against Mr. Nixon are evaluated and (as is quite possible) ultimately dismissed, he should be called on to step down from an office he can no longer occupy effectively."[38]

Watergate divided and demoralized conservatives. Between 1972 (when circulation stood at 115,000—already well below a previous high) and 1974, *National Review* lost more than 20,000 readers. *NR* veterans Linda Bridges and John Coyne later attributed this to opposing reactions among them, with the magazine satisfying neither side: "those who were disgusted by George Will's harshness toward Nixon and those who were disgusted by lingering traces of sympathy for Nixon (mostly from Jeff Hart, who liked the tough-guy persona)." When it was reported that one tape of a presidential conversation had an eighteen-and-a-half-minute gap, Rusher wouldn't let anyone jump to conclusions. "At one editorial conference after another, he presented ever more ingenious explanations of the gap, while Burnham and Will, and to a lesser degree Buckley, said basically, 'Oh, come *on*, Bill.'"[39]

The first annual Conservative Political Action Conference (CPAC) was held in January 1974 under the sponsorship of the ACU and YAF, which were still chaired by Rusher's friends Evans and Ron Docksai. Watergate was the most pervasive issue. "Panelists and speakers returned to it again and again," the ACU newsletter *Battle Line* reported, "in an attempt to analyze its causes and implications and to chart a conservative response." There were no easy answers. Rusher and John Ashbrook—the congressman had already urged resignation—led a session on the Nixon presidency. It was CPAC's best-attended presentation, drawing an overflow crowd. Rusher argued that Watergate resulted from a decades-long growth in presidential power and that technocrats, not real conservatives like themselves, had been running the White House.[40]

Writing two and a half years after Nixon's resignation, he concluded that the former president was "able, energetic, perceptive, undeniably; self-destructive, too, quite probably; vain, combative, and unscrupulous, no doubt; above all, perhaps, a man of his time and place: of an America that had temporarily forgotten, in its zeal to make things better, the fundamentally corrupting quality of power."[41]

## World Crisis

After Gerald Ford took office in August 1974, his choice for vice president was Nelson Rockefeller, who had resigned the previous year as governor of New York after nearly four terms. In his column and in his own mind, Rusher tried to argue that Ford saw himself as essentially a conservative and was balancing the ticket. But the choice made no sense to him, since Rockefeller "represented virtually everything that antagonized social conservatives" without bringing the Republicans any new voting bloc. It seemed to Rusher that the president, if he were going to run in 1976, either didn't want these voters or didn't recognize them as a factor. Clif White told him Rockefeller had simply been Ford's easiest choice, given the need for confirmation of the vice-presidential appointment by the majority-Democratic Senate.[42]

Buckley had urged Ford to nominate George Bush—a New England patrician by origin who was a former congressman from Texas, a UN ambassador in the Nixon years, and at the time chaired the RNC. But he thought the choice of Rockefeller was a laudable outreach, appealing to Democrats and independents. It would help stabilize the country after what Buckley called the "great dislocation" of Watergate. In a pro-Rockefeller editorial written by Burnham, *NR* praised the decision on similar grounds, noting specifically that it tended to bring the Midwest, represented by President Ford, and the Northeast together.[43]

During the first half-year of the new presidency, Rusher's anxiety about the movement deepened into a fear that conservatism was, as he told the editors, facing "quite possibly its supreme crisis." His concern reflected not just the Nixon disaster and the Republican collapse in the 1974 congressional elections but the current course of world events, of Western society, and of American society. "Even though he's an optimist by nature, he was very pessimistic about the future of the United States at that time," Rusher's friend Frank Shepherd recalls. "He had no confidence that the country was going to survive to the year 2000. I think he used that exact time, those exact words to me."[44]

He had begun to think about such questions in more religious terms. Not long before the fall of Saigon in early 1975, Rusher met Edward Teller, the father of the hydrogen bomb, for breakfast in New York. He suspected the hawkish physicist's reason for the invitation was to make him friendlier toward Vice President Rockefeller, to whom Teller was an informal adviser. But eventually their talk turned toward the world picture. "Let me tell you what I would like to see, and then what I predict," Rusher recalled saying in a contemporaneous memo:

> The United States isn't really afraid of the Russians. It is afraid of itself—of a world without God, in which it lacks any recognizable right-relation to reality, as it perceives reality. Subliminally, the American society wants to die. And the Soviet Union will accommodate its wish in this respect. What I want, therefore—what I would like to see—must be called a step backward: a retrograde motion, toward a revived belief in God, and in mankind's and this

nation's relation to Him. Now as to what I predict: I predict the exact opposite. As I said, I believe that America wants to die; and I believe America will get its wish.[45]

In a column about the deteriorating situation in Indochina at the beginning of 1975, Rusher argued that up to this point the Southeast Asians' continued "fierce resistance to the massive Communist effort to overrun them" had been among "the great success stories of the latter 20th century." Dismissing those who "scoff at the 'democratic' pretensions of these young and precariously viable nations," he urged that even at this late date, the Left must not be allowed to get its way. "Unfortunately those Americans who labored so long and hard to end U.S. military participation in the Southeast Asian war have almost a vested interest in seeing Communism overrun the peninsula . . . Anti-Communist governments [in the region] . . . constitute a vastly irritating reminder that the struggle was not, in fact, in vain." Continued aid for South Vietnam "is an absolute must," Rusher added, "if we are to keep faith with the tens of thousands of Americans who gave their lives to hold the line there against Communism."[46]

In early March, he wrote even more angrily of his contempt for liberals who wouldn't let the U.S. do this. "Certainly the motive cannot be frugality; Congress is capable of squandering ten times $222 million in a single afternoon. Nor is there even any pretense that our Cambodian allies seek anything but their freedom, and the peace in which to enjoy it. It is shells provided by the Soviet Union and Red China that are slamming into the market-places of Phnom Penh, ripping open the bodies of children whose parents made the unbelievable mistake of trusting the United States."[47]

After Congress refused new aid to Cambodia and South Vietnam and the countries fell to the communists in April, Rusher wrote that it remained important to look back and understand what went wrong. Lyndon Johnson's "catastrophic" conduct of the war began when "he lied about his intentions (in the campaign of 1964). Then he tried to minimize the whole thing by failing to ask for a declaration of war—which made it impossible to nail for treason the Jane Fondas and Ramsey Clarks who gave aid and comfort to the enemy. Worst of all, Johnson ordered a purely defensive strategy" resulting inevitably in "a war of attrition . . . In such a war, dictatorships have an enormous advantage, since they are largely immune to the frustrations and sheer fatigue that can erode the morale of a volatile democracy like ours." Although Americans' resentment over their "futile losses in blood and treasure" mounted in the Johnson years, Rusher thought Nixon was mistaken in believing "that a bold bid for victory . . . was by then [1969] already more than American opinion would support."[48]

Africa, too, presented an ugly prospect. Following the overthrow of Portugal's decades-old rightist regime, the last European colonial empire had been essentially abandoned. Rusher warned readers in December 1975 that thousands of Soviet-equipped Cuban troops were "spearheading and stiffening a drive by local Communist forces to take over all of Angola . . . If they succeed, communism will have reached the eastern shore of the Atlantic on a front nearly a thousand miles long, and Soviet naval vessels, including submarines, will enjoy secure bases directly astride the route of any tanker that tries (once the Suez Canal is closed) to carry oil from the Middle East to either the United States or Western Europe." Angola, in short, was "another notch in the butt of Comrade Brezhnev's gold-handled cane." Rusher cited other grim situations around the world: communist control in Mozambique on the other side of southern Africa, the fall of Southeast Asia, a "savage civil war" in Lebanon, impending chaos in Argentina "while Peru shifts quietly to the left and Panama agrees to wait—but only a year—for the Canal. Domino theory, anyone? That rumble you hear isn't dominoes falling. It's the roof caving in."[49]

Earlier that year, with little hope left for South Vietnam and Cambodia, the publisher had joined Bill and Priscilla Buckley, Senator Buckley, and columnist Kilpatrick for a luncheon meeting with Henry Kissinger, secretary of state since 1973. Kissinger was "in an extremely discouraged mood" and their meeting at the State Department was not without tension. Throughout, he "tended to refer to conservatives of our general type as 'purists'—presumably in contradistinction to 'realists' of his own type," Rusher recorded later for his own reference. He "acknowledged that America needs leadership today—then looked direct at me, pointing, and added, 'but not Reagan.' Ford, he said, is patriotic. As for Rockefeller (my suggestion, for discussion purposes), Kissinger avowed that at least Rockefeller 'would be ruthless in foreign policy—more ruthless even than Nixon. Nixon was ruthless sporadically.'" Rusher then asked "how he felt about the proposal of his ruthless friend's brother, David Rockefeller, for a trade deal with the Soviet Union, under which the United States would finance and provide the technology for the development of the Siberian natural gas fields." The secretary favored such a deal over perhaps ten years, along with regular policy concessions by the Soviets. "The question, Kissinger asserted, is simply: What country shall grant credits to the Russians? . . . it might as well be the United States."[50]

In a column in early 1976, Buckley hinted, without quite saying, that to some extent Kissinger believed "our civilization is ending." Agreeing with other conservatives that America had recently lacked "effective leadership," Buckley argued that Nixon deserved most of the blame, explaining: "It is the President who speaks to the public. His Secretary of State is a technician."

He cited Kissinger's hawkish record on Vietnam, on Chile's now-overthrown Marxist president Salvador Allende, on Angola, on the threat from the strong communist parties in politically unstable Portugal and Italy. These were "neither the words nor the deeds of a man who welcomes the day when his dark, private vision will be realized." Buckley then asked: "Can the leader who, convinced that history has spoken its sullen and irreversible judgment, understand himself to be capable of something other than merely stalling? Is that how best to characterize our foreign policy during the Kissinger years? And is there an alternative?" He concluded cryptically: "The trouble—and listen carefully—is this. There is an alternative. But it is a measure of our malady that it cannot be spoken by anyone who desires to be President."[51]

Rusher immediately criticized the Buckley column, telling *National Review* editors: "It simply doesn't follow that a pessimistic analysis based in large part on the internal weaknesses of the West leaves us no other choices. If Kissinger really blames the liberal establishment as much as he says he does, then at a minimum he has no business playing as much ball with it as he plays. He should be called upon to attack it frontally while there is still time."[52]

In his own column, Rusher told readers Kissinger used "his pessimism as an excuse for pursuing policies that simply make matters worse." It was certainly true "that this country is in deep trouble; and that large numbers of its citizens have lost their moral moorings and self-restraint and are out to rip off whatever they can pry loose, with precious little consideration for their fellow citizens or the nation [as] a whole, let alone the future." But Rusher also thought America could do much better:

> I know too that this opulent and self-indulgent land of ours is sur-rounded by hungry billions just aching to get their hands on its throat (and its wealth)—billions led by hard-eyed men who don't bother about the democratic niceties. Put that picture together and I get pretty much what Kissinger gets.
>
> It is precisely there, however, that the secretary and I part com-pany. For, by all accounts, Kissinger then proceeds to conclude that there is nothing he can do in the circumstances but make a carefully calculated series of concessions to the Soviet Union, in return for various delays in the coming of the inevitable.
>
> If America's doom were truly inevitable, rather than merely likely, there would be a respectable case for Kissinger's strategy. But our weaknesses are internal, self-generated, and reversible by a simple (though supremely difficult) act of will. The masters of the Kremlin are not ten feet tall, and there is no objective reason why

they must prevail. America's resources are as vast as theirs, or vaster, our population at least as clever, our cultural tradition one of the world's richest, our technology (for which they yearn) the finest on the planet. What we are suffering from is simply a decay of self-discipline and national will common in advanced and prosperous societies. If that decay could be reversed, the Soviet Union would cower in its Eurasian caves indefinitely.

Rusher noted in fairness that he disagreed with extremists who believed Kissinger (as they believed Rockefeller, and in some cases even Nixon as president) was a traitor, knowingly selling out to the communists. "I reject out of hand the kook-right suspicions of his loyalty; this man would do for America whatever he could bring himself to think possible." In further mitigation of his attack, Rusher added: "One shrewd student points to Kissinger's desperately insecure youth in a tottering Europe, followed by a lifetime in the still more poisonous atmosphere of postwar Harvard. 'Henry,' he concludes, 'has never had much chance to visit the United States.'" Replying directly to Buckley's recent column, Rusher added: "To argue that defeat at the polls awaits anyone who dares to call for a stronger and more resolute America is . . . presumptuous, because we will never know what the response might be unless the call is issued; and pointless, because if the response is not forthcoming we can suffer, at worst, only the fate Kissinger believes is inevitable anyway."[53]

His own choice, Rusher had told Edward Teller in their March 1975 meeting, was "to resist the inevitable as stoutly as one can." He gave two reasons: "In the first place, it may not be inevitable after all—my notion of the future may be mistaken. In the second place, as an individual the really important thing for me is not what happens in my particular historical epoch, but how I personally respond to it."[54] His other comments to Teller, about America's suicidal drift toward destruction by international communism and about the primacy of a spiritual rather than political crisis, were echoes of Whittaker Chambers in *Witness*, which had so impressed Rusher back in the early 1950s. They reflected his ability to consider and predict the worst possible outcomes at moments when he felt them likely. But they also reflected his determination to keep fighting. However often Rusher had such dire feelings about the future in 1975, he was working as if it were still within conservatives' grasp.

# 13

# How to Start a Party?

To movement conservatives, the brightest hope for national leadership in 1976 was Ronald Reagan, who had completed his second and final term as governor of California. But the GOP nomination wasn't there for the taking. Gerald Ford, the House minority leader who was appointed successor to Agnew and then became president after Nixon's resignation, would run for a term of his own. A mainstream Republican, Ford had been comfortable enough with ideological conservatives to sit on the dais at *NR*'s tenth-anniversary dinner in 1965. But in addition to doubting his political strength, the movement understood that the new president wasn't one of its own, as he showed repeatedly in the year after he took office in August 1974.

Reagan was the focus of its hopes, not just highly popular, because otherwise the movement lacked solid national candidates. Agnew had resigned in disgrace. Former Texas governor and former Treasury secretary John Connally had been indicted on a corruption charge, although he was later acquitted. Jim Buckley, whom many on the Right considered a presidential possibility when he was elected in 1970, had "earned the respect of his colleagues as an able and conscientious member of the Senate," Rusher later recalled, but unfortunately showed "no flair whatever" for publicity.[1]

Rusher, meanwhile, took an increasing interest in social issues—less in their intrinsic importance, which he had long recognized, than in their political power. In late 1971, as movement leaders denounced what they considered Nixon's betrayals in foreign and economic policy, he had readily admitted that their southern comrade Anthony Harrigan made a good point in suggesting social issues' special potency.

As he continued to watch the political scene, this perception strength-ened. In a memo written shortly after the president's landslide reelection in 1972, Rusher told the editors he was "struck by the rather careful distinc-tion Nixon seems to have made, over the past two years, in determining which conservative positions he would endorse and which he would jetti-son." The president tended to remain "solidly, almost noisily conservative on what might be called the 'Archie Bunker' issues—i.e., those which were visible and disturbing to lowbrow conservatives: busing, abortion, amnesty [for draft evaders] and the Supreme Court." Nixon had been "much more cavalier" with issues that "preoccupy (for example) small journals of con-servative opinion: wage and price controls, Red China policy, SALT agree-ments, etc."[2]

Now writing a regular column, Rusher pulled back from his work with the American Conservative Union. In mid-1973, he resigned from the chair-manships of its political action committee and Conservative Victory Fund, explaining that he no longer had time. The following February, Rusher left the ACU board, on which he had served from the beginning nearly a decade before. His engagement with the organization had long been less intensive than his previous roles in the Young Republicans and YAF. In board meet-ings, according to Bob Bauman, Rusher tended to give a "lawyer's summary" of the discussion and offer his own opinion briefly. Interested primarily in moving things along, he was less an advocate than a "political manager."[3]

But when it came to the presidency and to Reagan, whom he had first met in the midsixties, his interest remained as strong as ever. In a thank-you note for doing a "wonderful job" on an *Advocates* program in Los Angeles toward the end of 1970, Rusher had reiterated to Reagan his "allegiance to you and your purposes." He had also gotten the impression over the years that Reagan enjoyed talking with him. According to Jeff Bell, whom he suc-cessfully endorsed for a spot on the governor's political staff in 1974, Rusher "still had clout with the Reagans." It helped that "Nancy thought he was part of the sophisticated, eastern big world that she so looked up to. Bill had some of that cachet—because he knew how to tell the sommelier what to do about the wine, he had all those skills."[4]

Shortly after another visit with them in early 1974, Rusher warned that any national campaign shouldn't be left to Reagan's familiar circle. Many "professionals and semi-professionals," he reported, "are frankly nervous over the prospect that your 1976 activities may be managed by local peo-ple from California who, however well intentioned and loyal, are simply not qualified to conduct a national campaign as one has to be conducted if there is to be any serious chance of success." These professionals needed reassurance on the question, Rusher added, if they were to join the Reagan team. After all, they would be "gambling with their own future as well as on yours."[5] Given that Rusher rarely sounded so assertive in letters to Reagan, these remarks were probably intended to buttress or prepare a case for Clif White as 1976 campaign manager.

While Reagan considered how to remain as prominent and politically attractive as possible after his governorship ended, Rusher passed along recommendations from his friend Dan McGrath, media-buying director for the D'Arcy-MacManus advertising firm in New York. Reagan, McGrath recommended in July, should appear regularly on network television if possible and should therefore approach the major networks with a proposal to serve as a commentator two or three times a week. The idea was "a real long-shot," but Reagan was a "totally qualified broadcaster with unparalleled governmental experience." Although the network news departments "would prefer to fall down dead rather than help a conservative," McGrath added, "a star of Governor Reagan's magnitude hardly ever comes along." ABC, eager to break out of its close-third position among the Big Three, was a better bet than the stodgy NBC. Another possibility was a slot on CBS's *Sixty Minutes*. Failing that, Reagan should try radio syndication, which had advantages of its own.

Rusher read McGrath's memo over the phone to Peter Hannaford, the governor's public-affairs director, mailing it to him as well. A memo from Hannaford the following month made serious acknowledgements of McGrath's and Rusher's advice on the question. Rusher, he told the governor or staff, thought a radio series (suggested, too, by Hollywood radio producer and marketer Harry O'Connor) was an excellent idea. Hannaford recommended pursuing a full range of possibilities: radio, TV, a newspaper column, other venues.[6] Although CBS offered a twice-weekly commentary on the then preeminent Walter Cronkite newscast and aide Michael Deaver enthusiastically urged him to accept, Reagan turned down the more lucrative option, siding with Hannaford's preference for radio syndication. "People will tire of me on television," he explained. "They won't tire of me on the radio."[7]

Lunching with Deaver and chief of staff Edwin Meese that August in Sacramento, Rusher was told Reagan would stay on the political scene after leaving office at year's end. A month later, the select veterans of the Goldwater cadre known as the Hard Core, who had continued to meet over the years, gathered at Charlie Barr's farm near Chicago. Of the dozen or so people attending, some thought it would be best to back Ford, while others wanted to see what Reagan would do. Rusher was surprised to find significant sympathy among them for a possible new party. Similarly, members of the YAF national board showed a good deal of interest in this when he talked with them on October 12 at their meeting in New York.[8] These reactions encouraged Rusher to think Reagan might be persuaded to lead such a venture.

## The Making of the New Majority Party

Within months, Rusher became a national spokesman and spearhead for the new-party idea. Four days after his visit with the YAF leaders, he began to outline *The Making of the New Majority Party*. Working quickly, "as if I were simply transcribing a book already written in my mind," he finished a draft by the end of December.[9]

"I believe this particular ball had to be kicked off as promptly as possible," Rusher explained in a letter sent to various people, including Buckley. The short book's purpose was "to shape, insofar as I could, the general lines of the ensuing discourse on the subject . . . [and] to start people thinking—and acting" very soon. Seeking feedback on the draft from those he shared it with, he promised to "do my damnedest to incorporate your suggestions." After reading the manuscript, Buckley cited two main concerns: What Rusher had written was "very good and very useful" but lacked "a sense of having annihilated the Republican Party, and . . . a description of the catalyst that could bring the new party into being." It was "a handbook of sorts if the party does materialize."[10]

In addition to interest among conservative activists and respectful attention from Buckley, other rumblings were heard. Within the past year, George Wallace had said he might run as a third-party candidate "if the Democrats have a boss-controlled convention and a [very liberal] platform like 1972." At a dinner honoring conservative-movement elder Clarence Manion, Senator Jesse Helms, a freshman Republican from North Carolina, asked whether it was "time to forge new political parties, fashioned along the lines that the people are thinking, not along the existing lines of political power-seeking?"[11]

Reagan staff members Jeff Bell and Robert Walker, who had been a regional coordinator for the 1968 presidential effort under Clif White, were able to interest their boss in the idea. He acknowledged the possibility at a news conference in October 1974, although unlike Helms, he spoke vaguely and minimally. "I see the statements of disaffection of people in both parties—the loss of confidence," Reagan said. "And you wonder which is the easiest. Do you restore the confidence or do you change the name or something? I don't know. I really don't."[12]

Others thought they did know. One of Reagan's major and original fundraisers, Holmes Tuttle, told him: "You're a Republican, and you're going to stay one." Aides John Sears and Lyn Nofziger agreed. The day after the midterm election rout, the governor said he was "not starting a third party" and expressed confidence in the GOP.[13] Rusher, however, thought Reagan was the man to lead a new party and wanted his agreement to do so. "The book would be my selling tool." In early 1975, he sent the hoped-for candidate and party founder his second draft.[14]

Reagan was considering a Republican primary challenge against Ford, whom he not only disagreed with but disdained as a leader. Although Rusher wished him well in this, he expected the Reagan campaign would fail because the president, and those in the party who favored his centrism or deferred to incumbency, held too many advantages. In a memo to Reagan that spring, ACU chairman Stan Evans made the same point, stressing the strength of the "support-our-President mystique" as well as presidential patronage power. In addition, voters would "more or less correctly" interpret Watergate, the Vietnam disaster, and the nation's economic problems as Nixon's and Ford's legacy. As Republican nominee, Evans warned, Reagan would be considered the Nixon-Ford "heir apparent." As a third-party candidate, he could expect much of the antiadministration vote.[15]

In *The Making of the New Majority Party,* Rusher began by asserting the existence of a conservative majority. In a Gallup poll, only 23 percent of Americans called themselves Republicans. Yet 38 percent said they would prefer the conservative party if the two parties were ideologically aligned, while just 26 percent would choose the liberal party. Rusher pointed out that if one counted only people who gave an opinion on the question, or assumed that the poll's undecideds would favor the conservative party in the same proportion as those who answered the question—doubtful assumptions, as he did not acknowledge—then a large majority of the public would vote conservative. Admittedly, some people who called themselves conservative might really be thinking of their personal values. But if a party was, among other things, "specifically designed to express" such values, it could benefit from their votes.

The parties at the presidential level now stood for little. Republican and Democratic administrations had been virtually indistinguishable, a situation that caused "growing indifference to both parties." Behind this, Rusher believed, was the problem that liberals had too much influence in the GOP. Although a minority in the party and unable to dominate it, they could always hobble it as a conservative force. At Republican national conventions, the liberal bloc was consistently able to "force the selection of candidates and the adoption of platform planks calculated to offend its sensibilities as little as possible." The party had drifted into "essential meaninglessness," Rusher wrote. "No one can effectively lead or even work for the Republican party today, because no one can possibly say what it stands for."[16]

But the core analysis in *New Majority Party* went well beyond familiar complaints about the policy weakness of Republican presidents and convention vetoes by liberals and moderates. In Rusher's view, the GOP also failed to seriously pursue current conservative goals because it remained oriented toward an outdated conflict. It was still "designed to fight (and, one is tempted to add peevishly, to lose) a battle that ended, for most practical purposes, at least a quarter of a century ago." The battle against the New Deal was over, "as irrevocably as Antietam and Gettysburg." Instead, Rusher took the following perspective on the America of 1975:

> The basic economic division . . . is no longer (if it ever was) between the haves and the have-nots. Instead, a new economic division pits the producers—businessmen, manufacturers, hard-hats, blue-collar workers and farmers—against a new and powerful class of non-producers comprised of a liberal verbalist elite (the dominant media, the major foundations and research institutions, the educational establishment, the federal and state bureaucracies) and a semi-permanent welfare constituency, all coexisting happily in a state of mutually sustaining symbiosis. It is this new economic and social cleavage that has produced the imposing (though not yet politically united) conservative majority detected by Dr. Gallup; and it is the ineradicable presence in the Republican party of a liberal minority that either belongs to or is broadly sympathetic to this new class . . . that makes the Republican party, all else aside, so spectacularly unfitted to be the political vector of the conservative majority in the American society.[17]

The producing majority—a concept Rusher borrowed from Frank Meyer—had two kinds of conservatives, economic and social. Each already had a preeminent advocate among politicians, Ronald Reagan and George Wallace respectively. Rusher noted his general agreement with both types of conservative.[18] But he stressed the importance of integrating the populistic social conservatives, who would soon be known as the New Right, into the new majority party—and the need to respectfully accommodate their viewpoint. This would include compromises with a more moderate view of government's economic role, something at which Rusher had hinted in the National Press Club comments he proposed for Reagan back in 1968.

In addition to mostly agreeing with economic conservatives on the specific issues, Rusher admired their "illusionless grip on economic reality" and their "firm belief in the worth of individual effort." But unfortunately, they might not always understand or care about "the plight of those who, for whatever reason, cannot, or at any rate do not, put forth a winning effort." There was a sense, too, in which the social conservatives were the true realists. They seemed "closer to the needs and concerns of many Americans" and were "less prone to didacticism" on economic issues, less ready to "believe that ability and hard work will always receive their just rewards." Furthermore, Rusher wrote, social conservatives tended to understand that people of wealth and privilege "are not always, or perhaps even usually, kind to those less favored. It is a perception that colors their outlook on many things."

Rusher found a special value in that outlook's ability to "moderate the near-Puritan severity of traditional conservative economics without undermining its basic structure" and to keep "firmly before the American conscience the cause of this country's workers." He quoted approvingly from the late-nineteenth-century papal encyclical *Rerum Novarum*, which he urged all conservatives to read: "It is shameful and inhuman to treat men like chattels to make money by, or to look upon them merely as so much muscle or physical power . . . [The employer's] great and principal obligation is to give to everyone that which is just."[19] His grandfather, whom he never knew, had been a socialist follower of Eugene Debs. "Remember this, son," Rusher recalls his father saying, in a point drawn from an upbringing in southern Indiana. "Those coal mine owners didn't exactly wear white wings."[20]

While the social conservative placed an emphasis on "the desirability of collective efforts, both for affirmative achievement and for mutual protection," he was also "a stout individualist" at heart. Distrusting big business, such conservatives had "an almost equal distaste for bigness in any form—including even Big Labor, not to mention Big Media, and that largest monster of them all, Big Government." While they usually weren't interested in foreign policy, they knew (as little people, Rusher implied) the importance of strength and took understandable pride in belonging to the world's greatest power. Social conservatism also had possible dangers. While economic conservatism's negative aspect was its potential lack of understanding or compassion for the less fortunate, social conservatism's dark side was its potential for bigotry—and in regard to economics, a possible temptation toward "envious hatred" of the rich or successful.[21]

Rusher admitted that the "Great Coalition," as he called it, could conceivably occur within the Republican Party. But the history of newly Republican groups in his lifetime suggested difficulty in realizing that hope. When many people from one previously Democratic constituency—Catholic ethnics, many of them McCarthyites—moved into the GOP in the 1950s, established Republican leaders viewed them with near hostility. Similarly, blue-collar union members had been viewed with suspicion, and small farmers got "no very special welcome." For their part, social conservatives often felt wary of the Republicans given sectionalist attitudes toward the Civil War and memories of the Depression.[22]

The book advocated not just a presidential candidacy, but a full-fledged new party extending throughout the political system. Rusher proposed naming it the Independence Party, but only as a suggestion. Although new parties in America had largely been mere alternatives or dissenters, and had been limited mainly to presidential races, he told readers the Independence Party could be different. Many ambitious younger people in both parties would be willing to run as its candidates, especially since there would be no long apprenticeship, as with the Republicans and Democrats. More experienced people, too, who had kept away from politics because they found it "strife-ridden, self-seeking and often blatantly corrupt," might be inspired to become involved in a new party. Officeholders and former officeholders, including some of the many Republicans defeated in 1974, might be willing to join the Independence Party and run as its candidates. By their example, these established figures would bring in others.

In many cases, the new party should endorse incumbents for lesser offices in 1976. But thereafter, it should run its own full slates as soon as possible. The key to attaining major status below the presidential level, Rusher explained, was for the new party to offer positions to officials and volunteers who left the existing parties. He wanted it made as easy as possible "for both individual Republicans and whole Republican organizations to move into the Independence party without appreciable loss of status or other disadvantage." As a precedent he cited the "resignation rallies" of the Goldwater era, in which entire Democratic county central committees in the South, or large portions of them, simply resigned en masse and joined the GOP. To the extent possible, candidates should be current officeholders. That way, the new party would benefit from established people's experience. Running these incumbents would also signal the party's "basically familiar and non-'radical' character" to the public. Organizing the new party in such a way, Rusher conceded, would favor people who already held places in an existing party and therefore wouldn't be done easily: "This will require great diplomacy, and probably some sacrifice all around, but it will be eminently worth it in the long run."[23]

He also warned against fringe elements. Neither the new party's candidates nor its managers should be agents of "extreme-right organizations." In addition, its leaders must watch out for congenital malcontents— "personalities simply incapable of participating in a collective effort, especially if that effort requires them to subordinate their own preferences in any serious degree." There were also people who really didn't like to win, or even the prospect of winning.[24]

Rusher readily noted additional difficulties in establishing a new party. There was an increasingly large and "bewildering" mass of laws governing nominating processes, campaign finance, and other aspects of elective politics, so competent legal advisers would be important. In terms of money, corporate interests that hedged their bets by giving to both major parties wouldn't be likely to help the Independence Party in its early stages. But a combination of grassroots fund-raising from the Right's now-proven base of small donors, more-principled business sources who had always supported conservatism, and unions opposed to the Democrats' leftward evolution could provide a good financial base: the problem was "real but not insoluble." For organizing and organizational maintenance, specially-trained field representatives from the national party and already-experienced political "managers and technicians" who had served the major parties would be very helpful.[25]

Noting that the creation of the party shouldn't depend entirely on one individual, Rusher nonetheless pointed clearly to Reagan as the best nominee. He also cited difficulties with other figures whom readers might have considered. Bill Buckley, the only other "conservative spokesman" at all comparable to Reagan and Goldwater in national prominence, wasn't a viable candidate because his "often brilliant rhetorical and literary effects" came at "a fearful price in listener identification and sheer comprehension." Rusher was impressed, on the other hand, by Wallace's third-party showing in 1968 and his sizable vote in the 1972 Democratic primaries. The fact that the governor had changed his stance on segregation might improve his image, and his past shouldn't automatically disqualify him. On this point, Rusher cited the examples of the internationalist Senator Vandenberg's former isolationism, Robert Kennedy's onetime closeness with Joe McCarthy as a Senate counsel, Rockefeller's drift toward the center after a career as a liberal, and Reagan's rightward movement in the 1950s. "As he presents himself to the national electorate today," Rusher argued, Wallace was "entitled to attention for the issues he is stressing today."

Then he turned to Wallace's minuses. Rusher had no particular knowledge of his physical capacity after the 1972 assassination attempt that confined him to a wheelchair. But he noted that Franklin Roosevelt, also disabled, had managed the job. He expressed more concern about the governor's strong southern accent. It "immediately connotes 'otherness' to . . . non-Southern areas of the country," and in Wallace's case it gave an "impression of scruffiness that easily overpowers . . . whatever is being said." The "irrational" prejudice against such an accent must be taken into political account—and "serious politicians," Wallace among them, would do that. Also problematic was the fact that many people heard a shrillness in him, and if he hoped to become the new party's nominee, Wallace "must strive for a more reassuring and broadly acceptable public image." But all things considered, he probably had "a major role to play" in the new party. "He speaks for many millions who have been cynically disregarded by the dominant Eastern leadership of both major parties for decades," Rusher concluded, "and he deserves to be heard—and listened to."[26]

In acknowledging Wallace as a conservative leader, Rusher knew he was distancing himself from Buckley's hostility. In 1968, the editor had written to Nancy Reagan that Wallace was "a dangerous man" who abused "the rhetoric and analysis of conservatism." At the end of the campaign, *NR* told readers he had been "an enemy of conservatism since he first entered politics."[27] In 1972, Buckley maintained that Wallace was "distrusted by truly conservative Americans, and for good reason," since he was "forever defiled" by his segregationism or segregationist past. In a column at the end of 1974, he wrote warily of right-leaning populists in the context of the energy crisis, saying it was their nature to want "a villain." In the same column, though, he wished that someone—Reagan if possible—would visit Wallace and get him to help "seduce" his populist supporters "into the conservative camp." Buckley doubted this would work, given what he considered populists' and implicitly Wallace's lack of economic sophistication, but said it should be tried.[28] Thus, he agreed that unity on the broadly defined Right was an important goal but took an attitude different from Rusher's toward many of the new voters this would require.

Discussing Reagan in *New Majority Party*, Rusher emphasized his success as a governor and a conservative spokesman. His age, 65 in 1976, was a "vulnerable point" in political terms, although outstanding leaders in other countries had been much older. Reagan had a long record of fighting successfully "for more economical government, for higher efficiency, for freedom from the decisions of Washington bureaucrats, and for what he considered the long-range best interests of the people of California." At the same time, he had a gift for "negotiation and compromise." Reagan was also unequaled in articulating millions of Americans' concerns with "skill and good humor . . . Uniquely among conservatives of truly national prominence, he possesses the ability to put the conservative case in terms that automatically command majority assent."[29]

While Rusher wrote optimistically of prospects for organizing a new party and immediately making it a large factor in politics, he confessed to his dark feelings about American society, emphasizing especially the great political pressure for mounting deficit spending and the public's understandable difficulty in grasping economic policy. The founding of a new party couldn't wait for the 1980 presidential cycle. "The hour is late—perhaps too late,"

Rusher cautioned. "I do not want to pretend to an optimism I do not feel. But *if* there is still a chance, then the Great Coalition and a new major party based on it are its indispensable embodiments."[30]

Pat Buchanan, formerly of the Nixon White House, joined in the public consideration of a new party. His 1975 book, *Conservative Votes, Liberal Victories*, analyzed the Right's policy frustrations in more detail than Rusher's. Of all the movements characterizing the 1960s—civil rights, antiwar, women's liberation, environmentalism—only conservatism appeared to have no results on the policy level. After 1972, the GOP's new title as "spokesman of Middle America" had been lost in Watergate, more inflation, and a bad recession; right-leaning Democrats wouldn't easily be gotten to vote for it again. "The hour may be approaching," Buchanan wrote, "for conservatives to dissolve a popular front with the Republican Party that no longer seems to serve their political interests."[31]

The book also cited obstacles not discussed in Rusher's. Buchanan thought the "senior partner" in a new party would probably be Wallace, not Reagan, given the ballot status the former Wallace parties still held in some states. The most likely outcome of a rightward bolt from the Republicans in 1976 would be a Democratic president. Like Buckley when he responded to Rusher's manuscript, Buchanan didn't see a "conclusive prognosis" that the Republican Party was hopeless for conservatism. And finally: "The heart has reasons that the mind knows not. For conservatives who have long been loyal to the GOP, who believe deeply in the continuity of institutions, it would be a wrenching experience to abandon and attack the party of their youth, their hopes, their dreams." Still, Buchanan concluded: "Neither party today voices the concerns or defends the interests of the hardest working and most productive of citizens. Both parties are up to their elbows in this sordid business of bidding for votes with the tax dollars of the American people. And things need saying that are not being said."[32]

It was well known that Rusher, Buchanan, and others were not speaking in a vacuum. In early-1975 Gallup polls, 24 percent of both Republicans and Democrats said they would be likely to support a conservative third party the following year. Similarly, in a Harris poll, a Reagan-Wallace third-party ticket received 23 percent of the vote. After reading *New Majority Party* in draft or proof form, Peter Hannaford, formerly the governor's press and community relations director and now in private practice with Michael Deaver as half of Reagan's two-man publicity team, told Rusher he found the book "brilliantly reasoned, carefully substantiated, innovative in terms of platform." He added: "I hope it causes a stampede to the banner!"[33] *National Review* cooperated with its longtime publisher to the extent of running a long excerpt from his book in May, featuring it on a cover that announced:

"A NEW PARTY: Eventually, Why Not Now?" Buckley cautiously told *NR* supporter Roger Milliken that in his "current mood," he was attracted to the idea—if Reagan also won the Republican primaries. "I am not always in agreement with Bill Rusher," Buckley added, "but I find a lot in his book . . . most convincing."[34]

Meanwhile, Rusher failed in his "gentle pressures on Reagan and others" to line up a campaign role for Clif White. Reiterating his request more firmly, Rusher was told by close Reagan advisers that White had critics as well as friends in the party—a rather insignificant reason, he later wrote, considering that White had been active in the GOP for nearly a quarter-century. Rusher's continued urgings on behalf of his friend had an almost comical result, one that foreshadowed the frequent passivity in Reagan's campaigns and presidency that would irritate many conservatives. He got Reagan and White to meet for a private dinner in Washington that May. But to White's surprise, John Sears showed up too, and the conversation went little beyond the weather and baseball. The nonideological Sears would later head Reagan's 1976 campaign, announced that November. White, "vigorously wooed" by the Ford people, enlisted with them instead.[35] By saying essentially nothing to Rusher's old political partner and favorite political manager that evening, Reagan had said no.

Serious discussion of the new-party concept also meant serious criticism. In June, *NR* published a long review of Rusher's book. While conceding that the idea was intellectually respectable, journalist Bob Novak essentially dismissed it as a nonstarter for now. Rusher had made a "cogent and persuasive" case for the desirability of a new party. He was no "hothouse theoretician" but a credible figure, "a seasoned in-fighter of Republican and conservative politics." In addition, Rusher rightly stressed that the new party couldn't be ideologically pure. But unfortunately, the book didn't establish the idea's practicality. Novak doubted such a party could be a strong, durable institution, with internal differences safely subordinate to the main goal. He had seen a good example of this formidable challenge at conservative activists' second annual CPAC meeting in Washington several months before. Many of those attending seemed most interested in "their pet causes," Novak observed, while the "bitter debate over abortion cast doubt on both the common sense and seriousness of purpose of the putative party founders. Since then, talk of a new party has diminished to the point of inaudibility." Novak also predicted that few economic conservatives would be as willing as Rusher was to compromise with blue-collar interests in the new party, and thus to reliably support it.[36]

After his book got into the stores in early June, Rusher went on as many radio and television shows as possible—he knew dozens of hosts personally—to promote it. Richard Viguerie ordered 100,000 copies of the paperback edition for free distribution to people on some of his conservative mailing lists.[37] But colleagues at *National Review* generally took a cool attitude toward the new-party idea, although Jeff Hart was "broadly sympathetic," Rusher would recall, to the idea of unifying the economic and social conservatives. Rusher's "neopopulism" in this period, according to Hart, "tended to isolate" him at the magazine. More concretely, *NR* was quick to predict that a single uplifting event, the prompt retaking of the captured USS *Mayaguez* off Southeast Asia shortly after the fall of Saigon, would dampen third-party interest. Ford's potential 1976 campaign, it said, was greatly helped by this show of leadership. The odds had lengthened "against attempts . . . for this next period at least, to swing Republican conservatives . . . into an anti-Ford new party alignment."[38]

## Reagan or Wallace?

At CPAC that February, Rusher had introduced Reagan as "the next president of the United States. "The time-honored formula," he later recalled, "brought the several hundred conservatives in the ballroom to their feet, roaring their cheers and applause, and Reagan's speech didn't disappoint them." Listening carefully, Rusher was glad that he "left technically unanswered a question that he himself bluntly posed: 'Is it a third party that we need, or is it a new and revitalized second party, raising a banner of no pale pastels, but bold colors which make it unmistakably clear where we stand on all the issues troubling the people?'"

Rusher's sanguine reaction reflected his ability to interpret even a slight ambiguity favorably, much as he had done with Goldwater's refusals in early 1963. Where Rusher spotted a possible loophole for a third-party candidacy in Reagan's remark, others might see only an eloquent plea that conservatives work within the GOP and get it committed to their ideology. That is how the quotation is remembered today. But when Reagan told the activists it was time to reassert conservatism and "raise it to full view," he added: "If there are those who cannot subscribe to these principles, let us go forward without them." The *New York Times* called this comment "even more enigmatic." It might mean only that Reagan would be willing to live with defections by liberal Republicans if he won the nomination. Or it might signify a willingness to go third-party in some contingency.

At a press conference that day, Reagan's opaque comment—"I don't know whether there'll be a third party, but I would hope that the two-party system that has served us so well will continue to do so"—suggested no enthusiasm for the first of these options, regardless of what he might ultimately do. Rusher thought Reagan had done his best to leave the door open. But as a careful listener and reader, he must also have noticed that Reagan seemed to be disagreeing with much of his *New Majority Party* thesis: his argument that the political system was broken.[39]

It was the audience and membership at CPAC that proved to be fertile ground for third-party talk. When ACU chairman Evans said: "At the presidential level, we need a new political party in 1976," the response was loud applause.[40] Delegates approved a Committee on Conservative Alternatives, authorizing it to consider the new-party possibility. Rusher was named to it, along with a long list of other conservative leaders, including his old comrades Evans, Congressman Ashbrook, and Bob Bauman, the former YAF chairman who was now a Republican House member from Maryland. Among the other participants were Senator Helms, outgoing YAF chairman Ron Docksai, editor Tom Winter of *Human Events*, former Reagan gubernatorial aide Bob Walker, former Wallace adviser Eli Howell, and from New York, the Conservative Party's Dan Mahoney. Significantly, the committee also included grassroots leader Phyllis Schlafly, who was simultaneously a heartland social conservative and a veteran of internal GOP politics—and, given the success of her widely distributed pro-Goldwater and anti-Republican establishment tract *A Choice Not an Echo*, a household name among many on the Right for the past decade.[41]

Involvement in COCA didn't necessarily indicate commitment to the third-party idea. Although Evans and Docksai, like Rusher, had announced support for the idea, public officeholders Helms, Ashbrook, and Bauman had not committed to it. But the group immediately received funding from two prominent movement donors—South Carolina textile manufacturer Roger Milliken and Colorado beer baron Joseph Coors.[42]

Rusher discussed his forthcoming book with Reagan at the Madison Hotel before they left town. He could tell the former governor, after receiving the manuscript just a few days before, had at least dipped into it—because Reagan brought up his disagreement with the reference to his 1968 partial campaign as a real attempt at the Republican nomination. Rusher "didn't argue the point strenuously or change the manuscript much . . . No political figure, I decided, enjoys remembering in fond detail the battles he has lost."[43]

Buckley expressed sympathy with Rusher's idea but with a typically distanced analysis and caveat. In his February 27 column, he wrote that momentum for a new party would grow "as the program of President Ford fails"—which was bound to happen, he added, because its welfare-state premises were wrong. Generally more interested in economic policy than Rusher, Buckley was dismayed that Ford had proposed to fight inflation "by

spending more money." He was also distressed that the Soviets were apparently on track to gain massive strategic superiority in the coming years. But
he obliquely suggested that a truly conservative new party wouldn't be overwhelmingly popular. "I am no means convinced," Buckley wrote, "that a
majority of Americans yearn for principle." Those advocates who were motivated more by winning than by an ideological party's intrinsic value would
likely be disappointed.[44]

Several months later, Buckley also signaled continued hostility to George
Wallace. He understood that the people who had previously voted for him
were necessary in order to win the White House—adding, too, that only
Wallace could "deliver them." Implying that he feared the governor was still
a racist, however, he opposed any concession to him by third-party advocates if it were "philosophically disreputable . . . on the issue, for instance, of
metaphysical human equality."[45]

Buckley nonetheless made clear his sympathy with Rusher's premise
that the Republican Party was bankrupt as a conservative force. In a column written amid Reagan's victories in the later primaries—which also ran
a month later in National Review—he complained that liberals had controlled the party for a whole generation, adding: "Who cares, really, about
the Republican Party?" It was largely "an administrative convenience for
a few politicians." Buckley also estimated that if Reagan were to run as an
"independent," he would win more votes than any Republican nominee
except John Connally.[46]

Just after CPAC, Goldwater had admonished an audience of Young
Republican leaders that formation of a third party would virtually ensure
the destruction of the GOP, and that his fellow conservatives shouldn't take
a "rule or ruin attitude." He said much the same thing three years before, in
response to the Ashbrook candidacy. Undeterred, the Committee on Conservative Alternatives, or COCA, held its first meeting on March 7, chaired
by Jesse Helms. Rusher, with his legal background, agreed to head a subcommittee charged with researching the election laws of every state. That month,
thirty-three House Republicans reportedly failed to sign a pledge of GOP
loyalty, proposed in order to weaken any breakaway movement in its early
stages.[47] Clif White kept away from the project, telling Senator Helms and
presumably Rusher that he was against such parties. On Reagan's staff, Jeff
Bell made himself "kind of an odd man out" by writing memos explaining
that the GOP was hopeless and urging Reagan to form a third-party alliance
with Wallace.[48]

Despite the respect he had expressed for Wallace in his book, Rusher
told NR colleagues that Reagan was the only figure "who can plausibly carry
the conservative banner . . . in 1976." When friends in California indicated

to him that the former governor was increasingly opposed to the new-party route, Rusher determined to see him as soon as possible. He arrived at the Reagan house in Pacific Palisades for dinner on April 30, his newly published volume in hand. "I presented the book formally to Nancy," Rusher later recalled, "knowing her influence with her husband and hoping desperately that the new-party concept might appeal to her more powerfully than, I now suspected, it appealed to him." Reagan said "gently but quite clearly" that he was inclined against the idea. Economic and social conservatives should form a coalition, he agreed. But they should do it within the Republican Party. The GOP wouldn't nominate him in 1976, Rusher objected. "Well, now," Reagan answered, "that remains to be seen."[49]

Belief in his chances to win the nomination wasn't the only reason for Reagan to refuse the entreaties from Rusher. He also thought he might tarnish his reputation among the public by leaving the GOP just thirteen or

*Courtesy National Review*

*With Buckley and Reagan at* National Review's *twentieth-anniversary dinner*

fourteen years after officially leaving his first party, the Democrats. But Rusher's assumption that a challenge to Ford would fail had substantial support, because polls in 1975 showed Reagan well behind in that contest. In May, Rusher told William Loeb of the *Manchester Union Leader* in New Hampshire that Wallace would go third-party and that Reagan still might.[50]

On a *Face the Nation* broadcast on June 1, however, Reagan reiterated his strong preference for ideologically rectifying the GOP. Asked by David Broder of the *Washington Post* if he "absolutely" ruled out a third-party race, he philosophized that "no one in this day of flux can rule out anything"—but immediately added that he had been saying, and would repeat now, that third parties "usually succeed in electing the people they were set up to oppose."[51] Rusher, as it happened, had a chance to put in another word with him that afternoon. Over cold cuts and coffee at John Sears's law office a block from the White House, Reagan met with several of his aides, Rusher, and Evans. Calling the meeting a mere "gathering of the clan," he deferentially denied to reporters that they were "plotting the overthrow" of the president.[52]

Also meeting with the former governor in Washington that month were other figures on the Right—among them Buchanan, Viguerie, Joseph Coors, new-majority political analyst Kevin Phillips, the leaders of two New Right organizations founded in the past year or so: Howard Phillips of the Conservative Caucus and Paul Weyrich of the Committee for the Survival of a Free Congress, and two Wallace representatives. They urged Reagan to take the third-party plunge and were turned down. They also had sessions with Wallace, then Connally, with the same request and result.[53]

The fact that these activists met with three potential candidates, not just one, showed the inherent complexity of new-party organizing. While Rusher had a personal connection to Reagan, Viguerie had a more definite link to Wallace, having raised $2.6 million for the Alabama governor in the previous year and a half, as of early 1975.[54] In addition, their project faced the tough question of whether a genuine party was contemplated, or just a one-time revolt in a frustrating presidential situation. Rusher's book was urging a new party all the way down the ballot, albeit in hopes that many conservative incumbents would join it. In fact, his strong belief in the need to win control of the House and Senate was a major reason for his advocacy. The four-year Democratic presidency that might result from a split conservative vote in 1976 would be "a small price to pay," he told Governor Meldrim Thomson of New Hampshire, if the Right's later unity in the new party allowed what the GOP no longer attempted—a serious challenge to the entrenched Democratic majorities in Congress. But in advocating a third-party presidential campaign at the CPAC conference, Stan Evans had said the goal in congressional and other races should be to keep the Republican Party "as conservative as possible."[55]

The COCA members thought that if Reagan lost the nomination to Ford, he would choose the third-party alternative if one had been successfully built—and that other conservative leaders would support this when he did so. On June 10, Rusher and Evans were named to a five-member group that would decide which method of ensuring a ballot line was best in each state—a new party, filing an independent slate of electors, or co-opting a party already on the ballot. In addition, Rusher reported to Reagan, people in each state would be designated so they would be in place to take the necessary steps "when and if the signal is given." He also enclosed a favorable review of his *New Majority* book.[56]

Writing a month later, Reagan said nothing about this activity, but he emphasized that Rusher could count on real access to him. Noting that he missed "our regular get-togethers," he looked forward to continuing "our frequent communications" and to "any ideas or suggestions you deem worthy of passing along." Reagan added: "I have great confidence in your judgment, and wouldn't want to do without your input and counsel." He also wished to meet again soon, when Rusher was in Southern California. In early August, Rusher called Reagan to update him about the new-party project and was calmly reminded: "We have disagreed on this." But the ex-governor also expressed a "vague hope," in Rusher's words, that the new party might help him to win the votes of social conservatives if he got the GOP nomination.[57] The logical inference was that Reagan wanted such a party's endorsement, and a possible further inference was that he would welcome widespread ballot status for it, Rusher's intermediate goal.

On August 21, Rusher and Evans met with Governor Wallace in his office at the statehouse in Montgomery. They didn't make any proposal, according to Evans, and he may not really have known who they were. "We were just getting to know him . . . sort of an interview with him, to size him up—and he was very cordial to us." Wallace was also "a man of obvious intelligence, not in the least any kind of fanatic, a savvy politician." Rusher noted that the governor "indicated general approval" when they outlined their activities in anticipation of 1976. From this talk and from a meeting with Wallace's campaign manager, he got the impression that Wallace would be willing to run as vice-presidential nominee with Reagan. In addition, he might "accept the chairmanship . . . or something like that" of the new-party project.[58]

To actually place a third party—or independent candidate or electors—on the state ballots, another group was formed out of the Conservative Alternatives committee in September and soon had a full-time executive director. Rusher chaired this project, known as the Committee for the New Majority. It also included Viguerie, Howard Phillips, and Meldrim Thomson. The work was demanding. Rusher spent much time on it between August 1975 and August 1976, especially on pursuing ballot status for the already-existing American Independent Party in additional states.[59] The AIP was the most prominent member of a coalition of parties under various names, some of which had been around since the 1950s. After the 1968 election, a faction split off into the American Party, which placed a stronger emphasis on anticommunism. In 1972, however, the parties had joined forces to the extent of agreeing on a presidential nominee.[60]

Although the American Independent Party was being permitted a large role in the New Majority group's scenario if it chose to have one, the volunteers recruited for the nationwide drive were, according to Rusher, basically regular conservatives whom the committee members had known from the Goldwater campaign, YAF, the ACU, and other movement organizations. In almost every state, he knew someone who could be asked to get up a petition drive or other needed project.[61]

Meanwhile, little had seemed to result from the recent get-togethers with Wallace and his campaign manager, Charles Snider. Although he allowed an aide to facilitate contact with a possible donor for the new-party effort, "several weeks of fruitless phone calls in various directions," Rusher recalled later, "convinced me that Wallace and his staff were being approached by others with different notions of how to play the cards in 1976."[62] Snider told the media his organization was providing no money or manpower to the new-party activitists, explaining: "We're determined to keep good faith with the Democrats as long as possible." But on November 12, announcing his Democratic primary campaign, Wallace did not rule out a later third-party effort. He also announced a platform fairly close to Reagan's.[63]

## Strange Bedfellows

As Rusher proceeded with work for third-party ballot placement, he increasingly had to face the Right's familiar question of extremism. But people he and his comrades knew from the Goldwater movement, YAF, the ACU, and elsewhere were not only available but actually helping in the effort. Already, in May, Rusher had tentatively agreed with a suggestion to consider designating electors for their ultimate candidate, rather than organizing a party, in states where the law required parties to hold conventions. Conventions, he noted to Evans, risked the possibility that "our organization might get taken over by extremists."[64]

Rusher and his colleagues in the New Majority committee were determined not to have a fringe party and therefore kept "a rigorous distance from the few such types who tried to make common cause with us." Although, in contrast, the people who actually ran the existing American Independent Party and American Party were "not unsavory" to him, their 1968 support for Wallace was wrongly seen as clear evidence of racism. But despite the potential embarrassment of a relationship with people who had backed Wallace when he was more strongly identified with segregation, Rusher and his fellow organizers decided they couldn't fairly be criticized for "simply using" existing third parties to elect Reagan.[65]

In October, Rusher told Reagan the fifty-state plan was proceeding. It seemed increasingly clear that all three options his committee had in mind, including the use of an officially recognized minor party, would be employed depending on the state-level situations. He also made clear that Wallace might be the ultimate beneficiary of their efforts. "The Wallace people," he wrote, "have decided to put in [our] basket such third-party eggs as they have for 1976" and former Wallace adviser Eli Howell was the committee's vice chairman. The legal structure for a new-party campaign would be in place "when it may be needed, either by you or by Wallace, or both."[66]

Early in the primary season, Rusher reiterated—this time to both Reagans—that the New Majority group would, in fact, have to use the former Wallace parties in some states. But through "a series of lucky breaks . . . we have managed to split off and discard . . . the more extreme and irresponsible state organizations of this type." The others had "voted to work with us," which Rusher took to mean: "They realize that our joint effort will not merely be a new Wallace effort, but a combined effort to find the best possible ticket and take it to victory in November." In those states where his group was starting new parties or preparing to run independent electors, "there is of course no danger of extremism whatsoever, since we are choosing the leaders of these efforts from the ranks of the responsible conservatives we have worked with over the years."[67]

Similarly but more specifically, Rusher told Buckley in February 1976 that his group had begun to overcome difficulties arising from differences between the organizational heirs of the 1968 Wallace campaign. The American Independents (who with the American Party had nominated then congressman John Schmitz of California, a Birch Society member, for president in the last election and received a little over a million votes) seemed ready to cooperate. But the American Party, led by Schmitz's 1972 running mate, former farm-magazine publisher Tom Anderson, was more problematic. Anderson had apparently "come to dislike Wallace," Rusher reported. An anti-Wallace move on his part had enthusiastic support from Willis Carto, the founder of Liberty Lobby, a conspiracy-minded organization perennially suspicious of international bankers and widely considered anti-Semitic. Carto had also, Rusher informed Buckley, denounced the New Majority committee as "the Rusher-Viguerie-Rockefeller axis" and claimed it was "out to destroy the impact of the true conservative movement in 1976."

But Rusher remained optimistic despite these problems. More politically congenial people in the American Party had gotten most of its state affiliates to withdraw and start a new organization, friendlier to the New Majority project, in January. Then, after the annual CPAC in Washington, Rusher had convened a daylong meeting with representatives from the third parties, the ACU, YAF, Phyllis Schlafly's Eagle Forum, Howard Phillips's Conservative Caucus, and the New Majority committee. The agenda was to review the states individually and see where things stood. The work was going very well, Rusher told Buckley, and it was possible a third-party option would appear on every state ballot.

For various reasons, including the fact that much of the conservative Republican talent went into the Reagan primary campaign, the new-party project had taken a "heavily pro-Wallace slant." But that didn't bother him a great deal. For one thing, "it has always been more or less clear that Wallace could have the third-line nomination if he wanted it, assuming that Reagan didn't." In addition, the Alabama governor and his campaign manager Snider had always struck him as "extremely flexible and open-minded on the question of what to do, and with whom, if their venture in Democratic politics falls through." Still, Rusher added, he wished "we had a few marbles of our own to play with." It would help if the Conservative Party of New York could be enlisted.[68]

More concerned about close quarters with people suspicious of *National Review* and its editor, Buckley heatedly suggested that Rusher's reputation might be at stake. Describing a recent meeting he and other New Majority members held in Chicago with some of the activists, the publisher had noted: "One of the principal avenues of attack upon me was my association with you. I found myself in the unfamiliar and not terribly appealing position of having to 'prove' my own conservatism and 'justify' my association with you and other dangerous leftists." But movement journalist Medford Evans, Stan's father, had played "an extremely influential and helpful role in certifying my legitimacy as a conservative to doubters."[69]

Reading Rusher's brief description of the meeting "with great interest," Buckley wasn't amused. "I confess to finding it slightly undignified," he wrote from Switzerland in early March, "that you should have to explain your association with me as if to a Jacobinical court. You could after all have said, why don't you read his magazine, his columns, or his 13 books, but that would presume that they know how to read, and obviously with that gang, no such thing is safe. Medford Evans is of course a fine man and a scholar, but he is nuts. The whole situation sounds to me awfully close to the kooks, and I am troubled about it . . . In the last analysis, if you have to deal with people of that sort, a) you're not going to get anywhere; b) you are simply going to besmirch yourself."[70]

Rusher answered that Buckley's concern about his relationship with "some of these types" was indeed "perfectly understandable . . . I share it." But the new party wouldn't be defined by "whether this or that near-kook is associated with it." It would be defined by its nominee. "I will certainly not remain identified with it," Rusher added, "if it wanders too far afield in this respect." He then challenged Buckley on a personal level, with thoughts on the gap between *NR* conservatives and the third-party members he had met:

> For what it is worth, though, I did find it interesting to learn that there are people out there in the boonies who lead reasonably active and dedicated lives (politically speaking) without understanding or even knowing much about what you and I are doing. Worse yet, they note and absorb only the highly visible but largely irrelevant epiphenomena concerning you: the yachts, etc. It is of course easy to grow impatient or even angry with such people, but I suspect that in doing so we reveal a parochialism not unlike their own.
>
> On a related point, I remain permanently amazed at just how easy it is for the [John Kenneth] Galbraiths and the [Arthur] Schlesingers to associate with just about anyone, however odoriferous, on the left, while you and I are restricted to an extremely narrow social range on the right.[71]

Rusher had just quit as chairman of the New Majority committee—as "you will, I am sure, be relieved to know," he told Buckley—because the syndicate marketing his newspaper column was getting uncomfortable with his simultaneous roles as activist and commentator. He would, however, remain a presence throughout the group's efforts and deliberations. Because of the preexistence of the AIP and the American Party, the nominee "will either have to be Wallace or somebody Wallace consents to support." But Rusher thought he would gladly run as the vice-presidential candidate with Reagan.

He added that in truth he was dissatisfied with them. Praising the manuscript of an angrily written book by populist organizer Robert Whitaker, *A Plague on Both Your Houses*, to which he wrote a laudatory foreword, Rusher told Buckley it was "wonderfully stimulating and incisive in many ways" even though the author "is not always as kind as he ought to be to conservatives, specifically including thee and me." The book had caused him "to reflect that Reagan and Wallace probably both represent . . . political dead ends for the expression of American conservative thought: the one too soft and genial, and the other too Southern, parochial, etc."

Indeed, Rusher predicted: "If they play the rest of their respective hands as badly as they have played them hitherto, this will be the last year for both of them on the national political scene—and then the fun will really begin." He closed by teasing Buckley: "Who, do you suppose, will be the new leader of the social conservatives? If he is young, good-looking and articulate, and comes from the Southwest or West, treat him with respect, for you may be dealing with the new master of us all."[72]

The situation in which Rusher found himself wasn't entirely new. More than fifteen years earlier, Buckley had admonished him for sending out copies of the anti–Supreme Court booklet *Nine Men Against America* to law-school deans around the country and requesting their comments. He had noted his antiestablishment views frequently in internal *NR* correspondence and not backed away from them. Yet for all his New Right advocacy with Buckley, Reagan, and the public, Rusher had almost no experience with the political demographic he was now explicitly targeting. He said so plainly in his foreword to the Whitaker volume, noting that nearly all of his friends were conservative Republicans. "Of our proposed allies . . . I knew a fair amount by reputation and rumor, but practically nothing by way of direct contact. I had no populist friends—we agreed on many things, but simply didn't run in the same social circles." Rusher hadn't known where to find populists, what organizations they belonged to, who their leaders or spokesmen were.[73] Although he never became immersed in populist organizations or settings, his respect for the growing viewpoint and its issues proved permanent.

As Rusher had warned, Whitaker was tough on better-known figures in *Plague on Both Your Houses*—writing, for example, that Buckley "keeps respectable conservative noses to the old establishment grindstone." Although the *New Majority Party* book had admittedly inspired some people in the mainline movement, Rusher and others who aimed to build a new party were nonetheless offering "a cure they do not have," Whitaker wrote. "They have little or no input from populist [e.g., antibusing] protest groups. Their approach does not involve actually dealing with the masses, but merely appealing to them. Conservatives, it appears, will make policy, and then send out an invitation for populists to vote conservative."[74]

Wishing Reagan well in the primaries notwithstanding his alternative plans for him, Rusher was upset by Barry Goldwater's backing of Ford, a position long evident although not officially announced by Goldwater until June 30, after the primary season. In a February column, Rusher criticized him on two grounds: lining up with Ford, and publicly praising Rockefeller (rather theoretically by this time) as a "damn good" potential president. The likely explanation was that Goldwater's "grip on conservative principles just isn't . . . the absolutely dependable thing we believe it to be" and perhaps never was so dependable. Soon thereafter, liberal columnist Mary McGrory quoted the senator as calling Rusher and the also-critical Richard Viguerie "those sons of bitches."[75]

Rusher was further angered by comments on Reagan's opposition to the contemplated Panama Canal Treaties. In May, he wrote that conservatives in

1976 were learning "who their real friends are." Goldwater had always been a "centrist" in terms of nominations. There was his "Grow up, conservatives!" exhortation at the 1960 convention, his 1965 endorsement of Nixon three years in advance, and his continued Nixon support in 1968 even as many conservatives turned to Reagan. Now the senator was not only with Ford but also "doing his best to undermine Reagan" again. In particular, Rusher had been incensed when Goldwater, on a Sunday TV talk show, asked viewers: "Are you willing to go to war" over the Panama Canal, in stark opposition to Reagan's belief in holding it by force if necessary. Rusher pointed out that a 1963 book by Goldwater, *Why Not Victory?*, had "warned against concessions to Panamanian demagoguery" by noting that concessions in such a situation were easily seen as weakness and generated greater demands.

The recent comments from Goldwater were "carefully designed to injure Ronald Reagan, and . . . quite capable of doing so," he alleged. "There is a bitter irony in watching Goldwater, who was falsely maligned as an 'extremist' and deserted by millions of liberal Republicans . . . setting up Ronald Reagan for exactly the same treatment—an irony bitterer still when one reflects that Reagan first came to political prominence as a result of the brilliant television talk he gave for Goldwater during that same 1964 campaign."[76]

Goldwater wrote fumingly to Buckley the next month, enclosing a copy of a letter he was sending to an old and close friend. It was indicative, he told Buckley, "of the attitude that has been forced on me by the unconscionable attacks on me by men I thought were friends of mine, former conservatives, or at least those who called themselves conservatives." Much as he had warned enthusiastic backers at the 1960 convention against insisting on a "Russian-type veto" in the party, he now told Buckley conservatism was "far too vital a thing to be bandied around on the lips of those who see their way as the only way. I want to have a long, personal talk with you about this . . . This has to be brought to the attention of those people who are yours [*sic*] and my friends and who cannot see the wrongness in turning just as the communists do." Rusher, former aide Lee Edwards, and others, the senator complained to his friend in the letter shared with Buckley, had been reporting his positions on legislation "in as dishonest a way as can be done." Admitting that he had penned a "short diatribe," Goldwater added that the situation "has absolutely disgusted me" and could destroy the Republican Party by the end of the year.[77]

Buckley may have spoken with Rusher some weeks later. Sending along copies of Goldwater's two letters, he jotted: "Let's discuss." But the senator's complaint got no visible response in Buckley's column or in *NR* editorials—and a month before Goldwater wrote him, the editor had taken a position much closer to Rusher's. Both Goldwater and Reagan were partly responsible for the "destructiveness of the criticism . . . against Republicans by Republicans," he told readers, adding: "But I am required to say, because my affection for Goldwater would not permit me to dissimulate, that I think he has been the principal aggressor this time around, and for reasons I cannot fathom." Buckley then cited one of the quotations from *Why Not Victory?* that Rusher used in his anti-Goldwater column dated a week later.[78]

Even as Rusher fell out with Goldwater, praised Whitaker's articulate but cantankerous populism, and worked tenaciously to launch a new party, he showed his ingrained respect for conventional compromise when Reagan made an early vice-presidential choice that was quickly opposed by much of the Right. As the 1976 campaign continued into the spring, Reagan pulled out of an otherwise-fatal slump with the help of ACU activists and the Helms organization in North Carolina, winning the state's primary. Heavily using the Panama Canal issue and foreign policy, attacking Secretary Kissinger as well as President Ford, he continued to win primaries. His dramatically revived candidacy threatened the president's nomination, as it had much earlier in the season but not since. A few weeks before the Republican convention, Reagan decided to boost his chances further by making a vice-presidential pick. It was a man clearly to his left, Senator Richard Schweiker of Pennsylvania, with whom Rusher wasn't especially familiar.[79]

While giving a luncheon speech in California three days later, Rusher was called to the phone to speak with Reagan, who was contacting supporters to reassure them about Schweiker. A conservative almost had to choose a relative liberal in order to balance the ticket, Rusher said. Reagan told him "convincingly" that Schweiker wasn't as liberal as people were saying.[80] But the unhappy conservatives had evidence for their opposition. The liberal Americans for Democratic Action gave Schweiker's Senate voting record a score of 89; the AFL-CIO rated him at a perfect 100. Like many conservative columnists, George Will denounced the Reagan-Schweiker partnership, calling it "another subtraction from the dignity of the political vocation."[81]

Buckley judiciously held back, pointing out that the ADA rating stressed economic issues. Schweiker favored capital punishment and had introduced a constitutional amendment for school prayer, and he opposed abortion and gun control. He had also been "consistently critical of détente" and had often noted the desirability of the emancipation of Eastern Europe. Although Schweiker was quite guilty of big-government "Washingtonitis," Buckley hoped he might place a higher priority on his social and foreign-policy conservatism.[82] Of the figures on the New Right who opposed Schweiker, an unnamed ACU activist suggested they were forgetting its professed wish (voiced, for example, in Rusher's book) to compromise on economic issues in order to get non-Republican conservative votes: "They don't know their own program." But such points made little difference. The Schweiker choice badly reduced the enthusiasm among many key Reagan backers and produced no new delegates.[83]

## Denouement

Rusher certainly hoped Reagan would win the nomination. In Oregon, his friend and former YR ally Diarmuid O'Scannlain, who had worked for the Reagan candidacy in 1968, found the choice in 1976 difficult but thought "one should stick with the incumbent" and ended up as a Ford delegate. Inexperienced as a delegate, O'Scannlain requested advice about the upcoming convention. Rusher had just one word for him: "Switch!"[84] After the narrow loss at Kansas City, he wrote a column neatly combining his acute disappointment at Reagan's rejection of the new-party strategy with his deeper and long-standing reverence. God gave Reagan so many great qualities and talents but, sadly, hadn't endowed him with the imagination to see the promise of a new party and of his leadership of such a party. At 65, he knew there would be "no political tomorrows" for him. But writing now from the viewpoint of the tearful Reagan delegates, Rusher added that it was a privilege to have fought and lost with such a leader.[85]

Soon after the Republican convention, the American Independent Party met in Chicago at the Conrad Hilton Hotel. It was now on the ballot in about thirty-six states; several more seemed likely if a reasonably good candidate were found. In the week between the Republican and AIP conventions, Rusher called prominent conservatives—starting perfunctorily with Reagan—to see whether one would accept the nomination. Reagan wouldn't, having promised to back Ford. Ex-governor Connally, Senator Helms, and Governor Thomson also refused. The absence of a major candidate, according to Rusher, left the American Independent convention to the more extreme people among the Wallaceites. They had been willing, though in some cases reluctantly, to accept the nomination of Reagan or Helms. From the standpoint of later third-party strength, the situation was especially unfortunate. If its nominee won at least 5 percent of the vote in 1976, the AIP would get federal funds in 1980; a substantially better result would similarly increase those funds.

Rusher persuaded Bob Morris, his boss at the Senate Internal Security Subcommittee and a former president of the conservative-Catholic University of Dallas, to make himself available for the nomination. His onetime YAF ally and protégé Viguerie, a strong presence in the movement as a mass fund-raiser for the past decade and the founder of *Conservative Digest* as

*Rusher and Richard Viguerie, center, at the American Independent Party convention, with Louisiana state representatives Daniel Richey, left, and Woody Jenkins, right*

well, would be Morris's running mate. Also supporting the ticket were New Right leaders Howard Phillips and Paul Weyrich.[86]

The somewhat contrived candidacies didn't work. The convention's keynote speaker, John Couture, attacked the vast power of "murderous" and "atheistic political Zionism" to cheers and flag-waving from many of the delegates—a scene that depressed Rusher, Viguerie, and others at the outset. The disdain was mutual. People who already belonged to the AIP "resented the newcomers with their three-piece suits and slick campaign literature."[87] Although the convention included many delegates who identified with Reagan, their belief in "a more aggressive anti-Communist foreign policy" contrasted with the Wallaceites' tendency to isolationism, *Time* magazine reported. One group supported John Rarick, an ultraconservative former Democratic congressman from Louisiana. The "articulate" Bob Morris was the candidate of "the intellectuals," including Rusher.[88]

In any case, Reagan and Wallace weren't available. It became apparent that most delegates were ready to nominate former Georgia Democratic governor Lester Maddox, "a notorious racist," Rusher later lamented, whom they may have picked in hopes of generating enough publicity or excitement to win the party the 5 percent qualifying it for federal dollars. (Ironically, Buckley had hinted at a possible Maddox nomination in his perturbed comments to the publisher back in March.) At one point, the "fast-talking" and "flamboyant" Atlanta segregationist claimed Wallace had "joined the pointy-headed bureaucrats"—a borrowed Wallace epithet—by staying in the Democratic Party. Rusher, Morris, Viguerie, and most delegates who shared their vision of a new and "responsible" third party left the convention. The AIP also lost the potential support of the Conservative Party in New York and of organizations in some other states.[89]

Rusher told the press that the party had "turned inward, backward, and downward." Likewise, Viguerie said the nomination of Maddox "dashes our hopes." AIP founder William Shearer shrugged off their disappointment, saying Rusher and Viguerie represented "the super-educated, highly affluent, country-club people" who thought they were "too good to commune with the just-average George Wallace people." Shortly after the convention, a presumably embarrassed Rusher wrote Joe Coors to request help in paying off the New Majority project's debt.[90]

In a negative sense, he had stepped into the spotlight nationally and not just at the AIP gathering. As Priscilla Buckley recalls: "Garry Wills wrote the funniest column I ever read in my life about Bill Rusher and that Lester Maddox debacle. It was sort of *samizdat* around the *National Review* office. We were too polite to bring it up in person."[91] In his own column, Rusher noted that he had fully expected "a rough couple of weeks" and had "dreaded" what Buckley and Jack Kilpatrick would say. Without naming names or even mentioning the New Majority group, Buckley wrote of "genuine innocents, who expected the nomination of Snow White." Kilpatrick's column referred to them as "Boy Scouts" who got "the old heave-ho."

Mild though he agreed their condescension was, Rusher didn't like being portrayed as what he called "a little petunia in an onion patch." But despite the recent repudiation by the American Independents, he sought to counter descriptions of the party more than to defend his judgment. In the last eight or ten months, Rusher had gotten to know its chairman Bill Shearer fairly well—and "we have our differences, not least stylistic." Over a long career in "hard-right politics" in California, Shearer had "supported (I trust reluctantly) candidates that would make a vulture retch." But Rusher added: "I have never detected the slightest odor of racism, anti-Semitism or any other noxious doctrine in his personal ambiance, and the worst policy-plank I have ever discovered in his private portfolio is a rather outdated isolationism."

It wasn't true, he maintained, that the third-party convention "pitted the forces of rectitude, typified by me and longing hopelessly for a respectable presidential candidate, against a larger body of yahoos determined to go nuts at any cost." The American Independent leaders were "ready, willing and . . . able to lead their party into the endorsement of any prominent conservative Republican officeholder who would accept their nomination." Unfortunately, because none had left the Republican convention "angry enough," no such figure could be found. Rusher also thought the New Majority activists deserved much of the credit for the strongly conservative positions that Helms, among others, pushed into the GOP platform. These were probably allowed, he explained, "only because the Ford forces . . . knew and feared the possible outcome" of the AIP convention a week later.[92] The Republican delegates had adopted an anti-détente plank, somewhat rebelliously titled "Morality in Foreign Policy"—as well as planks endorsing antibusing, antiabortion, and pro-school-prayer constitutional amendments.[93]

*National Review* urged readers to take heart from the predominant conservatism at the convention—a main point Rusher had made in 1968, after Reagan lost to Nixon. Liberalism was now "virtually extinct" among Republicans. Despite Ford's nomination, "the natural evolution of the party can scarcely be aborted," especially because the convention had so many "young, bright, and energetic" people. The editorial also called it "curious" that some conservatives, including smart and principled ones, had decided to initiate a new party that year. The AIP convention was "an exotic exercise . . . it seems too unnecessary."[94]

At Kansas City and for a few weeks afterward, leading conservatives suggested publicly and privately that if Ford lost, a push would occur soon after the election to capture the GOP for conservative principles or conceivably try again for a new party. The second point proved to be empty talk. Equally empty for new-party advocates was Election Day, as a candidate they didn't want received one-fifth of 1 percent at the polls. The combination of Maddox and his minuscule vote was a "thoroughly miserable end," Rusher felt, "to our 1976 experiment with a new party . . . into which many good and earnest people had thrown themselves for over a year." He took more than a little "good-natured ribbing" from friends who had always predicted it would fail.[95]

Rusher would look back on his third-party advocacy ambivalently—as a "waste of time" yet also "sensible" in its context, given the situation conservatives faced. "Mark Twain, I think it was, said that 'every man with a new idea is a crank until the idea succeeds.' And since that particular idea didn't succeed, I guess I have to be convicted of being a crank on that particular subject." Rusher thought he had proved his point when the Republican convention picked Ford over Reagan. But Reagan "certainly proved his in 1980 . . . when he got the nomination and the presidency."[96]

## "Chronic Losers"

As he had done in 1972, Rusher left his presidential ballot blank. Writing the week before the election from Cairo as he hurried home to vote, he told readers Jimmy Carter was "probably a step in the right direction" compared with the last four decades of Democratic nominees. Sounding like Jim Burnham on John F. Kennedy, Rusher also wrote of the recent Georgia governor: "there travels with him the whole baggage-train of American liberalism— the spend-and-elect philosophy that bankrupted New York City, built the presidency into a Frankensteinean monster, dragged this country into two wars it had no plan for winning, and fastened Big Government on our necks forever. Try as he may, Carter cannot but help serve that party and policy."

Just a week before, Rusher had warmly applauded much of Ford's recent domestic policy. By the standards of the past half century, his economic team had a "truly outstanding" record, and the administration enforced fiscal discipline despite the unpopularity of doing so. But the president, he now wrote in his final election column, was "necessarily the product and prisoner of the party that nominated him: a moribund heap of chronic losers, serving a highly selective set of economic interests and little else . . . If the Republican party didn't exist the Democrats would have to invent it: seldom have so many owed so much to so few."[97]

Rusher's continued indictment of the Republican Party and his unwillingness even tepidly to endorse Ford were based on the reasons given in his 1975 book, which he still found compelling: the GOP's apparent lack of ideological willpower, its apparent unwillingness to adapt to new political circumstances, its low standing among voters. His disgust with the Republican Party, and his wish to destroy it even after his new-party project had failed, motivated him more than did policy judgments about the current presidency or Carter's potential one. Worsening his low opinion of the party was his perception that the Democrats actually seemed to be responding better to the more conservative postsixties era. Although even the highly ideological *Human Events* reluctantly backed Ford, calling Carter a "collectivist-liberal," Rusher wasn't alone in taking a scorched-earth attitude. Viguerie, for instance, said some of his New Right colleagues would actually be voting for the Democratic candidate because a new conservative party couldn't arise until the GOP died. He had "no strong recommendation" himself, because there was little at stake for conservatives in the election, but tentatively planned to write in Reagan.[98]

Two years of toil by Rusher ended in a note of serenity from his political hero. Visiting Reagan in California in late 1976, "I asked him if he had any plans for '80, and he said: 'On or off the record?' I said: 'Both.' 'Well,' he said, 'On the record: It's too early to tell. Off the record: You know, I never really had to have that job.'"[99]

# 14

# Commentaries

Rusher remained hostile to the Republican Party well into President Carter's term. Although Reagan never shared that viewpoint, he did agree that the GOP was tied too closely to business interests both in the public mind and to some extent in reality. Speaking to the Intercollegiate Studies Institute, a conservative academic organization, in January 1977, Reagan said the new Republican Party he envisioned "will not, and cannot, be limited to the country club–Big Business image that for reasons both fair and unfair it is burdened with today. It is going to have to have room for the man and woman in the factories, for the farmer, for the cop on the beat, and for the millions of Americans who may never have thought of joining our party before."[1]

At the CPAC conference early that year, Rusher was pleased that speakers spent significant time discussing the new-party idea. In calling for "a new, lasting majority" that combined social and economic conservatives, "something new . . . open and vital and dynamic," Reagan himself showed that he had "finally gotten around to studying the basic strategy." But he then made it clear that he meant a conservative-dominated GOP. Reagan was, Rusher complained, still trying to achieve the movement's goals "through that spavined, threadbare, disreputable old wreck . . . to squeeze the greatest coalition in American political history into the puny and discredited framework of the Republican party." Rusher seemed to give up on him, telling readers: "Ronald Reagan is a wonderful speaker and a wonderful man, but not that wonderful. If we're going to sell a new blend of wine, we're going to need a brand-new bottle."[2]

In addition to his frustration with Reagan, Rusher liked the new president in some respects, not only as an indicator of a potentially moderate Democratic Party but also for his "simplicity and outspoken morality." In March, after a recent visit to Georgia, he shared his thinking with readers. "Jimmy Carter isn't merely funnin' us . . . this is what he is truly like, and the irreverent cynics are just going to have to get used to the idea," Rusher wrote. "The America of the South and West—what the late Willmoore Kendall long ago called 'the great Baptist subculture of the United States'—has at last outnumbered and overpowered the America of the long-dominant Northeast, and it is imposing its own style and values on the nation by right of conquest." The president would "slowly earn the respect, and perhaps also the affection, of people all over the world who have never even heard of Baptism. The scrupulously amoral, 'realistic' politics of a Kissinger or a Nixon appeals strongly to deracinated intellectuals . . . But Jimmy Carter's characterizing way is the Way of the Gospel, which works powerfully in the hearts of men, and it may find echoes where the appeal of 'realism' would evoke only mirthless laughter."[3]

Although Buckley took a much cooler attitude, writing, "The general feeling . . . is that, with a little luck, the republic will survive a term in office by President Carter," Rusher's openness to the president wasn't idiosyncratic at *National Review*. "For a time," John Coyne recalls, "a lot of us shared Bill's hopes for Jimmy Carter. He'd served with distinction as a naval officer, he'd run a fiscally conservative administration in Georgia, his religious commitment was sincere . . . At the magazine, as I remember, this view was initially treated with respect."[4] Believing that nations couldn't be held to the standards of individuals, Burnham saw potential danger in the president-elect's moralizing on foreign policy—although he suggested, unlike Rusher, that it was probably a combination of demagoguery and mere sentimentality. Writing during the campaign, however, he had found it commendable that Carter spoke of religion "without embarrassment," which Burnham saw as a rejection of "the counterculture's obscenities and drugs and excesses." Carter was "a brand-new guy," notes Richard Brookhiser, who joined the magazine in 1976. "We were all trying to figure him out."[5]

Almost one-third of self-identified conservatives had voted for him in the general election, and numerous rural counties in the South and elsewhere had shifted massively in their presidential vote, from Republican to Democrat, since 1972. Rusher hoped to reach Democratic players who understood the implications of Carter's right-of-center support, could talk with the new president, and might then "influence his future course in a conservative direction." In 1977, he brought the idea to a well-connected Democratic friend. The Democrat initially thought he would arrange an introduction to Charles Kirbo, a close friend of the president's from Georgia, but changed his mind and set up an appointment with the new federal budget director, Bert Lance. Rusher met Lance, also a friend of the president's, at the Old Executive Office Building on July 13. Not knowing of the ethics charges that were in prospect for the budget chief, he told him the Democratic Party would gain votes by moving to the right as the country was doing and also suggested they set up a line of communications. Lance "listened carefully, did not take issue with my central point, and suggested amiably that we keep in touch."[6]

Carter's nomination, Rusher told readers about a week later, had returned the conservative Democrats to their party, and his election as president had ensured that most would remain there at least until 1984. The Democrats had abandoned their "long and passionate commitment to programmatic liberalism in favor of something much closer to the American center." Carter was "clearly open to conservative influences, and has among his closest friends and highest appointees men who are conservative by any fair definition." Certainly a new-party victory in 1976 would have been better, but the prospects for such a party now looked dismal. Conservatives should develop input into the Carter administration: "encourage it when we believe it is right, warn it when we feel it is wrong, and battle for its soul . . . exactly as we would have battled for Ford's if he had won."[7]

In an interview that spring, Rusher had said Carter did "surprisingly well" in his first hundred days. He was "a moralist." If his recent proposal to the Soviet Union for sharp bilateral cuts in nuclear arms were refused—or accepted but then cheated on—he would be "a moralist with a clear conscience" in dealing with the Russians, and thus from their standpoint "a very dangerous man indeed." Also very positive were the president's stress on balancing the budget within four years and his symbolic repudiation of the so-called imperial presidency. Wearing sweaters and cutting back on chauffeurs might be dismissed as public relations, but such gestures were "precisely what is needed." Absent some catastrophe, Carter would win a second term. He could "take his left wing for granted and bid toward the right center," and he was in fact doing that. Conservatives should "do more talking to Carter than to Republicans," Rusher urged, even though they wouldn't be very influential themselves—"as usual, I might add."[8]

In addition to praising the president's commitment to a balanced budget, Rusher liked his introduction of human rights in the shaping of foreign policy and indications that Carter would strengthen America's defense posture. All this, he wrote, had "grated on liberal sensibilities."[9] Rusher defended the beleaguered Bert Lance in August and again a month later. He saw the controversy over the budget director's former practices while a banker in Georgia as a power struggle, much as he had viewed Watergate. If the liberals forced Lance to resign, Carter's ability to go against their wishes would be limited. After a hearing in which the official firmly confronted two senators, Rusher wrote that there still was no credible evidence he had ever done anything wrong.[10] But two and a half months after their July meeting, his hoped-for conduit to Carter left the administration.[11]

In addition to his new interest in influencing the Democratic Party, Rusher continued to support the idea of conservative contact with unions, which he had suggested in *New Majority Party*. At the beginning of 1978, he urged as a good resolution for the year that conservatives "try not to be critical of unions or union members as such." He criticized "compulsory union membership" and constant increases in the minimum wage, also noting that organized labor's national lobbyists often lost sight of the general public interest. But he added that unions and their members were "among the most conservative forces in our society"—favorable toward the free-enterprise system, "stoutly patriotic and anti-Communist, contemptuous of welfare grifters, proud to be among America's 'producers.'" If the conservative movement "ever gets its act together and takes over the government," Rusher concluded, that would happen only once it began "recognizing the American union . . . as an ally and a friend."[12]

The following month, a large delegation including New Right organizers Viguerie, Weyrich, and Howard Phillips, conservative congressmen Philip Crane of Illinois and Mickey Edwards of Oklahoma, and state and local Republican leaders met with local union leaders in Youngstown, Ohio, where a major steel plant had recently been closed. The visitors proved right in their expectation that major overlaps in economic viewpoint existed between themselves and the unionists. In their private meetings, agreement emerged on several points: that the steel industry's economic climate had been damaged by unfavorable tax laws, excessive governmental regulation, the lack of sufficient energy production, the loss of capital availability due to excessive government spending and borrowing, and the Carter administration's failure to enforce antidumping laws involving imported products.[13]

These discussions, in which the conservatives listened more than talked, seemed to Rusher "one of the most original and promising political developments in years." Some of the union leaders, he noted in his column, said that to them, "the word 'conservative' meant a wealthy businessman with little comprehension of, or interest in, the problems of the average steelworker. But, questioned on issue after issue, these same spokesmen unwittingly came down on the conservative side." Although Rusher thought the Right shouldn't "expect too much too soon" in terms of a possible alliance to restore manufacturing employment, he suggested a cautious optimism.

Higher-level labor leaders, however, wouldn't go along. In 1977, for example, the AFL-CIO had produced and distributed a film called *The New Right Machine* warning union members against this new aspect of the conservative movement and describing it in lurid terms. As then congressman Edwards later recalled, such attitudes among union officials "quickly dissipated" his colleagues' efforts.[14]

## "The Credibility of the United States"

Even as Rusher began his abortive relationship with the new administration, he expressed concerns about its foreign policy. One such complaint was that the text of the proposed Panama Canal Treaties lacked a crucial point that the president, just weeks ago, had suggested it would have: "the permanent right [in Carter's words] to defend the neutrality of the canal from any threat, for an indefinite period," after the treaties gave control to Panama.[15] While Burnham, who decided to support the treaties, thought the United States could quickly seize the canal in any world crisis calling for such action, Rusher questioned whether a future American president would have the will to do this if Panama possessed sovereignty.[16] "What is really at stake is the credibility of the United States as a major power," he wrote, telling readers of his opposition. "A great many Americans sense this, and it accounts for the intense resistance these treaties are encountering."[17]

Although the Senate ratified them by a narrow margin in 1978, the strong opposition from Reagan, Rusher's allies on the New Right, and most of the movement helped to set the stage for conservatives' political triumph in 1980. Buckley's endorsement of the treaties on *Firing Line* and elsewhere—he debated Phyllis Schlafly as well as Reagan—caused many cancellations from *NR* readers. Addressing the disagreement frankly in a letter to subscribers, Rusher wrote: "You and I believe Bill Buckley was wrong about the Canal treaties. But I hope you will agree with me, on reflection, that this kind of occasional disagreement is inevitable among spirited personalities."[18]

Although he commented often on the treaties while they were a live issue, Rusher had a more long-standing interest in Taiwan. His relationship with the country had begun in the early 1960s, when its recently appointed New York representative Eugene Loh was cultivating *National Review*. The Taiwanese government eventually told Rusher he could visit at its expense anytime he liked, and he did so. He first traveled there in 1962 and by 1989 had gone about twenty times.[19] In addition to Taiwan's staunch anticommunism, Rusher was impressed by its economic progress, comparing the modernized society of the 1970s—"a smaller and more streamlined version of

*Greeting Taiwanese president Chiang Ching-kuo*

the Japanese miracle"—with the underdeveloped country he saw a decade-plus before. He liked the food, the art, and various characteristics of Chinese culture, such as its emphasis on family: the large dinner table with three generations around it, from the elderly matriarch to young kids in high chairs. He also liked the "infectious good humor" in Taiwan, especially notable on his earlier visits.[20]

Rusher was in a position to gain an inside perspective on Taiwanese policy and concerns, and at least occasionally he could tell the country's government something as well. In December 1976, he had written Frederick Chien, vice minister of foreign affairs, to report that Reagan—"still a very influential man"—seemed to remain solidly on their side. Over lunch in Los Angeles the previous week, Rusher had checked on his general attitude toward Taiwan and communist China. Vice Minister Chien had previously suggested that Reagan was softening his position on the mainland government and perhaps on Taiwan. But the ex-governor's "complete bewilderment" upon hearing this seemed fully convincing, Rusher told his friend.

Reagan planned to stay "very actively involved in future policy formulations for the Republican party, and I honestly do think you can count on him."[21]

Also fascinating to Rusher was South Africa, a country he thought was unjustly besieged and that impressed him with its "utter modernity." In 1965, with the conservative black journalist Dr. Max Yergan, he had cofounded the American-African Affairs Association, which published a series of monographs about Cuban and communist Chinese activities on the continent and sent leading conservatives on fact-finding trips to assess issues in southern Africa. Among those involved in the organization were Frank Meyer, former congressman and prominent conservative foreign-affairs expert Walter Judd, journalist John Chamberlain, and David Rowe, a political scientist at Yale.[22] Rusher persistently dissented from the liberal orthodoxy that opposed and attacked South Africa's "white minority" government and demanded immediate black rule in its next-door neighbor, the breakaway British colony of Rhodesia. He would stay in close touch with regional developments well into the 1990s, commenting on them frequently in his column. His controversial perspective was based on seven visits to South Africa between 1962 and 1987.[23]

The publisher and *National Review* were in comfortable agreement on Taiwan. But in the 1970s, as the magazine gradually became more liberal on South Africa, the positions Rusher took toward its government and racial policies grew more noticeable. He was "tireless" in debate about the country, Rick Brookhiser recalls, with arguments that were "often not good arguments . . . but if they would serve, he'd grab 'em."[24] Rusher believed the predominant American attitude toward South Africa was self-righteous and simplistic—another case of the heedlessly abstract moralizing that liberals, at great cost to everyone, imposed on social problems at home. South Africa, he wrote in 1987, "illustrates, as few other things can, the dictum that humility is the beginning of true wisdom." Rusher criticized "career liberals" who had "almost unconsciously been looking for new worlds to conquer" after the civil-rights agenda was enacted in the United States. "To such people, the cause of South Africa's blacks—perceived from a great distance, very largely misunderstood, but capable of generating gratifying quantities of cost-free moral indignation—was a godsend."[25]

The Soweto riots outside Johannesburg in 1976, which proved to be the beginning of the end for apartheid and white rule in the country, occasioned very distinct responses from Burnham and Rusher. The riots were clearly, Burnham wrote, "a mass protest by the blacks against the South African system"—though also "irrational" to an extent, since they had "destroyed much property that served their needs and provided their amenities" and in some cases attacked other blacks. As for the future, Burnham noted: "In today's world . . . no nation is an island. Left more or less to themselves, the white South Africans might preserve their bizarre system for generations. But they will not be left to themselves." Without precisely condemning apartheid and white rule, Burnham said the system couldn't survive and that Western governments, therefore, now understandably viewed the European-descended residents of southern Africa as "expendables."

Rusher responded angrily in the pages of *NR*. Although he mixed his criticism with much respect, he found Burnham's column more than irritating. "For a certain type of personality," he began, "realism can be as heady a drug as that more familiar stimulant, idealism. To pursue the metaphor cautiously, both potions can be beneficial when taken in moderation. But I am afraid that my valued friend and colleague Jim Burnham, whose cold-eyed realism about world affairs is surely one of the major assets of the American Right, overindulged in his column." Burnham hadn't said he *approved* of Western governments' writing off the whites as expendable, and this suggested he actually disapproved. But Rusher continued: "The kicks involved here are of a far more sado-masochistic variety: We are being invited, like so many white-smocked technicians, to observe (from a safe distance, of course) the imminent extinction—total, inevitable, and no doubt bloody—of several million people much like ourselves. Thus spake Zarathustra."[26]

In his column a month later, Rusher asked: "Why this savage worldwide hostility to the concept of apartheid?" He explained the distinction between what South Africans called "petty apartheid," or the pervasive and mandatory segregation in daily life, and "grand apartheid," or long-term segregation, which Rusher described as the "ambitious scheme to divide the country into one white and eight black nations." Without discussing the apartheid of daily life, he defended as an "ingenious idea" the eventual movement of the black population into the traditional homelands of the eight main tribal groupings. Although the eventual white nation would get 87 percent of South Africa under the policy, much of this was "barren desert," Rusher noted—and the borders of the black homelands "ought to be, and are, subject to further negotiation and expansion." As for the major cities, he regarded them as "culturally the achievement of the white population, which arrived in this part of southern Africa simultaneously with the blacks 350 years ago." The liberal-dominated international community's "real objection to the black homelands . . . is that [they] would enable white South Africa to survive."[27]

Rusher also frequently criticized the Carter administration's policy on Rhodesia. In 1977, he warned that State Department officials were aiming to replace the white government under Prime Minister Ian Smith, who had agreed in principle to a black-dominated democracy the previous year, with "a Moscow-backed enemy of Western influence in southern Africa." U.S. policy, he wrote in 1978, amounted to backing terrorists led by Joshua Nkomo and Robert Mugabe who were trying to "shoot their way to power." In contrast, a settlement had already been negotiated to provide majority rule with protections for white interests. The new Zimbabwe "would have a real chance of surviving and progressing under a democratically elected black government. Why not give it that chance?"[28]

Equally offensive to Rusher was Carter's sudden recognition of the communist mainland regime as China's legitimate government, withdrawal of diplomatic recognition from Taiwan, and abrogation of the American defense treaty with Taiwan. Holding back from a direct attack on Carter, he wrote that all this was inevitable once Nixon and Kissinger began to build a relationship with the mainland regime seven years earlier and made clear from the outset that the relationship must progress. But Rusher nonetheless considered these new steps in December 1978 outrageous—and outrageously executed.

The "repellent" set of decisions was announced with Congress adjourned and the public's attention on the holidays. There had been no time for public consideration or congressional discussion. Every poll showed a substantial majority opposed to Carter's recognition of Peking and his break with Taiwan. These decisions, Rusher added, were made "at the behest of foreign-policy pressure groups representing narrow interests frankly at odds with U.S. public opinion." America, he concluded, had been "truly diminished."[29] Describing the mood he found on a visit to Taiwan shortly thereafter, Rusher told readers there had been a feeling of shock, but no lasting economic impact. He praised the Taiwanese people for not panicking and applauded Congress for getting Carter to accept generous provisions that would maintain trade and other relations through nongovernmental channels. The government in Taipei, Rusher reported, was happy with these provisions.[30]

With debate under way on the proposed SALT II nuclear-arms treaty in mid-1979, Rusher acknowledged his and the public's inability to reach a fully informed conclusion about such a technical issue. But he was confident in saying the Soviet Union would "cheat on every aspect of the agreement" they could cheat on, whereas "we, being nice guys, won't." In addition, foreign-policy liberals would use SALT II ratification as an excuse to slash other defense spending. But an especially powerful argument from Rusher's perspective was that the treaty had been produced by the U.S. foreign-policy establishment and its "hardworking disaster factory." Delegitimizing and replacing this "arrogant, undemocratic, nearsighted and self-serving" government-big-business-academic alliance had, he told readers, become an essential goal of the Right.[31]

The Panama Canal, Chinese, and Soviet issues were not just cases of geopolitical weakness but also violations of American values, in the case of China, and of public opinion, in the case of both China and the Canal. "I am not saying the people are always right," Rusher told an activist acquaintance in 1978, "but I am damned if I see much point in letting such important matters as American foreign policy be run by a handful of multinational corporations, their lawyers, and their government friends."[32]

## Big Changes

Despite his strong criticism of Carter on foreign affairs, Rusher objected to the more general condemnations that were increasingly directed at him. In the summer of 1978, Buckley called the president "the last surviving ritualistic liberal, although I suppose . . . he shares the honor with George McGovern." There was "a very strong case for unworldliness," Buckley added, but "those who aspire to be Caesar are not those who are supposed to reject this world. Carter is doing that, and the world is requiting that rejection."[33] Three months before, regretting that the "savaging" of the president was looking like a "national pastime," Rusher had urged: "Let's give Mr. Carter at least two or three of his four years before going after him with an ax."[34] Conservatives calling for the president's resignation, he told readers in 1979, wanted a Democrat to be "smashed and destroyed as Nixon was smashed and destroyed." Given that the case against Nixon had been something of a "rickety jumble," he understood a desire for revenge, but "America simply cannot afford 'government by resignation.' We cannot afford . . . to appease the bloodlust of rival factions in our society." The country must "get used to having, and following, a president again."[35]

Rusher's gentleness toward Carter may have owed something to a new development in his life. In the spring of 1978, he was baptized as a Christian, specifically an Anglican. He had never been an atheist, and his childhood was vaguely Protestant. As an adult, Rusher was an agnostic sympathetic to religion but not much interested in it, then a moderate theist—or as John Thomson remembers, a "barely believing Christian." Thomson told his friend in the 1960s that he had "high hopes about God's guidance for you."[36] Rusher would sometimes explain: "I consider myself a Christian, but what I believe is very personal to me." Thomson would cite Jesus to the effect that a Christian should be in communion—which didn't mean "me, myself, and I." But Rusher disliked the informality of the evangelical church, while also finding Catholicism too hierarchical to be compatible with his commitment to individualism and personal freedom. In addition, according to Thomson, he was "not a joiner."[37]

His turn toward faith was gradual. Working at *National Review* over the years, Rusher had been "impressed by its explicit religiosity and implicit Catholicism." His own "developing view of the world" seemed increasingly consistent with this. The availability of a new branch of the Anglican communion made it easier. A theologically conservative faction had recently broken from the Episcopal Church—which was run, Rusher wrote, by "ultra-liberal" leaders, many of whom had directed it toward "crassly political purposes"—to organize the Anglican Church in North America. "I was sitting in my office one day after lunch at Paone's," he recalls, "and I realized that if the Lord had gone to all the trouble to make this new denomination just for me, maybe the least I could do was join it."[38] To his old friends Dave and Judy Fernald, who were strong Christians, he said the Holy Spirit had come to him quite suddenly—like a paper clip that "flew across the room and landed on his desk."

Now fifty-four, Rusher was baptized and confirmed in a simple ceremony—shared, as it happened, with "a little boy and girl on either side of me, dressed in white." Every Sunday he would take the train to suburban Port Chester, forty minutes each way, to attend church.[39] Although comfortable with his decision, he wrote about it only once, under the title "The Columnist Comes in from the Cold." He asked Thomson an occasional question about religion, but "never seemed to want to get too deep." Buckley remembers that "the subject never sort of arose" between him and Rusher, "and in situations like that, I usually tend to be very careful not to push."[40]

In November, several months after Rusher joined the church, *National Review* experienced a great loss when the semiretired Burnham—one of the founders and by far its oldest editor—had a severe stroke. Deprived of his short-term memory, he was unable to work for the magazine again. Rusher felt moved to cheer him up. Having kept in touch with his progress mainly through Priscilla Buckley, the publisher wrote in early 1979: "I have not been eager to add to your obligatory reading by sending you a letter. But I do want you to know that you are very much in all our thoughts here." He assured his old adversary, now seventy-three, that things were going well at the magazine. The newer editors Brookhiser and Sobran, and "all the other relative youngsters down on the second floor," made Rusher feel "very much better than I did a few years ago about the longer-range prospects for *National Review*." It had a "really strong team . . . in their early thirties, backed up with yet another strong team still in its early to mid-twenties."[41]

Also sounding optimistic about things in general, perhaps more than he had since 1963, Rusher observed to Burnham that "domestic liberalism seems to be in a state of near-total collapse." On a Virginia campus, he had recently debated liberal hero Eugene McCarthy, who "flatly refused to propose it as the proper course for America in the 1980s!" A few days before that, he had debated the left-leaning economic historian Robert Heilbroner, who wouldn't "recommend socialism to the audience . . . and added that he didn't even know what it was!"[42]

Through 1978, however, Rusher had continued to write about the Republican Party with a kind of grim finality. It wasn't clear, he told readers that June, why the GOP should even run a presidential candidate two years hence. If a Republican should be elected, "the most we can expect is four to eight years of debilitating squabbles with Democratic Congresses, spiced with a couple of dubious appointments to the Supreme Court and punctuated by the new chief executive's traditional sellout of all the principles for which he and his party campaigned." There were, he allowed, relatively "honorable" prospective candidates (among whom he presumably counted Reagan) who intended to get the public to pressure the Democratic Congress on behalf of their agendas. But Republican presidents, at least, had never succeeded in this. Judging by previous experience, the election of a Republican to the presidency "cures nothing . . . temporarily kills the pain" of the larger reality, Democratic rule. As late as October 1978, noting the Democrats' continued advantages on several major issues as indicated in recent polls, Rusher told readers he would like to see a new party along the lines laid out in his *New Majority* book. Such a party could win the next election handily. But he stopped short of an explicit call to form one.[43] After the midterm election, Rusher appreciated the gain of a few more conservatives in the Senate and of six additional Republican governorships but was far from convinced the GOP was in good shape for 1980, and his tone toward the party remained contemptuous.[44]

Along with his syndicated column, there was now another outlet for his opinions. From 1976 to 1979, Rusher appeared regularly on ABC's *Good Morning America* in its "Face Off" debate segment. At ABC and elsewhere, Neal Freeman recalls, his client "invariably impressed producers and editors as a well-prepared, thoroughly professional, and obviously intelligent spokesman for what most of them regarded as a bizarre but mediagenic point of view." Inspired by Rusher, appreciative viewers also conveyed their reactions. "By stirring the enthusiasm of vocal parts of their audiences, he emboldened the faithful and at least reminded media types of a large and underserved audience."[45]

## Reagan?

When Ronald Reagan made his second race for president, not every conservative preferred him. John Connally entered the 1980 Republican contest and initially sparked a bit of interest on the Right, as did Congressman Phil Crane. Senator Howard Baker of Tennessee was a candidate, as was the establishmentarian George Bush, whose long résumé now included the de facto ambassadorship to mainland China. A survey of leading Republicans in early 1979 showed about 32 percent for Connally and 18 percent for Baker, with Reagan and Bush well behind them at 11 percent each.[46] Rusher's preference among the alternatives to Reagan, at least initially, was Crane, a former history professor and a hard-core economic conservative who had impressed him even as a new congressman in 1969. When Crane declared his candidacy in the late summer of 1978, Rusher called it a "thoroughly healthy development." If Reagan didn't run, or his campaign somehow failed early, there had to be a serious conservative in his place.

Although Rusher favored Reagan, he did so ambiguously. The ex-governor would be "eminently worth electing at 85 in a wheelchair." But at sixty-nine, his age in the upcoming election, many people weren't in very good health—and for this reason, Rusher had written in late 1977, Reagan's chances of winning the nomination were "poor." It was also worrisome that Reagan might feel compelled to address the age issue by pledging not to seek a second term. He would still be "the class of the crop" among White House contenders, but the Right would react angrily when the vice-presidential nomination went to a liberal under such circumstances.[47]

While Reagan was "almost universally beloved and respected . . . on the Republican right," the Chicago-area congressman had become "recognized as quite possibly the ablest conservative spokesman in the younger generation of political leaders." That was important because conservative Republicans must look to this group "if their faith is to survive and succeed." Many of them "hope devoutly that they never have to make the choice" between Reagan and Crane.[48] Youthful in his late forties, the congressman was "handsome, articulate and scholarly," Rusher had written in 1977. In addition, as ACU chairman, he had been working hard to reduce the "debilitating rivalry" between the older Right and the populist social conservatives.[49] Rusher didn't understand why some conservatives saw the Crane campaign as treasonous. Reflecting his bias toward relative youth, he suggested the movement's newer national leaders probably had to come from the congressional generation now in its forties. Along with Crane, he mentioned upstate New York congressman Jack Kemp and the freshman senator from Utah,

Orrin Hatch. "And when will [the movement] get around to letting them stretch their legs? When they too are approaching 70?"[50]

Within months, Crane had enlisted a substantial corps of proven conservative activists. He was an "optimistic, energetic" candidate who loved the game of politics, according to a mainstream-media account at the time. But he wasn't using social issues, as Rusher had urged in *New Majority Party* and elsewhere—or the foreign-policy issues Rusher was deeply concerned about. On the campaign trail, Crane consistently delivered a "relentlessly economic" message. Also contrary to Rusher's strategy for conservatives, he didn't moderate on economics or in his economic rhetoric. "Reagan has moved to the center in recent years on such subjects as environmental protection and aid to the underprivileged," the *Washington Post* reported in early 1980. "But Crane still boasts to audiences about his votes against major environmental bills and his reputation as the 'biggest skinflint in Congress' on social programs." The political premise of his campaign, he explained in an interview, was that Reagan "would eventually be reduced to mortal dimensions . . . and when he got in trouble, his support would turn out to be soft."[51]

Buckley, who like Rusher had been a friend of the Reagans since the 1960s, was concerned about the ex-governor's age as well. The editor supported him in his speaking engagements but was noncommittal in his columns, and *NR* made no endorsement before the primaries. Buckley wondered whether Reagan could still handle the pace of a national campaign, also doubting his electability at sixty-nine. In addition, he admired George Bush, with whom he had attended Yale. As Rick Brookhiser later recalled: "Bill liked the all-American Ivy League type, which he wasn't, quite," and appreciated this quality in Bush.[52]

In early 1979, Rusher wrote a highly favorable column about Connally, which reflected the growing belief that the country needed a tougher international leader than Carter. By midyear, he was feeling better about Reagan, telling readers that he remained "King of the Hill" and would win the nomination unless someone "manages to topple him from that eminence . . . his strength is formidable and the case for nominating him is, in most respects, stronger than ever." The age issue would be resolved only in the early primaries, but "certainly he looks and acts perfectly capable of the presidency." Still, Rusher saw a possible deadlock in the party if stop-Reagan voters and forces were to coalesce behind one candidate, perhaps Senator Baker. In that circumstance, he could see Connally winning the nomination as a compromise choice.[53]

When Reagan officially entered the race that November, Rusher supported him. The most important thing in a president, he had written in

*New Majority Party* in 1975, was a certain type of character: "a temperament so balanced and serene that it can almost command its environment"
rather than reflect the environment, as most politicians did. Rusher had
also stressed that a conservative party's national nominee must come across
as "reassuring," with an "ability to communicate as a friend to the average American." Reagan did that.[54] After the New Hampshire primary, which
Reagan won by more than a two-to-one margin, Rusher stopped worrying
about his age. If the state's Republican voters showed no serious concern,
there was no reason to think other Americans would either.[55]

His backup choice, Phil Crane, proved to be a nonstarter despite his
intense campaigning—hurt by fund-raising problems, by losing most of
his original staff, and perhaps also by a set of investigative stories in the
*Manchester Union Leader* in early 1979 that alleged, in the words of a *Washington Post* account, that he "conceals a playboy's fondness for women and
whiskey beneath his clean-cut outward appearance." Crane strongly denied
the reports and blamed them on Reagan aides.[56] Rusher appeared to loyally
dismiss the paper's allegations when he wrote, several months later, that the
congressman remained a viable candidate, also quoting him to the effect
that being attacked by the *Union Leader* was perhaps a plus in New Hampshire.[57] Initially a high-profile conservative, Crane lost prominence in the
movement and party after 1980. He later admitted to a serious drinking
problem and in 2004 was defeated for reelection.

When the question became who Reagan's running mate should be,
Buckley suggested to his campaign manager, future CIA director William
Casey (who had drawn up the legal papers for *NR* at its founding), that sec-
ond-place finisher Bush be considered for vice president. He also urged that
Reagan consider Gerald Ford.[58] Reagan thought the ex-president would be a
quite helpful choice for the campaign—and he did not want Bush, whom he
considered weak under pressure, on the ticket. A complicated set of factors
sustained the possibility during the Detroit convention: Reagan's preference
for Ford, the strong interest of Republican leaders in the idea, widespread
opposition to Bush among Reagan's aides, the ambitions of ex-Ford officials
and eventually the former president himself, and Ford's desire to help defeat
Carter while reversing, in this sense, his narrow and painful 1976 loss. The
possible "dream ticket" dominated media coverage during much of the convention, also preoccupying the delegates and operatives. Under such circumstances, Reagan's reputation as a leader was at some risk—and so, at least as
far as noninsiders knew, was the substance of his prospective presidency.[59]

In his column, Rusher didn't quite say that, but he did tell readers a
"catastrophe" was narrowly averted and that "divine providence . . . must
have Ronald Reagan in its special care." The attempt to get the former

president on the ticket was "ill-conceived and worse-executed." Both the campaign and the country could well have been seriously harmed. For one thing, Rusher wrote, if Ford had been chosen with "major concessions," as his representatives reportedly demanded, he would have seemed "the convention's real winner—and a victor over Reagan, at that." Rusher did not believe Ford would have been an especially strong asset to the ticket, and he thought his presence on it would have given the Democrats a constant opportunity to "raise and re-argue the controversies of the mid-1970s." In addition, "inevitable rivalry" between the president and vice president would have become the administration's strongest and most lasting feature. And finally, Ford "would have become the natural rallying-point for the defeated 'moderate' wing of the GOP to which he has always belonged."[60]

With no real role in the campaign, Rusher couldn't do much about the possibility. Although it alarmed him that so many conservatives seemed willing to passively accept Ford, he had "no time or opportunity to convey my misgivings to Reagan or even to Clif White [Reagan's convention manager] in his trailer." The idea collapsed because officials from the Ford administration tried to negotiate a deal in which the ex-president, and presumably they, would largely control the Reagan administration, and because Ford offended Reagan by confirming to Walter Cronkite that it would be akin to a co-presidency. Although Reagan had gotten himself into this situation, he did not, in fact, want to make that kind of a deal. He reluctantly chose Bush—a decision with which Rusher felt "perfectly comfortable."[61]

Rusher happily shared with readers the sense of unity at the convention: "The ovation for Barry Goldwater, limping in on a crutch in deference to a bum hip, was long, deep and genuine. Most of the delegates are conservative to the core; many of them cut their baby teeth on the Goldwater campaign." The vast majority of the conservatives were "in too good a mood to be impolite," and Kissinger therefore got "a nice hand" from the delegates. In 1976, Ford's managers wouldn't let Kissinger "enter the hall, let alone speak, until Ford was safely nominated. This time he . . . gracefully made peace with his old foes by acknowledging, in this convention's most memorable phrase, that Reagan is now 'the trustee of all our hopes.'"[62] More important, the convention represented "the long-awaited marriage of economic and social conservatives." For the past sixteen years, Reagan had stood for expanding the GOP and for the idea that "the logical direction of its expansion is toward the social conservatives," Rusher wrote. If elected, he would have "a real chance to make permanent the coalition that has come in triumph to Detroit and given him the Republican nomination."[63]

In his column, Rusher was finally denouncing Jimmy Carter in broad rather than narrow terms. His response to inflation had been a "long, dreary chapter in the old story of Too Little and Too Late," and his attitude toward defense was "blemished by debilitating doubts as to what needed defending, and against whom." America had declined terribly in its international "moral leadership," Rusher wrote two weeks later, suggesting this was an even graver problem than the growing appearance of military weakness and irresolution.[64]

The *National Review* writers and editors watched the campaign against President Carter, which became a tight race until almost the end, with special interest. Reagan was one of their own. A real movement conservative, he was also a longtime subscriber to *NR* and read the magazine closely.[65] While in town to cover the Democratic convention at Madison Square Garden, former Washington editor George Will said of Reagan's prospects: "I'm not sure. But I'm worried about the country's chances if he's *not* elected." On October 28, the editorial staff watched the single Reagan-Carter debate at the managing editor's apartment—initially feeling, Bridges and Coyne later recalled, "as nervous as parents whose son had been chosen class valedictorian." Having apparently won the debate, Reagan seemed in good shape. "I think that did it," a confident Priscilla Buckley said.[66]

Rusher had recently warned that Carter was likely to make the last weeks of the campaign "ugly and quite possibly dangerous." He believed the president had panicked over the polls and was "ready to do just about whatever it takes" for reelection. "If that means pushing the [Iran-Iraq] war in the Persian Gulf to the brink of some sort of military confrontation between the United States and the Arab world, or even the Soviet Union, so be it." Saber-rattling might benefit Carter enormously by causing voters to reward his experience. Rusher also excoriated the president for his claim at a Chicago rally: "You'll determine whether or not this America will be unified or, if I lose the election, whether Americans might be separated—black from white, Jew from Christian, North from South, rural from urban." Rarely in modern American history, Rusher wrote, was there "so cheap and demagogic an attempt to arouse hostility among various segments of the population and focus it on a political opponent."[67] Brightening his mood, though, was his indirect access to the Reagan campaign. Rusher now had some inside knowledge of it, since White was a senior adviser to Bill Casey and worked closely with the campaign manager at the headquarters outside Washington. Rusher knew how well Reagan was doing, especially during the final week, when "each report from my friends . . . was better than its predecessor."[68]

The election, he would remember in *Rise of the Right*, "slaked at last and in full the burning thirst that first developed in me in 1936." There was "a sense in which, for me at least, 1980 was the year in which [radio commentator] H. V. Kaltenborn's famous prediction at last came true: The 'rural vote,' figuratively speaking, finally came in." It seemed that something extremely decisive had occurred. In a postelection column, Rusher wrote: "On November 4 conservatism's long battle—though to be sure only its first—was over."[69]

At his apartment near *National Review* two evenings after the election, he was watching a rerun of the president-elect's first press conference. The phone rang and the caller asked if he had Bill Rusher. "It was a man's voice, carefully neutral. 'Yes?' I replied inquiringly. 'Ronald Reagan.' I was so astonished that I literally stood up, as one is expected by protocol to do when the president of the United States enters the room." Reagan had spent several hours calling old friends, and Rusher guessed he probably enjoyed their surprise at hearing from him spontaneously. If so, "he certainly got his money's worth out of me!"[70]

Shortly after the election, *National Review* celebrated its twenty-fifth anniversary. The president-elect did not attend the dinner, although he had done so in 1975 and Buckley had invited him to this one several months previously. Campaign aides decided there was a schedule conflict, and Reagan may not have known about the repeated invitations to the dinner. According to Brookhiser, Buckley was the source of the confusion, since his reminders had been quirky and the Reagan staff didn't understand them. (One said: "Cinderella expects Prince Charming.") The editor was sorely disappointed. Brookhiser felt his two heroes had thrown him for a loop: Buckley by "bungling the invitation," Reagan by "dissing us." Rusher took the situation in stride, patiently explaining to his young colleague that "Reagan was about to become the most powerful man in the world, and did not have time to turn around."[71]

Given its relationship with the new president, *NR* jokingly pretended to have acquired the same level of responsibility, teasing readers after the election: "We have a world to run." But it still needed the type of careful attention Rusher had always been counted on to provide. He was "preternaturally careful," wrote an admiring Chris Simonds, who handled *NR*'s coverage of popular music in the hippie days the publisher had found so noxious. "Over the deficit Rusher presides, cheerfully Sisyphean, juggling premium offers, fund appeals, advertisers, rates, circulation figures, printing costs, and a myriad other factors with a grand aplomb and never a slip."[72] Reagan would continue to read the magazine carefully as president. "He was very anxious to get *National Review*," Rusher recalls. "We had to arrange a special way of getting it to his secretary's desk early, so that he would have it early."[73]

Long after the president had left office—a year after Reagan's funeral, to which he received no invitation—Rusher observed: "Most politicians will agree with you and not mean a goddamn word of it." Even in Reagan's case, he was prepared to be disappointed. And he was astounded, Rusher added, by how little that happened.[74]

# 15

# A Friend in the White House

Rusher began the 1980s with hope and apprehension, thinking the nation wouldn't recover from years of weakness anytime soon. The hostage crisis in Iran was nearly as much America's fault as the Ayatollah Khomeini's: "We labored for at least two decades to persuade the rest of the world that we are a paper tiger," Rusher wrote. "We succeeded, and the world is acting accordingly."[1] He also had serious doubts about the prospects for economic recovery—and about the character of the American people. "I honestly don't know whether there is still time to turn this country around," he told Nancy Reagan toward the end of the campaign, "but I do know that the man America will elect on November 4th intends to try," which was "the best news in many, many years."[2]

Conservatives took heart from Reagan's record as a public figure and as their advocate. He was, a scholar later noted, "probably the only twentieth-century president whose political career was so thoroughly devoted to contesting for the public philosophy."[3] But would the Reagan era leave a lasting legacy? A friend in California warned Rusher not to assume so. In his eight years as governor, Michael Djordjevich wrote, Reagan had failed to build a political organization or bring forward a new generation of conservative leaders. Because the new administration must not make that same mistake, it must "be prepared to channel, to solidify and . . . develop further" the conservative trends in American public sentiment. It must build up a new leadership, one with "vision and integrity and independence." It couldn't be dominated by power brokers and old faces. Its pragmatists should be pressured to look past the next election. People like Rusher must come up with ideas for maximizing the opportunity the Reagan presidency signified for conservatives.

Rusher admitted that he didn't really know whether Reagan would fulfill his friend's hopes. But the president-elect was a "thoroughly sincere man" and as close to a movement conservative as one could find in a politician. Although he would disappoint them at times, Rusher told Djordjevich, "his understanding of the world is basically like ours." As for officials from previous administrations, they were almost inevitable, wouldn't do harm, and might even prove helpful depending on circumstances.[4]

What Rusher hadn't acknowledged was that Reagan's aloof type of leadership heightened the risks in making such appointments. At issue were his accessibility, his aggressiveness, and his willingness to deal with specifics. "He was slow to anger but extremely stubborn," according to biographer Lou Cannon. "He detested arguments. He trusted everyone who worked for him and considered even mild criticism of the most incompetent subordinate to be a disguised attack on him or his policies."[5]

The man whom Rusher considered his main political hero contrasted sharply with his antihero, Richard Nixon, in more than devotion to principle. An aide to both presidents, economist and Reagan domestic-policy director Martin Anderson, would remember Nixon as "the kind of man who thinks seven or eight moves ahead in a chess game"—whereas Reagan "rarely planned and never plotted." As a manager, Anderson conceded in his memoir of the Reagan years, the president made no demands and gave almost no instructions, simply dealing with what was brought to his attention. He seldom asked probing questions and rarely insisted on knowing why something had or hadn't been done. But he did act quickly and decisively on things in front of him.[6]

Getting things in front of Reagan, getting his attention, would preoccupy many of the Right's leaders and many administration conservatives in the next eight years. In addition to his avoidance of personal conflict, hands-off management style, and determination to maintain country-club Republican support, they were up against the fact that Reagan was an unusually old president. He was also badly wounded in an assassination attempt two months into his term, perhaps with a lasting effect on his energy level despite a quick recovery. As speechwriter Peggy Noonan later recalled: "We wanted him to be young."[7]

Rusher had long regretted that the chance to elect a much younger Reagan was lost back in 1968, but came to see his presidency as a "golden age." He would find himself in the unaccustomed position of urging patience on the Right, even satisfaction. At the outset, *NR*'s Brookhiser recalls, Rusher decided to "defend Reagan on everything, on every single thing. His reasoning was: 'This is the best guy we're going to get. It will never be better; it will never be as good. So you have to back this guy up.' It's a very kind of practical calculation, but one also based on his perception—I think a correct perception—of what Reagan believed and where he was coming from."[8]

## "Ron's True Allies"

Hoping the president-elect would pay attention to cementing the Republican Party's relationship with its new voters, Rusher wrote to Mrs. Reagan, aware that she was her husband's great confidante: "There is a conservative majority in America today—probably a large one. This year it voted Republican, except for the House of Representatives. But the blue-collar and ethnic voters who swelled our totals this year have never felt comfortable in the GOP." Rusher knew—"because he told me so, in our private talks in the mid-1970's"—that Reagan would try hard to make the new alliance permanent. "It won't be easy, but very few things he attempts to do will be so important, or will yield such dividends in future elections."[9]

At the end of the campaign, Rusher had expressed his wish that a substantial share of the new administration's appointments would go to individuals who had backed Reagan all along, fully sharing his main beliefs. Otherwise things might be "taken over by the sort of people who are found in every campaign," by "political operators with various talents, but without any serious commitment to his conservative principles."

In making this point, he chose not to explicitly pit conservative Republicans against moderates. Instead, he artfully defined three categories of potential appointees: the "routine time-servers," the "hot-eyed philosophical zealots," and the "sensible and authentic conservatives." Because time-servers would tend to push harder in seeking key jobs, an active attempt to "find and bring forward Ron's true allies" was desirable. Rusher knew principled, loyal younger people from the campaign who were ready to help in recruiting such appointees. Calling two nights after the election with thanks for his support over the years, Reagan had said: "I want those names."[10]

Rusher immediately sent them, citing several movement conservatives as good additions to the transition team who would help the new president pick others for the permanent positions. Some were also available to work in the administration.[11] He had no Washington ambitions himself, telling the Reverend George Rutler, a young priest who was close to National Review: "When a man is in his thirties, the idea of serving in somebody else's presidential administration can be exciting; in one's fifties, it merely looks like an introduction to a lot of hassling that nobody needs."[12] Rather than become "the world's foremost authority on widgets" in a tightly defined administration post, Rusher recalls, he preferred to remain a commentator and "the world's foremost authority on anything."[13]

The column and *National Review* were just two of the claims on his time. Although he was no longer on *Good Morning America*, Rusher continued his public-speaking engagements and now did three radio commentaries a week for the Westinghouse Broadcasting Corporation (Group W), heard in major metropolitan areas throughout the country. In early 1982, he would turn down an appointment to the board of the Corporation for Public Broadcasting, explaining that he was falling further behind on *The Rise of the Right*. "If I don't find a hole in my schedule pretty soon," he told the president, "I will have to return the advance royalty payment . . . which, needless to say, I would hate to have to do!"[14]

Cabinet selections to date were mostly "very good," Rusher wrote Nancy Reagan as 1980 ended. He had previously become acquainted with the new secretary of state, Alexander Haig, and the new budget director, David Stockman, when he appeared with them on special one-time *Advocates* programs during the campaign. Both seemed impressive. But even as he made additional personnel recommendations, Rusher sounded a note of resignation: "I guess it is inevitable that most posts in government will be filled by the type of seaweed that drifts in and out with the tides of politics."[15]

Although movement conservatives were not well-represented in the really high-level appointments, they did get a few of these. They also received more jobs at lower levels in the coming months. Among the most prominently placed conservatives were former YAF members Richard Allen and Donald Devine, respectively the national security adviser and the director of the Office of Personnel Management—the arena of what became a successful battle to press reforms on the national bureaucracy. Ex-YAFers were prominent in the transition effort and in lesser appointments as well.[16]

The presence of Ed Meese, who had worked with Reagan since his Sacramento days and now held the title of counselor to the president, was especially important to Rusher because he was considered, along with moderate chief of staff James Baker and moderate aide Michael Deaver, among the top three officials or "troika" at the White House. In symbolic terms, it was good to see Meese on the Sunday interview programs in the Adam Smith neckties now popular among conservatives. Rusher, who had a complete set of them, usually wore one himself.[17] It delighted him, he told Reagan in May, to see "how thoroughly and vigorously you are living up to the highest expectations of your longtime supporters. Better yet, the American people as a whole are obviously delighted too."[18] But although Rusher and most conservatives understood Reagan to be their ideal president, his

White House was increasingly seen as a perpetual battleground between the Right and its country-club Republican skeptics and foes. Meese was quickly losing clout to Deaver, the deputy chief of staff and prime custodian of Reagan's public image, who like Meese was a Californian and a longtime Reagan aide.[19] Baker and Deaver were strongly in league with Mrs. Reagan, herself a pragmatist.

*National Review* now had just over 100,000 subscribers. Response from a list of Reagan supporters solicited by direct mail was excellent, Rusher noted, suggesting that the magazine's ideological tie to the administration be exploited further. In these new circumstances, some previously unproductive mailing lists might do better. An example was the readership of *Foreign Affairs*—a list that recently had performed well, Rusher told Buckley, because some "opportunists in that establishment crowd think it advisable to have *National Review* on their coffee tables now, or at least peek at it from time to time for guidance." But as always, finances remained difficult: "We will have to raise every nickel we possibly can."[20]

The magazine was made readily available to the administration. In addition to ensuring Reagan's prompt access to it, Rusher got the names and room numbers of "everybody who is anybody" in the West Wing of the White House and in the Old Executive Office Building, where most of the presidential staff worked. These seventy-seven people would receive *NR* at no cost. It seemed likely, therefore, that "anything written in *National Review* will get noticed in High Quarters."[21] At the beginning of 1982, after Buckley told him Reagan wasn't getting the magazine regularly, Rusher advised the president that it would now be mailed directly from the *NR* office "first class, addressed to you and with the [special] numerical code written over your name." A year later, not having received a reply from Reagan on the point, he inquired briefly in an unrelated letter, noting: "If it is *not* in fact reaching you, let's find the mole!"[22]

The president responded—"Shame on me and forgive me"—that he had indeed been getting the magazine and should have acknowledged this. But Rusher's "mole" remark, whether serious or not, reflected an understanding among the politically well-informed that some people around Reagan were not only adversarial toward ideological conservatives but also manipulatively so, and conceivably might try to prevent him from seeing *National Review*. It was rumored, after all, that Baker and others tried to keep *Human Events* away from the president. In addition, as Reagan's longtime secretary Helene von Damm would recall, Nancy Reagan and Deaver took it upon themselves to make him inaccessible to people they considered politically risky or unworthy of contact with him. Von Damm, who later became the director of presidential personnel, sometimes felt she had to bypass such decrees by handing Reagan a letter directly—and keeping him from putting it in the pile he would take up to the living quarters at the end of the day.[23]

## How to Win Arguments

The main personal event for Rusher in the early Reagan years was the publication in 1981 of *How to Win Arguments*, the only nonideological book among the five he would eventually produce, which concisely presented the wisdom acquired in two full decades of debate as a movement conservative and in what the author noted had been a lifetime of arguing.

Good debating wasn't reserved to a brilliant elite, Rusher stressed, and it was important to distinguish between natural and acquired skills. The key natural abilities included special mental quickness, like Buckley's, and a well-organized mind. In addition, some people had more forceful personalities than others. But it was the acquired skills that mattered most in debate: "poise, clarity of thought and expression, a basic understanding of logical processes, and willingness to state the case for a soundly considered view." A debater should rely more on substance than style. To the extent style mattered, the most important thing was one's voice. But a good voice could result from solid factual preparation, since that helped one to sound more sincere and authoritative. A person who trained himself properly, even without natural talent for it, should be able to win many of his arguments and even tie a world champion. Anybody who deserved to win *could* win.[24]

Rusher also stressed the easily overlooked point that a debater might have various objectives. Among the possible goals were strengthening an already-sympathetic audience's commitment, increasing the number of people who agreed with one's position whether or not they were a majority, and persuading part of the audience to take action. A debater who wanted a quick result and therefore aimed at popularity might leave out points some people might find offensive, or concede a few things he shouldn't, or avoid the use of ridicule. Such moderation came at a price. A debater could end up "letting falsehood off too easily for the audience's . . . long-range good." When the "admired personality is gone and his charm has worn off," Rusher explained, "the fallacious arguments of his opponent . . . may reestablish themselves in the minds he (temporarily) changed." Similarly, if the debater who persuaded or convinced them had pulled his punches, people might not know his case well enough to argue adequately later. Rusher also suggested that listeners must be broken out of their positions, not gently drawn away from them.

The book included a few confessions. Pointing out that courtesy required listening to the opponent and keeping any interruptions to a minimum, Rusher admitted he found it hard to follow that rule. "I am a born interrupter—not, I hasten to say, because I *want* to be discourteous, but because my mind has raced ahead . . . to some crushing response that I find it unbearably difficult to delay." Too much interruption was rude, and it irked listeners. Because an audience needed a moment to digest a point before hearing the other side's comeback, it resented a debater who pursued his adversary so aggressively that a listener didn't have time to think. "I have probably . . . lost or damaged more arguments in this way than in any other."[25]

Rusher even acknowledged that many liberals must have felt hurt by his debate tactics over the years. Most of his opponents had been used to "adversaries who believe (as they themselves do) that the future scarcely hinges on this particular encounter." In contrast, he had often "psyched myself into believing that the entire future did in fact hinge on this particular encounter, and that my opponent was, consciously or otherwise, the instrument of Satan. The resulting onslaught must have made more than one accomplished debater wonder what he had climbed into the ring with."

He felt "special remorse" over a debate on a civil-liberties issue with Professor Robert McKay of the New York University law school, who "as far as I was concerned at the time, was just one more designing leftist standing between America and salvation. I behaved—or rather misbehaved— accordingly," an especially unpleasant memory because the professor had responded so mildly. But they got to know each other better, and McKay proved to be among the "gentlest, most judicious . . . people I have ever met," also magnanimously arranging for Rusher to receive a Distinguished Citizen Award from the law school in 1973. It recognized, as the citation said, his "able articulation of the conservative viewpoint."[26]

## Drama on the Right

Owing partly to his anxiety about the country's moral life and partly to political considerations, Rusher strongly appreciated the newly active Religious Right: the forces favorable, as he explained in a column, to "the family as an institution" and to the "recognition of God's involvement in human affairs." Society's large differences over moral issues were increasingly apparent, Rusher thought, because television had gradually imposed a common culture of permissiveness throughout the country. This decadent culture included drugs in every high school, far more illegitimate births, and less emphasis on marriage. The Religious Right, which was defending the healthier older culture, "did not seek this confrontation," Rusher wrote. "It has been forced upon them, and I am sure many earnest Christians are turning to political action regretfully and prayerfully."[27]

Not every potential ally welcomed the social conservatives. David Brudnoy, a libertarian *NR* contributor who hosted a radio talk show in Boston, told Rusher that "family" had now become a code word for "ultra-rightwing hatred." Especially offended by hostility toward homosexuality on the Religious Right, he urged Rusher to read gay newspapers in order to understand how destructive such hostility could be. Rusher took exception to Brudnoy's angry dismissal of "family," telling him it wasn't only a euphemism for hatred. "It may be that too, but it is . . . more than just that. Family values *are* under heavy attack," and social conservatives could certainly use the word.[28]

He made a similar point after Senator Goldwater denounced the Religious Right for diverting attention from conservative economic issues and for its allegedly authoritarian tendencies. "From where," Goldwater had asked, "do they claim the right to dictate their moral beliefs to me?" He would "fight them every step of the way if they try to dictate their moral convictions to all Americans in the name of 'conservatism.'" Goldwater had also blurted out, after Moral Majority president Jerry Falwell was quoted as saying that "every good Christian should be concerned" about the nomination of Arizona judge and former state legislator Sandra Day O'Connor to a Supreme Court vacancy in mid-1981, that "every good Christian ought to kick Falwell right in the ass."

America had been on a "moral toboggan-slide" for years, Rusher wrote in response, and it was surprising that social conservatives had waited so long to counteract the trend politically. To be sure, many "ill-advised things" were being said by extremists. But the Religious Right consisted overwhelmingly of reasonable people who didn't "for a moment seek to impose their own religious views, or any religious views at all, on individual fellow citizens of a different mind."

At the same time, Rusher sought more understanding for Goldwater by giving context to his widely publicized remarks: "Actually he has always been an orthodox Republican economic conservative first and foremost, with grave doubts about the so-called social conservatives." The senator had also "bitterly resented the coercion" of an Arizona right-to-life group during his 1980 reelection campaign—in which he was nearly defeated—when it demanded and won his reluctant support for a constitutional amendment banning abortion. In addition, the results of an unsuccessful hip operation kept Goldwater in near-constant pain, another mitigating factor in his "angry tirade." Explaining that few top political leaders really grasped the significance of the Religious Right, Rusher predicted that those who did so would benefit.[29]

It was unclear, though, to what extent even Reagan considered the Religious Right important. It also had few, if any, strong allies in close proximity to him. Although Harris surveys indicated that such voters had been crucial in his 1980 landslide, aides to the president-elect, including his conservative pollster Richard Wirthlin, believed the constituency had already become strongly opposed to Carter regardless of political organizing or messaging. Harris's analysis to the contrary, they believed Moral Majority preachers and activists hadn't vitally influenced the vote. But the Religious Right could also point to the much higher turnout of evangelicals compared with 1976—two million more, by one estimate—owing partly to its voter-registration drives.

Social issues were deemphasized, according to Lyn Nofziger, a conservative longtime Reagan aide who served as the White House's lead political operative in the first year of the administration, because they were "hardly number one on our agenda" and were "highly divisive." The president himself said, in early 1981, that such issues "must wait while we dispose of this [economic] problem and . . . get economic recovery underway." At that point, Reagan added, "priorities with these other measures" could be discussed.[30] Accordingly, constitutional amendments against abortion and for school prayer were left to their promoters. And in addition to nominating O'Connor, who would eventually disappoint many conservatives as a strong defender of *Roe v. Wade* and a seemingly resulted-oriented moderate on the Court, Reagan disappointed some antiabortion advocates by not speaking in person to the March for Life held annually in Washington, after hinting during the primary campaign that he would.[31]

The New Right's direct-mail fund-raiser Viguerie, in his 1981 book *The New Right: We're Ready to Lead*, complained that just a few of the administration's key positions had gone to movement types. Reagan also hadn't seemed to make high-level representation for populist constituencies a priority. There wasn't a single "outspoken" born-again Christian in the cabinet, anyone representing working-class Democrats, anyone from the conservative women's movement led by Phyllis Schlafly, or a black conservative. Most policymaking positions went to people Viguerie saw as moderates and liberals. Nearly all the conservatives he had talked with were disappointed.[32]

Rusher got a strong dose of these sentiments in January 1982, when he attended an all-day meeting of sixty conservatives at the Mayflower Hotel in Washington that resulted in a public statement criticizing the administration's first year. Voicing "our deep concern about the present conduct and future prospects of the administration" and warning that the "result of such default, unless corrected, could be calamitous for our nation," the statement

said Reagan had surrounded himself with moderates and that more conservatives should be appointed. In economic policy, it sought an "all-out
effort" to cut entitlement programs. In foreign policy, the president should
purge "relics of the Kissinger era and the Carter administration" from the
State Department and aid anticommunist forces in Afghanistan, Poland,
Nicaragua, Cuba, and Angola. Instead, there was "continued pursuit of the
illusions of détente, restrained demeanor toward our communist opponents
and cavalier treatment of our friends."

The Mayflower statement actually represented a compromise between
less-critical and more-critical conservatives—and avoided strong personal
comments against Reagan, saying the basic problem was advisers who
weren't letting him follow his instincts. But Paul Weyrich of the Committee
for the Survival of a Free Congress gave the president only a C or C-minus
for carrying out his campaign pledges, while Viguerie said: "I would have
liked the guys to come down a lot harder."[33]

Although Rusher was among the forty-five attendees who signed the critique issued at the conference, he rejected its claim that Reagan's presidency
was comparable to those of the last three Republican presidents. In his column, he minimized it as "mildly critical" in tone and as merely conveying
"the sort of impatience any ideologue worth his salt will feel over the slow-
ness and imprecision of the political process." Rusher also suggested that the
president "privately welcomes" such pressures from the Right. They functioned, after all, as a counterweight to pressures from liberals.[34] To Reagan,
Rusher stressed that the statement wasn't highly critical on a personal level
and was "basically moderate and well-balanced," thanks to its drafter, Stan
Evans.[35]

In a mid-1982 column, Rusher mentioned a Washington social dinner he had recently attended at which some prominent older conservative,
neoconservative, and New Right figures had met for the first time. Many
of them sensed that Reagan was less ideologically forceful now than when
he ran in 1980. Without denying this, Rusher asked readers to consider the
differences between a president's situation and a candidate's; to understand
that a president had different perspectives, duties, and options. "Conservatives had better be grateful for Ronald Reagan, for my guess is that he is
unique. We shall not see his like again."[36]

Meanwhile, an issue of Viguerie's monthly magazine *Conservative Digest*
focused on what it called "the growing conservative disappointment with
the President." To *Time* reporter Laurence Barrett, who was writing a book
on the administration's early years, Reagan dismissed such criticisms partly
on personal grounds. Viguerie and other New Right leaders had initially
backed other candidates for the 1980 nomination, the president pointed out,

and perhaps there was also a lingering resentment among them stemming from his rejection of the third-party idea in the 1970s. Social issues were "very vital and very important," Reagan said, "but they're a periphery to a philosophy." "They are not the essence," Barrett asked, "of what you've been crusading about?" "No." "They are adornments, they are filigree, so to speak?" "Yes."[37]

Rusher's own concerns about Reagan had less to do with policy, more with his public relations and with the possibility the president might grow isolated. In early 1982, he suggested that the president give short television speeches, as Roosevelt had given effective radio speeches in the 1930s. He wrote a column proposing this and sent it to Nancy Reagan, noting that "several seasoned politicians whose advice I value highly have said virtually the same thing to me in the last week or two . . . it was from their comments that I got the idea." Bill Rickenbacker, who remained friendly with Rusher despite having left the *National Review* editorial board more than a decade before, told him he agreed. It was amazing that Reagan hadn't done more to exploit his ability as a world-class orator—"the one instrument that can place his administration beyond serious attack." In response, Rusher told Rickenbacker there was reason to think the president was considering the possibility.[38] As it happened, Reagan's weekly Saturday radio addresses, which continued throughout his time in office, began the following month, apparently at the suggestion of a veteran aide.[39]

Rusher also suggested that Reagan hold an informal dinner every two or three weeks with perhaps a dozen people from around the country, a different and "carefully chosen" group each time, who could provide a window onto what the public seemed to be thinking. It might include "a reasonably friendly labor leader, two or three businessmen (big and small), a sprinkling of civic leaders from communities around the country . . . plus a couple of intelligent and truly representative young college types." Because the president knew so well how to listen, he "wouldn't have to work hard at such a dinner . . . I do think the input would be tremendously valuable to him."[40]

Similarly, *American Spectator* editor Bob Tyrrell wanted to start a series of luncheons with representatives from the Right's leading publications, like ones the president was holding with conservative economists. These might, he thought, strengthen the relationship between Reagan and the conservative intellectual world. Such a meeting occurred in September 1982 between Reagan, some of his top staff, and representatives from *NR*, *Commentary*, the Heritage Foundation's *Policy Review*, and the neoconservative policy journal the *Public Interest*, as well as the *Spectator*. Tyrrell hoped people from other "responsible" conservative journals might be included at later get-togethers. Rusher enjoyed the luncheon and saw it, like Tyrrell, as the first in a hoped-for series of meetings that would give the president "regular . . . input from influential conservatives."

Writing to Reagan the next day, Rusher took care to describe the likely participants, and implicitly those who had been at the luncheon, as more supportive than critical. They were people "who are *not* furious at you for 'betraying the movement.'" That was very much his own perspective too: "You know that I am in your corner, and that I will continue to be there. Let me know if there is anything I can do." As the event drew to a close, Reagan had asked White House communications director David Gergen to schedule a series of such gatherings. He also reiterated his interest when responding to Rusher: "I agree with you about doing this more often." But the series never happened. According to Tyrrell's angry recollection, White House pragmatists thought the visiting intellectuals and journalists were attempting a power grab.[41]

After a substantial Democratic gain in the House in the 1982 midterm election, criticisms from movement leaders continued during the second quarter of the Reagan era. The administration, Viguerie wrote in another short book, *The Establishment vs. the People*, had given only lip service to the issues social conservatives deemed most important. Furthermore, its key figures "had little time for them." Reagan "turned his back on the populist cause" after the 1980 election, and the "failure to bring about a significant realignment . . . is one of the great tragedies of recent history," Viguerie contended. "After years of back-breaking work trying to push the Republican Party away from the country club set, populists are as far away from controlling the GOP as they ever were." There should be a new populist party, attracting all the constituencies "victimized by the establishment."[42]

President Reagan probably worried more about whether these claims had political traction than about their possible merits. After Viguerie and the New Right journalist John Lofton "blasted me as not a true conservative," he wrote in a 1982 diary entry, it did make him "wonder what my reception would be" at the upcoming CPAC conference. Reagan was a CPAC regular, continuing to speak at the movement's unofficial convention each year despite serious misgivings from moderate White House aides and the first lady. Upon returning from the 1982 dinner, the president recorded: "I needn't have worried, it was a love fest. Evidently R. V. & J. L. don't speak for the rank and file conservatives. Speech was well received." The comment in his diary after he addressed CPAC the following year was similar: "Evidently the Right Wing Rebels have had little effect. I was warmly received."[43]

Although he took a dismissive tone in these diary entries and in the interview with the *Time* writer, Reagan sometimes felt the sting of such activists' dismay. He told Rusher in early 1983 that he was especially troubled by Stan Evans's "intense and continued disapproval of me" because he was "a longtime fan and admirer" of the conservative journalist and former ACU chairman. In contrast, Reagan noted, "your own understanding and friendship warms my heart."[44]

In this ongoing drama, Rusher advocated a middle course to his *National Review* colleagues, much as he had with respect to the Birch Society question twenty years earlier. *NR* should indicate that it was "substantially less dissatisfied" than *Conservative Digest*. But it should also avoid "wounding remarks that would cause a serious rupture" with the New Right and its leaders. Because criticism from people to Reagan's right helped the president disregard constant pressures from his left, *NR* should say it intended to "keep the heat on Reagan where we think there is any danger of his wandering away from the true path." Rusher thought that conservatives more disappointed than himself raised an important question about chief of staff Jim Baker. Since he had tenaciously fought Reagan in the Ford and Bush camps in the 1976 and 1980 primaries, it wasn't certain that Baker could "really put his heart into a distinctively Reagan-type program . . . Maybe he can, but one is surely entitled to wonder."[45]

Rusher also wrote in early 1983 to Senator Paul Laxalt of Nevada—the member of Congress personally closest to Reagan—to express alarm at television coverage of a poorly planned visit to Pittsburgh during which the president was booed by thousands of unemployed steelworkers, at criticisms of Reagan leaked by unnamed aides, and at what he perceived as likely collusion between such aides and congressional Republicans opposed to parts of the president's program. Believing it was White House communications director Gergen's responsibility to prevent such situations, Rusher told Laxalt that he ought to be replaced.[46]

But even when he privately acknowledged problems in the White House or administration, he kept a distance from criticisms of Reagan. "I was too much of a politician, not quite enough of an ideologue, to condemn him the way they did," Rusher recalls. "I understood what he was going through, and he had to be cut a lot of slack that we wouldn't cut for the editor of *National Review* or somebody like that." Viguerie, in contrast, continued to believe "that we did not do our cause any good by remaining silent." Conservative cabinet officials sometimes told him to keep up the pressure because it was needed.[47]

In addition to disagreeing with some New Right criticisms of the president and rejecting the impatient spirit he thought they reflected, Rusher differed strongly with complaints from neoconservative Irving Kristol in 1983. Asked by Buckley for thoughts on an op-ed by Kristol in the *Wall Street Journal*, Rusher conceded there was some truth to his charge that the administration had often been too reactive or passive in foreign policy. But a blockade of Nicaragua to oust its fledgling Marxist dictatorship, as the piece seemed close to urging, might trigger the approval requirements in the War Powers Act. That, Rusher thought, would undesirably bring Congress further into the decision making on Central America.

On Social Security, he found it unrealistic to criticize Reagan for accepting a hike in the payroll tax. If Kristol meant to suggest a cut in Social Security benefits as the better alternative, that just showed why Reagan was president and he wasn't. The neoconservative leader also got it wrong, Rusher told Buckley, when he criticized Reagan's repeated use of bipartisan commissions to suggest broad compromises on issues the administration preferred not to address on its own. Given that the Democrats controlled the House and therefore held a large veto power, Rusher considered this a smart approach.[48]

Continuing to watch the progress of younger leaders, Rusher was especially impressed by the populist-leaning Weyrich and by a junior congressman from the Atlanta suburbs named Newt Gingrich. Asking Clif White to meet with both in 1982, he rated Weyrich as "by far the ablest nuts-and-bolts politician now operating on the New Right," and Gingrich as the most talented "polemical strategist" conservatives had. Gingrich was "a remarkable young man" who should be "cultivated and encouraged," Rusher urged as he sent White a packet of political material the thirty-eight-year-old congressman had put together, including a tough letter to chief of staff Baker.[49] He would remain impressed six years later, noting to a friend that Gingrich was among the movement's "most brilliant strategic thinkers"—even though not "quite as good a political leader," Rusher added, citing his "rather squeaky voice" as a minus. "I have told him more than once that he is wasted in the House of Representatives: He ought to have a spacious office at the Republican National Committee or the Heritage Foundation, with a map of the United States on the wall and all sorts of pins sticking in it."[50]

## "Ashore on a Continent"

Rusher stuck by his admiration for Reagan's performance even as the extent of the disappointment among some of his movement colleagues became especially clear in a symposium, "What Conservatives Think of Ronald Reagan," that ran in *Policy Review* at the beginning of 1984 in which his position was very much in the minority.

"It has been business as usual," wrote Evans, "not much different from any other Republican administration in our lifetime . . . populated by corporate executive types, and people with previous experience managing large government institutions, with the result that there has been no Reagan revolution." Howard Phillips, director of the Conservative Caucus, regretted that the president "is not well informed and defers to credentials, even to people who don't share his values. He shrinks from conflict . . . I wish he had more confidence in his own judgments."

Looking to the political implications, Congressman Gingrich warned that the administration had shown no capacity to launch "strategic offensives on behalf of Reagan's vision." After the impressive income-tax cut and the domestic-budget reductions were enacted in the summer of 1981, political debate again became "totally enmeshed in the rhetoric and values of the liberal welfare state," Gingrich wrote. The administration also hadn't acknowledged or responded effectively to its lack of real power. Given that Republicans didn't control the House and "didn't really" control the Senate, Reagan would have done better to focus "more on changing the nation than on governing." He should have been consistently "forcing a polarization of the country . . . running against liberals and radicals" in order to prepare the groundwork for his reelection campaign.

Rusher, in contrast, gave the president virtually unqualified approval: "Genuine conservatives are by and large overjoyed by Reagan, and rightly so. He has a great many accomplishments to his credit, and he has been remarkably loyal to the agenda of movement conservatism. What little he hasn't done, he hasn't forgotten that it needs to be done later." Once again, Rusher also stressed Reagan's ability to unite an electoral coalition of economic and social conservatives. He remained confident, too, that the president understood the coalition's crucial importance.

Furthermore, policy debate had been redefined by and under Reagan, Rusher argued. It now centered on how much the budget should be reduced, how much defense spending should grow. And although ideological conservatives were admittedly far from dominant in high positions, others were gaining invaluable experience that would prepare them for more powerful ones in future administrations. Nobody in the movement had been "postmaster of Dogpatch, Kentucky," before Reagan took office. "How can you have a reasonable agenda for redesigning the Environmental Protection Agency, when no conservative has ever served there? Reagan has been like Columbus. He has led us ashore on a continent many of us have never seen or been on."[51]

Rusher's column paid fairly close attention to policy developments, as it always had. In addition to applauding, as did all movement conservatives, the large income-tax cuts enacted in Reagan's first year, he thought the administration had gotten general fiscal and economic policy basically right. He also saw early grounds for optimism in foreign policy—not only because of Reagan's firmness on the nuclear- and conventional-defense buildup and his candor about international communism, but also because of what Rusher, like Reagan, understood to be the fundamental weakness of the Soviet Union. When its regime's leader, Leonid Brezhnev, died in late 1982, long before major reform in Moscow was widely anticipated, Rusher wrote: "Soviet society is simply too incongruent with the realities of human nature and the laws of economics to survive indefinitely. Already it is dependent for grain on the capitalist societies it professes to scorn. For advanced technology it must look to such windfalls as the pipeline it is getting from Western Europe, or even to ordinary theft, to supplement Russian research. As the noose of necessity draws tighter, the sounds of dissension within the Politburo will grow louder."[52]

With the 1984 election season under way, Rusher took special satisfaction in the seemingly limited effect of media hostility on the president's fortunes. Reagan had gone through an extended rough patch resulting mainly from the sharp recession in 1982. But now, in late 1983:

The scornful word "Reaganomics" has virtually disappeared from discussions of public affairs. Inflation has been whipped; interest rates are sharply down; the stock market . . . is joyfully registering new highs. Unemployment has dropped nearly two full percentage points; merchants are getting ready for the best Christmas season in recent memory; even the Detroit car manufacturers are posting impressive gains . . . All three of our key allies—Britain, Germany and Japan—are currently led by staunch conservatives very much in Mr. Reagan's own mold. He has just returned from a triumphant state visit to the Far East. The terrible blow of the Beirut car-bombing [at the barracks of a U.S. Marines peacekeeping force] was greatly softened, in terms of political fallout, by the invasion of Grenada which immediately followed, and which has proved so popular, according to the polls . . . Thanks in part to the shooting down of the Korean airliner [the Soviets had attacked a straying passenger jet in September, killing all on board], Mr. Reagan obtained from Congress the necessary funds to deploy the MX missiles, while in Europe the Soviet effort to block the deployment of NATO's new [Pershing II] missiles through popular protests was a failure. Even ABC-TV's own cynical contribution to the [nuclear disarmament] hysteria, "The Day After," turned out to be an anticlimactic bust.[53]

Still, Rusher remained anxious about the team around Reagan. When White House political-operations director Lyn Nofziger quit (as planned) in early 1982, he had written a column lamenting the loss. Now, in early 1984, he was sorry that Ed Meese would be leaving his counselor-to-the-president post once the Senate confirmed him as the new attorney general. Conservatives would no longer have a major "spokesman, confidant or source of input" close to the president "with whom they can feel really comfortable," and that situation should be remedied.[54]

In a phone conversation with Vice President Bush about a month later and a subsequent letter to him, Rusher similarly urged that after Meese's departure from the White House, conservatives should have a new "spokesman" there who enjoyed comparable access to the president. "As matters stand," he told Bush, "they feel excluded—which may be silly, given President Reagan's own feelings and inclinations, but . . . it's the perception that counts in these things." It would be in everybody's best interests, Rusher suggested, to ensure a high-level conservative presence.[55]

He also made the same request to the president that fall, writing shortly before the election that "conservatives feel unrepresented" at higher White House levels and adding that it would be ideal if William Clark could be brought over from his new position as interior secretary. In doing so, Rusher took pains to stay deferential. "I hope you will forgive me for bringing the matter up," he told Reagan. "I am not very fond of giving unsolicited advice, but I thought you wouldn't mind if I did it, just this once."[56] In late 1984, other conservatives, too, were strongly urging that Clark receive a major role in the president's second term, and an article in the *Wall Street Journal* reported that he might temporarily become chief of staff. But no such offer was made.[57]

"Judge Clark," who had been Governor Reagan's chief aide in the turbulent year of 1968, was a man of few words who did not enjoy politics. In 1981, he reluctantly left his working ranch and his seat on the California Supreme Court to fill a State Department post at the president-elect's urging. Reagan trusted him. Although he may not have been ideally suited to play the role of internal conservative spokesman that Rusher envisioned, Clark was able and inclined to "let Reagan be Reagan," as the oft-heard movement slogan went. Like Rusher, he believed in the president's essential competence. Serving as national security adviser after Richard Allen was forced out of the position, Clark had also been good at making firm, objective personnel decisions and at improving efficiency and morale among the National Security Council staff. Unlike Baker, he didn't leak to reporters—another likely plus from Rusher's standpoint. Without directly pushing his hard-line anticommunism, Clark reminded colleagues that Reagan's similar views were supposed to govern foreign policy.[58]

Nancy Reagan, however, had become hostile to her husband's longtime friend, believing that he was too anti-Soviet and contributed to the president's own image as such. Baker and Mike Deaver were also against him.

By late 1983, Clark had no White House allies but Meese, was increasingly losing battles with Secretary of State George Shultz and other foreign-policy moderates, and was seen internally as having lost his previous high standing with Reagan. His move to the secretary of the interior position at that point was a step away from the main action, toward a hoped-for retirement.[59] It was unlikely, therefore, that Rusher's recommendation of him for a high-level White House position would be heeded, or that Clark wanted the job.

Even so, the president felt close enough to Rusher to candidly express an unusual degree of anger toward opponents and weak Republicans. Writing him in mid-1984 to applaud a column in defense of Meese, who as the nominee for attorney general (replacing the moderate William French Smith, like Clark a friend of the president's who wanted to return to California) had come under persistent attack from the left-wing senator Howard Metzenbaum and others on ethics allegations, Reagan observed: "I can't recall having a greater antipathy to a fellow human equal to the one I have for Metzenbaum unless it was Hitler and Stalin. This lynching is Washington at its worst. Sadly, he might succeed. There are some on the [Capitol] hill who are rabbits when they should be tigers and they are on both sides of the aisle."[60]

Far from a peaceful reign reflecting a conservative or Republican consensus, Reagan's eight years were mostly a time of struggle for the party, for the Right, and for its president. Virulent opposition from congressional liberals, including Speaker Tip O'Neill and his comfortably sized—after 1982—Democratic majority in the House, and from reinvigorated liberal interest groups, succeeded in blocking large parts of the Reagan agenda while greatly complicating others. It also made many administration figures pay a high personal price for holding office.

But conservatives could take much satisfaction from Reagan's accomplishments in dramatically lowering income taxes and limiting (though not much reducing) the size and scope of government, rebuilding America's international strength, improving the nation's economy and morale, changing the emphases of the federal bureaucracy and the composition of the federal judiciary to partly reflect conservative principles, and denouncing both communism and statism more intensely than any other president. The Republicans would keep their small but useful Senate majority in 1984, while Reagan would be reelected in a 59 percent landslide in which he won all but one state, inspiring a further sense of political triumph.

Longings for a new party and sympathetic interest in previous signs of moderation among the Democrats were now just memories for Rusher. "What's a nice guy like you doing in a party like that?" he asked Bert Lance, the Carter official to whom, back in 1977, he had suggested a possible alliance between movement conservatives and the Democrats' moderate wing. "The Democratic party you have fought and bled for is gone."[61]

Conservatism, the GOP, the voters, and public policy were all broadly in sync at last. Rusher delighted in Reagan's successes, in the strong rebound in his popularity, in party unity behind not just a movement candidate but a movement president. His close friend, YR ally, and Goldwater-campaign comrade Roger Moore, now general counsel to the Republican National Committee, told him about a happy encounter at the convention in Dallas. Crossing paths with Senator Charles Mathias of Maryland, a leading liberal Republican, Moore asked: "Good morning, Senator. How are things going?" Shaking his head, Mathias answered: "You guys own the ocean."

Rusher was pleased to hear of the wry admission, with which he agreed. "We knew we were going to win hugely. We had the best of all possible presidents in the White House. He'd been there for four years. He was going to be there for four more. What more can you ask for in politics than that, except a great big convention, with lots of parties and cheering and a speech by Reagan? It was just paradise."[62]

# 16

# Éminence Grise

Much of Rusher's spare time the previous two years had been spent writing a medium-length book on the conservative movement, published in the spring of 1984. *The Rise of the Right* was "a little deceptive" as a title, he admitted to his aunt Mary Louise, since he "had intended a history of the conservative movement" and it was "turning into more of a personal memoir of my own participation in the movement."[1] The book nonetheless traced the history of postwar American conservatism, balancing accounts of *National Review* and other institutions with thoughts on historical trends, elections, and Republican nomination contests.

Rusher made clear his satisfaction with the movement's progress. The essential reality, he wrote, was that "conservatism cannot and will not be denied indefinitely the influence on American society that is dictated by its inherent strength." Meanwhile, it was "unmistakably *on the playing field* at last, as one of the two major contestants." Conservative analyses of issues were now "too numerous, too incisive, and too widely disseminated to be disregarded."[2]

A long-range perspective was also clear in Rusher's response to criticisms of Reagan for not achieving enough or not trying hard enough. The president, he wrote, had been wise enough to see that his election in 1980 wasn't a mandate for the entire conservative agenda or Republican platform. He was also a resilient master of the tactical retreat: "Like a skillful club boxer, Reagan moved into the attack, landed his punches, backed off, shifted his weight, parried, and attacked again. I came to feel that I was watching a protagonist who knew precisely what he wanted, enjoyed battling for it, and firmly intended to get it in the long run."[3]

Eventually, Rusher predicted, the conservative movement would disappear, like an ocean wave giving shape and force to the next one. Conservatism as such, though, because it was "a profound analysis of the nature of man and of human society" rather than a political operation, would survive. In the meantime, the movement's next battles were in the media and the academy—of which the latter was the most important and most difficult.[4]

In the *American Spectator,* Aram Bakshian, a former speechwriting director at the Reagan White House, praised the book as "tightly constructed yet wide-reaching . . . informative, highly readable, and largely candid." Rusher's relish for tactical politics, combined with his appreciation of different types of conservatism, made him the ideal person to write it. He had "mastered his subject and seen through the ephemeral to the significant." In *Policy Review,* editor Adam Meyerson called the book a "fascinating history" and an "indispensable guide."[5]

Unfortunately for its potential impact among nonconservatives, *Rise of the Right* got a hostile reception in the *New York Times* and its book-review section. One review misrepresented the author as the product of a privileged background whose youthful choice for conservatism was like "deciding to summer in Newport instead of Saratoga," while the other portrayed the teenaged Rusher as "suckled on the milk of paranoia" and abnormally interested in "political intrigue" rather than cars and girls. Reviewer Lewis Lapham, the editor of *Harper's,* inaccurately accused him of taking almost total credit for conservatism's success and presenting the reader with "an itemized bill." The book was also "humorless," Lapham complained, and characterized by a "juggling of abstractions." The review by Walter Goodman suggested that Rusher focused too much on the ideological conflict within the Republican Party and hadn't provided enough objective analysis or inside knowledge of the movement.[6]

Despite the positive reviews on the Right, the book's sales seemed to disappoint Rusher. In early 1985, responding to a query from Russell Kirk, he complained: "I seriously doubt that there are any good publishers. I have had several, and I would not credit any of them with the ability to sell the Holy Bible."[7] More uplifting was the response from Barry Goldwater, who immediately contacted the *Washington Times* book editor to express hope that *Rise of the Right* would get "its just review." Rusher was "one of the real founders of the modern conservative movement," Goldwater wrote. "Having read any number of books about the birth of the conservative movement . . . I think this is by far the best one that has been done on the whole subject." In a letter to Rusher, Goldwater said he had easily finished it in one sitting because it was "so intriguing." He had no disagreements, or certainly no serious disagreements, with the book and was thankful to Rusher for writing it.[8] The president, in response to a newspaper inquiry about what he was currently reading, listed *Rise of the Right* along with four other books.[9]

## "A Considerable Sense of Achievement"

Rusher continued to travel to speaking engagements, for which he typically earned an honorarium of two to three thousand dollars plus expenses. He was also heard even more frequently on the radio now, recording five ninety-second commentaries per week. Under the sponsorship of a conservative Ohio industrialist, Fred Lennon, they aired on hundreds of AP Radio Network stations around the country.[10] As of 1986, about 240 mostly small newspapers ran Rusher's column, equating to a potential audience of close to six million readers.[11]

As early as 1983, having purchased an attractive condominium in San Francisco and begun to rent it out for the time being, he was anticipating retirement from *National Review*. He felt "no pressure whatever" to leave, Rusher told his aunt, and undoubtedly could "sit right here . . . respectfully patronized by the oncoming generations, until I am 85 or 90." But it was his "rather strong feeling that, with the election of Reagan and the 'coming of age' of the conservative movement . . . an end of sorts has come to the quarrel upon which I embarked" in 1956–57. Rusher noted that he still felt "absurdly young." As long as interest in him continued, he would keep writing the column and books, continue his public speaking, and appear on the radio and occasionally TV. But five more years of "coping with *National Review*'s fairly trivial internal problems, and answering letters about our annual fund appeal, strikes me as just about enough."[12]

Admirers had occasion to reflect on Rusher's career in July 1985 when Neal Freeman, now a successful television producer, sponsored and arranged a Potomac River cruise aboard the former presidential yacht, *Sequoia*. (The mildly damaged boat had been inactive for a while, but Interior Secretary Donald Hodel, an old friend of Rusher's, allowed its use for the party.) Coinciding with Rusher's sixty-second birthday, the afternoon was a thank-you and a stock-taking, separate from the New York milieu where he was inevitably overshadowed by Buckley. Even some who couldn't be there participated in spirit. Sending his regrets, Attorney General Meese wrote: "Your role as sage and shepherd of the conservative movement has been a personal inspiration to me."[13] Rusher introduced Tom Farmer, a Washington attorney, with slight exaggeration as "the only Democrat I know" and with no exaggeration as "my oldest friend." At one point, Senator Helms drolly approached Farmer, who had lit up a cigar. "Thank you for smoking," the North Carolinian said. Pat Buchanan, now the White House communications director, told attendees about the tightly compressed bit of wisdom he received in the 1960s. "Pat," Rusher had warned, "Richard Nixon will break your heart."[14]

Rusher and Farmer later had a nightcap at the Madison Hotel downtown. The day on the river had been something of a revelation. People's remarks "really brought it home to me that you are one of the most important influences on present day American politics," Farmer noted, adding that it was "quite an accomplishment, and you should be well satisfied with your life's work." He was also impressed and a bit envious that his friend spoke with such "equanimity" about approaching retirement. Rusher replied that he did feel "a considerable sense of achievement" while doubting it was wholly justified, since in one form or another much of the conservatives' success probably would have occurred anyway. "I cherish our friendship very deeply," he wrote.[15]

For the past several years, one of Rusher's favorite people at *NR* had been Rick Brookhiser, who remembers him as "a great presence and a great friend." An in-depth political reporter at the time, Brookhiser was also enamored of literature and thus had two interests in common with Rusher, who read and recited poetry. When Brookhiser married Jeanne Safer in 1980, the publisher did a reading at their wedding. Rusher "would take us to some fancy restaurant that he liked, and then we would cook for him," Brookhiser recalls, "and those were just delightful occasions. It was very interesting: my wife's a liberal Democrat; she's also a psychoanalyst. Through me, she learned that conservatives could be quite pleasant people even if she disagreed with them on everything. And with Bill Rusher it was something more . . . In terms of his own life and what he'd been through, he was very insightful. He was very interested in the fact that my wife was a psychologist, and they just conversed about that at a very sympathetic level."[16]

Another person who learned to appreciate Rusher was his last secretary. Claire Wirth, hired in 1978, had previously worked in the ABC News department and in the 1950s had assisted Walter Winchell with his television news program and his variety show—a difficult man, she later recalled, so "paranoid" that he carried a gun. Wirth could take another challenging boss. Upon joining *National Review*, she received an encouraging note from former senior editor Bill Rickenbacker, who had stayed in touch with Rusher. He predicted that she would eventually come to know the publisher, who was "like a comfortable old shoe."

From the beginning, Rusher seemed "a terribly serious person" who was also "very proper and cordial . . . no-nonsense, pleasant, well-mannered, reserved, intellectual." All were qualities Wirth enjoyed. It was stimulating to work for him, and Rusher probably found it easy to talk with her because they were closer in age and she "understood a lot of situations," like his health problems. One day, New York was hit by torrential rains from a hurricane. Wirth lived in the city, closer than employees who lived in the suburbs, and felt obliged to come in because many others wouldn't be able to. After getting drenched on the way, she casually mentioned her trip through the downpour and Rusher neglected to sympathize, pointing out that she could have her raincoat waterproofed "as though I had never thought of that." But Rickenbacker's guess proved correct. "We did become friends."[17]

In addition to food, wine, and the opera, Rusher continued to enjoy cigars, sometimes after an especially satisfying lunch. "He smoked them at the office," Wirth recalls, "never at home. 'Don't foul your own nest' is the way he described it." When a younger friend urged him to exercise, Rusher responded that although anybody who wanted to was "entitled to do it," he wouldn't. "Exercising may make your day; it would assuredly ruin mine."[18] It was more diplomatic than his father's "Hell, that's not living," but the point and the stubbornness were the same. Nor did Rusher, "the mainstay of the taxi industry," walk the few blocks to work most days. Told once that "joy is the best medicine," he asked: "Does it cure arthritis?"[19]

For several years, not wanting to be "pushed around" by the computer age, Rusher resisted the now-ubiquitous word processor. Although he dictated his column into a tape recorder at the office, his books were written in longhand at his apartment. Rusher had always prided himself on the old-fashioned method, looking forward to "pushing a pen across a yellow pad until I toppled over." In 1986, as he reported in his column, he finally gave in because arthritis in his thumb made it too painful to continue doing so. But before getting a word processor, he tried thousands of dollars worth of treatments, including a copper bracelet and a Chinese herbal lotion.[20] His own tastes notwithstanding, Rusher saw that the magazine had to modernize technologically at some point, and in his last years as publisher he asked an employee to look into the question. Would significant changes be necessary before he left? The answer was no, not in that short time.[21]

His office remained as it had always been, "neat as a pin—constantly," with weights on the stacks of paper. Noneditorial staff members "treaded quietly when Rusher was around" and felt a little nervous when called into his office, according to Edward Capano, one of his successors as publisher and at the time Jim McFadden's assistant in the circulation department. Over the years, Capano had gotten the impression that the publisher might be "a very lonely man" at times, but now he seemed to have grown "more mellow and more sensitive." He came across rather like a headmaster with students, Wirth recalls, and everyone "respected him tremendously."[22]

*From the personal collection of William Rusher*

*At his* National Review *office*

Rusher's friend Frank Shepherd helped to look after his mother, Verna, living alone in Miami Shores, Florida. She had a personality much like her son's, "very precise and succinct," Shepherd recalls, and "very well-organized . . . very fastidious . . . a person of relatively few words." Rusher called her every Sunday morning and sent her his column, also visiting fairly often for two or three days. By early 1985, her financial resources were exhausted, and upon retirement Rusher would need a new source of income, in addition to his *NR* pension and his speaking fees, to pay for Verna's full-time practical nurse. He "saw to her every need," Wirth remembers. "He was a very dedicated son. He took it very seriously."[23]

Although Rusher never married, his secretary noted a couple of cases in which women showed romantic interest. One was a younger woman on the staff. Another time, a divorced lady he knew sat in the waiting room on the first floor, determined to catch him as he was leaving. Rusher got the building superintendent to let him out the back. Wirth thought he was "very happy being single. He had control of his life, and he did what he wanted to do. He was so devoted to the conservative movement . . . writing about it, being involved in it at meetings . . . promoting it."[24]

Rusher also continued to travel for pleasure. On an Asian tour in late 1985, he visited Nepal, where his friend Lee Weil now served as ambassador. Upon learning that he was scheduled to speak to the Katmandu Council of World Affairs on the rise of the conservative movement, Weil thought "this is crazy—who in Nepal is really interested?" but turned out to be "absolutely wrong. The room was filled, and there was great interest in what Bill was talking about." The audience asked many questions and kept him a long time. Still, Weil "gathered that Nepal wasn't quite his type of country" even though Rusher's comments about the brief stay were favorable.[25] Another old friend, John Thomson, was commercial counselor at the U.S. embassy in Saudi Arabia. Thomson and his wife invited Rusher to see them. As Rusher knew, his debating abilities might cause friction in the tightly controlled country, which Westerners couldn't easily enter. Acting as "his usual buttoned-up, formal, but respectful and courteous self" during the week-long visit, he knew "when not to be a debater . . . how to couch his ideas and views in nonthreatening ways." Although Rusher "engaged happily in spirited discussions with a cross-section of leaders on sensitive subjects as diverse as the Israeli-Arab dispute and women's rights," Thomson recalls, "I never heard a word of anything but praise for Bill and gratitude for his visit."[26]

Participating in another adventurous trip in early 1987 on a tour of southern Africa sponsored by the Reverend Sun Myung Moon's Unification Church, owners of the *Washington Times*, Rusher made an excursion to a remote part of Angola, where the anticommunist guerrillas led by Jonas Savimbi were headquartered. The journalists, including *NR*'s Brookhiser and Tom Bethell of the *American Spectator*, took a flight in a DC-3, landed on a dirt airstrip, and rode over bush trails to reach the secret site.[27]

## Old Habits, New Battles

Although Rusher's relationships with *National Review* colleagues, as with the political scene, were more relaxed than they had been previously and editorial conflicts were far milder, the permanent absence of Jim Burnham after 1978 had not increased his clout. Too much of a gap remained between Rusher's vision of *NR* and that of many others there. Rusher preferred something of a "Beltway entity," according to Brookhiser, a magazine more heavily political and news-oriented. The alternative was to present an entire conservative mental world, drawing readers into it with "all different kinds of bait."[28] When Rusher brought up his name for strategic missile defense— offered in preference to liberal opponents' derisive "Star Wars"—Buckley made fun of it, quipping that "Star Shield" sounded like a condom. But such dismissals were to be expected. By the 1980s, according to Joe Sobran, Buckley had "stopped listening to almost everybody."[29]

Sobran and Brookhiser both turned to Rusher about difficulties they had with the editor in the latter half of the decade. When Sobran sought his advice in 1986 after being accused by neoconservatives of writing anti-Semitic columns, Rusher indicated it was an "explosive and risky" situation but was "very generous to me and protective of me" during the controversy.[30] The publisher told an old political friend that Sobran was "a careful and thoughtful writer" who had "tangled quite as cheerfully with the ostentatious alleged spokesmen for 'women, blacks, Italians and others' quite as much as he has in the case of Jews." Rusher added: "Frankly, I am not sure that he *is* aware of just how sensitive some of this material is (i.e., how sensitive many minorities are, rightly or wrongly, to the least whisper of group criticism); but I am absolutely certain that Joe is not in any meaningful sense of the word anti-Semitic." He continued: "If the subject still bothers you, I would deeply appreciate it if you would drop me a note and say so. Joe respects my advice, and has already been the object of some of it."[31]

In mid-1987, Brookhiser learned that he would not be Buckley's successor, as they had long planned. Buckley dropped the news abruptly as he was leaving on vacation, in a confidential letter placed on Brookhiser's desk: "It is by now plain to me that you are not suited to serve as editor-in-chief of NR after my retirement." The then managing editor (Priscilla Buckley had retired at the end of 1985) lacked "executive" characteristics, Buckley explained, and nothing would distract him more from his true calling as a writer than bearing ultimate responsibility for a magazine. In view of the fact that he was breaking a previous understanding with Brookhiser, who would remain on the staff if he chose to, Buckley proposed special financial arrangements and asked the young editor to think these over for a week or so. Shocked and wounded by the news and the way it was communicated, Brookhiser asked Rusher for advice. Already aware of the decision, the publisher also knew Buckley's tendency to announce things by letter or through him. Brookhiser should think of a response soon, he urged, "before Buckley decides to consult his fifty closest friends."[32]

Although Rusher now wrote few editorially or politically substantive memos at *National Review*, his belief in a strong linkage to the movement and in supporting conservative leaders and projects remained about the same. So did his editorial tastes. He disliked some of the symbolic covers, mainly by a Czechoslovakian expatriate whose work Buckley used even if its relationship to the edition's material was unclear. It would "drive Bill crazy," Buckley recalls, "if he didn't see the connection between a particular photograph and the story it was supposed to illustrate."[33] A made-up cover featuring a Socialist Realist statue of a naked woman and headlined WHY REAGAN CAN'T WIN IN 1984 didn't fool him, although Claire Wirth reported that he paled for a second. He was amused and sent it to the president, who predictably found it funnier than some on the White House staff.

"Bill Rusher does not get as easily carried away as the editors by our wit and merriment," Priscilla Buckley explained at *National Review's* thirtieth-anniversary dinner in 1985. "He provides the needed ballast to our Ship of State, and takes our occasional ribbing with sunny good humor—because he knows he's right."[34] But Rusher's good humor coexisted uneasily with other aspects of the *NR* mental world, not only the artistic covers. In addition to his low regard for the satirical verses of the magazine's amateur poet W. H. von Dreele, he read just one of Buckley's many spy novels—a lesser-known one, *The Story of Henri Tod*—because he disliked mixing historical characters with fictional ones. Doing this in a novel, it seemed to Rusher as to Robert Frost on unrhymed poetry, was like "playing tennis with the net down."[35]

At the thirtieth-anniversary gala at the Plaza Hotel, President Reagan said he awaited his copy of *NR* "as anxiously as ever." It was to the West Wing of the White House "what *People* magazine is to your dentist's waiting room." He also paid homage to *NR's* wider influence: "I want to assure you tonight. You didn't just part the Red Sea—you rolled it back, dried it up, and left exposed, for all the world to see, the naked desert that is statism." Buckley was "perhaps the most influential journalist and intellectual in our era," the president said. "He changed our country, indeed our century." Rusher's own remarks were businesslike, with a plug for the conservative grass roots and an implied warning against forgetting them. The fact that the magazine had survived for three decades was "strictly a function," he told the audience, "of the steadfast and unstinting generosity of *National Review's* friends."[36]

Several months before, as Reagan's second term got under way, Rusher had told him conservatives were "delighted . . . with the recent personnel changes in the White House,"[37] the most prominent of which was the appointment of Pat Buchanan as director of communications. More important, he enjoyed the continued proliferation of conservative organizations and activities, telling Russell Kirk in a typical comment that the right-leaning *Washington Times*, founded in 1982, was doing "a splendid job" both journalistically and politically.[38]

To Brent Bozell III, a conservative activist and son of his former *NR* colleague, Rusher noted his "surprise and delight" that the movement had seen political triumph in his lifetime. It probably explained, he suggested, why he felt much more satisfied than people who viewed the president's performance as only a minimum standard for conservative policymaking. Rusher

found it a little sad to hear movement-oriented "youngsters of 20 say . . .
Reagan was a disgrace, etc.," and had cautioned one who took this attitude
that he could expect to feel "perfectly miserable in American politics, when
he realizes what will be coming along after Reagan." He was, according to
Bozell, "cracking the whip in defense of Reagan at all times."[39]

Such predictability could be irritating. "I used to joke about how Bill
was enamored of Reagan," Sobran recalls. "Well, I liked Reagan too, but I
didn't worship him, and I thought Bill came pretty close to worship." Sobran
and Brookhiser thought he could save himself the trouble of verbal comment by preparing a standard notice to pass out at editorial meetings when
the president's policies were discussed: "I support                    ."[40]

There were times, according to David Keene, who became ACU chairman in 1984, when Rusher "didn't really understand what might be going on"
in Washington and therefore viewed a Reagan-related matter "simplistically."
In such cases, he may have forgiven the president and those around him more
than was warranted, but he viewed himself as something of a political player,
which required a certain amount of loyalty. Politicians, Keene notes, like
people who "don't bitch at them all the time." They were inclined to listen
to Rusher because he seemed to have their best interests at heart while also
understanding the activists and ideologues. Rather than complain, he was
more likely to give advice about working with the movement.[41]

Despite his general respect for Republican politicians in the 1980s, Rusher's attitude toward former president Nixon, who now lived in New Jersey and
had an office in Manhattan, remained largely unchanged. The extent of a visiting South African's interest seemed dismally amusing. He was "wondering
if he could get to meet Nixon," Brookhiser recalls. "Could Rusher set that up?
Rusher said no, he couldn't do that . . . and then the guy was saying: 'What
do you suppose Nixon thinks of the life after death?' and Rusher said to me:
'Could you imagine, asking that cad about the life after death?'"[42]

Nixon had written respected foreign-policy books in his postpresiden-
tial years, also making himself available to conservative and Republican figures interested in seeing him, and in such ways had rehabilitated himself to a
significant extent. An anticommunist society called, in memory of the Hiss
case, the Pumpkin Papers Irregulars invited the ex-president as the featured
speaker at its annual dinner in 1985. Asked to give the introduction, Rusher
tactfully declined: "I don't think I am the man to introduce Mr. Nixon."
Claiming to have no personal objection, he noted that they had never "seen
eye to eye" politically and added a second reason, denying he felt hurt by it. In
recent years, Nixon had sometimes invited conservative columnists to dinner
while "pointedly" excluding him, most recently just a week before.[43]

In May 1986, Rusher taped a long-awaited interview with Reagan at the

White House for a ninety-minute PBS historical documentary, *The Conservatives*, produced by Freeman. As the lights were being adjusted, "we were talking about the Soviet Union" and the president said: "'You know, their economy is a basket case.' . . . In those days, the Soviet Union was regarded as twenty feet tall and too hard to pick on. Reagan didn't have that attitude at all. He had spotted their weakness, and he knew exactly what it was. Their economy was a basket case."[44]

Rusher's contacts with Reagan over two decades helped to maintain the unflagging confidence he was now well known for expressing. Criticisms on the Right during the president's second term, having previously tended to come from social conservatives, populists, or highly ideological small-government advocates, increasingly involved foreign policy and often appeared in *National Review*. In mid-1985, Rusher defended Reagan's handling of a drawn-out, volatile highjacking in the Mediterranean region after an editorial said his "dangerous tendency toward passive crisis management" was making the president look more and more like Jimmy Carter. In support of that claim, *NR* cited other terrorist situations the administration had faced, plus the 1981 declaration of martial law in Poland and the Korean airline massacre by the Soviets in 1983.

"We are at war" with Islamic terrorists such as those who captured TWA Flight 847, the editorial told readers, "and if the President does not know it, he should clear his mind of cant." Writing under the Open Question heading, Rusher objected that Reagan's response to the seventeen-day crisis in which one passenger was killed but the rest were ultimately freed had been "almost flawless," adding—not prophetically, it turned out—that "deadly retaliation" by the U.S. was likely. Steps called for in the editorial, like requiring other nations' airlines to boycott airports subject to terrorism, would have done nothing to free the hostages. The editorial was a mere venting of "the authors' impatience, frustration, and exasperation."[45]

Also disagreeing with those who believed Reagan was getting too soft on policy toward the Soviet Union, Rusher spoke to Buckley in mid-1986 about recent editorials on the question by Jeff Hart and Brookhiser and passed along points Reagan had made to him about such criticisms. He had urged Buckley "to keep a closer eye on the general tone" of critical editorials, Rusher told the president, and "Bill seemed to agree with me." Although he couldn't guarantee that unpleasant editorial comments about Reagan would never appear again, Rusher suggested *NR*'s continued appreciation of him was more important: "As I said over the phone, rest assured that our bark is far worse than our bite—even the writers who are most critical, from time to time, would cheerfully agree that no presidency in modern times can compare with yours."[46]

Immediately before the Reykjavik summit between Reagan and the seemingly reformist new Soviet leader Mikhail Gorbachev in October of that year, Rusher stood by the president in his column, dismissing "the hysterics who are trying to coach him from the sidelines." While some American conservatives, in addition to Gorbachev, thought Reagan might give up the Strategic Defense Initiative in return for major nuclear reductions, Rusher wrote: "Anybody who thinks the president is going to bargain away that possibility is sniffing glue."[47] The difference between himself and such critics, he later explained to a friend, was that "I know Reagan well enough personally to be absolutely confident that he hasn't changed his mind (and won't) on any of the essentials."[48]

After the Democrats regained their Senate majority in the midterm elections despite Reagan's continued popularity, the president was in the deflated position of Nixon, Ford, and Eisenhower—facing a Congress in which the opposition party controlled both houses. Simultaneously with the lost election, it was revealed that the administration had used Israel to sell weaponry to the fanatical Islamist regime in Iran, hoping to facilitate the release of several American hostages captured by terrorists in Lebanon. The profits, it was further reported, were sent to the "contra" fighters in Nicaragua despite a then current congressional ban on funds for the anticommunist forces. Reagan's opponents, and many in the media, quickly sensed in the Iran-Contra affair a major scandal that might destroy his presidency.

Initially worried about the appointment of former Senate majority leader Howard Baker as the new White House chief of staff, Rusher wrote a rare column questioning the president's judgment. It seemed that Reagan had chosen "a short-term gain at the price of what may prove to be a long-term loss." Baker was quite intelligent, and his moderate brand of Republicanism made him popular with Congress and the media. But he was "privately cool" to distinctively Reaganite policies and might well argue against pursuing them. After watching developments for three months, Rusher praised Baker in mid-1987 as "a first-rate choice." What mattered most wasn't where his heart lay politically, but what he did and how well. Rusher explained that the chief of staff had worked cheerfully for the remaining items on the president's agenda, used his Capitol Hill knowledge and bargaining skills effectively, helped to limit the political damage from the congressional Iran-Contra hearings—and "sought out leading conservative spokesmen and solicited their input." Thus, many conservatives thought he now qualified as a "loyal supporter of the Reagan Revolution."[49]

Rusher was among the movement leaders who had met with Reagan and Baker in March and urged the president to "seize the initiative," as he later described the point, "from those who want to concentrate on the Iran controversy forever." One possibility, they suggested, would be to announce termination of the Anti-Ballistic Missile Treaty negotiated in the Nixon years, which SDI opponents argued forbade the deployment of strategic missile defense. Rusher also agreed with Clif White that Reagan should start holding press conferences outside Washington—"to the total exclusion," he told the president, "of the prima donnas who are making their careers, and their fortunes, out of baiting you." In his response, Reagan indicated the ABM Treaty wouldn't be terminated while also assuring Rusher that SDI would go ahead. He didn't comment on the idea of press conferences outside the Beltway, but said he thought the meeting with the conservative representatives had been well worthwhile.[50]

Like his other media-related concerns, Rusher's suggestion about the press conferences was important to him. Various Reagan advisers, including some of the "oldest and shrewdest," had themselves strongly recommended what he was advocating. Outside the Beltway, Rusher explained in his column, such proceedings would have a better tone, Washington political reporters would be cut down to size, and a wider range of questions would be asked while major national topics could still be addressed.[51]

Rusher followed Iran-Contra with dutiful interest, seeing it as largely a political struggle featuring "heavy attack by a congressional investigating committee and impeachment clearly on everyone's mind if not (yet) on everyone's tongue," with the media "in the Democrats' corner once again."[52] As he had during Watergate, he challenged some elements of the dominant story line. Rusher disagreed that Reagan—as Buckley wrote in one of his own columns—had "given in to terrorists." He also rejected the assumption that the Boland Amendment, which banned governmental appropriations for the contras, necessarily forbade officials to solicit other sources of money for them.[53] The secret negotiations with "potential friends" in Iran and the arms sales, Rusher judged in August, after the story had played out for nearly a year, "began as a perfectly sound diplomatic initiative . . . and only gradually took on the aspect of a 'trade' of arms for hostages. It seems likely that . . . President Reagan believed that, far from dealing with the kidnappers, he was bringing heavy pressures to bear on them." And even if there was a deliberate arms-for-hostages deal, it seemed like "a crime of the heart . . . No doubt he ought to have been made of sterner stuff. But there is simply no denying that President Reagan is extremely sensitive to the human aspects of these grim events . . . Too much stress on the human element—that must count as a weakness in any president. But if Ronald Reagan has to have a weakness, I'm kind of glad it's that one."[54] Rusher was relieved that Iran-Contra didn't match Watergate in its political impact. Despite some damage to the president, there was no attempt to impeach him, and he again had a good job-approval rating. The media, it turned out, were "not invincible."[55]

In mid-1987, with the growing prospect of an Intermediate Nuclear Forces arms-control treaty with the Soviet Union, *NR* ran a symposium against the deal as it appeared to be taking shape. Although Buckley sent Reagan a copy in advance so he wouldn't be blindsided, the special issue hit the president hard, starting with its title: "Reagan's Suicide Pact." The lead essay was a contemptuous attack by political scientist John Roche, a Cold War liberal and former ADA chairman who now wrote pieces for *NR* as a disaffected Democrat. Buckley was fond of Roche and several years earlier had called him "arguably the wittiest polemicist alive." Another piece in the special issue, cowritten by Nixon and Kissinger, strongly urged a more careful approach than Reagan seemed to be taking. Evan Galbraith, a close friend of Buckley's and the American ambassador to France in the first Reagan term, warned about a treaty's likely impact on West Germany.

The response from Rusher in the next issue of *National Review* reflected his instincts as a lawyer, as a Reagan admirer, and as a movement conservative with a long memory. No actual treaty had yet taken shape, he pointed out, nor had Reagan made a statement outlining its provisions. Rusher also insisted that the many conservatives now making the "wholly gratuitous assumption that Reagan has lost his mind and intends to leave Europe defenseless" should weigh their anxieties against his impressive record on communism and defense. He implied that Nixon and Kissinger were discredited by history. Why, Rusher asked, should conservatives regard their advice as compelling? It was a point he would repeat in his column over the next several months, denouncing the former president and former secretary of state as cheap "Machiavellis" who lacked credibility in addressing a Soviet problem they had, in his opinion, done much to worsen. Finally, Rusher condemned the magazine's editorial as "wildly premature and affirmatively damaging to a man who, as of this date, deserves only our gratitude."[56]

In his subsequent newspaper columns, Rusher got more into the merits of the INF issue, taking a position not only against his magazine but against other conservatives. In addition, the only 1988 Republican presidential candidate who supported the treaty at the time was George Bush; several others opposed it.[57] Even with the elimination of intermediate-range land-based missiles from Europe, Rusher pointed out, there would still be sea-based nuclear weapons in addition to the nuclear-tipped artillery shells that could stop Russian tanks. NATO had formidable conventional strength as well, a consideration too easily overlooked in the debate. Rusher also suggested that a viable "space shield" defense against nuclear missiles was less than a decade away. Finally, he stressed that it was high time Western Europe made the sacrifices necessary to strengthen its conventional defenses instead of relying so much on American nuclear forces.[58]

Ideally, Rusher told readers, there should be no treaties with the Soviet Union because it was ruled by an illegitimate, murderous regime that was—as Reagan had called it several years before—"the focus of evil in the modern world." But treaties became inevitable because Americans, including some prominent conservatives, had given it many "admissions of legitimacy" by, for example, traveling to the country or respectfully hosting Kremlin spokesmen on television. In addition, Rusher was concerned that after Reagan left office, a future president or Congress would let the Soviets get away with cheating on the INF Treaty and that liberals would precipitously seize on the agreement as justification for slashing defense spending.

But on balance, he considered INF a good idea for two reasons. It was a small step toward eliminating reliance on the doctrine of mutual assured destruction and replacing MAD with "the far saner and more civilized concept of mutual defense by means of space satellites." Rusher also argued that Gorbachev's attempts to give his society small doses of political and economic freedom deserved American cooperation because "irresistible pressures for still more freedom" would follow. Lightening the regime's "crushing burden of armaments" even modestly, he explained, "may encourage the men in the Kremlin to hope that world conquest is not their only road to safety." Meanwhile, international opinion would not tolerate the MAD approach indefinitely "if an effective alternative based on space-satellite defenses is available."[59] Buckley, in contrast, thought it was foolish to count on the development of such defenses, warning Reagan that diplomatic developments like the INF Treaty would increase accommodationism toward the Soviets in Congress, causing it to "starve SDI to death after you have left the White House."[60]

In August 1987, Rusher justified the president's agreement to cosponsor a peace plan for Central America on two grounds. Given Reagan's nearly total dependence on "a hostile Democratic Congress to provide additional military aid to the freedom fighters," Rusher noted, he had a weak hand in the region. Furthermore, once the Marxist Nicaraguan regime led by Daniel Ortega refused to accept or honor democratic requirements in the peace plan, Reagan would again fight hard with the Democrats on behalf of the contras. The president's "head-ducking modesty and soft-spoken manner" were only superficial qualities and therefore nothing to worry about. Reagan had "won more victories for conservatism than all of his conservative critics put together—critics, in most cases, whose entire portfolio of winning strategies consists of the Thermopylae Defense."[61]

In a similar spirit, Rusher told his former colleague Rickenbacker the following month: "The truth, I suspect, is that he lives in the real world and most of his critics don't." At a recent editorial dinner, Buckley had "expounded his theory that Reagan ought to have warned the Soviet Union, very explicitly and early on, that installing a Communist regime in Nicaragua would result in invasion by American armed forces." As the editors unanimously agreed with "this sunburst of insight," Rusher sipped his soup, reflecting that such a threat "would have given the Democrats their happiest hours since Vietnam."[62]

## The Media Conundrum

Rusher's attention increasingly turned to problems of interest to conservatives but not, strictly speaking, political. In 1988, he published his final book, *The Coming Battle for the Media.* Along with his own content analysis, Rusher provided other detailed illustrations of political bias and drew heavily on research by nonconservative sources to establish the overwhelmingly liberal views of people in the major media outlets.

He disputed the accusation of "slanting the news," a concept conservatives often used when criticizing the media. "Almost every story worth reporting," Rusher explained, required the journalist to "adopt some 'theory' of its thrust that will enable him or her to distinguish the relevant from the irrelevant and the important from the unimportant. Quite often this process will involve value judgments as to which individuals may and do differ." Rather than try to artificially limit reporting to definite facts, a fair editor would simply ensure "that personal biases don't get out of control, and that the *mix* of stories (and thus 'theories') ultimately presented to the reader or viewer is reasonably well balanced."[63]

Believing that a reduction in large-scale bias and other media abuses was an urgent task in which the quality of American democracy was at stake, Rusher discussed possible remedies and lamented the demise of the National News Council (NNC), a project to which he had given considerable time in the 1970s. Founded in 1973 at the behest of a mainstream foundation, the NNC served for a decade as an unofficial investigator of complaints that individuals, organizations, and businesses could file against the media. The founders and members hoped council findings, in cases where they went against a media outlet, would exert pressure for better practices or policies. While most of the NNC's fifteen members were actually liberals, Rusher was asked to join in the interest of ensuring substantial conservative representation. Serving on the council from its founding through 1980, he was a member of its grievance committee, which received documentation and testimony, considered the merits of the complaints, and recommended findings to the full body.

Supporters of the council included CBS News president Richard Salant and Norman Isaacs, a prestigious liberal journalist who was an editor in residence at the Columbia University journalism school and also served as NNC chairman for several years. But *New York Times* managing editor and later executive editor A. M. Rosenthal was an implacable opponent while the paper's publisher, Arthur (Punch) Sulzberger, warned that the organization might encourage a pro-regulatory atmosphere leading to intervention by government. The council shut down in 1983 owing to a lack of continued funding and other problems—including the *Times*'s refusal to cooperate, which fueled or reinforced negative attitudes elsewhere in the industry. It was the NNC's bad luck, Rusher explained in *Coming Battle for the Media*, to begin its life just as Watergate was becoming a public issue. The media's celebrated role in exposing the scandal, he believed, made journalists increasingly arrogant and uninterested in self-criticism after a period in which attacks by Vice President Agnew and others had led to more serious consideration of media ethics or at least to anxiety about public disapproval.[64]

Rusher threw cold water on the idea—often brought up among conservatives—that sympathizers might win control of a major TV network by purchasing it. Buckley, he noted, had been equally skeptical when many people suggested this to him in the late 1950s. It would require vast amounts of money and be an "enormous drain . . . on the time and energies of the individuals qualified and willing to mount such a drive." Even if the takeover actually occurred, Rusher warned, liberal intellectuals and the media itself would try to discredit such a network; a term like "right-wing" or "ultra-conservative" would be permanently attached to it. He also doubted that the "basic thrust of a large news organization could be permanently transformed from liberal to conservative by a mere change of ownership" unless there were "fundamental shifts in the intellectual atmosphere of the entire society." And finally, the goal shouldn't be a conservative network anyway but a balanced one.[65]

Drawing on his perspective as a lawyer, Rusher gave serious consideration to governmental action against media abuses. He mildly hoped that in the future, a more conservative Supreme Court might weaken what he saw as the media's excessive protection against libel lawsuits. It might also recognize the authority of a president, as commander in chief, to restrain reporting on "military developments" in the interest of morale and other "familiar military considerations." Unlike many conservatives in the era of deregulation, Rusher still favored the Fairness Doctrine at least in extreme cases of bias. If it were "revived, taken seriously, and rigorously enforced, it could transform the performance of the major electronic news media over-night." Federal laws against media abuses seemed unlikely, since Congress was "closely allied with the media and itself involved in, or at least benefiting from" these abuses. But states could enact a right of reply in certain situations when a story made a person or entity look bad; they could also enact stronger protections for individual privacy.[66]

Despite these speculations, Rusher was at least as interested in the possibility that criticism, pressure, and even common sense might substantially affect the media. Because there were "receptive minds" among media officials and elsewhere, it would be "a serious mistake to assume that internal impulses toward change don't exist or cannot be generated."[67] One partial vindication of the point occurred several years later, in 1995, when Mike Wallace, the legendary lead reporter on CBS's *60 Minutes*, told a Harvard audience that Abe Rosenthal, CBS anchorman Walter Cronkite, and other opponents had characterized the National News Council unfairly. The idea, he said, had been a constructive one and was "worth a second shot." Cronkite also said in retrospect that he was probably wrong to oppose it.[68]

In addition to seeing hints of openness to change among some in the media and noting that pressure on the media was vitally important, Rusher was pleased that many right-leaning young people were trying to enter the news business. Some were graduates of regular schools of journalism, while others had worked for the conservative student papers established on various campuses in the 1980s. Still others came from the National Journalism Center, run by Stan Evans, and the Institute for Political Journalism at Georgetown University, founded by Lee Edwards. Conservative journalists could bring their employers "new and stimulating perspectives on events—perspectives that can complement, without replacing, those available on the left."[69]

The book received wide attention, with reviews in the *New York Times*, *Los Angeles Times*, *Washington Post*, *Wall Street Journal*, *Washington Journalism Review*, and *Publishers Weekly*. Vice President Bush, with whom Rusher had occasional correspondence, reported that Reagan very much liked *The Coming Battle for the Media*: "The president told me he has almost finished reading it and was raving about it. I'm [also] anxious to read it."[70] Brent Bozell III was impressed by Rusher's approach in the book and in columns dealing with media issues. He liked the message that there were "cracks developing," with real opportunities to take advantage of them. Rusher gladly accepted Bozell's invitation to join the board of his recently founded Media Research Center (MRC). He had a high opinion of the MRC's work, including its regular roundup of media bias, *Newswatch*—"the most important conservative project to come along in many a moon."[71]

Rusher's continued interest in helping conservatism, not merely enjoy-ing its new strength, also extended to Young Americans for Freedom even though YAF had fallen on hard times in recent years with financial crises, internal dissension, and difficulty in forming a galvanizing agenda on cur-rent issues.[72] Another problem for Sergio Picchio, its national chairman from 1986 to 1989, was that many senior conservatives had lost interest in the organization and didn't want to be associated with it. ACU chairman Keene was ready to exclude it from CPAC, the annual Washington confer-ence of movement activists.

"You've got to respect these guys," Rusher would say of the disaffected movement figures. "They've been here for a long time. You need to listen to them." In addition to general ideas about how to keep YAF going, he could explain what certain people liked and didn't like about YAF, where they fit in the Right's ideological catalogue, and how to deal with them. He would ask how the latest meeting with them went, interested in all the details. Along with his concern and insight, Rusher "had a great sense of humor," Picchio recalls. "But nobody really saw that when you first got to meet him. It would take a while, and then he'd crack a joke—and it was kind of hilarious when he would, because he seemed so serious most of the time."[73]

# 17

# All Good Things Must End

Rusher increasingly looked ahead to life after *National Review*, with plans that leaned toward the philosophical questions underlying politics and hopes that he might link up with a "quasi-academic" organization. In early 1986, the new chairman of the Institute for Contemporary Studies, former defense secretary Donald Rumsfeld, responded enthusiastically when its president, Lawrence Chickering—whom Rusher had once found irritating at *NR*—mentioned that he might be coming on board.[1]

In the post-Enlightenment era, Rusher told officials of the organization in 1987, it seemed that politics had become modern man's new method of deciding right and wrong. Through communist and fascist totalitarianism, this calamitous intellectual development caused "the bloodiest century in human history." As a solution to what Nietzsche called the death of God, political fanaticism had clearly failed. In addition, science—its enormous power another Enlightenment legacy—was now encountering what Rusher suspected were intrinsic limits to its knowledge. It seemed unlikely by itself, for example, to explain the origins of the universe or of life.

In the coming century, mankind would "turn elsewhere than to science alone for guidance on the truly fundamental questions." It was tempting to accept, with the great Russian anticommunist writer Aleksandr Solzhenitsyn, "that the answer must take the form of a reintegration of the West's Judeo-Christian religious heritage into the ongoing intellectual tradition of the Western world . . . But even if Solzhenitsyn is right, what form will the reintegration take? What modalities will be developed to combine our

Judaeo-Christian heritage with the will and the accumulated wisdom of 21st-century man? In particular, how can essentially religious insights and impulses be brought to interface successfully with science and the legitimate claims of science?"

Although modesty was required in addressing such questions, Rusher hoped there would be a "serious and systematic program for doing so" and suggested that the Far East, a region he had become familiar with, might play an especially important role in this. "There is simply too much intelligence," he told the ICS officials, "too much subtlety and sensitivity, and too much sheer intellectual energy latent in the Oriental peoples to deny them a major share in the shaping of man's future."[2]

Another California-based organization, the Claremont Institute, dedicated to the ideals of the American founding, also took an interest in Rusher. Its president, Larry Arnn, had been told well in advance that he would be retiring from *NR* and moving to the state. Arnn "liked Buckley a lot, so I was interested right away," and he also knew of Rusher as someone who had "done good work." They became acquainted over a couple of lunches and long talks at Paone's restaurant near the magazine. Arnn admired the fact that Rusher had given up a legal career "for conviction" and had then, as Buckley confirmed, "played a large role in the making of *National Review*." In addition, their personal chemistry worked well. "To know him is to like him," Arnn says.[3]

## Conservative Enough

Rusher had no clear favorite among the Republicans running to succeed Reagan: Vice President Bush, the president's own preference; Senate minority leader Robert Dole, who had been majority leader in 1985–86; and Jack Kemp, a relatively senior but still youthful congressman strongly associated with tax cuts, supply-side economics, and free-market opportunities for the poor. Having talked privately with each of them in the first half of 1987, he told Ken Rast, a friend with whom he had worked on the third-party project in the midseventies, that he was "more or less equally" favorable toward them all.[4]

He was personally closest, though, to the vice president. Rusher had sought to influence him as early as 1981, suggesting that he give a speech with "a kind word . . . about understanding the religious right" and that nothing "would more promptly open a great many conservative minds on the hitherto closed subject of George Bush." The vice president was receptive to Rusher's thoughts, noting in early 1984: "The door is wide open."

In 1982, at Bush's request, Rusher wrote or contributed heavily to the remarks he would make at the next meeting of the Southern Baptist Convention. From a platform shared with the Reverend Billy Graham, the short speech was given to a rally of perhaps forty thousand at the Superdome in New Orleans. The vice president was "so delighted at the enthusiastic response of the Baptists," Rusher told ex-colleague Rickenbacker, that he "phoned me the instant the *National Review* switchboard opened up" the next morning.[5]

He met with Bush in late 1984—"now is the time for a little serious skull practice," Rusher had suggested—in order to discuss his old theme of uniting the economic and social conservatives behind the same candidate, which he expected to be the main challenge facing the party in 1988. After that meeting—a visit Bush said he was "anxious to have"—Rusher sent photocopied pages from his *New Majority Party* book that described the two elements of the Right's coalition. "I read the pages," Bush responded. "I understand."[6] Two years before, in early 1983, Rusher had told Reagan that he foresaw a "moment of peril" when the president stepped down in 1988, because many Republican politicians would want to "inch back toward what they consider 'center,' abandoning . . . any serious attempt to hold onto the votes of the social conservatives."[7]

While Rusher stressed an economically moderate but socially conservative swing vote that had been apparent for at least fifteen years, Republican operative Lee Atwater, who later managed Bush's 1988 campaign, emphasized newer political forces. In December 1984, as Rusher sent the vice president his pages from *New Majority Party*, Atwater offered a forty-page memo based on a strategy largely envisaged by former White House political aide James Pinkerton and deriving in part from the insights of futurologist Alvin Toffler. It would be essential, he told Bush, to tap into such trends as high technology, "decentralization, demassification, and the entropy of giant institutions." Bush wrote that he was "staggered" by the memo's "thoughtfulness, its clarity . . . its brilliance" and that he agreed with its conclusions.

In a speech a few months later at a conference sponsored by the libertarian Cato Institute, Atwater focused on the baby-boom generation's growing political weight, arguing that economically conservative but socially more "liberal or at least open-minded" voters had become crucial and that education, health care, and the environment were highly important issues to them. In 1986, Atwater advised Bush to pursue "a combination of business-minded conservatives and baby-boom libertarians . . . rather than the 1980 Reagan coalition," with its voters inclined toward a governmental role in restoring traditional values.[8]

Still, in addition to maintaining his widely acknowledged loyalty toward the president, Bush worked to strengthen himself with family-values and southern voters. A genuinely religious man like Reagan and Carter but not necessarily known as one, he made friendly contact with social-conservative leaders and mass-audience televangelists such as Jerry Falwell, Pat Robertson, Jimmy Swaggart, and Jim Bakker—even telling Bakker that he watched his show "from time to time."[9]

When George Will wrote what became a famous anti-Bush column in early 1986, Rusher quickly defended the vice president with a gentler but unmistakable cynicism of his own. Will's column, "George Bush: The Sound of a Lapdog," had savaged a speech by the vice president at the New York Conservative Party's annual dinner as a "shambles," a "debacle," "rot," and "gibberish." By adopting a hysterical tone, Rusher told readers, Will had failed to maintain his "pleasantly ornate" style and his "general air of a periwigged courtier inhaling a pinch of snuff." Furthermore, as the liberal *Washington Post* publisher Katharine Graham's favorite conservative, he had no business calling anyone else a lapdog. Rusher added that the columnist's earlier attacks on Reagan had "systematically" faded in the late 1970s and that the same might well happen with Bush—if his political star rose high enough. An incoming President Bush might even be the guest of honor, as Reagan had been after the 1980 election, at an elegant party hosted by his former critic.[10] Bush was most appreciative, telling Rusher that his response would be sent to "every friend, every family member, every passer-by who was as stunned as I by the vicious *personal* nature of Will's column." Two months later, Bush followed up with a friendly postcard from Tunisia, signed: "Arf."[11]

As for Kemp, Rusher thought he would help himself most by identifying more clearly with the movement. Reaching out to the congressman with that advice, he asked if they could get together. But by the time they met for coffee in April 1987, Kemp had already urged stronger support for the contras, attacked abortion vigorously, and called for Secretary of State Shultz's resignation on the grounds that he had removed Reaganites in the State Department, not supported SDI, and been too solicitous toward a radical black leader in South Africa.[12]

Rusher now wrote in his column that Kemp was deservedly "conservatism's most prominent spokesman after Ronald Reagan's [impending] departure." But that role was different from a strong presidential candidacy. The movement was "extraordinarily healthy" in most respects, Rusher told readers. Its "infrastructure—the think tanks, legal foundations, financial resources, publications, cadres and training schools—is stronger than ever." But it was also adjusting to its new status and therefore wasn't ready for a second round of intense action. Similarly, the American people were generally satisfied with the Reagan tax cuts, the rebuilding of national defense, and the end to growth in domestic spending. They were not, in Rusher's view, eager for more major conservative policy directions in the near future.[13]

He gave Bush the same advice when they met for breakfast at his official residence, also repeating the point to Atwater. If he was right, Rusher told the campaign manager, both average citizens and the movement in 1988 might "actually prefer . . . a candidate who is determined to honor and preserve the Reagan legacy but not necessarily to try to run another 90 yards with the ball." Atwater told Rusher he strongly agreed.[14]

Although movement activists responded coolly to Bush, who won only 4 percent in the presidential straw poll at the CPAC conference in early 1987, he was perceived as being to Dole's right in a nationwide poll at the beginning of 1988. In his battle with Dole for the nomination, Bush stressed economic conservatism, including his opposition to tax increases and support for capital-gains tax cuts. The senator ran somewhat to the vice president's left on economic issues and went after social conservatives.[15] But they now had a candidate appealing more directly to their themes. Rusher praised televangelist Pat Robertson's grassroots campaign for ensuring the presence of "a powerful social-conservative voice" in shaping the GOP ticket and platform, which would, he predicted, probably help the party in 1988.[16]

Kemp's popularity on the Right stemmed from his optimistic zeal in promoting its less-government, lower-taxes vision as a good thing for all Americans, plus the strong potential among blue-collar voters the former professional quarterback had shown by easily winning reelection for nearly two decades in his Buffalo, New York, district. His campaign chairman Ed Rollins later recalled that Kemp loved giving speeches, "relished the intellectual combat of candidate forums and debates," and "had a magic with crowds," but was "impossible to discipline and simply wouldn't listen." His message wasn't focused enough to make clear what he would do as president.[17]

After Bush wrapped up the nomination, Rusher made no such criticisms of Kemp but stressed that voters had seen him as too conservative. In his column and in a letter to the congressman, he explained that Kemp had been "trying to persuade the python," the public, "to swallow another pig," another intensely conservative candidate like Reagan, when the python "simply wasn't in any mood or condition" for that. In contrast, Bush and Dole "were ready to defend and honor the Reagan legacy, but . . . not in a position of urging the American people to replicate the whole vast experience immediately." Neither was Kemp, Rusher added, but "I do think that's the way that you were perceived . . . [and] why you did not succeed."[18]

The conservative coalition as Rusher understood it appeared doubtful at the close of the primary season, with Bush lagging sixteen points behind

Democratic candidate Michael Dukakis in the Gallup poll. It seemed that one-third of the Democrats who backed Reagan in 1984 were about to return to their party.[19] In a column, Rusher worried about the vice president's weak numbers among Catholic voters, adding that he wasn't sure the Bush campaign understood how "absolutely indispensable" social conservatives were to victory and that "ignoring the subject would be Bush's swiftest and surest road to electoral disaster."[20] On Memorial Day weekend, he attended a meeting with political aides and advisers at the Bush family's vacation home in Kennebunkport, Maine, whose purpose was to begin work on the fall campaign. "I'm afraid I didn't have much to contribute," Rusher told the vice president, "since the level of expertise among the people who were briefing you was positively awesome. But it was a learning experience for me, and I am genuinely grateful to you for thinking to include me."[21]

One thing he could do was suggest a bit of advice about debating Dukakis, now the governor of Massachusetts, who had served as the moderator for the Boston-based *Advocates* programs when Rusher appeared regularly on the show. As an advocate for Reagan in an election special in 1984, he had the opportunity to cross-examine Dukakis. Watching the videotape of this encounter when Rusher sent it to him, campaign manager Atwater thought it showed how the Democratic nominee could be embarrassed "by someone who is aggressive and has complete command of the facts." When Rusher charged that Speaker O'Neill and the House of Representatives would spend all of Democratic candidate Walter Mondale's proposed tax increase rather than use it to help cut the deficit, his point "left Dukakis silent." Few if any of the candidate's adversaries had accomplished this feat in 1988, and Rusher's performance was "a good primer for what the Vice President needs to accomplish" in the upcoming debates. Agreeing that Dukakis was no pushover in such a forum, Rusher warned: "The man is pretty imperturbable and . . . very good at squeezing in all sorts of points that he wants to make. Bush must be careful not to let himself get, or even seem, overexcited by comparison."[22]

Having defended Reagan against New Right critics earlier in the decade and more recently disagreed with his magazine on the president's arms-control policies, Rusher was now at odds with some of the commentary on Reagan's successor in *National Review*, which suggested that the vice president was a questionable fit for serious conservatives and represented the Republican Party's country-club past. "Bush does seem rock hard in his embrace of the Reaganite anti-tax position," wrote Bob Novak. "But while the words are correct, the music is off-key." "The control of the GOP is now held by Establishment Republicans, not Reaganites," wrote the magazine's Washington editor, John McLaughlin. "George Bush," Rick Brookhiser observed, "is a dream . . . from which the postwar conservative movement has tried to wake."[23]

Rusher took a more hopeful view, telling readers in a column that spring that the vice president had "become substantially more conservative than he used to be on a good many issues," and that Bush "admires Reagan and has learned a great deal from him." He also conceded that the apparent nominee originally came from the establishment wing of the GOP and still had close ties to it. His performance as president would "swiftly disappoint those conservatives whom not even Reagan was able to please." In addition, it was possible that he could become strongly anticonservative should the Right's skepticism curdle into hostility. "If conservatives insist on treating George Bush as an enemy, they might—just might—turn him into one." The proper course was to "demand" a running mate from the conservative side of the party, maintain the ideological identity of the Republican platform, and seek substantial input into the new president's appointments. On the other hand, Bush was entitled to choose "people with whom he can work comfortably."[24]

Shortly before the convention, Rusher wrote that Bush needed to choose someone who could speak for the concerns of social conservatives—and was from the West, since every winning Republican ticket since the 1920s had included such a candidate. Seeing few good options among leading politicians in the region, he suggested his friend Donald Hodel of Oregon, whom he had first known as a Harvard Young Republican in the midfifties. In late 1984, Rusher had recommended Hodel, then secretary of energy, for an unspecified White House position. Instead, he was appointed to replace Bill Clark at the Interior Department.[25] Hodel had fifteen years of experience in federal office, Rusher pointed out. A former state Republican chairman who enjoyed an excellent reputation among party officials across the country, he was a strong supporter of the Reagan agenda. Even more important, he was a born-again Christian who had "spoken out strongly on every subject on the social-conservative agenda." Hodel was also "warm, friendly, and highly articulate."[26] Despite Rusher's advocacy, the fact that he had never held or sought elective office was—rightly, Hodel says—a major obstacle to placing him on a national ticket.[27]

When Senator Dan Quayle of Indiana was chosen for the vice-presidential spot, Rusher approved, telling readers it was a clear signal "that Bush is now solidly in the conservative camp and intends to lead America forward along soundly conservative lines." He no longer thought a western running mate was necessary. Reagan himself would fill this role, because he had stated his intention to campaign hard for the ticket and because Bush had made it clear that he would run as the president's "loyal disciple and heir."

In a slightly tougher tone, Rusher told his friend and former Goldwater ally Roger Moore that the choice of Quayle—along with the retention of the conservative party platform and Bush's acceptance speech—meant the vice president had "really learned his lesson."[28]

Early in the fall campaign, *NR* editorialized about Bush's lack of serious themes, saying he needed to persuade voters of the importance and the political fragility of Reagan's achievements, which Bush should seek to extend. The decade's successes were not simply the result of good governance but were, in fact, ideological and partisan. The vice president seemed not to understand these points, *NR* complained. "His campaign acts as if Reagan is an embarrassment from whom Bush must 'distance' himself." With his small nods—"spastic little 'progressive' gestures"—toward liberalism, he was failing to "enlist the resonance of the Reagan era."[29] Rusher thought Bush was doing well, and he either disbelieved or minimized points like Novak's, McLaughlin's, and Brookhiser's. He concentrated on attacking Dukakis and the media rather than holding the vice president's feet to the fire. Rusher enjoyed Dukakis's weak performance in the campaign, Bush's successful presentation of himself to the voters, and the inability of a blatantly biased media, as he saw it, to win the election for the governor. The Republicans, he wrote in November, had been right to demolish their opponent's false image as a nonideological technocrat by using such issues as furloughs for imprisoned murderers, his membership in the American Civil Liberties Union, and his liberal positions on the Pledge of Allegiance and the death penalty. The television ads created for Bush by Roger Ailes were "probably the best ever produced."[30]

The "wimp" label long attached to Bush—a "poisonous little piece of propaganda" in Rusher's opinion, "based on a widespread but wholly inaccurate perception of the man"—had disappeared well before the election, he reflected in January. Over the course of 1988, Bush transformed himself "into a relaxed, sure-of-himself national leader." Rusher praised him for having "kept his cool and his sense of humor" despite postelection hostility from the media and congressional Democrats. He even applauded Bush for naming to his cabinet "a series of old Washington hands who were widely known and respected, both among the media and on Capitol Hill." In doing so, the president-elect had further shown critics that his administration would be "a class act."[31] Rusher could also take satisfaction from Bush's success in holding the social conservatives—80 percent of evangelical Christian voters supported him in the election. About one hundred Religious Right leaders were invited to the White House to discuss issues with Quayle and senior aides to the incoming president.[32]

## Half-Full or Half-Empty?

An uncertain year had ended agreeably for Republicans as Bush took a solid 53 percent of the vote. But the party made history of a slightly embarrassing sort when it lost a few congressional seats even as its presidential candidate won. Expecting serious trouble with Congress, Rusher lamented that the people had chosen "four years of stalemate at best and chaos at worst" and would now "get what you voted for."[33] The fact that Reagan—and any Republican immediately succeeding him—would continue to have a Democratic House and quite possibly have a Democratic Senate was something Rusher had seen as a great problem for years. In his column, he rejected the idea that government did less harm when control of the White House and Congress was split, calling it a rather "primitive" notion. A president was elected in order to lead. Divided government meant "near paralysis on any issue big enough and controversial enough to require a united effort by the elected branches." Rusher also voiced this concern privately, telling Clif White in 1984 that it was the "most serious single problem" facing the country.[34]

Writing in 1987, with Democrats now a majority in the Senate, he saw the executive and legislative branches as locked in an "ongoing civil war." Countering what he called the excessive "self-congratulation" of the Constitution's bicentennial celebrations that year, Rusher told readers it was "scarcely working at all right now in some very important respects." He worried that the situation "may doom this country unless the problem is faced and corrected soon." In comparison with America's "zany formula," most democracies had a parliamentary system, in which the executive entered office with a favorable legislative majority and kept it until he faced the voters again. Although Rusher didn't call for a parliamentary system, he warned that separately elected branches made American government unworkable unless the same party controlled both.[35]

The hard fact, he knew, was that the Republican Party's progress in the previous decade hadn't produced a conservative government. Whether there would ever be one was anybody's guess. Analyzing the correlation of political forces early in the 1988 campaign season, political scientist Paul Allen Beck acknowledged that modest gains had occurred in GOP identification among voters since the party's disastrous period in the midseventies, although he cautioned that they resulted mainly from "Democratic losses and short-term rallies to a popular President." The party had also grown much stronger organizationally and financially. In addition, the Reagan presidency had "developed a new cadre" of leaders by bringing in new activists, encouraging existing ones, and giving many conservatives politically advantageous experience in the federal government. But Republican popularity looked "highly fragile" and hadn't broken Democratic dominance in Congress or the state legislatures. Although the GOP seemed "better positioned" than it had been since the New Deal to become the dominant party, Beck doubted it would find "a new Ronald Reagan" who would continue to "unite social and economic conservatives with moderates in presidential politics"—much less a leader who would build "a grand, majoritarian coalition."[36]

While Rusher's political commentary throughout the decade had been overwhelmingly positive in its evaluations of conservative strength, he remained aware that elections could have different results for the Republican Party and the movement. In a letter to his friend Peter Brimelow, a conservative journalist, in mid-1988, when the Democrats looked like a strong threat to win the White House, he had also indicated dissatisfaction with the available supply of well known politicians on the Right—without citing names, but presumably including Kemp. However unfortunate for the party and the nation, Rusher told Brimelow, losing the election "would be the healthiest imaginable result for the conservative movement. It would burn out this entire second growth of second-hand Reagans and give a tremendous boost to the new young saplings who are assuredly out there. It would also invigorate the infrastructure of the movement, which always thrives in opposition."[37]

Critical commentary on Reagan from conservatives, meanwhile, raised several questions. One was whether his political achievement would last. Pat Buchanan thought he would leave "a legacy of prosperity, reduced taxes, and new jobs" but that "the historic opportunity to displace the Democrats as America's governing party has passed." The GOP had failed to accomplish this "because its leadership class recoils from moral and religious issues that engage the passion of the people; and because it harbors a sense of guilt about race and, hence, is easily intimidated." Noting that the White House had presented its opposition to high taxes and big government quite effectively, Buchanan regretted that such "clarity and conviction" were usually absent on cultural issues.[38]

Reagan was also accused of being a weak manager, of failing to understand the importance of naming a top team that really cared about change in a rightward direction, of negligence in generating public and conservative support for his agenda, of lacking a serious plan for changing the country, and of softheartedness inappropriate in a president who meant to cut government substantially. He had been "a superb chief of state," said activist Howard Phillips, "and a deficient chief executive."[39] Reagan was "a successful president and perhaps a great one," former aide Lyn Nofziger reflected later, "but the tragedy is he could have been even more successful had his chiefs of staff understood and been willing to use all the resources at their command." Although Clif White had told him shortly after he took office: "You can't win a revolution with mercenaries," Nofziger recalled, over the years "it became obvious that Reagan never got the message."[40]

Rusher didn't take such critiques seriously, and never would, partly because he was so glad to have a real conservative and a friend in the White House and partly because he thought Reagan had produced truly great results. Among these, the growing prospect of victory in the Cold War took precedence. It seemed to Rusher that the president's geniality and patience were probably essential at this delicate stage of the triumph.

Despite negative reactions from some conservatives, he thought Reagan had been right to say, when answering journalists' questions at the 1988 Moscow summit with Mikhail Gorbachev, that he no longer considered the Soviet Union an "evil empire." In recent years, Rusher noted, its government had taken early steps on a course that might well result in "total elimination of the Soviet system and its replacement by market forces and democracy." There was "nothing to be gained by trying to push them all the way to the end of it immediately, or by denouncing them (falsely) for not making any significant changes at all." American leaders must "encourage the ailing Soviet system to (1.) sit down, (2.) lie down, and (3.) die, in that order. It has started to sit down. This is not the time to proclaim (or to forget) the terribly evil thing it has been." What worried Rusher wasn't Reagan's conciliatory recognition of Gorbachev-inspired openness and reforms, but rather the possibility that "greedy American businessmen" might bail out the communist system with more trade, greatly extending its life.[41] Again, Rusher and Buckley disagreed, as they had on the arms-control treaty the previous year. Reagan was right to "encourage changes" in the Soviet Union, Buckley wrote, and "wildly exciting" developments were indeed occurring there, but the president's rejection of his previous epithet amounted to an Orwellian "vaporization" of reality. Denying that the regime still had an evil character would "sow only confusion."[42]

Rusher's strongly positive view of the past decade also rested on a simple comparison. Having watched American politics for over half a century, he had seen no other president "who even comes close to Ronald Reagan in the degree to which he has delivered on the pledges he made to the American people," Rusher wrote in August, and "I don't expect to live to see his record approached."[43] In a column the following January, he concluded: "It is slowly becoming apparent that the Free World, after 40 years of grim persistence, has in fact won the Cold War." In addition, the nation was "entering an unprecedented seventh year of prosperity."[44]

Buckley saw the question in similar terms, agreeing with Rusher that a president could accomplish only so much and that this one had accomplished a great deal. About a year after Reagan left office, he told an audience: "No era associated with a single successful leader . . . is fairly evaluated by dredging up surviving delinquencies, deeds left undone. The 1980s are most certainly the decade in which Communism ceased to be a creed, surviving only as a threat. And Ronald Reagan had more to do with this than any other statesman in the world." He had also greatly influenced Americans' attitudes toward the state. Thanks to his rhetoric and policies, they had adopted a healthier "mood about life and about government."[45]

## Changing of the Guard

The Reagan era had been good for *National Review*'s economic position, as Rusher had hoped. In 1987, it earned more than $1 million in gross ad revenue—an "unheard-of" achievement for an opinion journal, according to a New York business columnist.[46] On the surface at least, Rusher's successor would be coming into a good situation. That successor would be Wick Allison, the editor, publisher, and owner of *Art & Antiques*. Forty years old in 1987, Allison had grown up as a conservative and was the Goldwater youth chairman in Dallas. Previously, he had noticed that his high-school library didn't have *National Review* and asked the librarian to subscribe to it. Told incorrectly that the library already had a diverse range of political journals, Allison went to his father, who wouldn't get involved but gave him a list of local Republican precinct chairs. After they spoke up at a school-board meeting, the library soon had the magazine.[47]

Allison had already sat on the *NR* corporate board for several years, invited to join because he was the only conservative publisher Buckley knew besides Rusher. He found it an unusual experience. Rusher distributed the twice-yearly financial statement with extreme caution, to prevent accidental exposure to the eyes of others. "By the time he finished handing it out," Allison recalls, "he would come around to the first person and collect them back." After the approximately fifteen-minute meeting came "a four-hour dinner at which . . . you just never knew who was going to show up," often followed by "the best after-dinner speeches by drunk people I have ever heard in my life." Buckley "knew everybody, and he just loved being surrounded by people all the time."[48]

Despite his limited opportunity to review its financial data—half a minute per meeting, one minute per year—Allison knew enough to fear the magazine would go under without Buckley and Rusher. *NR* was kept alive by their fame, by support from the readership that depended on their continued presence. It was important to "start thinking about this as a business," the junior board member urged, "because either one of these guys could get run over by a truck; and God forbid that the same truck hits both of them at the same time."

When Buckley asked to see him shortly thereafter and explained Rusher's plans to retire, adding that he wanted Allison to be the new publisher, "I don't think I could have been more thrilled—although it was a kind of complicated thing." Buckley also said he would like Allison to own the magazine at some point, and after a long discussion, "I agreed to do it."[49]

*National Review*'s 1987 fund-raising letter announced Rusher's planned retirement. In it, Buckley noted the sacrifice the publisher had made for decades. "His contributions to the magazine for thirty years," the editor pointed out, "have not been compensated by anything approaching what the Harvard Law School had equipped him to earn." But the amiable distance between them was evident in a small detail. In his draft, Buckley explained that Rusher would now "teach" in California. Rusher corrected this, replacing it with "write."[50]

For his part, Buckley decided to step back while remaining ultimately in charge. He would give a large share of his responsibilities to a new editor, John O'Sullivan, a British journalist who had held editorial positions at the London *Times*, the *Daily Telegraph*, and the *New York Post*, in addition to being a former editor of *Policy Review*. At the time he served as special adviser to Prime Minister Margaret Thatcher. Other conservatives praised him as "very literate," "extremely jolly," quick-witted, and an excellent political analyst. Allison and O'Sullivan would "bring a high degree of

*At Paone's with* NR *board members Tom Bolan, center, and Wick Allison*

professionalism to their jobs," Rusher said in an interview, adding that they had far more journalistic experience than either he or Buckley in the 1950s.[51]

The anticipated changes came against a backdrop of unfavorable or at least mixed publicity. In the first half of 1988, a detailed biography of Buckley, researched with his full cooperation, was published by the left-leaning journalist John Judis. Although the book was insightful and respectful, its final chapters described both *NR* and Buckley as having faded into a kind of classy mediocrity. "The magazine still printed well-written articles," Judis explained, "and its headlines and short items displayed the same panache as of old, but like Buckley's column, it appeared detached from national politics and exerted very little influence."

Key members of the *National Review* family testified to a decline. The magazine was no longer "very topical," Joe Sobran told Judis. Daniel Oliver, a friend of Buckley's now heading the Federal Trade Commission, a former junior writer at *NR* who had been its executive editor in the 1970s, said it had lost the "aura of being something that one takes out to read in the park in a brown wrapper." Oliver also predicted that "because Bill's establishment now," it would be impossible to recover this sense of excitement. Ernest van den Haag thought *NR* was "not as intellectually good as *The New Republic*" and needed "articles that are deeper, concerned with serious intellectual questions, better intellectual caliber." Buckley had increasingly become "a prisoner of his commitments," said scholar and friend Hugh Kenner, implying that he had little time for excellence.[52]

A *Christian Science Monitor* article on the leadership changes planned at the magazine, while not unfriendly, made several pointed observations. The climate for the intellectual Right had become less predictable and congenial; conservatives would be out of power to an extent even if Bush won the election. Although there might be a consensus "that O'Sullivan is the right man" to become editor, there was "rather less consensus on what the job is." *National Review* was sometimes criticized as "too 'journalistic,' or at least insufficiently 'serious,'" the article reported, also quoting Brookhiser as saying that some of the younger editors, himself included, had urged "more current coverage of things." Priscilla Buckley, retired from the managing editorship for two and a half years, had been "the glue that held the whole thing together," an anonymous source said. "Ironically," the writer suggested, "the Reagan years have not been altogether good for conservative intellectuals, in part, because they may have become complacent. 'After Reagan's election, we kind of put our feet up,' Brookhiser concedes, adding that it may have ushered in a 'narcotic phase' in conservative editorial offices."[53]

The message that *NR* was entering a new era offended Buckley, as did the concluding themes in the Judis biography. O'Sullivan would indeed have the title of editor, he explained to colleagues—but it was wrong to suggest that Buckley's new editor-in-chief title would be just "an honorific, permitting me to drift from the scene while still a formal presence." He was giving O'Sullivan specific duties, including reading and approval of the material to be published, and the new editor would serve as chief executive when Buckley was away. But the founder and owner had "no other retrenchments in mind." He also disliked the *Monitor* article's suggestion that people at and associated with *National Review* weren't wholly pleased with the magazine. Buckley blamed its "derogatory patter" on libertarian publications continually doubtful of *NR*'s commitment to freedom, biographer Judis's implication that "Buckley is through," and such intrafamilial kibitzing as "van den Haag's eternal quest for more ten thousand word articles." He seemed unwilling to invite any self-critiques. "I don't doubt that NR could be better," Buckley told the senior editors and staff. "So could the Bible."[54]

From Rusher's standpoint, these problems were for others. Although he was not among the critics quoted in the biography or the article, he didn't challenge them in the column he wrote about the book, where he objected only that it didn't "convey Buckley's most striking characteristic . . . his fun-loving quality . . . his almost manic need to be amused, and to amuse others." Addressing what he considered Judis's main thesis, that Buckley had long ago settled for celebrity status, Rusher pointed back to his "supreme accomplishment." It had occurred in the 1950s, when the young editor joined the "disparate strands of anti-liberal thought," weaving them "into a coherent intellectual movement." He speculated that Buckley, ill-suited in Rusher's opinion to politics and to giving political counsel, had been relieved in the past two decades to settle increasingly for "the good life" and the role of "patron saint."[55] For several years, Rusher had believed that he'd "done everything" he could at the magazine. "After Reagan's election and reelection," he wrote in early 1989, "it was as if a great curtain had descended on a long and successful play. It was time for me to find new channels for my energy."[56]

## Farewell

Rusher was headed to the West Coast and a continuing but much-reduced relationship with *NR*. He was eager to move into his prepurchased condominium apartment on Nob Hill in the scenic heart of San Francisco—and almost as eager to leave the city where he had lived, minus the Washington interlude, since 1948. The late 1980s were the "absolute pits" in New York's long decline. Although old roosts like *National Review*, his nearby apartment on East 37th, and the University Club were fine, most of the city had become "a terrible, terrible place." On one occasion shortly before moving to California in the second half of 1989, Rusher recalls, he left his club and passed a man bleeding on the sidewalk just a block up Fifth Avenue. Nobody was "doing a goddamned thing about it. It was just New York, and there was a lot of that going on." Noting that Ruth Messinger, a candidate for Manhattan borough president, had militantly vowed to take back the city for all the right causes, he conceded: "Ruth baby, you can have it. California, here I come."[57]

New York was growing "dirtier and meaner every year," Rusher had told his aunt in 1983, estimating that half the cab drivers didn't bother to thank him for a tip. During the winter and summer, its weather could be brutal. Rusher looked forward to San Francisco for several reasons. He liked the large population of "smart, hardworking Orientals." In such amenities as restaurants and the theater, he had found much of New York's cosmopolitanism. He loved its climate, "cool and clear and brisk." Above all, San Francisco was by far the most beautiful city on the continent.[58] Rusher told the gay conservative radio host David Brudnoy that although he knew the city had its minuses, he had, after all, lived within a half-mile of Times Square for forty years. "I doubt that San Francisco can shock me very greatly." He kept an index card listing the average weather in various cities. When Wick Allison asked: "Bill, why are you moving to San Francisco?" he pulled it out and said: "Here's why."[59]

Rusher's last year at *National Review* included a major health scare. In the early morning hours of June 16, 1988, he awoke with chest pains and was taken to the hospital, where he spent a precautionary week.[60] Doctors told him it was a heart attack, a very mild one. He received nitroglycerin pills for his angina, was advised to resume his normal schedule slowly, and took care to lose ten pounds.[61] Rusher wasn't surprised, and it was "not a terrifying experience." He had felt some cardiac symptoms in the past five years or so, and always knew the history on his father's side of the family: three deaths by heart attack before age sixty. In his case, the problem could be fixed before it became incapacitating or fatal. "Perhaps a good warning," wrote his old friend Wilma Sievertsen Rogalin, "and you'll probably outlive all of us!"[62]

On December 9, the *National Review* circle and Rusher's political and personal friends joined in proud recognition of his retirement at a dinner party on a chartered cruise around Manhattan. Three days later, Rusher entered the hospital for prescheduled heart surgery. President-elect Bush made a deeply appreciated call to wish him luck. He accepted the operation, a sextuple bypass, as another experience—taking it in good spirits that his close friends the Fernalds could see when visiting afterward. "He described it very articulately and proudly."[63] When Rusher left *National Review* on December 31, just three weeks before Ronald Reagan left the White House, it was a fitting coincidence after having so earnestly wished to nominate and elect, as he wrote to Goldwater back in 1963, "a conservative Republican president." In his last days in office, Reagan again complimented him on his columns, noting that he would "treasure" the latest. "I've been grateful and proud," the president wrote with his usual simplicity, "to have had your support over the years."[64]

In a farewell piece that ran in *NR* that month, Rusher said of his time at the magazine: "I can't imagine a job being more fun." He recalled the many dinners at the Buckleys' East 73rd Street townhouse, held mainly on alternate Mondays and attended by the senior editors and himself. Because Buckley liked so much to invite other guests, Rusher had enjoyed the company of "fabulously interesting people drawn from Bill's huge and highly eclectic circle of warm friends." Even more memorable was the food, thanks to Pat's outstanding culinary skill and kitchen staff. "To tuck my feet under the Buckley dinner table is one of my life's greatest satisfactions," Rusher wrote, "and one I hope to experience often in the years ahead when I return . . . to New York on visits."

Turning more serious, he felt compelled to teach one more lesson about movement consciousness, in this case stressing the need for independence from the establishment. It was an old point but still a vital one to Rusher. He repeated a complaint about the magazine he had made quite publicly in *Rise of the Right*. "Careful study of *National Review*'s editors over the years" had shown him his colleagues' "touching dependence on the *New York Times*." He saw a glaring inconsistency in this. "No magazine condemns the *Times* more roundly for its liberal biases—but none receives more of its information from that rightly suspect source, or is more resistant to information that has not received the imprimatur of publication there."

Rusher reflected on his departure from *NR* with a lyrical fatalism. "One might as well ask what makes a trumpeter swan leave its Canadian summer haunts for Texas when the first cool breezes of autumn whisper their intimation . . . It's an instinct of some sort, that's all—a serene acquiescence in the mysterious economy of nature." He explained that he would continue writing, speaking, "playing a little politics." But he also wanted to spend his remaining years "probing some of those deeper questions that will confront mankind in the twenty-first century, as the secular-humanist solutions that have been in vogue ever since the Enlightenment are seen, beyond argument, to have failed." In addition, Rusher hoped to "encourage the oncoming generations of youthful conservatives. They are the troops on which all else depends. We must seek them out, teach them everything we can, put their feet on the upward path, and cheer them on their way . . . They must dare greatly, building on what has been accomplished but demanding, and achieving, even more."[65] His own career lent weight to these exhortations. They represented what he had done.

To Rusher, a mostly bad era in world history was ending well. There was substantial promise now of a better one. "I agree with your long-range optimism," he had told Jack Kemp in mid-1988. "I find that many conservatives don't; but I honestly believe that the twenty-first century is quite likely to be a big improvement, in many respects, over the twentieth."[66]

# 18

# Rusher by the Bay

W hen Wick Allison took over as publisher of *National Review* at the beginning of 1989, he found the magazine still "operating in the 1950s," with carbon paper and "secretaries who were treated as secretaries." Like Rusher, he thought *NR* should give more space to politics and issues. Allison had more clout not only as the new publisher but as the "theoretical next owner," whereas Buckley and Rusher were in something like a "thirty-year marriage" in which they eventually "stopped listening to each other."[1] John O'Sullivan would remember Rusher's successor as good-natured and friendly while "extremely impulsive and a classic entrepreneur type," enthusiastically pushing ideas. *NR* would become more politically oriented and Washington-oriented under O'Sullivan's and Allison's leadership, and subscriptions rose by 50 percent.[2]

At *Art & Antiques* and at *D* magazine, which covered business and lifestyles in Dallas, Allison had published for "intense, passionate audiences." He knew they could support profitability. Believing the same should happen at *NR*, Allison doubled the subscription price, confident that readers would pay. He also raised two million dollars and modernized some inefficient operations, especially involving production. In a smaller illustration of Allison's new-broom approach, he ordered senior editor and Dartmouth professor Jeffrey Hart, a culture hero to young Ivy League conservatives, to get a computer. Rusher took little interest in most of these managerial changes, according to Allison, but did favor making *NR* self-supporting, although it surprised him that the new publisher thought it was possible. "His major concern was my relationship with Bill Buckley." Both Rusher and board members who were close friends of Buckley's warned that he would never change his mind after rejecting an idea. Therefore, Rusher advised, "get to Bill" before others did.[3]

Under O'Sullivan, who became editor at the end of 1990, *NR* dropped most of its regular columns in favor of more commissioned articles. It became "more editor-driven . . . livelier, more contemporary," changes of which Rusher was "extremely supportive," telling O'Sullivan about a year later that he thought it had become much better. Similarly, Rusher told Brookhiser there had been "too much rote in the magazine," that O'Sullivan was right to "shake things up."[4]

O'Sullivan, who had overlapped with Rusher in 1988, when he began as an editor in training, came to like the outgoing publisher as "a very, very good colleague—thoughtful, helpful, very anxious to help you succeed and help other people succeed." But when Rusher, after retiring, was in town for the board meetings held three times a year, he made little effort to urge any particular views upon the new leadership or ex-colleagues. "If Bill expressed an opinion, we paid attention," O'Sullivan notes. "We held Bill in high regard, so he could have played a bigger role." Had Rusher remained in New York, it might well have happened, but "fundamentally he was now a San Franciscan."[5]

## New Life on a New Coast

At the beginning of September 1989, Rusher moved to his apartment on the northeast side of Nob Hill near the elegant Fairmont Hotel, between Pacific Heights and Chinatown. The Powell Street cable car lent another picturesque touch, running in front of his building. Rusher had figured things out carefully, preparing drawings that allowed him to decide months in advance exactly where the bookcases should go, to see that his red leather sofa might be hard to place. He was two doors down from the University Club, to which he had always belonged in New York. In the club's understated dining room and reading room, using the latter for cigars and relaxed conversation, he frequently hosted people he knew or was getting to know.[6] His dwelling was about 1,200 square feet, much larger than the Manhattan apartment, while retaining a familiar character with a similar floor plan. The only view from his old apartment had been a bleak one of a building. Now Rusher had good views of San Francisco Bay and the Financial District. "I enjoy the place even more than I expected to," he told a friend, "and that's saying a lot!"[7]

He decided to keep tropical fish again, a hobby he had loved as a teenager and as a young attorney. Buying a four-foot-long aquarium, he found things had changed since the 1950s. With scientific pretension, gravel was now called "substrate." Breeding by dealers and hobbyists had altered many fishes' colors. But giving due weight to the positive side, Rusher described a "neat" new filtration system and explained that attractive fishes could still be found. "I have tracked down some recognizable old favorites, and I must hurry to feed them," he told readers. "Small as they are, they have taught me 'to see a world in a grain of sand . . . eternity in an hour.'"[8]

Drawn to the thought of hosting his own talk show in San Francisco, he considered various stations with Neal Freeman and a local friend, Larry Cott, who knew the area's radio scene and was politically sound, having edited *Combat*, an anticommunist newsletter published by *NR*. Although the notion went unfulfilled, Rusher continued with his AP network commentaries. He had asked listeners in the first half of 1989 to consider whether the homeless really wanted homes, applauded the choice of former Secretary of Education William Bennett as President Bush's drug czar, and contrasted the French Revolution with the American Revolution. Another radio talk, "Blasphemy for Profit," criticized both Salman Rushdie's book *The Satanic Verses*, offensive to orthodox Muslims, and Martin Scorsese's film *The Last Temptation of Christ*.[9]

As a senior fellow of the Claremont Institute, nearly an hour east of Los Angeles but easily reachable by a short flight from the Bay Area, Rusher was a valued counselor to its president, Larry Arnn, an idealistic Ph.D. with limited political experience, much younger than himself and working hard to establish the decade-old organization more prominently on the conservative map. Rusher "changed it and made it better," Arnn recalls, partly by bringing Claremont closer to other parts of the movement. In addition to his advisory role, he helped with fund-raising. The elderly and somewhat shy industrialist Fred Lennon in Ohio, whom Rusher knew well, was especially generous. Rusher also helped to get money from the Bradley Foundation, one of conservatism's major sources of financial support. For years, he served as master of ceremonies at Claremont Institute events, carrying himself with a fine "mixture of humor and dignity" as he moved a conference or dinner along.

Arnn learned much from Rusher about the movement's origins and early years, also gaining greater respect for the work that went into building it. The institute had been impatient with Reagan at times. Arnn, who met Reagan on several occasions, once argued with him throughout dinner, starting out by saying: "You know, Mr. President, you're the greatest man I've ever known, but . . ." Rusher offered a different view based on his own familiarity with Reagan, cautioning Arnn that he probably represented a peak for conservatives in terms of presidential power: "My boy, you're going to remember this time as a golden age." Arnn, now president of Hillsdale

College, finds himself "much less impatient with Reagan today than I was back then—as Bill predicted I would be."[10]

*Yana Bridle, photographer; courtesy Claremont Institute*

*With Larry Arnn and Jack Kemp*

Rusher also began a long association with the *California Political Review*, a conservative monthly journal founded soon after he moved to San Francisco. In a tangible acknowledgment of the new Californian's stature on the Right, editor and owner John Kurzweil ran a lengthy interview with him in the first issue in 1990 that reflected Rusher's good cheer. "He was always very positive and optimistic," Kurzweil recalls, when many active conservatives "were down in the dumps" after Reagan left office. "I'm not worried about the conservative movement," Rusher told readers, pointing to what he called its great luck. Goldwater had served as its early champion, and "no sooner was he defeated in 1964 than Ronald Reagan rose out of the ashes and became twice president of the United States. That is not the way the world generally works." Admittedly, no "knight in shining armor" had appeared as the movement's new leader, but it had grown much larger, and "numerous contenders" could be expected from now on.

With the future of the *California Political Review* uncertain, Rusher soon obtained a substantial grant, which Kurzweil used for its first direct-mail solicitation. The mailing got a good response and succeeded in building readership. The roster of California residents who subscribed to *NR* proved to be among the most productive mailing lists, another resource made possible by Rusher. "In many ways . . . we wouldn't have survived, even past that first year, if it hadn't been for Bill," Kurzweil says. Having spent most of his adult life among the leadership of a national publication, Rusher gladly continued to assist the state-level journal. Over the years, he did "a great deal to make himself available" and made sales pitches to donors at events. "A lot of this stuff, I could tell—it was a strain on him. He was no young man anymore, and he was tired. But he always came, and he always had some very pithy and useful, interesting and absorbing comments to make." Like Arnn, Kurzweil appreciated his ability to "put things in perspective" as they discussed conservative politics and activity.[11]

In addition to his roles with the Claremont Institute and the *California Political Review*, Rusher had become board chairman for the Media Research Center, incorporated in 1986 by Buckley's nephew Brent Bozell III. Because the MRC began with minuscule resources, difficulties in the first three years meant that "everything had to be done correctly." Without Rusher's assistance as chairman, "I suppose it would have made it anyway. But it would have been much, much, much harder."

Rusher's idiosyncrasies came through at times, appreciated by Bozell in one case and accepted in another. The Media Research Center board meetings were generally held in Washington, which now meant a cross-country trip. "He would send these meticulous receipts for every penny," Bozell recalls, "showing how he had gotten the most inexpensive flight and stayed at an inexpensive hotel room so he wouldn't cost the organization any money. He could have thrown his weight around: 'I'm a member of this board. I am Bill Rusher. I go first-class.'" They had a running dispute over the advisability of the annual April Fool's edition of the MRC newsletter, which featured made-up quotations from liberal journalists. "Brent," Rusher pronounced heavily, "you have inherited your uncle's sense of humor." Every year they would debate the question, Rusher urging him to reconsider.[12]

In 1989, Rusher took on another commitment by agreeing to chair the board of the John M. Ashbrook Center at Ashland University in Ohio. Headed by his old friend Clif White, the center sponsored a public-affairs lecture series, an annual dinner in the late congressman's memory that drew big-name speakers, a scholar-in-residence program, a scholarship program for undergraduates, and a corporate seminar that drew on White's experience in educating businessmen about politics and government.[13] Rusher would also serve on the boards of the Pacific Research Institute, a free-market policy organization in San Francisco, and the Pacific Legal Foundation, a conservative public-interest law firm. In addition, he continued to do some lecturing. He was "working somewhat harder than I did before."[14]

## Family Relationship

Wishing his old magazine well, Rusher may have stopped an impending purchase of *National Review* in the early 1990s by the international media mogul Rupert Murdoch. One day, Allison and O'Sullivan were told to come to Buckley's house in Stamford. "We got there," Allison remembers, "and we were ushered into a room and given—Bill loved to communicate this way— an eight-page memo to read . . . The upshot of the memo was that Rupert Murdoch had offered five million dollars for *National Review*, and promised to keep it exactly the way it was." O'Sullivan didn't mind. Having worked for Murdoch previously, "I knew him, I liked him, and he treated me very well. So I was perfectly happy for Rupert to take it over." He also assumed it was a sure thing.[15]

Allison strongly opposed the deal. Buckley was "naïve," he thought, and probably understood the proposal as "the solution for *National Review*'s future because it would have five million dollars in the bank." But because nothing, according to Allison, would have prevented Murdoch from taking the money back, he suspected the new funds would "last till the day after closing." In addition, he believed such a jarring change in ownership would be devastating to the magazine's reputation. Allison disliked what he considered Murdoch's vulgarity and the "salaciousness" of parts of his media conglomerate. "It didn't fit with Bill Buckley, and it didn't fit with *National Review*."

Also in attendance were Rusher and Evan Galbraith, Buckley's Yale class-mate and a longtime *NR* board member. "Bill presented this as a fait accom-pli," Allison recalls. "He explained that he had shaken hands with Murdoch and it was a done deal. I looked at Bill Rusher, and Rusher just looked at me like a shrug . . . So I said: 'This is the wrong thing to do.'" It was Allison's impression that Buckley wasn't interested in his opinion. Rusher then asked him to explain what his objection was. Allison said Murdoch, upon becom-ing the owner, could simply withdraw the five million he'd given in order to obtain the magazine. "The conservative movement, your subscribers who have supported you for these thirty-five years," he remembers saying, "are going to be outraged that you gave *National Review* to somebody like Rupert Murdoch." Nor was there any reason for it, Allison told Buckley, because the magazine was doing fine.

"You'd have thought Bill would have a heart attack. I said: 'Well, if you're going to do the deal, I quit.' 'What if you became part of Murdoch's publishing empire?' 'I don't want to become part of Rupert Murdoch's publishing empire. I joined this thing to do *National Review*.' Then Bill Rusher joined in and said . . . 'It's true that people are not going to be happy about Rupert Murdoch tak-ing over *National Review*, and that . . . especially considering . . . his reputation, and the other things he owns, and his business interests—it's not going to be looked on favorably.' He's being very gentle with Bill Buckley. I say, because I'm a little bit more hotheaded: 'It's a violation of the public trust.'"[16]

It was the only time, Allison recalls, that he ever saw Buckley change his mind, as they learned the next day had happened. Because Rusher was present, "I kind of knew there was a chance . . . Rusher being in the room means Bill was worried [about] how it was going to be received by the public. There's some twinge in Bill Buckley's mind about this—and so that's what I played upon, and Rusher supported me, and it was over."

There was concern that readers wouldn't approve, O'Sullivan agrees, partly because they felt "in some sense . . . that they were the owners of the magazine. It wasn't just another magazine. It had an intimate relationship, a family relationship also, with its readers . . . This was the view that won out, I think."[17]

Although Rusher continued to keep a distance from internal *National Review* issues, he disagreed with Buckley's unexplained decision in 1997 to remove O'Sullivan as editor. According to O'Sullivan, he responded with "general moral support and regrets" upon hearing the news. "He said: 'I can't understand why Bill has done this. I don't like what he's done. But we both know him, and we just have to live with the guy . . . He is the kind of wayward, impulsive person, and when he reaches these kinds of decisions you can't change his mind.' I had already reached that conclusion." They both "admired Bill on many other grounds," O'Sullivan notes, but "we both knew he had a whim of iron."[18] Rusher liked the deposed editor. "We got along very well. I was very sorry when Buckley replaced him. I thought he was doing a good job. I never had any trouble with John at all . . . I have no idea what Bill's calculations were. He didn't tell me."[19]

## Elder Statesman

Rusher linked up with yet another project, the George Washington Society, led by William Allen, a government professor at the Claremont Colleges and an expert on the first president. Billing itself hopefully as the "West Coast Headquarters of the Conservative Movement," the group was envisioned partly as an ongoing discussion of issues in light of American founding principles, partly as an attempt to expand conservative activity in California and neighboring states. It would also "mediate differences" among conservatives while encouraging and educating new candidates and connecting them with political professionals.[20] These ambitions made the George Washington Society a good forum for Rusher's combination of talents.

Much of its impetus, according to Sergio Picchio, a member whose tenure as YAF chairman had ended in 1989, was post-Reagan anxiety about where the organized Right was headed and about the more ambiguous situation under President Bush, generally seen by movement people as a nonconservative. But although Rusher wouldn't heavily criticize Bush in the group's dinner discussions held at Southern California restaurants, even its strong libertarians tended to respect his views. Usually "people would listen to him a lot."[21]

In these years, Rusher's satisfaction with the political situation could cause him to overgeneralize. The conservative movement "controls the GOP" and "has a lock on the presidency," he wrote in an outline for an address at the 1989 national YAF convention in San Diego. But such opinions were no excuse to ignore problems. Power for conservatives had "brought disillusionment," Rusher knew. There was also some inevitable disunity in the movement that bore watching. As a result of the movement's problems—and increasingly prominent challenges like the condition of the underclass, homelessness, and drugs, so difficult to address effectively—the Right had lost the "moral initiative." Rusher urged by way of response that it apply conservative analysis, "speak the hard truths," and recover its "capacity for indignation." In the long run, things nonetheless looked good.[22]

Books written later by some of the Bush administration's small minority of ideological conservatives expressed contempt for a White House staff dominated by passive establishmentarians with no sense of obligation to the Right. These accounts argued that the president hadn't made his real departure from conservative principles when he agreed to the tax-raising 1990 budget deal with Democratic congressional leaders, violating his main campaign pledge. Once elected, rather, he had quickly signaled an unwillingness to engage in conflict with the Democrats as well as a lack of identification with the movement or the outgoing Reagan administration. "Bush and most of his White House aides . . . preferred to define areas in which they and their adversaries could agree while often denigrating their natural allies," wrote Charles Kolb, a deputy presidential assistant for domestic policy. "Over time, this stance caused the Reagan coalition to fray and ultimately collapse . . . The President caved in repeatedly, first on taxes, then on quotas in the [1991] civil rights bill, on spending, on regulatory policy."[23]

It took Rusher longer to stop identifying with Bush. The president, he judged in late 1989, "has tended the coalition with loving care."[24] Even in mid-1991, Rusher insisted that Bush was filling a role "almost as valuable" as Reagan's—that of "a genuine political leader who is not ashamed to follow through on a course of action initially defined by someone else." Although conservatives, being perfectionists, would bemoan inevitable disappointments, Rusher thought that when looking back on the whole record, they

If Not Us, Who?

would be glad Bush had been there.[25] Less controversially, he joined most conservatives in praising the president for the Gulf War that drove Iraqi forces from Kuwait. Bush had carried out "one of the most successful and diplomatically significant major military operations in American history." Otherwise, due to the ambitions of Iraq's dictator Saddam Hussein, America would have faced an Arab nuclear power before long. With the Gulf War, Bush had "nailed down, beyond doubt or dispute, the predominant role of the United States in the world now emerging."[26]

Agreeing with the entire conservative movement that the collapse of communist rule in Central and Eastern Europe in late 1989, and two years later in the Soviet Union, was a thrilling victory for freedom and civilization, Rusher wrote that he had never expected to live to see it. He only regretted that Frank Meyer wasn't around to witness the great events.[27] In a nutshell, "the shrewdest minds in the communist world ultimately realized that their side was losing." Recognizing "communism's basic misconceptions concerning the nature of man and the most efficient way to organize society," they "decided to cut their losses and try to salvage what they could." With happy finality, Rusher noted "the official abolition of the Soviet Communist Party and the legal extinction of the Union of Soviet Socialist Republics"—both ending, like a grand opera's last act, "in a welter of smoke and flame."[28]

In many of his public talks, people asked how the end of the Cold War would affect the Right or the Republican Party. Addressing the question, Rusher denied that anticommunism had been the main unifier of the conservative coalition (which, distinguishing more carefully among its elements than many observers, he defined as "the traditionalists, the moderate libertarians, the Cold Warriors, the neoconservatives, the Religious Right"). The real unifying factor had been "antiliberalism," which would remain necessary and was a strong motivator, giving the movement "good reason to survive."[29]

Rusher reacted warily to commentator Pat Buchanan's right-wing populist challenge in the 1992 Republican primaries. Without denouncing it, he urged Buchanan to be a team player. Depending on how it was conducted, the insurgent's primary campaign could either weaken Bush in the general election or set Buchanan up well for 1996. Writing in March, Rusher pointed out that Buchanan would be "Mr. Conservative" at the convention in Houston. It was in his interest to make a cooperative speech. He should give "a rousing salute to conservatism" while playing "the Happy Loser, preparing to do battle" for the endangered president. That fall, Rusher gamely served as Bush's advocate at a debate on a Texas campus with George McGovern.[30]

The aftermath, not the campaign, was the time to take a hard look. Just after the president's humiliating defeat, Rusher told a Council for National

Policy audience that the movement "had little to gain—or lose—from the election." The Republican campaign had "failed to demonize Congress" or to use family values effectively. Rusher worried about Democratic success in mobilizing minorities, gays, and environmentalists. He urged that the Republicans pursue Asian voters. The movement must "avoid fatal internal divisions" and needed a leader who could keep it together as Reagan had. Still, Rusher believed conservatism was winning. "Victories over Communism and socialism were tremendous," he jotted in the tiny but legible handwriting he used for his lecture notes. "At bottom, *ideas* count most . . . We still have the intellectual initiative."

Rusher's thoughts turned to the theme he had adopted in recent years: "The basic unresolved issue is the relation of society to religion. The courts have made atheism the state cult, but this will change." He seemed resigned to a long-term struggle against secularism: "So what if it takes 50 years?" To the board of the Media Research Center, Rusher gave essentially the same presentation, adding that conservatives "must stop scaring people—e.g. on abortion." One reason why the movement needed a leader similar to Reagan was his "non-threatening" quality.[31] Attending the CPAC conference in Washington as Arkansas governor Bill Clinton moved into the White House in January, Rusher was encouraged to find high spirits among the participants, who believed most voters hadn't repudiated conservative positions, and by his impression that these activists were generally willing to compromise on questions dividing conservatives.[32]

In the post-1989 world, Rusher could finally set aside his refusal to visit communist countries. The ones he was interested in seeing, other than mainland China, were no longer communist. In 1993, he spent his seventieth birthday on a trip to the former Soviet Union, where he was photographed in Red Square next to the Kremlin, raising two fingers inconspicuously in the Churchillian "V for Victory" salute. In a buttoned sweater and his trademark heavy-rimmed glasses, Rusher resembled George Smiley as played by Alec Guinness, the diffident but trusted old professional at the British espionage headquarters in John le Carré's *Tinker, Tailor, Soldier, Spy*. He had sometimes said, in a hyper-rhetorical mood, that he would visit Moscow only if he could ride through "its radioactive ashes in a Sherman tank." Now he dined with two American conservatives who were on political business in the country.[33]

Rusher was also pleased by the fulfillment of his hopes for a major conference on the legacy of the Enlightenment, which he had begun to plan on his own several years before. Its purpose was to identify more clearly the positive and negative aspects of the Enlightenment, questions Rusher believed modern man must understand in order to successfully navigate the twenty-first century. Russell Kirk, the godfather of the traditionalist wing of American conservatism and a prolific independent scholar, had encouraged this interest back in 1987: "Your mission it is, William of Nob Hill that shall be, to undo Voltaire and all his works. To your folios!" Kirk wasn't just indulging in flattery. In his letter, he provided a long list of books Rusher might profitably read in the area. Rusher hinted to an acquaintance that it might be too ambitious: "Lord knows when, or whether, I will have time to read all the books he recommends." But to Kirk, he wrote that he found the input "extremely stimulating." Rusher had previously read the abridged version of Arnold Toynbee's *A Study of History*. He was now reading Christopher Dawson, another historian recommended by Kirk, who had written extensively on the relationship between religion and culture. Dawson, he thought, was "fascinating."[34]

The Claremont Institute took on the project with major assistance from the Bradley Foundation, which had also provided the funds for Rusher's senior fellowship with the organization. With Rusher as the lead organizer, three closely related conferences were held in Southern California in 1990 through 1992, grouped under the name "Project 21," a reference to the coming century. Participants included a long list of political-philosophy scholars and a shorter but impressive list of scientists and conservative intellectual luminaries.[35] Writing after the second conference, philosopher of science Leon Kass told Rusher: "I can't remember the last time I was in the company of such intelligent, thoughtful, and deeply serious people, unashamed to admit that they were, above all, interested in the truth. You set a simply marvelous tone: high-minded, judicious, and weighty."

Although the Claremont Institute later published a selection of papers from the three conferences in a volume Rusher edited, *The Ambiguous Legacy of the Enlightenment*, he had planned to write his own book-length summary as well. "The trouble," Rusher told another participant, was that "the closer I get to this project, the less confident I become of my own educational background and hence of my ability to deal with the subject effectively." Still, he would try.[36]

Rusher next became heavily involved in the California Civil Rights Initiative, a ballot measure passed by the voters in 1996 that banned racial and gender preferences on the part of state and local government. It was "in its infancy" and therefore needed "a solid endorsement by you," he wrote Buckley in 1994.[37]

Later that year, when he prodded the initiative's founders to professionalize their nascent petition drive, Rusher's disarming courtesy was as evident as it had been in memos to Buckley thirty years before. "I apologize," he wrote academics Glynn Custred and Thomas Wood, "if I seem to have become a bit of a Johnny One-Note recently, stressing the urgency of taking early steps to insure that CCRI is on the California ballot in 1996 . . . I figure you will forgive me if I occasionally seem to be a bit of a pest." He advised the political novices to draw up a firm timeline and recommended sharing management responsibility with a larger, well-connected committee. This would provide more of a focus on the actual tasks, encourage productive specialization among those involved, and "make the whole operation more significant in the eyes of observers." Rusher assumed Custred and Wood weren't eager to give others a large, perhaps dominant say in things. That was natural. "But either this is a major project, requiring the attention of powerful people, or you two may be known in a few years as 'those guys who had that initiative against quotas, but flapped around and never got anywhere.'"[38] Rusher also urged Larry Arnn, the founding chairman of the project, to "issue a memo . . . decreeing that the CCRI campaign will never . . . use the term 'affirmative action,' but always speak only of 'race preferences' or, if necessary, 'race and gender preferences.' Frequent quotation of the exact words of the initiative is always helpful, since it makes our case for us."[39]

Rusher was thrilled by the Republicans' capture of Congress in the 1994 election and approved of the Contract with America spearheaded by Speaker Newt Gingrich. Writing in 1995, he commented that the House Republicans' program sought to fulfill a "rare moment" in history wherein "an impressive number of voters [had] decided to resist and if possible reverse the constant and often blind expansion of federal power that has been the central theme of American politics for more than 60 years." Such an opportunity might never come again. But looking back on the 104th Congress a year and a half later, Rusher regretted that its leaders had called their program a "revolution." He saw it as a term that many potentially supportive voters had probably disliked.[40]

In May 1996, Rusher was delighted to be the keynote speaker at a Princeton conference on the development and success of modern American conservatism, organized by two graduate students in history there, Benjamin Alpers and Jennifer Delton. Neither was a conservative, but both were perplexed that historians seemed to be neglecting "the biggest story of the late twentieth century," and they wanted to hear from someone who had "played a role in the events in question," according to Delton, now a professor at Skidmore College. They also wished to provide a balance to the other experts, most of whom would be "speaking from a liberal or left perspective."[41]

In his address, Rusher told the audience that "the serious work of historiography on this subject has scarcely even begun." He stressed the centrality of two things at the early *National Review*. One was a *"sense of mission"* its editors felt to "provide the ideas for a conservative transformation of American politics, precisely as *The New Republic* had provided the new ideas that led to the New Deal." The other was a *"sense of embattlement,"* in which Rusher and his colleagues "believed . . . we were taking on a powerful and determined intellectual orthodoxy that we called 'the Liberal Establishment,' and that it would do its best to destroy us—preferably, of course, by ignoring us." Most of them had never thought they would "live to witness the realization of our dreams." Rusher recalled that when he was at Princeton, "it was almost universally assumed, even by those of us who resented it bitterly, that socialism was the wave of the economic future all over the world. Today, even the senescent Communist bosses of China have adopted market principles." Conservatism's first and second battles, the destruction of communism and the revival of predominantly market-oriented economics, had been won.

In conclusion, Rusher raised the subject of the Enlightenment's legacy. The issues involved would occasion "modern conservatism's 'final conflict'— and the foe will be the remaining defenders of the Enlightenment's commitment to secular humanism." Noting that he wouldn't live to see it, Rusher predicted conservatism would win this one too, "the most important battle of them all. In ways now hidden to us, but congenial to the mind and spirit of twenty-first-century man, we will find our way to the upward path again."[42]

## Diminuendo

While Rusher remained notably active, he had become less urgent about things. Having fought in the political and *National Review* trenches for so long, he seemed to enjoy not being "on" all the time. In 1995, he told readers the past six years had been "the happiest of my life."[43] Rusher "seemed to show more interest in people on a personal level," according to political consultant Arnold Steinberg, who occasionally saw him at conservative events in California. Disputes among conservatives were largely off his agenda. After decades as "a fire-breathing champion for his beliefs on matters both major and minor," Neal Freeman recalls, Rusher in the 1980s had "elided with remarkable grace into his role as an elder statesman. He burnished the good memories, brushed away the bad, and refused to become involved in criticism of the new people and the new order. He was, front to back, a class act."[44]

Although he saw less of the people he knew in New York, his friend Jack Casey, the conservative lawyer, had moved to San Francisco as well. In addition, Rusher could more easily visit with Diarmuid O'Scannlain, who had practiced law and held appointive offices in Oregon since the midsixties and was appointed to the U.S. Court of Appeals for the Ninth Circuit in 1986. Because the court had its headquarters in San Francisco, O'Scannlain came down from Portland quite often. When he and Rusher had dinner every month or two, the judge would share "war stories . . . and horror stories" about liberal victories on the Ninth Circuit. Listening sympathetically to these accounts of losses for judicial conservatives, Rusher also took a real interest in the federal appellate process, according to O'Scannlain, who gave his friend copies of many of his dissents.[45] In 1997, there was better news when a Ninth Circuit panel upheld Proposition 209, the voter-approved California measure Rusher had assisted that barred the state from engaging in reverse discrimination. The opinion, written by Judge O'Scannlain, was promptly faxed to him.[46]

Even as he enjoyed the company of out-of-town friends and politically congenial San Franciscans, Rusher was losing some of those closest to him. Roger Moore, several years younger than himself, and Clif White, several years older, died of cancer early in the decade. He also lost his closest family members, in 1990 his mother and in 1994 his aunt. Reaching the age of seventy-five in 1998, Rusher mentioned to readers his health troubles over the past several years: a hernia, an ulcer, a cataract, and early-stage prostate cancer. All were treated successfully, "but only to make way for the next nuisance: arthritis in my right hip, which makes me limp and will no doubt require replacement surgery." What he didn't know yet was that the aggressive treatment for his prostate cancer would have lasting, gradually debilitating side effects.[47]

Overall, Rusher's thoughts on turning seventy-five were happy. "Life remains interesting, and very much worth living." He had lived to see "the two greatest evils of my lifetime—communism and socialism—consigned to the ash-heap of history." Although much remained to be done, and always would, "no one who has seen the miracles I have witnessed will doubt that American conservatism can do it. Vibrant, energetic and positively awash with new ideas, it has resources—both human and material—that we never dreamed of 40 years ago." Rusher added: "Cheer up, young conservatives! You are the inheritors of a great tradition, with a long series of notches in its belt. But be glad that every day brings new challenges."[48]

One old challenge, media bias, would partly elude his cautious optimism. In 2001, Rusher told readers that he no longer expected much self-recognition and reform in the news industry, owing to its "contempt for conservatives" and eagerness to help liberalism. His hopes for countering bias now rested entirely on the emergence of new outlets, plus public pressure that might yet grow in strength. Rusher was glad to see the media giants weakened by cable TV and talk radio. In a similar spirit, he admired Rush Limbaugh for "pounding hard" against liberals and their positions.[49] He also noticed the new vehemence from many liberals during the George W.

Bush administration. They had, Rusher wrote in late 2003, "started pushing back at the conservatives with impressive ferocity." With talk radio incessantly attacking liberalism, with the Fox News Channel giving "full and equal voice to conservative spokesmen and dominating TV news as a result," with divisions at major publishing houses now focused on right-leaning books, Rusher thought liberals had decided they could no longer "afford to give conservatism the silent treatment." The public discourse was growing harsher, but "I welcome the change." As liberals grew louder, he explained, their arguments were becoming easier to discredit.[50]

Despite his serious reservations about what was often called President Bush's "big-government conservatism," Rusher remained upbeat about the strength of both the conservative philosophy and the movement. In discussions with Diarmuid O'Scannlain, he distanced himself a bit from current concerns. The shape of ideological conflict remained far better, Rusher suggested, than it was when he joined the emerging movement and for a long time thereafter. Without defending the president's fiscal record, he was saying that in general the policy debates remained on conservative terms. O'Scannlain found it "another example of Bill's fundamental optimism."[51] Even so, that optimism had never been unalloyed. In a column in early 2004, Rusher noted Bush's failure, even relative to other presidents, at budgetary restraint. The widespread belief "that they are financially more responsible than their opponents, and less inclined to expand government" had historically been among the GOP's and conservatives' major assets. "If Bush squanders those assets in pursuit of 'bolder, more inspirational ideas,' he will bear a heavy responsibility for the future fates of the party and the movement."[52]

In late 2004, at the age of eighty-one, Rusher decided to move from his condominium apartment into a retirement home with independent living. He would be giving up a spacious dwelling, with an inspiring view, where he had spent fifteen years. He would also miss his personal library, deeply regretting that he must unload 1,000 of his approximately 1,200 books, "the hardest thing I ever did." They went to an educational project of his church. "I told the priest that I thought there might be one or two books that would not be appropriate. I said: 'I don't think you would particularly want Baudelaire's *Flowers of Evil.*'"[53]

The retirement facility to which Rusher moved—San Francisco Towers at Van Ness Avenue and Pine Street—was "the Cadillac" of such places in the city, a cab driver remarked when he went over for a look. The fairly new, classically designed building had beautifully furnished common areas, a glass-ceilinged atrium with a finely polished stone floor in the lobby, good food, a dignified little library where Rusher read newspapers (certainly including the *New York Times*) at leisure, a notably courteous staff, well-mannered and affluent residents. It was spotlessly clean. A danger arose that the rule requiring men to wear ties at dinner in the main dining room might be dropped. When it wasn't, Rusher expressed thanks for upholding standards, sending the appropriate staff person what he quaintly recalled as "a mash note."

No smoking was allowed, of course, at a San Francisco retirement home, but Rusher soon noticed that a tiny café with a couple of sidewalk tables sat on the block. He then found that he could more suitably take advantage of a little-used outdoor terrace, even though it meant carrying a hidden ashtray from his small apartment through a couple of hallways. While living on Nob Hill, Rusher had gone to the nearby University Club most afternoons for a cigar, sitting in a particular chair near the magazine table with a large window overlooking the city just behind him. Within a few years after moving, he resigned from the club, according to Frank Shepherd, because "when they cut out smoking he got very upset about it."[54]

Until about 2007, Rusher still ate out often, noticing a mildly irksome decline in proper dress. New Yorkers hadn't been completely formal even at the opera, but "certainly they weren't as resolutely down-at-the-heels as people are nowadays—where I am, in San Francisco, usually the only person in the restaurant wearing a necktie." He got along well with the San Francisco Towers residents, even though he found conservatives somewhat underrepresented among those he met. In addition, only a small handful of the residents he knew were knowledgeable enough about politics that he could truly enjoy discussing it with them. He continued to see San Francisco friends and occasional out-of-town friends but eventually found it easier to meet them in the dining room.[55] Rusher and his college classmate Ted Meth, who had begun corresponding in their later years, got together for a "lovely evening" in Princeton. Although Meth, a staunch liberal, felt "disgusted" by conservatives' political success, he liked much of Rusher's personality. He also noted a striking consistency. Dinner with Bill in 2005 was "not much different from having lunch with him in Freshman Commons."[56]

A consistency of personality was also evident to ACU chairman David Keene. One evening, Rusher called him about a cruise the organization was cosponsoring. Because there were friends in Rome and elsewhere in the Mediterranean region he wanted to see, it made sense to combine these visits with the cruise. Keene urged him to do so. Citing old age, Rusher said he would need someone to assist him, explaining: "You're elected." Keene agreed. As the passengers boarded, Rusher presented him with a paper listing a name and number in San Francisco. "Bill, what's this?" Keene asked. "That's if I die. That's my lawyer." A shipboard panel featured Keene and Rusher discussing movement history. At one point, the ACU chairman told or reminded the audience of Rusher's rationale for a new party in the midseventies.

*Courtesy Claremont Institute*

*In his living room at San Francisco Towers*

He would recount the episode with a chuckle. "I said: 'Bill took the position, then, that the Republican Party would never nominate someone like Ronald Reagan, and therefore we needed a third party.' Bill just looked at me, and he said: 'Yeah—in 1968, you were one of only two members of the YAF board that supported Nixon.' I said: 'Well, Bill—maybe we should just move on.'"[57]

As *National Review* planned its fiftieth-anniversary celebration, to be held in Washington in October 2005, Rusher worried that Buckley might recycle the famous toast the editor had given back in 1969 at the appreciation dinner in his honor—and had used again in 1988 for most of his talk at Rusher's retirement party. In it, the publisher was described as a lovable but highly eccentric colleague, laughably meticulous and precise and predictable, high-strung, obsessively ideological. Most of the lengthy toast had been reprinted as recently as 2004 in *Miles Gone By*, the editor's autobiographical collection. Rusher never especially liked it, Buckley noted a few weeks before the dinner: "He's lived with it so long, and people poked fun at him about it." *NR* put together a slideshow, presenting the magazine's history and noting its key personalities. As plans for the event proceeded, Rusher wrote Buckley a letter "begging me not to restrict [the] notice given to him to the prolongation of that caricature. So we fussed with it."[58]

## Passages

In October 2007, Rusher sadly confided that Buckley, Van Galbraith, and others of their generation seemed to have aged considerably when he saw them at a recent *NR* board meeting. Buckley, who suffered from emphysema and diabetes, had just four months to live, as it turned out. He died of a heart attack in his study next to the Stamford house on the morning of February 27, 2008, his short book on Reagan nearly complete. At 8:15 A.M. Pacific time, *NR* publisher Jack Fowler called with the news. Rusher "thanked him very much for thinking of me, and at 8:30, ABC or something called . . . I was glad that Fowler got to me before ABC. But I can't say that I felt a terrible blow in the pit of the stomach, or anything like that. He had been in not the best of health . . . Pat had died in April of last year. I wasn't expecting it, exactly, but I cannot say I was surprised. Bear in mind: while we were very close there for thirty-one years, it's been nineteen that I've been away, so there's been a good deal of distance between us in that time."[59]

A special issue of *National Review* soon appeared in tribute. Reminiscences of various lengths ran in the order of people's seniority in Buckley's life. First was a piece by his older sister Priscilla, explaining what "Billy" was like as a boy in the 1930s. Next was a contribution from British historian Alistair Horne, who had known Buckley since their time together at Millbrook, an upstate New York prep school, just before the war. The third was from Henry Kissinger, who met Buckley in 1954. Among their many contacts, they had spent many Thanksgivings together. "I cannot bear it," Kissinger had said when Buckley's son, Christopher, called to tell him.

Fourth was a conspicuously short piece from Rusher, who met Buckley toward the beginning of 1956, in *NR*'s first months. It was about the difficulties of keeping an unprofitable magazine afloat for decades—stressing, as Rusher had in *Rise of the Right* and elsewhere, the crucial importance of donations from loyal readers—and said almost nothing about Buckley. With some chagrin, Rusher noticed the contrast between his impersonal contribution and the emotional, detailed appreciations from so many others, mainly people in the *NR* family. It was, he said, a "rather misbegotten" piece. He had been asked to write on exactly that topic, and what he sent was shortened in the editorial process.[60] Rusher was unable to attend Buckley's memorial service in April at St. Patrick's Cathedral in Manhattan, which drew a capacity crowd of more than two thousand. "Bill asked me to tell everyone he could not make it because of health . . . wanted me to really convey that," recalls Arnie Steinberg, who flew out from California.[61]

Despite his many friends in the city and elsewhere, Rusher felt a certain loneliness—partly, perhaps, because he had never liked to talk long on the phone. In terms of family, there was a cousin whom he occasionally wrote but couldn't necessarily picture in his mind. He would often tell people: "I don't have a blood relative that I would recognize if he or she walked into the room." With a visitor in 2008, he momentarily recalled his lifelong bachelor status and the many weddings in which he was "Rusher the Usher." He had been a godfather to twelve, among them children of Judy Fernald, Roger Moore, and Bill Runyeon.

None of his closest friends from his generation survived. In addition to the previous deaths of Moore and White, Charlie McWhorter was killed in an auto accident in 1999. Jack Casey, who moved to San Francisco but developed Alzheimer's disease, was now gone. Runyeon had passed away in 2005. Rusher felt the departures of these "wonderful people" as great losses. Having kept in touch with Runyeon consistently since their Princeton years, he traveled to Pennsylvania for the funeral, where he delivered a eulogy. Tom Farmer in Washington was his last remaining octogenarian friend, as distinct from friendly acquaintance. He pointed this out to his high-school classmate, urging him to take care of himself.[62]

For the first time in his adult life, Rusher now looked as old as he was. He would step down as chairman of the Media Research Center, knowing he could no longer make the trip to Washington three times each year for board meetings. Although getting around had become more of a problem, he continued at eighty-four to walk with an impressively straight posture, aided by an elegant wooden stick he had long used. His voice, though weaker now, remained unmistakably his.

He still read some poetry. Among his favorites were Shakespeare, Swinburne, Yeats, Robert Browning, A. E. Housman, Robert Frost, T. S. Eliot, and the satirical poems of Hilaire Belloc. He enjoyed limericks. Poetry aside, he cited *Moby Dick* and Boswell's *Life of Samuel Johnson* as two favorites over the years. Rusher had always regretted not being able to read as much as he wished. "I would like to have another whole life," he said, "in which I'd read books." On television, he occasionally saw something on the History Channel but mainly watched Fox News.[63]

Although he had given up most of his books, Rusher continued to read many conservative and some liberal magazines, receiving an early copy of each *National Review*. One favorite was *First Things*, a high-toned conservative religious journal dealing with social, ecclesiastical, and theological issues. Faith had become "an integral aspect of my life" after his baptism in 1978, he reflected, "and I regard it as an important one. I expect to live and die in the church, and I'm very glad that this is so . . . It has become a comfortable, congruent part of my world outlook, without necessarily changing it a lot. No reason why it should change it. It fitted in very well." On matters such as "forgiveness and things like that," ones having "a clear religious aspect . . . I think to some degree it influenced me." Rusher had happily attended the small, traditionalist St. Thomas Anglican Church about a mile west of his old apartment, but later he made the effort only on special occasions like Easter—a Day of Holy Obligation, he noted. Still, he met for lunch every six weeks with its rector, James Eugene Provence, an archbishop in the break-away Episcopal church whose formation he had welcomed in the 1970s.[64]

Even with a slower life, Rusher remained happy with the city he had chosen. "San Francisco has a dreadful reputation among conservatives," he noted, "and New Yorkers are forever raising the subject, mostly New Yorkers. I just dismiss it. I'm not in the least interested in what the majority of people in San Francisco think. I like the weather, I like the food, I like the ambiance. It's where I want to live. If they want to live there too—good luck."[65]

## Enduring Faith

Rusher still took some interest in the political scene, guessing in 2007 that former Massachusetts governor Mitt Romney, George Romney's son, would probably be the best Republican nominee in the following year's election, at least against Hillary Clinton. Romney could contrast favorably with her in debates, he thought, by using a gentle condescension in response to Mrs. Clinton's shrillness. In early 2008, after John McCain had apparently won the nomination, Rusher noted that the Arizona senator seemed like a man of substance and a strong general-election candidate. But he still expected it would be, as he often said, "a Democratic year."[66]

A sense of the larger forces in politics shaped his view of what many conservatives now perceived as George W. Bush's failure. "Presidents wear out their welcome," Rusher said, and "each president is denounced as the worst president we have ever had. I heard that about literally every president of the United States, so I don't take it all that seriously. Bush is no 'great cosmic breakthrough,' as Buckley would put it, but neither is he the worst president we have ever had." Rusher hadn't developed a settled opinion of Bush, only a "moving assessment," thinking that he didn't completely understand him even after seven years. Bush had been "a bit disappointing," but mostly in the sense of an "inability to conceptualize his presidency and its policies in a way that the American people could understand and approve of."[67]

After the 9/11 attacks in 2001, Rusher had written that although he certainly supported Bush's goals of eliminating international terror organizations and punishing the regimes that harbored them, this wouldn't come close to solving the jihadist challenge. "Ultimately the whole Islamic world must be brought into accord with the trends that dominate the globe . . . toward democracy and free markets. Only then will it know the prosperity that the Western world enjoys today, and be able to resist the forces of envy and resentment."[68] Now, in 2008, he wasn't "as upset as most people" by the drawn-out conflict in Iraq, noting that "wars tend to go badly." He had no doubt that the American effort there could prevail, "and should, and will." Agreeing that democratization in some countries "probably should not be attempted prematurely" and that America ought not to make war precipitately, Rusher rejected claims that the decision to invade Iraq in 2003, and the long occupation aimed at democratization there, constituted betrayals of conservatism.

He looked differently at immigration. "We are so deep in the dilemma over immigration, there's no getting out of it," Rusher lamented. "I have written columns in which I said: 'Conservatives, grow up. We've lost this one. We're being overrun; we will continue to be overrun. We have the businessmen of America in league with the left wing of the Democratic Party, which between the two of them is an overwhelming political force in favor of inundating the United States with immigrants, legal or otherwise, for cheap labor and votes.'" The result, Rusher predicted, would be "a profound change in the nature of the society, in its ethnic composition, and with the cultural implications that go with that . . . The power of America to assimilate is enormous and has been tremendously influential in the past. We are, however, pushing it beyond its manageable limits." But Rusher also believed that the English language and other major aspects of American society would remain dominant—and that "there will always be conservative things that can be done in any situation . . . some things that are better to do than others."

In regard to the movement in which he had spent most of his life, he strongly disagreed with activists and observers who saw a collapse in the latter half of the decade. Of a recent remark that Buckley had both created the movement and lived to see its disappearance, Rusher said: "That's nonsense . . . I don't worry about it at all. I think it's going to be around for a long, long time." He felt encouraged by the movement's proliferation of advocates and by its "tendency . . . to create new organizations and new personalities," noting that it had repeatedly shown such an ability. As for the perception that anticommunism and Reagan were really what held conservatives together, Rusher said: "I sometimes wonder how we get along without them. But here we are. We've been without them for quite a while, and I don't see that the movement has disappeared, or is fading, or anything like that." Another reason for his faith in its future, one also stressed in *Rise of the Right*, was that he believed the conservative viewpoint was fundamentally the truth, that its principles remained "perfectly sound and perfectly applicable."[69]

In February 2009, Rusher gave up his column after thirty-five and a half years, telling readers he was now eighty-five and couldn't keep writing it.[70] His friend O'Scannlain was among those saddened to see a man of such vitality having to "deal with the effects of age." In mid-2009, when he forgot dinner plans with the judge and his wife, Rusher "was so apologetic. God bless him, he said: 'You know, I think it's the failings of an old man. I'm sorry—I wrote it down in a book, but then I didn't check it.'"[71]

When Frank Shepherd—who came out from Miami as often as possible on professional business in order to visit Rusher—saw him that July, he still showed his characteristic hard-boiled optimism although he was no longer the conversationalist he had been. He reminisced a bit about his life, and they briefly discussed the new president. What about Obama? "Well, I've seen it all before," Rusher said. He's very glib, Shepherd persisted. "I'm not all that impressed with him," Rusher replied, conceding nothing. How did he compare with Franklin Roosevelt? Answer: Obama was no FDR. On a visit several months before, Rusher had told his friend not to take the political situation too hard. "He said: 'Don't worry; there's a yin and a yang to politics.' Conservatism will come back, in his view."[72]

In mid-2010, Rusher fell in his apartment. Although not seriously injured, he now needed a full-time nurse and had already begun to lose a previously normal appetite. A few months later, he was moved to his retirement home's onsite nursing unit. Painful abdominal complications had crept up on Rusher, and he was unable to absorb enough nutrition or undergo the necessary operation. Bedridden and badly emaciated, he retained some of his long-term memory and was able to communicate sparsely, recognizing friends. He still wanted to live—urging a visitor on Thanksgiving weekend, in the strongest voice he could muster, to tell everyone he would make it. A slight improvement in early 2011 offered some hope, but Rusher was fighting the odds. Conscious until very nearly the end, he passed away peacefully at about 10 A.M. on Saturday, April 16.

Under a clear sky at noon, Rusher was buried five days later in what he knew would be a tiny private ceremony, next to his mother and aunt in Independence, Kansas. Friends attended a requiem Mass on April 28 at St. Thomas in San Francisco. Around the country, many who couldn't be there wrote moving public tributes.[73]

# Conclusion

# "The Truth Will Prevail"

For want of me the world's course will not fail:
When all its work is done, the lie shall rot;
The truth is great, and shall prevail,
When none cares whether it prevail or not.

Rusher recited these lines at the end of nearly all his serious talks over the past thirty years. The quatrain of the nineteenth-century British poet Coventry Patmore "isn't a Pollyanna poem," he explains. "It is a harsh poem. What it says is that the truth will damned well prevail, whether you like it or not . . . or whether we like it or not. We had better get in accord with it, and then have confidence in it. It will not fail us. In the long run, the lie will rot. The truth will prevail. It's a tough message."[1]

Yet in contrast to the hard-boiled optimism Rusher shared with Patmore, his political life was an extraordinarily lucky one, for it was exceptionally well timed. In his teen years, he looked to Walter Lippmann, the great newspaper commentator of the day, as the kind of political figure he might become. Lippmann was the ultimate journalistic insider, a title no one at *National Review* could ever really claim. In a conversation toward the end of his life, during Watergate, he reflected that "presidents in general are not lovable," because they "had to do too much to get where they are." But there was one exception in his lifetime, Teddy Roosevelt: "I loved him."[2] These thoughts on the presidency were not unlike Rusher's cautionary remarks over the years about politicians, and the exception for the first Roosevelt was also Rusher's for Reagan. But Walter Lippmann's favorite

434

president held office in the journalist's early youth, even before he worked at the *New Republic*. All who came later were something less. William Rusher's favorite president dominated American politics in the last decade he spent at *National Review*. Politically speaking, modern America's golden age as Rusher saw it coincided with the culmination of his own professional life. In Lippmann's case it was rather the opposite.

Dividing his time among deliberations at a magazine of ideas, meetings aimed at political action, personal mentoring, debates, speeches, conferences, and eventually columns meant a complicated and somewhat unclear identity for Rusher. "I used to say that I was Janus-faced," he recalls. "I looked both ways. I could interpret the politicians like Clif White to the intellectuals like Buckley, and the intellectuals like Buckley to the politicians like White. I stood in-between. And I guess, depending on where you came from, I might have looked like an extremely energetic organizer—particularly if you were a literary type that hadn't been interested in organizing before. And maybe to other people, I would have looked altogether like a literary dilettante who wasn't doing nearly enough; I don't know."[3]

Rusher's career was unconventional in this sense, yet it garnered great respect. "I think of him as bright, well-read, resolute, committed; and a good wordsmith, good orator," Buckley says. "I've had decades of personal experience with him, so I've seen him in a number of roles, and he is all of the things that I've mentioned. I don't think anybody would disagree with that." The goodwill for him across the fractious spectrum of American conservatism is something Rusher has "earned" for several reasons, according to Buckley: "his attachment to his cause; the ingenuity of his resources; the time he's prepared to give to other people to help solve common problems; plus personal amiability."[4]

A large part of Rusher's example, Lee Edwards suggests, lies in "the importance of preparation—of marshaling all of your facts and figures, and all the various elements of a particular situation, so that you don't go into a meeting unprepared, you don't leave anything to chance. Perseverance: this is not a 100-yard dash, this is a marathon—and be prepared to keep working, keep working, keep working." Priscilla Buckley adds: "He got things done because of his impatience."[5] In comparison with today's TV and radio controversialists, Barry Farber says, Rusher was "lightning versus the lightning bug." On Farber's New York radio programs over the decades, he was "so smart, and so serious, and so focused, full-time . . . superior in feeling, preparation, energy." By that daunting set of criteria, there are "no Bill Rushers out there."[6]

Rusher was simultaneously a relentless voice in the public arena and a force on the Right. For conservatives, he was an inspiration toward political seriousness—persistence, discipline, imagination, careful understanding of the American people, realism about the political process, and prompt action. He was also a symbol of increasingly unfashionable, yet still appreciated, standards of elegance and taste. Even when wrong, he was worldly, shrewd, and exceptionally well spoken. He was a standard-setter, mainly by example.

The amiability Buckley cites was inconsistent; it could be turned on and off. There was a harsh side to Rusher. He "could be a rough character in these internal arguments" at the magazine, Jeffrey Hart remembered in 2005, and "could be slashingly take-no-prisoners" in public debate. Rusher distinguishes between the two. "I wasn't particularly interested in fighting" within the conservative movement. "But certainly I regarded fighting the liberals as the thing I most wanted to do, and that most needed doing; and I did as much of it as I could, in as many media as would allow it."[7]

Despite their varying personalities and perspectives, the keen sense of responsibility felt by the leading *National Review* figures bound them together in obligation to the conservative cause as much as did Buckley's inspiration and diplomatic abilities. When Bill Rickenbacker told them in 1964, "We are willing, I take it, ultimately to sacrifice our lives in the cause of Christian civilization," it may have been hyperbolic. But he wrote this in a businesslike memo, trying to persuade colleagues to share his and Rusher's and Frank Meyer's urgent commitment to Goldwater. He believed, then, that the statement wouldn't be laughed off or taken amiss. With all their differences, the leaders of *NR* were comrades. Although they often disagreed about the appropriate role for the magazine, they all shared a belief in the great importance of *NR*'s mission. It was, after all, the relatively moderate, relatively pro-elite James Burnham who claimed in the same year that modern liberalism was "the ideology of Western suicide."[8]

Rusher clearly diverged from others on the central question of what sort of magazine *National Review* should be. While Burnham consistently and Buckley generally believed in having an outstanding magazine first, a useful political product second, Rusher could remind strong people that his political knowledge, and the movement's need for leadership, should influence their decisions more often than they might think. He could say unpopular things to colleagues and others because of his widely conceded knowledge and because of his wit, good manners, and sheer sincerity. Even Hart, whose history of *National Review* is partly an extended endorsement of the Burnham-Buckley position, does not dismiss the more political Rusher: "I admired his intelligence, which is formidable." Like others, he also found Rusher "great company, always lively."[9]

Strength in difference also characterized the men, largely of Rusher's generation, who sat down at a Chicago motel on October 8, 1961, and began inching toward a conservative takeover of the Republican Party. Even well before his most populist phase, Rusher could work with and gain the confidence of people as different as Roger Allan Moore, who presented himself convincingly as an upper-class Bostonian, and Frank Whetstone of Montana, who looked (White would recall) like "a gigantic frontiersman who had accidentally put on a business suit." When the Draft Goldwater campaign nearly fizzled from discouragement and again when Goldwater said he opposed it, Rusher reacted viscerally against that, helping to keep the project alive. Without his stubbornness and presence of mind in preserving the Goldwater movement at these junctures, it is plausible to consider that Ronald Reagan's ultimate election might never have happened. Much the same can be said for Rusher's efforts at the early *National Review*: without his prudence as a manager, according to Priscilla Buckley, "there's a good chance" the magazine "might not have succeeded."[10]

Just as the continuance of *NR* remained uncertain, the leaders of the conservative movement had to proceed, at least until the election of Reagan, without knowing where it would all end up. "In my own life," reflects Larry Arnn, president of Hillsdale College and former president of the Claremont Institute, "I've done all kinds of things that I marvel at what success they've had. And of course, I also am old enough to know that I don't know how they're going to do tomorrow. Well, those guys lived their lives that way, and happily so—and made sacrifices along the way, and couldn't think other than that they would make them . . . You learn that, if you hang around Bill Rusher for a while."[11]

Dan McGrath, a friend of more than forty years, points to confidence as a key factor. "Self-doubt didn't seem to be a major affliction with Bill Rusher," he notes. "That was, I think, a major part of his success."[12] Yet with that self-confidence, Rusher remained focused on the things and people he believed in, much less on himself. "He wasn't one of these big-ego guys," says John Kurzweil of the *California Political Review*. "He did a heck of a lot of work out of sight, and without getting a lot of plaudits . . . and that didn't seem to bother him in the least." Such people are "much freer in their spirit, they're much more creative, they get a lot more done, they accept what comes in life and make the most of it. It's the key to his optimism, for instance, I think, about the movement, and [his] seeing that there's always a great deal that's positive there—because there is."

For Kurzweil, Rusher illustrates well the lesson often cited by Reagan: "There's no limit to what you can accomplish if you don't care who gets the credit." He seemed to have escaped the "trap of getting wrapped up in your own emotional reactions," Kurzweil suggests, and concentrated instead on "the objective situation." Perhaps "some people are just kind of born that way. Clearly, I think, he's one of them. They never lose their childlike fascination with the world around them. They see the charm and the opportunities in everything that pops up . . . They look out upon the world, they find it fascinating, and they go forward, and they try to do what they can."[13]

# Notes

Introduction: "The Most Underrated Major Conservative Leader"

1. Interview with William F. Buckley Jr., November 14, 2007. Although Buckley, Rusher, and a few other sources have since passed away, I have decided to maintain stylistic consistency by citing my interviews with them in the present tense.
2. Interview with Priscilla Buckley, August 5, 2006.
3. F. Clifton White with William J. Gill, *Suite 3505: The Story of the Draft Goldwater Movement* (New Rochelle, NY: Arlington House, 1967), 26.
4. Interview with Jeffrey Bell, September 5, 2009.
5. Twentieth-anniversary dinner remarks, *National Review*, December 5, 1975.
6. William F. Buckley Jr. interviews, September 17, 2005, and November 14, 2007.
7. Interview with Richard Viguerie, November 15, 2007.
8. Interview with M. Stanton Evans, November 16, 2007.
9. Interview with Eugene Meyer, August 28, 2009.
10. Author recollection. I have known Rusher since late 1992.
11. Jeffrey Hart, *The Making of the American Conservative Mind:* National Review *and Its Times* (Wilmington, DE: ISI Books, 2005), 149.
12. Interview with William Rusher, April 17, 2006.
13. William A. Rusher, *Special Counsel* (New Rochelle, NY: Arlington House, 1968).
14. William A. Rusher, *The Rise of the Right* (New York: William Morrow, 1984).
15. Interview with Kevin Lynch, November 16, 2007; interview with Linda Bridges, July 26, 2005.
16. Interview with Richard Brookhiser, January 5, 2009.
17. Rusher interview, April 15, 2005.
18. Interview with Lee Edwards, July 31, 2006.
19. William A. Rusher, *The Making of the New Majority Party* (New York: Sheed and Ward, 1975).
20. Rusher interview, August 23, 2005.
21. Rusher interview, April 16, 2005.
22. Rusher interview, August 5, 2003.

23. *From Max Weber: Essays in Sociology*, ed. and trans. H. H. Gerth and C. Wright Mills (New York: Oxford University Press, 1946), 128.

24. Buckley interview, July 26, 2005.

25. Remarks at Rusher testimonial dinner, April 10, 1969, in William F. Buckley Jr., *Miles Gone By: A Literary Autobiography* (Washington: Regnery, 2004), 293.

26. Priscilla Buckley interview.

## Chapter 1: Enter This War Now

1. *Arista* (Great Neck High School yearbook), 1940; Rusher interview, April 15, 2005; *New York Journal and American* clipping, undated November 1938, in Rusher's possession.

2. Rusher interview, April 15, 2005; Steve Neal, *Dark Horse: A Biography of Wendell Willkie* (Garden City, NY: Doubleday, 1984), chs. 9–10; Charles Peters, *Five Days in Philadelphia: 1940, Wendell Wilkie, and the Political Convention that Freed FDR to Win World War II* (New York: PublicAffairs, 2005), 36–82.

3. Quoted in William Allen Rusher, "The Progressive Element in the Republican Party from 1936 to the Present" (senior thesis, Princeton University, School of Public and International Affairs, May 1943), 61.

4. Rusher interviews, April 17, 2006, and August 24, 2005.

5. Rusher, *The Rise of the Right*, 16.

6. Rusher interviews, April 15, 2005, and August 24, 2005.

7. Rusher interview, April 15, 2005; Army officer's service book for Evan Rusher; Evan Rusher, *A Success Formula for Advertising Salesmen*, 1947. All Evan and Verna Rusher items are in Rusher's possession.

8. Verna Rusher, taped interview by William Rusher, October 25 and 27, 1975.

9. Verna Rusher to William Rusher, 1976.

10. Rusher interviews, April 15, 2005, and March 23, 2006; radio program: Rusher, *Special Counsel*, 138.

11. William A. Rusher, "Fond Memories of Innocent Times," syndicated column, July 25, 1991.

12. Rusher interviews, April 17, 2006, and August 24, 2005.

13. Piano-accordion: Rusher, "A Long Life Over," syndicated column, March 8, 1990; description of Evan: Rusher interviews, April 15, 2005, and August 24, 2005.

14. Evan Rusher, manuscript for *Winning Promotion in a Retail Store*, 1947; "Making Money in Retailing," promotional booklet for Standard Store Service Co., 1931.

15. Evan Rusher, *Earning More Money as a Retail Salesperson*, 1947; promotional flier for Evan Rusher.

16. Propper-McCallum Hosiery Co. newsletter, 1934.

17. Rusher interview, March 23, 2006; Evan Rusher, *Winning Promotion* manuscript; Evan Rusher medical records; Evan Rusher, *Success Formula*.

18. *Nassau Herald* (Princeton University yearbook for class of 1944), 1943; Evan Rusher, *Earning More*.

19. Rusher interviews, April 15, 2005, and March 23, 2006.

20. Interview with Judy Fernald, August 7, 2009.

21. Interview with Barry Farber, July 21, 2009.

22. Robert R. Selle, "William Rusher: Crafter of Conservatism," *The World & I*, June 1999.

23. Rusher interview, August 24, 2005.

24. Rusher, "Gone Fishing? Well, Not Exactly . . . ," syndicated column, May 22, 1990.

25. Fernald interview.

26. Richard Kluger, *The Paper: The Life and Death of the* New York Herald Tribune (New York: Knopf, 1986), 346.

27. Rusher interview, April 17, 2006.

28. Kluger, *The Paper*, 284*n*, 353.

29. Rusher interviews, March 23, 2006, August 24, 2005, and April 15, 2005; *New York Journal and American* clipping, November 1938. Lippmann, who had been associated with the Progressive movement as a young writer, remained mostly liberal in his later politics. But he was highly critical of Roosevelt beginning in 1935, opposing what he called the New Deal's "collectivist side" as the administration went beyond its early emergency measures and seemed to him increasingly authoritarian. He reluctantly supported Republican candidate Alf Landon in order to "check Roosevelt." In foreign policy, he saw the 1938 Munich agreement with Hitler by the British government as an enormous defeat and became, like Rusher, an interventionist. Ronald Steel, *Walter Lippmann and the American Century* (Boston: Little, Brown, 1980), 316–22, 371, 387.

30. Rusher interview, April 15, 2005; Landon buttons: interview with Thomas Farmer, October 8, 2005; Rusher interview, August 5, 2003.

31. "Strongly Republican": Farmer interview; "skipped second grade": Rusher interview, April 15, 2005.

32. Farmer interview.

33. Ibid.

34. *Nassau Herald* yearbook.

35. Farmer interview.

36. Ibid.

37. *Arista* yearbook; Rusher interviews, August 24, 2005, and March 23, 2006.

38. Farmer interview.

39. Rusher interview, March 23, 2006. Rusher proudly memorialized his mother for readers upon her death at age ninety-two. After the divorce, Verna remained in New York for a time. Soon, thanks to the "relative absence of male competition" during the war, she became a department head at a major branch of National City Bank in Manhattan. She later married and moved to Charlottesville, Virginia, then in 1953 to Miami. There she "decided to become an entrepreneur" and began buying space in local newspapers, which she filled with a shopping column she wrote that included paid endorsements of merchants who couldn't afford to run display ads. Always a "superb cook," she began to win lucrative prizes in cooking contests in the 1960s. Rusher was also impressed by Verna's courage as a young girl in southeastern Kansas. "When the oil company was about to bring in a gusher, she would vie with the other kids to see who dared get nearest to the well—then run like the wind when it blew." Rusher, "A Long Life Over" column.

40. Rusher interview, April 15, 2006; Marcia Graham Synnott, *The Half-Opened Door: Discrimination and Admissions at Harvard, Yale, and Princeton, 1900–1970* (Westport, CT: Greenwood, 1979), 5, 221–22.

41. F. Scott Fitzgerald, *This Side of Paradise* (New York: Scribner's, 1920, reissued by Mac-Millan, 1988), 25.

42. Alexander Leitch, *A Princeton Companion* (Princeton: Princeton University Press, 1978), 374, 4.

43. Ibid., 115–18, 385–86, 498.

44. Rusher interview, August 24, 2005; interview with Theodore Meth, December 16, 2005.

45. Meth interview.

46. Rusher interviews, August 24, 2005, and March 23, 2006.

47. Interview with Konrad Mueller, December 17, 2005; Rusher interview, August 24, 2005.

48. Leitch, *A Princeton Companion*, 504–6.

49. Rusher interview, March 23, 2006; "In the Limelight," *Princeton Hall-Mark*, March 9, 1943, 4, in Rusher's possession; Mueller interview.

50. "In the Limelight," *Princeton Hall-Mark*, March 9, 1943.

51. Meth interview; Princeton University Class of 1944, *Reflections: 60 Years Out* (2004), 32.

52. *Nassau Herald* yearbook; Rusher, *The Rise of the Right*, 18.

53. *Nassau Herald* yearbook; Rusher interview, August 24, 2005.

54. "Princeton for Willkie," *New York Times*, November 4, 1940, 10; Rusher, *The Rise of the Right*, 17.

55. William A. Rusher, *How to Win Arguments* (Garden City, NY: Doubleday, 1981), 68; Rusher interview, August 24, 2005.

56. Rusher, "How We Got into World War II," syndicated column, November 25, 1999.

57. On the motives and diversity of the isolationists, see Manfred Jonas, *Isolationism in America 1935–1941* (Ithaca, NY: Cornell University Press, 1966), chs. 1–3. "Isolationist" is the word most familiar today, but the more accurate term, at least in discussing the 1939–41 debate, is "anti-interventionist." True isolationism was the belief that the United States should have only minimal relations with other countries. The "isolationists" differed significantly among themselves on this question, while agreeing that America should not take steps that might lead to war.

58. John B. Judis, *William F. Buckley Jr.: Patron Saint of the Conservatives* (New York: Simon and Schuster, 1990), 33–34; Buckley interview, September 17, 2005; interview with Robert Douglas Stuart Jr., Appendix B in Ruth Sarles, *A Story of America First: The Men and Women Who Opposed U.S. Intervention in World War II*, ed. Bill Kauffman (Westport, CT: Praeger, 2003), 209–14.

59. Meth interview.

60. Rusher to Frank Runyeon, December 27, 1971, William A. Rusher Papers, Library of Congress, Box 78, File 1. The description Rusher quoted and applied to himself referred to Whig-Clio members in general.

61. Cigarettes: Rusher, "Another Target for the Trial Lawyers," syndicated column, May 8, 1997; Meth interview.

62. *Nassau Herald* yearbook; Mueller interview; *Nassau Herald* yearbook.

63. Rusher, "Once Foe, Japan Is Now Admirable Friend," syndicated column, December 5, 1991.

64. Ibid.; Rusher, "How We Got into World War II" column.

65. *Nassau Herald* yearbook.

66. "Yale in War Sets Year-Round Basis," *New York Times*, December 16, 1941, 33; Rusher interviews, April 15, 2005, and March 23, 2006; Princeton academic transcript, in Rusher's possession.

67. *Nassau Herald* yearbook; Meth interview; Mueller interview.

68. Rusher, "Progressive Element," iii, 6–7.

69. Ibid., 15–16.

70. Ibid., 10, 6.

71. Ibid., 71, 2, 6, dedication page.

72. Ibid., 16, 108, 17, 38.

73. Donald Bruce Johnson, *The Republican Party and Wendell Willkie* (Urbana, IL: University of Illinois Press, 1960), 42; Raymond Moley, Perspective column, *Newsweek*, February 26, 1940, 13, and March 4, 1940, 56; Rusher, "Progressive Element," 49.

74. Rusher interview, August 24, 2005; Rusher, "Progressive Element," 52, 71.

75. Wendell L. Willkie, "We, the People: A Foundation for a Political Platform for Recovery," *Fortune*, April 1940, 64–65, 168–71. According to one Willkie expert, the response to this article among business leaders "was immediate and extensive" as it was "widely circulated and discussed, and along the eastern seaboard, bankers, industrialists, and financiers began to think about what they could do . . . to foster the Willkie movement." Johnson, *The Republican Party and Wendell Willkie*, 63.

76. Peters, *Five Days in Philadelphia*, 172–73; Neal, *Dark Horse*, 159; Joseph Barnes, *Willkie: The Events He Was Part Of—The Ideas He Fought For* (New York: Simon and Schuster, 1952), 225–27.

77. Rusher, "Progressive Element," 70.

78. Johnson, *The Republican Party and Wendell Willkie*, 125; Peters, *Five Days in Philadelphia*, 24.

79. Neal, *Dark Horse*, 122.

80. Disorganized campaign: ibid., 149.

81. Wendell L. Willkie, *One World* (New York: Simon and Schuster, 1943), 158–62, 180, 101–2.

82. Rusher, "Progressive Element," 84, 108.

83. Johnson, *The Republican Party and Wendell Willkie*, chs. 5, 7–8; Ellsworth Barnard, *Wendell Willkie: Fighter for Freedom* (Marquette, MI: Northern Michigan University Press, 1966), chs. 16, 18, 20.

84. Rusher, "Progressive Element," 83; Neal, *Dark Horse*, 316–18; Rusher interview, April 17, 2006.

85. Rusher interviews, April 15, 2005, and March 23, 2006; vision: Army Air Force record, in Rusher's possession.

86. Rusher interview, April 17, 2006; twenty-one: Rusher, "On Turning 75," syndicated column, September 3, 1998.

87. Rusher interview, April 17, 2006.

88. Rusher interviews, March 23, 2006, and April 17, 2006; interview with Daniel McGrath, November 14, 2007.

89. Major-General S. Woodburn Kirby, *The War Against Japan*, vol. 2, *India's Most Dangerous Hour* (London: Her Majesty's Stationery Office, 1958), 259, and vol. 3, *The Decisive Battles* (1961), 120–21; Wesley Frank Craven and James Lea Cate, eds., *The Army Air Forces in World War II*, vol. 7 (Chicago: University of Chicago Press, 1958), 139.

90. Rusher interview, March 23, 2006.

91. Barry Goldwater to Rusher, July 19, 1985, Rusher Papers, Box 35, File 2.

92. Rusher interview, April 17, 2006.

93. Rusher interviews, April 17, 2006, and April 15, 2005.

94. Barry Goldwater, *With No Apologies: The Personal and Political Memoirs of United States Senator Barry M. Goldwater* (New York: William Morrow, 1979), 37; Alice Rogers Hager, *Wings for the Dragon: The Air War in Asia* (New York: Dodd, Mead, 1945), 250; Albert Mayer, "Americans in India," *Survey Graphic*, March 1947, 204, 206.

95. Date of departure: Rusher to General George E. Stratemeyer, November 12, 1958, Rusher Papers, Reel 2; William Rusher to Evan Rusher, undated May 1945.

## Chapter 2: Young Republican

1. Rusher interview, April 17, 2006. Rusher was later a reserve officer in the Air Force. Appointment and honorable discharge documents, December 17, 1954, and September 28, 1957, personal papers in the possession of Alfred Tong.

2. Rusher interviews, August 24, 2005, and April 17, 2006.

3. Richard O. Ulin, "You Can't Tell a Harvard Man," *Christian Science Monitor*, May 1, 1948, magazine section, 4; Bayard Hooper, "Political Network Controlled by Few," *Harvard Crimson*, May 1, 1948. All *Crimson* articles were accessed online from the archive at www.harvard.edu.

4. "Rusher to Chair Political Forums in Spring Term," *Harvard Crimson*, January 22, 1947; Harold E. Stassen, "Stassen Explains His Town Meeting Idea," *New York Times Magazine*, May 12, 1946, 10, 45; Lewis Wood, "Stassen Creates Open Party Forums," *New York Times*, March 30, 1946, 16.

5. Rusher interviews, August 24, 2005, and April 17, 2006.

6. John T. Flynn, *The Roosevelt Myth* (San Francisco: Fox & Wilkes, 1998), 385. Originally published in 1948.

7. John Earl Haynes and Harvey Klehr, *Venona: Decoding Soviet Espionage in America* (New Haven: Yale University Press, 1999), 337.

8. James Burnham, *The Struggle for the World* (New York: John Day, 1947).

9. Rusher interview, April 17, 2006.

10. Rusher, *The Rise of the Right*, 19. While in law school, Rusher, representing his Republican club, participated in a broadly based "Harvard-Radcliffe Committee to Save the Marshall Plan." It urged that the American program for European economic recovery be amply funded in order to provide genuine reconstruction, not merely relief. "Plan to Save" and "Moravec to Head 'Save Marshall Plan' Project," *Harvard Crimson*, February 13, 1948. On postwar isolationism among congressional and other leading Republicans, see Justus D. Doenecke, *Not to the Swift: The Old Isolationists in the Cold War Era* (Lewisburg, PA: Bucknell University Press, 1979), chs. 3, 5–6.

11. Rusher interviews, August 5, 2003, and April 17, 2006.

12. Rusher interview, August 24, 2005; Lee H. Simowitz, "William Rusher," *Harvard Crimson*, April 2, 1965. According to John Thomson, who was HYRC president in the midfifties, although Rusher and Charlie McWhorter later spoke of each other as the club's cofounders, "there's no doubt that Bill was the driving force" in its establishment. Interview with John Thomson, July 10, 2009.

13. "New Republican Club for Leftist Opposition Recruits This Evening," *Harvard Crimson*, November 4, 1947.

14. "Political Network," *Harvard Crimson*; Rusher interview, April 17, 2006; "Club History," Harvard Republican Club home page, www.harvard.edu, accessed August 31, 2006.

15. "Political Network," *Harvard Crimson*.

16. "HYRC Boosts Membership Over 400," *Harvard Crimson*, April 9, 1948; "Political Network," *Harvard Crimson*; "Republicans Meet HYD Over Radio, Plan New Drive," *Harvard Crimson*, January 24, 1948.

17. "Political Network," *Harvard Crimson*; "GOP Mock Convention Nominates Vandenberg," *Harvard Crimson*, April 30, 1948; Rusher interview, April 17, 2006.

18. Rusher interview, August 24, 2005; *GOP Newsletter*, Harvard Young Republican Club, March 18, 1948, in Rusher's possession; "Douglas Backers Claim Supremacy," *Harvard Crimson*, April 12, 1948.

19. Rusher, "The Mole Caper: Now It Can Be Told," syndicated column, July 6, 1995. For some reason, Rusher did not name the mole.

20. "Democratic Leader Repudiates Truman," *Harvard Crimson*, October 20, 1948; "Former Chief Will Be Tried for 'Treason,'" *Harvard Crimson*, October 21, 1948; "out of their minds": Rusher, "The Mole Caper" column.

21. "serious problem," "putting you to work": Rusher interview, August 24, 2005; William Rusher to Evan Rusher, October 3 and October 4, 1947.

22. Rusher interview, April 15, 2005.

23. Evan Rusher to William Rusher, November 8, 1947; Rusher interview, August 24, 2005.

24. Class standing: Rusher's Federal Bureau of Investigation (FBI) file (77–70977), 1956, personal papers; William Rusher, "One Cheer (and Four Rules) for New York" article manuscript, October 1971, personal papers. Rusher passed the New York State bar exam in March of 1949 and was certified as a member of the bar in June (FBI file).

25. Rusher interview, August 24, 2005.

26. Ibid.; Rusher, *How to Win Arguments*, 11.

27. Rusher interview, August 24, 2005; interview with Frank Shepherd, August 4, 2009.

28. Rusher, "One Cheer" manuscript; Rusher interview, March 29, 2008; Rusher, "Gone Fishing? Well, Not Exactly . . ." column.

29. Rusher, "Another Target for the Trial Lawyers"; Rusher interview, March 29, 2008.

30. Richard Norton Smith, *Thomas E. Dewey and His Times* (New York: Simon and Schuster, 1982), 360–66, 39, 410.

31. "ability to win": Warren Moscow, *Politics in the Empire State* (New York: Knopf, 1948), 31–32; Dewey's background and orientation: Michael Barone, *Our Country: The Shaping of America from Roosevelt to Reagan* (New York: Free Press, 1990), 172–73.

32. Rusher interview, April 17, 2006. In his book on *National Review*, Jeffrey Hart uses the phrase "added a kind of astringency" to describe, in part, Rusher's contribution to the atmosphere at the magazine—a style that "helped keep things on the tracks." Hart, *The Making of the American Conservative Mind*, 148.

33. Smith, *Thomas E. Dewey and His Times*, 30, 24–26, 371.

34. Ibid., 21, 35, 507–8, 527. A particularly rough attack came in a speech in Chicago before a huge crowd on October 25. "In our time," Truman said, "we have seen the tragedy of the Italian and German peoples, who lost their freedom to men who made promises of unity and efficiency and sincerity . . . and it could happen here." He warned of "powerful reactionary forces which are silently undermining our democratic institutions" and accused Dewey of being a "front man" for the kind of people who had supported Hitler and Mussolini. Ibid., 535.

35. Gary A. Donaldson, *Truman Defeats Dewey* (Lexington, KY: University Press of Kentucky, 1999), 209–10; Rusher interview, April 17, 2006.

36. "Democrats Storm Mem Hall to Cheer Party Gains," *Harvard Crimson*, November 3, 1948; Rusher interview, April 17, 2006; "Election Night," *Harvard Crimson*, November 3, 1948.

37. Malcolm Moos, *The Republicans: A History of Their Party* (New York: Random House, 1956), 520; Donaldson, *Truman Defeats Dewey*, 212–13.

38. William A. Rusher, "Thomas E. Dewey, RIP," *National Review*, April 6, 1971, 358.

39. Moscow, *Politics in the Empire State*, 129–130; Rusher interviews, August 24, 2005, and April 17, 2006.

40. Rusher interview, April 17, 2006.

41. Interview with Leon Weil, July 16, 2009.

42. Hometown, Distinguished Flying Cross: Bruce Lambert, "F. Clifton White, 74, Long a Republican Strategist," *New York Times*, January 10, 1993; White, *Suite 3505*, 28.

43. F. Clifton White with Jerome Tuccille, *Politics as a Noble Calling: The Memoirs of F. Clifton White* (Ottawa, IL: Jameson Books, 1994), 55–61, 72, 102–03; congressional race, building political base, status in 1952: White, *Suite 3505*, 28.

44. White, *Politics as a Noble Calling*, 101; "sense of responsibility": White, *Suite 3505*, 29.

45. Interview with Ned Cushing, July 31, 2009; Fernald interview.

46. Rusher, *The Rise of the Right*, 20.

47. Ibid., 100, 17; interview with Wilma Sievertsen Rogalin, August 15, 2009.

48. White, *Politics as a Noble Calling*, 73–74.

49. Fernald interview.

50. Rusher, *The Rise of the Right*, 17–18, 20–22, 28–30.

51. Rusher interview, April 17, 2006.

52. Ibid.

53. Whittaker Chambers, *Witness* (New York: Random House, 1952), 4–17.

54. "already agreed": Rusher interview, April 17, 2006; "no religious beliefs," "philosophical case": Rusher, *The Rise of the Right*, 17, 24–25; "Alpha and Omega," "every published account": Rusher, *Special Counsel*, 17.

55. Rusher, *The Rise of the Right*, 19.

56. Taft's personality: James T. Patterson, *Mr. Republican: A Biography of Robert A. Taft* (Boston: Houghton Mifflin, 1972), 533.

57. Ibid., 530, 560–62.

58. Smith, *Thomas E. Dewey and His Times*, 590, 594.

59. Patterson, *Mr. Republican*, 556; Rusher quoted in Michael Kramer and Sam Roberts, *"I Never Wanted to Be Vice-President of Anything!": An Investigative Biography of Nelson Rockefeller* (New York: Basic Books, 1976), 239.

60. William F. Buckley Jr., *Getting It Right* (Washington: Regnery, 2003), 5.

61. Rusher, *The Rise of the Right*, 19; Rusher interview, March 29, 2008; Rusher, *Special Counsel*, 14.

62. Robert Morris, *No Wonder We Are Losing* (New York: Bookmailer, 1958), 4–38, 82.

63. Ibid., 98–117, 156. Morris and McCarthy committee: Thomas C. Reeves, *The Life and Times of Joe McCarthy: A Biography* (New York: Stein and Day, 1982), 462; Morris cited in David M. Oshinsky, *A Conspiracy So Immense: The World of Joe McCarthy* (New York: Free Press, 1983), 252–53.

64. Howard Rushmore, "Robert Morris," *American Mercury*, March–April 1953, 85; Whittaker Chambers to Buckley, July 17, 1959, in William F. Buckley Jr., ed., *Odyssey of a Friend: Whittaker Chambers' Letters to William F. Buckley, Jr., 1954–1961* (New York: Putnam's, 1969), 257.

65. Weil interview; Rusher, *Special Counsel*, 26–27. Morris's father was known as an active opponent of Hudson County, New Jersey, political boss Frank Hague (Constance L. Hays, "Robert J. Morris Is Dead at 82; Crusader Against Communists," *New York Times*, January 2, 1997). The obituary quoted Chambers's compliment about Morris's work, sourced in note 64, but misrepresented it as a negative contention that Morris "may have been more McCarthyesque than the Senator himself." In fact, Chambers was saying that Morris accomplished more of a constructive nature than McCarthy, whom he believed had harmed the Right more than the Left.

66. Rusher, *The Rise of the Right*, 26, 23–24; Rusher, *Special Counsel*, 14, 17; Rusher interview, August 24, 2005.

67. Farmer interview; Rusher interview, April 17, 2006.

68. Rusher, *How to Win Arguments*, 116–17. Taylor "leaned back against a blackboard . . . lowered his eyes to half-mast, and replied, 'That question is not germane to my topic today.'"

69. Rusher, *The Rise of the Right*, 22.

70. Ibid., 26–27; "disaffection," "quiet participation": Rusher interview, April 17, 2006.

71. Arthur Herman, *Joseph McCarthy: Reexamining the Life and Legacy of America's Most Hated Senator* (New York: Free Press, 2000), 238–52.

72. W. H. Lawrence, "Nixon Says 'Questionable Methods' and 'Reckless Talk' of Red Hunters Are Diversion from GOP Program," *New York Times*, March 14, 1954, 1; "Text of Nixon Reply to Stevenson Attack on the Administration," *New York Times*, March 14, 1954, 44.

73. "McCarthy Says He'll 'Get Rough' No Matter 'How High' His Critics," *New York Times*, March 14, 1954, 1.

74. Rusher, *The Rise of the Right*, 27–28, 31. Similarly, Rusher later recalled to his former *National Review* colleague Brent Bozell that "the first two or three years of the Eisenhower administration had destroyed my faith in the significance of the game I had so carefully schooled myself to play." By 1955, he knew as much as he wanted and thought he needed to know about "the mechanics of American politics." He also felt "fully capable of achieving just about any reasonable personal goal in that field—say, a position of high influence in a Republican administration." Rusher went on to explain that by 1956, he believed—and this proved to be a permanent conviction, he added—that politics could never "really do what needed to be done." His later political activity was simply based on "my personal duty to use that hard-won and otherwise wholly wasted expertise to press the conservative case in political terms whenever and wherever I could." Rusher to L. Brent Bozell Jr., March 6, 1969, Rusher Papers, Box 11, File 13.

  In short, Rusher was saying that although he considered political work a poor second to the Right's intellectual battle in terms of its ultimate value, he knew politics was where he could best contribute. Given that Bozell by the end of the 1960s was himself alienated from politics and was rejecting the conservative movement in his new religious journal *Triumph*, it is possible that Rusher overstated the point in this letter—either as a matter of personal sympathy or as an attempt to explain attractively to a distressed friend why, as he concluded, "I propose to struggle on." During his career at *National Review*, Rusher stressed politics tirelessly, whatever his deepest or occasional thoughts about its value may have been.

75. Herman, *Joseph McCarthy*, 283, 291–93; Rusher interviews, April 16, 2005, and August 24, 2005.

76. Meth interview.

77. Rusher, *The Rise of the Right*, 67.

78. Rusher interview, August 24, 2005; Rusher, *The Rise of the Right*, 56.

79. John L. Hess, "Isador Lubin Dies, 82; In 'Brain Trust,'" *New York Times*, July 8, 1978, 22; "Biographical Sketches of Commissioners of the BLS," *Monthly Labor Review*, January 1955, 50; "Two Good Appointments," editorial, *New York Times*, January 1, 1955, 12.

80. Rusher, *The Rise of the Right*, 56; Rusher interview, August 24, 2005.

81. Leo Egan, "Lubin Confirmed as GOP Yields," *New York Times*, March 2, 1955, 1; Rusher interview, August 24, 2005.

82. "Lubin Confirmed as GOP Yields," *New York Times*, March 2, 1955; "Mr. Lubin Confirmed," editorial, *New York Times*, March 2, 1955, 26.

83. Rusher interview, August 24, 2005.

84. Family history: Rusher interview, March 29, 2008; conversation: Fernald interview.

85. Interview with Diarmuid O'Scannlain, July 22, 2009.

86. John Thomson to author, July 6, 2009.

## Chapter 3: Investigating Communism

1. Weil interview.

2. Morris, *No Wonder We Are Losing*, 194.

3. Rusher, *The Rise of the Right*, 56; Rusher interview, August 24, 2005.

4. Thomson interview; Thomson to author. Lockwood was the governor's "jack of all trades, political ambassador, confessor, and alter ego." Smith, *Thomas E. Dewey and His Times*, 364–65.

5. Rusher, *Special Counsel*, 13, 18–19; "right thing to do": Thomson to author.

6. Rusher, *Special Counsel*, 17–19.

7. Ibid., 14–15.

8. "Investigations: The Eagle's Brood," *Time*, July 11, 1955; "The Press: Eastland v. the Times," *Time*, January 16, 1956; several journalists fired: Edward M. Alwood, "The Hunt for Red Writers: The Senate Internal Security Subcommittee Investigation of Communists in the Press, 1955–56" (Ph.D. diss., University of North Carolina at Chapel Hill, 2000), abstract (http://proquest.cmi.com, document ID 732002801).

9. Rusher, *Special Counsel*, 286.

10. Ibid., 28–29, 62.

11. Ibid., 20–25. Watkins had chaired the special panel that inquired into Senator McCarthy's conduct and recommended censure in 1954. Jenner, a small-town lawyer and a former state legislative leader in Indiana, served in the Senate from 1947 through 1958, holding the ISSC chairmanship in 1953–54 (with Morris as chief counsel). Majority Leader Taft and other Republican colleagues may have given his committee primary responsibility for anticommunist investigation in hopes of reducing McCarthy's prominence. Jenner was McCarthy's most outspoken ally in Congress, or nearly so. Perhaps the best-known example of Jenner's zealotry and temper was his reference, in a 1950 speech, to General George Marshall, former secretary of state and at the time nominated for secretary of defense, as a "front man for traitors." A lengthy and critical study of his career notes that some liberal senators "attested to Jenner's fairness" in actual investigations, and that he correctly believed "his investigations were more workmanlike and less emotional" than McCarthy's. On the other hand, although Jenner's ISSC was "more considerate than McCarthy, its practice of exposing 'Fifth Amendment pleaders' and its interpretation of [Fifth Amendment] use as evidence of communist membership and activity were disturbing at best." Michael Paul Poder, "The Senatorial Career of William

E. Jenner" (Ph.D. diss., University of Notre Dame, 1976), 244–46 (http://proquest.umi. com, document ID 761399391).

12. Rusher, *Special Counsel*, 29, 238–39, 34.

13. Ibid., 31–34; Rusher to J. Anthony Panuch, May 28, 1956, personal papers. Panuch was forced out of the State Department position in 1947 (Herman, *Joseph McCarthy*, 95).

14. Rusher, *Special Counsel*, 29–30.

15. Robert D. Novak, *The Prince of Darkness: 50 Years Reporting in Washington* (New York: Crown Forum, 2007), 39.

16. Rusher, "They're Trying to Rewrite History," syndicated column, June 15, 1989.

17. Rusher, *Special Counsel*, 277–79.

18. Ibid., 138–44.

19. Ibid., 160–69, 180–82.

20. Ibid., 169–73.

21. Ibid., 183–90. Emmerson later described Morris as rude and inquisitorial when they met on March 11 (the day before the first hearing at which he testified that month) despite his expressed full willingness to testify. He also complained that the transcripts of his March 12 and March 21 hearings were released to the press despite the fact they had been held in executive session; the State Department's permission for their release was, he wrote, a cowardly response to "Jenner, Morris, and company." About his own position concerning the relationship between U.S. authorities and Japanese communists, Emmerson recalled that Sanzo Nosaka, head of the Japanese Peoples Emancipation League and cofounder of the Japanese Communist Party, knew the communists wouldn't take over postwar Japan but wanted the party to have the freedom to participate in politics. "In the recommendations that he described to us," Emmerson added, "Nosaka's ideas were mainly consistent with the postsurrender directives already being hammered out in the State Department," such as punishment of war criminals, civil-liberties guarantees, breakup of industrial monopolies, and land reform. "We also knew that our interests would not remain compatible, that a parting of the ways would come sooner or later." John K. Emmerson, *The Japanese Thread: A Life in the U.S. Foreign Service* (New York: Holt, Rinehart and Winston, 1978), 333–40, 203.

22. Rusher, *Special Counsel*, 193–214. Despite the negative publicity from the Norman incident and the earlier ISSC investigation of the press, the American Bar Association's house of delegates in 1959 commended the subcommittee for the professional quality of its work over the years. Ibid., 28.

23. Ibid., 183, 215–27.

24. Ibid., 226–30, 234. Writing in 1978, Emmerson recalled thinking, after the suicide, that Norman "could never have been a conspirator secretly concocting Communist plots against his government and mine." Although he learned many years later that "Norman had joined the Communist party while a student at Cambridge University in March 1935," the scholar-diplomat "loathed totalitarianism" when they knew each other in postwar Japan. Emmerson implicitly agreed with Pearson's explanation that Norman acknowledged that in the prewar years "'he had had mistaken beliefs and had been following a false ideology.'" Emmerson, *The Japanese Thread*, 338–41, 272.

A purportedly thorough review conducted for the Canadian foreign ministry in 1990 concluded that Norman was never an actual member of the American, Canadian, or British Communist Party—"perhaps because the Party preferred it that way"—but had been a communist in the ideological sense and a Soviet sympathizer: "Openly and enthusiastically while a student at Cambridge, 1933–35; less openly but perhaps more dogmatically while in Toronto 1936–37, and Harvard 1936–38. His emancipation from communism was gradual and cannot be pinpointed. After joining the public service in 1939, he cut his Party associates but kept up several friendships among Marxists that he had formed during the 1930s." To superiors in the foreign ministry, Norman "understated . . . the degree of his commitment [in previous years to communism] and also his knowledge of the views and activities of his left-wing friends." The report concluded, however, that he had never been either a spy or an "agent of influence" for the Soviet Union and that there was no evidence to that effect. In addition, his "known services to the Party were trivial." As for his suicide, Norman "did not appear to fear serious new revelations" but nonetheless dreaded a "McCarthyite . . . ruthless" investigation by a subcommittee determined, in the author's view, "to 'get' Lester Pearson as well as himself." Peyton V. Lyon, "The Loyalties of E. Herbert Norman," report prepared for External Affairs and International Trade Canada (foreign ministry), March 18, 1990, 220–21, 229 (http://www.jstor.org; also published in *Labour/LeTravail* 28 [Fall 1991], 219–59).

Rusher told readers in 1986, however, that a new book by professor James Barros of the University of Toronto (*No Sense of Evil—Espionage: The Case of E. Herbert Norman*) established that the diplomat "was a lifelong communist and probably an agent of Soviet intelligence as well." Rusher, "Ottawa's Red-Hot Potato" and "The 'Redbaiters' Were Right," syndicated columns, November 25 and October 30, 1986.

25. Rusher, *Special Counsel*, 248, 239–41. Arthur Herman's relatively recent biography concludes that McCarthy was probably manic-depressive, and that the mild-mannered personality Rusher saw may have been explained by prolonged depression after the senator was politically marginalized (Herman, *Joseph McCarthy*, 329–31).
26. Rusher, *Special Counsel*, 249–50.
27. Rusher interview, April 17, 2006.
28. Moos, *The Republicans*, 518.
29. Rusher, *The Rise of the Right*, 68.
30. White, *Politics as a Noble Calling*, 72; "can openers," "Little states": Rusher interview, April 17, 2006.
31. Rusher interview, April 17, 2006.
32. Rusher to Mr. Hochwald, August 1, 1955, personal papers; Rusher, *The Rise of the Right*, 68.
33. Rusher and Bostwick: Rusher, *The Rise of the Right*, 69; Richard E. Mooney, "Young G.O.P. Hits Eisenhower Stand on 4 of 5 Issues," *New York Times*, June 23, 1957, 1. The fifth contested issue—on which the delegates overwhelmingly agreed with the administration—was Eisenhower's modest civil-rights program. The YRs actually went further, declaring: "We favor an unceasing program of positive policies in civil rights."
34. Rusher, *The Rise of the Right*, 69; headline: Mooney, "Young G.O.P. Hits Eisenhower Stand on 4 of 5 Issues"; Rusher interview, April 17, 2006.
35. McWhorter's personality: Thomson interview. By the time he was fifty, Thomson estimates, "he must have had five hundred of the darned things."
36. Ibid.
37. Rusher interview, April 17, 2006.
38. Chambers to Duncan Norton-Taylor, March 2, 1954, in Whittaker Chambers, *Cold Friday* (New York: Random House, 1964), 221; Chambers to Buckley, Christmas Eve 1958, in Buckley, ed., *Odyssey of a Friend*, 229.
39. Regnery and Buckley quotations: George H. Nash, *The Conservative Intellectual Movement in America Since 1945* (Wilmington, DE: Intercollegiate Studies Institute, 1998), 129, 134; "thinking of . . . a magazine": Judis, *William F. Buckley Jr.*, 114.
40. Rusher, *The Rise of the Right*, 46; Rusher interview, August 24, 2005; William A. Rusher, "Cult of Doubt," *Harvard Times-Republican*, November 3, 1955, personal papers.
41. Buckley interview, July 26, 2005; William F. Buckley Jr., The Ivory Tower, *National Review*, January 11, 1956, 24.
42. William F. Buckley Jr. to Rusher, December 28, 1955, personal papers; Rusher interview, April 17, 2006; visit to Stamford: Rusher, *Special Counsel*, 159. Thanking Moore for putting them in touch, Buckley remarked that meeting Rusher "has already meant a great deal to me." Buckley to Roger Moore, February 28, 1956, William F. Buckley Jr. Papers, Sterling Memorial Library, Yale University, Box 3, File: Moore, Roger 1956–57.

43. William A. Rusher, "The Rebellion Against the Eggheads" manuscript, January 19, 1956, personal papers. Rusher recalled later that in the first half of 1956, "I realized the existence of God had become necessary to my comprehension of the world, and tried—awkwardly at first, but persistently, and at last regularly—to pray to Him." Rusher, "The Columnist Comes in from the Cold," syndicated column, August 4, 1978.

44. Frank Barnett to Rusher, November 10, 1955, personal papers; Malcolm Wilson to Rusher, January 27, 1956, personal papers; *Congressional Record*, January 9, 1956, personal papers; Panuch to Rusher, May 23, 1956, personal papers. Panuch told Rusher his essay was "a trenchant diagnosis of the political malaise of our pseudo-intellectuals who, lacking the courage to embrace Communism openly, have been its most efficient 'carriers' in the United States." He added: "For two decades, the Popular Front coalition of your 'Cult of Doubt' and the Totalitarian Liberals have been the real Fifth Column in the Kremlin's grand design for the political conquest of the United States. In that strategy, the activities of the American card-carrying Communists are essentially a diversionary tactic." In the same letter in which he wrote of his pride in assisting Bob Morris, Rusher replied: "I agree with all you say about the 'real Fifth Column.'" Rusher to Panuch, May 28, 1956, personal papers.

45. Dennis Lyons to Rusher, January 31, 1956, personal papers; Rusher to James E. Bacon Jr., February 15, 1956, personal papers.

46. Rusher to Ernest van den Haag, December 7, 1970, Rusher Papers, Box 94, File 8.

47. Rusher to Charles McWhorter (bc: Clif White), July 26, 1966, and "Notes for a conversation with Charlie McWhorter," undated 1957, Rusher Papers, Reel 33. Similarly, Rusher told another friend, Harvard Young Republican leader Donald Hodel, that his "growing sense of disgust with traditional political methods and personalities" had led him to join *National Review*. He saw his new job as "a terrific challenge, and an opportunity to contribute effectively in the one area that is transcendently important." Rusher to Donald Hodel, August 2, 1957, Rusher Papers, Box 40, File 2.

48. Rusher, *Special Counsel*, 251–54.

49. Ibid., 284; conversation with Buckley: ibid., 285, and Rusher interview, April 17, 2006. Morris ran for the Senate in the New Jersey Republican primary in 1958, finishing a distant third.

50. Buckley interviews, July 26, 2005, and September 17, 2005; Rusher interview, April 17, 2006.

51. Rusher, *Special Counsel*, 285; financial concerns: Rusher, "A Fond Farewell to National Review," syndicated column, April 27, 1989, and Rusher interview, April 17, 2006; "uncomfortable . . . feeling": Rusher, *Special Counsel*, 285.

52. Rusher interview, April 17, 2006; Buckley interview, July 26, 2005.

53. Rusher, *Special Counsel*, 294; date: William A. Rusher, "Now It Can Be Told" (recollections of *National Review* career), *National Review*, January 27, 1989, 36; Rusher interview, April 15, 2005.

## Chapter 4: The Right Publisher

1. Buckley, *Miles Gone By*, 284; Priscilla L. Buckley, *Living It Up at* National Review: *A Memoir* (Dallas: Spence, 2005), 11; "rabbit hutch": Judis, *William F. Buckley Jr.*, 131.

2. Priscilla L. Buckley, "Notes on a Fifth Birthday," *National Review*, November 19, 1960, 307; Priscilla Buckley, *Living It Up at* National Review, 12.

3. Buckley to Gerrish Milliken, undated 1958, Buckley Papers, Box 5; Rusher interview, October 29, 2007.

4. "Began to impose": remarks at Rusher testimonial dinner, in Buckley, *Miles Gone By*, 293.

5. "learned the ropes": Rusher, "Now It Can Be Told," 36.

6. Judis, *William F. Buckley Jr.*, 141–42.

7. Catholic War Veterans announcement, undated circa October 1957, Rusher Papers, Reel 2.

8. Rusher interview, December 22, 2006.

9. "flashing smile": Lee Edwards, *The Conservative Revolution: The Movement That Remade America* (New York: Free Press, 1999), 78; Rusher, *How to Win Arguments*, 63.

10. "Stupid": Rusher interview, August 5, 2003.

11. Debate with Eleanor Roosevelt: Buckley to Rusher, undated 1973, Rusher Papers Box 121, File 6.

12. "Publisher's Statement," *National Review*, November 19, 1955, 5.

13. Rusher, *The Rise of the Right*, 34.

14. Edwards, *The Conservative Revolution*, 77–78; Rusher, *The Rise of the Right*, 34–35.

15. "Apology for a New Review," *Modern Age* 1:1 (Summer 1957), 2–3.

16. Money from Buckley's father: Judis, *William F. Buckley Jr.*, 118; compliment from Chambers: Chambers to Buckley, January 1, 1955, in Buckley, ed., *Odyssey of a Friend*, 95.

17. William H. Brady Jr. to Rusher, January 23, 1961, Rusher Papers, Reel 4.

18. Dan Wakefield, *New York in the Fifties* (New York: Houghton Mifflin, 1992), 264–65.

19. Rusher interview, August 5, 2003.

20. Rusher, *The Rise of the Right*, 44, 112.

21. "Report from the Publisher," *National Review*, July 27, 1957, 101.

22. Bozell: Judis, *William F. Buckley Jr.*, 56–57.

23. Rusher interview, December 22, 2006.

24. Nash, *The Conservative Intellectual Movement*, 133.

25. Buckley to James Burnham, undated 1964–1975, James Burnham Collection, Hoover Institution Archives, Stanford University, Box 5, File 5.26.

26. Judis, *William F. Buckley Jr.*, 117, 148–51, 155–57.

27. "damned thing": ibid., 62; janitor anecdote: William F. Buckley Jr., foreword to John A. Murley and John E. Alvis, eds., *Willmoore Kendall: Maverick of American Conservatives* (Lanham, MD: Lexington Books, 2002), xi.

28. "The Editors of National Review Believe," *National Review*, November 19, 1955, 8.

29. Buckley to Henry Regnery, quoted in Nash, *The Conservative Intellectual Movement*, 371 *n*176.

30. Quoted in Priscilla Buckley, *Living It Up at* National Review, 216.

31. Daniel Kelly, *James Burnham and the Struggle for the World: A Life* (Wilmington, DE: ISI Books, 2002), 34–39; "real world": quoted recollection from Lucius Wilmerding, a close friend of Burnham's.

32. Ibid., 85.

33. Ibid., 99–101.

34. "James Burnham and the Managerial Revolution," in Sonia Orwell and Ian Angus, eds., *The Collected Essays, Journalism, and Letters of George Orwell*, vol. 4 (New York: Harcourt, Brace, 1968), 172–73, 175. Originally published as "Second Thoughts on James Burnham," 1946.

35. Kelly, *James Burnham and the Struggle for the World*, 138–39, 147.

36. Ibid., 149–55, 174–77.

37. Ibid., 195; Judis, *William F. Buckley Jr.*, 122–23. In a resignation letter, Burnham explained that he was neither pro- nor anti-McCarthy. He favored many things the senator had done, and some of his methods, while disapproving of others. He considered the "McCarthyism" label a semantic evasion of the real issue.

38. Reading on honeymoon: Buckley interview, September 17, 2005; Kelly, *James Burnham and the Struggle for the World*, 209–10.

39. Rusher interview, December 22, 2006.

40. Quotations: L. Brent Bozell Jr. to the editors, February 23, 1961, Rusher Papers, Reel 3; Evans interview; interview with David Keene, August 17, 2009; Rusher interview, December 22, 2006.

41. Kevin J. Smant, *Principles and Heresies: Frank S. Meyer and the Shaping of the American Conservative Movement* (Wilmington, DE: ISI Books, 2002), 6–34.

42. "Collectivism Rebaptized," in Frank S. Meyer, *In Defense of Freedom and Related Essays* (Indianapolis: Liberty Fund, 1996), 3–13. Originally published in *Freeman*, July 1955.

43. See Frank S. Meyer, *In Defense of Freedom: A Conservative Credo* (Chicago: Regnery, 1962).

44. Quoted in Smant, *Principles and Heresies*, 129.

45. Hart, *The Making of the American Conservative Mind*, 44; Rusher interview, December 22, 2006.

46. Quoted in Smant, *Principles and Heresies*, 60–61.

47. Interview with John Meyer, August 29, 2009.

48. Chambers to Buckley, undated November 1958 and January 12, 1960, in Buckley, ed., *Odyssey of a Friend*, 216, 280.

49. Rusher interview, August 5, 2003.

50. Sam Tanenhaus, *Whittaker Chambers: A Biography* (New York: Random House, 1997), 500–501, 504–5; Rusher quoted in Judis, *William F. Buckley Jr.*, 159–60.

51. Buckley, *Miles Gone By*, 311 (recollections originally published as "The End of Whittaker Chambers," *Esquire*, September 1962); Tanenhaus, *Whittaker Chambers*, 506.

52. Buckley interview, November 14, 2007.

53. Buckley, 1962 article in *Miles Gone By*, 317; Rusher interview, August 5, 2003.

54. Chambers to Buckley, Christmas Eve 1958, in Buckley, ed., *Odyssey of a Friend*, 229–30.

55. Judis, *William F. Buckley Jr.*, 44–46.

56. Albert Jay Nock, *Our Enemy, the State* (Delavan, WI: Hallberg, 1983), 98, 46–47, 107. Originally published in 1935.

57. Albert Jay Nock, "Isaiah's Job" (originally published in 1933), in William F. Buckley Jr. and Charles R. Kesler, eds., *Keeping the Tablets: Modern American Conservative Thought* (New York: Harper & Row, 1988), 431–41.

58. Willmoore Kendall, "How to Read Richard Weaver: Philosopher of 'We the (Virtuous) People,'" in Nellie D. Kendall, ed., *Willmoore Kendall Contra Mundum* (New Rochelle, NY: Arlington House, 1971), 394.

59. Hart, *The Making of the American Conservative Mind*, 162, 38.

60. Rusher interviews, August 5, 2003, and October 29, 2007.

61. Rusher interviews, August 5, 2003, and October 29, 2007.

62. Rusher, *The Rise of the Right*, 113.

63. Willmoore Kendall to Buckley, undated January 1961 and January 25, 1961, Buckley Papers, Box 15, File: Kendall, Willmoore 1961.

64. Nash, *The Conservative Intellectual Movement*, 230.

65. Comments (originally published in *National Review*'s 1980 anniversary issue) in Buckley, *Miles Gone By*, 290; Kelly, *James Burnham and the Struggle for the World*, 224.

66. Priscilla Buckley, "Notes on a Fifth Birthday," 308.

67. General recollections: Priscilla Buckley, *Living It Up at National Review*, 216–18.

68. Ibid., 5–8; Judis, *William F. Buckley Jr.*, 148.

69. Rusher interview, August 5, 2003; Hart, *The Making of the American Conservative Mind*, 64.

70. Rusher interview, August 5, 2003.

71. Priscilla Buckley, *Living It Up at National Review*, 14; William F. Buckley Jr., "J. McFadden, RIP," *National Review*, November 9, 1998.

72. Rusher interview, October 29, 2007.

73. Rusher interview, December 22, 2006.

74. Buckley, testimonial dinner remarks in *Miles Gone By*, 293.

75. Priscilla Buckley interview; Priscilla Buckley, "Notes on a Fifth Birthday," 308.

76. Not "colossal": Rusher interview, August 5, 2003.

77. Rusher interview, October 29, 2007.

78. Priscilla Buckley, *Living It Up at* National Review, 47–49; condition of building: Rusher to Frederick Scholem, January 13 and January 25, 1966, January 27, 1969, and August 22, 1983, Rusher Papers, Box 113, File 1.

79. Priscilla Buckley, *Living It Up at* National Review, 67; Priscilla Buckley interview.

80. Priscilla Buckley, *Living It Up at* National Review, 99–101.

81. Burnham to Buckley, undated (early 1963), Buckley Papers, Box 26, File: Interoffice January–March 1963.

82. Priscilla Buckley interview.

83. Buckley, testimonial dinner remarks in *Miles Gone By*, 293.

84. Priscilla Buckley interview.

85. Priscilla Buckley, *Living It Up at* National Review, 49–50.

86. Priscilla Buckley interview.

87. Ibid.

88. Rusher, *Special Counsel*, 13; Buckley interview, July 26, 2005.

89. Rusher to "All editors and would-be editors," July 9, 1964. Rusher Papers, Reel 19.

90. Buckley to the editors, November 19, 1957, Buckley Papers, Box 2, File: Interoffice 1955–57; Buckley to Rusher, June 15, 1961, Rusher Papers, Reel 4.

91. Buckley to Rusher, undated 1959–62, Rusher Papers, Reel 4.

92. Buckley interview, November 14, 2007.

93. Rusher to Buckley, March 2, 1962, Rusher Papers, Reel 4.

94. Buckley interview, November 14, 2007.

95. Rusher interview, August 5, 2003.

96. Interview with David Franke, July 28, 2006.

97. Buckley interview, July 26, 2005.

98. Background: "Nixon Said to Find Oppenheimer a Risk," *New York Times*, December 23, 1957. The item briefly reported on Buckley's interview with Nixon, hence the title. Preparation for interview: Rusher, *How to Win Arguments*, 97–99.

99. Rusher, *How to Win Arguments*, 99–100; "hills and dales," "bucking and dodging": Rusher interviews, April 16, 2005, and August 23, 2005. De Toledano was also present at the meeting.

100. Rusher, *How to Win Arguments*, 101; Buckley to Richard Nixon, December 26, 1957, Buckley Papers, Box 3, File: Nichols-Nixon 1955, 1957.

101. Priscilla Buckley interview.

102. Buckley interview, September 17, 2005; Buckley to Rusher, undated 1961–62, Rusher Papers, Reel 4.

103. Buckley interview, September 17, 2005.

104. Gerhart Niemeyer to Buckley, November 4, 1958, Rusher Papers, Reel 11.

105. Rusher to Buckley, November 6, 1958, Rusher Papers, Reel 11.

106. Priscilla Buckley, *Living It Up at* National Review, 187.

107. Rusher interview, December 22, 2006.

108. Garry Wills to Rusher, undated circa 1958–59, Rusher Papers, Reel 2.

109. Buckley interview, November 14, 2007.

110. Nash, *The Conservative Intellectual Movement*, 138.

111. Bertrand de Jouvenel to Buckley, Easter Thursday 1962; Buckley to Jouvenel, July 17, 1962, Buckley Papers, Box 20, File: Jouvenel 1962.

112. Judis, *William F. Buckley Jr.*, 140.

113. Rusher to Buckley, November 21, 1957, Buckley Papers, Box 2, File: Interoffice 1955–57.

114. Rusher to John L. ("Jack") Easton Jr., January 24, 1958, Rusher Papers, Reel 2.

115. Erwin N. Griswold to Rusher, January 21, 1958; Vernon X. Miller to Rusher, January 17, 1958, Rusher Papers, Reel 2.

116. Buckley to Bozell and Rusher, February 4, 1958, Buckley Papers, Box 5, File: Interoffice.
117. Rusher to Wills, February 26, 1958, Rusher Papers, Reel 2.
118. Rusher to William Knowland (recently retired senator from California), February 2, 1959, Rusher Papers, Reel 2; Elizabeth C. Barnes (chair, DAR National Defense Committee) to Rusher, November 7, 1960, Rusher Papers, Reel 3; Rusher to E. E. Moore (vice president, U.S. Steel), August 11, 1958, Rusher Papers, Reel 2; Rusher to Sean L. O'Scannlain, January 23, 1961, Rusher Papers, Reel 12.
119. Katharine C. Briggs to the editors, November 8, 1958, Rusher Papers, Reel 2.
120. *National Review Newsletter* editions, April, May, and July 1958. Rusher Papers, Box 117, File 1.
121. Rusher, *The Rise of the Right*, 72.
122. *National Review Newsletter*, October 1959, Rusher Papers, Box 117, File 1; Rusher to Buckley, November 6, 1958, Rusher Papers, Reel 11.
123. *National Review Newsletter*, October and December 1958, Rusher Papers, Box 117, File 1.
124. Jeffrey Hart, *The American Dissent: A Decade of Modern Conservatism* (Garden City, NY: Doubleday, 1966), 31*n*; "counted down": Keene interview.
125. M. M. [Michael] Mooney to Rusher, Buckley, and James McFadden, August 8, 1962, Buckley Papers, Box 20, File: Interoffice.
126. Frequent problems included long-delayed subscription orders, "a great deal of carelessness" in processing such orders, serious billing errors, and failure to promptly answer customers' letters of complaint. Because the circulation offices were in terrible disarray, letters and checks could be almost anywhere. Causes of these problems included inadequate storage space, poor coordination of operations, too much use of part-time personnel, and too much shifting of employees from one job to another. There was also inadequate instruction or supervision. Buckley to McFadden, May 10, 1962; R. S. (Rosemary) Vance to McFadden, May 16, 1962, Buckley Papers, Box 20, File: Interoffice.
127. Rusher to Buckley, February 27, 1964, Rusher Papers, Reel 18.

## Chapter 5: Speaker, Debater, Advocate, Mentor

1. Cushing interview; Fernald interview.
2. Buckley interview, July 26, 2005.
3. Rusher to William D. Carroll (Democratic club), November 12, 1957, Rusher Papers; Helen Dryhurst (president, New England Women) to Rusher, March 5, 1959, and May 20, 1959, Rusher Papers, Reel 1.
4. Rusher to C. Mildred Pafundi (Brooklyn Heights Republican club), January 14, 1960, Rusher Papers, Reel 1; M. N. (Mrs. A. E.) Bonbrake to Rusher, December 17, 1958, Rusher Papers, Reel 2.
5. Farber interview.
6. James J. Hall to Rusher, March 6, 1962, Rusher Papers, Reel 8.
7. Bell interview.
8. Rusher, *How to Win Arguments*, 68; Rusher interview, October 29, 2007.
9. Farber interview.
10. Rusher, *The Rise of the Right*, 77; Judis, *William F. Buckley Jr.*, 175–76.
11. Rusher, *The Rise of the Right*, 77–78.
12. Rusher interview, October 29, 2007.
13. William F. Buckley Jr., "Disorganized We March," syndicated column, February 3, 1963. The Buckley columns cited are generally accessible through the "Buckley Online" archive, www.hillsdale.edu.
14. Importance of Agony meetings to Meyer-Rusher faction: Smant, *Principles and Heresies*, 136–40.

15. John Meyer interview.
16. Burnham to Buckley, undated (early 1963), Buckley Papers, Box 26, File: Interoffice January–March 1963.
17. James Burnham, *Suicide of the West: An Essay on the Meaning and Destiny of Liberalism* (New Rochelle, NY: Arlington House, 1964), 32, 297, 301–2.
18. Frank S. Meyer, "Conservatism and Crisis: A Reply to Father Parry," in Meyer, *In Defense of Freedom*, 174–79. Originally published in *Modern Age*, Winter 1962–63. Meyer actually equivocated on the power of liberalism in Congress and the state legislatures. In the same piece, he said those institutions were only a "partial" exception to liberal predominance at "the heights of our society."
19. Buckley interview, September 17, 2005.
20. Buckley to Rusher, April 14, 1964, Buckley Papers, Box 30, File: Interoffice January–July 1964; Buckley, remarks in *National Review* twenty-fifth anniversary issue, in Buckley, *Miles Gone By*, 289.
21. Bell interview.
22. Rusher interview, December 22, 2006.
23. Buckley interview, September 17, 2005.
24. Rusher interview, October 30, 2007.
25. Smant, *Principles and Heresies*, 136, 140; Rusher interviews, December 22, 2006, and August 5, 2003.
26. Priscilla Buckley interview.
27. Rusher to Buckley, February 9, 1962, Rusher Papers, Reel 4. Although Rusher's memos and nearly all of his correspondence were typewritten, the Rusher Papers for the 1960s are generally on microfilm and were sometimes poorly reproduced. Sometimes a word, sentence, or paragraph—and very occasionally an entire letter or memo—is unintelligible.
    David Franke, a national and New York–area YAF leader, remembers that Burnham not only approved of the organization's activities but also was quite interested in hearing about them. Franke interview.
28. Buckley interview, September 17, 2005.
29. Priscilla Buckley interview; Kelly, *James Burnham and the Struggle for the World*, 221–22.
30. Priscilla Buckley interview.
31. Judis, *William F. Buckley Jr.*, 173–74; description of new policy: Buckley to "Writers for National Review," April 1, 1959, Rusher Papers, Reel 4.
32. Positions of Schwarz and Judd: Donald T. Critchlow, *The Conservative Ascendancy: How the GOP Right Made Political History* (Cambridge, MA: Harvard University Press, 2007), 58–59.
33. Frank Meyer to Buckley, April 23, 1961, Buckley Papers, Box 14, File: Interoffice; Judis, *William F. Buckley Jr.*, 198.
34. Ibid., 194–96.
35. Rusher to the editors, April 3, 1961, Rusher Papers, Reel 4.
36. Rusher to Bozell (cc: Buckley and Meyer), September 28, 1961, Rusher Papers, Reel 3.
37. Meyer to the editors, January 17 and February 4, 1962, Buckley Papers, Box 20, File: Interoffice.
38. Judis, *William F. Buckley Jr.*, 198–99.
39. Rusher to Buckley, February 20, 1962, Rusher Papers, Reel 4.
40. Judis, *William F. Buckley Jr.*, 199–200.
41. Ibid.
42. Ibid., 186–87.
43. Survey result: Rusher to Sean O'Scannlain, January 23, 1961, Rusher Papers, Reel 12.
44. Rusher to Buckley, August 14, 1961, Rusher Papers, Reel 4.
45. Rusher to Buckley, May 23, 1963, Buckley Papers, Box 26, File: Interoffice April–December 1963.
46. Ibid.

47. Hugh W. Barber Jr. to Rusher, January 11, 1961, and Rusher to Barber, January 16, 1961, Rusher Papers, Reel 3.

48. Fernald interview.

49. Interview with Tom Van Sickle, August 27, 2009.

50. Bell interview.

51. Interview with Anne Edwards, November 18, 2007.

52. Viguerie interviews, July 28, 2006, and November 15, 2007.

53. Gregory L. Schneider, *Cadres for Conservatism: Young Americans for Freedom and the Rise of the Contemporary Right* (New York: New York University Press, 1999), 43–44; Viguerie interview, July 28, 2006.

54. Viguerie interview, July 28, 2006.

55. John A. Andrew III, *The Other Side of the Sixties: Young Americans for Freedom and the Rise of Conservative Politics* (New Brunswick, NJ: Rutgers University Press, 1997), 67–68; Franke interview. The loyalty-oath issue arose from the National Defense Education Act of 1958, which increased spending on scientific and technical training in schools and universities. It required students who received loans from the government under its programs to swear loyalty to the Constitution and to sign an affidavit certifying they were not members of any subversive organization. The presidents of Harvard and Yale announced that this provision was unacceptable to them, and Senator John F. Kennedy sponsored a bill to repeal it. Caddy and Franke formed their group to defend the controversial provision. It started chapters on thirty campuses and lobbied members of Congress on the issue. Kennedy's bill passed the Senate but died in a House committee. Schneider, *Cadres for Conservatism*, 21–23.

56. Franke interview.

57. Interview with Stanley Goldstein, December 13, 2005; Cushing interview.

58. Goldstein interview; interview with Robert Bauman, August 15, 2009.

59. Andrew, *The Other Side of the Sixties*, 54–55, 67; Schneider, *Cadres for Conservatism*, 27–33.

60. Marvin Liebman, *Coming Out Conservative: An Autobiography* (San Francisco: Chronicle Books, 1992), 151.

61. Rusher, *The Rise of the Right*, 89–90.

62. Andrew, *The Other Side of the Sixties*, 83; Schneider, *Cadres for Conservatism*, 40.

63. Wakefield, *New York in the Fifties*, 270; Franke interview. Franke headed YAF's Greater New York Area Council until 1963. The council, which claimed sixty active chapters, was a particularly active part of YAF. In this period, it "organized an anticommunist demonstration in Washington, marched in support of HUAC hearings, picketed embassies and consular offices, held meetings to discuss important issues, and helped in local political campaigns." The New York–area chapters, according to Franke, were "pretty antagonistic toward things the national group were doing because we were in the trenches doing stuff and they were issuing press releases." Schneider, *Cadres for Conservatism*, 38.

64. Bauman interview.

65. Lee Edwards interview, July 31, 2006.

66. Interview with William Cotter, September 4, 2009; Rusher, *The Rise of the Right*, 115.

67. Schneider, *Cadres for Conservatism*, 41–42.

68. Ibid., 41–43; "access . . . puppeteers": Cotter interview. Cotter told Gregory Schneider, the author of a substantial book on YAF, that Liebman was (in Schneider's words) "a pushover in disputes, which was why he needed Rusher, a tougher infighter, to help him through this." Schneider, *Cadres for Conservatism*, 200 *n*59.

69. Interview with Douglas Caddy, July 29, 2009.

70. For Phillips's account—undisputed in both books—see Schneider, *Cadres for Conservatism*, 43–44; and Rick Perlstein, *Before the Storm: Barry Goldwater and the Unmaking of the American Consensus* (New York: Hill and Wang, 2001), 155–56. For Caddy on Liebman's allegedly self-serving relationship to YAF, see Schneider, *Cadres for Conservatism*, 47.

71. Rusher to Bozell (cc: Buckley and Meyer), September 28, 1961, Rusher Papers, Reel 3; Schneider, *Cadres for Conservatism*, 53–54.

72. Ibid.; "keep the meeting going": Lee Edwards interview, July 31, 2006.

73. Rusher to Buckley, Marvin Liebman, and Meyer, September 5, 1961, Rusher Papers, Reel 3.

74. Cotter interview.

75. Carol Dawson to author, September 3, 2009.

76. Rusher to Bozell (cc: Buckley and Meyer), September 28, 1961; Rusher, *The Rise of the Right*, 115.

77. Lee Edwards interview, July 31, 2006; Caddy interview.

78. Schneider, *Cadres for Conservatism*, 49, 202 *n*95.

79. Caddy interview; Bauman interview.

80. Schneider, *Cadres for Conservatism*, 47–48.

81. Andrew, *The Other Side of the Sixties*, 115, 122–25; Schneider, *Cadres for Conservatism*, 52–54.

82. Viguerie interview, November 15, 2007; Franke interview.

83. Rusher to Bozell (cc: Buckley and Meyer), September 28, 1961, Rusher Papers, Reel 3.

84. Niemeyer to Buckley, July 20, 1961, Buckley Papers, Box 15, File: Niemeyer.

85. Meyer to the editors, September 3, 1961, Buckley Papers, Box 14, File: Interoffice; Rusher to Buckley, September 14, 1961, Rusher Papers, Reel 4.

86. Rusher to Bozell (cc: Buckley and Meyer), September 28, 1961, Rusher Papers, Reel 3. The event was hosted by the YAF of Bergen County, New Jersey.

87. Ibid.

88. Ibid.

89. Perlstein, *Before the Storm*, 151–52, 156–57; Critchlow, *The Conservative Ascendancy*, 63; Andrew, *The Other Side of the Sixties*, 155–62.

90. Rusher to Buckley, March 2, 1962, Rusher Papers, Reel 4.

91. Rusher to Buckley, March 12, 1962, ibid.

92. Rally description: Schneider, *Cadres for Conservatism*, 52, and Perlstein, *Before the Storm*, 164; cheers for *National Review*: Rusher to Buckley, March 12, 1962, Rusher Papers, Reel 4.

93. Conservative Party prospectus: Judis, *William F. Buckley Jr.*, 190–91; 1956 national effort: ibid., 145; "plain racists": quoted in Kelly, *James Burnham and the Struggle for the World*, 228.

94. Discussion of rationale and immediate plans for a conservative party in New York: Buckley to "All Concerned," January 22, 1957, Buckley Papers, Box 1, File: Buckley—Conservative Activity; 1957 meeting, Rusher given responsibility: Judis, *William F. Buckley Jr.*, 190.

95. Rusher interview, August 23, 2005.

96. Rusher, *The Rise of the Right*, 98.

97. J. Daniel Mahoney, *Actions Speak Louder* (New Rochelle, NY: Arlington House, 1968), 15.

98. Conservative Party press release, July 26, 1962, Rusher Papers, Reel 8.

99. Viguerie interview, November 15, 2007.

100. Rusher to Bozell (cc: Buckley and Meyer), September 28, 1961, Rusher Papers, Reel 3.

101. Conservative Party press release, June 28, 1962, Rusher Papers, Reel 8; Kramer and Roberts, "*I Never Wanted to Be Vice-President of Anything!*," 239; Rusher, *Special Counsel*, 108.

102. Rusher to Buckley, October 3, 1962, Buckley Papers, Box 20, File: Interoffice.

## Chapter 6: The Insurgent

1. Communist threat worse: Rusher to James L. ("Lew") Kirby Jr., February 17, 1958, Rusher Papers, Reel 2.

2. Eisenhower on Warren: Stephen E. Ambrose, *Eisenhower*, vol. 2, *The President* (New York: Simon and Schuster, 1984), 128–29. Decades later, most conservatives would think better of Eisenhower. In addition, his lack of conservatism was a matter of degree and perspective. Ike was really a conservative and became more of one in office, according to relatively liberal former speechwriter and counselor Emmet John Hughes. He accepted the New Deal and Truman's Fair Deal "as a matter of political necessity" and was best understood, more generally, as a man of strong will who "reserved his greatest force for keeping unwanted things from being done." But in Hughes's opinion, Eisenhower's "grasp did not seem firm; his manner was kind, but uncertain; his words were benign, but unclear." His foreign policy was "beset by . . . inner contradictions." Emmet John Hughes, *The Ordeal of Power: A Political Memoir of the Eisenhower Years* (New York: Atheneum, 1963), 333, 360, 343–44.

3. Arthur Larson, *A Republican Looks at His Party* (New York: Harper, 1956), 10, 19, 197.

4. "The Magazine's Credenda," *National Review*, November 19, 1955, 6.

5. Burnham to Buckley, August 25, 1956, Buckley Papers, Box 2, File: General Correspondence 1954–57.

6. "So Long, Ike," editorial, *National Review*, January 14, 1961, 9.

7. L. Brent Bozell, "The 1958 Elections: Coroner's Report," *National Review*, November 22, 1958, 334–35.

8. James J. Kilpatrick, "Down to the Firehouse," *National Review*, December 20, 1958, 397–98.

9. Rogalin interview; Thomson interview; Rusher, *The Rise of the Right*, 78; Rusher encouraged Jenner: Rusher, *Special Counsel*, 23–24; Novak, *Prince of Darkness*, 41; Thomson interview.

10. "New Jersey Verdict for Liberalism," *New York Herald Tribune* editorial, April 21, 1960; Joseph Alsop, "Nixon and the 'Conservatives,'" *Herald Tribune* column, undated 1960, Buckley Papers, Box 10, File: Morris, Robert.

11. Quoted in Andrew, *The Other Side of the Sixties*, 28.

12. Critchlow, *The Conservative Ascendancy*, 46–47, 297 *n7*. According to another account, Manion got a more favorable reception from Goldwater at this initial meeting: the senator seemed to be losing ideological confidence in Nixon and seemed to think the party couldn't win with either the vice president or Rockefeller. Goldwater felt that he had political disadvantages as a candidate himself and that he was unqualified to be president given his limited education. But in addition to not repudiating his visitors' plan, he seemed rather pleased with it. Lee Edwards, *Goldwater: The Man Who Made a Revolution* (Washington: Regnery, 1995), 106.

13. Edwards, *Goldwater*, 112–15.

14. Perlstein, *Before the Storm*, 51; Robert Alan Goldberg, *Barry Goldwater* (New Haven: Yale University Press, 1995), 139.

15. Goldberg, *Barry Goldwater*, 104–11.

16. Perlstein, *Before the Storm*, 36–39.

17. Ibid., 39–42.

18. Rusher interview, December 22, 2006.

19. Robert D. Novak, *The Agony of the G.O.P. 1964* (New York: Macmillan, 1965), 27.

20. J. William Middendorf II, *A Glorious Disaster: Barry Goldwater's Presidential Campaign and the Origins of the Conservative Movement* (New York: Basic Books, 2006), 29.

21. Perlstein, *Before the Storm*, 58; Russell Kirk to Buckley, December 20, 1961, Buckley Papers, Box 15, File: Kirk, Russell, General Correspondence.

22. Liebman, *Coming Out Conservative*, 166.

23. Goldberg, *Barry Goldwater*, 164; Judis, *William F. Buckley Jr.*, 221.

24. Stephen E. Ambrose, *Nixon: The Education of a Politician 1913–1962* (New York: Simon and Schuster, 1987), 553–54.

25. White, *Suite 3505*, 23–24; Goldberg, *Barry Goldwater*, 145–46.

26. Goldberg, *Barry Goldwater*, 145–46. According to former YAF leader Carol Dawson, there was a good deal of movement sentiment in the Youth for Nixon organization at the convention. Many of its members were also "strong Goldwaterites." She and others "were not all that naïve" about Nixon, but were nonetheless "happy to have Nixon rather than Nelson Rockefeller." Dawson to author.

27. L. Brent Bozell, "Goldwater's Leadership: An Assessment," *National Review*, August 13, 1960, 74–75; Rusher, *The Rise of the Right*, 87–89.

28. Earl Mazo, *Richard Nixon: A Political and Personal Portrait* (New York: Harper, 1959), 282, 294. The biography, although independent rather than a Nixon product, was written, published, and read in the context of his likely presidential campaign. Specific foreign-policy positions: Ambrose, *Nixon: The Education of a Politician*, 617.

29. Rusher interview, April 17, 2006.

30. Chambers to Buckley, March 16, 1960, in Buckley, ed., *Odyssey of a Friend*, 284–85.

31. Perlstein, *Before the Storm*, 76.

32. Bozell to Hubbard Russell, July 24, 1962, Rusher Papers, Reel 3.

33. Priscilla Buckley interview.

34. Rusher interview, October 30, 2007.

35. Comment on Casey: O'Scannlain interview.

36. Meyer to the editors, May 10, 1960, Buckley Papers, Box 10, File: Interoffice.

37. Rusher to Buckley, October 10, 1960, ibid.

38. Rusher to Buckley, September 14, 1960, ibid.

39. Burnham to Buckley, October 9, 1960, ibid.

40. Priscilla Buckley to Buckley, undated 1960, ibid.

41. Buckley to Burnham, October 11, 1960, ibid.

42. "National Review and the 1960 Elections," editorial, *National Review*, October 22, 1960, 233–34.

43. Rusher to Arthur W. ("Nick") Arundel, November 14, 1960, Rusher Papers, Reel 3.

44. "Who Lost the Election?," editorial, *National Review*, November 19, 1960, 300.

45. Meeting: Thomson interview; election irregularities and White's desire to contest the election: White, *Suite 3505*, 24–25.

46. L. Brent Bozell, "The Challenge to Conservatives, Part 1": *National Review*, November 19, 1960, 343; Frank S. Meyer, "Only Four Years to 1964," ibid., 344; "Senator Goldwater Speaks His Mind: An Interview with L. Brent Bozell," *National Review*, January 14, 1961, 13–14. Bozell told readers it would be dangerous for a conservative to win the nomination under the wrong circumstances. If Kennedy and the Democrats were too popular in 1964, a losing Goldwater campaign could "deliver the conservative movement a crippling, 'We told you so' defeat." The real chance for the movement might occur in eight years, not four. Bozell, "The Challenge to Conservatives, Part 2," *National Review*, January 14, 1961, 12.

47. Rusher to William K. Runyeon, November 14, 1960, quoted in Andrew, *The Other Side of the Sixties*, 77–78.

48. Rusher, *The Rise of the Right*, 98.

49. Rusher to Bozell, March 23, 1961, Rusher Papers, Reel 3. In a similarly negative spirit, he told Stan Evans two months later: "A serious interest in conservatism is simply incompatible with success in the Republican party today." Andrew, *The Other Side of the Sixties*, 150.

50. "Appalled": Rusher quoted in White, *Suite 3505*, 27; "darkest days": Rusher, *The Rise of the Right*, 95.

51. White, *Suite 3505*, 27.

52. Ibid., 30–31, 33.

53. Rusher, *The Rise of the Right*, 78–79.

54. Ibid., 98–100; Rusher to John Ashbrook, July 13, 1961, Rusher Papers, Reel 3. "I have just discovered," he wrote happily, "that I am a good personal friend of at least four

Republican state chairmen." Rusher to Daniel G. Buckley Jr., July 13, 1961, Rusher Papers, Reel 4.

55. White, *Suite 3505*, 32; Rusher, *The Rise of the Right*, 100–101.

56. White, *Suite 3505*, 32–33; Stephen Shadegg, *What Happened to Goldwater? The Inside Story of the 1964 Republican Campaign* (New York: Holt, Rinehart and Winston, 1965), 38. Shadegg's son, also named Stephen, was elected to the House in 1994 and served through 2010.

57. White, *Suite 3505*, 32–35.

58. Rusher interview, December 22, 2006.

59. White, *Suite 3505*, 37–38.

60. Van Sickle interview.

61. Rusher interview, December 22, 2006.

62. White, *Suite 3505*, 37–39; Rusher interview, December 22, 2006; Rusher, *The Rise of the Right*, 101–102, 107.

63. White, *Suite 3505*, 40–42. The fourth game of the World Series had been played that day. "All afternoon," a participant in the meeting told White, "not one of those guys ever even asked who was winning the ball game." Ibid., 42. The complexity of the task they faced, whether it be nominating Goldwater or simply maximizing conservative clout at the national convention, was well expressed in this observation: "There are fifty such independent systems of law on delegate choice, and as they change from year to year, only a political technician with staff can keep in mind all their intricacies, dates, sharp and pointed legal distinctions, and dominant personalities." Theodore H. White, *The Making of the President 1964* (New York: Atheneum, 1969), 131.

64. Rusher to Goldwater, May 3, 1961, Rusher Papers, Reel 16. Goldwater did tell Rusher that he considered White a useful asset to the party: "It turns out that everyone I speak to knows Cliff [*sic*] White and has a high regard for him and his political judgment." At the moment, the RNC was too poor to hire him. Otherwise, "I feel certain we could use this man." Goldwater seemed to mean that White either expected or would expect too high a salary, although he might have meant that the RNC couldn't afford to create a position for him. Goldwater to Rusher, May 16, 1961, Rusher Papers, Reel 16.

65. White, *Suite 3505*, 43–44; Rusher, *The Rise of the Right*, 104–6.

66. White, *Suite 3505*, 44–48.

67. Rusher interviews, August 5, 2003, and December 22, 2006.

68. White, *Politics as a Noble Calling*, 141–42; Rusher, *The Rise of the Right*, 110.

69. Goldberg, *Barry Goldwater*, 164. At midyear, a *Time* article had described Goldwater as "the hottest political figure this side of Jack Kennedy." No other Republican was in greater demand. Since March alone, Goldwater's Senate office had received more than 650 written invitations, and hundreds of telephone requests, for appearances. Visitors crowded around the office, "hoping to earn a passing handclasp or a hastily scrawled autograph." White wasn't surprised, having begun to hear reports from around the country of Goldwater's increasing popularity. White, *Suite 3505*, 30–31.

70. White, *Suite 3505*, 52–54.

71. Rusher interview, October 29, 2007.

72. Rusher, *The Rise of the Right*, 140–42. Campaign chronicler Theodore White remembered him in the 1960 Nixon campaign: "a pale young man with China-blue eyes, given to jaunty bow ties, very courteous yet quite tense." T. H. White, *The Making of the President 1964*, 91.

73. Lee Edwards interview, November 16, 2007.

74. Rusher, *The Rise of the Right*, 111.

75. Ibid., 112.

76. "Each other's enthusiasm": Shadegg, *What Happened to Goldwater?*, 58.

77. White, *Suite 3505*, 75–76; Rusher interview, December 22, 2006; Lee Edwards interview, November 16, 2007; "Rusher's . . . optimism": Edwards, *Goldwater*, 146. Rusher told

Bozell after the cadre's next national meeting, in December, that $250,000 "was pledged then and there." He added: "More important, the finance boys did not blanch when we told them we would need $3,200,000 for the whole period 1963–4." Rusher to Bozell, December 21, 1962, Rusher Papers, Reel 3.

78. Quoted in Rusher to *New Individualist Review* (letter to the editor), undated 1965, Rusher Papers, Reel 31.

79. Ambrose, *Nixon: The Education of a Politician,* 670. As if in direct contradiction to Nixon's take on the midterms, Meyer wrote that the campaign had signified "a basic shift in the structure of American politics," because media commentators analyzed the results in terms of "conservative-Liberal confrontation," not parties. "This is new political language, a coming-of-age of conservatism." Frank S. Meyer, "The 1962 Elections: The Turning of the Tide," *National Review,* December 4, 1962, 434.

80. Rusher to Burnham, October 21, 1958, Rusher Papers, Reel 11.

81. White, *Suite 3505,* 85–88.

82. William A. Rusher, "Crossroads for the GOP," *National Review,* February 12, 1963, 109–12. Adding to Rusher's case for Republican growth in the South prior to 1964 is the fact that party "identification" in the region had changed very substantially during the past decade. Polls indicated that white southerners' partisan ID—the party a voter says he generally supports—was 9 percent Republican in 1952 and 21 percent Republican in 1960. In those eight years, Democratic ID also declined significantly, from 78 percent to 60 percent. Earl Black and Merle Black, *The Rise of Southern Republicans* (Cambridge, MA: Harvard University Press, 2002), 209. As Rusher suggested in his comments on southern social developments, the more competitive results in a few presidential elections and the 1962 House races were only part of the case for a large Republican opportunity.

The change in southern party ID is especially interesting in light of the fact that President Eisenhower appointed Chief Justice Warren, who wrote the *Brown v. Board of Education* school integration decision in 1954—to which southern political leaders, nearly all of whom were still Democrats, pledged what became known as "massive resistance"; signed the modest Civil Rights Act of 1957; and angered many southerners in the latter year by sending federal troops to enforce desegregation at a Little Rock, Arkansas, high school. While Eisenhower did not generally favor mandatory integration or strong civil-rights laws, neither did his Democratic opponent in 1952 and 1956, Adlai Stevenson. In addition, although Kennedy won a larger majority of the black vote in 1960 than Stevenson had, Nixon was substantively about as supportive of the civil-rights agenda as his opponent. In view of all this, the changing party ID numbers since 1952 would seem to suggest the soundness of Rusher's argument that a new southern demographic, not vehemently opposed to civil-rights liberalization, was doing much to strengthen the GOP.

83. Evans interview. Rusher did not know, a year and a half beforehand, that Goldwater would vote against the Civil Rights Act—or whether he would vote on it: President Johnson and Senate allies had to bypass the Judiciary Committee to obtain a floor vote in 1964. Thus, he couldn't assume what certainly became a large bonus for Goldwater in the Deep South in the general election—his 87 percent in Mississippi, for instance—resulting from such a stark division between the senator and Johnson. In addition, Rusher's essay was written months before civil rights rose from a major issue to an enormous issue in the South, with the Birmingham demonstrations and police violence, and Kennedy's endorsement of the Civil Rights Act, in the spring of 1963. Finally, it should be noted that he referred not just to 1964, when civil rights clearly would be of political importance, but also to 1968 "and all the years beyond."

The liberal journalist Theodore White, in his book on the 1964 election, cited the existence of a new southern middle class that "felt a deep and abiding contempt . . . for the one-party courthouse politicians who have chained the White South to the past by promising, in recompense, only to shackle the Negroes in an endless segregated servitude." Although he lamented the Goldwaterite capture of the southern GOP as a "distortion" of this otherwise healthy trend toward two-party politics, he also described the region's Goldwater leaders in respectful terms: "men between thirty and forty years old, city people, well-bred, moderate segregationists, efficient, more at ease at suburban cocktail parties than when whiskey-belting in courthouse chambers." T. H. White, *The Making of the President 1964*, 136–37.

84. "The Folly of Factionalism, Or How to Fail Without Even Trying," *New York Herald Tribune*, editorial, December 5, 1962, 26, Rusher Papers, Box 154, File 7.

85. White, *Suite 3505*, 102–12.

86. Rusher to F. Clifton White, January 10, 1963, Rusher Papers, Reel 17.

87. White, *Suite 3505*, 115–18.

88. Rusher to Buckley, January 14, 1963, Rusher Papers, Reel 16.

89. Shadegg, *What Happened to Goldwater?*, 46.

90. Goldberg, *Barry Goldwater*, 169; Goldwater, *With No Apologies*, 161. Goldwater recalled here that he also saw a large difference between merely being president and having a strong impact as president. There was, in particular, the "stubborn resistance inherent in the bureaucracy" and the difficulty of getting Congress to act. Edwards, a biographer and former aide, would conclude that a major part of Goldwater's reluctance was his concern about the effect an "overwhelming loss" would have on the conservative movement, should it occur. Edwards, *The Conservative Revolution*, 112. Bozell had, in *National Review* after the 1960 election, made the same point about the hazard of such a campaign.

91. Goldwater to Rusher, June 8, 1984, Rusher Papers, Box 35, File 2.

92. Goldberg, *Barry Goldwater*, 78.

93. Rusher interview, December 22, 2006.

94. Quoted in Rusher, *The Rise of the Right*, 142–43.

95. Goldwater to Rusher, January 22, 1963, Rusher Papers, Reel 16.

96. Rusher to Goldwater, January 23, 1963, Rusher Papers, Reel 16. Rusher's letter also touted his forthcoming *National Review* essay about the Republican opportunity in the South, saying its "general strategic view" was being "adopted by many, many professional Republicans, including potential delegates."

## Chapter 7: Goldwater Feels a Draft

1. Rusher to Buckley, February 5, 1963, Buckley Papers, Box 26, File: Interoffice January–March 1963. But Bill Middendorf, also present at the meeting, recorded in his notes that Goldwater explicitly left open the possibility he might run for president. Middendorf, *A Glorious Disaster*, 30–31.

2. White, *Suite 3505*, 120–23; Rusher, *The Rise of the Right*, 144–45.

3. Rusher, *The Rise of the Right*, 145; White, *Suite 3505*, 123.

4. White, *Suite 3505*, 123–25; Rusher, *The Rise of the Right*, 145.

5. White, *Suite 3505*, 125, 128.

6. Rusher to Buckley, February 20, 1963, Rusher Papers, Reel 16.

7. Meyer to Buckley, February 27, 1963, Buckley Papers, Box 26, File: Interoffice January–March 1963.

8. Rusher to Buckley, March 1, 1963, Rusher Papers, Reel 16.

9. Rusher, *The Rise of the Right*, 145–46.

10. Perlstein, *Before the Storm*, 190.

11. Book review manuscript, February 5, 1965, Rusher Papers, Reel 31.

12. James Jackson Kilpatrick, "Goldwater Country," *National Review*, April 9, 1963, 282.

13. L. Brent Bozell, "Goldwater for President: Part 2. Is it Feasible?" *National Review*, April 23, 1963, 313.

14. Interview with Peter O'Donnell, July 27, 2009; Cushing interview.

15. Novak, *The Agony of the G.O.P.*, 144.

16. Book review manuscript, February 5, 1965, Rusher Papers, Reel 31.

17. Rusher to Peter O'Donnell, June 11, 1963, Rusher Papers, Reel 17.

18. Ibid.

19. Rusher to the editor, *New York Herald Tribune*, July 3, 1963, Rusher Papers, Reel 17. The latest editorial warned that "highly vocal groups" at a recent RNC meeting and a recent YR convention had seemed to favor a candidate and platform "that will be soft on civil rights." The intent was "a 'lily-white' party . . . as immoral a political act as any by a major party in American history." It would be "treason to all the party has stood for." The *Trib* further raised the prospect of a Republican national convention that "courts the White Citizens' Councils and the Ku-Klux Klan." This would alienate independents and "write off much of the heart and brain of Republicanism, leaders and followers alike." "Keep the Party Republican," *New York Herald Tribune*, editorial, July 2, 1963, 18, Rusher Papers, Box 154, File 7.

20. Rockefeller statement: quoted in Perlstein, *Before the Storm*, 224; statement quoted and Goldwater's reaction: Novak, *The Agony of the G.O.P.*, 207–11; Rockefeller on not backing Goldwater, ibid., 216. In response to Buckley's request for thoughts on the civil-rights issue from the senior editors and the publisher, Rusher suggested that the Commerce Clause, the constitutional warrant for the public-accommodations provisions of the eventual 1964 Civil Rights Act, did not authorize an antidiscrimination law for hotels, restaurants, and the like—facilities Rusher considered for the most part "purely local." He added that perhaps the president could bring "his *moral force* (if any) to bear" against discrimination in public accommodations, but that he saw no reason why *National Review* shouldn't "go right on … warning that federal force is the poorest of all possible ways to enforce integration" in such facilities. More broadly, Rusher remarked here that liberal white politicians should be careful not to exploit the civil-rights issue or to promote unrealistic expectations among blacks. He believed the more moderate black leaders—"their pastors" and those in agreement with them—were focused on the sort of legislation under discussion, a position Rusher considered realistic although he opposed it himself. Rusher to Buckley, June 18, 1963, Rusher Papers, Reel 16.

21. Rusher to Buckley, September 24, 1963, Rusher Papers, Reel 16.

22. William A. Rusher, "The Draft Goldwater Drive: A Progress Report," *National Review*, September 10, 1963, 187.

23. Bell interview.

24. Judis, *William F. Buckley Jr.*, 222–24.

25. T. H. White, *The Making of the President 1964*, 320n.

26. Middendorf, *A Glorious Disaster*, 51.

27. Lee Edwards interview, July 31, 2006; Barry M. Goldwater with Jack Casserly, *Goldwater*, (New York: Doubleday, 1988), 148.

28. Novak, *The Agony of the G.O.P.*, 219, 220 n2.

29. Robert A. Goldwin to Meyer, with marginal notation, October 22, 1963; Rusher to Buckley, Burnham, and Meyer, November 22, 1963, Rusher Papers, Reel 16. Percy, then chairman of the Bell & Howell Corp., headed the Republican platform committee in 1960.

30. Rusher, *The Rise of the Right*, 159; Goldwater on running against Kennedy and Johnson, initial decision not to run: Edwards, *The Conservative Revolution*, 115–16.

31. Goldberg, *Barry Goldwater*, 179.

32. Middendorf, *A Glorious Disaster*, 65.

33. Goldberg, *Barry Goldwater*, 182; Shadegg, *What Happened to Goldwater?*, 171. Kitchel also had "no real sensitivity for politics," according to Goldwater's Senate comrade John Tower. According to Shadegg, his fellow Arizonan actually "disliked politics and politicians."

34. Van Sickle interview; Bauman interview; Fernald interview.

35. Goldwater, *With No Apologies*, 166; White, *Suite 3505*, 304.

36. O'Donnell to Rusher, January 20, 1964, Rusher Papers, Reel 19.

37. Rusher to Buckley, February 27, 1964, Rusher Papers, Reel 18.

38. White, *Suite 3505*, 276–79.

39. Burnham to Buckley, February 16, 1964, Buckley Papers, Box 30, File: Interoffice January-July 1964.

40. Comment on Rockefeller: Theodore H. White, *The Making of the President 1960* (New York: Atheneum, 1961), 66–67.

41. Rusher interview, October 29, 2007.

42. Hart, *The Making of the American Conservative Mind*, 25.

43. Neal Freeman quoted in Judis, *William F. Buckley Jr.*, 225–26.

44. William Rickenbacker to the editors, March 2, 1964, Buckley Papers, Box 30, File: Interoffice January–July 1964.

45. Rusher to the editors, December 30, 1963, Rusher Papers, Reel 19.

46. Rusher to Buckley, February 3, 1964, Rusher Papers, Reel 18. The publisher carefully noted that his recollection of the talk with Burnham was "taken from notes I made contemporaneously."

47. Buckley to Rusher, February 14, 1964, Buckley Papers, Box 30, File: Interoffice January–July 1964.

48. Buckley to the editors (cc: Rusher and Priscilla Buckley), March 5, 1964, Buckley Papers, Box 30, File: Interoffice January–July 1964.

49. Rusher to Buckley, March 6, 1964, Rusher Papers, Reel 18.

50. Rusher to the editors, February 25, 1964, Rusher Papers, Reel 19.

51. Rusher to Buckley, February 3, 1964, Rusher Papers, Reel 18; Buckley to Rusher, February 14, 1964, Buckley Papers, Box 30, File: Interoffice January–July 1964.

52. Rusher to Buckley, February 17, 1964, Rusher Papers, Reel 18.

53. Buckley to Rusher, March 3, 1964, Rusher Papers, Reel 18.

54. Rusher to Jerry Harkins Jr., March 2, 1964, Rusher Papers, Reel 19. Harkins had complained about the striking ineptness of Goldwater's campaign staff, the absence of "coordination" and "confidence" between his personal aides and the political professionals who had been joining the team—and the lack of even a word of thanks or encouragement to any of the Missouri Draft Goldwater leaders from the candidate or Kitchel at a recent event, despite the state committee's excellent early performance. Goldwater came across to Harkins's colleagues as "cold and aloof. (I thought he was shy)." He "just doesn't act like a man trying to get elected," and he was "not articulating his positions so that [uncommitted] people can understand them." Buckley replied that his friend's observations gave him "chills." Goldwater, he noted, had very uncharacteristically not acknowledged two "important letters" he wrote him after the Kennedy assassination. Buckley also speculated that the senator had declared his candidacy in the belief that he wouldn't have to fight for the nomination, had quickly learned that he would indeed have to fight for it, and was now reacting with a negative attitude. The editor would immediately write Rusher "and a couple of others, to see if there's anything we can do." Harkins to Buckley, February 4, 1964, and Buckley to Harkins, February 26, 1964, Buckley Papers, Box 30, File: Harkins. In a second letter—written at Rusher's request, after the recent leadership meeting in Chicago attended by Rusher and himself—Harkins reported that Goldwater's attitude was much better there and "certainly recharged my battery." Still, he was more ambivalent about the staff. Buckley responded, very briefly, that the letter "perked me up." Harkins to Buckley, February 20, 1964, and Buckley to Harkins, March 3, 1964, Buckley Papers, Box 30, File: Harkins.

55. White, *Suite 3505*, 297–98.

56. Rusher to Buckley, March 12, 1964, Rusher Papers, Reel 18.

57. Rusher to Denison Kitchel, March 12, 1964, Rusher Papers, Reel 19.

58. Rusher to William Runyeon, March 17, 1964, Rusher Papers, Reel 19.

59. Buckley, "How Does It Go for Goldwater?," syndicated column, February 26, 1964.

60. Robert L. Sprinkel to Rusher, January 23, 1964, Rusher Papers, Reel 20.

61. Ted Hicks to Rusher, April 23, 1964, Rusher Papers, Reel 19.

62. Rusher to Hicks, April 27, 1964, Rusher Papers, Reel 19.

63. Evans interview.

64. Buckley interview, September 17, 2005.

65. James Burnham, "Political Notes from the Prairies," *National Review*, April 7, 1964, 278.

66. James Burnham, "A Landslide View," *National Review*, April 21, 1964, 317–18; James Burnham, "Bread, Butter and Abstractions," *National Review*, May 5, 1964, 350.

67. Rusher to the editors (not distributed), April 7, 1964, Rusher Papers, Reel 19.

68. Cushing interview.

69. Goldberg, *Barry Goldwater*, 189–91. "School chums . . . army buddies": Clif White quoted.

70. White, *Suite 3505*, 346; Goldberg, *Barry Goldwater*, 190–91.

71. White, *Suite 3505*, 348–50.

72. Edwards, *Goldwater*, 215.

73. Rusher, *The Rise of the Right*, 163; Judis, *William F. Buckley Jr.*, 228.

74. Buckley interview, September 17, 2005; Rusher, *The Rise of the Right*, 164.

75. "Thirteen of sixteen": Perlstein, *Before the Storm*, 356; Dewey anecdote: T. H. White, *The Making of the President 1964*, 158.

76. "Reflections on California," editorial, *National Review*, June 16, 1964, 478–79; Buckley, "Blues, Blues, Go Away" and "Mr. Scranton's Ploy," syndicated columns, June 16 and June 18, 1964.

77. Rusher to Buckley, June 16, 1964, Buckley Papers, Box 30, File: Interoffice January–July 1964.

78. Buckley, "Why Goldwater Will Lose, Maybe," syndicated column, July 2, 1964.

79. Frank S. Meyer, "The Republican Platform," *National Review*, June 30, 1964, p. 535.

80. Meyer to the editors, July 6, 1964, Buckley Papers, Box 30, File: Interoffice January–July 1964.

81. Rusher to White, June 16, 1964, Rusher Papers, Reel 20.

82. William A. Rusher, "Lessons of the Nomination Drive," *National Review*, July 28, 1964, 641–43.

83. Ibid., 643.

84. Schneider, *Cadres for Conservatism*, 82.

85. Perlstein, *Before the Storm*, 371–74; "flatbed truck": Bauman interview.

86. Bauman interview.

87. Lodge at hotel: Perlstein, *Before the Storm*, 374; John Dos Passos, "The Battle of San Francisco," *National Review*, July 28, 1964, 640, 652.

88. Rusher, *The Rise of the Right*, 165.

89. T. H. White, *The Making of the President 1964*, 200–201. Upon his election as governor in 1958, Rockefeller had asked Rusher's friend Wilma Sievertsen Rogalin to be vice chairman of the state party and president of its women's federation, positions she would hold until 1970. Naturally, at the San Francisco convention, she was a Rockefeller delegate. "You know, Governor," she said, sitting next to him in the delegation, "they think that we have horns just because we're from New York." Rogalin interview.

90. White, *Suite 3505*, 398.

91. Ibid., 13–15; Bauman interview.

92. White, *Suite 3505*, 15–16.

93. Donald G. M. Coxe to Rusher, undated (late July or early August) 1964; Rusher to Coxe, August 7, 1964, Rusher Papers, Reel 18.

94. Rusher, *The Rise of the Right*, 168; Rusher interview, December 22, 2006.

95. White, *Suite 3505*, 406; Rusher, *The Rise of the Right*, 170; importance of RNC chairmanship: Goldwater with Casserly, *Goldwater*, 188.

96. Rusher, *The Rise of the Right*, 170.

97. Middendorf, *A Glorious Disaster*, 133–34; Rusher interview, December 22, 2006. Middendorf describes the emotions at the gathering as "mixed," with some of the activists "jubilant" and others "perplexed by Barry's appeal to coarse passions" in his acceptance speech.

98. Rusher, *The Rise of the Right*, 170.

99. Coxe to Rusher, undated (late July or early August) 1964, Rusher Papers, Reel 18.

100. Perlstein, *Before the Storm*, 392–93.

101. Rusher to Kitchel, July 23, 1964, Rusher Papers, Reel 19.

102. Rusher to Dean Burch, September 1, 1964, Rusher Papers, Reel 18.

103. Middendorf, *A Glorious Disaster*, 155.

104. Ibid., x–xi.

105. Rusher interview, December 22, 2006.

106. Edwards, *The Conservative Revolution*, 132; Perlstein, *Before the Storm*, 453.

107. White, *Suite 3505*, 415; Perlstein, *Before the Storm*, 480–82.

108. Perlstein, *Before the Storm*, 484, 494.

109. Ibid., 485–87, 495; White, *Suite 3505*, 414; Shadegg, *What Happened to Goldwater?*, 255.

110. White, *Suite 3505*, 414–15. Shadegg agreed with White that the film was respectable: "Since the election I have shown my copy . . . to many people. While the viewers have not all been enthusiastic and many have said the intended message was somewhat obscured, not a single critic has classified the documentary as racist or vulgar." Shadegg, *What Happened to Goldwater?*, 255.

111. Rusher, *The Rise of the Right*, 155.

112. Perlstein, *Before the Storm*, 459.

113. Goldwater, *With No Apologies*, 170–71, 179.

114. Middendorf, *A Glorious Disaster*, 170.

115. Rusher to L. Richard Guylay, September 16, 1964 (Burnham's script attached); Guylay to Rusher, September 18, 1964, Rusher Papers, Reel 19.

116. James Burnham, "Goldwater as Omen" article manuscript, sent August 28, 1964, Burnham Collection, Box 4, File 4.5.

117. Judis, *William F. Buckley Jr.*, 230–32.

118. Rusher to Richard L. Noble, October 2, 1964, Rusher Papers, Reel 19.

119. Rusher, *The Rise of the Right*, 171–72.

120. Edwards, *The Conservative Revolution*, 136.

121. Rusher to Noble, December 9, 1964; Rusher to Walter J. Mahoney, December 8, 1964, Rusher Papers, Reel 19.

122. Buckley, "Republican Hangover," syndicated column, November 10, 1964.

123. Book review manuscript, February 5, 1965, Rusher Papers, Reel 31.

124. Rusher to John L. Casey Jr., October 2, 1964; Casey, "Some Notes on the Presidential Election of 1964," Rusher Papers, Reel 18.

125. Goldberg, *Barry Goldwater*, 234, 237.

126. Novak, *The Agony of the G.O.P.*, 468.

127. Rusher interview, December 22, 2006.

128. Rusher interview, August 5, 2003.

129. Rusher, *The Rise of the Right*, 169, 172–73.

## Chapter 8: The Conservative Message

1. Rusher to *New Individualist Review* (letter to the editor), undated mid-1965; Rusher to Charles Thone, December 14, 1964, Rusher Papers, Reel 31.

2. Frank S. Meyer, "What Next for Conservatism?" *National Review*, December 1, 1964, 1057; Rowland Evans and Robert Novak, *The Reagan Revolution: An Inside Look at the Transformation of the U.S. Government* (New York: E. P. Dutton, 1981), 29–30.

3. Bauman interview; Judis, *William F. Buckley Jr.*, 233; Rusher, *The Rise of the Right*, 182.

4. Rusher to Buckley, February 2, 1965, Rusher Papers, Reel 31. After the election, Goldwater and Baroody established the Free Society Association, headquartered in Phoenix, with former campaign manager Kitchel as its president. It was intended to promote conservatism through pamphlets and other materials but had no major conservative intellectuals on its advisory board. Although the Free Society Association had the potential to become significant in the movement because it controlled some of the mailing lists the campaign had generated, Goldwater closed it down within a year after it ran short of funds. Rusher, *The Rise of the Right*, 181–82; Schneider, *Cadres for Conservatism*, 88–89.

5. Andrew, *The Other Side of the Sixties*, 213–14; Judis, *William F. Buckley Jr.*, 233.

6. Rusher to Buckley, March 3, 1965, Rusher Papers, Reel 31.

7. Donald Bruce to Rusher, June 18, 1965, Rusher Papers, Box 123, File 6; Rusher to Buckley, February 9, 1965, Buckley Papers, Box 35, File: Interoffice January–June 1965; "shoved down his throat": Rusher to Buckley, March 3, 1965, Rusher Papers, Reel 31.

8. Rusher to the editors, August 26, 1965, Rusher Papers, Box 132, File 6.

9. Ashbrook considered resigning, "our boys . . . pressing too hard": Rusher to Buckley, March 1, 1966, Rusher Papers, Reel 33; "childish behavior": Rusher to Ashbrook, March 4, 1966, ibid.; Rusher to the editors, May 22, 1967, Rusher Papers, Box 132, File 9; Stephen Hess and David S. Broder, *The Republican Establishment: The Present and Future of the G.O.P.* (New York: Harper & Row, 1967), 76–77.

10. Judis, *William F. Buckley Jr.*, 237.

11. Rusher, *The Rise of the Right*, 187; Neal Freeman to author, July 10, 2009.

12. Rusher interview, October 30, 2007.

13. Rusher to Arthur F. Thompson, January 6, 1966, Rusher Papers, Reel 33.

14. Rusher to Roger W. Jones Jr., October 4, 1966, Rusher Papers, Reel 33. Having also found Lindsay distasteful as an "extremely elegant, aristocratic East Side Republican," Rusher was "surprised later, when he retired and subsequently died, to read in the papers that he actually did not ever have much money and lived quite modestly." Rusher interview, October 30, 2007.

15. Rusher, *The Rise of the Right*, 187.

16. Bell interview.

17. Judis, *William F. Buckley Jr.*, 239–41.

18. Bell interview.

19. Judis, *William F. Buckley Jr.*, 242.

20. Bell interview.

21. Judis, *William F. Buckley Jr.*, 248–49.

22. Knowing New York politics, gave advice: Freeman to author, July 10, 2009; comments on radio appearance: Rusher to Buckley, September 24, 1965, Rusher Papers, Reel 32.

23. Rusher to Buckley, Liebman, J. Daniel Mahoney, Neal Freeman, et al., September 15, 1965, Rusher Papers, Reel 32.

24. Rusher to Buckley, Liebman, Freeman, et al., September 2, 1965, Rusher Papers, Reel 32.

25. Freeman to author, July 10, 2009.

26. Rusher, *The Rise of the Right*, 188–89; hard to beat: Rusher to Roger Jones, October 4, 1966, Rusher Papers, Reel 33.

27. Rusher interview, March 28, 2008.

28. Judis, *William F. Buckley Jr.*, 255–57. In addition to running for mayor in 1965, Buckley decided in 1967 to challenge Robert Kennedy, then a senator from New York, when his seat came up three years later. There was, he said in a later interview, "a lot of pressure" to run in 1970 against Senator Charles Goodell, a liberal Republican who was appointed to replace Kennedy. Four things kept him from doing so, Buckley explained: "the gruesome prospect of campaigning"; the probable loss of his *Firing Line* program and his column due to tightening conflict-of-interest standards in the media, his distaste for Washington, and finally, the fact that as a candidate or senator he would miss the "considerable free-

dom of expression" he was used to. Buckley interview, *Playboy*, May 1970, Rusher Papers, Box 121, File 3.

29. Judis, *William F. Buckley Jr.*, 265–67; Simowitz, "William Rusher"; Rusher interview, April 17, 2006.

30. Buckley to Rusher, February 3, 1965, Buckley Papers, Box 35, File: Interoffice January–June 1965.

31. Rusher to Buckley, February 20, 1963, Rusher Papers, Reel 16.

32. Rusher to Buckley (bc: Rickenbacker), June 23, 1965, Rusher Papers, Reel 31; Rusher to Buckley, July 12, 1965, Rusher Papers, Reel 32. The memos were written at the beginning of the editor's mayoral campaign. "What happened," Buckley had written in an example Rusher cited in the second memo, "is that enough of them to make the difference have been persuaded to align themselves against the Amendment not because on reflection they are persuaded that it is undesirable, but because they have been intimidated by the civil rights lobby, which claims that the Dirksen Amendment would release to the southern states a means by which to nullify the effect of the voting rights bill." A sentence, Rusher admonished, shouldn't "be launched as a kind of open-ended plaything, to be festooned with dependent clauses or to serve as a convenient *point d'appui* for still other sentences born after the launching: or broken up by inappropriate punctuation in a desperate attempt to remedy the irremediable: a process that gives a reader the sensation that he is clambering among the gigantic boulders of the Khumbu Icefall."

33. Rusher to Buckley, February 27, 1964, Rusher Papers, Reel 18.

34. Rusher to Buckley, April 6, 1965, Rusher Papers, Reel 31.

35. Rusher to the editors, August 26, 1965, Rusher Papers, Box 132, File 6; Buckley to Rusher, April 14, 1964, Buckley Papers, Box 30, File: Interoffice January–July 1964.

36. Remarks at tenth-anniversary dinner, *National Review*, November 30, 1965, 1123.

37. James Burnham, "Rhetoric and Medicare" (Open Question), *National Review*, August 24, 1965, 720.

38. Meyer to All Concerned, May 23, 1966, Buckley Papers, Box 39, File: Interoffice May–December 1966.

39. Rusher to the editors, January 31, 1966, Rusher Papers, Reel 33.

40. Buckley to Rusher, February 10, 1966, Buckley Papers, Box 39, File: Interoffice January–April 1966.

41. Judis, *William F. Buckley Jr.*, 264.

42. Ibid., 309–10. "Became tolerant": John Buckley Jr. quoted.

43. Ibid., 269–70.

44. Rusher to the editors, September 1, 1965, Rusher Papers, Reel 32.

45. Rusher to the editors, September 24, 1965, ibid.

46. Rusher to the editors, September 30, 1965, ibid.

47. Rusher to Sam H. Long, February 1, 1966, Rusher Papers, Reel 33; Rusher to the editors, December 6, 1966, ibid.; Rusher to the editors, January 25, 1966, ibid.

48. Neil McCaffrey to Buckley, Rusher, and McFadden, April 19, 1966, Buckley Papers, Box 39, File: Interoffice January–April 1966.

49. Rusher to the editors, December 6, 1966, Rusher Papers, Reel 33; Kelly, *James Burnham and the Struggle for the World*, 315–16. The lawsuit came to trial but was dismissed on the grounds that Pauling and the other plaintiff had not made their case.

50. Rusher to the editors, December 6, 1966, Rusher Papers, Reel 33.

51. Rusher to Buckley, December 13, 1966, Rusher Papers, Reel 33.

52. Hess and Broder, *The Republican Establishment*, 78.

53. Rusher to Ripon Society (bc: Ronald Reagan, White, and Buckley), June 17, 1966, Rusher Papers, Reel 33.

54. Rusher to Thomas Farmer, July 8, 1966, Rusher Papers, Reel 33.

55. Rusher to Nixon (cc: Rowland Evans and Robert Novak, columnist Bruce Biossat; bc: *National Review* editors and White), November 2, 1965, Rusher Papers, Reel 32.

56. Rusher, *The Rise of the Right*, 198–200.

57. Rusher to Bonbrake, March 4, 1966, Rusher Papers, Reel 33.

58. Rusher to Buckley, McFadden, and McCaffrey, December 6, 1966, Rusher Papers, Reel 33.

59. Rusher to the editors, January 3, 1967, ibid.; "1968—A Tentative Prognosis," undated Rusher memo, late December 1966 or early January 1967, Rusher Papers, Reel 33.

60. Rusher to John R. Thomsen [*sic*], February 10, 1967, Rusher Papers, Reel 33.

61. Thomson interview.

62. Rusher to Thomsen [*sic*], February 10, 1967, Rusher Papers, Reel 33.

63. Buckley, "Ronald Reagan for Prez?" syndicated column, December 1, 1966.

64. Hess and Broder, *The Republican Establishment*, 288.

65. Buckley, "Ronald Reagan's Opener," syndicated column, January 17, 1967.

66. Lou Cannon, *Governor Reagan: His Rise to Power* (New York: Public Affairs, 2003), 176–77; interview with Thomas Reed, August 27, 2009; Rusher, *The Rise of the Right*, 203.

67. Cannon, *Governor Reagan*, 258.

68. Rusher, *The Rise of the Right*, 203–4.

69. Reed interview; "caution and ambition," Nofziger and Clark: Cannon, *Governor Reagan*, 259.

70. Reed interview. The Republican Party in California, as Reed notes, had been wracked by internal conflict since 1958. Reagan insisted there must be a unified delegation at the national convention and that he would lead it, saying this "to everybody at all times. Whether it was because he wanted those delegates himself, or whether he did not want to go through [something like] this Goldwater-Rockefeller bloodshed that he had helped to repair—it depends on what time frame these conversations were held."

71. Thomas Reed to Rusher, November 8, 1967, private papers.

72. Rusher, memo to file, August 29, 1966, Rusher Papers, Reel 33.

73. Judis, *William F. Buckley Jr.*, 280; Rusher interview, October 30, 2007.

74. Judis, *William F. Buckley Jr.*, 280.

75. Buckley interview, November 14, 2007; Rusher to the editors, October 20, 1967, Rusher Papers, Reel 21.

76. Rusher to the editors, July 10, 1967, Rusher Papers, Reel 21.

77. Rusher, *The Rise of the Right*, 204–5.

78. Rusher to the editors, October 20, 1967, Rusher Papers, Reel 21.

79. Judis, *William F. Buckley Jr.*, 280; Rusher interview, October 30, 2007.

80. Bell interview.

## Chapter 9: Reagan vs. Nixon

1. Rusher to Bonbrake (bc: Buckley), March 4, 1966, Rusher Papers, Reel 33.

2. Buckley to Rusher, March 14, 1966, Buckley Papers, Box 39, File: Interoffice January–April 1966.

3. Buckley, "How to Help Romney" and "The Presidency and the Polls," syndicated columns, September 19 and October 14, 1967; William F. Buckley Jr., "Reagan: A Relaxing View," *National Review*, November 28, 1967, 1324.

4. Judis, *William F. Buckley Jr.*, 282.

5. Buckley interview, November 14, 2007.

6. Meyer to Buckley, March 9, 1968, Buckley Papers, Box 50, File: Interoffice January–March 1968.

7. Quoted in Rusher, *The Rise of the Right*, 210–13; impact of Kennedy announcement: ibid., 212–13, Reed interview.

8. Cannon, *Governor Reagan*, 260.

9. Mike Sholer, "Viet War, Election Forecast Topics of Rusher Talk," *Anthill* (UC-Irvine student paper), January 19, 1968, Rusher Papers, Reel 24.

10. Rusher to Norman ("Skip") Watts, March 28, 1968, with enclosed remarks, Rusher Papers, Reel 24.

11. Rusher to White, April 17, 1968, Rusher Papers, Reel 25.

12. Rusher to the editors, May 3, 1968, Rusher Papers, Reel 21.

13. Rusher to White (bc: Reed and Dave Nichols), May 6, 1968, Rusher Papers, Reel 25.

14. Meyer to the editors, May 25, 1968, Buckley Papers, Box 50, File: Interoffice April–June 1968. Senior editor Bill Rickenbacker was especially unhappy with Buckley's approach to the Republican contest and ended up resigning after the general election. Rickenbacker later said he had "started laying plans for a graceful departure from the top rank at *NR*" when Buckley began publicly signaling his Nixon support in late 1967, "long before the editors ever had a chance to discuss it." Judis, *William F. Buckley Jr.*, 282.

15. Rusher to Buckley, February 1, 1968, Rusher Papers, Reel 22; suggestion that Buckley write an article for each issue, Notes & Asides was "not Buckley at his best": Rusher to Buckley (cc: editors), January 9, 1968, Rusher Papers, Reel 22.

16. Buckley to Rusher, undated February 1968, ibid.

17. Rusher to Stephen A. Nye, July 12, 1966, Rusher Papers, Reel 33.

18. Interview with Shawn Steel, July 23, 2009.

19. Pam Sellers, "Kalish Fears Nuclear War; Rusher Favors Freedom Opportunity," *UCLA Daily Bruin*, January 22, 1968, Rusher Papers, Reel 24.

20. "'Review' Publisher Here Defends U.S. War Morality," *Anthill*, January 19, 1968, Rusher Papers, Reel 24; Sholer, "Viet War, Election Forecast," ibid.

21. M. Dunn, "Publisher Defends War Effort," *The Occidental* (Occidental College student paper), January 19, 1968, Rusher Papers, Reel 24.

22. "Kalish Fears Nuclear War; Rusher Favors Freedom Opportunity," *UCLA Daily Bruin*, January 22, 1968, Rusher Papers, Reel 24.

23. Steel interview.

24. Shepherd interview.

25. Rusher to McCaffrey, December 21, 1966, and Rusher to Ruth Matthews, December 21, 1966, Rusher Papers, Reel 33.

26. Rusher, *Special Counsel*, foreword, 7–8.

27. Ibid., 32, 249.

28. Ibid., 293.

29. Rusher interviews, October 30, 2007, and April 17, 2006.

30. Cannon (and Broder quoted), *Governor Reagan*, 259.

31. Rusher interview, October 30, 2007.

32. Reagan's chances, "tragedy": ibid.

33. Rusher, *The Rise of the Right*, 214, 209; "frantic conversation": Rusher to William Timmons, August 22, 1968, Rusher Papers, Reel 24; Steel interview.

34. Interview with Ronald Docksai, May 26, 2009.

35. F. Clifton White and William J. Gill, *Why Reagan Won: The Conservative Movement 1964–1981* (Chicago: Regnery Gateway, 1981), 121; White, *Politics as a Noble Calling*, 177.

36. Donald Hodel to author, July 4, 2009; Reed interview.

37. White and Gill, *Why Reagan Won*, 122; White, *Politics as a Noble Calling*, 178.

38. Docksai interview.

39. Rusher to Hodel (cc: Don Pearlman and Diarmuid O'Scannlain), August 28, 1968, Rusher Papers, Reel 21; Rusher to Reagan, August 23, 1968, and Reagan to Rusher, September 3, 1968, private papers.

40. Rusher to Patrick Buchanan, August 20, 1968; Buchanan to Rusher, August 24, 1968, Rusher Papers, Reel 22.

41. "McWhorter Fallacy": Rusher to Earl M. Kulp, January 11, 1966, Rusher Papers, Reel 33.

42. Rusher to McWhorter, August 22, 1968, Rusher Papers, Reel 21.

43. Rusher to "My valued colleagues, the editors," August 12, 1968, ibid.

44. Buckley interview, November 14, 2007; Freeman to author, July 10, 2009.

45. Rusher to "My valued colleagues, the editors," August 12, 1968, Rusher Papers, Reel 21.

46. Lee Edwards to Rusher, October 17, 1968, ibid.

47. Rusher to Charles B. Goldberg, November 22, 1968, ibid.

48. Confrérie des Chevaliers du Tastevin announcement, December 10, 1968, Rusher Papers, Reel 22.

## Chapter 10: Neither Nixon nor Woodstock

1. Buckley, "Mr. Nixon's Cabinet," syndicated column, November 16, 1968.

2. Rusher to Buckley, November 21 and November 20, 1968, Rusher Papers, Reel 22.

3. Judis, *William F. Buckley Jr.*, 300–303.

4. Participation in International Seminar: Henry Kissinger to Rusher, June 30 and August 18, 1964, Rusher Papers, Reel 20; Kissinger to Rusher, April 24, 1968, and Benjamin H. Brown (acting director) to Rusher, July 12, 1968, Rusher Papers, Reel 21. In his August 1964 note, Kissinger remarked: "you did an extremely skillful job under difficult conditions." Comment on Kissinger: Rusher to Robert W. Naylor, December 4, 1968, Rusher Papers, Reel 22.

5. Rusher to Buckley, February 12, 1969; Buckley to Rusher, February 20, 1969, Rusher Papers, Box 121.

6. Rusher to Buckley, March 4, 1969; Buckley to Rusher, March 17, 1969, ibid; Buckley, "Restiveness on the Right" and "A New Blacklist?," syndicated columns, March 11 and March 15, 1969.

7. Toast reprinted in Buckley, *Miles Gone By*, 292–95.

8. Notice to friends, undated 1969, Buckley Papers, Box 61, File: Interoffice March–April 1969. Rusher noted that there were many requests for a copy of the poem, so he prepared one and sent it to all who had attended.

9. Kevin P. Phillips, *The Emerging Republican Majority* (New Rochelle, NY: Arlington House, 1969), 25–42, 461–74.

10. Rusher to Meyer, August 1, 1969; Rusher to the editors, August 12, 1969, Rusher Papers, Box 122, File 8.

11. Dan T. Carter, *The Politics of Rage: George Wallace, the Origins of the New Conservatism, and the Transformation of American Politics*, 2nd ed. (Baton Rouge: Louisiana State University Press, 2000), 379–80.

12. Stephen E. Ambrose, *Nixon: The Triumph of a Politician 1962–1972* (New York: Simon and Schuster, 1989), 308–11.

13. Robert Mason, *Richard Nixon and the Quest for a New Majority* (Chapel Hill: University of North Carolina Press, 2004), 64. Similar terms had been used in the 1968 Republican campaign: "quiet center," "quiet Americans," "quiet majority"—and most optimistically, "new majority." William Safire, *Before the Fall: An Inside View of the Pre-Watergate White House* (Garden City, NY: Doubleday, 1975), 175.

14. Safire, *Before the Fall*, 352; Mason, *Richard Nixon and the Quest for a New Majority*, 65.

15. Rusher to the editors, August 12, 1968, Rusher Papers, Box 6, File 6.

16. Rusher interview, October 30, 2007; Rusher, *The Rise of the Right*, 230–31. The vice president's friendly notes to Rusher were signed with his nickname, "Ted." Spiro Agnew to Rusher, August 12 and September 24, 1970, January 5 and December 20, 1971, Rusher Papers Box 6, File 6. Rusher later wrote: "I always find these conversations tremendously instructive, as well as pleasant." Rusher to Agnew, August 2, 1973, ibid.

17. Keene interview.

18. Judis, *William F. Buckley Jr.*, 306–7; "useful service": *Playboy* interview, Rusher Papers, Box 121, File 3.

19. Burnham to Buckley, March 6, 1970, Buckley Papers, Box 165, File: Interoffice March–June 1970.

20. Rusher interview, October 30, 2007; *Playboy* interview, Rusher Papers, Box 121, File 3.

21. Judis, *William F. Buckley Jr.*, 299.

22. Rusher interviews, April 16, 2005, and October 30, 2007.

23. Rusher to Buckley and Burnham, August 6, 1965, Rusher Papers, Reel 32.

24. Rusher to the editors, August 22, 1967, Buckley Papers, Box 43, File: Interoffice July–December 1967. Rusher reiterated his belief in the "domino theory" in a guest column written two years later. He suggested that people who laughed at the theory were trying to have it both ways, since they weren't willing to defend any country in the region should they be proven wrong. Rusher also saw very dangerous implications for Indonesia, and for India under its left-leaning prime minister Indira Gandhi, if greater Southeast Asia fell. In addition, a "bugout" from Vietnam would place dangerous pressure on Japan, the Philippines, South Korea, and Taiwan. Advocates of U.S. withdrawal, he concluded, were "engaging in the greatest leap-before-you-look maneuver in human history." Rusher, "Let's Play the 'Domino Theory' Game," syndicated These Days column (substituting for John Chamberlain), September 12, 1969, private papers.

25. Rusher to Buckley, March 26, 1968, Buckley Papers, Box 50, File: Interoffice January–March 1968. Rusher may have been worrying here about Charles Percy as a long-shot prospect for the Republican nomination. A year before, in early 1967, Buckley had negatively described the freshman senator as the "foremost Republican dove"—albeit, he thought, opportunistically so. In recent weeks, Percy had called for a unilateral end to hostilities in Vietnam. Buckley, "The Emerging Percy," syndicated column, March 21, 1967.

26. Rusher to the editors, June 3, 1969, Rusher Papers, Box 122, File 8.

27. Rusher to Reagan, February 14, 1969; Rusher to Mrs. Ronald Reagan, July 17, 1969; Mrs. Reagan to Rusher, July 21, 1969, private papers.

28. Rusher to Mrs. Reagan, July 17, 1969, private papers.

29. Rusher to Priscilla Buckley, January 12, 1970, Rusher Papers, Box 123, File 1.

30. Cotter interview.

31. Freeman to Buckley and Rusher, February 11, 1970, Rusher Papers, Box 123, File 1.

32. Rusher to the editors, February 16, 1970, Rusher Papers, Box 123, File 1; Rusher to Buckley, February 19, 1970, Rusher Papers, Box 121, File 3.

33. Priscilla L. Buckley, "Notes on a Fifteenth Anniversary," *National Review*, December 1, 1970, 1294.

34. Rusher to the editors, September 2, 1971, Rusher Papers, Box 123, File 2.

35. Buckley interview, September 17, 2005.

36. Interview with Joseph Sobran, August 5, 2009.

37. Rusher to Buckley, October 9, 1968, Rusher Papers, Reel 22.

38. Schneider, *Cadres for Conservatism*, 121–40; "flag-burning . . . Rusher advised": Docksai interview.

39. Rusher to Buckley, January 7, 1970, Rusher Papers, Box 121, File 3.

40. Buckley to Goldwater, March 2, 1971, Rusher Papers, Box 173, File 6.

41. Schneider, *Cadres for Conservatism*, 151–52.

42. Docksai interview.

43. Ron Docksai to Rusher, September 6, 1971, Rusher Papers, Box 173, File 6.

44. Rusher to James J. Capra, June 7, 1965, Rusher Papers, Reel 31.

45. Rusher to the editors, April 26, 1968, Buckley Papers, Box 50, File: Interoffice April–June 1968.

46. Rusher, "The New Barbarians," address to Chicago Society, January 31, 1969, reprinted in *Religion and Society*, June 1970, 18–25, private papers. Rusher had been considering writing a book on the growing division between the old and new cultures in America, seeing "an urgent need" for one. But in response to a note from Arlington House president McCaffrey, he suggested that it might need to ripen in his mind first. He hadn't yet been able to find the time, or to develop his thoughts with sufficient clar-

ity. McCaffrey to Rusher, August 25, 1969, and Rusher to McCaffrey, August 26, 1969, Rusher Papers, Reel 21.

47. Rusher to Steven Binder (Merv Griffin Productions), April 29, 1970, Rusher Papers, Box 219, File 7.

48. Tom McSloy letter and responses (under Notes & Asides), *National Review*, April 7, 1970, 347–51.

49. Rusher to the editors, November 12, 1969, Rusher Papers, Box 122, File 8. He had been "dimly aware" of *The Alternative* for about a year, Rusher noted, "and I gather that several of you know them far better than I do. But better late than never. . . ."

50. William A. Rusher, "Vintage Goldwater," *National Review*, October 20, 1970, 1117–118.

51. John R. Coyne Jr., to author, July 1, 2009; Sobran interview.

52. Rusher to the editors, September 9, 1968, Rusher Papers, Reel 21.

53. Richard Brookhiser, *Right Time, Right Place: Coming of Age with William F. Buckley Jr. and the Conservative Movement* (New York: Basic Books, 2009), 42; Priscilla Buckley, *Living It Up at* National Review, 197.

54. Bridges interview.

55. Priscilla Buckley interview.

56. Priscilla L. Buckley, "Notes on a Twentieth Anniversary," *National Review*, December 5, 1975, 1371.

57. Rusher interview, October 29, 2007; Buckley to Rusher, August 8, 1967, Buckley Papers Box 43, File: Interoffice July–December 1967.

58. Rusher to Thomas A. Stalker, January 3 and January 14, 1966, Rusher Papers, Reel 33.

59. Rusher to Buckley, January 21, 1972, Rusher Papers, Box 121, File 5; Rusher, "The Fallen Giants of Easter Island," syndicated column, January 27, 1978.

60. McGrath interview.

61. Rusher, "One Cheer (and Four Rules) for New York." Although Rusher was often subsidized on his travels, his income from *National Review*, speaking engagements, and beginning in 1970 his appearances on *The Advocates* was adding up and increasingly able to support fine dining. For 1966, he had a wages/salary income of slightly over $17,000 and a speaking- and writing-related income of almost $4,500. For 1970, his wage/salary income was slightly under $44,000, and his net profit from speaking and writing was about $8,400. Internal Revenue Service Form 1040 with accompanying schedules, 1966 and 1970, private papers.

62. McGrath interview.

63. Rusher interview, October 29, 2007.

64. "Profile in Courage: Ted Sorensen's Finest Hour," *National Review*, April 7, 1970, 345–47.

65. Rusher to C. Dickerman Williams, November 3, 1970, Rusher Papers, Box 97, File 8. Before starting on *The Advocates*, Rusher was already becoming, it seemed to him, the "house conservative" on the *Today* show with his occasional appearances there. Rusher to G. MacKenzie (Ken) Rast, July 29, 1970, Rusher Papers Box 75, File 5. Impressed by Rusher's "wonderful" skill as a television debater, Williams later cited it as a major reason why he should run against Senator Javits. David Keene, the former YAF chairman and Agnew aide, now an aide to Senator James Buckley, had told the attorney on his recent visit to Washington that Rusher could have the Conservative Party nomination if he wanted it. Bill Buckley, Williams added, had "greatly enhanced his reputation" by running for mayor a decade earlier. "Win or lose, you would become a great deal more of a national figure than you already are." Williams to Rusher, May 28, 1974, Rusher Papers, Box 97, File 8.

66. Buckley to Rusher, March 16, 1971, Rusher Papers, Box 121, File 4.

67. Rusher, *How to Win Arguments*, 30. Miller enjoyed the description and agreed with it. Interview with Howard Miller, August 26, 2009.

68. Miller interview.
69. M. A. Jones to Mr. Bishop, Federal Bureau of Investigation memo, May 26, 1971; Rusher to J. Edgar Hoover, June 9, 1971, in FBI summary ("References to name of William A. Rusher Appearing in Miscellaneous Files . . ."), private papers.
70. Rusher, *How to Win Arguments*, 121–22; "thirty-three times": ibid., 157*n*; Miller interview.
71. Lee Edwards interviews, July 31, 2006, and November 16, 2007.
72. Miller interview.
73. Lee Edwards interview, November 16, 2007.
74. Miller interview; Rusher interview, August 5, 2003.
75. Rusher to Buckley, February 24, 1971, Rusher Papers, Box 121, File 4.
76. Peter S. McGhee to Rusher, July 16, 1971, and Rusher to McGhee, July 21, 1971, Rusher Papers, Box 222, File 1.
77. William A. Rusher, *The Coming Battle for the Media: Curbing the Power of the Media Elite* (New York: William Morrow, 1988), 113; Priscilla Buckley interview.
78. Van den Haag to Rusher, November 20, 1970, and Rusher to van den Haag, December 7 or 8, 1970, Rusher Papers, Box 94, File 8.
79. Van den Haag to Rusher, December 14, 1970; Rusher to van den Haag, January 11, 1971; van den Haag to Rusher, January 13, 1971, Rusher Papers, Box 94, File 8.
80. Description of Rusher's voice and apartment: D. Keith Mano, "America's Number-Two Conservative Spokesman," *New York* magazine, July 14, 1975, 39–40, private papers; "square . . . whatever he could do": Lynch interview.

## Chapter 11: Running Right

1. flag lapel pin: Safire, *Before the Fall*, 413; Ambrose, *Nixon: The Triumph of a Politician*, 250–51, 325–26, 659.
2. Safire, *Before the Fall*, 341–43.
3. Ibid., 480, 484, 557–58.
4. Buckley on Nixon and Chambers: Judis, *William F. Buckley Jr.*, 305.
5. A. James Reichley, *Conservatives in an Age of Change: The Nixon and Ford Administrations* (Washington: Brookings, 1981), 114–16, 125.
6. Garry Wills, *Nixon Agonistes: The Crisis of the Self-Made Man* (Boston: Houghton Mifflin, 1970), 272.
7. Judis, *William F. Buckley Jr.*, 311–12.
8. Weil interview; Liz Doyle (James Buckley campaign) to William F. Buckley Jr., with notation, June 30, 1970; Rusher to James Buckley and David Jones, July 15, 1970, Rusher Papers, Box 169, File 3.
9. Judis, *William F. Buckley Jr.*, 311–13; Nixon and Goodell's financial support: Nicol C. Rae, *The Decline and Fall of the Liberal Republicans: from 1952 to the Present* (New York: Oxford University Press, 1989), 104–105.
10. Farber interview.
11. Fernald interview; Judis, *William F. Buckley Jr.*, 313.
12. Safire, *Before the Fall*, 544–47.
13. Buckley, "The Patience of Mr. Nixon," syndicated column, May 29, 1971.
14. Reichley, *Conservatives in an Age of Change*, 206, 229; Safire, *Before the Fall*, 509, 528.
15. Bell interview; Schneider, *Cadres for Conservatism*, 148.
16. Judis, *William F. Buckley Jr.*, 329–30.
17. Statement quoted in Rusher, *The Rise of the Right*, 239–40; "Evans refused": Edwards, *The Conservative Revolution*, 170.
18. Allen Drury, "Richard—And the Elves," *New York Times*, September 29, 1971; William A. Rusher, "See Here, Mr. Drury," *New York Times*, October 20, 1971.

19. Rusher to Binder (Merv Griffin Productions), April 29, 1970, Rusher Papers, Box 219, File 7.

20. Rusher to the editors, September 2, 1971, Rusher Papers, Box 123, File 2; Buckley, "The Economic Problem," syndicated column, July 29, 1971.

21. Rusher to Buckley, March 9, 1972, Rusher Papers, Box 121, File 5; Rusher, *The Rise of the Right*, 241.

22. Rusher, *The Rise of the Right*, 243–44.

23. David W. Reinhard, *The Republican Right Since 1945* (Lexington, KY: University Press of Kentucky, 1983), 224–25; Rusher interview, October 30, 2007.

24. The Ripon Society and Clifford W. Brown Jr., *Jaws of Victory: The Game-Plan Politics of 1972, the Crisis of the Republican Party, and the Future of the Constitution* (Boston: Little, Brown, 1973), 302; Judis, *William F. Buckley Jr.*, 332.

25. Rusher to Buckley, March 9, 1972, Rusher Papers, Box 121, File 5.

26. Meyer to the Manhattan Twelve, October 16, 1971, Rusher Papers, Box 167, File 12.

27. Anthony Harrigan to Buckley, Randal Teague, Tom Winter, et al., undated (late October or early November) 1971, Rusher Papers, Box 167, File 12; Rusher to Harrigan, November 12, 1971, ibid.

28. "In Re New Hampshire" editorial, *National Review*, December 31, 1971, 1449; Ripon Society and Brown, *Jaws of Victory*, 302.

29. Ripon Society and Brown, *Jaws of Victory*, 302–303.

30. Rusher, *The Rise of the Right*, 244–45. Ashbrook had recently listed the same points, plus a demand that Nixon visit Taiwan after his mainland China trip, as the conditions under which he would drop his plans to run. But according to an Ashbrook supporter who later wrote a detailed account of the campaign, the congressman's resolve soon "hardened," and Buchanan's conditions, as cited by Rusher, were insufficient for him. Charles A. Moser, "Promise and Hope: The Ashbrook Presidential Campaign of 1972" (Free Congress Foundation, 1985, available at www.ashbrook.org), 15.

31. Moser, "Promise and Hope," 13.

32. Rusher, memo to file, December 21, 1971, Rusher Papers, Box 123, File 2.

33. Ripon Society and Brown, *Jaws of Victory*, 303–304.

34. Goldwater press release, December 29, 1971, Rusher Papers, Box 168, File 6; Reagan's reaction: Moser, "Promise and Hope," 20.

35. Keene interview.

36. Rusher interview, October 30, 2007.

37. Buckley, "Enter Ashbrook" and "Why John Ashbrook?," syndicated columns, January 4 and June 20, 1972.

38. Announcement of candidacy, quoted in Ripon Society and Brown, *Jaws of Victory*, 301.

39. Rusher, *The Rise of the Right*, 244–45; specifics of Rusher's campaigning in New Hampshire: Moser, "Promise and Hope," 28.

40. "In Re New Hampshire," editorial, *National Review*, December 31, 1971, 1449.

41. Buckley to Peter Flanigan (cc: John Mitchell, Henry Kissinger, Robert Haldeman, Frank Shakespeare, and James Buckley), January 3, 1972, Rusher Papers, Box 168, File 6. The letter also included a reference to an ambassadorial appointment Buckley had endorsed, which may explain why it went to some of the others.

42. Buckley, "The Conservatives and New Hampshire," syndicated column, December 28, 1971.

43. Buckley, "Enter Ashbrook," syndicated column, January 4, 1972; Judis, *William F. Buckley Jr.*, 334.

44. *National Review* endorsement: "The Ashbrook Candidacy," *National Review*, January 21, 1972; Rusher to Buckley, January 31, 1972, Rusher Papers, Box 121, File 5.

45. Burnham to Buckley, February 7, 1972, Buckley Papers, Box 166, File: Interoffice 1972; inability to air TV ads: Ripon Society and Brown, *Jaws of Victory*, 304; lack of support from elected officials: Moser, "Promise and Hope," 19. Only a handful of House

members, including Reps. Philip Crane of Illinois and John Schmitz of California, supported Ashbrook.

46. Rusher to Buckley, February 9, 1972, Rusher Papers, Box 121, File 5.

47. Rusher to Buckley, February 25, 1972, ibid.

48. Moser, "Promise and Hope," 27; radio spots: Judis, *William F. Buckley Jr.*, 336.

49. Buckley, "Senator Goldwater's Reassurance" and "Capitulation in Peking," syndicated columns, March 9 and February 28, 1972 (the latter, written in Peking, was mailed on that date, appearing in newspapers soon thereafter).

50. "implausible": Judis, *William F. Buckley Jr.*, 338.

51. Edwards, *The Conservative Revolution*, 173–74. According to Edwards, the Ashbrook campaign "almost certainly" had these effects on Nixon.

52. Mason, *Nixon and . . . New Majority*, 139.

53. Steven F. Hayward, *The Age of Reagan: The Fall of the Old Liberal Order 1964–1980* (Roseville, CA: Forum/Prima, 2001), 286; Buckley, "A Right-Wing Formulation," syndicated column, March 23, 1972. The column quoted at length from a letter to this effect, identifying it as coming from "a middle-aged American conservative." The author of the letter was Rusher.

54. Judis, *William F. Buckley Jr.*, 341.

55. Reprinted in Rusher, *The Rise of the Right*, 247–49. About a month before the 1972 election, Rusher told *National Review* writer D. Keith Mano that after four years of a McGovern presidency, if somehow there were one, 80 percent of Americans would move rightward politically. Mano, "America's Number-Two Conservative Spokesman."

56. "Nixon-Agnew in 1972," editorial, *National Review*, September 1, 1972, 934.

57. Linda Bridges and John R. Coyne Jr., *Strictly Right: William F. Buckley Jr. and the American Conservative Movement* (Hoboken, NJ: Wiley, 2007), 145; John Meyer interview.

58. Rusher, *The Rise of the Right*, 250.

## Chapter 12: Years of Doubt

1. Meyer anecdote: McGrath interview; Hart, *The Making of the American Conservative Mind*, 254. Hart's recollection arguably underestimates his interest in politics. His syndicated newspaper column, for example, actually preceded Rusher's, which began in the summer of 1973.

2. Rusher interview, August 5, 2003.

3. Nash, *The Conservative Intellectual Movement*, 292–94.

4. Rusher to the editors, January 22, 1973, Rusher Papers, Box 123, File 4.

5. Rusher, memo to file, March 5, 1973, Rusher Papers, Box 123, File 4.

6. Rusher to Buckley, February 21, 1973, Rusher Papers, Box 123, File 4; Buckley, "The Upcoming Strikes," syndicated column, February 10, 1973.

7. Rusher to Buckley, February 21, 1973, Rusher Papers, Box 123, File 4.

8. Kelly, *James Burnham and the Struggle for the World*, 356–57.

9. Rusher to the editors, April 17, 1973, and Burnham to Rusher, April 17, 1973, Rusher Papers, Box 123, File 4.

10. Rusher to the editors, April 30, 1973, Rusher Papers, Box 123, File 4.

11. Coyne to author.

12. Judis, *William F. Buckley Jr.*, 349.

13. Keene interview.

14. Judis, *William F. Buckley Jr.*, 348–49.

15. Nixon's view of Connally: Safire, *Before the Fall*, 497–98, and Ambrose, *Nixon: The Triumph of a Politician*, 585–86.

16. Rusher to the editors, March 15, 1973, Rusher Papers, Box 123, File 4.

17. Rusher to the editors, April 30, 1973, Rusher Papers, Box 123, File 4; Keene interview.

18. Judis, *William F. Buckley Jr.*, 350.

19. Ibid., 350–51. Buckley's dissatisfaction: Buckley to George Will (bc: Priscilla Buckley, Rusher, Burnham, and Jeffrey Hart), June 25, 1973, Rusher Papers, Box 97, File 7. At a recent Agony meeting, Buckley told Will in this letter, everyone had expressed admiration for his talent but everyone also agreed he had violated their understanding, carefully worked out several months before, that he must, in Buckley's words, "observe certain restraints in your treatment of Mr. Agnew." Will's columns gave the impression of "unsparing criticism of Agnew fueled by a personal animosity." In addition, he hadn't really gone after liberal beliefs, attitudes, and spokesmen—which was "a journalistic delinquency." Buckley judged that Will's overly negative comments about the vice president were a mistake "under the pressure of general events" rather than a deliberate flouting of his agreement with the editors, and he noted that the writer was free to criticize Agnew within limits. But he also told Will to start coming to New York for most of the fortnightly editorial meetings. This would allow him and the editors to communicate better. In addition, he would be able to "hear from us ... the meaning of the enterprise to which several of us have devoted our lives."

Will replied that he thought the agreement had allowed "reasoned" criticism even if it was strong. He felt he had now been placed in a position in which he could satisfy Buckley only by not writing about Agnew—who could, given that the Watergate scandal might drive Nixon from office, be president within half a year. It seemed to Will that Buckley had decided to subordinate *National Review*'s role as an opinion journal to "its role as instrument of a political movement (and, increasingly, as the instrument of a candidate)." He concluded: "I am, now more than ever, convinced that the only acceptable guidelines for a writer are: defend liberty and good taste. Nothing more (there is hardly anything more); nothing less (a candidate, an administration, a 'movement' is much less)." Will to Buckley, June 27 [1973], Rusher Papers, Box 97, File 7.

20. Rusher to the editors, August 1, 1973, Rusher Papers, Box 123, File 4.

21. Kelly, *James Burnham and the Struggle for the World*, 357; Coyne to author.

22. Judis, *William F. Buckley Jr.*, 360; Priscilla L. Buckley, "Notes on a Twentieth Anniversary," 1371.

23. Judis, *William F. Buckley Jr.*, 377; interview with Jeffrey Hart, January 8, 2009.

24. Rusher to Mary Louise Self, July 17, 1973, Rusher Papers, Box 81, File 6.

25. Rusher, *The Rise of the Right*, 232–34.

26. M. Stanton Evans to Don Lipsett, April 18, 1974, Rusher Papers, Box 133, File 3; Sobran interview.

27. Rusher interview, August 5, 2003. Looking back on three decades of column-writing, Rusher also observed that he had soon realized he "couldn't hope to compete" in his political reporting with Washington-based columnists Will and Robert Novak. "They were 'where the action was,' and able to communicate daily with the key actors. I would have to settle for commenting, I hoped intelligently, on events as they unfolded." Rusher, "Thirty Years of Columns," syndicated column, August 5, 2003.

28. Rusher, "Man of the Year," syndicated column, August 29, 1973.

29. Rusher to van den Haag, January 8, 1974, Rusher Papers, Box 94, File 8. Rusher was once asked about possibly working for Nixon. At some point when the Watergate scandal was "getting pretty thick," he remembered in an oral history interview: "a fellow in the White House . . . called me on some pretext and said—as if it had just occurred to him—'I don't suppose you would be interested in becoming special counsel to Mr. Nixon.' I felt the wings of history rustling by. I replied that I had been out of the practice of law for about twenty years, so he let it pass." In this recollection, Rusher suggested the idea probably stemmed from his having developed a reputation "as a kind of conservative bully boy of a legal disposition." Gerald S. Strober and Deborah H. Strober, *Nixon: An Oral History of His Presidency* (New York: HarperCollins, 1994), 424. Interview conducted September 20, 1993.

30. Burnham to Buckley, Priscilla Buckley, Hart, and Rusher, July 16, 1973, Rusher Papers, Box 123, File 4.

31. "Where Do We Go from Here?," editorial, *National Review*, November 9, 1973, 1221–222.

32. Kelly, *James Burnham and the Struggle for the World*, 340; Rusher, "The Managers Around Nixon," syndicated column, December 2, 1973. With Nixon, Rusher wrote, men who took a "coldly antiseptic approach" and were lacking in "gratitude, tradition, principle—the whole ancient currency of politics" finally "got their hands on the White House."

33. Coyne to author.

34. Buckley, "Procedure and Mr. Agnew," syndicated column, October 4, 1973. Shortly after Agnew's resignation, Buckley criticized unnamed conservatives "who, for old times' sake, and in veneration of their ideals as so trenchantly defended" by the vice president, "will say now: *I'm standing behind Agnew—Agnew was framed.* Mr. Agnew, reaching for self-justification, was no more plausible than Alger Hiss." Buckley, "Farewell to Agnew," syndicated column, October 23, 1973. Rusher and the former vice president kept casually in touch. In 1975, Rusher noted that he would like to meet "for a chat" and tell about his recent political activities, presumably the new-party work. He apparently visited or had a friendly conversation with the Agnews several years later. As late as 1988, Agnew wrote that he was eager to talk politics the next time he was in New York. Rusher responded favorably. Rusher to Agnew, November 7, 1975; Rusher to Agnew, May 7, 1980; Agnew to Rusher, August 25, 1988; and Rusher to Agnew, August 31, 1988, Rusher Papers, Box 6, File 6.

35. Rusher, memo to file, November 12, 1973, Rusher Papers, Box 123, File 5. Agnew had asked Rusher "with particular emphasis" not to repeat his opinion about what Nixon would do to him in the House. In the memo, Rusher explained that he now considered the request "inoperative, in view of his subsequent resignation." He continued to defend Agnew in mid-1974 after a book on the case against him came out, *A Heartbeat Away* by Richard M. Cohen and Jules Witcover. After *National Review* published a review by Bob Novak, Rusher told the editors: "it simply won't do to give Agnew the old dark-alley treatment in America's leading journal of conservative opinion, however predictable such a performance might be in the 'Washington Post.'" The review hadn't even hinted that Witcover was no more objective about Agnew than "John Wilkes Booth on the subject of Lincoln." Rusher also criticized Novak for calling the evidence against Agnew "irrefutable" when it came from "self-confessed . . . felons" who were given important immunities in exchange for testifying against him. Rusher to the editors, May 22, 1974, Rusher Papers, Box 123, File 5.

36. Rusher to the editors, April 26, 1974, Rusher Papers, Box 123, File 5.

37. Buckley, "The Unholy Impeachment Process," syndicated column, April 9, 1974.

38. Rusher, "Is Nixon Mortally Wounded?" syndicated column, May 19, 1974.

39. Bridges and Coyne, *Strictly Right*, 160–62.

40. Jim Roberts, "Who's Who of American Conservative Movement Attend '74 Conference," *Battle Line* (American Conservative Union newsletter), February 1974, Rusher Papers, Box 133, File 3.

41. Rusher, "Was Nixon 'An Evil Man'?" syndicated column, February 2, 1977.

42. Rusher, *The Rise of the Right*, 263–64.

43. Judis, *William F. Buckley Jr.*, 368–69; Hart, *The Making of the American Conservative Mind*, 223–24.

44. "Supreme crisis": Rusher to the editors, April 10, 1975, Rusher Papers, Box 123, File 6; Shepherd interview. Two of Rusher's grimmer columns in this period were "End of the Line for Democracy?" and "When Nations Fall," March 15, 1974, and March 19, 1975. In the first, he explained that once the right to vote is "extended to a society's lowest economic levels," its resources eventually "prove insufficient to cover its real needs (e.g., its military defense) in addition to the escalating promises of the politicians to the vot-

ers." In the second column, Rusher strongly doubted that Americans still had the will to defend their country militarily. He also suggested that a refusal to make economic sacrifices was indicative of a "gaseous cynicism" that "will penetrate every crack in the body politic, making all idealism, all effort, seem futile."

45. Rusher, memo to file, March 31, 1975, Rusher Papers, Box 123, File 6.

46. Rusher, "South Vietnam: No Time to Quit Now," syndicated column, January 24, 1975.

47. Rusher, "Congress, Cambodia and Catastrophe," syndicated column, March 7, 1975.

48. Rusher, "Vietnam: Epilogue," syndicated column, May 9, 1975.

49. Rusher, "Communist Take-Over in Angola," syndicated column, December 14, 1975.

50. Rusher, memo to file, July 21, 1975, Rusher Papers, Box 123, File 6. He took extensive notes on the meeting that afternoon while flying back to New York but only later had the time to write them up in a five-page, single-spaced memo. The quotations, Rusher explained, should be "understood . . . as a near paraphrase."

51. Buckley, "Understanding Kissinger," syndicated column, April 10, 1976.

52. Rusher to the editors, April 9, 1976, Rusher Papers, Box 124, File 1.

53. Rusher, "Kissinger's Pessimism—and Policies," syndicated column, April 18, 1976. Rusher recalls Kissinger asking him at some point in the 1960s, when he was in Cambridge to address the latter's International Seminar: "Do you realize how difficult it is to be the only Republican on the Harvard faculty?" Rusher interview, October 29, 2007.

54. Rusher, memo to file, March 31, 1975, Rusher Papers, Box 123, File 6.

## Chapter 13: How to Start a Party?

1. Rusher, *The Rise of the Right*, 265–66.

2. Rusher to Priscilla Buckley (for consideration at editorial meeting), November 17, 1972, Rusher Papers Box 123, File 3.

3. Rusher to Evans, June 5, 1973, and February 20, 1974, Rusher Papers, Box 133, File 3; Bauman interview. The ACU, Rusher told its chairman Evans in the second letter, had a good staff and was "clearly here to stay."

4. Rusher to Reagan, December 1, 1970, private papers; "enjoyed talking": Rusher interview, March 28, 2008; Rusher to Reagan, April 5, 1974, private papers; Bell interview. The day before the *Advocates* taping, Rusher spent two and a half hours with the governor at his home (Rusher to Mrs. Ronald Reagan, November 30, 1970, private papers). In his conversations with Reagan over the years, Nancy probably "went along . . . without necessarily enjoying it as much as he did," Rusher recalls. Rusher interview, March 28, 2008. In the letter thanking the governor for the *Advocates* performance, he singled out Reagan's "basic reasonableness and obvious good will," adding that his regular liberal opponent Howard Miller "was a rather subdued advocate when I had a drink with him after the show . . . observing resignedly that you are the ablest politician in America today." In addition, Rusher wrote, Reagan had made a "tremendous impact" on staff people for the show. They were loyal to Rusher, doing good work for his side on *The Advocates*, but nearly all of them were "pretty explicitly liberal" and Reagan "charmed them utterly." Rusher to Reagan, December 1, 1970.

5. Rusher to Reagan, April 5, 1974, private papers.

6. Dan McGrath to Rusher, July 9, 1974; Rusher to Peter Hannaford, July 11, 1974; Hannaford memo, "Communications Strategy for 1975," August 2, 1974, private papers.

7. Cannon, *Governor Reagan*, 400.

8. Rusher, *The Rise of the Right*, 265–66. YAF had refused to endorse Nixon in the 1972 general election, although many of its members campaigned against McGovern. Schneider, *Cadres for Conservatism*, 153.

9. Rusher, *The Rise of the Right*, 266–67.

10. Rusher to Buckley, February 10, 1975, and Buckley to Rusher, undated February 1975, Rusher Papers, Box 121, File 8.

11. Jody Carlson, *George C. Wallace and the Politics of Powerlessness: The Wallace Campaigns for the Presidency, 1964–1976* (New Brunswick, NJ: Transaction, 1981), 191; William A. Link, *Righteous Warrior: Jesse Helms and the Rise of Modern Conservatism* (New York: St. Martin's, 2008), 147.

12. Bell and Walker: Evans and Novak, *The Reagan Revolution*, 44; Reagan comment: Cannon, *Governor Reagan*, 400–401. According to Cannon, the governor was "impressed" by Rusher's "thoughtful exposition" of the new-party idea and possible candidacy, but it is unclear whether this refers to the book or to some previous discussion.

13. Cannon, *Governor Reagan*, 401.

14. Rusher, *The Rise of the Right*, 269.

15. Evans to Reagan (perhaps a draft), undated circa May 1975, Rusher Papers, Box 133, File 3.

16. Rusher, *The Making of the New Majority Party*, xiii–xxii; "essential meaninglessness": 103.

17. Ibid., xxi–xxii.

18. Ibid., 163, 171.

19. Ibid., 35–38.

20. Rusher interview, April 15, 2005. He told an interviewer at the time that his grandfather, Charles Rusher, had also been an organizer for the United Mine Workers. Mano, "America's Number-Two Conservative Spokesman."

21. Rusher, *The Making of the New Majority Party*, 36–37.

22. Ibid., 25.

23. Ibid., 160–62, 189–91, 162.

24. Ibid., 158–59.

25. Ibid., 183–90.

26. Ibid., 169–76.

27. Judis, *William F. Buckley Jr.*, 283; "A Vote for Wallace Is . . . ," editorial, *National Review*, November 5, 1968, 1098.

28. Buckley, "The Prospects for George Wallace" and "How to Approach the Wallaceite," syndicated columns, May 25, 1972, and December 3, 1974.

29. Rusher, *The Making of the New Majority Party*, 164–69.

30. Ibid., 200–202.

31. Patrick J. Buchanan, *Conservative Votes, Liberal Victories: Why the Right Has Failed* (New York: Quadrangle, 1975), 15–16, 169–70.

32. Ibid., 176–77.

33. Carlson, *George C. Wallace and the Politics of Powerlessness*, 194, 199; Hannaford to Rusher, March 24, 1975, Rusher Papers, Box 37, File 8.

34. Rusher, *The Rise of the Right*, 274–75; Judis, *William F. Buckley Jr.*, 380.

35. Rusher, *The Rise of the Right*, 273–74.

36. Robert D. Novak, "Producer's Party," *National Review*, June 6, 1975, 622–24.

37. Rusher, *The Rise of the Right*, 274–75.

38. Ibid., 274–75 and 275*n*; Hart, *The Making of the American Conservative Mind*, 242, 238.

39. Rusher, *The Rise of the Right*, 270–71.

40. Cannon, *Governor Reagan*, 401.

41. Rusher, *The Rise of the Right*, 271.

42. Sara Diamond, *Roads to Dominion: Right-Wing Movements and Political Power in the United States* (New York, Guilford, 1995), 129; Kim Phillips-Fein, *Invisible Hands: The Making of the Conservative Movement from the New Deal to Reagan* (New York: W. W. Norton, 2009), 219.

43. Rusher, *The Rise of the Right*, 271.

44. Buckley, "The Desire for a New Party," syndicated column, February 27, 1975.

45. Buckley, "A Voice from Philistia," syndicated column, July 24, 1975. The title referred to Kevin Phillips—who had recently attacked Buckley in an essay—as a philistine, low-brow and vulgar.

46. Buckley, "The GOP Triumphant," syndicated column, *National Review*, June 25, 1976, 699. The title of the column, originally dated May 20, was ironic. *National Review* reprinted selected Buckley columns, usually three per edition.

47. Rusher, *The Rise of the Right*, 272; House Republicans: Mason, *Nixon and . . . New Majority*, 217–18.

48. White and Gill, *Why Reagan Won*, 168; Bell interview.

49. Rusher to the editors, April 10, 1975, Rusher Papers, Box 123, File 6; Rusher, *The Rise of the Right*, 273.

50. Craig Shirley, *Reagan's Revolution: The Untold Story of the Campaign that Started It All* (Nashville: Thomas Nelson, 2005), 36; polls and Rusher's expectations: Critchlow, *The Conservative Ascendancy*, 145.

51. CBS News partial transcript, *Face the Nation*, June 1, 1975, private papers.

52. Robert Shogan and Richard Bergholz, "Reagan Gathers 'Clan' to Talk '76," *New York Post*, June 4, 1975, private papers.

53. Shirley, *Reagan's Revolution*, 37. Rusher told New Hampshire Governor Meldrim Thomson that Connally had been saying privately "he is going to look into the possibility of a 'third force'," which perhaps suggested that he would try to lead it. In addition, various "splendid senators and governors like yourself" deserved "careful attention" as possible presidential standard-bearers—and should give it "serious thought." Rusher to Meldrim Thomson, July 28, 1975, Rusher Papers, Box 91, File 10.

54. Carlson, *George C. Wallace and the Politics of Powerlessness*, 194.

55. Rusher to Meldrim Thomson, July 28, 1975, Rusher Papers, Box 91, File 10; Cannon, *Governor Reagan*, 401.

56. Rusher, *The Rise of the Right*, 275; Rusher to Reagan, June 23, 1975, private papers.

57. Reagan to Rusher, July 24, 1975, private papers; Rusher, *The Rise of the Right*, 275.

58. Evans interview; Rusher, memo to file, September 3, 1975, Rusher Papers, Box 123, File 6. In deciding to meet with Wallace, they believed his "approval of our overall strategy . . . would be useful . . . Certainly his opposition was to be avoided if possible." Rusher, *The Rise of the Right*, 276.

59. Rusher, *The Rise of the Right*, 275–76.

60. Diamond, *Roads to Dominion*, 145.

61. Rusher, *The Rise of the Right*, 278.

62. Ibid., 277. Rusher later suggested that one of the people talking to Wallace or his staff was probably Tom Anderson, the third-party vice-presidential candidate in 1972 who would be nominated by the American Party in 1976. Ibid., 277*n*.

63. Carlson, *George C. Wallace and the Politics of Powerlessness*, 199, 203.

64. Rusher to Evans, May 21, 1975, Rusher Papers, Box 133, File 3. The suggestion came from Eli Howell, the former Wallace adviser on the Conservative Alternatives exploratory committee.

65. Rusher, *The Rise of the Right*, 279.

66. Rusher to Reagan, October 7, 1975, private papers.

67. Rusher to the Reagans, January 30, 1976, private papers.

68. Rusher to Buckley, February 19, 1976, Rusher Papers, Box 121, File 9.

69. Ibid. Rusher tried hard to reassure Buckley on this score. Referring to a six-page summary, apparently written for some of the suspicious activists, he noted: "if you will read Medford's report of my remarks . . . I think you will feel that I managed to discharge my task [defending his association with Buckley] reasonably well. You will probably also be amused at some of the broken-field running I had to do!"

70. Buckley to Rusher, March 4, 1976, Rusher Papers, Box 121, File 9.

71. Rusher to Buckley, March 16, 1976, ibid.

72. Ibid.

73. William A. Rusher, foreword to Robert W. Whitaker, *A Plague on Both Your Houses* (Washington and New York: Robert B. Luce, 1976), ix.

74. Whitaker, *A Plague on Both Your Houses*, 198–99. Rusher later recalled that in "desperation" he turned to Whitaker—a friend who was living in Washington but had participated in intensive protests against school textbooks in West Virginia—to help find people there who could help organize third-party preparations, since the state had no substantial movement organizations to draw them from. Whitaker tried, but without success. Two of the three possibilities, he reported, were running for governor and Congress in the Democratic primary. The third had just been indicted for dropping a bomb from a helicopter. Rusher, *The Rise of the Right*, 278n.

75. Rusher, *The Rise of the Right*, 280–82.

76. Rusher, "Problems Ahead for Reagan," syndicated column, May 16, 1976. In this column, Rusher also wrote contemptuously: "It is true that as a conservative spokesman Goldwater, as someone said of that ungainly beast the camel, 'was put together by a committee'; but he allowed himself to be described as the author of 'Why Not Victory?,' no matter who actually wrote it, and the public is entitled to wonder whether, if that book didn't reflect his true sentiments, his present campaign oratory does either." The New Right magazine *Conservative Digest* had also been highly critical of Goldwater. A 1975 article by Richard Viguerie and Lee Edwards described him as "a serious problem for conservatives" because his "image continues to be used and misused by others, in and out of the media." Goldwater, they also complained, was "content to vote conservative, but not to lead any conservative opposition or counterattack." Alan Crawford, *Thunder on the Right: The 'New Right' and the Politics of Resentment* (New York, Pantheon, 1980), 114–15.

77. Goldwater to Buckley, with marginal notation, June 18, 1976; Goldwater to Mr. B. F. (Bucky) Harris III, June 18, 1976, Rusher Papers, Box 35, File 2. The pain in the letter to Harris—a friend of Goldwater's going back to their days at Staunton Military Academy in the 1920s—was obvious. Goldwater wrote that he "felt it was absolutely incumbent upon me to take Ronald Reagan to task for saying that he would, in effect, send troops to Panama, likening Panama to Alaska, or any state carved out of the Louisiana Purchase." In classic Goldwater style, he explained: "Now, I don't give a hoot who the man is running for President, my brother, myself, or my best friend or worst friend. But when I see a person putting himself in that ridiculous position I would, one, be doing a discredit to the feeling to my country if I didn't call his attention to it and, two, I wouldn't be much of a friend if I let him go on using it." At this point, "thousands . . . who have always called themselves conservatives and probably are, began taking old Goldy on." In a reference to worries about his drinking "that my good, old conservative friends have circulated across this country," Goldwater added: "I have cut down my drinking drastically this whole year."

78. Buckley, "Messrs. Goldwater and Reagan," syndicated column, *National Review*, June 11, 1976, 640. The original column was dated May 8, about a week before Rusher's more hard-hitting piece.

79. Attacks on Kissinger: Critchlow, *The Conservative Ascendancy*, 148.

80. Rusher, *The Rise of the Right*, 284–85.

81. Ratings for Schweiker: Evans and Novak, *The Reagan Revolution*, 55–57; columnists and Will: Shirley, *Reagan's Revolution*, 280.

82. Buckley, "Schweiker as Ideologue," syndicated column, August 7, 1976.

83. Crawford, *Thunder on the Right*, 119; Evans and Novak, *The Reagan Revolution*, 55–57.

84. O'Scannlain interview; Diarmuid O'Scannlain to Rusher, June 30, 1976, and Rusher to O'Scannlain, July 7, 1976, Rusher Papers, Box 70, File 2.

85. Rusher, "Farewell to Ronald Reagan," syndicated column, August 25, 1976.

86. Rusher, *The Rise of the Right*, 287–89; Phillips and Weyrich: Diamond, *Roads to Dominion*, 130.

87. Keynote speech: Edwards, *The Conservative Revolution*, 190; hostility from AIP members: Crawford, *Thunder on the Right*, 237.

88. "Conclave in Chicago," *Time*, September 6, 1976.

89. Rusher, *The Rise of the Right*, 288; Maddox as possibility: Buckley to Rusher, March 4, 1976, Rusher Papers, Box, 121 File 9; description of Maddox and his anti-Wallace comment: "Conclave in Chicago," *Time*, September 6, 1976.

90. Convention quotes: Allan J. Lichtman, *White Protestant Nation: The Rise of the American Conservative Movement* (New York: Grove, 2008), 327; Rusher and Coors: Phillips-Fein, *Invisible Hands*, 220, 314 *n*15.

91. Priscilla Buckley interview. Rusher was unlikely to care much about this column, as distinct from reactions to it at *National Review*. Although Wills was a friend in his early *National Review* years, he had sided with liberal politics and at times with the Left since the 1960s.

92. Rusher, "Footnotes to History," syndicated column, September 10, 1976. According to an expert on right-wing activism, Shearer had been a founding leader of the racist California Citizens' Council. Diamond, *Roads to Dominion*, 130, 351 *n*104. Rusher later recounted to a friend: "Senator Helms told me shortly after the convention that, when Ford's representative on the platform committee flatly refused to accept the Helms amendment implicitly criticizing Kissinger by calling for 'morality in foreign policy', Helms threatened him bluntly: 'Either I get that plank or I go straight to Chicago.' The Ford forces got the point—and Helms got the plank." Rusher to Kirby, June 16, 1977, Rusher Papers, Box 49, File 2.

93. Critchlow, *The Conservative Ascendancy*, 149–50.

94. "Campaign 1976 (IV. Third Party)," editorial, *National Review*, September 17, 1976, 995.

95. Rusher, *The Rise of the Right*, 293, 289. American Party candidate Tom Anderson got a comparable vote in November. Rusher told his aunt that after the Republican convention, Reagan "strongly hinted to me that he would be ready for a new party if the GOP lost . . . But I phoned him again about a week after the elections, and to my disgust he has apparently decided against such a course." Rusher to Mary Louise Self, December 2, 1976, Rusher Papers, Box 81, File 6.

96. "Looking back on new-party project": Rusher interview, August 5, 2003; "certainly proved his": Rusher interview, August 23, 2005.

97. Rusher, "Homeward Bound" and "Salute to Ford's Economic Team," syndicated columns, October 31 and October 22, 1976. Rusher's dismissal of the GOP, in the October 31 column, as representing little but "a highly selective set of economic interests" seemed inconsistent with his praise, in the October 22 column, for the administration's adherence to conservative economic principles as both courageous and good for the country. Among other things, he wrote, Ford's proven "capacity to learn that hard but important lesson" of the futility of wage-price controls stood in clear contrast to Nixon's "cynical resort" to them in 1971.

Buckley praised Ford after the convention, in more general terms, as having quickly earned the Reaganites' votes. He also compared Carter to George McGovern. Both were "nice, good, intelligent men" but appeared to be "addicts of the most insidious delusion of the century, namely that the state can do it better, and that a republic can remain free by subjugating its people. These junkies control the language of reality . . . they get away with statements like 'free health' and 'free education,' which is like talking about square triangles, or rectangular circles." Ford had attacked such "hallucinations" with "plain but heroic prose." Buckley, "And Now the Good News," syndicated column, September 4, 1976.

98. *Human Events* and Viguerie: Laura Kalman, *Right Star Rising: A New Politics, 1974–1980* (New York: W. W. Norton, 2010), 171–72.

99. Reagan quote: Rusher interview, March 28, 2008; see also Rusher, *The Rise of the Right*, 293. Rusher would forget whether the conversation occurred before or after the election, but it was probably in December, over lunch in Los Angeles.

## Chapter 14: Commentaries

1. White and Gill, *Why Reagan Won*, 196.
2. Rusher, "Can the G.O.P. Be Expanded?" syndicated column, February 18, 1977. Reagan's publicity director Hannaford told Rusher at the time: "I think it is a good idea to keep this subject open for continuing discussion." Although he agreed with Reagan that the Republican Party was probably still the best arena for conservatives, Hannaford added that "it may not always be so and, furthermore, the active advocacy of a new party by serious students of the subject such as yourself will tend to nudge the GOP more into the conservative mainstream and away from the 'yes, but' orthodoxy of the old Republican Establishment." Hannaford to Rusher, February 16, 1977, Rusher Papers, Box 37, File 8.
    A continuing sense that the party might have been terminally wounded in recent years was fairly common. Early in 1977, *National Review* ran three essays on the question: "Is the Republican Party Dead?" Closest to Rusher's view was Hart, who admitted the Republicans might sink into oblivion but thought the public might back the right kind of conservative party, one that didn't convey an "almost total identification with business, and especially big business." Author and socialite Clare Boothe Luce, widow of the news magazine baron Henry Luce, argued that neither the GOP nor limited-government principles had a future, since most Americans no longer gave "a damn" for those principles. She foresaw a permanent majority tyranny by "the have-nots, the need-mores, and the want-mores." Ernest van den Haag, in the most nearly optimistic of the pieces, wrote that although the party had failed to implement conservative policy and voters wouldn't rally around a mere attempt to slow the socialistic drift, it wasn't possible to predict the nation's political course. Nothing, he insisted, was inevitable. "Is the Republican Party Dead?" symposium, *National Review*, March 18, 1977, 326–29, 347.
3. Rusher, "Mr. Carter's Presidential Style," syndicated column, March 11, 1977.
4. Buckley, "Carter After a Fortnight," syndicated column, February 1, 1977; Coyne to author.
5. Kelly, *James Burnham and the Struggle for the World*, 351; Brookhiser interview.
6. Almost one-third: Critchlow, *The Conservative Ascendancy*, 154; Republicans' rural losses, discussion with Lance: Rusher, *The Rise of the Right*, 291–94. A small but telling incident that argued against perceptions of a more conservative Democratic Party occurred at its 1976 convention. During the roll call confirming Carter's nomination, the state legislator chairing the Alabama delegation "tried to say a few words in praise of Wallace. Before he could declare that Alabama was on the team, he was shouted down. There was so much noise raised in protest that many did not hear [Senator] Wilson announce that all but a handful of the Alabama delegates had switched to Jimmy Carter. Some of the Alabama delegates walked out of the convention, and later DNC chairman [Robert] Strauss declared from the podium that Wilson's remarks had been 'seriously misinterpreted.'" Carlson, *George C. Wallace and the Politics of Powerlessness*, 218–19.
7. Rusher, "New Majority Party Unlikely Now," syndicated column, July 24, 1977.
8. "Q & A" interview, *City Dispatch* newsletter, May 15, 1977, private papers.
9. Rusher, "Behind the Attack on Lance," syndicated column, August 28, 1977.
10. Ibid., and "Lance: The Real Battle," syndicated column, September 23, 1977.
11. Rusher, *The Rise of the Right*, 294.
12. Rusher, "A Kind Word For Unions," syndicated column, January 1, 1978.
13. Rusher, "The New Right's Bid to Labor," syndicated column, February 12, 1978; Crawford, *Thunder on the Right*, 250–51; Mickey Edwards, *Reclaiming Conservatism:*

*How a Great American Political Movement Got Lost—and How It Can Find Its Way Back* (Oxford: Oxford University Press, 2008), 38–39.

14. Description of meetings: Rusher, "New Right's Bid" column; AFL-CIO attitude and film: Crawford, *Thunder on the Right*, 252; quashing of potential alliance: Edwards, *Reclaiming Conservatism*, 38–39.

15. Rusher, "Reject the Canal Treaties," syndicated column, September 16, 1977.

16. Kevin J. Smant, *How Great the Triumph: James Burnham, Anticommunism, and the Conservative Movement* (Lanham, MD: University Press of America, 1992), 149; Buckley, *Miles Gone By*, 376–78 (debate excerpt). Reagan, Buchanan, and Latin American specialist Roger Fontaine of Georgetown University had a friendly *Firing Line* debate on the issue with Buckley, Burnham, and George Will.

17. Rusher, "Reject the Canal Treaties" column.

18. Buckley's debate with Schlafly and Rusher's letter to subscribers: Donald T. Critchlow, *Phyllis Schlafly and Grassroots Conservatism: A Woman's Crusade* (Princeton: Princeton University Press, 2005), 258.

19. Rusher interview, October 29, 2007; William A. Rusher, *The Meaning of Taiwan* (privately printed pamphlet, 1989), 1.

20. Rusher, "The Taiwan Miracle," syndicated column, February 2, 1975; Rusher interview, October 29, 2007.

21. Rusher to Frederick Chien (bc: Gene Loh), December 23, 1976, Rusher Papers, Box 19, File 9.

22. "utter modernity": Rusher interview, October 29, 2007; American-African Affairs Association: Rusher to All Concerned, undated 1966, Rusher Papers, Reel 33, and Diamond, *Roads to Dominion*, 118–19, 346 n46.

23. Visits: William A. Rusher, *A Short Course on South Africa* (privately printed pamphlet, 1987), 1–2.

24. Brookhiser interview.

25. Rusher, *A Short Course on South Africa*, 12, 30.

26. James Burnham, "The Expendables" (The Protracted Conflict column), *National Review*, July 23, 1976, 776; Rusher, "Cold Eyeball to Cold Eyeball on Southern Africa" (Open Question piece), *National Review*, August 6, 1976, 839.

27. Rusher, "The Fear of Apartheid," syndicated column, September 8, 1976.

28. Rusher, "The Woes of Cyrus Vance" and "Stop Backing the Rhodesian Terrorists," syndicated columns, September 2, 1977, and March 5, 1978.

29. Rusher, "Apology to Free China," syndicated column, December 22, 1978. Rusher was also offended by the State Department's treatment of his friend Gene Loh, Taiwan's New York representative since 1963 and an energetic advocate for it in the media. After he wrote a statement for the *New York Daily News* deploring the "shabby treatment" of Taiwan that the new American policies amounted to, the mainland government insisted that he be told to leave the U.S.—meaning he wouldn't be able to continue, as the Taiwanese government had planned, as its now-unofficial representative in New York. Although Loh remained accredited to the Taiwanese embassy with ministerial rank and the embassy had not yet closed, he was forced to leave the U.S. on one week's notice. By getting the State Department to order his ouster, Rusher noted, Peking had succeeded in "paralyzing . . . the intricate network of friendships and contacts upon which much of Taiwan's remaining influence here depended." Rusher, "Farewell to a Friend," syndicated column, February 4, 1979.

30. Rusher, "Taiwan: Planning for the Future," syndicated column, May 13, 1979.

31. Rusher, "SALT II, At Last," syndicated column, May 27, 1979.

32. Critchlow, *Phyllis Schlafly and Grassroots Conservatism*, 258–59.

33. Buckley, "Misunderstanding Carter," syndicated column, August 1, 1978.

34. Rusher, "Just How Awful Is Carter?" syndicated column, May 5, 1978. In December, Rusher would write: "as presidents go, Jimmy Carter deserves a certain amount of cautious but serious approbation from conservatives." He was working to boost NATO's

strategic armory and had made progress toward peace in the Middle East without Russian participation. Carter had also declared an inflation-adjusted freeze on domestic spending for 1979, and his fiscal prudence was responsible for the fact that the "whole vast array" of proposals for new welfare-state spending had been shelved. Rusher, "Does Carter Deserve Conservative Praise?" syndicated column, December 13, 1978.

35. Rusher, "A Warning to Conservatives," syndicated column, July 25, 1979.

36. Thomson to author.

37. Thomson interview.

38. Rusher interview, March 29, 2008; "ultra-liberal . . . crassly political": Rusher, "Found: The Third Bishop," syndicated column, January 15, 1978. The founders of the new church, Rusher wrote in the January column, several months before his baptism, had "sworn" to keep it away from liberal activism and direct it "back toward the faith of their fathers, for whom 'the Gospel' was gospel enough, without putting the word 'social' in front of it."

39. Fernald interview; Rusher interview, March 29, 2008; Rusher to Mary Louise Self, July 31, 1978, Rusher Papers, Box 81, File 6.

40. Thomson interview; Buckley interview, November 14, 2007.

41. Rusher to Burnham, March 27, 1979, Rusher Papers, Box 13, File 8.

42. Ibid.

43. Rusher, "Will Ford and Reagan Replay 1976?" and "Is There an Alternative to the Democrats?" syndicated columns, June 2 and October 13, 1978.

44. Rusher, "What G.O.P. Comeback?," syndicated column, November 15, 1978.

45. Rusher, *How to Win Arguments*, vi; Freeman to author, July 16, 2009.

46. Craig Shirley, *Rendezvous with Destiny: Ronald Reagan and the Campaign That Changed America* (Wilmington, DE: ISI Books, 2009), 36.

47. Rusher, "Crane's Candidacy a Healthy Step" and "New Leader for Conservative Republicans?" syndicated columns, August 11, 1978, and November 25, 1977. Rusher had told Buckley a decade before that Crane, then a newly elected member, "is much the best thing that has happened to Congress in half a dozen years." Rusher to Buckley and Priscilla Buckley, December 16, 1969, Rusher Papers, Box 121, File 3. He now remarked to a friend: "Phil is . . . in many ways a more serious conservative than Reagan, let alone Goldwater, ever was." Rusher to Michael Djordjevich, October 16, 1978, Rusher Papers, Box 26, File 2. Rusher wasn't merely speculating about the possibility that Reagan would seek just one term. He had "every reason (to put it mildly) to believe that Reagan, when he declares his candidacy, will proclaim that he is running for one term *only*." Rusher to Rast, August 17, 1978, Rusher Papers, Box 75, File 5.

48. Rusher, "Congressman Crane Enters 1980 Race," syndicated column, July 26, 1978.

49. Rusher, "New Leader" column, November 25, 1977.

50. Rusher, "Crane's Candidacy" column, August 11, 1978. Although Kemp was already becoming popular on the Right for his hard-charging, upbeat style and his simultaneous advocacy of free-market economics and outreach to non-Republican voters, Hatch was less prominent. In a column, Rusher explained in detail why he was impressed with the new senator. As an attorney who had never run for office, Hatch had defeated a liberal but seemingly secure Democratic incumbent in 1976. He then flouted "the hoary tradition that freshmen senators maintain a low profile," worked hard, showed impressive parliamentary skills, and earned an essentially perfect ACU rating. Rusher thought Hatch would be a plausible presidential candidate in later years, and a good choice for vice president if a moderate won the nomination in 1980. Rusher, "New Boy in the Senate," syndicated column, September 10, 1978.

51. T. R. Reid, "'Early Bird' Crane Stalking for Republican Supporters" and "Crane Keeps GOP Right Guard Up," *Washington Post*, December 20, 1978, and February 23, 1980.

52. Judis, *William F. Buckley Jr.*, 413–14; Brookhiser, *Right Time, Right Place*, 83.

53. Rusher, "Connally in 1980?" syndicated column, March 11, 1979; Rusher, "Republican Scenarios for 1980," syndicated column, June 6, 1979. In an interview earlier that year,

Rusher praised Connally as "a strong, energetic leader" who might be just what America needed to "re-assert its prestige in the world." Crawford, *Thunder on the Right*, 138. He was, however, subject to damaging perceptions. Fellow Texan George Bush detested the ex-governor and considered him corrupt. A chronicler of the 1980 campaign later wrote: "Connally did not even grasp what conservatism meant . . . He believed government could solve most problems," also favoring abortion rights and the SALT II agreement. Shirley, *Rendezvous with Destiny*, 56–58. Connally's campaign would be remembered mainly for spending a then large amount of money and winning just one delegate.

54. Rusher, *New Majority Party*, 152–55.

55. Rusher, *The Rise of the Right*, 301.

56. T. R. Reid, "Salvo from Editor Loeb Ignites a Crane-Reagan Fracas," *Washington Post*, March 9, 1979. Most of the sources for the *Union Leader* stories, which consisted largely of "generalized observations," were conservative Republican political operatives.

57. Rusher, "Crane: Hanging in There," syndicated column, September 21, 1979.

58. Judis, *William F. Buckley Jr.*, 418.

59. Cannon, *Governor Reagan*, 471–75; Shirley, *Rendezvous with Destiny*, 350–52.

60. Rusher, "Convention Afterthoughts," syndicated column, July 23, 1980.

61. Rusher, *The Rise of the Right*, 304; Shirley, *Rendezvous with Destiny*, 353–64. Several weeks before the convention, Rusher had suggested that Reagan choose Sam Nunn, a junior Democratic senator from Georgia. He pointed out to readers that more voters were independents now and that Democrats continued to greatly outnumber Republicans. If Reagan did a good job of explaining such a choice, the Republican convention would go along. Given communist aggression around the world, the growing Soviet nuclear threat, and the possibility that economic troubles would worsen, Rusher suggested that perhaps Republicans and Democrats should be asked to "pull together." Nunn had already earned high respect in the Senate as a defense specialist. His ACU rating was 54; his AFL-CIO rating only 38. Choosing him would send "a clear signal . . . that Reagan is dead serious about reversing the current trends toward military inferiority, global retreat and economic collapse." It "might also pave the way . . . toward that broader coalition of conservative Americans that has long hovered just below the political horizon." Rusher, "A Democratic Veep for Reagan?" syndicated column, June 4, 1980.

62. Rusher, "Convention Notes," syndicated column, July 16, 1980.

63. Rusher, "The Real Meaning of Detroit," syndicated column, July 15, 1980.

64. Rusher, "Carter's Failure of Leadership" and "America: No Hero Anymore," syndicated columns, May 23 and June 8, 1980.

65. Judis, *William F. Buckley Jr.*, 414, 416.

66. Bridges and Coyne, *Strictly Right*, 217–18.

67. Rusher, "Mr. Carter's Forthcoming Maneuver," syndicated column, October 12, 1980.

68. White, *Politics as a Noble Calling*, 7; Rusher, *The Rise of the Right*, 305.

69. Rusher, *The Rise of the Right*, 16; Rusher, "When Did It All Begin?" syndicated column, November 16, 1980.

70. Rusher, *The Rise of the Right*, 306–307.

71. Judis, *William F. Buckley Jr.*, 242; Brookhiser, *Right Time, Right Place*, 89–90.

72. C. H. Simonds, "A 25 Year Frolic: The First Twenty Years," *National Review*, December 31, 1980, 1606.

73. Rusher interview, August 5, 2003.

74. "No invitation": author recollection; "Most politicians": Rusher interview, April 16, 2005.

## Chapter 15: A Friend in the White House

1. Rusher, "Reviewing the Lessons of the Hostage Crisis," syndicated column, October 24, 1980.

2. Rusher to Nancy Reagan, October 31, 1980, Rusher Papers, Box 75, File 7.

3. Hugh Heclo, "Ronald Reagan and the American Public Philosophy," in W. Elliot Brownlee and Hugh Davis Graham, eds., *The Reagan Presidency: Pragmatic Conservatism and Its Legacies* (Lawrence, KS: University Press of Kansas, 2003), 17–18.

4. Djordjevich to Rusher, November 5, 1980, and Rusher to Djordjevich, January 19, 1981, Rusher Papers, Box 26, File 2.

5. Lou Cannon, *President Reagan: The Role of a Lifetime* (New York: PublicAffairs, 2000), 18.

6. Martin Anderson, *Revolution* (Stanford, CA: Hoover Institution Press, 1990), 278–79, 289–90.

7. Lasting effect of assassination attempt: Novak, *The Prince of Darkness*, 367–69; "wanted him to be young": Peggy Noonan, *What I Saw at the Revolution: A Political Life in the Reagan Era* (New York: Random House, 1990), 345.

8. "Regretted": Rusher, *The Rise of the Right*, 293; Brookhiser interview.

9. Rusher to Nancy Reagan, November 7, 1980, Rusher Papers, Box 75, File 7.

10. Rusher to Nancy Reagan, October 31, 1980, Rusher Papers, Box 75, File 7; "I want those names": Rusher interview, March 28, 2008.

11. Rusher to Nancy Reagan, November 7, 1980, Rusher Papers, Box 75, File 7. Among the people he recommended was Tony Dolan, a former *National Review* writer and prize-winning newspaper reporter who should, Rusher suggested, be put in charge of a White House unit for "pinpointing issues, ferreting out opposition weak spots," and the like. He also advised Mrs. Reagan that Clif White, who had worked as a senior consultant to campaign manager (soon to be CIA director) Bill Casey in the 1980 general election, would probably like to serve as a political counselor to the president while also establishing, and perhaps running for a year, an office focused on obtaining the "most effective support" for Reagan from the RNC, congressional Republicans, and state party organizations. Dolan, recommended by Buckley as well as Rusher, was appointed to head the speechwriting team. White was not brought onto the staff.

12. Rusher to the Reverend George Rutler, December 10, 1980, Rusher Papers, Box 78, File 3.

13. Rusher interview, March 28, 2008.

14. Rusher to Nancy Reagan, July 31, 1981, and Rusher to Ronald Reagan (bc: Helene von Damm), February 11, 1982, private papers.

15. Rusher to Nancy Reagan, December 31, 1980, Rusher Papers, Box 75, File 7.

16. Schneider, *Cadres for Conservatism*, 170.

17. Rusher to Edwin Meese, June 9, 1981, Rusher Papers, Box 31, File 4.

18. Rusher to Reagan, May 5, 1981, private papers.

19. Helene von Damm, *At Reagan's Side: Twenty Years in the Political Mainstream* (New York: Doubleday, 1989), 195–99.

20. Rusher to Buckley, March 9, 1981, Rusher Papers, Box 122, File 2.

21. Ibid.

22. Rusher to Reagan, January 11, 1982, and February 28, 1983, private papers.

23. Receipt of *National Review* confirmed: Reagan to Rusher, March 15, 1983, private papers; difficulties with staff and first lady: von Damm, *At Reagan's Side*, 181–82.

24. Rusher, *How to Win Arguments*, 9–10, 14–16.

25. Ibid., 43–44, 179.

26. Ibid., 60.

27. Rusher, "The Collision Ahead," syndicated column, October 17, 1980.

28. David Brudnoy to Rusher, January 8, 1981, and Rusher to Brudnoy, January 20, 1981, Rusher Papers, Box 12, File 10.

29. Rusher, "Goldwater and the Religious Right," syndicated column, September 23, 1981; Falwell on O'Connor, Goldwater on Falwell: Goldberg, *Barry Goldwater*, 315.

30. Evans and Novak, *The Reagan Revolution*, 214–17, 225; evangelical voters' participation in the 1980 election: Diamond, *Roads to Dominion*, 233.

Reagan was nonetheless "more interested in Moral Majority questions than his political aides." He understood that social issues were now an important part of the movement. Moral Majority leaders, members, and sympathizers remained supportive of the president, knowing that "Reagan was with them in spirit as no other president of the last half century had been." Evans and Novak, *The Reagan Revolution*, 217–18, 225.

31. Cannon, *President Reagan*, 722–23. Apparently agreeing with aides in mid-October 1980, when his poll standing seemed to have flattened, that such an announcement would help to revive his campaign, Reagan said he would name a woman to "one of the first" Supreme Court vacancies. On the extent of social-conservative opposition to the O'Connor nomination, see also Critchlow, *Phyllis Schlafly and Grassroots Conservatism*, 282. Rusher defended the nomination, explaining among other things that O'Connor had been an active "conservative Republican" and had backed Reagan in 1976 despite her fellow Arizonan Goldwater's backing of Ford. She was therefore quite probably sympathetic to the country's more conservative mood on many issues over the past decade. Rusher, "Mrs. Justice O'Connor?" syndicated column, July 22, 1981.

32. Richard A. Viguerie, *The New Right: We're Ready to Lead*, rev. ed. (Falls Church, VA: Viguerie Co., 1981), 176. In the fall of that year, Rusher wrote that while he believed Reagan should "support the social issues from a prudent distance" rather than become strongly involved in them, it troubled him that recent comments by Baker and David Gergen—and recent appointments he attributed to Baker—suggested a revival of the old, ignorant Republican misconception "that conservative economics alone can woo and win a majority of American voters." It was partly for this reason that he lamented the loss of veteran Reagan aide Lyn Nofziger, whom Rusher thought had a strong understanding of social conservatives' importance, from his White House political post. Rusher, "White House Blunder in the Making" and "Nofziger's Departure," syndicated columns, October 2, 1981, and January 17, 1982.

33. Statement quoted in Rusher, "How Mad Are Conservatives At Reagan?" syndicated column, January 29, 1982, and Bill Peterson, "Conservative Critique Charges Administration with Moderation," *Washington Post*, January 22, 1982; Weyrich and Viguerie comments: Peterson, "Conservative Critique," ibid.

A week and a half later, Reagan met with what he called "hard nosed conservative friends" who were anxious about the administration's direction. But the difficulty of making a lasting impression on a president is illustrated by the fact that in this short period, in addition to more official business, Reagan also met with, among others: U.S. Chamber of Commerce and small-business representatives; black Republican leaders; Republican mayors; the Clemson University football team; members of the Franklin Roosevelt family and veterans of his administration in connection with the hundredth anniversary of Roosevelt's birth ("The press is dying to paint me as now trying to undo the New Deal. I remind them I voted for F.D.R. 4 times. I'm trying to undo the 'Great Society.' It was L.B.J.'s war on poverty that led to our present mess"); Urban League president John Jacobs ("I believe we can continue communicating & establish a good relationship"); and a group of Youth Senate program participants ("I told the B-17 story and again choked up so I could hardly finish"). Entries and editor's summaries for January 19–February 2, 1982 in Douglas Brinkley, ed., *The Reagan Diaries* (New York: HarperCollins, 2007), 64–66.

34. Rusher signed Mayflower statement: summary of statement with names of signers, enclosure with fund-raising letter sent by Richard Viguerie, February 15, 1982, Rusher Papers, Box 95, File 1; comments on statement: Rusher, "How Mad Are Conservatives at Reagan?" column, January 29, 1982.

35. Rusher to Reagan, February 11, 1982, private papers.

36. Rusher, "Washington Tidbits," syndicated column, June 23, 1982.

37. Laurence I. Barrett, *Gambling with History: Ronald Reagan in the White House* (Garden City, NY: Doubleday, 1983), 61–62.

38. Rusher to Nancy Reagan, March 3, 1982, private papers; Rickenbacker to Rusher, March 11, 1982, and Rusher to Rickenbacker, March 26, 1982, Rusher Papers, Box 76, File 8. Rusher's column advocated that Reagan try televised "fireside chats." He warned that if the president's voice wasn't "raised regularly," it wouldn't get through a hostile media to the people, which was necessary if Reagan was "to win ... the battle to change America's direction." Rusher, "Let's Have Fireside Chats," syndicated column, March 5, 1982.

39. William Ker Muir Jr., *The Bully Pulpit: The Presidential Leadership of Ronald Reagan* (San Francisco: ICS Press, 1992), 22, 225*n*.

40. Rusher to Nancy Reagan, March 3, 1982, private papers.

41. R. Emmett Tyrrell Jr., *The Conservative Crack-Up* (New York: Simon and Schuster, 1992), 106–107; Rusher to Reagan, September 23, 1982, and Reagan to Rusher, September 27, 1982, private papers.

Tyrrell remembered the episode as a case of prominent conservatives' frustrations in dealing with the Reagan White House. "The lunch was very agreeable, except when I would accidentally lock eyes with one of these grim assistant presidents . . . Only the President seemed to share my enthusiasm, and in his 'gosh-goll-darn-it' demeanor he asked Dave Gergen to schedule a series of these pleasant luncheons." After the coffee was finished, Gergen nervously told Tyrrell "that I probably would be more comfortable dealing with a staff member friendlier to me . . . [in my opinion] Dave had thrown in with the Country Clubbers, and all my talk of Ideas imperiled the Process. He enlisted the overworked but 'friendlier' Ed Meese to schedule further meetings and we were lost in Ed's congested briefcase. Our group never met again. The White House had been saved for [socialite Betsy Bloomingdale] and Nancy, the designers and interior decorators and, of course, the Country Club Republicans." Tyrrell, *Conservative Crack-Up*, 107–108.

42. Richard A. Viguerie, *The Establishment vs. the People: Is a New Populist Revolt on the Way?* (Chicago: Regnery/Gateway, 1984), 219–26.

43. February 26, 1982, and February 18, 1983, entries in Brinkley, ed., *The Reagan Diaries*, 71–72, 132.

44. Reagan to Rusher, March 15, 1983, private papers.

45. Rusher to Buckley (cc: senior editors), July 28, 1982, Rusher Papers, Box 122, File 3.

46. Rusher to Paul Laxalt, April 8, 1983, Rusher Papers, Box 52, File 4.

47. Rusher interview, March 28, 2008; Viguerie interview, November 15, 2007.

48. Rusher to Buckley, October 17, 1983, Rusher Papers, Box 122, File 3.

49. Rusher to White, March 1, 1982, Rusher Papers, Box 97, File 5. Rusher also praised Gingrich for having shown, in recent speeches, "an exceptional ability to visualize the future in practical conservative terms." Rusher, "A Georgian's Vision of the Future," syndicated column, February 7, 1982.

50. Rusher to Hodel, September 8, 1988, Rusher Papers, Box 40, File 7.

51. "What Conservatives Think of Ronald Reagan: A Symposium," *Policy Review*, Winter 1984, 15–18.

52. Economic policy: Rusher, "Mr. Reagan Stands Firm," syndicated column, February 1, 1983; Soviet Union: Rusher, "The Soviet Succession," syndicated column, November 18, 1982.

53. Rusher, "Reagan on a Roll," syndicated column, December 1, 1983.

54. Rusher, "Nofzinger's Departure" column, January 17, 1982; Rusher, "Ed Meese Steps Out," syndicated column, January 26, 1984. Helene von Damm later suggested that Nofziger's departure in early 1982 probably "marked a turning point in the Reagan Administration." He had known Reagan for years, "understood his weaknesses as well as his strengths, and would speak plainly to him when necessary. Lyn knew when Ronald Reagan was allowing himself to be talked into something which went against his gut instincts . . . He also knew how to protect his political base. But President Reagan never seemed to grasp what a void was created when Lyn left." von Damm, *At Reagan's Side*, 226.

55. Rusher to George Bush, March 6, 1984, private papers.

56. Rusher to Reagan, October 19, 1984, private papers.

57. Paul Kengor and Patricia Clark Doerner, *The Judge: William P. Clark, Ronald Reagan's Top Hand* (San Francisco: Ignatius Press, 2007), 291–92.

58. Barrett, *Gambling with History*, 234, 329–33; Edmund Morris, *Dutch: A Memoir of Ronald Reagan* (New York: Random House, 1999), 455–56.

59. Cannon, *President Reagan*, 373–74. Clark, who was "winning fewer and fewer of his battles" as national security adviser by late 1983, also "had a restless streak," according to Cannon. "Now he was ready to step out . . . return to his ranch in California without giving the appearance of abandoning the Reagan administration. Many of the conservatives, especially Meese and [Defense Secretary Caspar] Weinberger, urged him to stay. While Clark was agonizing, an unexpected opportunity [James Watt's resignation as Interior Secretary] intervened that provided an outlet for his troubleshooting talents."

60. Reagan to Rusher, May 8, 1984, private papers. The day before, Reagan met with his old Southern California backer Holmes Tuttle about the Meese situation for half an hour. "I think he'd like to have me push him overboard," the president wrote. "I can't do that." May 7, 1984, entry in Brinkley, ed., *The Reagan Diaries*, 238. The president had already told Rusher of his anger at the treatment of Meese a month before. In a note mentioning that he read *National Review* "cover to cover," he confided: "In my nightly prayers, I have to ask forgiveness for what I've been thinking about those villains all day. It's not an easy thing to do." Reagan to Rusher, April 9, 1984, in Kiron K. Skinner, et al., eds., *Reagan: A Life in Letters* (New York: Free Press, 2003), 560.

61. Rusher to Bert Lance, August 7, 1984, Rusher Papers, Box 52, File 1.

62. Rusher interview, March 28, 2008.

## Chapter 16: Éminence Grise

1. Rusher to Mary Louise Self, June 20, 1983, Rusher Papers, Box 81, File 8.

2. Rusher, *The Rise of the Right*, 310, 318–19.

3. Ibid., 309, 313.

4. Ibid., 320, 323.

5. Untitled review by Aram Bakshian Jr., *The American Spectator*, December 1984, 41; Adam Meyerson, "Rusher to Judgment," *Policy Review*, Fall 1984, 71. In 1988, Rusher recalled that he had needed to "make a federal case" in order to get *The Rise of the Right* reviewed in the *Spectator*. Rusher to Wick Allison, November 29, 1988, Rusher Papers, Box 6, File 10.

6. Walter Goodman, "Books: Right Face," *New York Times*, June 15, 1984, C25; Lewis H. Lapham, "Present and Active at the Creation," *New York Times Book Review*, July 15, 1984, 9.

7. Rusher to Kirk, January 30, 1985, Rusher Papers, Box 112, File 4.

8. Goldwater to Colin Walters (book editor, *Washington Times*), June 8, 1984; Goldwater to Rusher, June 8, 1984, Rusher Papers, Box 35, File 2.

9. Reagan to *Baltimore Sun*, June 26, 1984, in Skinner, et al., eds., *Reagan: A Life in Letters*, 285.

10. Speaking fees: Rusher Papers, Boxes 216 and 218; radio broadcasts: Rusher to F. A. Lennon, October 2, 1983, and October 24, 1988, and Freeman to Lennon, December 2, 1983, Rusher Papers, Box 52, File 7.

11. Rusher to Pearlman, March 6, 1986, Rusher Papers, Box 71, File 5.

12. Rusher to Nancy Reagan, December 21, 1983, private papers; Rusher to Mary Louise Self, September 8, 1983, Rusher Papers, Box 81, File 8.

13. Hodel allowed use of *Sequoia*: Freeman to author, July 24, 2011; congratulations: Meese to Rusher, July 19, 1985, Rusher Papers, Box 58, File 8.

14. Birthday party recollections: Farmer interview. In 1981, 1985, and during the Reagan-

Bush transition, Rusher unsuccessfully recommended his friend for a position on the president's Foreign Intelligence Advisory Board. A former general counsel to the Agency for International Development, Farmer had worked as a covert-operations case officer at the CIA from 1951 to 1954, specialized in international finance as a lawyer, and chaired the Intelligence Oversight Board, a body set up by the Carter administration to advise the president on the legal and political propriety of CIA and FBI operations. "Tom is an eminently sensible and moderate gent," Rusher told CIA director Casey, "and by no means the kind of partisan who would seek to get in the president's way." To Meese, he suggested that "a moderate Democrat with Tom's fund of experience would be vastly preferable to somebody with only political qualifications." Farmer to Rusher, June 8, 1981, Rusher to Meese, June 9, 1981, Rusher to William Casey, June 23, 1981; Rusher to Admiral Daniel Murphy (Office of the Vice President), March 18, 1985, Rusher to Donald Regan (White House chief of staff), November 8, 1985; Rusher to Congressman Henry Hyde, December 1, 1988, Rusher to John Sununu (incoming White House chief of staff), December 7, 1988. Rusher Papers, Box 31, File 4.

15. Farmer to Rusher, July 21, 1985, and Rusher to Farmer, July 25, 1985, Rusher Papers, Box 31, File 4.

16. Brookhiser interview.

17. Interview with Claire Wirth Russhon, March 3, 2009.

18. Ibid.; Rast to Rusher, March 31, 1986, and Rusher to Rast, April 4, 1986, Rusher Papers, Box 75, File 6.

19. Rusher interview, March 29, 2008; Russhon interview.

20. Dictated columns: Russhon interview; "pushed around," writing with pen and paper: Rusher, "Author Meets Computer," syndicated column, July 10, 1986.

21. Brookhiser interview.

22. Interviews with Edward Capano, July 28 and September 2, 2009; Russhon interview.

23. Shepherd interview; financial situation: Rusher to T. Clarke Conwell (San Francisco tenant), March 12, 1989, personal papers; Russhon interview.

24. Russhon interview.

25. Weil interview.

26. Thomson interview; Thomson to author.

27. Rusher, *A Short Course on South Africa*, 1; Brookhiser, *Right Time, Right Place*, 102–3.

28. Editorial conflicts were milder: Rusher to Jack Kemp, August 8, 1985, Rusher Papers, Box 48, File 2; Brookhiser interview.

29. Brookhiser, *Right Time, Right Place*, 100; Sobran interview.

30. Sobran interview.

31. Rusher to Goldberg, May 20, 1986, Rusher Papers, Box 34, File 11.

32. Brookhiser, *Right Time, Right Place*, 137–39; Buckley to Richard Brookhiser, July 5 [1987], private papers. Rusher's warning that Buckley might consult his "fifty closest friends" was apparently not borne out. According to Brookhiser, Buckley didn't share the news widely, if at all.

33. Brookhiser, *Right Time, Right Place*, 95; Buckley interview, September 17, 2005.

34. Priscilla L. Buckley, "The Last Five Years: The Staff at Work and Play," *National Review*, December 31, 1985, 117–18; "The Party at the Plaza," coverage of thirtieth-anniversary dinner, ibid., 126.

35. Rusher interview, April 16, 2005; author recollection; Rusher interview, March 29, 2008.

36. "The Party at the Plaza," *National Review*, December 31, 1985, 127–29.

37. Rusher to Reagan, March 22, 1985, private papers. Rusher told the president he had said the same thing to the first lady at the recent CPAC dinner, at which he was seated next to her on the dais. They had also "managed to get caught up on a lot of things."

Hoping for a personal channel of communication with the administration, Rusher met with National Security Adviser Robert McFarlane and began corresponding with him shortly after the 1984 election—apparently at Nancy Reagan's suggestion. In doing so, he told McFarlane, he wished in particular to help make the administration "the success that it deserves to be." Rusher gently noted that Reagan had been a *National Review* reader for a quarter of a century and that he and the president had always shared the same agenda. McFarlane wrote in response that he appreciated Rusher's "interest in keeping me informed of developments and priorities" among conservatives and was glad he would be able to "look to you from time to time for ideas on ways to build and sustain that support." Rusher to Nancy Reagan, November 16, 1984, private papers; Rusher to Robert McFarlane, December 13, 1984, and McFarlane to Rusher, January 4, 1985, Rusher Papers, Box 57, File 11.

Their correspondence seems to have been cursory, although the national security adviser applauded the "Star Shield" suggestion, telling Rusher: "I like it!" and noting that the administration had been considering the problem of finding a good popular name for missile defense for quite a while. McFarlane to Rusher, June 17, 1985, Rusher Papers, Box 57, File 11. Although it is unclear why Mrs. Reagan would have steered Rusher to McFarlane, foreign-policy pragmatists in the administration had increasingly come to count on him as an ally. "Nicaragua aside, McFarlane had won the plaudits of the White House staff and the first lady for the importance he attached to improving U.S.-Soviet relations." Cannon, *President Reagan*, 526.

38. Rusher to Kirk, January 30, 1985, Rusher Papers, Box 112, File 4.

39. Rusher to L. Brent Bozell III, June 25, 1986, Rusher Papers, Box 153, File 9; interview with Bozell, July 9, 2009.

40. Sobran interview; Brookhiser interview.

41. Keene interview.

42. Brookhiser interview.

43. James Barros to Rusher, July 15, 1985, and Rusher to Barros, July 23, 1985, Rusher Papers, Box 10, File 2.

44. Rusher to Reagan, March 22, 1985 (bc: Freeman), and May 27, 1986, private papers; Rusher interview, March 28, 2008. In a brief diary note on the taping, the president referred to Rusher as a "long time friend." May 23, 1986, entry in Brinkley, ed., *The Reagan Diaries*, 413–14.

45. "Perdicaris Alive, Raisuli Alive," editorial, *National Review*, July 26, 1985, 16–17; William A. Rusher, "In Reagan's Defense," *National Review*, August 9, 1985, 41. Looking back later, then Secretary of State Shultz wrote that the president's decision for the administration to maintain "relative silence" resulted in "a threatening aura" that effectively served American purposes in the crisis. George P. Shultz, *Turmoil and Triumph: My Years as Secretary of State* (New York: Scribner's, 1993), 668. Rusher sent McFarlane his piece in defense of Reagan, also noting that the *National Review* editorial and critical pieces by George Will and neoconservative Norman Podhoretz came out before he had time to alert McFarlane. These critics were "full of hot air," Rusher wrote, but he did hope the White House would "plan a really grisly retaliation" against the terrorists. Rusher to McFarlane, July 8, 1985, Rusher Papers, Box 57, File 11. No such action occurred. Although Reagan authorized an air raid on the capital of Libya in 1986 in response to other terrorist incidents, for the previous five years he "talked tough about terrorism but did virtually nothing in the way of retaliatory action to stop it." Cannon, *President Reagan*, 539.

46. Rusher to Reagan, August 19, 1986, private papers. The president, vacationing at his ranch, called the following day about items in *National Review* "that echo the errors in the press about our position on arms control & SDI," and Rusher was "pleased to get the inside info." August 20, 1986, entry in Brinkley, ed., *The Reagan Diaries*, 433. Sensitive to concerns that overly personal jabs at Reagan on foreign policy had occasionally appeared in the magazine, Buckley later promised that "*no personal criticism of this sort, i.e., questioning your motives, will be published . . . your motives are beyond question.*" Buckley to Reagan, October 18, 1987, in William F. Buckley Jr., *The Reagan I Knew* (New York: Basic Books, 2008), 205.

47. Rusher, "Reagan's Not About to Blink," syndicated column, October 9, 1986.

48. Rusher to Rast, December 17, 1987, Rusher Papers, Box 75, File 6.

49. Rusher, "The White House, Revised" and "New Baker in the Kitchen," syndicated columns, March 12 and June 4, 1987. Two months after Rusher's column praising Baker came the most important domestic battle of Reagan's last two years, the nomination of the conservative judge Robert Bork to the Supreme Court as a replacement for the centrist justice Lewis Powell. Baker was "unenthusiastic about Bork" and did little for him in the crucial early stages. Also in 1987–88, many experienced conservatives left the Reagan administration in part because they believed their ideas had little chance with Baker in charge. John Ehrman, *The Eighties: America in the Age of Reagan* (New Haven: Yale University Press, 2005), 145, 142. While Rusher blamed liberal activists and Democrats on the Senate Judiciary Committee for Bork's defeat, *National Review* editorialized that the White House "was out to lunch," additionally blaming the Republican National Committee and the party's complacent "master strategists." Rusher, "Mudslinging from the Swamp," syndicated column, October 1, 1987; "The Bork Disaster," editorial, *National Review*, November 6, 1987, 16. More generally, the magazine's Washington reporter wrote that the White House under Baker was systematically avoiding political risks in the delusional hope this would strengthen Reagan's diminished clout. John McLaughlin, "Reagan's No-Risk Regimen," *National Review*, November 6, 1987, 26.

But according to Ed Rollins, a conservative who was the national director of the 1984 campaign and for a time the director of White House political and intergovernmental affairs in the second term, Baker succeeded—after the two-year tenure of former treasury secretary Donald Regan as chief of staff—in restoring "confidence, dignity, and a sense of common decency to the West Wing." With his deputy Kenneth Duberstein, Baker "stopped the bleeding" in a beleaguered administration. Ed Rollins with Tom DeFrank, *Bare Knuckles and Back Rooms: My Life in American Politics* (New York, Broadway Books, 1996), 176–77.

50. Rusher to Reagan, March 27, 1987, and Reagan to Rusher, April 1, 1987, private papers.

51. Rusher, "Bullring in the East Room," syndicated column, April 2, 1987. Although Reagan did not hold outside-the-Beltway press conferences as Rusher and others recommended, he had met with non-Washington reporters throughout his years as president. Those press conferences increased substantially in his first term, from just three in 1981 to ten in 1982 and fourteen in 1983. But thereafter, they declined to three and four per year in 1986 through 1988. Muir, *The Bully Pulpit*, 171–72.

52. Rusher, *The Coming Battle for the Media*, 147.

53. Rusher, "He Didn't Yield to Terrorists" and "What Did Congress Ban?" syndicated columns, February 10 and May 21, 1987.

54. Rusher, "A Crime of the Heart," syndicated column, August 18, 1987.

55. Rusher, *The Coming Battle for the Media*, 148–49.

56. Advance copy to Reagan: editors' note in Skinner, et al., eds., *Reagan: A Life in Letters*, 418; Buckley on Roche: Buckley, "Red-Baiting," syndicated column, December 18–19, 1982; symposium on INF issue: "Reagan's Suicide Pact," *National Review*, May 22, 1987, 27–35; response: William A. Rusher, "Reagan's No Suicide," *National Review*, June 5, 1987, 36. Buckley refused to run the initial version of Rusher's piece, in which the publisher called Nixon and Kissinger "dime-store Machiavellis," because he considered the "dime-store" adjective unfair. Brookhiser, *Right Time, Right Place*, 131–32. Rusher's contempt for Nixon's and Kissinger's stance in the debate was also expressed, for example, in "Reagan, the Great Strategist" and "Conservatives and the Treaty," syndicated columns, December 3 and December 10, 1987. In the first of these columns, he accused them of opposing the treaty "in a desperate effort to restore their credentials as strategists after their disastrous experiments with détente."

57. James Mann, *The Rebellion of Ronald Reagan: A History of the End of the Cold War* (New York: Viking, 2009), 264. Candidates Jack Kemp, Pat Robertson, Pete du Pont, and

Alexander Haig, Reagan's first secretary of state, all opposed the treaty; Senator Robert Dole was noncommittal. Two prominent critics in regard to Reagan's Soviet policy at the time, in addition to Buckley, were George Will and Charles Krauthammer. Ibid., 264, 51, 98–99.

58. Rusher, "Nuclear Wimps and Naysayers," "The Zero Option's Dangers," "Europe, Arm Thyself," and "NATO Is No Pushover," syndicated columns, June 2, July 28, July 30, 1987, and January 5, 1988.

59. Rusher, "Make That Deal with the Devil" and "Another Battle in the Cold War," syndicated columns, September 24 and November 5, 1987.

60. Buckley to Reagan, October 18, 1987, in Buckley, ed., *The Reagan I Knew*, 205–206.

61. Rusher, "Will Reagan Ax the Contras?" syndicated column, August 27, 1987.

62. Rusher to Rickenbacker, September 23, 1987, Rusher Papers, Box 76, File 9.

63. Rusher, The Coming Battle for the Media, 217.

64. Ibid., 115–18. A study of the NNC later faulted it for not making its own ethical criteria clear but also noted that the Council operated under a presumption of innocence and concluded that it showed no pattern of hostility toward the media or toward any particular outlet, including the New York Times, despite the paper's refusal to provide documentation in support of itself for complaints filed against it or otherwise to participate in the NNC process. Differences in the conclusions reached by the Council's media and nonmedia members were not large, the study found, and most of its decisions were unanimous. The NNC "represented, at least potentially, an antidote to the insider approach that has predominated in the debates over journalism ethics." Erik Ugland, "The Legitimacy and Moral Authority of the National News Council (USA)," *e-Publications@Marquette*, College of Communication, Marquette University, June 1, 2008. Originally published in *Journalism: Theory, Practice & Criticism*, 9:3 (June 2008). On the NNC's founding and its work, see also Norman E. Isaacs, *Untended Gates: The Mismanaged Press* (New York: Columbia University Press, 1986), ch. 7.

65. Rusher, *The Coming Battle for the Media*, 182–85.

66. Ibid., 207–11. Asked in an interview the following year whether the Fairness Doctrine long enforced by the Federal Communications Commission but repealed in 1987—which had required radio and TV outlets to present controversial issues of public importance in a balanced way that reflected opposing views—was really consistent with his small-government principles, Rusher said it "isn't my prescribed solution" to the problem. Transcript of television interview with Richard D. Heffner on *The Open Mind*, January 14, 1989, www.thirteen.org, accessed February 8, 2011.

67. Rusher, *The Coming Battle for the Media*, 213–15.

68. Mike Wallace, "Why My Mind Has Changed about the Value of a National News Council," excerpt from 1995 remarks at Harvard upon receipt of the Goldsmith Award, www.news-council.org, accessed February 8, 2011.

69. Rusher, *The Coming Battle for the Media*, 216–17.

70. William A. Rusher, "Reviewing the Reviewers," *Arete: Forum for Thought*, August/ September 1988, 22, private papers; Bush to Rusher, May 11, 1988, private papers.

71. Bozell interview; Rusher to Bozell, September 4, 1986, Rusher Papers, Box 153, File 9.

72. Schneider, *Cadres for Conservatism*, 175.

73. Interview with Sergio Picchio, August 3, 2009.


## Chapter 17: All Good Things Must End

1. Rusher to A. Lawrence Chickering, May 17, 1985, and Chickering to Rusher, April 24, 1986, Rusher Papers, Box 19, File 8.

2. Rusher to Robert Hawkins and Chickering (Institute for Contemporary Studies), November 16, 1987, ibid.

3. Interview with Larry Arnn, July 20, 2009. In 1987, Rusher expressed interest in a then-planned Reagan Institute of Politics if any of its work would be in or near San Francisco. Several months later, he told Mrs. Reagan, without citing the Claremont Institute by name, that although it had offered to designate him as a senior fellow and pay him a salary, he would prefer to work for the Reagan Institute. Rusher to Nancy Reagan, August 26, 1987, and March 2, 1988, private papers.

4. Rusher to Rast, July 6, 1987, Rusher Papers, Box 75, File 6.

5. Rusher to Bush, October 23, 1981, and Bush to Rusher, March 15, 1984, private papers; Rusher to Rickenbacker, November 25, 1985, Rusher Papers, Box 76, File 9; location of speech, shared platform with Graham: "Bush Lauds Christians' Role," *New York Times*, June 14, 1982, B11. The acquaintanceship between Rusher and the vice president also included several meetings during the Reagan years. On one of these occasions, Rusher recalls, Bush "said: 'The president thinks very highly of you,' and then he repeated that a little bit later in the conversation." Rusher mentioned the compliment to someone "who ruined it for me by saying: 'Maybe he says that to everybody.'" Bush had, however, said this at least twice on the same visit. He was presumably "quite impressed with the fact, or at least wanted me to be impressed . . . that he was impressed with the fact." Rusher interview, March 28, 2008.

6. Rusher to Bush, November 14, 1984; Bush to Rusher, November 30, 1984; Rusher to Timothy J. McBride (Office of the Vice President), December 13, 1985 [*sic*: 1984]; Bush to Rusher, January 8, 1985, private papers.

7. Rusher to Reagan, February 28, 1983, private papers.

8. John Brady, *Bad Boy: The Life and Politics of Lee Atwater* (Reading, MA: Addison Wesley, 1997), 135–36, 143–46.

9. Herbert S. Parmet, *George Bush: The Life of a Lone Star Yankee* (New York: Scribner, 1997), 302–303.

10. Rusher, "Tory Tantrum," syndicated column, February 2, 1986.

11. Bush to Rusher, February 10, 1986, and April 2, 1986 postcard, private papers.

12. Rusher to Kemp, May 23, 1988, Rusher Papers, Box 48, File 2. Reasons for opposing Shultz: David S. Broder, "Conservatives Cheer Kemp's Call for Shultz to Quit," *Washington Post*, February 21, 1987.

13. Rusher, "The Molting of a Movement," syndicated column, June 16, 1987.

14. Rusher to Lee Atwater, June 16, 1987, and Atwater to Rusher, undated 1987, private papers. Opinion polls at the time tended to support Rusher's argument that average voters were uninterested either in continued ideological activity by the next president or in abandoning Reagan's main policies. Bush's pollster Robert Teeter "sensed that the nation's general unease masked an overall satisfaction with individual voters' own personal lives. Surveys throughout 1987 and 1988 revealed that the public was unmoved by any single issue; Americans worried about drugs, crime, education, and the environment, but their concerns resembled a low-grade fever." Michael Duffy and Dan Goodgame, *Marching in Place: The Status Quo Presidency of George Bush* (New York: Simon and Schuster, 1992), 18–19.

15. Bush's low CPAC support: Broder, "Conservatives Cheer Kemp's Call for Shultz to Quit"; perceptions of candidates, characterizations of campaigns: Ellen Hume and David Rogers, "Moderate Conservatives Bush and Dole Woo a Right Wing that Doesn't Quite Trust Them," *Wall Street Journal*, January 28, 1988, 1.

16. Rusher, "Pat Robertson, the Powerful," syndicated column, October 8, 1987.

17. Rollins, *Bare Knuckles and Back Rooms*, 181–85.

18. Rusher to Kemp, May 23, 1988, Rusher Papers, Box 48, File 2.

19. Parmet, *George Bush*, 334.

20. Rusher, "George Bush at Midpoint," syndicated column, May 24, 1988.

21. Rusher to Bush, June 8, 1988, private papers.

22. Rusher to Atwater, May 16, 1988; Atwater to Rusher, July 11, 1988; Rusher to Atwater,

July 19, 1988, private papers. Recalling his other experiences with him on *The Advocates*, Rusher told readers Dukakis was "a thoroughly decent guy" but played the role of moderator "with all the dash and elan of a traffic light." Rusher, "Yes, I Do Know Mike Dukakis," syndicated column, July 7, 1988.

23. "The Reagan Legacy" symposium, *National Review*, August 5, 1988, 38; John McLaughlin, "Yearning to Be Free," *National Review*, March 18, 1988, 24; Richard Brookhiser, "Bush on the Brink," *National Review*, February 5, 1988, 60.

24. Rusher, "Bush and the Conservatives," syndicated column, April 7, 1988.

25. Rusher, "Ticket, Please? Bush-Hodel!" syndicated column, August 9, 1988; Rusher to Nancy Reagan, November 16, 1984, private papers. Hodel, a president of the Harvard Young Republican Club in the 1950s, was an "old protégé." Rusher to Goldberg, March 16, 1984, Rusher Papers, Box 34, File 11. In 1986, Rusher had even suggested that Hodel could become the movement's new "political spokesman," telling him the role was "about to be vacated" when the Reagan presidency ended in two years. There was "no other evident contender" for it, "and I have high hopes that you can nail down the honor." He drafted a speech intended to position his friend as the leading conservative voice, hoping that Clif White, Roger Moore, and Donald Pearlman—Hodel's old political ally, now his top aide at the Interior Department—would make suggestions for it as well. Rusher to Hodel (cc: Pearlman, White, and Moore), November 24, 1986, Rusher Papers, Box 40, File 3. A few months later, with Hodel's input on the answers, Pearlman prepared a first draft of an "interview" that would run in *Human Events*, a procedure agreed to by editor Tom Winter. Pearlman sought Rusher's advice on the "subject matter of the questions; thrust and tone of the answers; and [the] specific wording" of both. Pearlman to Rusher, February 6, 1987, Rusher Papers, Box 40, File 4.

26. Rusher, "Ticket, Please? Bush-Hodel!" column. Hodel, who was available for the vice-presidential nomination while understanding the "incredible sacrifices" it would mean for his family and privacy, attended the convention in New Orleans with Pearlman. They "virtually made me a member of their official family," Rusher told his friend Moore, happily noting that he was driven around in an air-conditioned limousine. Availability for the ticket, concerns about running: Hodel to author; Hodel, Pearlman, and Rusher at convention: Rusher to Roger Moore, August 19, 1988, Rusher Papers, Box 59, File 8.

27. Hodel to author.

28. Rusher, "Right Choice, Mr. Bush!" syndicated column, August 23, 1988; Rusher to Roger Moore, August 19, 1988, Rusher Papers, Box 59, File 8.

29. "Where *Is* George?," editorial, *National Review*, September 2, 1988, 12, 14.

30. Rusher, "Where Michael Dukakis Went Wrong," syndicated column, November 15, 1988. Bush was genuinely troubled by the extent of Dukakis's social liberalism and believed it was right, not just politically expedient, for the campaign to make this liability clear to the public. Parmet, *George Bush*, 341.

31. Rusher, "George Bush Begins His Presidency," syndicated column, January 19, 1989.

32. Diamond, *Roads to Dominion*, 249.

33. Rusher, "Vote Splitting Limits Bush's Power," syndicated column, November 17, 1988.

34. Rusher, "Giving It One More Try" and "Divided We Fall," syndicated columns, September 29, 1983, and February 14, 1984; Rusher to White, May 4, 1984, Rusher Papers, Box 97, File 5.

35. Rusher, "A Vote for a One-Party State," syndicated column, November 26, 1987. Rusher told readers he was shocked by the title his syndicate, the Newspaper Enterprise Association, gave to this column. He had merely urged a return to government "by a president and Congress of the same party." Explanatory note in syndicated column of December 8, 1987.

36. Paul Allen Beck, "Incomplete Realignment: The Reagan Legacy for Parties and Elections," in Charles O. Jones, ed., *The Reagan Legacy: Promise and Performance* (Chatham, NJ: Chatham House, 1988), 152–69.

37. Rusher to Peter Brimelow, June 29, 1988, Rusher Papers, Box 12, File 5.
38. "The Future of the GOP" symposium, *National Review*, September 16, 1988, 34.
39. Phillips comment: Edwards, *The Conservative Revolution*, 239.
40. Lyn Nofziger, *Nofziger* (Washington: Regnery/Gateway, 1992), 278–79.
41. Rusher, "'Evil Empire' Sits Down" and "Go Slow on U.S.-Soviet Trade," syndicated columns, June 7 and June 9, 1988.
42. Buckley, "So Long, Evil Empire," syndicated column, *National Review*, July 8, 1988, 56–57 (originally published June 1).
43. Rusher, "Hail to President Reagan," syndicated column, August 11, 1988.
44. Rusher, "George Bush Begins His Presidency" column.
45. Buckley, *The Reagan I Knew*, 240–41.
46. Philip H. Dougherty, "Shifts at Top of National Review," *New York Times*, June 3, 1988, Rusher Papers, Box 6, File 10.
47. Goldwater youth chairman: Allison to Rusher, September 17, 1985, Rusher Papers, Box 6, File 10. Library anecdote: interview with Wick Allison, July 22, 2009.
48. Allison interview.
49. Ibid.
50. *National Review* fund-raising letter draft with notations, undated 1987, Rusher Papers, Box 113, File 7.
51. James H. Andrews, "National Review Tries a Transatlantic Tack," *Christian Science Monitor*, July 18, 1988, 21, Rusher Papers, Box 122, File 6.
52. Judis, *William F. Buckley Jr.*, 438–43.
53. Andrews, "National Review Tries a Transatlantic Tack."
54. Buckley to senior staff (Hart, Joseph Sobran, Brookhiser, et al.), July 26, 1988, Rusher Papers, Box 122, File 6.
55. Rusher, "Let's Consider Bill Buckley," syndicated column, May 31, 1988.
56. Rusher, "A Fond Farewell to National Review" column.
57. Rusher interview, March 29, 2008; Rusher, "Ta-Ta, N.Y. California, Here I Come," syndicated column, September 7, 1989. "I require an urban—yes, and a cosmopolitan—environment," Rusher noted. "Country or small-town living would send me straight up the nearest wall."
58. Rusher to Mary Louise Self, September 8, 1983, Rusher Papers, Box 81, File 8.
59. Rusher to Brudnoy, September 9, 1988, Rusher Papers, Box 13, File 3; Allison interview.
60. Rusher to John McConnell, July 8, 1988, Rusher Papers, Box 57, File 9.
61. Rusher to Monsignor Eugene V. Clark, October 18, 1988, Rusher Papers, Box 19, File 2.
62. Rusher interview, March 29, 2008; Rogalin to Rusher, July 5, 1988, Rusher Papers, Box 77, File 4.
63. Rusher to Bush, January 9, 1989, private papers; Fernald interview.
64. "Conservative Republican president": Rusher to Goldwater, January 23, 1963, Rusher Papers, Reel 16. Thank-you note: Reagan to Rusher, January 17, 1989, in Ralph E. Weber and Ralph A. Weber, eds., *Dear Americans: Letters from the Desk of Ronald Reagan* (New York: Doubleday, 2003), 366.
65. Rusher, "Now It Can Be Told," *National Review*, 41–42.
66. Rusher to Kemp, May 23, 1988, Rusher Papers, Box 48, File 2.

## Chapter 18: Rusher by the Bay

1. Allison interview; Rusher on *NR*'s focus: Rusher interview, August 23, 2005.
2. Interview with John O'Sullivan, July 25, 2009; Allison interview.
3. Allison interview.
4. O'Sullivan interview; Brookhiser interview.

5. O'Sullivan interview.

6. Planning for apartment: Rusher to Astrid Flood, April 12 and July 28, 1989, private papers.

7. Size of Rusher's apartments, lack of view in New York: conversation with Alfred Tong (housekeeper), September 1, 2010; enjoyment of new apartment: Rusher to Harrigan, June 11, 1990, private papers.

8. Rusher, "Gone Fishing? Well, Not Exactly . . ." column.

9. Inquiries into radio show: Freeman to Rusher, October 23, 1989, and Larry Cott to Rusher, November 9, 1989, private papers; AP network radio talks: scripts, January–May 1989, private papers.

10. Arnn interview.

11. Interview with John Kurzweil, July 29, 2009.

12. Bozell interview.

13. John M. Ashbrook Center for Public Affairs, board of advisers meeting notes, May 18, 1989; Report of Activities by F. Clifton White, director, May 12, 1989, private papers.

14. Working harder: Rusher to Harrigan, June 11, 1990.

15. Allison interview; O'Sullivan interview; O'Sullivan to author, September 13, 2009.

16. Allison interview.

17. Ibid.; O'Sullivan to author.

18. O'Sullivan interview; O'Sullivan to author.

19. Rusher interview, March 28, 2008.

20. George Washington Society flier, circa 1990, private papers.

21. Picchio interview.

22. Handwritten notes for "The Future of Conservatism," address at Young Americans for Freedom convention, San Diego, CA, August 12, 1989, private papers.

23. Charles Kolb, *White House Daze: The Unmaking of Domestic Policy in the Bush Years* (New York: Free Press, 1994), 343.

24. Rusher, "Why Bush Didn't Yield on Abortion," syndicated column, November 28, 1989.

25. Rusher, "Bush Is Now Good for Conservatives," syndicated column, July 16, 1991. Rusher had, however, publicly warned that there could be "a rebellion in 1992 that will spell the end of his presidency." More than centrist policies, it was the sense of "directionless drift" on Bush's part that was now, he noticed, beginning to disaffect the "serious conservatives" who might make that happen. Rusher, "Dear Mr. President: Please Read This," syndicated column, November 20, 1990.

26. Rusher, "Bush's Iraq Decisions Defy Scrutiny," syndicated column, August 8, 1991.

27. Rusher, "In Praise of the Cold War Generation," syndicated column, January 23, 1990; Rusher interview, August 5, 2003.

28. Rusher, "The Cold War *Was* World War III" and "1991 Was a Great Year for America," syndicated columns, March 20, 1990, and December 31, 1991.

29. Rusher, "Will Abortion Debate Split the GOP?" syndicated column, May 1, 1990.

30. Rusher, "Where Is Pat Buchanan's Bid Going?" syndicated column, March 5, 1992; Keely Coghlan, "On the issues: McGovern agrees with Rusher that jobs tops election," *San Angelo Standard Times*, October 7, 1992, 1, private papers. In a column, Rusher had sketched an acceptance speech he thought Bush should deliver at the convention. It focused on the Democratic Congress's obstructions and urged voters to elect a Republican Congress. Rusher, "Dear George: Say This in Houston," syndicated column, July 30, 1992.

31. Handwritten notes for "Conservatism and the Election," address at Council for National Policy meeting, Williamsburg, VA, November 7, 1992, and "Conservatives and the Future," address at board meeting of Media Research Center, Washington, DC, November 12, 1992, private papers. Rusher's own pro-life position was tempered by a sensitivity to pro-choice and ambivalent voters. Right-to-lifers, he had written in 1981,

"don't always realize ... how unreasonably intransigent and offensively smug we sometimes appear." Adding that such a "highly pluralistic" democracy as America "requires constant compromise among people who differ passionately," he went on to warn that "a position that by its very nature cannot be compromised is therefore a constant menace to the health and stability of the body politic." The abolitionists ultimately succeeded in ending slavery "not because anybody came to like them," but because the American people knew deep down that they were right. The decisive factor wasn't the abolitionists' agitation, but the absolute truth of their belief that the slave was a human being, "created equal." Rusher concluded that abortion too would eventually be outlawed, and without a civil war. Rusher, "The Problem—and Strength—of Right to Life," syndicated column, December 6, 1981.

32. Rusher, remarks in *George Washington Society Newsletter*, March/April 1993, private papers.

33. Rusher, "Celebrating 70 with a Former Foe," syndicated column, July 29, 1993; photo in Red Square, dinner with American conservatives: author recollections. Rusher spent one week each in Russia and Ukraine. Rusher, "Snapshots of Contemporary Russia," syndicated column, August 5, 1993.

34. Kirk to Rusher, March 31, 1987; Rusher to M. J. Rossant (Twentieth Century Fund), April 3, 1987; Rusher to Kirk, June 12, 1987, personal papers.

35. Larry Arnn to Michael Joyce (executive director, Lynde and Harry Bradley Foundation), December 15, 1991; Joyce to Arnn, January 17, 1992; conference schedules for "The Ambiguous Legacy of the Enlightenment," "The Permanent Limitations of Science," and "Progress or Return? Beyond Enlightenment" conferences, Claremont, CA, January 25–27, 1990, February 15–16, 1991, and February 28–29, 1992, private papers.

36. Leon Kass to Rusher, February 20, 1991; Rusher to Walter McDougall, March 23, 1992, private papers.

37. Rusher to Buckley, January 5, 1994, private papers.

38. Rusher to Glynn Custred and Tom Wood, August 17, 1994, private papers.

39. Rusher to Arnn and Arnie Steinberg, July 27, 1995, private papers.

40. Rusher, "A Plea to Moderate GOP Senators," syndicated column, September 21, 1995; "Word Games," syndicated column, February 20, 1997.

41. Jennifer Delton to author, August 28, 2009.

42. Rusher, "Reflections on the Rise of the Right," keynote address at "From Redemption to Reaganism" conference on American conservatism, Princeton University, May 3, 1996 (Claremont Institute publication).

43. Appreciation of ability to relax: O'Scannlain interview; "happiest years": Rusher, "Can San Francisco Survive Brown?" syndicated column, December 21, 1995.

44. Interview with Arnold Steinberg, July 28, 2009; Freeman to author, July 16, 2009.

45. O'Scannlain interview.

46. Opinion faxed to Rusher: author recollection.

47. Health problems: Rusher, "On Turning 75" column; side effects of cancer treatment: author recollections.

48. Rusher, "On Turning 75" column.

49. Rusher, "Who Says the Media Are Biased?" syndicated column, December 27, 2001; comment on Limbaugh: Rusher interview, August 5, 2003.

50. Rusher, "The Liberals Fight Back," syndicated column, November 6, 2003.

51. O'Scannlain interview.

52. Rusher, "How Conservative is Bush?" syndicated column, February 12, 2004.

53. Books: Rusher interview, March 29, 2008.

54. Author recollections; cigars at University Club: Shepherd interview.

55. Rusher interview, March 29, 2008; Rusher on San Francisco Towers residents: author recollections.

56. Meth interview.

57. Keene interview.

58. Buckley interview, September 17, 2005. Rusher also objected to Jeffrey Hart's reference to him as a "Dickensian" character in the draft version of *The Making of the American Conservative Mind*. The author agreed to drop the word. Hart interview.

59. "Sadly confided": author recollection; reaction to news of Buckley's death: Rusher interview, March 28, 2008.

60. William F. Buckley Jr., memorial edition, *National Review*, March 24, 2008; "rather misbegotten": Rusher interview, March 28, 2008; asked to write, shortened: author recollection.

61. Steinberg to author, July 21, 2009.

62. Rusher interview, March 28, 2008; Jack Casey: O'Scannlain interview.

63. Author recollections; literature, reading, television: Rusher interview, March 29, 2008.

64. Ibid.; met for lunch: conversation with the Most Rev. James Eugene Provence, April 19, 2011.

65. Rusher interview, March 29, 2008.

66. Romney a good candidate, McCain a man of substance: author recollections; McCain a strong candidate, "Democratic year": Rusher interview, March 28, 2008.

67. Rusher interview, March 28, 2008.

68. Rusher, "The Battle of the 21st Century," syndicated column, November 15, 2001.

69. Rusher interview, March 29, 2008.

70. Rusher, "The Final Column," syndicated column, March 3, 2009, www.townhall.com.

71. O'Scannlain interview.

72. Shepherd interview.

73. Conversations with Shepherd, Tong, and Roger Mertz (Rusher's attorney), July 2010–April 2011; Rusher's appearance, "tell everyone he would make it": author recollection.

## Conclusion: "The Truth Will Prevail"

1. Rusher interview, March 29, 2008.

2. Steel, *Walter Lippmann and the American Century*, 597.

3. Rusher interview, October 29, 2007.

4. Buckley interview, July 26, 2005.

5. Lee Edwards interview, July 31, 2006; Priscilla Buckley interview.

6. Farber interview.

7. Hart, *The Making of the American Conservative Mind*, 63; Rusher interview, August 23, 2005.

8. Burnham, *Suicide of the West*, 26.

9. Hart interview.

10. Priscilla Buckley interview.

11. Arnn interview.

12. McGrath interview.

13. Kurzweil interview.

# Acknowledgments

I n writing a complex biography while its subject and many who knew him are still living, an author draws on others' time. The unfailing assistance and goodwill of the dozens of people interviewed, and especially of William Rusher, were essential.

Neal Freeman conceived and financially sponsored this project and thus deserves much credit for it. In addition, I appreciate the fact that neither he nor Rusher sought any editorial control. At key stages, Brian Kennedy of the Claremont Institute provided a quiet work space there that was most helpful. The Institute also took care of most travel and research expenses.

Substantial portions of this book doubled as my doctoral dissertation in political science at Claremont Graduate University. I am grateful to my dissertation chairman, Charles Kesler, for his consistent calm and good cheer in the face of frustrating delays. Jack Pitney's research leads relating to the Senate Internal Security Subcommittee were useful as well. To Fred Lynch, thank you for some suggestions from a sociological standpoint.

At the Library of Congress and Sterling Memorial Library at Yale University, Jeff Flannery, William Massa, and their staffs were industriously helpful. I also note the permission of the late William F. Buckley Jr. to examine his papers at Yale, and of his son, Christopher, to quote freely from them. At ISI Books, editor in chief Jed Donahue and managing editor Jennifer Fox have been most patient, especially in accommodating a multitude of additions and refinements. ISI editors also pruned much that was inessential, and they came up with a wonderful cover. Any mistakes or interpretive shortcomings are mine alone.

The assistance of Rusher's former housekeeper Alfred Tong in many hours of accessing and photocopying what are cited as "private papers," and in lending photos stored with those papers, was essential and is gratefully acknowledged. Linda Bridges and Thomas Bolan at *National Review* were of much help in locating and identifying some of the other pictures. Pulling together a reasonably good range of illustrations was no small task. Thanks to all who aided in this.

To my friends Carl Aschmann, Matt Ausfahl, Lee Cheek, Bill Cuddihy, Steve Dolson-Andrew, Tim Finlay, Adam Fuller, Marcia Godwin, Stannie Holt, Chris Hovick, Tom Lorincz, Jim McNabb, Karen Robbins, Steve Schwartzberg, and Dave Thoits—thank you for all the encouragement, which I needed. Bob and Theresa Anderson gave me a place to stay on two of my research trips to Washington. Dave Roberts either came up with or crucially encouraged the idea, back in 1992, of starting a conservative journalists' conversation club in San Francisco with Rusher, we hoped, as its centerpiece—an excellent introduction to a remarkable man.

It was my brother Jerome Frisk, now of the University of California–Santa Cruz, whose enthusiastic example was the key factor in setting me on what proved to be an academic path when I was a teenager more than thirty years ago. Finally, I wish to stress the integrity and love of learning exemplified by my late parents, Richard M. and Marjorie Brown Frisk, and the commitment to the politics of freedom exemplified especially by my father—a Goldwater Republican who was the party's candidate for the State Assembly in Berkeley in 1964.

My disappointment in not completing the final draft of this biography while Bill Rusher clung to life these past two years—probably in hopes of seeing the published product—is balanced, although not canceled, by his appreciation of its title and by his faith in its author.

Claremont, California
December 21, 2011

# Index